Edited by Russ Kick

ABUSE YOUR ILLUSIONS

THE DISINFORMATION GUIDE TO MEDIA MIRAGES AND ESTABLISHMENT LIES

This collection Copyright © 2003 The Disinformation Company Ltd.

All of the articles in this book are Copyright © by their respective authors and/or original publishers, except as specified herein, and we note and thank them for their kind permission.

Published by The Disinformation Company Ltd.
163 Third Avenue, Suite 108
New York, NY 10003
Tel. +1.212.691.1605
Fax +1.212.473.8096
www.disinfo.com

Editor: Russ Kick
Publisher: Gary Baddeley

Designer: Leen Al-Bassam

First Printing April 2003

Library of Congress Control Number: 2002114915

ISBN 0-9713942-4-5

Printed in USA

Distributed in the USA and Canada by Consortium Book Sales and Distribution
1045 Westgate Drive, Suite 90
St Paul, MN 55114
Toll Free: +1.800.283.3572
Local: +1.651.221.9035
Fax: +1.651.221.0124
www.cbsd.com

Distributed in the United Kingdom and Eire by:
Turnaround Publisher Services Ltd.
Unit 3, Olympia Trading Estate
Coburg Road
London, N22 6TZ
Tel.: +44.(0)20.8829.3000
Fax: +44.(0)20.8881.5088
www.turnaround-uk.com

Attention colleges and universities, corporations and other organizations: Quantity discounts are available on bulk purchases of this book for educational training purposes, fund-raising, or gift giving. Special books, booklets, or book excerpts can also be created to fit your specific needs. For information contact Marketing Department of The Disinformation Company Ltd.

Disinformation is a registered trademark of The Disinformation Company Ltd.

ACKNOWLEDGMENTS

Thanks of a personal nature are due to Anne, Ruthanne, Jennifer, and (as always) my parents, who give me support in many ways. The same goes for that unholy trinity of Billy, Darrell, and Terry, who let me vent and make me laugh.

I'd like to thank Richard Metzger and Gary Baddeley for letting me edit the anthology series and taking a *laissez-faire* approach. Also, many thanks go to Leen Al-Bassam, who turned a bunch of computer files into the beautiful object you now hold in your hands. And thanks also head out to the many other people involved in the creation and distribution of this book, including everyone at Disinformation, Consortium, Turnaround, Bookspan, the printers, the retailers, and elsewhere. It takes a lot of people to make a book and get it into your hands!

Many more people played a role in helping me locate and secure material for this book: Kristina Borjesson, Mads Brügger, Alex Burns, Michael Ellsberg, Edward Hammond, Ina Howard, Kalle Lasn, John Oakes, Preston Peet, Marcia Rogers, Fredda Weinberg, Penmarin Press, the *Globe and Mail*, and many others I'm unfortunately forgetting as the deadline looms.

I also greatly appreciate all the readers out there who buy, borrow, or steal my books. Your direct and indirect feedback keeps me going. And to the person who spray-painted the titles of the first two Disinformation Guides on the student center at the University of New Hampshire—keep spreading the meme!

Last but definitely not least, I express my gratitude toward all the contributors, without whom there would be no *Abuse Your Illusions*. None of you will be able to retire early because of appearing in these pages, so I know you contributed because you believe so strongly in what you're doing. And you believed in me, which I deeply appreciate.

— R.K.

CONTENTS

PREFACE
RICHARD METZGER

Welcome to another Disinformation anthology, again edited by Russ Kick. A lot has happened since the publication of the first two books in this series, *You Are Being Lied To* and *Everything You Know is Wrong*, and once again, we at The Disinformation Company, are pleased to be publishing a book that we feel is an important and vital contribution to help make sense of the swirling media space of these, as the famous Chinese curse goes, "interesting times."

_SOUND AND FURY SIGNIFYING NOTHING

"To be corrupted by totalitarianism one does not have to live in a totalitarian country."
–George Orwell

"For a variety of reasons, including the desire to avoid charges of liberal bias, most reporting is carefully hedged. And the public, reading only praise or he-said-she-said discussions, never grasps the fundamental disconnect between problem and policy."
—Paul Krugman, *New York Times*

One of the things I find most satisfying about these anthologies is how ably Russ steers clear of falling too much into this camp or that. I am often left open-mouthed in astonishment at the notion that anyone would want to label themselves as "conservative" or "liberal" and consider this a ridiculous non-issue. I can understand why someone might feel pride of race or religion, but to *identify oneself* as a "Democrat" or as a "Republican" to me seems utterly ridiculous and worthy of contempt. It's just plain stupid. There are good ideas and there are bad ideas. Some of them might be "conservative" and some of them might be "liberal"—but if a good idea is a "conservative" idea or birthed by the "conservative" camp, does this mean that this good idea must be rejected out of hand by people who have decided that they are "liberals," or vice versa?

The two major political parties are proving grounds from which all political ambitions must be realized and channeled, so in other words, if you want to rise up from within them, you have to toe the party line. If you are a Republican, you'd *better* be against a woman's right to choose and spending on social programs, or else. If you're a Democrat, of course, you're 100 percent for abortion rights and butter, not guns (at least *rhetorically*). Go against the grain on this issue, in either subculture, and you're disqualified instantly. Try to take off the intellectual straightjacket, and you're *toast.*

In my own analysis—and I realize this is simplistic—at heart, "conservatives" seem to be sex-negative, while "liberals" (like Bill Clinton, although a look at his record will reveal him to be to the right of Ronald Regan) seem to be a little more on the randy side—like who in their right mind would find Ann Coulter sexy, if you know what I mean? It always amuses me, this *pack mentality* that politicos, especially conservatives, seem to have. Simply put, these people are the campus nerds, the ones on the debate team. Wimpy little guys who have gotten the crap kicked out of them their entire lives; now getting their kicks verbally jousting with others. Arguing in public, in other words. And *getting their revenge!*

Go to a Young Republicans meeting, and you'll see what I mean—visually—in two seconds flat. They all look alike, and few of them look like they've ever been laid. It doesn't mater what race or religion they are, they all look alike. Dinesh D'Souza? Ralph Reed? Trent Lott? See the difference? Neither do I. If you can't tell a Republican from a Democrat, you're as blind as a bat.

It may seem like I'm indulging in "conservative bashing" here (and I am), but please don't assume that Noam Chomsky speaks for me, either! And who exactly are the liberals these days, anyways? Point 'em out to me, please! As mentioned above, anyone who thinks Clinton is a liberal has *no idea* what he or she is talking about!

And don't get me started about the supposed liberal bias in the media; if there actually were one, *then we wouldn't be hearing about it.* This is the "big lie" the Republicans would have you believe, but look at who owns the newspapers and television networks in this country! Repeat something loud enough and long enough, and it becomes true. But it's 180 degrees out of whack with reality, as you know and I know and *they know it, too.*

The more you begin to detach from it, the more cosmically absurd American politics becomes. These people are the grown-up versions of the same people you hated in high school and college, and now *they* are running things. How did this happen? Why? It's *because they can.* You and I allowed this to happen. It doesn't matter to which party they belong anymore. It doesn't. The biggest difference, as I see it anyways, is that the Republicans aren't afraid to fight dirty, and the Democrats seem to have no fight left in them at all. The superficial styles and the personalities may differ, but it's long ceased to be about issues, and politics now solely concerns itself with the one issue to which all others must be subsumed: *Gaining and holding on to power at all costs.* Public interests are lowered to the level of *spectator sports*, and politics has become simply a brawl, a nationally televised pie-fight.

As a result civic affairs programs and news hours have slid to an epic level of buffoonery and idiocy. Ann Coulter is emblematic of what's occurred. She has, almost single-handedly, dragged political discourse down to the level of *name-calling*. Forget about ideas: Coulter's *relentlessly self-promoting* ascent to the top of the best-seller charts underscores my point: It's all about shouting down your opponents, but Coulter's a fine example of what the right does best and what the left has never gotten right—she's entertaining. She's entertaining in the same way that Anna Nicole Smith is entertaining, but she does command your attention even if the sight of her makes you want to puke…

It's worth mentioning that I was recently fooled by a satirical piece making the rounds on the Internet saying that Ann Coulter had written a kids' book for the children of conservative parents. The alleged book was titled *I Know You Are, But What Am I?* and purported to be a guide for Republican kiddies to "fight back" *with name-calling* against the "liberal poopyheads." And yes, I believed it was real.

What does this say about my credulity, about Coulter's shopworn "Rush Limbaugh with tits" shtick, and about the media space we inhabit? Or does it *not say anything at all*, and is this the entire point?

We're being shouted at by idiots everywhere we turn!

In an interesting article that appeared in the *LA Times* op-ed page, Neal Gabler argued that what we're seeing here is not the dichotomy between conservative and liberal so much as the difference between two styles of reporting: "objectivity" of the sort taught in journalism schools versus "advocacy," e.g., Rush Limbaugh/Bill O'Reilly/Ann Coulter-style polemic and general nastiness. These days as tabloid television, "reality TV" (and I use that term loosely), and the grotesque sham of "no spin zones" dominate the media, there is a need for heroic muckraking and no-nonsense *tell it like it is* reporting in America.

Paraphrasing something Jeff Cohen of Fairness and Accuracy in Reporting (FAIR) said at a 1991 speech in Los Angeles (referring to then-Police Chief Darryl Gates): "A reporter told me, 'I know the Chief of Police is lying, you know the Chief of Police is lying, and *the Chief of Police knows he is lying*—but I can't *say* 'The Chief of Police is a liar!'"

Why not?

_WE LIVE IN THE GOLDEN AGE NOW

"Without censorship, things can get terribly confused in the public mind."
—Gen. William Westmoreland

"Fascism should be more properly called corporatism, since it is the merger of state and corporate power."
—Benito Mussolini

But I digress.

Recently, I've felt compelled to peel my eyes off of the post-9/11 reporting and vowed to limit my intake of televised news. I don't need the pounding soundtrack with the martial drumbeat and the Wagnerian flourishes. I don't need CNN's graphics package of fighter jets taking off and American flags being burned by angry mobs in the Middle East, and I especially don't need a *noted liar* like Henry Kissinger explaining the "necessity" of bombing an Arab country back to the stone age when I know full well he's on the board of directors of several companies that will stand to make a *mint* once the action starts.

But still, there is hope. It's not *all* bad, and some signs are actually encouraging. Here's what Michael Powell, the Chairman of the FCC (and son of Colin Powell) said in the *New York Times* about media diversity: "When I look at the trends in television over the last 20 to 50 years, I see a constant and increasing explosion in variety. In the purported golden age of television there were three networks."

He's right.

A few years ago, I found myself in the library of the Museum of Television and Radio in New York, and I requested several tapes of the CBS Evening News with Walter Cronkite from the time of Nixon's reelection campaign against Senator George McGovern. I have long been fascinated by this race due to it probably being the last time that there was such a *stark* choice between the candidates in America. (McGovern was as close to a socialist ever to make the top of a major-party ticket. Nixon, well, we all know about him, now don't we?)

Having been long accustomed to listening to the "liberal" argument (as opposed to the conservative version) that there isn't enough diversity in media, I was astonished at what I saw: One white man behind a desk with static, over-the-shoulder graphics, and an occasional film clip—not video, mind you, *film*, the kind that you have to shoot, develop, and have shipped from where it was shot before you can put it on the air. Satellites were around back then, but not in common use like they are today, so it might have taken days before even important events reached America's living rooms.

What was also striking was how little time people were given to "speak for themselves." We always hear commentators decry how everything has been reduced to sound bites on the news these days, but back then even sound bites were a rarity! Most of the time it was just a paraphrase by the newsreader of what was really said and then, bang, on to the next story. The nightly news broadcasts were only 22 minutes long.

And there were, as Powell points out, only three networks. Compare what we had in 1971 with what we have now—several 24-hour news channels, even 24-hour local coverage in New York with NY1, and new "progressive" media networks like Free Speech Television offering radically different infotainment on a mass level, and it seems like we have an embarrassment of riches today. It really does.

And consider the fact that fully two-thirds of American homes now have Internet access. This means that millions upon millions of people, no matter how isolated they might be geographically, have nearly speed-of-light access to most of the major newspapers from any country in the world. It's astonishing to think where communications technology has taken us, and if you truly want to be well informed and if you want to hear opinions other than Bill O'Reilly's or Pat Robertson's or some other establishment shill's, you don't have to leave your home to get them. It is *easier* now to be "well informed" than at any time in the past.

There is more free speech today than at any time before in human history! But it's difficult to remember this sometimes, especially when you're watching Ann Coulter idiotically shouting someone down on FOX News...

_DON'T COMPLAIN ABOUT THE MEDIA—BECOME THE MEDIA

"We are taught you must blame your father, your sisters, your brothers, the school, the teachers—you can blame anyone but never blame yourself. It's never your fault. But it's always your fault, because if you wanted to change, you're the one who has got to change. It's as simple as that, isn't it?"
—Katherine Hepburn

As Marx once said, freedom of the press belongs to those who own the printing presses, but it's ridiculous to think this will ever change, especially now with all of the major media mergers and the FCC relaxing ownership rules. So what is the solution?

Infiltrate the system.

You wanna change the way the media works? Then become a journalist. You'd like to see an issue dear to you find its way onto the national radar screen, then make a documentary about it, organize a PAC, or enter politics yourself. As the saying goes, "It's not brain surgery," and if you've become frustrated with marches and political protests of the old-fashioned sort (although they can be dramatic and I don't want to discourage anyone from doing their part, I do question how meaningful even the biggest marches are these days), then *do something different!* Don't wait for others to take the lead for you, *do it yourself.* Educate others in a manner that will entertain them. It's the only way, really, to change something in our mass-mediated culture. Nothing else is as effective as wrapping your message in a funny, sexy, candy-coated shell and shooting that bullet deep into the culture where it can replicate like the common cold (see Douglas Rushkoff's classic *Media Virus* for more on this topic).

Of course, it's difficult enough to start your own band, let alone a political party or a newspaper, but many self-contained projects are well within the realm of possibility... And what of the possibility of joining (infiltrating!) a political party or *running for office yourself?* If the idiots who are in office now can do it, why can't *you*? (When FOX announced the reality program called *The American President* where "real-life" people with aspirations of living in the White House can bypass the political parties and go directly to the people (*American Idol* meets the primary season), I thought it was the most subversive thing I'd ever heard.)

If you have a message, get it out there in an entertaining way so that the idea can really take off and grow. But for God's sake, do something!

If you don't (or won't) do it, who will?

Ann Coulter, Rush Limbaugh and Bill O'Reilly...the list can go on and on, obviously.

Don't let this happen! Overcome your cynicism; things *can* change. It's about time for the culture of complaining in America to come to an end. Educate yourself. Seek out contrarian news sources, and find other people who think the same way you do, and get off your ass and make your world a better place.

Lose your illusions and *abuse theirs!*

And who knows, you might even have fun!

Richard Metzger
Los Angeles, Winter 2003

INTRODUCTION
RUSS KICK

Abuse Your Illusions[1] is the third anthology I've edited for Disinformation in as many years. When I started on the first volume (*You Are Being Lied To*) in 2000, people knowingly said, I bet you'll never run out of material, you'll be able to create these anthologies forever, and other words to that effect. As I suspected, they were right. The problem, as always, is not whether I'll get enough material to fill such a big book, but how I'm going to winnow down the number of possible subjects, contributors, articles, etc. The sheer volume of hidden information, suppressed facts, distortions, lies, myths, and misconceptions that washes over us is astounding.

Every day I read more material that undermines the consensus, harpoons big lies, sweeps dirt *back* out from under the rug, and shows the way things could be. My own assumptions are challenged regularly, sometimes hourly. There are days when I wonder if, as the title of the second volume said, literally everything I know is wrong.

Keeping up with the deceptions is an ever increasing challenge. It's like digging a hole while a bulldozer keeps shoving the dirt back in. And it's getting worse. The current administration is more fond of secrecy and repression than any in living memory, and that's saying something. Each President does what he can to up the ante, clamping down harder and keeping more secrets than his predecessor. These days, government Websites are quietly removing or changing thousands of pages. The Attorney General has ordered agencies to deny Freedom of Information Act requests more often. More information is considered "unclassified but sensitive" and, thus, restricted. Some types of statistics are no longer gathered. Money for printing government documents is scarcer. Libraries are being defunded.

And then we have the menace of pressure groups. You don't like that someone has revealed an embarrassing fact or expressed an uncomfortable opinion? Threaten them with boycotts, litigation, bad publicity, criminal prosecution (especially in Europe), and maybe even hint at harsher forms of retribution. It's all the rage. Simply everyone's doing it, darlings—the right, the left, Muslims, Jews, veterans, feminists, and so on. Apparently a lot of people haven't learned that the proper reaction to speech you don't like or agree with is counter-speech of your own, not trying to silence the other person.

The Internet has helped tremendously in freeing information. At the same time, it's unleashed so much info that it's forced us to sharpen our critical thinking skills. Who created the material we're reading? What are the sources they've used? Is what they're saying internally consistent? These are some good questions to ask about any material. But we mustn't go too far in the other direction by disbelieving everything we read on the Net. In what appears to be a backlash against the online info-flood, certain people would have you believe that *nothing* you read on the Net can possibly be true. Some of these people are simply being arrogantly dismissive, but others have an agenda. And beware the reviewers on Amazon who write, "Don't waste your money on this book." Translation: "This book has facts and opinions that upset me, so I don't want you to read it."

And speaking of books, they're part of the info-glut, as well. The number of worthwhile books with important revelations grows by leaps and bounds literally every single day. But who has time to read them? A 500-page exposé on some corporation, government agency, or political figure is great, but you'll be lucky to make it through one, never mind dozens upon dozens, in a reasonable amount of time. The same goes for that 600-page book that dramatically challenges our ideas about an historical event. And that 300-page tome on the latest scientific theory or technological breakthrough.

So why are we contributing to the info-overload, the pile of books stacking up beside your nightstand? (Not to mention that three-foot list of bookmarks in your Web browser.) Because we're hoping to gather some of the best of that far-flung material and put it in one place. It's still just a fraction of the good stuff that's out there, but it's a start.

At the same time, the anthologies offer an antidote to restrictions on the flow of information. Pretty much every article between these covers deals with a sensitive topic, and some of them are completely radioactive. De Beers has purportedly suppressed Janine Roberts' film on the dark, hidden aspects of the diamond trade. Doubleday contracted her for a book on the topic, even paid her an advance, then refused to publish it. (It'll be issued in 2003 by The Disinformation Company.) With the goading of the military establishment, the press pilloried April Oliver for her report on Operation Tailwind—yet they refuse to report on the evidence in her favor that keeps piling up. When the Sunshine Project issued a press release about declassified government documents which prove that the US is developing illegal bioweapons, every major media outlet in the country called co-founder Edward Hammond to find out more. But none of them ran the story. Only two alterative news sources covered the revelations—Pacifica Radio and the *Village Voice* (the latter with an online article by yours truly). Hammond told me that a reporter for the *New York Times* interviewed him for 45 minutes and was hot to do the story, but the editors at the *Times* killed it. Gary Webb's governmental report on racial profiling was immediately shelved by the California State Assembly. They didn't even put it online, apparently hoping that it would be forgotten, becoming rat food in their dusty archives.

Yep, even in the age of information overload, some facts have a hard time making it into the light. And of those many facts that do skitter out, how does one even know where to begin?

I humbly suggest that *Abuse Your Illusions* is a good place to start.[2]

Endnotes

1. If you were born too early or too late, you might not get the reference. Those of us skating somewhere in the middle recognize it as a play on the Guns n' Roses album *Use Your Illusions*. **2.** Should any of these articles pique your curiosity, you'll find sources for further information in the endnotes, the contributors' biographies and their Websites, and, of course, the articles themselves.

EXILE ON MAINSTREAM
WHY AN AMERICAN REPORTER HAD TO LEAVE THE COUNTRY TO REPORT THE NEWS
GREG PALAST

One: Stupid.

No, you're not stupid.

They just talk to you that way.

Two: Loony. Dangerous. Disgusting.

Have you heard about Cynthia McKinney, the former US Congresswoman?

According to National Public Radio...

...McKinney's "a loose cannon" (quoting a media expert).
..."The people of Atlanta are embarrassed and disgusted" by McKinney (quoting a politician).
...McKinney's "loony" and "dangerous" (quoting a Senator from her own party).

Yow! And *why* is McKinney dangerous/loony/disgusting? According to NPR, "McKinney implied that the [Bush] Administration knew in advance about September 11 and deliberately held back the information."

The *New York Times* revealed her comments went even further over the edge: "Ms. McKinney suggest[ed] that President Bush might have known about the September 11 attacks but did nothing so his supporters could make money in a war."

That's loony, all right. As an editor of the highly respected *Atlanta Journal Constitution* told NPR, McKinney's "practically accused the President of murder!"

■ ■ ■ ■ ■ ■ ■ ■ ■ ■

Problem is, McKinney never said it.

That's right. The "quote" from McKinney is a complete fabrication. A whopper, a fabulous fib, a fake, a flim-flam. Just freakin' *made up*.

_"ALL OVER THE PLACE"

A transcript of my phone call.

Times: New York Times.

Could you connect me to the extension of Lynette Clemetson?

Times: Hello.

Hi, Lynette. My name is Greg Palast, and I wanted to follow up on a story of yours. It says, let's see, after the opening—it's about Cynthia McKinney—it's dated Washington byline August 21—quote: McKinney's [opponent] capitalized on the furor caused by Miss McKinney's suggestion this year that President Bush might have known about the September 11 attacks but did nothing so his supporters could make money in a war. End quote. Now, I have been trying my darndest to find this phrase.... I can't....

THE "QUOTE" FROM MCKINNEY IS A COMPLETE FABRICATION. A WHOPPER, A FABULOUS FIB, A FAKE, A FLIM-FLAM. JUST FREAKIN' *MADE UP*.

Times: Did you search the *Atlanta Journal Constitution?*

Yes, but I haven't been able to find that statement.

Times: I've *heard* that statement—it was all over the place.

I know it was all over the place, except no one can find it and that's why I'm concerned. Now did you see the statement in the Atlanta Journal Constitution?

Times: Yeah....

[Note: No such direct quote from McKinney can be found in the *Atlanta Journal Constitution*.]

And did you confirm this with McKinney?

Times: Well, I worked with her office. The statement is from the floor of the House [of Representatives].... Right?

*So did you **check** the statement from the Floor of the House?*

Times: I mean I wouldn't have done the story.... Have you looked at House transcripts?

*Yes. Did **you** check that?*

Times: Of course.

You did check it?

[Note: No such McKinney statement can be found in the transcripts or other records of the House of Representatives.]

Times: I think you have to go back to the House transcripts.... I mean it was *all over the place* at the time.

Yes, this is one fact the *Times* reporter didn't fake: The McKinney "quote" was, indeed, all over the place: in the *Washington Post*, National Public Radio, and needless to say, all the other metropolitan dailies—everywhere but in Congresswoman McKinney's mouth.

Nor was it in the Congressional Record, nor in any recorded talk, nor on her Website, nor in any of her radio talks. Here's the Congresswoman's statement *from the record*:

"George Bush had no prior knowledge of the plan to attack the World Trade Center on September 11."

Oh.

■ ■ ■ ■ ■ ■ ■ ■ ■ ■

I should say *ex*-Congresswoman McKinney.

She was beaten in the August 2002 Democratic primary. More precisely, she was beaten to death, politically, by the fabricated quote.

_BLACK-OUT IN FLORIDA

Months before the 2000 presidential elections, the offices of Florida Governor Jeb Bush and Secretary of State Katherine Harris ordered the removal of 90,000 citizens from the voter rolls because they were criminals, evil-doers, *convicted felons*...and felons can't vote in Florida. There was one problem: 97 percent of those on the list were, in fact, innocent.

They weren't felons, but they were guilty...of being black. Over half the list contained names of non-whites. I'm not guessing: I have the list from out of the computers of Katherine Harris' office—and the "scrubbed" voter's race is listed with each name.

And that's how our President was elected: by illegally removing tens of thousands of legal African American voters before the race.

But you knew that...at least you did if you read the British papers—I reported this discovery for the *Guardian* of London. And I reported again on the nightly news. You saw that...if you live in Europe or Canada or South America.

In the USA, the story ran on page zero.

Well, let me correct that a bit. The *Washington Post* did run the story on the fake felon list that selected our President—even with a comment under my byline. I wrote the story within weeks of the election,

while Al Gore was still in the race. The *Post* courageously ran it...seven months after the election. The *New York Times* ran it...well, never, even after Katherine Harris confessed the scam to a Florida court after she and the state were successfully sued by the NAACP.

I HAVE THE LIST FROM OUT OF THE COMPUTERS OF KATHERINE HARRIS' OFFICE—AND THE "SCRUBBED" VOTER'S RACE IS LISTED WITH EACH NAME.

So, I can't say the *New York Times* always makes up the news. Sometimes the news just doesn't make it.

■ ■ ■ ■ ■ ■ ■ ■ ■ ■

At BBC Television, we had Florida's computer files and documents, marked "Confidential"—stone-cold evidence showing how the vote fix was deliberately crafted by Republican officials. Not a single major US paper asked for the documents—from the state nor from the BBC. Only one US Congressperson asked for the evidence and made it public: Cynthia McKinney of Atlanta.

That was her mistake.

The company that came up with the *faux* felon list that determined the presidency: a Republican-tied database company named "ChoicePoint," one of the richest, most powerful companies in Atlanta.

_FOXES ON THE CHICKEN TUBE

Before I started with the BBC in London, I took a one-day television training course with the Washington correspondent for Fox News.

We filmed Al Gore. Specifically, we filmed the eleven seconds of Gore's impromptu remarks...which we'd been given two hours earlier by his advance ladies. They wore blue suits.

The man for the Associated Press newswire wrote a lead paragraph of Gore's impromptu remarks one hour before Al walked in and said them. The network reporter copied down the AP lead line. I copied down the AP lead line.

After we got Al Gore's eleven seconds and footage of someone in the crowd saying, "Wow, Al Gore really talked different from the way Al Gore usually talks," we set up in front of the hotel where Al Gore talked. The important network reporter looked sternly into the camera and spoke in a very important voice. I squinted into the camera and spoke in a very important voice.

I can't remember what I said.

He can't remember what he said.

No one can remember what we said.

No one should.

_A PICTURE WORTH A THOUSAND LIES

The same week in June 2002 that NPR warned you that McKinney was dangerous and a wacko, another story caught my eye. There on page one of the *San Francisco Chronicle* was this Associated Press photo of demonstrators:

"TENS OF THOUSANDS OF VENEZUELANS OPPOSED TO PRESIDENT HUGO CHAVEZ..."

The caption let us know this South American potentate was a killer, an autocrat, and the people of his nation wanted him *out*. The caption continued: "[Venezuelans] marched Saturday to demand his resignation and punishment for those responsible for 17 deaths during a coup in April. 'Chavez leave now!' read a huge banner."

There was no actual story in the *Chronicle*—South America simply isn't worth wasting words on—just the photo and caption. But the *Chronicle* knew no story was needed. Venezuelans hated their terrible President, and all you needed was this photo to prove it.

And I could confirm the large protests. I'd recently returned from Caracas and watched 100,000 march against President Chavez. I'd filmed them for BBC Television London.

But I also filmed this: a larger march, easily over *200,000* Venezuelans marching *in support of* their President, Chavez.

That picture, of the larger pro-Chavez march, did not appear in a single US newspaper. The pro-Chavez marchers weren't worth a mention.

_"ALL THE NEWS THAT FITS THE PRINT"

By the next month, when the *New York Times* printed a photo of anti-Chavez marchers, they had metastasized. The *Times* reported that *600,000* had protested against Chavez.

Once again, the larger pro-Chavez demonstrations were, as they say in Latin America, "disappeared." I guess they didn't fit the print.

_GOLDFINGER

Did I mention to you that (ex-)Congresswoman McKinney is black? And not just any kind of black. She's the *uppity* kind of black.

What I mean by uppity is this:

After George Bush Senior left the White House, he became an advisor and lobbyist for a Canadian gold-mining company, Barrick Gold. Hey, a guy's got to work. But there were a couple of questions about Barrick, to say the least. For example, was Barrick's Congo gold mine funding both sides of a civil war and perpetuating that bloody conflict? Only one Congressperson demanded hearings on the matter.

You've guessed: Cynthia McKinney.

That was covered in the...well, it wasn't covered at all in the US press.

McKinney contacted me at the BBC. She asked if I'd heard of Barrick. Indeed, I had. Top human rights investigators had evidence that a mine that Barrick bought in 1999 had, in clearing their Tanzanian properties three years earlier, bulldozed mine shafts...burying about 50 miners alive.

I certainly knew Barrick: They'd sued the *Guardian* for daring to run a story I'd written about the allegations of the killings. Barrick never sued an American paper for daring to run the story, because no American paper dared.

The primary source for my story, an internationally famous lawyer named Tundu Lissu, was charged by the Tanzanian police with sedition, and arrested, for calling for an investigation. McKinney has been trying to save his life with an international campaign aimed at Barrick.

That was another of her mistakes.

_FITS IN PRINT

The *New York Times* wrote about McKinney that Atlanta's "prominent Black leaders—including Julian Bond, the chairman of the NAACP and former Mayor Maynard Jackson—who had supported Ms. McKinney in the past—distanced themselves from her this time."

Really? Atlanta has four internationally recognized black leaders. Martin Luther King III did not abandon McKinney. I checked with him. Nor did Julian Bond (the *Times* ran a rare retraction on their Website at Bond's request). But that left Atlanta's two other notables: Vernon Jordan and Andrew Young. Here, the *Times* had it right; no question that these two black faces of the Atlanta Establishment let McKinney twist slowly in the wind—because, the *Times* implied, of her alleged looniness.

But maybe there was another reason Young and Jordan let McKinney swing. Remember Barrick? George Bush's former gold-mining company, the target of McKinney's investigations? Did I mention to you that Andy Young and Vernon Jordan are both on Barrick's payroll? Well, I just did.

Did the *Times* mention it? I guess that wasn't fit to print.

_BROWN-OUT

Look at the *Chronicle*/AP photo of the anti-Chavez marchers in Venezuela. Note their color. White.

And not just any white. A creamy *rich* white.

I interviewed them and recorded in this order: a banker in high heels and push-up bra, an oil industry executive (same outfit), and a plantation owner who rode to Caracas in a silver Jaguar.

And the color of the *pro-Chavez* marchers? Dark brown. Brown and round as cola nuts—just like their hero, their President Chavez. They wore an unvarying uniform of jeans and T-shirts.

Let me explain.

For five centuries, Venezuela has been run by a minority of very white people, pure-blood descendants of the Spanish conquistadors. To most of the 80 percent of Venezuelans who are brown, Hugo Chavez is their Nelson Mandela, the man who will smash the economic and social apartheid that has kept the dark-skinned millions stacked in cardboard houses in the hills above Caracas while the white live in high-rise splendor in the city center.

Chavez, as one white Caracas reporter told me with a sneer, "gives them bricks and milk, and so they vote for him."

Why am I explaining the basics of Venezuela to you? If you watched BBC TV, or Canadian Broadcasting, you'd know all this stuff. But if you read the *New York Times*, you'll only know that President Chavez is an "autocrat," a "ruinous demagogue," and a "would-be dictator," who resigned when he recognized his unpopularity.

Odd phrasings—"dictator" and "autocrat"—to describe Chavez, who was elected by a landslide majority (56 percent) of the voters. Unlike *our* President.

_"RESIGNED"

On April 12, 2002, Chavez resigned as President of Venezuela. It said so, right there in the paper—*every* major newspaper in the USA, every single one. Apparently, to quote the *New York Times*, a typical story, Chavez recognized that he was unpopular, his time was up: "With yesterday's resignation of President Hugo Chavez, Venezuelan democracy is no longer threatened by a would-be dictator."

Problem was, the "resignation" story was a fabulous fib, a phantasmagoric fabrication. In fact, the President of Venezuela had been *kidnapped at gunpoint* and bundled off by helicopter from the presidential palace. He had not resigned; he *never* resigned; and one of his captors (who secretly supported Chavez) gave him a cellphone from which he called and confirmed to friends and family that he remained alive—and President. Working for the *Guardian* and the BBC, I was able within hours of the kidnapping to reach key government people in Venezuela to confirm that this factoid of the resignation was just hoo-doo nonsense.

But it was valuable nonsense to the US State Department. The *faux* "resignation" gave the new US-endorsed leaders the pretense of legitimacy—Chavez had resigned; this was a legal change of government, not a *coup d'etat*. (The Organization of American States bars recognition of governments who come to power through violence.)

Had the coup leaders not bungled their operation—the coup collapsed within 48 hours—or if they had murdered Chavez, we would never have known the truth. The US papers got it dead wrong—but how? Who was the source of this "resignation" lie? I asked a US reporter why American news media had reported this nonsense as stone fact without checking. The reply was that it came from a reliable source: "We got it from the State Department."

Oh.

_ELECTRONIC LOONY BIN

"He's crazy," shouts a protester about President Chavez on one broadcast. And if you watched the *60 Minutes* interview with Chavez, you saw a lengthy interview that had been cut to a few selective seconds, which, out of context, made Chavez look loony...crazy like McKinney.

In the old Soviet Union, dissidents were packed off to insane asylums to silence and discredit them. In our democracy we have a more subtle—and more effective—means of silencing and discrediting dissidents. Television, radio, and print press obligingly sequester enemies of the state in the media's madhouse. McKinney is "loony"; Chavez a mad "autocrat."

■ AND THE COLOR OF THE PRO-CHAVEZ MARCHERS? DARK BROWN.

It's the electronic loony bin. You no longer hear what they have to say because you've been told by images, by repetition, and you've already dismissed their words...if by some chance their words break through the television Berlin Wall.

Try it: Do a Google or Lexis search on the words *Chavez* and *autocrat*. Autocrat? True, there are hundreds of people held in detention without charges, but that's in George Bush's USA; in Venezuela there are none.

This is not about Venezuela but about the Virtual Venezuela, created for you by America's news wardens. The escape routes are guarded.

_THE PAPER OF RECORD

January 5, 2003, New York City. Picked up bagels on Delancey Street and the Sunday *Times*. Looks like that s.o.b. Chavez is at it again: Here was a big picture of a half-dozen people lying on the ground. The *Times* story read: "Protesters shielded themselves from tear gas during an anti-government rally on Friday in Caracas, Venezuela. In the 33rd day of a national strike, several protesters were shot."

That was it—the entire story of Venezuela for the Paper of Record.

Maybe size doesn't matter. But this does: Even this itty-bitty story is a steaming hot bag of mendacity. Yes, two people were shot dead—those in the *pro-Chavez* march.

I'd be wrong to say that every US paper repeated the *Times*-agenda. Elsewhere, you could see a photo of the big pro-Chavez march and a photo of the "Chavista" widow placed within an explanatory newswire story. Interestingly, the fuller and correct story ran in an outlet that's none too friendly to Chavez: *El Diario*, New York City's oldest Spanish-language newspaper.

Lesson: It's possible to get the news in the USA. But not in English.

■ ■ ■ ■ ■ ■ ■ ■ ■ ■

Friday, January 3, 2003. The *New York Times* ran a long "News Analysis: Venezuela Outlook." Four experts were quoted. For balance, two of them don't like Chavez, while the other two *despise* Chavez.

The *Times* reporter wrote that "the president says he will stay in power." *"In power"?* What a strange phrase for an elected official. Having myself spoken with Chavez, it did not sound like him. He indicated he would stay "in office"—quite a different inference than "in power." But then, the *Times*' phrasing isn't in quotes. That's because Chavez never said it.

■ ■ ■ ■ ■ ■ ■ ■ ■

I suppose it's my fault, McKinney's electronic lynching. Unlike other politicians, McKinney, who's earning her doctorate at Princeton's Fletcher School of Diplomacy, enjoys doing her own research, not relying on staff memos. She's long been a reader of my reports from Britain, including transcripts of BBC Television investigations. On November 6, 2001, BBC *Newsnight* ran this report with a follow-up story in the *Guardian* the next day:

Wednesday, November 7, 2001

Probes Before 11 September

Officials Told to 'Back Off' on Saudis Before September 11.

FBI and military intelligence officials in Washington say they were prevented for political reasons from carrying out full investigations into members of the Bin Laden family in the US before the terrorist attacks of September 11. US intelligence agencies have come under criticism for their wholesale failure to predict the catastrophe at the World Trade Centre. But some are complaining that their hands were tied.

FBI documents shown on BBC *Newsnight* last night and obtained by the *Guardian* show that they had earlier sought to investigate two of Osama bin Laden's relatives in Washington and a Muslim organisation, with which they were linked.

YES, TWO PEOPLE WERE SHOT DEAD—THOSE IN THE *PRO-CHAVEZ* MARCH.

And so on. There was not one word in there that Bush knew about the September 11 attacks in advance. It was about a horrific intelligence failure. This was the result, FBI and CIA/DIA (Defense Intelligence Agency) insiders told us at BBC, of a block placed on investigations

of Saudi Arabian financing of terror. We even showed on-screen a copy of a top-secret document passed to us by disgruntled FBI agents, directing that the agency would not investigate a "suspected terrorist organization" headed in the US by a member of the bin Laden family. The FBI knew about these guys before September 11 (with their office down the street from the hijackers' address).

The CIA also knew about a meeting in Paris, prior to September 11, involving a Saudi prince, arms dealers, and al Qaeda. Although the information was in hand, the investigation was stymied by Bush's intelligence chiefs. *This* is what McKinney wanted investigated.

Why were the Saudis, the bin Ladens (except Osama), and this organization (the World Assembly of Muslim Youth) off the investigation list prior to September 11, despite evidence that they were reasonable targets for inquiry? The BBC thought it worth asking; the *Guardian* thought it worth asking—and so did Congresswoman McKinney. Why no pre-September 11 investigations of these characters?

And what was the reason for the block? According to the experts we broadcast on British television, it was the Bush Administration's fanatic desire to protect their relations with Saudi Arabia—a deadly policy prejudice which, according to the respected Center for Public Integrity of Washington, DC, seems influenced by the Bush family ties, and Republican donors' ties, to Saudi royalty. McKinney, a member of the House Foreign Relations Committee, thought the BBC/*Guardian*/*Observer* investigation worth a follow-up Congressional review.

According to NPR, her "loony" statement was made on the radio news show *Counterspin*. (Not incidentally, *Counterspin* is produced by an NPR competitor, the nonprofit Pacifica Radio Network.) I have the transcript; it's on the Web. Her charge that Bush knew about the September 11 attacks in advance and deliberately covered it up can't be found.

What can be read is her call for a follow-up on the revelations from the BBC and *USA Today* on the information about a growing terror threat ignored by Bush...and whether the policy response—war, war, war—was protecting America or simply enriching Bush's big arms industry donors and business partners. Fair questions. But asking them is dangerous...to one's political career.

■ ■ ■ ■ ■ ■ ■ ■ ■

The BBC report which got McKinney in hot water mentioned the Bush Administration's reluctance to investigate associates of the World Assembly of Muslim Youth (WAMY), which the FBI secret document termed "a suspected terrorist organization." They may be. They may not be. McKinney's question was only, Why no investigation?

Just after McKinney's defeat, the courier of Osama bin Laden's latest alleged taped threat against the US was busted in Africa: He was on the staff of WAMY. Shortly thereafter, Prince Abdullah, the Saudi dictator, invited WAMY leaders to his palace and told them, "There is no extremism in the defending of the faith."

So if you listen to US radio and read US papers, you are told this: Abdullah's protector and godfather, George W. Bush, is sane and patriotic, and McKinney, who wants to investigate these guys, is loony and a traitor. Got it?

■ ■ ■ ■ ■ ■ ■ ■ ■

In 2002, the BBC and the *Guardian* teams got an award from the California State University School of Journalism for our Bush/bin Laden story, the one that buried McKinney, as one of the ten most important stories of the year *censored in the US press.* Thanks a lot. Unfortunately, the journalism school does not give out little trophies to the Project Censored winners. I suggest they make one up, like for the Oscars, except ours would be little gold-plated replicas of Dan Rather...bound, gagged, and blind-folded.

> "NOW IT IS THAT FEAR THAT KEEPS JOURNALISTS FROM ASKING THE TOUGHEST OF THE TOUGH QUESTIONS, AND TO CONTINUE TO BORE IN ON THE TOUGH QUESTIONS SO OFTEN." — DAN RATHER

_"TELL ME WHERE TO GET IN LINE"

Dan Rather was on my show—that is, he was interviewed by one of my colleagues on BBC's *Newsnight.* This is the program that ran the bin Laden story at the top of the nightly news, blacked out in the USA.

Dan Rather said:

What is going on to a very large extent, I'm sorry to say, is a belief that the public doesn't need to know, limiting access, limiting information to cover the backsides of those who are in charge of the war. It's extremely dangerous and cannot and should not be accepted, and I'm sorry to say that up to and including this moment of this interview, that overwhelmingly it has been accepted by the American people. And the current Administration revels in that, they relish and take refuge in that.

And Dan Rather said:

It is an obscene comparison—you know, I am not sure I like it—but you know there was a time in South Africa that people would put flaming tires around people's necks if they dissented. And in some ways the fear is that you will be neck-laced here, you will have a flaming tire of lack of patriotism put around your neck. Now it is that fear that keeps journalists from asking the toughest of the tough questions, and to continue to bore in on the tough questions so often. And again, I am humbled to say, I do not except myself from this criticism.

And finally Dan said:

And one finds one's self saying, "I know the right question, but you know what—this is not exactly the right time to ask it."

Of course, Dan said all these things to a British audience. Back in the USA, Dan told America:

George Bush is the President. He makes the decisions. He wants me to line up, just tell me where.

Dan Rather: Profile in courage.

_HAIRPIECE: THE TED KOPPEL STORY

Let's not pick on Dan. Hell, he's one of the *better* ones.

Instead, let's work on Ted Koppel, a man with a reputation for reporting many important stories, though no one can recall any of them.

Yet, one of *Nightline*'s stories I did find unforgettable. It was a kind of follow-up to the BBC elections story. Our BBC team discovered that of the 180,000 votes never counted in the Florida 2000 presidential race, a sickeningly disproportionate number came from black counties. In Gadsden County, where more than half the population is black, *one in eight ballots* was marked "spoiled" and, thus, never counted.

Koppel's team got on the case, flying down to Florida to find out why thousands of black votes were never counted. They talked to experts, they talked to important white people, and Koppel reported this: Many Blacks are new to voting and, with limited education, have a difficult time with marking the sophisticated ballots. In other words, ABC concluded, *African Americans are too fucking dumb to figure out how to vote.*

Hey, if true, then you have to report it. But it wasn't. It was a fib, a tall tale, made-for-TV mendacity, polite liberal electronic cross-burning intellectual eugenics.

Here's the real scoop: All races of voters make errors on paper ballots. But in white counties like Leon (Tallahassee), if you make a stray mark or other error, *the vote machine rejects your ballot, and you get another ballot to vote again*. But in black counties like Gadsden, you make a mistake and the machine *quietly accepts and voids your ballot*.

In other words, it wasn't that African Americans are too dumb to vote but that European American reporters are too dumb to ask, too lazy to bother, too gutless to tell officialdom to stop lying into the cameras.

■ ■ ■ ■ ■ ■ ■ ■ ■

So they lied to you about McKinney; they lied to you about Venezuela; they lied to you about September 11; they lied to you about the election. But I don't want you to get the wrong impression with these examples: They lied to you about a whole lot more. And they lied to you when they said they weren't lying.

_"90 SECONDS"

Back in the edit room with Mr. Washington Network TV Reporter, we were ready to bake the cake, the Gore story. We had all the ingredients.

"Take out your watch," said the Fox man.

"You get 90 seconds," he said. "That's what you get. You got an intro, 40 seconds of narration, two sound bites, and end with a stand-up to camera."

I repeated, "Forty seconds narrate, two sound bites, stand-up."

He said, "Two sound bites and a stand-up. Every story. Every time."

He said, "What do you think?"

I said, "I think I'm leaving the country."

Oliver Shykles, Fredda Weinberg, Ina Howard, and Phil Tanfield contributed research for this report.

WATERGATE REDUX
THE *WASHINGTON POST* AND THE PARTY LINE
JIM HOUGAN

It's like that mob-guy on *The Sopranos* said, quoting Al Pacino's character in *The Godfather, Part III*: "Just when I thought I was out, they *pulllll* me back in!"

More than 20 years ago, I set out to write an article for *Harper's Magazine* about a Washington private-eye who'd fallen upon hard times. Once the chief investigator for the House Committee on Un-American Activities, Lou Russell had been fired for soliciting "loans" from witnesses. Cut loose from the inner sanctum of the Cold War, he turned to booze and call-girls, working freelance for whomever would hire him.

All in all, it would have been an interesting piece about the capital, with lots of noirish details. But there was a problem with the story. Russell turned out to be a little too interesting. It was rumored that he'd gone to work for Watergate burglar James McCord in 1971, and that he was at the Watergate when five spooks were arrested inside the headquarters of the Democratic National Committee.

If true, the rumors would have turned my profile into a hard-news story, an investigative piece that would have required a lot more work than I wanted to do. But not to worry, I told myself. I was sure I could dispel the rumors with a little work over the course of a weekend.

Five years later, I'd written a "revisionist" history of the Watergate affair, laying waste to the received version of the story (as promulgated by the *Washington Post*).[1] Accordingly, I now find that I've become a part of the story in a way that I never intended.

Decades after setting out to write an article about a washed-up private-eye, a steady trickle of unwanted email still finds its way to my Yahoo! mailbox, cluing me in to the release of new transcripts and documents made public under the Freedom of Information Act (FOIA). Forever a lint-trap for conspiracy theories linking Watergate to the CIA, I am routinely alerted to Internet colloquies that are as arcane as they are ferocious and *en point*: Was James McCord a double-agent—or just a saboteur? As interesting as these arguments can often be, it is difficult not to be annoyed by the quinquennial calls from television hacks seeking to commemorate the affair's anniversary by reprising its contradictions with a skeptic.

I suppose I should be grateful they still care. But that's not where it ends. Where it ends is in court, with me having to give evidence in someone else's defamation suit.

That's what happened in 2001 when a Mississippi schoolmarm sued Watergate burglar G. Gordon Liddy. To my family's chagrin (and my own sense of wonder), I found myself testifying in the right-wing Liddy's behalf. And though that testimony went well, I and a great many others were left with a sense of astonishment when, soon after the verdict came in, the *Washington Post* published an editorial, attacking the jury for having the temerity to think for itself.

At issue was the jury's 7-2 vote in a defamation action brought by Ida "Maxie" Wells. Instigated by John Dean's attorneys in a related matter, the suit accused Liddy of slandering Wells during the questions-and-answers portion of a speech he'd given at James Madison University. In the opinion of the jurors, Liddy's revisionist view of the Watergate break-in was sufficiently plausible as to deserve the protections given to free speech. The judge agreed, dismissing the suit with the assertion that "no 'reasonable jury' could have found in favor of the plaintiff," Maxie Wells.[2]

> IN THE OPINION OF THE JURORS, LIDDY'S REVISIONIST VIEW OF THE WATERGATE BREAK-IN WAS SUFFICIENTLY PLAUSIBLE AS TO DESERVE THE PROTECTIONS GIVEN TO FREE SPEECH.

Stung by the verdict, the *Washington Post* declared:

Courts are a capricious venue for arguments about history. Sometimes, as when a British court last year resoundingly rejected the Holocaust denial of "historian" David Irving, litigation can help protect established history from those who would maliciously rewrite it. But conspiracy theorizing generally is better addressed in the public arena by rigorous confrontation with facts. That's true both out of respect for freedom of speech—even wrong-headed speech—and because historical truth does not always fare so well in court. A jury in Tennessee in 1999 embraced the looniest of conspiracy theories concerning the assassination of Martin Luther King Jr. And this week, in a federal court in Baltimore, the commonly understood and well-founded history of the Watergate scandal took a hit as well.

The forum was the defamation case of G. Gordon Liddy... Mr. Liddy has argued that the burglary was not an attempt to collect political intelligence on President Nixon's enemies, but an effort masterminded by then-White House counsel John Dean to steal pictures of prostitutes—including Mr. Dean's then-girlfriend and current wife—from the desk of a secretary at the Democratic headquarters. The secretary...is now a community college teacher in Louisiana and was understandably offended by the implication that she was somehow involved in a call-girl ring. She sued Mr. Liddy, and the battle has dragged on for four years.

The jury failed to reach a unanimous verdict, but it split overwhelmingly in favor of Mr. Liddy; the majority of jurors felt that Ms. Wells' lawyers had failed to proved his theory wrong. They found this in spite of the fact that Mr. Liddy relies, for his theory, on a disbarred attorney with a history of mental illness. The call-girl theory "is possible," one juror [said]... "It sure makes me more curious." "We'll never know" what happened, said another.

The danger of such outcomes as this one is that this sort of thinking spreads. For whether or not Mr. Liddy's comments legally defamed Ms. Wells, we do know what happened at Watergate—and it had nothing to do with prostitutes.[3]

The *Post*'s alarm at "this sort of thinking" was compounded more than a year later, when the judge's verdict was overturned on appeal. A new trial was ordered.

In *Wells v. Liddy* redux, Wells sought to bolster her case with the testimony of Sam Dash, chief counsel of the Senate Select Committee on Presidential Campaign Activities in 1973.[4] Having led the Senate's investigation of the Watergate affair, Dash ought to have been an impressive witness. But under cross-examination from Liddy's very astute attorneys, John Williams and Kerrie Hook, the Senate's chief investigator seemed pompous and strangely unprepared—characteristics he shared with Wells' own attorney, David Dorsen (himself a former deputy of Dash's). After listening to the witnesses, the jury returned a verdict in Liddy's behalf. This time, the jury was unanimous.

There were no further appeals and no more editorials. The *Post* buried the verdict on an inside page of the Metro section and turned its attention to other matters.

But the "established history" of the Watergate affair had suffered a grievous blow. And this, because one jury after another did what the *Post* prescribed, but which the *Post* itself has never done in 30 years: They confronted the facts in a rigorous way.

One of the most crucial of those facts was a key to Maxie Wells' desk, which Det. Carl Shoffler grabbed from Eugenio Martinez, a veteran CIA operative and one of the Watergate burglars. Though Shoffler was subsequently eulogized by the *Post* as "a police legend," he didn't grasp the significance of the key until long after the Watergate arrests—when he realized that it spoke volumes about

the purpose of the break-in.

That subject—*Why did they pick the Democratic National Committee headquarters (DNC) as a target?*—has been debated for decades, though one might not know it reading the *Washington Post*. Most accounts of the affair suppose that the break-ins (there were two successful efforts, one at the end of May 1972, another on June 17) were mounted to obtain "political intelligence." James McCord, the former CIA officer who led "the Cubans" into the DNC, told the Senate that DNC Chairman Larry O'Brien was the target. Accordingly, McCord installed a bug in O'Brien's office. Or so he *said*.

Howard Hunt and his Cuban cohort offered an entirely different reason for the break-in. According to them, they were sent into the DNC to find evidence of illegal campaign contributions from Fidel Castro.

In reality, neither explanation is supported by the evidence. If the burglars were looking for financial data, they certainly chose some strange places to search. DNC Treasurer Robert Strauss' office was untouched, as were the offices of the DNC's Comptroller. As for the bug in Larry O'Brien's office—it was never found, despite repeated and even desperate searches by the FBI and the telephone company.

Of course, even if there had been a bug, it wouldn't have yielded anything. O'Brien's office was part of an interior suite at the DNC and, as such, it was shielded from McCord's "listening post" in the Howard Johnson's motel across the street. Moreover, as Liddy himself pointed out, the subject of the reputed surveillance wasn't even in Washington. Nor was he expected to return anytime soon. More than a month before the break-in, the DNC's Chairman had moved to Florida, where the Democratic Convention was to be held.

Not that it mattered. In 1973, the burglars' motives weren't of much interest to anyone. Their trial was over, and the story had moved on. The Senate Watergate Committee was a political creation. It sought to establish responsibility for the break-ins and to deconstruct the cover-up. Accordingly, the Committee's attention was focused on the culpability of higher-ups in the Nixon White House and, in particular, in the Oval Office. Everything else was just a detail.

> THAT SUBJECT—*WHY DID THEY PICK THE DEMOCRATIC NATIONAL COMMITTEE HEADQUARTERS (DNC) AS A TARGET?*—HAS BEEN DEBATED FOR DECADES, THOUGH ONE MIGHT NOT KNOW IT READING THE *WASHINGTON POST*.

Things might have been different, of course, had Maxie Wells been more candid in her executive session testimony before the Watergate Committee. Instead, she neglected to mention that the FBI had questioned her about the key to her desk and the circumstances under which the key had been found. According to Howard Liebengood, who served as the Committee's minority counsel, the Committee's investigation might have taken a dramatic turn if he had learned of the key's existence and of Wells' interview with the FBI.

But he did not.[5]

The issue of the burglary's purpose was even raised in *Blind Ambition*, the John Dean memoir ghost-written by the well-regarded historian Taylor Branch. In that book, we're told that Dean raised the issue with Charles Colson in 1974, when both of them were doing time in federal prison:

> "Chuck, why do you figure Liddy bugged the DNC instead of the Democratic candidates? It doesn't make much sense. I sat in [Attorney General John] Mitchell's office when Liddy gave us his show, and he only mentioned Larry O'Brien in passing as a target....

> "It looks suspicious to me.... [I]t's incredible. Millions of dollars have been spent investigating Watergate. A President has been forced out of office. Dozens of lives have been ruined. We're sitting in the can. And still nobody can explain why they bugged the place to begin with."[6]

Though Dean subsequently repudiated his own memoir,[7] the anecdote makes a good point. The Watergate affair can only remain a mystery so long as the break-in's purpose remains hidden.

Fortunately, we know today what the Senate Watergate Committee did not: that Detective Shoffler wrested a key from one of the burglars. As much as a confession, that key is *prima facie* evidence of the break-in's purpose. Clearly, the burglars were after the contents of whatever it was that the key unlocked.

The FBI seems to have understood this because the Bureau's agents went from office to office after the arrests, trying the key on every desk until they found the one that it fit. This was Maxie Wells' desk, and Shoffler, for one, wasn't surprised. When he took the key from Martinez, Shoffler said, photographic equipment was sitting on that same desk.

But what was in it? What did the burglars hope to find?

It was precisely this question that was so embarrassing to Wells. Through her suit against Liddy, Wells sought to suppress discussion of the key because, she said, it unfairly implicated her in allegations about a call-girl ring.

A call-girl ring?

Well, yes. Although the *Post* prefers to ignore any and all evidence on the matter, links between call-girls and the DNC—and, therefore, between call-girls and the Watergate affair—have been rumored or alleged for years. The connection first surfaced in a book by a Pulitzer Prize-winning *New York Times* reporter, J. Anthony Lukas. According to Lukas, secretaries at the DNC used a telephone in the office of Wells' boss, Spencer Oliver, Jr., to make private calls. They did this because Oliver's office was often empty—he traveled a lot—and his telephone was thought to be among the most private in the Democrats' headquarters.[8] (In fact, Oliver had two phones, one of which was a private line that did not go through the DNC switchboard.)

"They would say, 'We can talk; I'm on Spencer Oliver's phone,'" Lukas wrote. Quoting Alfred Baldwin, who eavesdropped on these conversations at the direction of James McCord, Lukas reported: "Some of the conversations were 'explicitly intimate.'" Baldwin was even more specific in a deposition that he later gave. According to the former FBI agent, many of the telephone conversations involved dinner arrangements with "sex to follow." And while he never heard "prices" being discussed, Baldwin testified, he guessed that "eight out of ten" people would have thought the calls involved prostitution.

But he himself did not. As an ex-FBI agent, Baldwin knew that for prostitution to occur, there has to be a promise of money. But money was never discussed, Baldwin said, or at least not in his hearing. And since McCord told him that he was eavesdropping on telephone conversations emanating from the DNC, Baldwin assumed that the women must be amateurs. As incredible as it seems, it did not occur to him that McCord might have lied to him about the bug's location. To Baldwin, it was entirely plausible, or at least possible, that one secretary after another would go to a private telephone to engage her boyfriend in a conversation that was "extremely personal, intimate, and potentially embarrassing."[9]

The more sophisticated Anthony Lukas was skeptical of the idea. As he reported, "So spicy were some of the conversations on the phone that they have given rise to unconfirmed reports that the telephone was being used for some sort of call-girl service catering to congressmen and other prominent Washingtonians."[10]

The same rumors were overheard by others, including the DNC's Robert Strauss. In a 1996 deposition, Strauss testified that he recalled stories about "some of the state chairmen [who] would come into [Oliver's] office and use the phone to make dates..." Strauss added that "in connection with the use of the telephones, some of the calls...could have been embarrassing to some of the people who made them."

The DNC's Treasurer was even more specific in a 1996 interview with John Mitchell's biographer, a White House correspondent named James Rosen. As Rosen testified in *Wells v. Liddy* (I), Strauss told him, "Democrats in from out of town for a night would want to be entertained.... 'It wasn't any organized thing, but I could have made the call, that lady could have made the call'—it was a reference to Maxie Wells in the context of the interview—'and these people were willing to pay for sex.' Those were his exact words."[11]

"[I]t was a reference to Maxie Wells..." Indeed, it was. According to Sally Harmony, who typed the Gemstone reports for Gordon Liddy in 1972, "There were two names" that were particularly memorable from the reports: "Spencer Oliver and another name, given as 'Maxie.'"[12]

> FORTUNATELY, WE KNOW TODAY WHAT THE SENATE WATERGATE COMMITTEE DID NOT: THAT DETECTIVE SHOFFLER WRESTED A KEY FROM ONE OF THE BURGLARS.

In an interview with Liddy's attorneys, DNC secretary Barbara Kennedy Rhoden acknowledged that she, too, had overheard whispers about prostitution and the DNC. "One of the rumors was that Spencer Oliver and Maxie Wells were involved in some type of underhanded business, and that Spencer Oliver was running a call girl operation."[13] Asked if Rhoden had said "it was likely that Spencer Oliver and Maxie Wells were running a call-girl operation," Rhoden testified: "I might have said that..." But, she added, "I have no knowledge that they were."[14]

That a relationship may have existed between a call-girl service and the DNC was dissed and dismissed by Wells and her attorneys, and by Spencer Oliver and *his* attorneys—just as it was by the *Washington Post*. According to them, the only evidence of such a relationship is the testimony of Phillip Bailley, a disbarred lawyer with a history of mental illness.

But that isn't true. One man who knew a lot about the relationship between call-girls and the DNC was the private-eye that I mentioned earlier: Lou Russell. A former FBI "apprehensions agent," Russell was a tough-guy who knew a lot about electronic eavesdropping. And even more about whores.

THE NAMES IN BAILLEY'S ADDRESS BOOKS INCLUDED THE SECRETARIES AND WIVES OF SOME OF WASHINGTON'S MOST PROMINENT MEN—AS WELL AS THE NAMES OF THE JOHNS THEY SERVICED.

In the months leading up to the Watergate break-ins, Russell was working for James McCord and moonlighting for Bud Fensterwald, a Washington lawyer who'd founded the Committee to Investigate Assassinations. In the evenings, Russell hung out with call-girls at the Columbia Plaza Apartments, barely a block from the Watergate. According to Fensterwald and two of his employees, Russell told them he was tape-recording telephone conversations between the prostitutes and their clients at the DNC. The women didn't mind, and the taping was a source of amusement to Russell, who seems to have regaled anyone who'd listen with anecdotes about the calls.[15]

Not that Democrats were the only ones to avail themselves of the pleasures to be taken at the Columbia Plaza. Nixon biographer Anthony Summers quotes a longtime Nixon aide as saying that Nick Ruwe, then Deputy Chief of the Office of Protocol and himself a longtime Nixon aide, "was always using those call girls at the place next to the DNC."[16] Ron Walker, Nixon's top advance man, was a second source. According to Walker, he knew of the brothel next to the DNC because "I had colleagues that used call girl rings."[17]

In April 1972, the seamy side of Washington was exposed when FBI agents raided the office and home of the Phil Bailley, a Washington defense attorney whose clientele included prostitutes. Coded address books, photographs, and sexual paraphernalia were seized, and what began as a simple violation of the Mann Act metamorphosed into a grand-jury investigation with ramifications throughout the capital.

Assistant US Attorney John Rudy was placed in charge of the investigation. Soon, Rudy found himself looking into the Columbia Plaza call-girl ring and its connections to the DNC—where a secretary was suspected of arranging liaisons.

It was at about this time that Lou Russell appeared in Rudy's office. According to Rudy, Russell tried to divert his attention from the Columbia Plaza operation to another one that serviced lawyers and judges on the other side of town.

But it didn't work. On June 9, Bailley was indicted on 22 felony counts, including charges of blackmail, racketeering, procuring, and pandering. That same afternoon, the *Washington Star* published a front-page story headlined, "Capitol Hill Call-Girl Ring." According to the article:

The FBI here has uncovered a high-priced call girl ring allegedly headed by a Washington attorney and staffed by secretaries and office workers from Capitol Hill and involving at least one White House secretary, sources said today.

The article did not go unnoticed on Pennsylvania Avenue. Within an hour of its publication, Bailley's prosecutor received a telephone call from the President's counsel John Dean, ordering him to the White House. "He wanted me to bring 'all' the evidence but, mostly, what I brought were Bailley's address books," Rudy recalled. "Dean said he wanted to check the names of the people involved, to see if any of them worked for the President."[18]

It was, after all, a presidential election year, and the names in Bailley's address books included the secretaries and wives of some of Washington's most prominent men—as well as the names of the johns they serviced.

At first, Dean wanted Rudy to leave the address books with him, but Rudy demurred, pointing out that the books were evidence. As a compromise, Dean's secretary was permitted to photocopy the books, while Rudy and Dean discussed the case. When the secretary returned, Dean went through the copies page by page, circling names with a Parker pen.[19]

It wasn't the first time that Dean had shown an interest in such matters. As Dean recounts in *Blind Ambition,* he'd dispatched a White House investigator to New York some months before. The sleuth was to look into a call-girl ring run by a madam named Xaviera Hollander.[20] Like the Bailley case, the Hollander investigation was generating headlines. One, in the *New York Times*, blared:

POSSIBLE BLACKMAIL OF NIXON OFFICIALS CHECKED HERE

The story began:

At least two high-ranking officials in the Nixon administration are among the people the Manhattan District Attorney's Office intends to question about the possibility that they were blackmailed because of their association with an East Side brothel.

■ ■ ■ ■ ■ ■ ■ ■ ■ ■

Dean's meeting with John Rudy occurred on a Friday. On the following Monday, Jeb Magruder summoned Liddy to his office and told him that he had to break into the DNC a second time. The bugging device that James McCord had supposedly placed on Larry O'Brien's telephone had yet to work, and a second bug was generating little or nothing of political value.

Magruder told Liddy that he wanted the bug in O'Brien's office repaired, and even more important, he wanted to know if O'Brien was sitting on information that could damage the Nixon re-election campaign. It wasn't put in so many words, but that was Liddy's understanding of the brief that he'd been given.

If the purpose of the break-in was somewhat vague, the provenance of the order was even more so. Magruder was former Attorney General John Mitchell's deputy at the Committee to Re-Elect the President (CRP). Accordingly, Liddy *assumed* that Magruder was conveying an order from Mitchell, his boss. But Mitchell always denied that, and Magruder has given conflicting accounts. At first, young Jeb claimed that Liddy had acted on his own.[21] Later, he insisted that the order was Mitchell's. Even more recently, he told an interviewer (on tape) that it was John Dean who ordered the break-in.[22]

Whatever its purpose, the burglary took place in the early morning hours of June 17. McCord and four of his accomplices had not been inside the DNC for more than a few minutes when the police arrested them. Baldwin watched the arrests unfold from his seventh-floor aerie in the motel across the street, while Hunt and Liddy packed their bags and fled from the Watergate Hotel.

In the weeks that followed, John Rudy's investigation suddenly came a cropper. In the aftermath of the Watergate arrests, Rudy's probe of links between the Columbia Plaza call-girl ring and the DNC might appear to be politically motivated. Worried about that perception, Rudy's boss, US Attorney Harold Titus, told him to ice it.

And so he did.

Bailley was remanded to St. Elizabeth's Hospital to undergo psychiatric tests. This was an unwelcome and surprising development, inasmuch as he had been practicing law before that same court only a few weeks earlier. Eventually, he was certified sane and encouraged to plead guilty to a single felony. When he did, he was bundled off to a federal prison in Connecticut where, ironically, he served on the Inmates Committee with Howard Hunt and other Watergaters. The case-file, thick with interviews and evidence, was sealed and, soon afterwards, "lost."

Which was unfortunate because, a few doors down the hall, others in the US Attorney's office were putting together a case in which sexual blackmail was said to be the central motive in the Watergate break-in. Assistant US Attorney Earl Silbert was convinced that "Hunt was trying to blackmail Spencer [Oliver]."[23] Charles Morgan, who represented Wells and Oliver at the burglars' trial in early 1973, quoted Silbert on the subject in an effort to block any testimony about the contents of the conversations that Baldwin overheard. According to Morgan, Silbert told him over lunch in December 1972 that "Hunt was trying to blackmail Spencer, and I'm going to prove it."[24] Wells and Oliver didn't want to go there. Taking a page from John Dean's book, Morgan railed that "Mr. Silbert's blackmail motive had been woven

THE CASE-FILE, THICK WITH INTERVIEWS AND EVIDENCE, WAS SEALED AND, SOON AFTERWARDS, "LOST."

from whole cloth."[25] For that reason, he asked the court to bar any testimony about the conversations Baldwin overheard.

Judge John Sirica demurred, but Morgan's motion was granted on appeal.

■ ■ ■ ■ ■ ■ ■ ■ ■ ■

But what of Bailley? When I interviewed him in the early 1980s, he seemed normal enough: well-dressed, articulate, and intelligent, if bitter about the events that led to his downfall. In particular, he was curious to know what I knew about Watergate and how it related to him. I insisted he "go first," and so he did.

Bailley told me that he had been having an affair with a call-girl at the Columbia Plaza Apartments, a woman who used the alias "Cathy Dieter." She prevailed upon him to establish a liaison arrangement with the DNC. A hard-partying young Dem who knew a number of workers at the DNC, Bailley told me that one of his acquaintances was a secretary in Spencer Oliver's office. With her help, he said, the liaison arrangement was established. Here's how it worked:

According to Bailley, if a visitor to the DNC wanted companionship for the evening, the secretary would show the visitor photographs that she kept in her desk. If the man was interested, Bailley continued, he'd be sent into Spencer Oliver's office to await a telephone call. When the phone rang for the first time, he was not to answer it. A minute later, it would ring again and, on this occasion, he *was* to answer it. The caller would be the woman (or one of the women) whose picture the visitor had just seen. Knowing that the woman was a call-girl across the street, the visitor would make whatever arrangements he pleased.

As I testified in Wells' defamation suit, Bailley told me that the secretary was Maxie Wells. Wells denies that, as she always has, just as she denies keeping pictures of call-girls in her desk.

And one would like to believe her. But a letter that Wells wrote to a friend in September 1972, just after she'd been told that it was her telephone that had been tapped, gives us reason to wonder. In that letter, Wells reported that she'd "developed a crisis":

[T]he Republicans are going to try to discredit Demo. witnesses on moral grounds. They've got the makings for a good scandal in my case…. The FBI has a file on me a mile long now,…& I may have to bare (or bear) all in court, which…isn't so terrible—but I am really afraid the press will take off & run with all of this when they smell gossip. The other records will be private, & I don't think I've broken any laws, but you can understand my nerves…. If you talk to God in the next few days remind him about your friend who needs help keeping her nose clean.

Why would Wells, who left the DNC soon after the Watergate arrests, think that the Republicans had "the makings of a good scandal in my case"? What had she done that made her think that she might have broken the law? And why would the

FBI have a file on her, let alone a file that was "a mile long"? And what are "the other records" that seemed to worry her so much?

Clearly, Wells was panicked.

■ ■ ■ ■ ■ ■ ■ ■ ■ ■

And what about "Cathy Dieter," Phil Bailley's pal at the Columbia Plaza? Who was she?

According to Gordon Liddy and Carl Shoffler, Dieter's real name was Heidi Rikan. Liddy testified that he learned this from a seemingly authoritative source: Walter "Buster" Riggin, a sometime pimp and associate of Joe Nesline, himself a notorious organized-crime figure in the Washington area.

Formerly a stripper at a seedy Washington nightclub called the Blue Mirror, the late Erica "Heidi" Rikan was a friend of Nesline's and, more to the point, of John Dean and his then-fiancée, later wife, Maureen. Indeed, Rikan's photograph appears in the memoir that "Mo" wrote about Watergate.[26]

> ACCORDING TO BAILLEY, IF A VISITOR TO THE DNC WANTED COMPANIONSHIP FOR THE EVENING, THE SECRETARY WOULD SHOW THE VISITOR PHOTO-GRAPHS THAT SHE KEPT IN HER DESK.

While admitting their friendship with Rikan, the Deans deny that she ran a call-girl ring or that she used "Cathy Dieter" as an alias. Beyond Buster Riggin's assertion to Liddy, evidence on the issue is slim or ambiguous. One writer who attempted to verify the identification is Anthony Summers. As the Irish investigative reporter wrote in his massive biography of President Nixon:

> Before her death in 1990, Rikan said in a conversation with her maid that she had once been a call girl. Explaining that a call girl was "a lady that meets men, and men pay them"—the maid had grown up in the country and knew nothing of big-city sins—she added, tantalizingly: "I was a call girl at the White House."[27]

This would appear to confirm assertions that Rikan was a prostitute. But Summers undercuts the confirmation by reporting in that same book—strangely, and in a footnote—that he "found no evidence" of Rikan working as a call-girl.[28]

■ ■ ■ ■ ■ ■ ■ ■ ■ ■

In the litigation with John Dean and Maxie Wells, Liddy took the position that a secret agenda was at work in the break-ins, and that this agenda was unknown to him at the time that the break-ins occurred. Here's how the Fourth Circuit Court of Appeals summarized the issue:

> Liddy stated that the burglars' objective during the Watergate break-in was to determine whether the Democrats possessed information embarrassing to John Dean. More specifically, Liddy asserted that the

burglars were seeking a compromising photograph of Dean's fiancé that was located in Wells' desk among several photographs that were used to offer prostitution services to out-of-town guests.[29]

Dean and his wife challenged Liddy's account, which was first reported in *Silent Coup*—whose authors (among many others) the Deans sued.[30] While this writer does not find John Dean's account of his own role in the affair to be credible, neither does he think it likely that anyone would break into the DNC to retrieve a picture of his girlfriend, assuming that such a picture existed and that it was somehow "compromising." What would—what *could*—anyone do with such a photograph?

One question leads to another. If the instigator of the break-in (whether Dean, Magruder, or someone else) was not after pictures in Maxie Wells' desk, what *was* he after? The matter is necessarily speculative, but it seems useful to point out that men who make dates with call-girls seldom use their real names. Instead, they use handles like "Candyman" or resort to aliases like "George Washington." (One john at the Columbia Plaza—almost certainly a Democrat—used "Richard Nixon" as a *nom de guerre*.)[31] For that reason, the only person in a position to know who was dating whom was the person facilitating the liaisons. Whether that person kept a record of such contacts is unknown. But the instigator of the break-in may have suspected that she did. It seems reasonable, then, to suppose that the burglars may have been looking for a kind of calendar, or log, rather than a handful of dirty pictures that would be of little use to anyone.[32]

■ ■ ■ ■ ■ ■ ■ ■ ■ ■

The key to Maxie Wells' desk is obviously central to any "rigorous consideration" of the facts pertaining to Watergate. But it isn't the only important fact that the *Washington Post* and other media have done their best to ignore. A second and equally fundamental one is this: The only bugging device ever recovered from the headquarters of the DNC was likened to a broken "toy" by the FBI, whose agents seemed to believe that the device had been planted in order that it could be found. And it *was* found, but not until nearly three months after the Watergate arrests, and a few days after Baldwin went public with his testimony about eavesdropping on the DNC.

But what did it all mean? Did James McCord lie about bugging Larry O'Brien and Spencer Oliver? And if so, why? And if Alfred Baldwin wasn't listening to telephone conversations emanating from the DNC, what *was* he listening to?

These were the questions on Earl Silbert's mind as he prepared his case against the burglars in the summer of 1972. They were questions of which the public knew nothing. In secret correspondence with the Justice Department and the FBI, Silbert railed against the Bureau's inability to locate a listening device inside the DNC. The Bureau replied, coolly, that while it recognized the difficulties this presented for Silbert's case, it was a matter of fact. The DNC was clean.

Because the burglars ultimately pleaded guilty, obviating a need for a trial at which the evidence would be presented and contested, the discrepancy never came to the public's attention. Indeed, David Dorsen, who represented Wells in her defamation suit and Dean in *his,* seemed stunned by the information when it came out on cross-examination in Liddy's trial. If this was true, Dorsen asked, what did it mean? Who was bugged?

I suggested that there were only two possibilities: Either the bugs were removed from the DNC prior to the break-in on June 17—or Baldwin was listening to telephone conversations emanating from a bugging device at another location. Another location? What location? Dorsen wondered. The most likely place, I replied, was the call-girls' apartment in the Columbia Plaza, a block from the Watergate and in line-of-sight of Baldwin's motel room.

This testimony was so discombobulating to Wells' attorney that we did not get into the question of McCord's motives. Why would the former CIA officer lie about bugging Oliver and O'Brien?

It is an intriguing and important question, but it was not one that the jury was obliged to answer. Neither was it asked to decide if Liddy (or I) is correct in the belief that John Dean ordered the June 17 break-in because he'd learned of the relationship between the Columbia Plaza call-girl ring and the DNC. In essence, the jury was asked to decide if these issues, and their corollaries, are sufficiently plausible that fair-minded people can disagree about them. So, too, with Wells. Was she involved in facilitating arrangements between visitors to the DNC and call-girls at the Columbia Plaza, as Phil Bailey claimed? The evidence persuades me that she was, but, once again, it is a matter of opinion.

■ ■ ■ ■ ■ ■ ■ ■ ■ ■

In the first trial, the one that caused the *Post* to squeal, the court ruled in behalf of Liddy. This is not to say that the judge and jurors decided that the "alternative theory" of Watergate is correct. Rather, they seemed to be saying that the received version of the Watergate affair, as promulgated by John Dean and the *Washington Post,* is open to question, and that there is enough evidence in support of the alternative theory that it can (and should) be freely discussed.

The unanimous verdict in Liddy's behalf in the second trial was similarly oblique. As one attorney put it, "The jury never addressed the question of truth/falsity or even negligence. It took the easiest route it could, which was to decide that the statements Liddy made were not defamatory to Wells (an essential element of her case)."[33]

Ultimately, the real issue transcends Watergate and the who-shot-who of Washington politics. Rather, it has to do with the arrogance and intransigence of media such as the *Washington Post,* which pretend to an infallibility that they do not have. For decades, the *Post* and its cousins have refused to tolerate (much less undertake) a re-examination of the Watergate affair—or any other major story in which they may be said to have a stake.

Watergate, after all, was journalism's finest hour (or so we're told). Courageous editors and intrepid young reporters risked their careers in a brave effort to save America from a White House ruled by Sauron and the hordes of Republican Mordor. To question the received version of the story is, therefore, a kind of heresy. And that is why the *Post* stoops to name-calling, labeling its critics "conspiracy theorists" while warning the public against the "danger" of such thinking. Clearly, the *Post* would rather we let them do our thinking for us. Presumably, it's safer that way.

If there wasn't so much blood on the floor, it would be funny.

Endnotes

1. Hougan, Jim. *Secret Agenda: Watergate, Deep Throat and the CIA.* New York: Random House, 1984. **2.** Civil Case No. JFM-97-946, "Memorandum" by District Judge J. Frederick Motz, 19 March 2001, US District Court for the District of Maryland. **3.** The editorial appeared in the *Post* on 4 Feb 2001. **4.** Headed by Senator Sam Ervin, the committee was informally known as "the Watergate Committee." **5.** The Watergate Committee lacked direct access to the FBI's investigative files, and so knew nothing about such topics as the key to Maxie Wells' desk or the Bureau's inability to find any bugging devices inside the DNC. The exception to this was the single day that Sam Dash was permitted to look at the files. Years after the hearings had ended, the FBI's Watergate file was made public by this author. Using the Freedom of Information Act, I was able to obtain the release of more than 30,000 pages of investigative files, memoranda, and air-tels that Senator Ervin's committee had never seen. **6.** Dean, John. *Blind Ambition.* Simon & Schuster, 1976: 388-91. **7.** *Blind Ambition* was written in 1975, while Gordon Liddy was in prison, refusing to talk about Watergate. When Liddy came out with *Will,* and when other books began to appear, Dean's inconsistencies and "errors" became as glaring as they were numerous. Accordingly, Dean dismissed the book he had once embraced with pride, claiming that he hadn't actually read it from "cover to cover," and insisting that parts of the memoir were "made up out of whole cloth by Taylor Branch." A Pulitzer Prize-winner, Branch denies the allegation. **8.** Lukas, J. Anthony. *Nightmare.* Viking, 1976: 201. **9.** "Nomination of Earl J. Silbert to be United States Attorney, Hearings before the Senate Committee on the Judiciary," 93d Cong., 2d sess., Part I, April-May 1974: 52. **10.** *Op cit.,* Lukas: 201. **11.** Testimony of Rosen in the first *Wells v. Liddy* trial. **12.** It is widely, but incorrectly, believed that Alfred Baldwin taped the telephone conversations that he overheard in the listening post at the Howard Johnson's. In fact, he did not, but made notes on the conversations, which McCord then edited before giving to Liddy. For his part, Liddy calls McCord's technical excuse for not taping the conversations "unbelievable." **13.** From an unpublished manuscript by Liddy's attorney, John Williams, of Collier Shannon Scott, PLLC. **14.** Testimony of Barbara Kennedy Rhoden in the first *Wells v. Liddy* trial. **15.** *Op cit.,* Hougan: 118. **16.** The Office of Protocol makes arrangements for White House social events and for the visits of foreign dignitaries to the nation's capital. **17.** Summers, Anthony. *The Arrogance of Power.* Viking, 2000: 422. **18.** *Op cit.,* Hougan: 172-3. **19.** *Ibid.* **20.** Hollander subsequently wrote a book with Robin Moore, *The Happy Hooker.* **21.** Ehrlichman, John. *Witness to Power.* Simon & Schuster, 1982: 380. **22.** This was said to Len Colodny, coauthor (with Robert Gettlin) of *Silent Coup.* St. Martin's Press, 1991: 148. **23.** *Op cit.,* "Nomination": 52. **24.** "A Report to the Special Prosecutor on Certain Aspects of the Watergate Affair, June 18, 1973." (Published in *op cit.,* "Nomination": 42, 53.) **25.** *Ibid.:* 42. **26.** Dean, Maureen, with Hays Gorey. *Mo: A Woman's View of Watergate.* Simon & Schuster, 1975. **27.** *Op cit.,* Summers: 422. **28.** *Ibid:* 530. **29.** *Ida Maxwell Wells v. G. Gordon Liddy,* No. 98-1962, US Court of Appeals for the Fourth Circuit, decided 28 July 1999. **30.** Dean brought suit against Liddy, St Martin's Press, Len Colodney, Robert Gettlin, myself, and more than 100 others, charging a conspiracy to defame him and his wife. In particular, the Deans accused the defendants of malice for suggesting that he was "guilty of criminal conduct in planning, aiding, abetting and directing the Watergate break-ins, and gave perjured testimony...with catastrophic consequences to alleged innocent persons, was a traitor to his nation as was Benedict Arnold, and that all...historical writings by John Dean...have been and are a self serving, ongoing historical fraud." After years of legal wrangling, the case was settled out of court among the Deans, the authors, and their publisher. Terms of the settlement have not been disclosed. Both sides claimed victory. (This writer was dismissed from the case soon after it was filed.) For his part, Liddy refused to back down, wishing to take the case to court so that he could get Dean on the witness-stand. In that, Liddy was unsuccessful. The case against him was dismissed. **31.** A copy of a trick-book from one of the call-girl operations at the Columbia Plaza was given to this writer by Detective Shoffler. **32.** In fact, Bailloy told me that the photographs were in no way obscene, but were, instead, discreet pictures of attractive women—no more and no less. **33.** Correspondence between the author and Kerrie Hook.

MAINSTREAM MEDIA: THE DRUG WAR'S SHILLS

MICHAEL LEVINE

> Editor's note: This article originally appeared in *Into the Buzzsaw: Leading Journalists Expose the Myth of a Free Press*, edited by Kristina Borjesson (Prometheus Books, 2002).

Everything you need to know about mainstream media's vital role in perpetuating our nation's three-decade, trillion-dollar War on Drugs despite overwhelming evidence that it is a fraud you can learn by watching a three-card monte operation.

Three-card monte is a blatant con game where the dealer lays three cards on a folding table, shows you that one of them is the queen of spades, turns them over, shuffles them quickly. You're sure you know where the queen is, and you saw the guy before you win easily a couple of times, so you bet your money. If that dopey-looking guy can win, so can you. But, incredibly, you've guessed wrong. You lost. You've been taken for a sucker.

The suckers in three-card monte cannot possibly win—it's an obvious and well known con game, yet, as you walk away, you see a whole line of other suckers, eyes gawking, jaws slack, hands deep in their pockets, mesmerized by the show and ready to lay down their money as fast as the dealer can get to them. Why? Because they also saw the same dopey guy win, too. What they don't know is that he's a shill.

IN THE DRUG WAR MONTE GAME, MAINSTREAM MEDIA ARE NOTHING LESS THAN SHILLS.

Shills are the con men (and women) who entice suckers into the phony game by putting on a show intended to convince those watching that the game is honest, that if you keep playing you can actually win. A good shill also helps cover up the operation by distracting the police away from the illegal action. In a court of law, where three-card monte dealers are considered crooks and thieves, shills are considered their "co-conspirators." They are liable to an equal penalty if indicted and found guilty after trial. In the Drug War monte game, mainstream media are nothing less than shills.

Media's success as shills is unparalleled in the history of scams, con jobs, and rip-offs, and can best be measured by how effectively they continue to sell us a fraud so obvious and so impossible to win that it makes South Bronx Gold Mine certificates look like a conservative investment.

Here's some of the true history that—thanks to excellent shilling—most of you are unaware of:

When President Nixon first declared war on drugs in 1971, less than half a million hard-core addicts were in the entire nation, most of whom were addicted to heroin, with the problem being centered largely in inner city areas (the largest percentage of heroin addicts was found in the New York City metropolitan area). Only two federal agencies were charged with any significant enforcement of the drug laws—US Customs and the Bureau of Narcotics and Dangerous Drugs, two agencies that were greater enemies to each other than they ever would be to any drug cartel. The total Drug War budget was less than $100 million.

Three decades later, despite the expenditure of $1 trillion in federal and state tax dollars, the number of hard-core addicts is shortly expected to exceed five million. Our nation has become the Wal-Mart of the drug world, with a wider variety and more drugs available at cheaper prices than ever before. The problem now not only affects every town and hamlet on the map, it is difficult to find a family anywhere that is not somehow affected. There are now 55 federal and military agencies involved in federal drug enforcement alone (not counting state and local agencies), and US military troops are now invading South and Central American nations under the banner of the Drug War. The federal Drug War budget (not counting state and municipal budgets) is now well over $20 billion a year, and my personal quest to find one individual anywhere in the world who could honestly testify that the trillion-dollar US War on Drugs had somehow saved him or her from the white menace has thus far been fruitless.

Do you need a cop to tell you that this is evidence of an overwhelming fraud? If your stockbroker invested your money the way our elected leaders have with our Drug War monte dollars, you'd have jailed or shot him before 1972, yet the game continues.

Why?

Because mainstream media, as they did during the Vietnam War, shill us—by means of an incessant flow of fill-in-the-blanks bullshit "victory" stories—into believing that Drug War monte is a real war that our leaders intend to win. Media shills, which now include Hollywood and "entertainment" television and the publishing industry, are continuously conning us into believing that, if in a fit of sanity, we really tried to end the costly and deadly fraud, some unspeakable horror would be loosed upon us, like Mexican and Colombian drug dealers led by the latest media-created "Pablo Escobar" invading across our (forever) insufficiently protected borders to force-feed our kids heroin and cocaine. We might even have to arm the Partnership for a Drug Free America with missiles and rockets.

Unless of course our kids "just say no," as Nancy Reagan's billion-dollar media boondoggle campaign taught them.

And when mainstream media haven't directly shilled us into supporting Drug War monte, as they do to this day, they have aided in its perpetuation with their censorship, by conscious omission, of scandalous events that—had they been reported with the fervor the *Washington Post* showed during the Watergate era—would have brought the whole deadly and costly charade crumbling to the ground three decades ago. I know this firsthand because I took part in some of the most significant of those events as a federal agent and/or court-qualified expert witness and/or a journalist. The following are my personal experiences on both sides of the Drug War monte table.

_THE VIETNAM WAR

The undercover case that brought me into Southeast Asia during the Vietnam War was the most dangerous of my career, only the source of that danger was not just the dealers. It was the case that first brought me face-to-face with the fact that, like the Vietnam War, the War on Drugs was never intended to be won—it's a deadly fraud perpetrated against the people paying for it. It was also the first case that taught me that a runaway, corrupt federal bureaucracy could count on the mainstream media to shill for it. Ironically, it began on July 4, 1971.

At that time President Nixon had recently declared war on drugs. Our political leaders had already begun brainwashing Americans through media megaphones into believing that our growing drug problem was the fault of evil foreigners and that—other than the Vietnam War—the drug problem was our number-one national security concern. I was a young agent with US Customs assigned to the Hard Narcotics Smuggling Unit in New York City. My 25-year-old brother, David, at that point had been a heroin addict for ten years, and I was a TB (True Believer).

It was on that July 4 that I arrested John Edward Davidson at JFK International Airport in New York City with three kilos of 99-percent pure, white heroin hidden in the false bottom of a Samsonite suitcase. The investigation known as *US v Liang Sae Tiew, et al.* began.[1]

By nightfall the investigation had brought my team deep inside a desolate swamp on the outskirts of Gainesville, Florida, where a lone trailer was parked at the end of a barely visible trail. During the pre-dawn hours we raided the trailer and arrested the US-based financier of the smuggling operation, Alan Trupkin, and his heroin-addicted gofer, 22-year-old John Clements (remember this name; we'll see him again). By the following day I had all the details I needed to destroy one of the biggest heroin import operations on the globe. But there was one major problem to contend with that neither

I nor any of the senior officers to whom I reported could, in our wildest dreams, have imagined: The CIA.

Two years earlier, Davidson, stationed with the Army in Vietnam, had taken R&R leave in Bangkok. There he had connected with a Chinese heroin dealer, Liang Sae Tiew (a/k/a Gary). The prices were the cheapest in the world, the supplies unlimited. After Davidson's discharge, all he had to do was smuggle the stuff into the US, and he and his partners would be rich. Seven trips and 21 kilos later, his luck ran out and I arrested him.

Now, to do my job in accordance with my training and the very (supposed) philosophy of the entire War on Drugs, I had to take the next step and go for the source.

One month later I arrived in Bangkok, posing as Davidson's heroin-dealing partner. Within days I made contact with his heroin connections—Gary and someone called "Mr. Geh." At first my presence in Bangkok was kept secret from the Bureau of Narcotics and Dangerous Drugs, the sworn enemy of US Customs. The war between the two agencies for budget dollars and media attention had reached the level of fistfights, the arrests of each others' informants, and had, in fact, even come close to a shoot-out. But that's another story.

My presence in Bangkok was also kept secret from the Thai police, whose only competition for the most corrupt police force in recorded history, in my experience, was their Mexican counterparts. And, the fact was, I was in their country illegally. At the time undercover operations were illegal in most of the world. It was unthinkable that cops would be permitted to commit crimes to catch criminals. I'd already been warned by my own bosses that if the Thai police got wind of me being there to do a drug deal, undercover or otherwise, they would bust my ass and disappear me, and my own country would disavow all knowledge. In short, my butt was way out on a limb and I knew it, but I did not know the half of my problems.

After a week of hanging with the dopers, I had managed to convince them that I was the capo di tutti fruti of the Mafia hooked into individual Mafiosi across the US, each looking for large quantities of drugs. I was the Main Man. I told them that I needed a new supplier because my previous source, the French Connection, had been busted.

> THE UNDERCOVER CASE THAT BROUGHT ME INTO SOUTHEAST ASIA DURING THE VIETNAM WAR WAS THE MOST DANGEROUS OF MY CAREER, ONLY THE SOURCE OF THAT DANGER WAS NOT JUST THE DEALERS.

At the time the largest heroin seizure in history was in the neighborhood of 200 kilos, part of the original French Connection. I knew the case well, since I'd played a small role in it. The two Chinese heroin dealers were as aware of the American market as I was and assured me that these amounts were child's play compared to their operation. They had a "factory" in Chiang Mai run by Mr. Geh's uncle that was churning out a couple hundred kilos a week. What didn't go to the soldiers in Vietnam was going into the veins and brains of American kids. Like my own brother.

I cut a deal: I would buy a kilo of Dragon Brand for $2,500 cash and send it to my US Mafia customers as "samples." I'd then remain in Thailand awaiting their orders. I gave Gary and Mr. Geh an estimate that I might need as much as 300 kilos as a first order. The dopers' price for a 300-kilo load: $2,000 per kilo for a very paltry $600,000. That amount of heroin, at that time, could have met the entire US demand for about two to three weeks. The cost to our nation in death, destruction, and taxes was incalculable; the potential profits to the dopers was breathtaking.

French Connection heroin was then selling wholesale, delivered in the US, at $20,000 a kilo. The purity of the Dragon Brand heroin I was buying in Asia was as good or better. It was close to 100 percent pure, meaning that you could cut (dilute) the stuff up to fourteen times for the street. The US street price per ounce was $2,000, meaning that a single kilo (40 ounces) of Asian heroin at $2,000 could theoretically gross $1,120,000. Just multiply that by 300 kilos, and your original investment of $600,000 has now yielded more than $300 million.

At the moment I had everything I needed to destroy the operation *except* its location, but I knew how to remedy that. I made one proviso: I demanded to personally inspect their heroin-producing facilities in Chiang Mai—"the Factory"—before finalizing the deal. If they agreed, I would be one step away from destroying them.

Within days, the two dealers made contact with the factory's owner, Mr. Geh's uncle. He agreed to go forward with the transaction and authorized me to inspect the Factory after I bought the first sample kilo.

Sitting in my room at the Siam Intercontinental that night, alone, I replayed the words of the heroin dealers on a mini-recorder. The implication of what I had just learned to our nation, to my own heroin-addicted brother, mixed with the bullshit exhortations of our political leaders, seemed to sink deep inside of me. I felt as if I were playing some hero role in a John Wayne (now Tom Clancy) movie. I was in position to do what our leaders and mainstream media had psyched me to do: strike at the heart of America's greatest enemies.

I was on a mission from God.

I was a naïve idiot.

Bam! The adrenaline was pumping. I was moving. I made contact with my control officer, Customs Attaché Joe Jenkins. At a pre-dawn meeting I brought him up to date. He was as excited as I was but a lot more reserved. I could tell there was something he wasn't telling me, but at the moment I had a pressing need. I was almost broke. I needed cash to maintain my cover as a big-time dope dealer, $2,500 cash for the first kilo of heroin. Hell, I didn't even have enough money left to pay my hotel bill. I was already receiving notes under my door from the management asking me to bring it current.

Jenkins instructed me to meet him later at a girlie bar on Sukamvit. By that time, he assured me, he'd have headquarters and—more important—embassy approvals for the operation to proceed. And—most important—he'd have money.

Late that night I met Jenkins again. As three butt-naked, Asian doll-women in four-inch spike heels performed a somnambulistic, wriggle-writhe-squat over beer bottles on the bar above us while a Rolling Stones album blasted on monstrous speakers, Jenkins shouted that he had neither approvals nor money. From that point on, things got strange. Very strange.

The suddenly nervous Jenkins, his eyes jerking at every movement in the shadows around us, gave me Kafkaesque, bureaucratic reasons for the delays, saying he needed specific signatures from specific bureaucrats in Washington who were, for some reason or other, unavailable. He fed me other bullshit that only a brain-numbed, government employee would find normal.

I went back to my room and began stalling both the hotel and the drug dealers. My people are being cautious; they are sending me a courier. They take no chances. Etc., etc., ad nauseam.

At first the dopers thought that the caution of "my people" was admirable, but when more than a week had passed and the delays continued, I found myself out of excuses and in serious danger. For the first time in my life I heard myself utter the threat: "I'm going to the press." Jenkins looked at me and just rolled his eyes. He recognized an idiot when he saw one.

Some time before dawn, I was called into the embassy for a meeting with the first CIA officer I'd ever knowingly met. He gave no name, and I didn't ask for one. Joe had told me he was CIA; that was all I needed to know. The guy was short, stocky, bald, and wearing what I would come to know as a typical CIA uniform: a khaki leisure suit. He looked at me with a mixture of bemusement and disdain that I would also learn was typical.

THIS WAS YEARS BEFORE THE CIA WOULD COME TO BE KNOWN AMONG DEA AGENTS ASSIGNED OVERSEAS AS THE CRIMINAL INEPT AGENCY AND LATER THE COCAINE IMPORT AGENCY.

"You're not going to Chiang Mai," he said. "We just lost a man up there. It's dangerous."

"But I'm an undercover," I protested. "Already certified crazy. I didn't take this job to be safe."

Like I said: a naïve idiot.

After not much discussion, the spook looked at his watch and cut the conversation short. "You served in the military, right?" He didn't wait for my answer. "Well, our country has other priorities [than the Drug War]." He was firm—I was not going to Chiang Mai and that was it. The CIA had made the decision for us—a harbinger of things to come. My instructions were to buy the single kilo of heroin and set up the arrest of whomever delivered it. Then I was to leave the country ASAP. Case closed.

This was years before the CIA would come to be known among DEA agents assigned overseas as the Criminal Inept Agency and later the Cocaine Import Agency. Years before anyone with a government job questioned the judgment of the gang that can't spy straight. Years before I would state on my own radio show that the CIA seal at Langley, instead of reading, "...and the truth shall set you free," ought to read, "...and the truth shall piss you off."[2]

I'd stumbled into a quick look at an ugly truth that would haunt me for the rest of my life, but at that moment I was not prepared to believe it. I had served three years in the military as an Air Force sentry dog handler—combat-trained military police. I'd been an undercover federal agent for six years. I was a good soldier, trained to follow orders. I believed in the virtue and morality of my leaders. Like the devoted husband who catches his beloved wife exchanging a torrid look with the pizza delivery boy, the truth was too emotionally charged for me to absorb. It was much easier for me to accept that the CIA man knew more than I did and that it was in our national interest for me to simply follow orders.

And that's what I did. I ordered the kilo of heroin and busted the two Chinese dealers on the spot. Back in the US I received a Treasury Act Special Award for the first case of its kind, one agent traveling the globe to "destroy" a heroin operation. Another "victory" for the US media shill factory to tout.

For a while I was lost in my own press notices.

But I was no longer the same unquestioning young undercover agent. My cop instinct nagged at me, told me something was wrong. Within a year I would learn that the Chiang Mai "factory" that I'd been prevented from destroying by the CIA was the source of massive amounts of heroin being smuggled into the US in the bodies and body bags of GIs killed in Vietnam.[3] All I could do was pray that the CIA knew what it was doing. At that time I rather foolishly believed that they had the best interests of the American people at heart, but how competent were they? And if they weren't competent, who do you turn to in order to blow the whistle? Congress? The media?

I was a well trained, experienced undercover operative who, when in doubt, observes closely, documents what he sees, but takes no action—one of the reasons, I believe, that I survived my career. And in the early 1970s, there were very few in a better position than I was to observe the development of Drug War monte.

My unit, the Hard Narcotics Smuggling Squad, was a small group of men (sixteen to twenty of us) charged with the investigation of all heroin and cocaine smuggling through the Port of New York, the home of the majority of our nation's hardcore drug addicts. By necessity my unit became involved in the investigation of every major smuggling operation known to law enforcement. We could not avoid witnessing CIA protection of major drug dealers.

In fact, throughout the Vietnam War, while massive amounts of heroin emanating from the Golden Triangle Area were documented by us as flooding into the US, and tens of thousands of our fighting men were coming home addicted, not a single important heroin source in Southeast Asia was ever indicted by US law enforcement. This was no accident. Case after case, like *US v. Liang Sae Tiew, et al.*, was

killed by CIA and State Department intervention, and there wasn't a damned thing we could do about it.

It was also during those years that we became aware that the CIA had gone well beyond simply protecting their drug-dealing assets. Agency-owned proprietary airlines like Air America were being used to ferry drugs throughout Southeast Asia, allegedly in support of our "allies." (With friends like these...) CIA banking operations were used to launder drug money. The CIA was learning the drug business and learning it well.

Those of us on the inside, who were aware of the these glaring inconsistencies between Drug War policy as reported through mass media and its reality, were afraid to turn to either Congress or the media for help. It seemed impossible that anyone with any knowledge whatsoever of our growing drug problem would not have noticed the absence of enforcement in Southeast Asia. It was just too big, too out in the open. During those years, I believe a good journalist would have had many frustrated "inside sources" to quote from, yet no stories appeared.

It was also during those waning years of Vietnam that CIA protection of drug dealers spread to other areas under our watch. As cocaine traffickers grew in economic and political importance in South and Central America, so did their importance to the CIA and other covert US agencies.

For example, in 1972, being fluent in Spanish, I was assigned to assist in a major international drug case involving top Panamanian government officials who were using diplomatic passports to smuggle large quantities of heroin and other drugs into the US. The name Manuel Noriega surfaced prominently in the investigation. Surfacing right behind Noriega was the CIA, to protect him from US law enforcement.

After President Nixon declared war on drugs in 1971 and all of our political leaders began bleating about how drugs were our number-one national security threat, Congress began to raise our taxes and the Drug War budget on a regular basis that continues to this day.

> LIKE THE DEVOTED HUSBAND WHO CATCHES HIS BELOVED WIFE EXCHANGING A TORRID LOOK WITH THE PIZZA DELIVERY BOY, THE TRUTH WAS TOO EMOTIONALLY CHARGED FOR ME TO ABSORB.

Meanwhile, the CIA and the Department of State were protecting more and more politically powerful drug traffickers around the world: the Mujihideen in Afghanistan, the Bolivian cocaine cartels, the top levels of the Mexican government, top Panama-based money launderers, the Nicaraguan Contras, right-wing Colombian drug dealers and politicians, and others.[4]

Under US law, protecting drug trafficking was and still is considered "conspiracy to traffic in drugs"—a felony violation of federal and state laws. The first President George Bush once said: "All those who look the other way at drug trafficking are as guilty as the drug dealer." Ironically, not too many years earlier, as head of the CIA, Bush had authorized a salary for Manuel Noriega as a CIA asset, while the little dictator was listed in as many as 40 DEA computer files as a drug dealer. Seems only fitting that the CIA named its

AS HEAD OF THE CIA, BUSH HAD AUTHORIZED A SALARY FOR MANUEL NORIEGA AS A CIA ASSET, WHILE THE LITTLE DICTATOR WAS LISTED IN AS MANY AS 40 DEA COMPUTER FILES AS A DRUG DEALER.

headquarters after Bush.

In any case, it was clear to us on the inside of international drug enforcement that Congress was either well aware of what was going on or was guilty of terminal ineptitude. It was also clear to us that CIA protection of international narcotic traffickers depended heavily on the active collaboration of mainstream media as shills.

The media's shill duties, as I experienced them firsthand, were twofold: First, keep silent about the gush of drugs that was allowed to continue unimpeded into the US. Second, divert the public's attention by tricking them into believing the Drug War was legitimate by falsely presenting those few trickles law enforcement was permitted to stop as though they were major "victories," when in fact we were doing nothing more than getting rid of the inefficient competitors of CIA assets.

I began to notice the fill-in-the-blanks drug stories. Every week another "drug baron," another drug-corrupted government was (and continues to be) presented by the media as a new "threat" to American kids. Every case, many of which I took part in, was headlined in the media: "US Authorities Announce Major Blow Against (fill in the blank) Drug Cartel." Every country and national leader that the CIA and the State Department wanted to slander (e.g., Castro, the Sandanistas, and leftist guerrillas anywhere) got the same headline: "US Sources Say (fill in the blank) Poses New Narco-Trafficking Threat." Foreign leaders and nations whose images the CIA and the State Department wanted to keep clean (e.g., Manny Noriega for two decades, and Mexico and every one of its Presidents since NAFTA) got the headline: "(fill in the blank)'s New Anti-drug Efforts Win Trust of US Officials."[5]

_THE "COCAINE COUP"

On July 17, 1980, for the first time in history, drug traffickers actually took control of a nation: Bolivia, at the time the source of virtually 100 percent of the cocaine entering the United States.[6] The "Cocaine Coup" was the bloodiest in Bolivia's history. It came at a time when the US demand for cocaine was skyrocketing to the point that, in order to satisfy it, suppliers had to consolidate raw materials and production and get rid of inefficient producers. Its result was the creation of what came to be known as *La Corporacion*—The Corporation—in essence, the General Motors or OPEC of cocaine.

Immediately after the coup, production of cocaine increased massively until, in short order, it outstripped supply. It was the true beginning of the cocaine and crack "plague," as the media and hack politicians never tire of calling it. July 17, 1980, is truly a day that should live in infamy along with December 7, 1941. There are few events in history that have caused more and longer lasting damage to our nation.

What America was never told, in spite of mainstream media having the information and a prime, inside source who was ready to go public with the story, was that the coup was carried out with the aid and participation of Central Intelligence. The source would also testify and prove that, in order to carry out that coup, the CIA and the State and Justice Departments had to combine forces to protect their drug-dealing assets by destroying a DEA investigation—*US v. Roberto Suarez, et al.* How do I know? I was that inside source.[7]

All the events I am referring to are detailed in my book *The Big White Lie*, a book that, to date, has been virtually ignored by mainstream media—with good reason, as I hope this article makes clear.[8] The documentation of the events portrayed was carried out in accordance with accepted techniques and practices of evidence-gathering as taught in each of the four federal law enforcement training academies I attended. I took precisely the same precautions I would have taken were I preparing a case for a jury, backing up every assertion with solid evidence in the form of reports and tape-recorded conversations.

The Big White Lie is, at present, out-of-print, but it is available in libraries. I can only urge the reader, particularly those in law enforcement and the legal professions, to read it and judge its evidentiary value for yourself.

During the months after the Bolivian coup, I watched the massive news coverage with astonishment. Nothing even came close to the true and easily provable events. All of it was accurate insofar as it frighteningly portrayed the new Bolivian government as one comprised of expatriate Nazis like Klaus Barbie and drug dealers like Roberto Suarez, and that the power and influence of the drug economy was much greater than all the US experts had imagined. But it left out the most important fact of all: It was directed by the CIA, and US taxpayer-dollars had put these guys in power.

As I detailed in the book, the failure of the US media to cover what was arguably the most significant event in Drug War history was enough to push me over the edge. I was no hero, believe me. I was an undercover operative who knew well how to play the angles, not someone who took unreasonable chances. But this was not that long after Woodward and Bernstein and the *Washington Post*'s concentrated, full-court attack on the Watergate affair that resulted in real indictments and prison sentences for crimes a lot less serious than what I was about to report. The media still seemed to offer some hope. I could not believe that the failure to accurately cover the Cocaine Coup was intentional. I would provide them with the missing pieces. I would be the Drug War's Deep Throat.

The smoking gun evidence of the CIA's role in the Bolivian coup could be found in the Roberto Suarez case, a complicated DEA covert operation that I had run only two months before the Coca Revolution. Media shills had trumpeted it as the greatest undercover sting operation in history. Its finale occurred when Bolivian cartel leaders Roberto Gasser and Alfredo Gutierrez were arrested outside a Miami bank after I had paid them $8 million for the then-largest load of cocaine in history. Some of the facts of the case were used in the screenplay for Al Pacino's *Scarface*.

What America was never told before the publication of my book was that within weeks of their headlined arrests, both Gasser and Gutierrez were released from jail. When I learned from my post in Argentina that these two men and their drug cartel were key players in the Cocaine Coup and that the whole thing was CIA-inspired and -supported, I wrote anonymous letters to the *New York Times*, the *Washington Post*, and the *Miami Herald*.

In spite of the fact that the letters contained enough information to convince them that I was in fact "a highly placed source" and furnished them with information and leads that would quickly and easily lead a true investigative journalist to the truth, nothing happened. The only journalists who were at all curious about the sudden disappearance of the case from mainstream media news and the DEA's reluctance to even talk about it were working for *High Times*. They wrote this about the Suarez case: "The Drug Enforcement Administration will confirm that the arrests were made but will go no further. This is curious, because [the operation] may have been the all-time great sting operation...."

The other message mainstream media began to deliver with shill-like efficiency was the unquestioned bleating of politicians, bureaucrats, and media-anointed "experts" about how, as a result of the Coca Revolution, it was more urgent than ever that more money be budgeted and more federal enforcement agencies and military branches tasked to fight the War on Drugs. President Carter even mandated that the CIA get involved in fighting drugs.

THE SMOKING GUN EVIDENCE OF THE CIA'S ROLE IN THE BOLIVIAN COUP COULD BE FOUND IN THE ROBERTO SUAREZ CASE, A COMPLICATED DEA COVERT OPERATION THAT I HAD RUN ONLY TWO MONTHS BEFORE THE COCA REVOLUTION.

When this last fact hit the news, I ran a little test at the embassy in Buenos Aires, just so that I could say that I did it. I asked the CIA station chief to lend me a spy camera to cover an undercover operation I had going in Buenos Aires. "I'm back into the Bolivian cartel," I told him. The top spook didn't hesitate nor even blink an eye when he said he didn't have one single camera available. The CIA was simply not going to help me in any way that might, no matter how remotely, jeopardize their "assets."

How, I wondered, could any international DEA agent who took his job and oath seriously be considered anything but a threat by the CIA? In my Secret Country Report for the year, I put the "paradoxical" situation in as diplomatic terms as I could muster, pointing out that our policy makers, where the War on Drugs was concerned, seemed to be at odds with each other. Of course, as I expected, I received neither answer nor comment.

Then the "news" story hit that pushed me over the edge, the story that would change my life. Larry Rohter and Steven Strasser of *Newsweek* had just authored a feature piece on the Bolivian Cocaine Coup that was, in my opinion, the hydrogen bomb of Drug War scare stories. Maybe the greatest Drug War monte story of all time. It detailed how drug money had not only funded the Cocaine Coup but was now funding revolutions around the world. How many of these revolutions, I wondered, were backed by the CIA and

American taxpayers' dollars? But then how, I wondered, could the journalists know the truth unless they had a Deep Throat to steer them straight?[9]

I flew into action without thinking. I should have heeded the words of the CIA Chief played by Cliff Robertson in *Three Days of the Condor*—a warning that should be issued to all potential real-life government whistleblowers. Near the end of the movie, after a CIA employee played by Robert Redford had escaped two hours of Agency attempts to kill him to prevent him from blowing the whistle on some typically depraved CIA plot—although Hollywood CIA plots are always so much more clever than the real, goofball variety—he is about to enter the front door of a major newspaper (think *New York Times*, *Washington Post*). There waiting for him is the head of the CIA, who smiles shrewdly and utters the last line of the movie: "What makes you think they'll print the story?" Fade to black.

But my mind was full of Woodwards and Bernsteins. I sat down at my desk in the American embassy and wrote the kind of letter that I never in life imagined myself writing. After fully identifying myself, I detailed, in three typewritten pages on official US embassy stationary, enough evidence of my charges to feed a wolf pack of investigative journalists, along with my willingness to be a quotable source. I addressed it directly to Strasser and Rohter, care of *Newsweek*. I sent it registered mail with return receipt requested. Within a couple of weeks, I received the receipt (which I still have) and waited anxiously to hear from them. Two sleepless weeks later, I was still sitting in my embassy office staring at the phone. Three weeks later, it rang.

It was DEA's Internal Security. They were calling me to notify me that I was under investigation. I had been falsely accused of everything from black-marketing and having sex with a married female DEA agent during an undercover assignment to "playing loud rock music on my radio and disturbing other embassy personnel." The investigation would wreak havoc with my entire life for the next four years.[10] My days as the whistle-blowing diplomat were cut short. I would end up a lot luckier than most high-level government whistle-blowers. I would survive. When push came to shove, I was a well trained undercover operative with the survival skills of a Bronx roach.

_DEA HEADQUARTERS

Back in the "Palace of Suits," I decided that to survive the ongoing and ever expanding onslaught from Internal Security, I would follow the sage advice of a veteran suit: "A bureaucracy has a short memory. Keep your mouth shut, and the suits will forget you even exist." And that's exactly what happened. To survive, I became a Drug War monte player.

On my first day back at DEA headquarters in DC, assigned to the cocaine desk, I fielded a phone call from a wire service journalist. The newsie wanted to know what percentage of drugs being smuggled into the US was intercepted at the borders. During my negotiations with the Bolivian Cartel, the top cocaine producers in the world at the time, I was told that they factored in a loss of less than one percent at the US borders. Before I could answer, one of the other desk officers overheard the conversation and said: "Tell him ten percent. That's the [official] number." I repeated the number, and ten percent was the statistic published in the story.

It was that easy. The same phony percentage was used over the next two decades without a single so-called journalist ever asking the logical questions: How can you possibly know that you are intercepting ten percent? Who is doing the calculations? It is interesting to note that the magic number has recently been drastically increased, and it is Hollywood now helping with the con job.

I noticed what I recognized as a "rigged" scene in the hit movie *Traffic*. (It's important to note that the movie was shot with both the cooperation and collaboration of the Drug War monte suits.) The "Drug Czar" played by Michael Douglas is visiting a US-Mexican border crossing. He asks a real-life Customs officer (drafted for the movie role) what percentage of drugs are intercepted at the border. The answer, blasted in an unnaturally loud voice, is "48 percent."

Ten percent to 48 percent in 20 years, and there are more drugs on the streets than ever before? An Academy Award-winning movie? If this isn't shilling, I don't know what is.

But you have to remember that dealers and shills have no shame at all. And I suppose you could say that neither did I, because for the next five or so years, I took an active and conscious part in Drug War monte.

_OPERATION HUN AND SOUTH FLORIDA TASK FORCE

I spent much of 1983 shuttling between an undercover assignment on "Operation Hun" and a temporary post as a supervisor in Vice President Bush's South Florida Task Force. Operation Hun, ironically, was aimed at bringing down the same Bolivian drug-trafficking government that the CIA had put into power three years earlier. As I detailed in *The Big White Lie*, the operation, which could have truly been one of the most successful in the DEA's history, was still controlled by the CIA and was ultimately destroyed in order to hide the fact that protected CIA assets were the guys responsible for producing and distributing almost all of the world's cocaine at the time. I can only urge everyone with an interest to read it as if it were one of my prosecution case reports.

> I PERSONALLY TIPPED OFF AT LEAST A DOZEN "JOURNALISTS" WHO CALLED FOR INFORMATION AND KNOW OF OTHER AGENTS WHO DID THE SAME.

When I wasn't working undercover in Hun, I filled two consecutive assignments in Vice President Bush's task force. My first was as watch commander, which basically meant that during my watch, I was to notify Washington of every drug seizure so that press releases could be written and television appearances scheduled for Bush's first-in-history "Drug Czar," Admiral Daniel J. Murphy. My second task force assignment was as supervisor of Miami Airport operations. I had fourteen to sixteen DEA and Customs agents under my command. Our job was mostly to conduct follow-up inves-

tigations of Customs' drug-smuggling arrests at the airport. The trouble with both jobs and the whole South Florida Task Force concept was that it was all an expensive Drug War monte publicity stunt.

Vice President Bush and his Drug Czar, through the ever reliable media, would bamboozle the public into believing that drug seizures in South Florida had doubled. On any Sunday morning you couldn't avoid seeing Drug Czar Murphy—the "Little Admiral," as we used to call him—on two, three, and four popular news shows, waving the Drug War victory flags. The media-driven shilling of the public during this period was relentless. Check it out for yourself. It's easy to research on the Internet. There was only one problem with the claims of Drug War victories: They were purely bogus and easily disproved.

The same drug seizures that the DEA, Coast Guard, and Customs were normally making in South Florida prior to the existence of the task force were now being turned over to the task force and trumpeted as "victories," when in reality there were no more seizures than before.

What was even more fraudulent, if this were possible, was that the seizures were now being double-counted for congressional budget hearings. Customs would seize 1,000 pounds of marijuana and turn it over to the task force. Both the task force and Customs would count the seizures on their yearly statistics for Congress. The media points all went to the VP's task force. The bill, as always, went to the US taxpayer. And thanks to media shilling, everyone but the American taxpayer was aware of the fraud, and the perpetrators were made to look like heroes.

Did the media know the truth and hide it?

I personally tipped off at least a dozen "journalists" who called for information and know of other agents who did the same. It would not have taken much investigation to verify what we were saying—no more than a couple of phone calls to the agencies involved—yet nothing ever surfaced. Shills don't tell marks anything, do they?

_AFGHAN AND CONTRA WARS

While a barrage of media headlines continued to misdirect America's attention toward Vice President Bush's South Florida Task Force as a valiant and effective Drug War effort—the sucker card—the real action that was consciously omitted from news coverage was that some of the biggest drug dealers in the world were funneling drugs directly into the veins and brains of America's children with the protection of the CIA and the State Department. Namely, the Nicaraguan Contras and the Mujihideen rebels in Afghanistan.

For the entire duration of the Contra war, we in the DEA had documented the Contras—those "heroes," as Ollie North called them—putting at least as much cocaine on American streets as the Medellin Cartel. We had also documented the Mujihideen as vying for first place as America's source of heroin. Yet not a single case of any significance was allowed to go forward to prosecution against either entity. All were effectively blocked by the CIA and the State Department.

The media's shilling and misdirection were relentless and effective. As an example, Ollie North was voted in a media poll as one of the "ten most admired people" in the nation in spite of the fact that his efforts to protect major drug dealers and killers like Honduran army General Bueso-Rosa from prosecution had been well documented by Congress. Astoundingly, North, a CIA station chief and a US Ambassador, has been banned from entering Costa Rica for running drugs through that democratic nation into the US (among other crimes) by that country's Nobel-winning President, Oscar Arias, yet the news barely surfaced in the US. Now compare this to Monica Lewinsky coverage.[11]

THERE WERE A FEW OF US WHO, IN SUDDEN FITS OF MADNESS OR NAÏVETÉ, DID RISK OUR LIVES AND CAREERS TO BLOW THE WHISTLE.

Even drug-dealing Contra supporters in other countries were being protected. In one glaring case, an associate of mine was sent into Honduras to open a DEA office in Tegucigalpa. Within months he had documented that as much as 50 tons of cocaine had been sent into the US by Honduran military people who were supporting the Contras. Enough cocaine to fill a third of the US demand. What was the DEA response? They closed the office.[12] The tip-offs—both anonymous and straight out—to journalists continued to fly from sources within the DEA and other agencies, yet not one significant, truthful story ever surfaced.

_BACK IN THE BIG APPLE—THE DRUG WAR MEDIA CAPITAL

In 1984 I received a hardship transfer back to New York. My daughter living there now had a drug problem. By this time my brother David, a nineteen-year heroin addict, had committed suicide in Miami, leaving a note that said: "I can't stand the drugs any more." I was going to do whatever it took to save my little girl.

In New York City I was assigned as the supervisor of an active squad that was constantly being called out to stage raids for television news—CBS, ABC, etc., all the big players. On a slow news day the SAC would get a call: You guys got anything going down we can put on the eleven o'clock news? We could always come up with something. What was good for their ratings was good for our budget.

During those years, if you linked every doper the media shilled as a member of either the Medellin or Cali Cartels, hand in hand, the chain would reach the moon. The cartels were so effectively painted as devils that even the normally level-headed Mayor Ed Koch called for the bombing of Colombia. (Ironically, that is exactly what we're doing now.) I played the game, led the bogus raids, gave the newsies whatever they needed to sell papers or raise ratings. As an insider I learned the secret of the Drug War generals' control over the media shills.

Drug stories sold newspapers, got media ratings, and made great screen stories for Hollywood and television—as they still do. To get "access" to a police agency—that is, to get the "inside story" and "credibility"—the media executives, producers, and editors have to play the game. They can't broadcast or write an unfriendly story and expect an open door the next day. You don't make a tell-all movie and expect to film it with US government cooperation, do you?

The bottom line is money. No one in the mainstream media has taken an oath to protect anything but their jobs—not a criticism, just a fact. The fourth estate might as well be fifth, sixth, or seventh estate—it's all bullshit. For the money, mainstream media could (and can) be counted upon to shill the Drug War monte game as if their collective bank accounts depended on it. But this was only part of the media economic story. It would get worse. Much worse.

There were a few of us who, in sudden fits of madness or naïveté, did risk our lives and careers to blow the whistle. More often than not we'd find ourselves telling some incredulous Columbia School of Journalism-trained newsie that the current "news" release issued by (fill in the blank) Drug War monte agency talking about the "new political hope" in Mexico and/or Colombia and/or (fill in the blank) who was going to "clean up" government drug corruption, was just a repeat of the same bogus story that's been printed every couple of months since the beginning of time. And if they didn't believe us, all they had to do was check their own archives.

We'd tell them that our firsthand experience on the front lines had taught us that, as long as Americans spent hundreds of billions on illegal drugs, there could be no new hope, and that to ignore this history and to print or broadcast that bullshit was no different than shilling for Three Card monte.

The typical newsie answer would be a blank stare. Blank because they didn't have the slightest idea what we were talking about, nor the curiosity to research it. Blank because while they've been trained in sound bites, ellipses, and correct language, they haven't the slightest notion of the history or inner workings of Drug War monte. They don't even know that "conspiracy" is the federal law responsible for the majority of humans in cages. Their editors tell them that whatever "credentialed government spokespeople" say (usually some public affairs officer) *is* the story. They are assigned to be reporters, not investigative journalists.

Meanwhile, these encounters leave you, the potential whistle-blower, with a sinking feeling in the pit of your stomach that makes you wish you'd kept your damned mouth shut.

But back then, except for those few fleeting moments of sheer madness, I no longer had the slightest desire to play the Robert Redford role in my own movie. I had a daughter on drugs, a mortgage, and a debt-financed life. The only thing between myself and ruination was my job. I had learned the *Three Days of the Condor* lesson well: They most definitely would not print the story.

Then, in 1987, I was once again pushed over the edge. There would be no turning back.

_OPERATION TRIFECTA—DEEP COVER

I'd kept my mouth shut, and, as the DEA suit had predicted, by 1987 my "sins" had been forgotten. DEA Headquarters was now asking me to play a lead role in a deep-cover sting operation that would become my *New York Times* best-selling book, *Deep Cover*.

Posing as a Puerto Rican-Sicilian Mafia chief, myself and a small cadre of DEA and Customs undercover agents managed to penetrate the top of the drug world in three countries: Bolivia, Panama, and Mexico. The DEA called it "Operation Trifecta." Customs' name for it was "Operation Saber." Our fictitious little "Mafia" managed to make a fifteen-ton cocaine purchase and smuggling deal with the Bolivian drug cartel *La Corporacion*, the same group that the CIA helped take over Bolivia, the same group responsible for most of the cocaine base being processed in Colombia to this day.

Hidden video cameras rolled as I negotiated the price and quantity of the drugs with top representatives of the cartel. The deal done, I sent undercover pilots into the jungles of Bolivia to verify that the cocaine was on the ground and ready for delivery. Then I arranged with top Mexican government officials for military protection of the drug shipments as they transited through Mexico into the United States. Among those with whom I negotiated directly were Colonel Jaime Carranza, grandson of Mexico's former President Venustiano Carranza, and Pablo Giron, a bodyguard of Mexico's President-elect at the time, Carlos Salinas de Gortari.

> ## FOR THE ENTIRE DURATION OF THE CONTRA WAR, WE IN THE DEA HAD DOCUMENTED THE CONTRAS—THOSE "HEROES," AS OLLIE NORTH CALLED THEM—PUTTING AT LEAST AS MUCH COCAINE ON AMERICAN STREETS AS THE MEDELLIN CARTEL.

To verify that the Mexican government was keeping its part of the deal, "Mafia" representatives (undercover officers) were dispatched to Mexico to observe military units preparing our landing field. As part of the deal, my first drug payment—$5 million in cash—would be made to Remberto Rodriguez, chief money launderer for the Bolivian and Colombian cartels. His operation, as the cartel leaders told me, was protected by then-CIA asset Manuel Noriega. I personally went to Rodriguez's headquarters in Panama City, where we made arrangements for the first transfer of the down payment of $5 million cash and shook hands on the deal.

During this harrowing assignment our undercover team gathered hard evidence in the form of secretly recorded video and audio, firsthand observations, and secret government intelligence reports that clearly indicated that members of the military and staff of incoming President of Mexico Carlos Salinas de Gortari were planning to open the Mexican border for drug smuggling once he took office and NAFTA (North American Free Trade Agreement) was passed. We had hard evidence that they had already begun to put their plan into action.

We had also stumbled onto evidence indicating that the corrupt Mexican officials we were negotiating with were also directly involved in training CIA-supported Contras. We uncovered uninvestigated, personal links between US government officials (including at least one DEA officer) and corrupt Mexican government officials, some of whom may have been involved in the torture/murder of DEA agent Enrique "Kiki" Camarena and/or its cover-up.

And we had proof that the US paramilitary operation in the Andean Region (then Operation Snowcap, now Plan Colombia and/or the Andean Initiative) was a premeditated fraud on the American people, never intended to have any effect on the supply of drugs.

As I detailed in *Deep Cover*, once top officials in our government became aware of what we had uncovered, the CIA became involved. We had gone too far and had to be stopped. The top drug dealers, the Panama based money-laundering operation, and the high-ranking corrupt Mexican government officials that we had snared were effectively protected from prosecution. Operations Trifecta and Saber were destroyed.

Once again, I can only urge the reader of this article to read my book and judge it for its factual value, keeping in mind that the information in it was never intended to be a book. I detail how all the revelations listed above were first presented to the DEA's Internal Affairs division in one lengthy memorandum that I named the "Memo Bomb." I was hoping—naïvely—that it would end up in the hands of someone in government with a conscience, some bureaucrat or politician who took his/her oath to defend the Constitution seriously. When I learned that it was going to be covered up, I didn't even consider turning to the media. I began writing *Deep Cover*, which was published three months after I retired.

The book made the *New York Times* bestseller list despite being virtually ignored by mainstream media and Congress. What little media coverage it did receive portrayed me as a disgruntled whistleblower. Why? Because that is what "credentialed government spokespeople" said I was.

DEA and Justice Department officials refused to comment on any of the specifics. Not one single mainstream media journalist undertook what attorneys for my publisher (Delacorte Press) had done: conduct a libel reading or a detailed examination of how I had documented my facts. I was a man whose words in courts across the land were credible enough to convict and sentence thousands of people to tens of thousands of years in prison. My book screamed in a loud, clear voice that the Drug War was a premeditated fraud, yet no one in media was interested in investigating the story.

In 1991, "Project Censored" called *Deep Cover* one of America's ten most censored stories. During the taping of a show with Bill Moyers, he commented to me that he'd heard that *Deep Cover* was "the best read and least talked about book between the [Washington DC] beltways." I had already heard the same thing from my own sources inside DEA and other agencies.

I pointed out to Moyers that what I found both frightening and depressing about the whole affair was that, despite the fact that a team of US undercover agents had uncovered hard evidence of massive Mexican government drug corruption and involvement in the torture/murder of a DEA agent, our Congress had granted them "cooperating nation" status in the Drug War, meaning that they would be rewarded with US taxpayers' dollars for their betrayal. I also told Moyers that I was deeply disturbed that despite the book's well-documented revelations showing that Operation Snowcap was a premeditated fraud, Congress was expanding the militarized

South American drug war without even making a single inquiry.

All Moyers could do was shake his head the way a streetwise cop does when he watches the suckers line up to play three-card monte

The Plan Colombia war body count continues to mount, including the shooting down of an aircraft belonging to religious missionaries. Could this have happened if the mainstream media had pursued the facts and leads revealed in *Deep Cover* with the aggressive persistence shown during the Watergate and Monica Lewinsky affairs? I think not. Instead, they averted their collective gaze and continued the barrage of fill-in-the-blanks Drug War monte stories. And the suckers watched the show and continued to pay.

_TEN YEARS OF JOURNALISM

After my retirement and the publication of *Deep Cover*, I wrote *Fight Back: How to Take Back Your Neighborhood, Schools, and Families From the Drug Dealers*,[13] followed by *The Big White Lie* (co-written with Laura Kavanau-Levine). Whatever I thought I knew about Drug War monte and how to fight it was now in book form, but I still had a lot to learn, only now from the opposite angle.

THE TOP DRUG DEALERS, THE PANAMA BASED MONEY-LAUNDERING OPERATION, AND THE HIGH-RANKING CORRUPT MEXICAN GOVERNMENT OFFICIALS THAT WE HAD SNARED WERE EFFECTIVELY PROTECTED FROM PROSECUTION.

Beginning with my retirement from the DEA on January 1, 1990, up to this moment, I have been active as a freelance print journalist, media consultant, and on-air drug and crime expert, as well as an expert witness in federal and state courts on all matters related to drug trafficking and the use of deadly force. Since 1997, I have been the host of the *Expert Witness Radio Show*, which airs on WBAI, 99.5 FM, in New York City and KPFK, 90.7 FM, in Los Angeles. The show features interviews with front-line participants in major Drug War monte events and other crime and espionage stories that the mainstream media have either misrepresented or consciously ignored.

The screaming need for the show was best illustrated during a three-hour interview of four veteran federal agents called "100 Years Experience."[14] It was a roundtable discussion with Ralph McGehee (25 years with the CIA), Dennis Dayle (27 years with the DEA), Wesley Swearingen (25 years with the FBI), and myself (25 years with the DEA, Customs, IRS Intelligence, and the Bureau of Alcohol, Tobacco and Firearms). All of us had taken part in some of the highest profile events in law enforcement, military, and espionage history. All of us easily agreed that not a single one of these events—from the Vietnam War and the Cointelpro domestic spying program to the entire War on Drugs—had been reported honestly by the mainstream media.

Dennis Dayle, a principal subject in James Mills' best selling book *Underground Empire*, stated that the CIA had interfered with and/or destroyed every major international drug dealing investigation he had ever conducted. You remember seeing that anywhere in the news?

Now, as a journalist, I want to give you details on some of the most important events that I experienced firsthand and the media shilling that went on as they unfolded.

Drug War Invasion of Panama.[15] As I've already said, it was as early as 1971, when I was serving in the US Customs Hard Narcotics Smuggling Unit, that I became personally aware that both US Customs and the Bureau of Narcotics and Dangerous Drugs knew very well that Manuel Noriega was heavily involved in drug trafficking to the United States, and that he was protected from prosecution by the gang that can't spy straight.

This wacky little drug dealer, like countless other criminals doing damage to America, was on the CIA payroll. He'd even had lunch with George Bush. Ollie North had been assigned to "clean up his image." The protection had been going on for so long and was so well known that no one in the CIA had bothered to tell DEA agent Danny Moritz and federal prosecutor Richard Gregorie that the dude was off limits.[16]

So the same CIA that didn't know that the Berlin Wall was coming down until the bricks were hitting them in the head, didn't learn that their two-decade, drug-dealing asset Manny "Pineapple Face" Noriega was getting indicted until it was too late. Now there was a problem, a problem that only media shills could handle.

On the evening of December 20, 1989, I watched with a mixture of horror and wonder as Noriega's fortress of a home was blown to smithereens along with Chorillo, Panama City's entire inner city. It was the opening shot of America's first full-scale Drug War invasion. Hundreds, perhaps thousands (depending on whom you believe), of Panamanians died. Women, children, tiny babies. Burned, shot, mutilated by our finest and most advanced weaponry. It was a great opportunity to try out our stealth bombers and fighter planes. I could not help but be reminded of the Nazi bombing of Guernica, Spain.

I guess the stuff really works.

Twenty-six American soldiers also died, many of them by friendly fire. All this awesome firepower and death to arrest a man whose drug dealing the CIA had been protecting for almost two decades. How, I wondered, were the Drug War generals and the CIA going to hide the truth behind this grotesque atrocity?

Media shills to the rescue.

Within months, the media coverage had omitted, obliterated, minimized, and/or trivialized Manuel Noriega's true history and reputation with the CIA and DEA, instead turning the event into a major Drug War "victory." So effective was the media's scam that instead of being indicted as a co-conspirator, George Bush Sr. enjoyed a massive surge in his popularity ratings. Lee Atwater, the Chairman of the Republican Party, called the monstrous atrocity a "political jackpot."

The damage this did to those in law enforcement with a conscience was incalculable. Whatever faith we still had in the media fulfilling their alleged Fourth Estate role was gone. The "political jackpot" comment was the final straw for me. I had just retired and felt (again, albeit foolishly) relatively safe from retribution, so I began firing off a barrage of articles to every media outlet I could think of. It was really a futile attempt from the beginning, and I knew it, but I had to try and keep trying. It was only through alternative media and the then-nascent Internet that the truth surfaced, but who paid any attention to that? As long as alternative media had no effect on the polls, it would have no effect on American politicians.

I am close to many men and women who have spent their lives in law enforcement. All of them, when sitting in comfortable living rooms after having a couple of drinks, will lower their voices and admit that if any cop had done what those involved with the Noriega cover-up and the subsequent phony invasion had done, they'd have been buried under a federal jail. They'll say the words that no shill journalist would ever print, that anyone who was responsible for that invasion ought to be tried as a war criminal. It was the realization that our silence was the ugliest part of history repeating itself that kept me at my computer trying to out the true Noriega story. But the wall of media liars was impenetrable.

It was after my son, Keith Richard Levine, a New York City police sergeant, was killed by crack addicts on December 28, 1991, that the *New York Times* published one of my Noriega pieces.[17] I was never sure whether it was my son's very public murder or the upcoming Clinton-Bush election that changed their attitude, but I was grateful, even hopeful. My Bush-Noriega article—an op-ed piece—was a tiny drop in a media tidal wave going the other way, but it made an important point. There was some hope in the media. It was not monolithic. While it was, by and large, controlled by easily frightened and manipulated little people of little courage, there were editors, producers, and journalists out there who were still willing to risk taking a moral stand against the criminal and/or criminally inept exercises of power.

I was also learning another hard lesson: To force real congressional action against corruption and/or criminal ineptitude at the highest levels of government, one article or one television special is far from enough to combat the ocean of media shills. What's needed is a Watergate/Lewinsky-like wave of investigative journalism. A sprinkling won't work. A sprinkling will only be used to trick us into thinking we really have a free, aggressive media.

It was after the mass murder of women and children in Panama that, as a journalist, I began to notice a distinct increase in the militarization of the Drug War in the US. There was, and continues to be, a very clear acceptance by our elected "protectors" and the public of an increase in the use of deadly force in the Drug War, affecting all aspects of police-community relations.

This, too, could never have happened without the mainstream media, television, and Hollywood shilling us with bullshit-based Drug War monte movies like *Clear and Present Danger*, television Drug War specials and so-called "reality"-based programs like *Cops*, and the incessant flow of fill-in-the-blanks drug stories with headlines like, "New Threat in Drug Supply Discovered in (fill in nation of your choice)," "New Link in Opium Trail Discovered in (fill in the blank)," "The Hunt for (fill in the blank), New Leader of the (fill in the blank)

Cartel," "Government Sources Alarmed by Increase in Flow of (fill in the drug of your choice)," "Government Sources Allege Drug Corruption in (fill in some nation in which the CIA wants to initiate some dangerous, foolish, and very expensive action)," "Startling Rise in Drug Use Predicted by (fill in the name of agency that wants a budget increase)."[18]

_AS AN EXPERT WITNESS

Since my retirement, I've worked as an expert witness for attorneys defending people from the excesses of a Drug War monte game gone wild. I've been directly involved in a continuous flow of atrocities perpetrated on innocent citizens that, thanks to the reliable practice of censorship via omission by mainstream media shills, never get mainstream media exposure.

From my point of view, the use of the word "atrocities" is no hyperbole. As a front-line participant, I've watched the Drug War evolve from the point where, in 1973, DEA agents who raided premises in Collinsville, Indiana, in honest error were prosecuted for that error in federal court, to the current point where the killing of innocent Americans in their own homes is now not only condoned under the Drug War banner but actively covered up by Drug War generals with the acquiescence of media flim-flam artists.

> ALL OF THEM, WHEN SITTING IN COMFORTABLE LIVING ROOMS AFTER HAVING A COUPLE OF DRINKS, WILL LOWER THEIR VOICES AND ADMIT THAT IF ANY COP HAD DONE WHAT THOSE INVOLVED WITH THE NORIEGA COVER-UP AND THE SUBSEQUENT PHONY INVASION HAD DONE, THEY'D HAVE BEEN BURIED UNDER A FEDERAL JAIL.

Here's an example. Donald Carlson, a Fortune 500 company executive in San Diego who couldn't distinguish cocaine from garden mulch, was gunned down in his own home, in 1992, by a federal-state, multi-agency Drug Enforcement Task Force SWAT team that had conducted a military-style invasion using machine guns and grenades. They were acting on allegations made by a criminal informant who claimed that Carlson was concealing in his house 5,000 pounds of cocaine and four Colombian hitmen who had sworn never to be taken alive.

The very gringo Carlson, despite the drug agents' best efforts to stop his clock, miraculously survived three gunshot wounds. He decided to sue the government. I was hired by his attorneys to examine the government's reports related to the investigation and to provide an expert opinion—a job I had been trained to do as a DEA Inspector of Operations.

After reviewing more than 5,000 pages of government reports, transcripts of interviews, and statements, I came to the conclusion that the government agents had based their probable cause for the search warrant on the uncorroborated words of a street-level criminal informant whom the telephone company did not trust enough to furnish with a telephone. I concluded, citing specific examples from the government's own reports and statements, that the agents and prosecutors were not only criminally negligent but that they had knowingly violated all of Carlson's constitutional rights against unlawful search of his home, and that they then compounded this crime by perjuring themselves in an effort to cover up their misdeeds. My recommendation was, as it would have been had I been doing the job for the Justice Department, that the evidence be put before a federal grand jury with an eye toward a federal indictment of the agents and prosecutors.

Instead of giving US citizens, in the form of a grand jury, the opportunity to review what had actually happened and make their own choice as to whether the agents and prosecutors themselves deserved to be prosecuted, United States Attorney Allan Bersin, a

HOW IN HELL CAN THE SUITS GET AWAY WITH CLASSIFYING THE EVENTS LEADING UP TO THE SHOOTING OF AN AMERICAN CITIZEN IN HIS OWN HOME?

recent Clinton appointee, called a press conference for the Drug War shills. He proclaimed that "the system failed, but [that] the agents [and prosecutors] had done their job." This proclamation was the "news" broadcast as far and wide as the mainstream media could reach.

The system failed? What the hell does that mean? Only Drug War accomplices, not real journalists, would accept a statement like this on face value.

The bottom line of the whole adventure came soon after I turned in my report. The government settled for $2.7 million in damages to Carlson, and all government reports were classified.

Classified? How in hell can the suits get away with classifying the events leading up to the shooting of an American citizen in his own home? I kept waiting for some Woodward or Bernstein to even ask the question. Never happened. The media shills did their by then customary penguin walk, one following the other off the end of a rock, their gazes rigidly pointed away from the truth.

Once again, I tried to tell the story through any mainstream media outlet that would listen. *60 Minutes*, which in my opinion is one of the few remaining hopes in mainstream media, was the only entity interested. The Carlson debacle was run as part of a special called "Informants" during the summer of 1993. Unfortunately, the cover-up was omitted. Here again, I re-learned the lesson that, as much of a media powerhouse as *60 Minutes* is, a single story does not a change in government policy make. As devastating as the "Informant" piece should have been to Drug War monte, it was only another drop against the mighty torrent of mainstream media shilling.

The big question that the Fourth Estate should have been asking was: If our drug warriors and prosecutors could get away with acting so criminally in the case of a Fortune 500 executive, what can the average citizen expect?

Ezekiel Hernandez is the answer. In 1997, the 18-year-old recent high-school graduate was gunned down by a Marine sniper on "anti-drug" patrol while herding his family's goats in his own backyard. The young man probably never knew what hit him, since the shot was fired from a distance of more than 250 yards. I couldn't help wondering whether or not they were trying out a new weapon.

No one in Hernandez's community of MacAllen, Texas, was aware that those odd moving bushes out on the range were Marine snipers in camouflage outfits assigned to patrol the Texas-Mexico border—in direct violation of the Posse Comitatus Act.

As a radio journalist who also happens to be a court-qualified expert in the use of deadly force, I began my own investigation of the case, which, in my opinion, was at best a clear-cut case of negligent homicide and/or manslaughter. At worst, it was an execution.

While mainstream media continued to sell the death of young Ezekiel as an unfortunate but justifiable error, I tried to get a government spokesman to come on my show and explain the government's position on the young man's murder to a court-qualified expert. No one was willing.

I watched the media—television, newspapers, and magazines—closely. No government spokesman would field questions on the matter. Only self-serving, vague, and misleading statements were released. Why should the Drug War generals explain the murder of an American citizen that occurred during an alleged anti-drug action, as long as mainstream media willingly cover for them?

In this case, like the Carlson case, no government official admitted any wrongdoing. Why should they? The settlement with the Hernandez family was $1.7 million—significantly less than the very white and still living Carlson's $2.7 million—but then again, why should that fact interest a shill?[19]

_DRUG WAR MONTE BILLIONS PAID DIRECTLY TO THE SHILLS

A new level of the Drug War monte con game began when President Clinton and Republican majority leader Newt Gingrich raised each other's hands in victory to announce a new billion-dollar "Say No to Drugs"-style ad campaign. The money would be deposited directly into the coffers of every Hollywood and mainstream media entity on Wall Street's big board. The first $60 million would go to Disney Studios. All the full-page "anti-drug" ads you see in the *New York Times* (for instance) are paid for from this taxpayer-funded pot.

I received a tip from an inside person in the upper ranks of government who finds me cheaper to talk to than a psychiatrist and a lot more reliable than anyone in mainstream media. "Fraud," this person declared. "Go get 'em, Mike."

So I flew into investigative action. Do you think some mainstream media journalist is going to investigate the source of his/her company's millions? Particularly at a time when advertising income is on the decline?

My investigation, buttressed by research that I had done for my book *Fight Back*, revealed that neither the Partnership for a Drug-Free America, nor anyone else for that matter, had done any research into the effectiveness of this kind of advertising. In fact, according to psychological studies conducted by neurolinguistic experts, there was a growing body of evidence indicating that the ads weren't just ineffective—they *increased* drug use by suggestion. They actually put the idea of using drugs into the minds of kids to whom the idea had never occurred.

A lone article in *Brand Week*, the highly respected Madison Avenue trade magazine, pointed out that the full amount of taxpayer dollars that the Partnership for a Drug-Free America was about to give away was $2 billion, making them the biggest advertiser on Madison Avenue. The article called the giveaway "very suspect." My own DEA source pointed out that $2 billion would have been enough to buy up every coca leaf produced in South America that year. It could have surpassed all law enforcement and military operations in effectiveness.

If you put three-card monte dealers and shills in the can for ripping off hundreds of dollars from innocent suckers, what do you think these guys deserve?

_CIA DRUG SMUGGLING: THE VENEZUELAN NATIONAL GUARD CASE

What would be the appropriate action of a truly independent, mainstream media if say, the Central Intelligence Agency was caught red-handed actually smuggling as much cocaine into the US as the Medellin Cartel, in direct violation of federal law and with no political excuse?

Well, precisely that did happen.

Sometime in 1990, US Customs intercepted a ton of cocaine being smuggled through Miami International Airport. An investigation by Customs and the DEA quickly revealed that the smugglers were the Venezuelan National Guard headed by General Guillen, a CIA "asset" who claimed that he had been operating under CIA orders and protection. A fact that was soon, albeit very reluctantly, admitted by the CIA. Once again, as in the Noriega case, it seemed that the gang that can't spy straight had failed to notify the DEA and Customs of what they were up to. That would turn out *not* to be the case. If the CIA is good at anything, it is the complete control of American media. So secure are they in their ability to manipulate media that they even brag about it in their own in-house memos.

> "GOVERNMENT SOURCES ALARMED BY INCREASE IN FLOW OF (FILL IN THE DRUG OF YOUR CHOICE)."

CIA pimps and shills by far outnumber and outclass the Drug War monte variety, but in this case both con games—CIA monte and Drug War monte—were at grave risk. The CIA Public Information Office—referred to by CIA insiders as "the Mighty Wurlitzer"—flew into action. Result: The story appeared nowhere in media for the next three years.

The *New York Times* actually had the story almost immediately in

1990 and did not print it until 1993. It finally became news that was "fit to print" when the *Times* learned that *60 Minutes* also had the story and was actually going to run it. The *Times* ran the story on Saturday, one day before the *60 Minutes* piece aired. There were, however, serious differences between the *Times* report and the one aired by *60 Minutes*. The *Times* piece said:

> No criminal charges have been brought in the matter, which the officials said appeared to have been *a serious accident* rather than an intentional conspiracy. But officials say the cocaine wound up being sold on the streets in the United States. [Emphasis mine]

The highlight of the *60 Minutes* piece is when Federal Judge Robert Bonner tells Mike Wallace:

> "There is no other way to put it, Mike—[what the CIA did] is *drug smuggling*. It's *illegal*." [Emphasis mine]

Judge Bonner further revealed that his assertion came as a result of a secret joint investigation conducted by the internal affairs divisions of the DEA and the CIA. As if that weren't enough, Annabella Grimm, the DEA agent and attaché in Venezuela when the incident occurred, was interviewed on camera. She, too, said that the CIA had simply smuggled drugs in violation of lots of US laws.

You don't have to be a police detective to note that there are some serious differences in the two reports or to suspect media shilling in the first degree. I once again flew into action, doing what I thought a real journalist should do—investigate the story.

Accompanied by my life partner, wife, and cowriter, Laura Kavanau, I flew out to the coast to meet with Annabella Grimm, an ex-colleague of mine whose work and forthrightness I had always admired. After speaking with Annabella, Laura and I talked to another DEA officer who was directly involved in the incident.

The sum total of my investigation was that the CIA had not only been smuggling a lot more cocaine—around 27 tons—than the one ton they were caught with, but it had been warned by the DEA not to do it, that what they were proposing as an "intelligence gathering operation" was not only a "whacko idea" but a felony violation of US law punishable by life in prison.

The identities of at least two top-level CIA personnel who had chosen to ignore the DEA's warning and had gone ahead with the massive smuggling operation had been turned over to the DEA for indictment, but instead of focusing on these criminals, the investigation had turned on Grimm and others.

As I investigated the incident, I noticed that James Woolsey, the then head of the CIA, was appearing on every mainstream media television and radio "news" show that would have him (including National Public Radio), broadcasting the claim that no criminal act had taken place and that the event had all been a "snafu....a joint investigation between CIA and DEA that had gone awry."

Woolsey's public statement directly contradicted that of Federal Judge Bonner. The overwhelming evidence, my DEA sources assured me, showed that Woolsey, an attorney, was lying and that the mainstream media was helping him. Any real journalist could have done what I was doing, but none—other than *60 Minutes*—dared. Was there ever a news story more important than one that should have read something like: "CIA Betrays Nation - Caught Red-handed Smuggling More Drugs onto US Streets Than the Medellin Cartel," or, "Drug War a $ Trillion Fraud"?

The facts behind the case seem to be proof positive that the whole War on Drugs has been the longest running, deadliest con game in the history of American mis-government. In the Venezuelan National Guard Case, there were top-level, credentialed government spokespeople ready to speak openly, to tell a devastating truth about the worst kind of treason possible being committed by the CIA against its own people, yet no mainstream media entity, other than *60 Minutes*, deemed this news fit to pursue with the same in-depth zeal devoted to investigating the shape of President Clinton's penis.

Censorship by omission? Drug War monte shilling? I would say so. Unfortunately for America, my *Expert Witness Radio Show* was among the very few places that this important truth could be heard.

I should mention that when I called the Miami US Attorney's office in charge of prosecuting General Guillen, *et al.*, I was told that "national security" interests prevented them from providing me with a case status, or any statement whatsoever, for that matter.

A fitting postscript for this event, and the whole Drug War monte game for that matter: I was recently made aware that John Clements, the 20-year-old addict "gofer" featured in the Bangkok heroin investigation referred to at the beginning of this article, is about to be released from federal prison after having served most of his 35-year prison sentence. Young Clements was convicted of "conspiracy" to traffic in heroin for driving a drug dealer (Alan Trupkin) to a single meeting to pick up drugs. Of course, the rest of the story is that the media, while ignoring the massive flow of heroin coming into the US at the hands of CIA assets, had shilled the case to the point where there was no way the kid was going to get anything but the max. Unfortunately, I was as guilty as they were.

I can only hope this helps make up for it.

_BLACK TUESDAY: THE PREDICTION

By September 4, 2001, I had already completed and submitted this essay for its first publication in *Into The Buzzsaw*, edited by Kristina Borjesson. On that evening, from 7-8 PM, Kristina, the producer of my radio show *The Expert Witness*, aired an interview with ex-Clinton White House advisor Dr. Richard Nuccio, whose career had been publicly destroyed by the CIA and the State Department when he tried to blow the whistle on a CIA that was operating against America's best interests. The interview—which seemed to be the culmination of four years of our on-air warnings that a criminally inept CIA, like volunteer firemen who start their own fires and then can't control them, were supporting, training, and arming America's worst enemies and that some horrific terrorist act was inevitable.

Near the end of the hour-long show, Kristina, outraged at the mainstream media's complete abdication of their alleged role of government watchdog, blurted out: "We should not be surprised when they blow up the World Trade Center."

> "THERE IS NO OTHER WAY TO PUT IT, MIKE—[WHAT THE CIA DID] IS *DRUG SMUGGLING.* IT'S *ILLEGAL.*" — FEDERAL JUDGE ROBERT BONNER ON *60 MINUTES*

One week later, that is precisely what happened.[20]

By the end of this chapter, if you are convinced of the possibility that the mainstream media have spent the last three decades shilling the American taxpayer into believing in the efficacy of a War on Drugs that was in its every aspect as fraudulent as a game of three-card monte—as I hope you will be—then you must also ask yourself the following questions: Did mainstream media also shill for an inept and bumbling FBI and CIA in a successful campaign to convince Americans that our homeland defense was in the most capable hands possible, when in fact the Boy Scouts of America might have done a better job? And, did this shilling play a role in making us vulnerable to the events of Black Tuesday?

Hard to believe, right? Well, the fact is that—as federal court records verify—seven months *before* the first attempt at blowing up the World Trade Center in 1993, the FBI had a paid informant who had already infiltrated the bombers and had told the FBI of their plans to blow up the Twin Towers. An FBI supervisor—apparently without notifying the NYPD or anyone else, for that matter—"fired" the informant. Seven months later, after the bomb went off, they had to find the informant, who then helped them catch all those responsible.

And that's not all they missed. When the FBI, with the aid of their fired-and-rehired informant, finally did catch the actual bomber, Ramsey Yousef—a man trained by CIA funds during the Russian-Mujihideen war—they found indications on his PC of plans to use hijacked US plans as fuel laden missiles (as early as 1993), which they also ignored. The plans were code named "Bojinka."[21]

If at this point you are scratching your head and asking yourself why you hadn't heard about this, you can thank mainstream media "coverage," which for the most part gave the FBI "credit" for "solving" the case. The media then went on to convince us that the FBI "solved" the Unabomber case as well, when in fact the only way the madman (think anthrax now) was caught was when his own brother turned him in.

Had the media done a professional job of reporting the amateurish failures of the FBI and the CIA, this should have had our elected protectors working feverishly on revamping a human intelligence system that was in competition with the Three Stooges in the respect it commanded from our enemies.

In writing this piece, many of the anecdotes and incidents were taken from events captured in my nonfiction bestseller *Deep Cover*, subtitled: "The Inside Story of How...Infighting, Incompetence and Subterfuge Lost Us the Biggest Battle of the Drug War."

If you go back to the beginning of this chapter and substitute "the

World Trade Center" for "Drug War," hopefully you will understand the very dangerous shill game that is being run on us right now and where it will lead.

Endnotes

1. Goddard, Donald. *Undercover*. New York: Random House/Times Books, 1988. **2.** *The Expert Witness Radio Show*. WBAI, New York City, and KPFK, Los Angeles. <www.expertwitnessradio.com>. **3.** *US v. Herman Jackson, et al.* **4.** See Levine, Michael. *Deep Cover*. Delacorte, 1990. **5.** A typical example, "Mexico's New Anti-drug Team Wins the Trust of US Officials," was taken from the *New York Times*, July 18, 2001. **6.** Testimony of Felix Milian-Rodgriguez, convicted Medellin Cartel money launderer, in Executive Session before the Kerry Committee, June 1986. **7.** Levine, Michael, and Laura Kavanau. *The Big White Lie*. Thunder's Mouth Press, 1993; *op cit.*, Levine. **8.** *Op cit.*, Levine and Kavanau. **9.** *Ibid.* **10.** *Ibid.*: 103-4. **11.** Levine, Michael. "I Volunteer to Kidnap Ollie North." *Journal of Law and Social Justice* (Penn State University), and elsewhere. Available at <www.expertwitnessradio.com>. **12.** Scott, Peter Dale, and Jonathan Marshall. *Cocaine Politics: Drugs, Armies, and the CIA in Central America*. University of California Press, 1991, 1998. **13.** Levine, Michael. *Fight Back*. Dell Publishing, 1991. **14.** For ease of research, all articles, books, and radio interviews referred to are available at <www.expertwitnessradio.com>. **15.** <www.expertwitnessradio.com>. See, particularly, interviews with David Harris (author of *Shooting the Moon: The True Story of an American Manhunt Unlike Any Other, Ever*, Little, Brown, 2001) and DEA supervising officer Ken Kennedy, a participant in the arrest and prosecution of Manuel Noriega. **16.** *Ibid.* **17.** Levine, Michael. "The Drug War, Let's Fight It at Home." *New York Times*, 16 Feb 1992. **18.** <www.expertwitnessradio.

ANY REAL JOURNALIST COULD HAVE DONE WHAT I WAS DOING, BUT NONE—OTHER THAN *60 MINUTES*—DARED.

com>. See numerous interviews with front-line participants under "Drug War Media Mess." **19.** Expert Witness Radio Show. Interview with Ezekiel Hernandez, Aug 1997. Available on audio at <www.expertwitnessradio.com>. **20.** A recording of the actual interview, now titled "The Prediction" is available through <www.expertwitnessradio.org>. **21.** The actual tape-recordings of the FBI agent firing the World Trade Center informant and an FBI agent admitting that the indications of al Queda plans to use plans as "missiles" were ignored were played on *The Expert Witness Radio Show*, 4 Dec 2001, and are available through <www.expertwitnessradio.org>.

UNANSWERED LETTERS
SETTING THE RECORD STRAIGHT REGARDING TAILWIND

APRIL OLIVER

In June 1998, I co-produced an investigative story for CNN now widely known as the Tailwind report. The exposé detailed a covert operation launched into southern Laos in September 1970 by elite American commandos. The mission was top secret, and the soldiers were told to deny the raid had ever occurred. The CNN news story revealed, supported by taped on-camera statements by soldiers who participated, that sarin nerve gas was utilized to help extract the American commandos, and that the target of the combined operation was a village base camp where American defectors were being held. An article was also published in *Time* magazine, CNN's corporate sister, with my byline and that of correspondent Peter Arnett.

The story triggered an uproar, with prominent Nixon-era officials predictably asserting that such a scenario involving nerve gas and defectors was impossible. Henry Kissinger called CNN's top boss, CEO Tom Johnson, to assert the story was a malicious fabrication. News conferences were conducted by *Soldier of Fortune* magazine and the Special Forces Association, loudly demanding a retraction and the dismissal of all senior personnel involved. Some veterans launched an email campaign to pressure CNN's executives, demanding a retraction to clear their honor—even though many of those engaged in the pressure campaign had not participated in the mission. A section of the Website Ranger Bob's Command Post <www.greenberet.net> was set up encouraging the public to protest the Tailwind report and assigning projects to help discredit the Tailwind report.

> **THE EXPOSÉ DETAILED A COVERT OPERATION LAUNCHED INTO SOUTHERN LAOS IN SEPTEMBER 1970 BY ELITE AMERICAN COMMANDOS.**

Quickly, the disinformation campaign spread from the Internet to the mainstream press. The theme, promoted by Special Operations veteran John Plaster, was that sarin nerve gas was not survivable in combat, therefore, the Tailwind report was ridiculous because all the American soldiers would've been killed.[1] This is a demonstrably inaccurate thesis. US records of nerve gas experimentation on American soldiers reveal the survivability of exposure, and field manuals regarding weaponry suggest the same.[2] Further, the American commandos on the Tailwind raid were properly equipped with cutting-edge protective equipment, including the nerve gas antidote atropine and sophisticated face masks to protect against nerve gas exposure.[3]

But Plaster's disinformation themes, involving sarin-as-not-survivable and an impressionable young female on the Special Ops beat (i.e., me), were seductive to armchair reporters, unwilling to crack a chemical weapons manual.[4] Instead of national security reporters unearthing the depth and breadth of the American nerve gas program, the press pack instead cast the Tailwind story as a media misfire, with an inept, pregnant female to blame.

Further exacerbating the attack were the histrionic statements of General Perry Smith, CNN's talking-head military analyst. General Smith did not participate in the Tailwind mission, nor did he fly for the elite Special Operations Wing of the Air Force. In attacking the Tailwind broadcasts, General Smith promoted the work of John Plaster in the CNN executive suite, including Plaster's ten points about Tailwind—all of which were provably inaccurate. General Smith quit CNN amidst claims that the Tailwind story should have been cleared through him first and that he could have established that such a scenario was inaccurate. Prior to the Tailwind report, none of my earlier reporting on military issues had ever been cleared with General Smith, nor was this standard procedure within the investigative unit. Later, General Smith proclaimed to the *New York Post* that the Tailwind report, based on the actual words of combat veterans, was "almost Hitlerian."

Less than four weeks after the story was broadcast, CNN retracted it and fired me and my co-producer, veteran newsman Jack Smith. Ted Turner made the public comment to the Associated Press that the producers erred because "we didn't have evidence beyond a reasonable doubt."[5] Opinion editorials throughout the mainstream media cheered the retraction. The Green Beret Website that had helped stir up the cybersmear against the Tailwind report celebrated by featuring graphics of my coproducer, Jack Smith, and myself with knives through our heads, blood spurting out, in body bags.[6] General Perry Smith bragged in the *Wall Street Journal* that he would ensure that CNN would not receive cooperation with the military until reporter Peter Arnett was fired as well. Arnett departed CNN within the next eight months.

In justifying their actions of retracting and firing the producers, CNN's corporate executives cast us as rogue reporters who ineptly construed the words of our sources. CNN hired corporate lawyer Floyd Abrams to write an "independent" report—even though his coauthor was CNN's corporate counsel, who had vetted and approved the Tailwind report for air.[7] This created an inescapable conflict of interest (which is strongly prohibited by the legal ethical canons).

Floyd Abrams asserted that Jack Smith and I were true believers in the story, even though Abrams never once interviewed Smith or me on our "beliefs." Rather, our brief visits with him concentrated on our confidential sources. Further, CNN initially represented to us that Abrams was there to protect *our* interests—including First Amendment assistance and help with the relations of the Pentagon—not to conduct an investigation of us.[8] Ultimately, Abrams' spin of true belief was a useful legal stratagem to CNN, however inaccurate, as such purported true belief created a valid defense during the soldiers' libel suits certain to follow a high-profile retraction.

In retracting the story, Abrams never asserted that the Tailwind story was inaccurate. To the contrary, he stated that the story was exhaustively researched, with considerable supportive data, and that nothing was fabricated. Rather, Floyd Abrams asserted that the Tailwind report was flawed by overzealous reporting and editing, and also by not featuring enough naysayers. Abrams, however, was well aware that many of those purported naysayers, including Henry Kissinger and former CIA Director Richard Helms, had been offered opportunities to speak on CNN but had declined participation. In his report, Abrams also omitted quoting from a crucial final interview with a former Chairman of the Joint Chiefs of Staff, Thomas Moorer, thus creating an impression that some of our strongest evidence simply did not even exist.

But what CNN and Floyd Abrams attempted to cover up could not be entirely squelched. Sure enough, the soldiers' lawsuits were docketed. The sources who on tape and in reporters' notebooks had confirmed the Tailwind story now hired lawyers and sued for defamation—over a story for which many of them had offered on-camera confirming, corroborating, or supporting information. The lawsuits, however, provided one useful avenue: to put before the public the actual transcripts, sourcing, and factual basis of the Tailwind story, which CNN had actively attempted to squelch to ensure their access to the military during the ratings bonanzas of war-time.

One crucial Tailwind source deposed during the litigation was former Chairman of the Joint Chiefs of Staff Thomas Moorer. During a January 2000 videotaped deposition, Admiral Moorer proceeded to reaffirm the Tailwind story, reviewing and citing as accurate my original notes line by line. Among these notes were the crucial statements made by Moorer which Floyd Abrams had actively suppressed: that defectors were indeed targeted as part of the Tailwind mission and that sarin was the standard weapon used on covert operations in last-resort scenarios.

Moorer, however, went even further in the deposition. He tied a handwritten note on Joint Chiefs of Staff stationary—dated during the Tailwind timeframe—to a request for "poison gas," noting that seeking White House approval was standard procedure for the use of the secret weapon. Such a statement reveals why Henry Kissinger, then Nixon's National Security Adviser, might have a personal agenda in vigorously denying the Tailwind story.

CNN quickly settled my lawsuit for fraud and defamation after Moorer's reconfirmation of the Tailwind story under oath. Few in the press, however, covered the revelations of Moorer, even though I attempted to distribute the deposition widely.[9] CNN also settled with dispatch my co-producer's lawsuit, which had lodged specific complaints of fraud and wrongful dismissal against CNN. The Georgia judge in that case, in an early motion, found for the record that Floyd Abrams' statements were potentially defamatory to the producers, and that Jack Smith had a viable suit against Abrams himself for breach of fiduciary duty.

One soldier who sued for defamation was John Singlaub, former head of Special Operations.[10] Initially, Singlaub had denied involvement with the Tailwind report, asserting to the press that I must pick my sources up off the floor of a bar.[11] Later, Singlaub admitted in court papers that he was interviewed for the Tailwind report, even acknowledging that he had made confirming statements. However, this highly decorated veteran of Special Operations asserts in interrogatories that he was "intimidated" into saying statements he did not mean. A close reading of the interview notes establishes no such pattern of intimidation.

Alternatively, Singlaub has also explained the paper trail of his confirming statements as due to his own confusion over the call numbers for the sarin cluster bomb. In the same court papers, Singlaub attempted to distance himself from the sarin story, by claiming under oath that he has never been a commander at Rocky Mountain Arsenal, where this country's sarin supply was created. However, an official résumé establishes that John Singlaub indeed occupied such a posting during the Vietnam era.[12]

That posting is also reflected in contemporaneous notes during my reporting when Singlaub discussed his experiences there. Although Singlaub apparently did not want to sign the interrogatories, and getting his signature took multiple requests, his signature under oath creates the specter of perjury. Despite awareness of Singlaub's troubling inconsistencies, CNN also ultimately settled the suit with Singlaub.

During the litigation process of the past four years, I have alerted the editorial suites of major publications with updates and requests for corrections of the factual record. Such pleas have fallen on deaf ears. Few in the press have bothered to correct the Tailwind record, even after the Pentagon in May 2002 admitted to sarin nerve gas experiments on US soldiers.

Only one journalistic enterprise has formally retracted its Tailwind coverage. The McCormick Tribune Foundation withdrew a published speech by General Perry Smith, filled with inaccuracies and personal smears. Unfortunately, it is not the journalists who are correcting the factual record regarding Tailwind, but, on some level, the court system.

In March 2002, the Ninth Circuit Court issued an eighteen-page opinion regarding the Tailwind report, authored by Circuit Judge Bright. After reviewing seven hours of unedited tape of a prime source's words, the Ninth Circuit issued two holdings: First, that the Tailwind report was not defamatory to the commando, who served as an officer on the mission. The court found that the CNN story accurately depicted the officer's on-camera statements regarding nerve gas use, defectors killed, and women and children as casual-

DURING A JANUARY 2000 VIDEOTAPED DEPOSITION, ADMIRAL MOORER PROCEEDED TO REAFFIRM THE TAILWIND STORY, REVIEWING AND CITING AS ACCURATE MY ORIGINAL NOTES LINE BY LINE.

THE COURT FOUND THAT THE CNN STORY ACCURATELY DEPICTED THE OFFICER'S ON-CAMERA STATEMENTS REGARDING NERVE GAS USE, DEFECTORS KILLED, AND WOMEN AND CHILDREN AS CASUALTIES.

ties. The court found that the statements were reported in relative context and were uncoerced. In other words, my reporting was accurate regarding the source, a huge victory after press allegations that had suggested otherwise.

In a second holding, the Court slammed corporate lawyer Floyd Abrams and CNN's retraction statement. The Court asserted that Abrams potentially smeared the source by making the commando appear unreliable in an unwarranted manner. The Court stated that CNN, in its "zeal" to "shift the blame" for the Tailwind report, "sought to portray [the commando] as unreliable by any means available." This was the second court to hold that Floyd Abrams' *retraction* of the Tailwind report was potentially libelous.

Few in the media reported the Ninth Circuit decision, though I distributed it widely by email. CNN's investigative unit has been dismantled. *Time* magazine managing editor Walter Isaacson, who vetted the Tailwind report and praised it prior to broadcast, is now the head of CNN. Floyd Abrams continues to hold a position of prestige and is widely considered this country's preeminent First Amendment attorney, despite his demonstrable suppression of the facts girding the Tailwind report. My co-producer Jack Smith and I have left the field of journalism.

I undertook a legal education, in part in an effort to defend myself during the Tailwind litigation. Despite being busy with law school, I nonetheless stumbled upon yet more nerve gas documentation in the public domain. In pursuing a law review article regarding a Cold War case on radiation therapy, I found documents in a report released by the White House indicating that American soldiers were exposed to nerve gas in experiments as early as 1953. I distributed this article, with citations to the nerve gas records,[13] to approximately 100 journalists during the winter of 2001 but did not receive a follow-up call from a single reporter.

The specials ops soldiers from Operation Tailwind.

Starting in January 2002, however, the Pentagon went public to acknowledge Vietnam-era sarin experiments. Four years after the

Tailwind report, thousands began to receive Pentagon-sanctioned letters stating that they were exposed to sarin nerve gas at the hands of the US government during Vietnam-era experiments. Sporadic news coverage has reported that experiments took place in the open air, from Maryland to Hawaii, including experiments on servicemen.[14] The experiments were part of Project 112, a subset of which, known as Project SHAD, involved exposing US warships and their crews to chemical and biological weapons, including sarin.[15] (Other servicemen had received letters two years earlier alerting them to sarin exposure during the Persian Gulf War, although the exposure was explained as being caused by Saddam Hussein's inventory.)

Below is a series of letters written to various editors during the past four years of litigation. The letters depict the state of awareness of the editors as to the facts surrounding the Tailwind report and their reluctance to correct the record. None of these letters was published, and none received a formal response. (One letter did receive an offhand email response that the ombudsman would look into it, but I never heard from him again.)

To this day, nerve gas continues to be depicted as the weapon of a heinous enemy, despite the facts that the US has a vast nerve gas arsenal and that American experimentation on humans stretches back to 1953.

■ ■ ■ ■ ■ ■ ■ ■ ■ ■

To: *Washington Post* editors Leonard Downie, Jr. and Robert G. Kaiser, authors of *The News About the News: American Journalism in Peril* (Knopf, 2002).
From: April Oliver
Date: March 11, 2002

Dear Mr. Downie & Mr. Kaiser:

I am writing out of respect for the paper that broke the Watergate story. Certainly you understand the pressure of a smear campaign against your reporters by powerful people of the Nixon era.

Your book on the news industry has a few short paragraphs decrying the state of cable news. While you are correct in stating that many people at CNN are underpaid, the ensuing revelation that they are thus inexperienced or bad reporters is inaccurate.

The two fired producers of the Tailwind report had a combined experience of 50 years in the news industry. This includes a substantial amount of print experience, where the maxim was held dear: If your mother says she loves you, check it out. You err by not acknowledging that both Tailwind producers stand by the story and that substantial monetary settlements were made after they sued CNN for fraud and defamation.

Your criticism of CNN places you in a curious position. You condemn the network's investigative ability with almost no analysis, and yet you sanction Howie Kurtz's status there as a talking head. You dismiss the Tailwind report, implying strongly that it was inaccurate by stating it "had to be retracted." As Admiral Moorer's deposition has established, however, it never "had" to be retracted. That was CNN's political fix to a difficult public relations problem, so in contrast to the tradition established at the *Washington Post*. Furthermore, documents have been sitting at the *Washington Post* now for many months establishing the Tailwind report's essential accuracy.

Had Kurtz done the slightest bit of critical reporting on this story, this would have been easy to establish. However, not only did Kurtz wholly ignore the Tailwind producers' position, he became party to CNN management's kill job. Consider the following timeline.

May 1970. The *New York Times* breaks the story that sarin (GB) is in Vietnam on an American base, and that a soldier has heard reports of its use in combat.

August 1970. The CIA files a report placing a training camp with a large number of American prisoners in the vicinity of Chavanne, Laos.

September 11-14, 1970. Tailwind takes place in the vicinity of Chavanne, Laos. Admiral Moorer writes a note on JCS stationary which he later ties to a request for poison gas, stating the White House will have to decide what is to be done.

April 1972. *Earth Magazine* reports that American Special Forces used the highly lethal nerve gas VX in Cambodia

June 7, 1998. The Tailwind report appears on CNN, after 44 drafts of the script with management involvement, and nearly two years of reporting.

| MAY 1970. THE *NEW YORK TIMES* BREAKS THE STORY THAT SARIN (GB) IS IN VIETNAM ON AN AMERICAN BASE, AND THAT A SOLDIER HAS HEARD REPORTS OF ITS USE IN COMBAT.

Mid-June 1998. The Special Forces Association and author John Plaster start an Internet smear campaign against CNN, Ted Turner, and April Oliver.

June 14, 1998. A follow-up Tailwind report, with further evidence and voices.

Mid-June 1998. CNN counsel David Kohler writes Tom Johnson, CNN's head, buttressing the sourcing on Tailwind and admitting he approved the use of the word "confirmed" on Admiral Moorer.

June 18, 1998. The Special Forces smear campaign hits the *New York Times* in an op-ed by John Plaster. Nearly all of his "facts" are inaccurate, including that American soldiers would be dead if exposed to sarin. NYT fails to identify Plaster as author of the *Ultimate Sniper* and *Extreme Ultimate Sniper* books and videos, available through Paladin Press.

June 18, 1998. Henry Kissinger calls Tom Johnson directly to state that the Tailwind story was a malicious fabrication.

June 19, 1998. Floyd Abrams, who has served on CNN's payroll before, is hired. His hiring is explained to the Tailwind producers as

in their defense, to help them with confidential sources, relations with the Pentagon, and First Amendment issues.

June 21-23, 1998. The Tailwind producers meet with Floyd Abrams & David Kohler, primarily about confidential source issues. This includes what to do with Singlaub, who publicly smeared the story but privately confirmed it.

Evening, June 23, 1998. CNN manager Jim Connor, who has been intimately involved in the Tailwind story, calls April Oliver. He states that Floyd Abrams' role is changing. Instead of serving as the producers' lawyer he will be their investigator. Oliver states she smells a rat. Jim Connor states the following: I know you didn't make anything up, but it doesn't matter. Everyone in the back hall is putting you in with Steven Glass. It's only the perception that counts, not the truth.

Late June 1998. Kurtz is the first in the mainstream media to go to print comparing April Oliver with the fabricator Steven Glass. In Kurtz's report(s), Abrams is featured as an "independent investigator," and Kohler's conflict-of-interest as Abrams' coauthor (who had approved the Tailwind reports) is not explored. A speedy outcome is predicted.

July 2, 1998. The Tailwind report is retracted. Jim Connor is caught on tape instructing the CNN staff that the corporate goal was to kill the Tailwind story so it is dead and gone forever. The justification for the retraction by Abrams/Kohler does not state that the story was wrong but that the story had three essential flaws: Moorer's characterization as a confirming source (vetted and approved by Kohler); the deletion of Art Bishop, a pilot (done by Jim Connor and Pam Hill); and the failure to include the views of Doc Rose (who actually made the statement that the Tailwind story was accurate post-broadcast, but then during the pressure campaign changed his story). April Oliver (8 months pregnant) is mentioned almost exclusively in the report as being the blameworthy employee.

July 3, 1998. Kurtz reports the CNN retraction, without mentioning his own role at CNN. He compares the Tailwind story to the fabrications of the *Dateline* story on truck crashes.

July 12, 1998. The *Washington Post* prints an op-ed by April Oliver, which the NYT had turned down. The NYT never prints any op-eds or letters by Oliver, despite multiple submissions to counter the Plaster attack.

Mid-July 1998. Dana Priest reports on a Pentagon news conference where Defense Secretary Cohen says exposure to sarin is not survivable and that no evidence exists of sarin being in theater in 1970. Priest notes, however, that 2,000 entries of a sarin CBU deployment do exist, but that the Pentagon has explained the paper trail as a coding error.

Mid-July 1998. The *Washington Post* fails to report on the Smith/Oliver rebuttal to the Abrams/Kohler report, as does the *New York Times*, despite a press conference at the Freedom Forum with approximately 300 people in attendance.

August 1998 (approximately). Howard Kurtz is promoted to anchor of *Reliable Sources* at CNN.

November 11, 1998. The *Washington Post* gives ample coverage to "*Jag* Tears into CNN Nerve Gas Story," ridiculing the Tailwind report in a TV drama series.

November 29, 1998. The *Washington Post Magazine* prints a lengthy feature, "April's War," heaping ridicule on the Tailwind sourcing, while acknowledging that the Tailwind story is not as far-fetched as most reporters have made it sound. The freelancer, who had access to Adm. Moorer's confirming statements that the Abrams/Kohler report omitted, does not include Moorer's confirming statements.

May 1999. April Oliver sues CNN.

Spring 1999. Floyd Abrams is hired by CNN and featured on CNN airwaves as a "CNN lawyer" during the Clinton imbroglio.

January 2000. Adm. Moorer reconfirms the accuracy of the Tailwind story, confirming Oliver's notes line by line in a deposition. CNN settles with Oliver soon after.

Spring 2001. Reese Schonfeld writes a book about CNN, describing CNN's retraction of the Tailwind report as premature, cowardly, and dead wrong. He quotes Moorer's deposition extensively. Moorer's confirming statements had been available to the *Washington Post* since the fall of 1998, when the freelancer had access to it. Nonetheless, Kurtz continues to harp on TV and in columns that the Tailwind report was a dreadful mistake.

Winter 2001. April Oliver contacts the *Washington Post* ombudsman as to why the paper is printing the Pentagon story that 100,000 Americans were exposed to sarin in the Gulf War but should not worry about its effects. This seems strange to Oliver, given the Pentagon's previous insistence during its Tailwind news conference that any exposure would be lethal.

February 2002. Tom Johnson gives an interview to the *Atlanta Journal-Constitution*, acknowledging fierce depression that gripped him during his CNN years, making it difficult for him to face the morning papers. Kurtz does not report this story, which is perhaps relevant regarding Johnson's actions in the face of the Tailwind pressure campaign.

Spring 2002. Various newspapers, including the *Chicago Tribune* and *Hartford Courant*, expose that the Pentagon undertook nerve gas experiments on US soldiers in field trials during the 1960s and up to 1970.

Spring 2002. April Oliver will graduate magna cum laude from law school, in the top 5 percent of her class. Any hopes of returning to journalism seem dashed by an industry that continues to spin the Tailwind report as wrong, her reporting as sloppy, and the Abrams/Kohler retraction justification as independent.

I continue to believe that Kurtz's dual position as CNN talking head and *Washington Post* media critic damages the integrity of your paper. Your paper missed a good opportunity to take the *New York Times* to task on Tailwind: How could they print the Plaster editorial without checking their own files or the validity of his scientific assertions? If, as was noted by your paper recently, the end of the evening news is upon us, Kurtz's conflict of interest is only accentuated.

Thank you for your time and attention.

April Oliver

■ ■ ■ ■ ■ ■ ■ ■ ■ ■

To: *Washington Post's* ombudsman
From: April Oliver
Subject: Gulf War story in *Post*
Date: November 16, 2000

Dear Sir:

It is with great interest that I read your story two weeks ago regarding gas exposure in the Gulf. You reported 100,000 soldiers were exposed to nontoxic levels of sarin nerve gas, about which Americans should not be alarmed.

It is rather ironic to see this in print. Two years ago you and nearly every paper in this country reported the retraction of the Tailwind story, regarding the use of aerosolized sarin in Laos. Your paper brought heavy pressure on CNN, ridiculing its producers in news articles and op-eds. One article by Howie Kurtz compared me to fabricator Steven Glass. CNN retracted the story after Henry Kissinger and Colin Powell complained. You later covered the Pentagon press conference where Defense Secretary Cohen announced that sarin nerve gas was not survivable, period, and that therefore the Tailwind story could not possibly be true.

Apparently the press corps did not bother to crack the NATO Field Manual, which plainly states that sarin nerve gas on the battlefield is survivable and requires merely a gas mask (which the Tailwind commandos had).

Six months ago I supplied your paper with lots of documents. These included documents showing the US had been experimenting for years with sarin to develop incapacitating doses. The tests were on so-called human volunteers. I supplied a deposition with a former Chairman of the Joint Chiefs of Staff reconfirming the entire Tailwind story. I supplied documents putting incapacitating gas in the special operator's arsenal at the time of Tailwind. The documents also included a CIA memo placing a large training camp with Americans in the Tailwind area of operations just before the mission was launched. Your paper has not corrected the record.

Only one news outlet has covered the Moorer deposition—

NEARLY ALL OF HIS "FACTS" ARE INACCURATE, INCLUDING THAT AMERICAN SOLDIERS WOULD BE DEAD IF EXPOSED TO SARIN.

Law.com. Two weeks after their publication on Moorer reconfirming the Tailwind story under oath, CNN executive Rick Kaplan was fired, CEO Tom Johnson demoted, and lawyer David Kohler let go. These three executives perpetuated the Tailwind cover-up on the American public, pretending CNN didn't have the goods, when the record plainly established we did, as the legal record has reestablished. Howie Kurtz did not manage to link these firings to CNN's cut-and-run strategy on Tailwind and continues to suggest that the Tailwind retraction was a noble gesture. His paycheck from CNN taints his views, and calls into question your paper's integrity by allowing him to double-dip when such important journalistic truths are at stake.

If you would like further documentation on the debate among the JCS re: human testing of nerve gas, I recommend rereading the White House report on radiation testing, put out in 1995. Buried in Appendix number 1, you will find relevant documents regarding the need for testing on soldiers. This was 1953.

...

April Oliver

■ ■ ■ ■ ■ ■ ■ ■ ■ ■

To: The *New York Times*
From: April Oliver
Date: April 28, 2001

I am writing to applaud the *New York Times* in its coverage of the Bob Kerrey story [the former Senator and Vietnam vet admitted killing civilians, including women and children], but at the same time to pose some questions. The Greg Vistica piece empathetically portrayed the anguish and remorse of the ex-Senator. Kerrey deserves credit for putting the story forward. His frank talk will be cathartic for many veterans of Special Forces operations, who patriotically served our nation, but have born their pain in silence.

I would like to point out some interesting inconsistencies in both Mr. Vistica's and the *New York Times*' coverage of Special Forces missions during the 1969-70 timeframe in Indochina.

Nearly three years ago both Mr. Vistica, then at *Newsweek*, and the *New York Times* attacked the producers of the Tailwind story. You may recall this CNN/*Time* story related a 1970 Special Forces hatchet-force mission into Laos, with orders to kill everything the commandos came across. Mr. Vistica wrote with derision regarding the impossibility of such a scenario. He and Evan Thomas, his coauthor, relied on a sterilized after-action report that Tailwind—the largest Special Forces mission into Laos ever—was merely an innocuous mission to blow up a bridge (which for some reason, was never found or blown up), and that only enemy soldiers were killed. CNN retracted the story after *Newsweek* and the *New York Times* both attacked the Tailwind story, claiming the producers erred in not proving the story beyond a reasonable doubt.

Today, Mr. Vistica demonstrates newfound savvy that military docu-

ments detailing covert operations, such as Mr. Kerrey's after-action report, were routinely sterilized during the Vietnam War to omit civilian casualties and other troublesome details. However, in his Tailwind coverage, Mr. Vistica displayed no such sophistication about the practice of sterilizing documents, plausible deniability, or the no-holds-barred tactics of Special Forces missions. Instead, Mr. Vistica perpetuated military disinformation to smear the Tailwind producers.

Furthermore, three years ago both Mr. Vistica and the *New York Times* inaccurately reported that the Tailwind story was based on one man's "repressed memory" of the event. This was demonstrably wrong. The story was based on multiple on-camera sources, all of whom had fairly graphic recall. The soldier whom Vistica and Thomas discredited as suffering from "repressed memory" had actually written a book detailing Tailwind in a chapter long before he was ever interviewed by me, which stressed the potency of the vomit gas (a prime side effect of aerosolized sarin at incapacitating levels).

> **THE DOCUMENTS ALSO INCLUDED A CIA MEMO PLACING A LARGE TRAINING CAMP WITH AMERICANS IN THE TAILWIND AREA OF OPERATIONS JUST BEFORE THE MISSION WAS LAUNCHED.**

In your magazine Mr. Vistica and the *New York Times* rely on Mr. Kerrey's distant memory, even though he too claims to have attempted to repress the events. Where are the articles questioning Vistica's reliance on such a repressed memory of distant events? Vistica merely employed the same reportorial tactics that we did on the Tailwind trail—persistent, aggressive reporting to nail a big story. The words of Bob Kerrey strikingly echo the videotaped statements of some of the Tailwind veterans in terms of confusion, sadness, and remorse.

Hopefully, Mr. Vistica's three-year odyssey on the Kerrey reporting trail will make him and others in the press reassess what really went down on Special Forces missions in Indochina. Now that a retired Chairman of the Joint Chiefs of Staff has reaffirmed the Tailwind story in a sworn deposition dated January 2000, such a public reassessment is in order. While the men who provided the original support for the Tailwind story may not have Bob Kerrey's stature, they were equally courageous to put their stories forward for the public record.

April Oliver

■ ■ ■ ■ ■ ■ ■ ■ ■ ■

To: The *New York Times* and columnist Thomas Friedman
From: April Oliver

Dear Mr. Friedman:

I understand you spoke on C-Span this weekend, suggesting that Tailwind was a bogus story and that General Perry Smith saved the day through his Internet campaign. Surely you have read that CNN settled the lawsuit I filed against them for fraud and defamation on the basis of the phony Abrams report?

Since you have studied Tailwind enough to speak about it publicly, you must then too know that Admiral Moorer reconfirmed the Tailwind story in a deposition under oath. The deposition has been sitting at the NYT for nearly a year, as have documents describing the US nerve gas experiments on human volunteers to develop incapacitating doses of sarin. Your willingness to publicly attack fellow journalists as charlatans, and put a military spokesperson on a pedestal, is rather peculiar, and smacks of reckless disregard in light of the information at your disposal.

I issued an invitation to Felicity Barringer [media reporter for the *Times*] last spring to read tens of thousands of documents from the Tailwind files. This invitation was ignored. The NYT has failed to correct the public record. They did not acknowledge our rebuttal to Abrams, and they did not acknowledge the settlement of my suit, the deposition with Moorer, the various documents I sent, or the filing by eminent journalist Jack Smith of a suit against CNN on similar grounds. Could it be that Floyd Abrams is a factor?

....

AO

■ ■ ■ ■ ■ ■ ■ ■ ■

To: *USA Today*
From: April Oliver
Subject: Peter Arnett
Date: May 03, 2001

Peter Arnett has written a thoughtful piece about Bob Kerrey. However, he fundamentally mischaracterizes the sourcing of the Tailwind story, as well as his role in it.

CNN did not exhibit "gullibility" in believing a "pair" of veterans. As Mr. Arnett knows from his involvement, the Tailwind broadcasts of June 7 & 14, 1998 were based on the on-camera statements of at least six Tailwind veterans. The story was buttressed by many more off-camera sources. Furthermore, a Chairman of the Joint Chiefs of Staff, Admiral Thomas Moorer, read the script and conceded its accuracy prior to broadcast. Admiral Moorer has since reconfirmed the essence of the Tailwind story in a January 2000 deposition, as surely Mr. Arnett knows.

Finally, Mr. Arnett did not merely passively read the story. He traveled cross-country to interview key sources on camera, including one in Missouri and one in California. This does not constitute mere narration, but is the active blood and guts of reporting.

Mr. Arnett seems hell-bent on discrediting the Tailwind story, as his infamous (and wrong) statement that he did not add a comma to it underscores. Curiously, however, it was a young Peter Arnett who was among the first to report the use of poison gas by the US in Indochina. Contrary to what has been stated in the press about his gas reports, Mr. Arnett did not just report the use of mere tear gas but instead reported that the US was concocting strange "mixtures" of gas. The symptoms? Vomiting and exploding bowels. Such symptoms indicate exposure to incapacitating levels of sarin, not tear gas. Perhaps a young Peter Arnett did not know the magnitude of the

story he was breaking. It's apparent that he still doesn't today.

April Oliver

■ ■ ■ ■ ■ ■ ■ ■ ■

To: The editors of *Scientific American*
From: April Oliver
Date: August 7, 2001

Dear Editors:

I am writing to express my dismay regarding your latest article on Laos. Your reporter, Daniel Lovering, inaccurately states that the Tailwind story was erroneous. You might recall that at the time of its retraction, the assertion by CNN was that it was insufficiently sourced for a story that serious, not that it was "erroneous" or false, as your reporter implies. Since that time, a Chairman of the Joint Chiefs of Staff has reaffirmed the Tailwind story in a deposition and CNN has settled a lawsuit with me and my co-producer Jack Smith. We continue to stand by our story as an accurate report. The retraction was political, not editorial.

> **SURELY YOU HAVE READ THAT CNN SETTLED THE LAWSUIT I FILED AGAINST THEM FOR FRAUD AND DEFAMATION ON THE BASIS OF THE PHONY ABRAMS REPORT?**

....

Furthermore, the statement regarding CBU-15 embedded in your story defies logic. A top secret sarin weapon just happens "temporarily" to have the same numerical call sign as a common cluster-bomb unit? For what purpose? Why then were the Tailwind commandos told to put on their special NBC [nuclear, biological, chemical] masks, told to carry extra atropine, and briefed that the gas could kill them? All this—to protect them from shrapnel?

If your reporter had bothered to look at the [weapons] manuals of the era, he would find that CBU-15 is a dedicated sarin munition, and not a "temporary" non-gas cluster bomb. The data trail indicates that sarin in the form of the dedicated CBU-15 was used more than once, just as the Chairman of the JCS indicated in his public deposition....

Laos was the theater of the special operators. Your reporter needs to dig a little deeper to cut through the triple canopy cover stories.....

April Oliver

1. Plaster, John L. "*Vietnam the Way It Wasn't.*" *New York Times*, 18 June 1998. **2.** Document released by Pentagon upon subpoena by April Oliver during Tailwind litigation. "*Fact Sheet on Exposure Limits for Sarin (GB): Occupational and General Population Exposure to Sarin (GB) Air Concentrations and Summary of How They Were Derived*" <www.gulflink.osd.mil.dugway/low_lv_chem_fact.html> (noting on page four that the "incapacitation dose was derived from experiments with human volunteers and lab animals"). Also, a current NATO Field Manual addresses protection from nerve agents, stating in paragraph 204 that "[n]erve agent vapour in field concentrations is absorbed through the skin very slowly, if at all, so that where a vapour hazard exists alone, the respirator may provide adequate protection without the use of an NBC [nuclear, biological, chemical] suit." **3.** Indeed, the Tailwind medic has asserted in a press conference sponsored by *Soldier of Fortune*, as well as in email messages, that he was required to carry "extra atropine" on the Tailwind mission. Furthermore, the M-gas masks come equipped with atropine. During the post-broadcast disinformation campaign, Rose tied the "extra atropine" to a need for snakebite antidote, as opposed to nerve gas antidote. **4.** Had reporters done so, they would have found that sarin was heavily weaponized in aerosol form during the Vietnam era, including in such manuals as the 26 February 1971 field reference guide of the Department of the Army, Naval Warfare Information Publication, Department of the Air Force Manual, and Fleet Marine Force Manual. **5.** Elber, Lynn. "Turner Apologizes for Flawed Report." Associated Press, 10 July 1998. **6.** This Webpage has now been withdrawn, although self-congratulatory references remain regarding the attack against the Tailwind report. However, a description of the violent page was posted by *Salon* in an article by Francis Pisani, "Vets Declare War on CNN" (24 July 1998), which called the Website an "impressive, if somewhat frightening site. The dark background resembles camouflage fatigues or a range of mountains at night—a perfect environment for specialists in covert and dangerous operations. Flashing yellow letters invite the newcomer to visit the 'Operation Tailwind Information Center'.... The core feature of the site is a 'Body Count': 14 squares with name tags. Three of them correspond to the dismissed journalists, and 11 squares remain to be filled. The visitor willing to sign up is then served [a] 'Declaration of War'." **7.** The original document is signed on the cover sheet by lawyers Floyd Abrams and David Kohler, CNN's then-general counsel. David Kohler was also present at most meetings with Abrams. In later distributions of this report, however, CNN dropped the reference to Kohler from its cover, inaccurately casting the authorship as solely the work of Floyd Abrams. **8.** Abrams even provided us with direct legal advice. I asked him if I could sue General Singlaub, who had privately confirmed the story but publicly denied it. Abrams provided such advice, stating that in Britain one could sue your sources, but in America it wasn't done. **9.** Among those newspapers and magazines that received access to the Moorer deposition in full or in part are the *New York Times*, the *Washington Post*, the *Boston Globe*, and *The Nation* magazine. **10.** General Singlaub was not the commander in charge of the Tailwind mission. However, he is generally known as being an expert regarding special operations and is the purported mentor of the SOG commander who had been in charge of the Tailwind mission. **11.** Singlaub made this statement at a *Soldier of Fortune* press conference. That Singlaub would publicly deny his involvement as a confirming Tailwind source had been predicted by me in a formal sourcing memo to CNN and *Time* management prior to broadcast, consistent with the plausible deniability built into special operations. Nonetheless, editors at both institutions cleared the story for publication, with Singlaub couched as an off-the-record confirming source. **12.** Official résumé of Service Career of John Kirk Singlaub, Major General, 551-10-2506, as of 13 December 1973, stating: "Present Assignment: Commanding General, United States Army Readiness Region VIII, Rocky Mountain, Arsenal, Denver, Colorado, since August 1973" (on file with author). **13.** See: Oliver, April A. "Human Experimentation at the Brink of Life." George Mason Law Review (Summer 2001): footnote 94. **14.** Kelley, Matt. "Chemical Weapons Tests by US in 60s." Associated Press, 8 Oct 2002; unsigned. "US Tested Sarin in Hawaiian Rain Forest: 5000 Troops Involved in 1967 Experiments Are Urged to Contact Pentagon." Reuters. Appeared in *Washington Post*, 1 Nov 2002: A15. **15.** For declassified documents and other information about Projects 112 and SCHAD, see <deploymentlink.osd.mil/current_issues/shad/shad_intro.shtml> and <www.va.gov/shad/>.

LETHAL NERVE GAS IN VIETNAM CHARGED

Special to The New York Times

BOSTON, May 7—A former Army officer said today that he had seen lethal nerve gas stored at a United States air base in Bienhoa, South Vietnam, while on duty there in 1967 and 1968.

Larry Rottman, a former first-lieutenant, said, however, that he had never seen the gas used.

"I heard reports of its being used," he said.

Mr. Rottman, now a 27-year-old school teacher in Watertown, said the gas was stored in containers marked with the code name "GB." He produced an Army document that describes GB as a so-called nerve agent that causes death.

Mr. Rottman made his statement at a news conference of the National Committee for a Citizens Commission of Inquiry on United States War Crimes in Vietnam. The committee, a group of private citizens, is investigating alleged war crimes.

Critics charge that there were no accounts of poison gas in Southeast Asia. In this article from the *New York Times* (May 8, 1970), a soldier who had been stationed in Vietnam says that he saw containers of "GB" (another name for sarin) and heard reports of its use.

Table 2-II. Likely Signs and Symptoms of GB Poisoning Shown in Terms of Vapour Exposure and Approximate Blood Acetylcholinesterase Depression

Short term Ct mg.min.m^{-3}	Approximate AChE depression	Symptoms and signs*	
		Vapour	Systemic exposure only eyes protected
<2	<5%	Incipient miosis (miosis produced at Ct=2, t=30 min), slight headache.	Nil.
5	20% ±10%	Increased miosis, headache, eye pain, rhinorrhoea, conjunctival injection, tightness in chest.	Tightness in chest.
5-15	20-50% ±10%	Eye signs maximal. Bronchospasm in some subjects.	Symptoms beginning to appear. Bronchospasm.
15	50%±10%	Bronchospasm and all the effects already described.	Wheezing, salivation, eye effects, nausea, vomiting. (Local sweating and fasciculation in liquid contamination of the skin.)
40	80%±10%	Symptoms and signs as for systemic exposure.	Weakness, defecation, urination, paralysis, convulsions.
100	100%	Respiratory Failure Death	Respiratory Failure Death

* All symptoms and signs will be subject to very considerable inter-subject variation.

"Table 2-II" from *NATO Handbook on the Medical Aspects of NBC Defensive Operations, AMedP-6(B)*. Those who attacked the Tailwind report—including then-Defense Secretary William Cohen—flatly declared that sarin couldn't have been used because any exposure to it is always lethal. This NATO field manual—which is also used by the US Army, Navy, and Air Force—shows the effects of various amounts of sarin (a.k.a. "GB") on people who are either 1) unprotected or 2) wearing only eye protection (i.e, no full face mask and no body suit). Notice that at the lower levels, the symptoms are relatively minor. Things get really bad at 40 milligrams per cubic meter, and death only occurs once the concentration reaches 100 milligrams per cubic meter. The claim of 100 percent lethality is false.

> Normal clothing is penetrated by these agents whether contact is with liquid or vapour and specialised clothing including a respirator, nuclear, biological, and chemical (NBC) suit, gloves and overboots are required for protection when liquid agent is present. The respirator protects the eyes, mouth and respiratory tract against nerve agent spray vapour and aerosol. Nerve agent vapour in field concentrations is absorbed through the skin very slowly, if at all, so that where a vapour hazard exists alone, the respirator may provide adequate protection without the use of an NBC suit.

Section 204.b of *NATO Handbook on the Medical Aspects of NBC Defensive Operations, AMedP-6(B)*. Notice that the last sentence says that when exposed to sarin and other nerve gases in concentrations usually found in field situations, a gas mask is probably sufficient to protect the wearer from any harmful effects, never mind death. Again, this puts the lie to the claim that sarin is 100 percent lethal.

To: Dr. Kissinger
From: Sheila
Date: May 21, 1998
Re: CNN/Time SOG interview request   UPDATE

With a delayed response to our previous request, April Oliver of CNN now advises that the information to which she would like you to respond regards Operation Tailwind, Sept. 11-14, 1970. She says they have learned a great deal about the mission, "about both the hard target and the unusual tactics used to rescue the SOG team."

Previously you wrote, "Do not accept blackmail. Answer is now definitely no." I told her no earlier, but this woman just will not accept it. She really wishes to speak with you directly, which I explained would be highly unlikely due to the few hours you are in the office.

I just wanted to inform you of these most recent developments to make sure that you still wish to regret this interview.

Yes, regret interview ___✓___

This email to Kissinger from a staffer advises him of April Oliver's continuing requests for interview or comment on the Tailwind matter. The handwritten note at the bottom right (presumably from Kissinger), says: "Ask Rodman what he knows." This is a reference to Peter Rodman, who, at the time, was Director of National Security Studies at the Nixon Center. Rodman served in the Reagan and Bush I Administrations in various high-level positions regarding national security, and he is currently the Assistant Secretary of Defense for International Security Affairs.

The note scribbled in the upper right says:

"Per Peter Rodman
commando raid
[illegible] 10th
in North V. prison - Win Lord know [?]
nobody will watch it
right to stay away from it
can always reply later"

Thus, a former National Security Adviser and current Assistant Secretary of Defense has acknowledged that Tailwind was a commando raid on a prison run by the North Vietnamese. This directly contradicts those who claim that Tailwind was merely an operation to gather reconnaisance, or blow up a bridge, or something else along those lines.

Interview with Admiral Thomas Moorer, Chairman of the Joint Chiefs of Staff, 1970-74

May 2, 1998, 10 AM to 12:15 PM
Interview by April Oliver

April Oliver: Admiral, I wanted to fully brief you on our research. Our program airs on June 7th, and we have learned a lot in the past few months since we first met. The most important point we have learned has to do with defectors. You yourself told us on camera that this Tailwind mission was about defectors. Since then we have learned it was specifically to target them, to kill them. Is that your understanding of this specific mission?

Adm. Moorer: Generally SOG's objectives was to locate personnel such as defectors, or Laotian military, or track NVA movements within Laos. Tactics—I did not get involved with exactly how they did it. I knew what they were trying to do. But I was too busy. I had the Israeli problem to worry about. I didn't go into detail on exactly how they would do it. It was not the only such mission of its kind.

Compartmentalization is key here. I didn't even tell General Abrams when I was going to mine Haifong Harbor because I was too worried about leaks. That would have been disastrous. Leaks were always a problem. I can also remember talking about the Christmas bombing with Nixon. He asked me if it would leak or not. And I promised him it wouldn't—

Oliver: Yes, but back to the Tailwind mission. I understand about compartmentalization. That was common in SOG ["Studies and Observation Group," a secret commando unit]. Now, you had told us before the CIA was involved in this operation. Was it the CIA's job to track defectors?

Moorer: Yeah, trying to track defectors was one of its jobs, but it had several jobs. Again, I knew the general, overall task on this mission. But I did not know about the tactics.

Oliver: But was the mission at hand here, to try and kill these defectors—that they were creating a real military problem that had to be eliminated?

Moorer: I told you before that I would not hesitate to use any tactic or any weapon to save American lives.

Oliver: But defectors were a grave problem, one that was costing American lives?

Moorer: Yes. They had generally gotten mixed up in Laos doing various things.

Oliver: One of the breaks we have had in the past few weeks is locating several SOG recon teams who were sitting on the ridgeline surrounding the village base camp where the defectors were. They report back to HQ that there are "round-eyes" or "long-shadows" in that village. At least one person we have talked to observing the camp says they were walking around unfettered, freely mixing with the locals. Is that intelligence accurate?

Moorer: One of the prime factors in such a decision on a mission would be the confidence you have in the accuracy of the information obtained in the field. If it is an unconventional operation, and you did not have absolutely accurate intelligence, then you would hesitate about doing it. For such a mission to occur, you would have to have complete confidence in its accuracy. And then you would have to go ahead and do whatever it takes to protect American lives.

Oliver: So killing these defectors was the mission? And it was done to protect American lives?

Moorer: Yeah, I have no doubt about that. Now, I was not looking through the field glasses. But I assume the information was corroborated somewhere and that the recon teams saw what they saw.

Oliver: And then the correct decision in your view was to eliminate them?

Moorer: Yeah.

Oliver: Why not capture them?

Moorer: Well, you would have to examine that possibility. You would have to see if it was possible to capture them and bring them out. If it was impossible, then you can't leave them out there. You would have to eliminate them.

Oliver: And elimination was successful in this case?

Moorer: Yes. But, again, I do not remember exactly, but I do not think there was just one such incident. That there was a large group makes it a big incident. But, again, I do not remember the specifics of this action. I was aware of the fact that there was this objective in Laos.

Oliver: Our understanding when you mention a large group, is that there were as many as 20 in this village. Isn't 20 a large group, and isn't that memorable?

Moorer: That's a very large group. Probably others had been picked up by the Russians. They really liked electronic repairmen. The NVA [North Vietnamese Army] really liked getting their hands on them. They would treat them nicely.

Oliver: Our understanding is that these defectors might have been doing signal intelligence, etc. Is that your understanding?

Moorer: The problem at the outset of the operation—now, again, I did not get an exact rundown on the tactics of it—but that there were people mixed up with the locals. It is very difficult to capture such people as a group. Especially if it is a big group. Now, I am sure that there would be an effort to capture them alive; if they could capture them alive, they would do it. Because we would want to interrogate them about the other side. But at the same time they were of no assistance to what we were doing over there. If they caught, say, a senior sergeant, then the enemy would soon find out just what school they had gone to or what communications they knew or what codes. They would interrogate them and treat them real well and get them on their side.

Oliver: But is communications, codes, signal interpretation what was going on in this specific village?

Moorer: I think it could have been. The enemy would interrogate them in detail. But the enemy would get useful information out of them and do anything to get them to turn. And if they could get them to do something useful, they would do anything to keep them cooperative, even serve them ice cream.

Oliver: You mean drugs, women, etc.?

Moorer: Drugs, yes. Women, I don't know about. Have you ever seen the women over there?

Oliver: We have been told that when the Tailwind hatchet-force team hit the ground, the defectors went scrambling into a defensive perimeter around the base camp. Does that make them enemy?

Moorer: If they are participating in a defense and you are on the offense, then of course. No holds barred.

Oliver: Wouldn't the White House have to approve such an operation to go after the defectors?

Moorer: There's a lot of people in the White House.

Oliver: Specifically, did NSA [National Security Adviser] Kissinger know and approve it?

Moorer: He would be generally aware. There would be a member of the National Security Council staff that would know.

Oliver: Haig?

Moorer: Not Haig. He was just Kissinger's aide, really. Whether he really knew, I don't know.

Oliver: Now, I can imagine a scenario where the military comes to the White House and says, We have a problem, a nest of defectors costing us lives. We could go capture them. And the politicians say, No way, you can't bring those boys home. We can't go through 20 court-martials. Do whatever is necessary. Did that occur?

Moorer: No (sharply). At least I don't think so. I really don't know. That might be a conversation I normally might not know about on a CIA operation.

Oliver: So who would know?

Moorer: The CIA gives the President a report every day on what they do. They give him the key points in intelligence. There could have been a CIA action officer on the National Security Council that would have had that conversation. I don't know.

Oliver: So you didn't know the details about this operation before?

Moorer: I did not before. Afterwards, yeah.

Oliver: Was it your understanding that the SOG team achieved their objective?

Moorer: I don't know about "achieve." I knew about the problem. And I knew when the operation was finished. I didn't analyze the details. There was no hooray, hooray, we've won again.

Oliver: Now, about the mission completed. It's got to be a difficult choice. On the one hand, those defectors are somebody's father or child. On the other hand, they are a huge military headache and need to be taken care of. Is there a moral choice here, any ambivalence?

Moorer: I think that the second attitude you describe is more like it. When you go into a fight, it is life or death. You can't ease up on an operation. You can't go in with sentiment. You can't go in with no drive and aggression. If you are going in and need to do a job, you really have to put your heart and soul into it. Otherwise you might get yourself killed if you are fighting only halfway. I suspect in general you participate tooth and nail.

Oliver: So you were aware the problem had been taken care of?

Moorer: I don't think I was ever given an after-action report about that particular incident. After all, these were only ten or fifteen soldiers out of 100,000 or so. I do not remember the specifics. I do remember that it was executed, and it was finished.....

Oliver: How can you be sure there were not POWs there? The hatchet-force team was told to go in and shoot anything that moves. They wouldn't be told that if there were POWs there, would they?

Moorer: Now you are getting into the rules of engagement. Every combat force gets information on the rules of engagement. We had terrible rules of engagement during the Vietnam War. The rules of engagement tell you who to shoot and who not to shoot. Sometimes it comes down that, all right, all targets are okay.

Oliver: And it must have been concluded that the target in this case were all defectors and not POWs?

Moorer: Let's say that they were evaluated, and the conclusion was reached that they were defectors.

Oliver: On this specific operation?

Moorer: Yeah.

Oliver: Is our number of about fifteen defectors killed about right?

Moorer: I do not know for sure. You will have to talk to someone who was there. I do not know if there were 20 or fifteen. But there was a group.

Oliver: What do you think they were doing out there?

Moorer: I think they were people who were disenchanted with the way the war was going and what they were doing. They had the hope that they would someday escape and give up back to the American armed forces and get back to the US and Mr. Carter.

Oliver: You make it sound as if they are more like deserters.

Moorer: Defectors are deserters. And they were out there seeking the best way to stay alive until they could escape and go home. They were in my opinion probably deserters that—after all, this war was unique. There was no public support for it. Soldiers came back in uniform and were booed. These people apparently couldn't take it anymore. They said: I'll escape. Going into Laos is not the same as the Germans. They endeavored to make their way back home through Laos. And they were picked up by Laotian military people. And they were biding their time until the war was over. And they could make an escape back to the US.

Oliver: So there is this kind of gray area between defectors and POWs. They are kind of in the middle—

Moorer: In order to survive, they were cooperating with the enemy, doing things, to get through this stage and achieve their hope of getting home. They had set about doing things that would not displease their captors. They were collaborators. They did not wave the Laotian flag, but they did not want to be eliminated. They were taking the long-range view. They all got together and somehow decided how to survive until they could get out. They knew it would not have been effective to have attacked their captors. They did not have the equipment, and in that situation they could not escape. If they had to in some way assist their captors, then they would do it to survive.

Oliver: How exactly would they support the enemy?

Moorer: They would be interrogated. With the view to see if that individual had a talent or capability to be used. And if they did, the enemy would give them a job that they were fully conversant with and also give them food. And they would do anything to survive until the war was over. Conditions change.

Oliver: They were just getting by?

Moorer: Yes, just getting by. Until sometime later. Again, there weren't a lot, given the large number of soldiers we had over there.

Oliver: How many were there in general? Singlaub has given us a figure of 23, and someone else has told us 300.

Moorer: I think there is no way that I can really give you accurate figures on that. Even today, several bodies are disputed. I tell you this—one figure is too low, and the other too high. It is someplace in the middle. Many of the missing on the missing list are truly missing. Not every missing person is a defector. There is not a reliable source of figures on this. It depends on who is computing the information and how they handle the inferences.

Oliver: Did conventional forces have different rules of engagement for defectors than SOG?

Moorer: I think so. But it would be on a case-by-case basis.

Oliver: We've been told, including by Singlaub, that killing defectors—that defectors were always a top-priority target for SOG.

Moorer: Yes, I think so. You can rely on Singlaub. He was heavy into this from the start. He would have no reason to misinform you. You can believe him.

Oliver: But the conventional forces might be more apt to take a defector prisoner.

Moorer: It's on a case-by-case basis. You get into the PR game here. You can't have soldiers writing home, Dear mom, yesterday I saw a defector and he was American, but we had to shoot him. That would hit the papers sooner or later, and LBJ would be mad.

Oliver: So a big PR problem?

Moorer: Sure.

Oliver: So this was sensitive.

Moorer: It's very sensitive subject matter. Many mothers and fathers do not believe their sons would defect. If you kill a defector, it's a big PR problem.

Oliver: Because of the PR problem with defectors, that is why this operation was given to a black operation like SOG?

Moorer: Yeah.

Oliver: Isn't it unusual to conduct such a large operation against a large group of defectors?

Moorer: Yeah

Oliver: You said earlier that there was more than one such operation. What others?

Moorer: I can't name them. But I do not think that an organization such as SOG would be justified if there was just one such operation. There was a longstanding effort to find out the ground movements of the enemy and intelligence.

Oliver: But this is more than a recon job. This is a hatchet-force or exploitation force.

Moorer: Well, what do you do after you have the recon? You have to exploit what reconnaissance you get.

Oliver: So obviously the intel in this case was deemed accurate?

Moorer: Yeah. Intelligence is the origin of all operations. You have to have intelligence at the outset.

Oliver: Ever heard of Salt and Pepper?

Moorer: No.

Oliver: Turning now to another subject matter—the gas. We discussed CBU-15—which is GB, which is sarin—when we last met. I have been talking to lots and lots of Air Force people. And specifically to about 30 different A-1 pilots based at NKP [Nakhon Phanom,

Thailand]. And they say they had this weapon and used it a lot on Search and Rescue, SARs. The Sun is going down. The pilot is surrounded. In moments he will be captured and killed. They drop the CBU-15. But what is dramatic is that sometimes the pilot on the ground might not have a gas mask. How would it be decided to use such a weapon in that situation?

Moorer: Well, the weapon had to be on the airplane to begin with. The pilots would have to have had sufficient information that this weapon was needed to remove this threat. But the pilot would not want to kill his objective—the downed airman. You can't go dropping weapons like that willy-nilly.

Oliver: How do you decide whether to drop the weapon?

Moorer: It depends on good communication with the man on the ground. Hopefully the pilot can tell you I am just behind the big oak tree, up the hill. The pilots would have to know they have a good chance of attacking without killing him. There is no point in killing him while trying to save him. The key to that decision depends on sufficient communication to pinpoint his position. And if that is the case, and they are confident, then the attack should take place and the helicopter should make the pickup while the results of the attack is debilitating the enemy.

Oliver: But maybe not. Some describe a situation in which the gas would be dropped on the enemy. The Sun is going down. The gas could prevent the capture of another POW, who would then not give info to the enemy. And it would kill a lot of enemy and keep them from gaining the radios and other weapons on the aircraft. So the pilots would drop the weapon in the hope of preventing a capture, as sort of a prophylactic, even if it killed the airman.

Moorer: Well, one important factor here is the wind. It's important to talk to the pilots to make sure you drop the weapon downwind. You obviously want to drop downwind from where he was. You want to make sure the wind is not blowing over him. But the decision to use the weapon or not is an on-the-scene decision. There are three or four vital pieces of information that determine what to do. And if the wind is right and communication is good, I would be inclined to go ahead with the attack. I would try and rationalize as much as I could towards a possible attack. It's not just wind but time of day that matters, too. But the decision may have to be made on the spur of the moment. I have said to you a couple of times in my mind if that weapon gives the best chance of rescuing an American boy, that's what you do.

Oliver: I know this is a bit exacting, but I just want to make sure we know what we are talking about here. CBU-15 is GB is sarin is nerve gas. Agreed?

Moorer: I think everybody knows that.

Oliver: Not everybody. Not some of the men on the ground. They know GB, but they don't know it's sarin. Think they are just play-acting?

Moorer: I think everyone associated with those kinds of weapons knows their effects.

Oliver: Ever hear of a program of VX [an extremely potent variety of nerve gas] lobbed into Cambodia?

Moorer: No. When you are trying to make the decision to use the weapon, you try to determine whether it could kill the pilot or not. But of course that depends on the degree of exposure. Germans first used gas in World War I. Their two major innovations were the tank and the gas. But the worldwide reaction to the pain the victims of gas suffered was abhorrence. And now people try to make it like the nuclear bomb. There is always a public movement to eliminate nuclear weapons, eliminate gas, eliminate mines. But the problem is there is no assurance the enemy will do the same thing. So one side ends up doing away with the weapon, and then the other side is in a hell of a fix. The opponent finds out and exploits it.

Oliver: Now turning to Tailwind for a moment, one of the new pieces of information we have is that the A-1s had prepped the camp where the defectors were based the night before the SOG team attacked. We've been told CBU-15 was used in prepping the camp. Are you aware of that? Does that fit with what you said earlier about any weapon, any tactic is justified in saving an American life?

Moorer: I do not know this for sure. I knew what they were trying to do there. I do not know exactly how they did it. But the fact that this was an unconventional operation, yes, I tried to use every capability and facility to ensure success. I think you have to check that off the list in the planning. And in fact you have to use every capability you have.

Oliver: And so prepping the camp with gas was a part of the battle plan?

Moorer: Fundamentally, what you described is aimed at saving American lives. I have no problem with it. So is collecting intelligence, eliminating defectors. I come back to the point—if an operation is necessary to keep the losses of Americans to an absolute minimum, and if that capability ensures a significant reduction or elimination of American casualties, I'd use it.

Oliver: One pilot told me he flew the weapon fifteen different times. There are 60 or so pilots at NKP who fly A-1s. Could this weapon have been used more than a hundred times?

Moorer: I don't have the figure.

Oliver: But it was used a lot?

Moorer: Then again, did that pilot use it every time he flew it?

Oliver: I don't know.

Moorer: Well, I can comfortably say that if a pilot was involved in a SAR operation, then he probably flew it. I think it could be useful in a lot of those operations. I am not aware of how many times it was used.

Oliver: But it was always available on SARs?

Moorer: By and large it was available, yup. Whether or not it could be carried as easily as a 500-pound bomb, I don't know.

ABUSE YOUR ILLUSIONS

Oliver: "By and large" means what?

Moorer: If the rules of engagement included it. And that decision would be made at the squadron command level or area command level. It would be stipulated in the rules of engagement.

Oliver: We have heard the weapon was generally available from 69 to 70—

Moorer: (Rolls his eyes, as if to say, way too low). I do not know the exact dates of the weapon in the area. I am not aware specifically. Let me say this. It was definitely available in the Vietnam War. This is a much bigger operation than you realize. It takes authorization to move the weapon into Southeast Asia. That is only step one. And there are many steps to make it available to the pilots.

Oliver: Who gives authorization to move it to Southeast Asia?

Moorer: The Secretary of Defense would probably authorize it, or at least be advised.

Oliver: And to use it?

Moorer: The weapon itself would not be located in the area if it wasn't contemplated it would be required.

Oliver: Would the White House be aware?

Moorer: Someone on the NSA staff would be aware. [In this case, "NSA" stands for National Security Advisers.]

Oliver: Kissinger?

Moorer: I am sure he had a briefing. He was generally briefed on all weapons in Southeast Asia. I am not sure he thought about it seriously. It was just another weapon in war. He was told what its characteristics are. But in the broadest sense, the US was not to initiate gas warfare.

Oliver: But you told me before the NVA didn't use gas.

Moorer: That's true. What I mean is that we would not initiate in terms of regiment versus regiment or division versus division. But when you get into special operations, that's another question. If the weapon could save American lives, I would never hesitate to use it.

Oliver: And it did save American lives in Laos?

Moorer: Yes, uh-hum.

Oliver: How many American lives were saved by this weapon?

Moorer: I would not want to speculate on that.

Oliver: Estimate. One hundred or more?

Moorer: Well, it wasn't used every time a helicopter was shot down. I don't know.

Oliver: Was it ever used in South Vietnam?

Moorer: (Hesitates.) I do not recall using it in South Vietnam.

Oliver: Two pilots who flew in Tailwind swear they were briefed that the debilitating gas in this strange, boxy dispenser was in fact tear gas. Now, does that make sense to you? Would the pilots in general operating the aircraft know exactly what they carried?

Moorer: I think by and large the pilots would know. Before he would fill his bomb racks with an exotic weapon, he would want to know what it was before he took off. I don't know of a pilot that would take off with a mysterious weapon on his plane.... If it's a small-scale operation, the pilot is going to find out. He's got to know how best to use it so he doesn't do the wrong thing.

Oliver: Are you aware that a lot of yards [Montagnards, a mountain people of Vietnam] died in this operation? All the Americans on the SOG team get out alive. But the yards' masks were too large.

Moorer: I remember a general discussion of these people. I cannot say whether their gas masks fit them or not. I always felt we never discharged our full obligation to these little people. They did help quite a bit. One gave me a happy house....

Oliver: Soon after, I am told, the US started making smaller M-17 gas masks.

Moorer: I knew the yards were involved in this operation. I do not know the details about the gas masks. I can't say we instituted a smaller gas mask because of this. I do not remember. I am surprised we didn't have them sooner.

Oliver: There could be a lot of politics in the next few weeks, and I just want to be sure that you are comfortable with the candid nature of our discussions. If need be, would you take a call from the head of my company to verify again what we have talked about?

Moorer: Yes, of course. And now frankly I am more interested in how your baby is doing....

WHY UN INSPECTORS LEFT IRAQ IN 1998
WHAT A DIFFERENCE FOUR YEARS MAKES
JIM NAURECKAS

_ABC

"The UN orders its weapons inspectors to leave Iraq after the chief inspector reports Baghdad is not fully cooperating with them."

—Sheila MacVicar, *ABC World News This Morning*, December 16, 1998

"To bolster its claim, Iraq let reporters see one laboratory UN inspectors once visited before they were kicked out four years ago."

—John McWethy, *ABC World News Tonight*, August 12, 2002

_NBC

"The Iraq story boiled over last night when the chief UN weapons inspector, Richard Butler, said that Iraq had not fully cooperated with inspectors and—as they had promised to do. As a result, the UN ordered its inspectors to leave Iraq this morning."

—Katie Couric, NBC's *Today*, December 16, 1998

"As Washington debates when and how to attack Iraq, a surprise offer from Baghdad. It is ready to talk about re-admitting UN weapons inspectors after kicking them out four years ago."

—Maurice DuBois, NBC's *Weekend Today*, August 3, 2002

_ASSOCIATED PRESS

"The chief UN weapons inspector ordered his monitors to leave Baghdad today after saying that Iraq had once again reneged on its promise to cooperate—a report that renewed the threat of US and British airstrikes."

—Associated Press, December 16, 1998

"Information on Iraq's programs has been spotty since Saddam expelled UN weapons inspectors in 1998."

— Associated Press, September 7, 2002

_LOS ANGELES TIMES

"Immediately after submitting his report on Baghdad's noncompliance, Butler ordered his inspectors to leave Iraq."

—*Los Angeles Times*, December 17, 1998

"It is not known whether Iraq has rebuilt clandestine nuclear facilities since UN inspectors were forced out in 1998, but the report said the regime lacks nuclear material for a bomb and the capability to make weapons."

—*Los Angeles Times*, September 10, 2002

_NPR

"The United Nations once again has ordered its weapons inspectors out of Iraq. Today's evacuation follows a new warning from chief weapons inspector Richard Butler accusing Iraq of once again failing to cooperate with the inspectors. The United States and Britain repeatedly have warned that Iraq's failure to cooperate with the inspectors could lead to air strikes."

—Bob Edwards, National Public Radio, December 16, 1998

"If he has secret weapons, he's had four years since he kicked out the inspectors to hide all of them."

—Daniel Schorr, National Public Radio, August 3, 2002

_CNN

"This is the second time in a month that UNSCOM has pulled out in the face of a possible US-led attack. But this time there may be no turning back. Weapons inspectors packed up their personal belongings and loaded up equipment at UN headquarters after a predawn evacuation order. In a matter of hours, they were gone, more than 120 of them headed for a flight to Bahrain."

—Jane Arraf, Cable News Network, December 16, 1998

"What Mr. Bush is being urged to do by many advisers is focus on the simple fact that Saddam Hussein signed a piece of paper at the end of the Persian Gulf War, promising that the United Nations could have unfettered weapons inspections in Iraq. It has now been several years since those inspectors were kicked out."

—John King, Cable News Network, August 18, 2002

_USA TODAY

"Russian Ambassador Sergei Lavrov criticized Butler for evacuating inspectors from Iraq Wednesday morning without seeking permission from the Security Council."

—USA Today, December 17, 1998

"Saddam expelled UN weapons inspectors in 1998, accusing some of being US spies."

—USA Today, September 4, 2002

_NEW YORK TIMES

"But the most recent irritant was Mr. Butler's quick withdrawal from Iraq on Wednesday of all his inspectors and those of the International Atomic Energy Agency, which monitors Iraqi nuclear programs, without Security Council permission. Mr. Butler acted after a telephone call from Peter Burleigh, the American representative to the United Nations, and a discussion with Secretary General Kofi Annan, who had also spoken to Mr. Burleigh."

—New York Times, December 18, 1998

"America's goal should be to ensure that Iraq is disarmed of all unconventional weapons.... To thwart this goal, Baghdad expelled United Nations arms inspectors four years ago."

—New York Times editorial, August 3, 2002

_WASHINGTON POST

"Butler ordered his inspectors to evacuate Baghdad, in anticipation of a military attack, on Tuesday night—at a time when most members of the Security Council had yet to receive his report."

—Washington Post, December 18, 1998

"Since 1998, when UN inspectors were expelled, Iraq has almost certainly been working to build more chemical and biological weapons."

—Washington Post editorial, August 4, 2002

_NEWSDAY

"Butler abruptly pulled all of his inspectors out of Iraq shortly after handing Annan a report yesterday afternoon on Baghdad's continued failure to cooperate with UNSCOM, the agency that searches for Iraq's prohibited weapons of mass destruction."

—Newsday (New York), December 17, 1998

"The reason Hussein gave was that the UN inspectors' work was completed years ago, before he kicked them out in 1998, and they dismantled whatever weapons they found. That's disingenuous."

—Newsday (New York) editorial, August 14, 2002

THE PENTAGON'S NEW BIOCHEMICAL WARRIORS
US ENGAGED IN DEVELOPMENT OF ILLEGAL, TREATY-BUSTING BIOLOGICAL AND CHEMICAL WEAPONS
THE SUNSHINE PROJECT

Many biological weapons are rapidly destroyed by bright sunlight. The Sunshine Project works to bring facts about biological weapons to light! We are an international nonprofit organization with offices in Hamburg, Germany and Austin, Texas, USA. We work against the hostile use of biotechnology in the post-Cold War era. We research and publish to strengthen the global consensus against biological warfare and to ensure that international treaties effectively prevent development and use of biological weapons. All of the documents referred to in this article are on our Website <www.sunshine-project.org>.

_US ARMED FORCES PUSH FOR OFFENSIVE BIOLOGICAL WEAPONS DEVELOPMENT

US Navy and Air Force biotechnology laboratories are proposing development of offensive biological weapons. The weapons, genetically-engineered microbes that attack items such as fuel, plastics, and asphalt, would violate federal and international law. The proposals have been made by the Naval Research Laboratory (Washington, DC) and the Armstrong Laboratory (Brooks Air Force Base, San Antonio, Texas). They date from 1997 but were recently submitted by the Marine Corps for a high-level assessment by a panel of the US National Academies of Science (NAS).

The uncovering of these proposals for an offensive biological weapons program comes at a critical political juncture. The US has rejected a legally-binding system of United Nations inspections of suspected biological weapons facilities. At the same time, the Bush Administration is aggressively accusing other countries of developing biological weapons and expanding its so-called "Axis of Evil" based in large part on allegations of foreign biological weapons development.

But it is increasingly apparent that there are serious questions about the United States' own compliance with the Biological and Toxin Weapons Convention (BTWC). While US allegations against other countries are generally undocumented, the proposals described here were released to the Sunshine Project under the Freedom of Information Act and have been placed on the Project's Website for independent analysis.

Explicitly for Offense. In the murky world of biological weapons research, many technologies are "dual use"—that is, they have both offensive and peaceful applications. The alleged transfer of dual-use technologies, such as vaccine research, is a basis of charges made against Cuba by US Under Secretary of State John Bolton on May 6, 2002. The US military documents released to us, however, are not about "dual-use" technology—they are explicit proposals for offensive weapons-making.

According to the Naval Research Laboratory: "It is the purpose of the proposed research to capitalize on the degradative potential of…naturally occurring microorganisms, and to engineer additional, focused degradative capabilities into [genetically modified microorganisms], to produce systems that will degrade the warfighting capabilities of potential adversaries." The Air Force proposes "genetically engineered catalysts made by bacteria that destroy.... Catalysts can be engineered to destroy whatever war material is desired." The proposals indicate these weapons might be used by all the armed forces, including the Special Forces and in peacekeeping and anti-narcotics operations.

Additional Documents Suppressed. These proposals are probably only the tip of the iceberg. For well over one year and counting, the Marine Corps has delayed response to a Sunshine Project Freedom of Information Act request that now includes 147 *unclassified* documents. The two proposals described here are part of a first release of eight items from that request. One hundred and thirty-nine related legal and weapons development documents remain unreleased. The Marine Corps says the delay is due to a lack of manpower.

> WHILE US ALLEGATIONS AGAINST OTHER COUNTRIES ARE GENERALLY UNDOCUMENTED, THE PROPOSALS DESCRIBED HERE WERE RELEASED TO THE SUNSHINE PROJECT UNDER THE FREEDOM OF INFORMATION ACT.

The National Academies of Science are also suppressing related documents (see sidebar). As part of the Marine Corps-commissioned study, in 2001 at least 77 apparently chemical and biological weapons-related documents were deposited in the NAS Public Access Records File, a library open for inspection and copying by all persons. After the Sunshine Project requested copies of these documents on March 12, 2002, the National Academies placed a "security hold" on the public file. High-ranking NAS officials have refused to explain who ordered the hold or to offer a credible explanation as to why it exists.

The set of reports includes papers on synthetic opiate weapons of the class reported to have killed more than 100 people during the infamous "rescue" of hostages in a Moscow theater in October 2002. The Sunshine Project's Edward Hammond said: "The world has an urgent need to better understand what happened in Moscow and what other countries, including the US, are doing with these kinds of weapons. The National Academies' ongoing refusal to release the documents is very troubling." Hammond adds: "NAS has critical information for understanding the chemical agents used in Moscow, but is refusing to release it because it wants to avoid embarrassing the Pentagon, which denies that this type of research exists in the United States."

The Sunshine Project believes that NAS is under pressure from high-ranking US officials to "Enron" the public record in order to avoid release of politically sensitive material. Rather than assist a purge of the public record, NAS—a leading US non-profit scientific body—must condemn and release the proposals for illegal weapons that is has received.

Legal Implications. The research proposed by the Air Force and Navy raises serious legal questions of a national and international nature. Under the US Biological Weapons Anti-Terrorism Act, development of biological weapons, including those that attack materials, is subject to federal criminal and civil penalties. The Biological and Toxin Weapons Convention, which the US and 143 other countries have ratified, prohibits development, acquisition, and stockpiling of any biological agents not justifiable for peaceful or prophylactic purposes. There is no such justification for the offensive research proposed by the Navy and Air Force.

Weapons Already Developed? The military's proposals reveal that, as of 1997, they *already* had developed similar bioweapons. The Navy lab says that it has developed a fungus that breaks down polyurethanes. In the Air Force document, Armstrong Laboratories declares that it's been doing "biotechnological research at the molecular level" for eight years. Specifically, it's created a bio-agent that quickly destroys rocket fuel, plastic, and other organic and artificial polymers "without fire or explosion." This indicates the strong possibility that US federal law and the international convention have already been broken.

Third Document Released. On May 10, 2002, the National Academies of Science released "Biofouling and Biocorrosion," a 1994 document from the National Security Programs Office of the Idaho National Engineering Laboratory (INEL), a facility of the US Department of Energy. In the paper, the INEL proposes US development of offensive biological weapons that destroy materials. Like the Air Force and Navy proposals, the INEL document has recently been distributed to government officials by the Marine Corps-directed Joint Non-Lethal Weapons Program (JNLWP) and in 2001 was submitted for consideration by the National Academy of Sciences' panel "An Assessment of Non-lethal Weapons Science and Technology" (NAS Study NSBX-L-00-05-A).

In "Biofouling and Biocorrosion," INEL specifically proposes "selection of particularly active [microbe] strains" and "consideration of genetic techniques for further optimization and control." INEL also proposes "investigation of probable scenarios for

Some of the Public Documents on "Non-lethal" Weapons Being Withheld by the National Academies of Science

"Antipersonnel Calmative Agents." US Army Edgewood Research, Development and Engineering Center, Aberdeen Proving Ground, MD. 1994.

"Antipersonnel Chemical Immobilizers: Synthetic Opioids." U.S. Army Edgewood Research, Development and Engineering Center, Aberdeen Proving Ground, MD. 1994.

"Metabolic Engineering." National Security Programs, Idaho National Engineering Laboratory. 1995.

"Sticky Slicky Weapons." China Lake, CA. 1994.

"Marine Corps Sticky Foam Gun Support." Sandia National Laboratories, Albuquerque, NM. 1997.

"Enhanced Lethality KE [kinetic energy] Warhead." Lawrence Livermore National Laboratory, Livermore, CA. 1994.

"Spider Fiber Entangler." Naval Surface Warfare Center, Dahlgren Division, VA. 1997.

"Crow's Feet Area Denial System." US Army TACOM-ARDEC, Picatinny Arsenal, NJ. 1998.

"Vortex Ring Gun." Army Research Laboratory, Aberdeen Proving Ground, MD. 1997.

"Non-Lethal Land Mines." Army Research Laboratory, Aberdeen Proving Ground, MS. 1997.

"Corneal Irritation Laser (Sandman)." Armstrong Laboratory. 1994.

"Pulsed Impulsive Kill Laser." ARDEC, LANL, and Armstrong Laboratory. 1994.

"Thermal Gun." Oak Ridge National Laboratory, Oak Ridge, TN. 1994.

"The Covert Destruction of Aluminum and Aluminum Alloy Structural Members Using Gallium-Mercury Projectiles." Sandia National Laboratories, Albuquerque, NM. 1994.

"Are You Sure It's Nonlethal?" Naval Institute Proceedings. April 2001.

"Pulsed Energy Projectile (PEP) Program." AFRL/HEDO, Brooks AFB, TX. 30 April 2001.

"Human Behavior Modeling." Sandia National Laboratories, Albuquerque, NM. 2 May 2001.

[microbe] employment" and development of "organisms with faster rates of degradation and production of fouling agents, as well as novel methods for introducing the organisms to their targets."

US Attorney Contacted. In two letters, one on May 16 and another on May 23, the Sunshine Project has provided copies of these three documents to Mr. Johnny Sutton, the United States Attorney for the Western District of Texas. Letters accompany the documents requesting Department of Justice action pursuant to the Biological Weapons Anti-Terrorism Act of 1989, the US law that implements the Biological and Toxin Weapons Convention (BTWC), to which the United States is a contracting party. The Act was passed unanimously by both houses of the US Congress and signed into law by the elder President George Bush. It creates a general prohibition punishable by imprisonment and/or civil penalties on the development, production, stockpiling, transfer, acquisition, or possession of biological weapons (Section 175), and permits the United States Attorney to seek injunctions against preparation, solicitation, attempt, or conspiracy to engage in prohibited conduct (Section 177). The Act defines biological agents to include anti-material agents, specifically including those that cause deterioration of food, water, equipment, supplies, or material of any kind (Section 178).

A Fourth Document Surfaces. The US Special Forces have issued a brief but explicit request for US scientists to make proposals to create genetically-engineered offensive biological weapons. The US Special Forces' solicitation came in January 2002 as part of "Scientists Helping America," a cooperative effort between the Special Forces, the Defense Advanced Research Projects Agency (DARPA), and the US Naval Research Laboratory (NRL). Playing heavily on the US reaction to the September 11th attacks, "Scientists Helping America" asked researchers to show their patriotism by turning their talents to weapons, including bioweapons, specifically, 1) genetically-engineered bugs that eat materials and 2) stealthy modified organisms (called "taggants") that can be used to invisibly "paint" a target so that it can later be destroyed with other weapons.

The Special Forces' desire was initially identified in a short May 1999 document by its Future Technology Working Group. The document identifies the military appeal of "a bio-engineered organism [that] can become a weapon by acting as a corrosive agent after a certain period of time or by a remote command." The same document sets out the uses of a "bio-organism that can be placed on a building and then grow across that building to act as an illuminator for target identification, or precision attacks" (taggants). The document indicates that these bioweapons would be used covertly, stipulating that they "should be innocuous in appearance so that they can be carried and placed by Special Operations Forces without detection."

Following the May 1999 paper, the March 2001 report "Special Operations Technology Objectives" provided an overview of the wide range of military technologies required by the Special Forces. This report includes descriptions of many military technologies and reiterates the request for genetically-modified anti-material bioweapons and taggant bioweapons. In January 2002, as part of "Scientists Helping America," the Special Forces posted the March 2001 report on the Internet and requested that US scientists forward proposals to DARPA. In early 2002, DARPA vetted the ideas and invited the authors of promising proposals to come to Washington and present them to military officials.

On January 25, 2002, the Sunshine Project requested these proposals from DARPA under the Freedom of Information Act. DARPA acknowledges that the proposals are neither classified nor contain confidential business information, yet it responded to the request by refusing to provide any of the more than 300 biotechnology-related proposals it received and reviewed. Citing the "deliberative process of government" FOIA exemption, DARPA claimed that if the proposals were released, foreign intelligence agencies would target the scientists "helping America." The real reason, however, appears to be that DARPA prefers to keep its relationships with academic and commercial scientists confidential, and values secretive relationships above compliance with the Freedom of Information Act. The denial is under appeal as of November 2002.

Preventing genetically-engineered disasters is a common concern of arms control and biosafety. The Special Forces propose to covertly introduce difficult to detect genetically-modified organisms (GMOs) into other countries. The nascent international safety system for movement of GMOs across borders (the Cartagena Biosafety Protocol) creates the fundamental requirement of consent. That is, deliberate introduction of GMOs into the environment must have the advanced informed agreement of a competent government agency in the receiving country which reviews the safety and desirability of each new introduction on its soil. The Special Forces obviously will not seek permission from a country they are attacking. Moreover, the Special Forces have virtually no knowledge or ability to predict the ecological impacts of use of such environment-modifying weapons. As such, the proposed weapons not only pose arms control problems but are a direct affront to international biosafety efforts.

_PENTAGON PROGRAM PROMOTES PSYCHOPHARMACOLOGICAL WARFARE

In The Futurological Congress (1971), Polish writer Stanislaw Lem portrayed a future in which disobedience is controlled with hypothetical mind-altering chemicals dubbed "benignimizers." Lem's fictional work opens with the frightening story of a police and military biochemical attack on protesters outside an international scientific convention. As the environment becomes saturated with hallucinogenic agents, the protesters (and bystanders) descend into chaos, overcome by delusions and feelings of complacency, self-doubt, and even love. If the Pentagon's Joint Non-Lethal Weapons Directorate (JNLWD) has its way, Lem may be remembered as a prophet.

"The Advantages and Limitations of Calmatives for Use as a Non-Lethal Technique," a 49-page report obtained in June 2002 by the Sunshine Project under US information freedom law, has revealed a shocking Pentagon program that is researching psychopharmacological weapons. Based on "extensive review conducted on the medical literature and new developments in the pharmaceutical industry," the report concludes that "the development and use of [psychopharmacological weapons] is achievable and desirable." These mind-altering weapons violate international agreements on chemical and biological warfare, as well as human rights. Some of the techniques discussed in the report have already been used by the US in the "War on Terrorism."

The team, which is based at the Applied Research Laboratory of Pennsylvania State University, is assessing weaponization of a number of psychiatric and anesthetic pharmaceuticals, as well as "club drugs" (such as the "date-rape drug" GHB). According to the report, "the choice administration route, whether application to drinking water, topical administration to the skin, an aerosol spray inhalation route, or a drug filled rubber bullet, among others, will depend on the environment." The environments identified are specific military and civil situations, including "hungry refugees that are excited over the distribution of food," "a prison setting," an "agitated population," and "hostage situations." At times, the JNLWD team's report veers very close to defining dissent as a psychological disorder.

The drugs that Lem called "benignimizers" are called "calmatives" by the military. Some calmatives were weaponized by Cold War adversaries; this includes BZ, described by those who have used it as "the ultimate bad trip." Calmatives were supposed to have been deleted from military stockpiles following the adoption of the Chemical Weapons Convention in 1993, which bans any chemical weapon that can cause death, temporary incapacitation, or permanent harm to humans or animals.

"Calmative" is military, not medical, terminology. In more familiar medical language, most of the drugs under consideration are central nervous system depressants. The majority are synthetic, while some are natural. They include opiates (morphine-type drugs) and benzodiazepines, such as Valium (diazepam). Antidepressants are also of great interest to the research team, which is looking for faster-acting versions of drugs like Prozac (fluoxetine) and Zoloft (sertraline).

Powerful Drugs. Most of these drugs have hallucinogenic and other effects, including apnea (stopped breathing), coma, and death. One class of drugs under consideration is fentanyls. (The report's cover even features a diagram of fentanyl, the same—or a very close relative—of the agent that killed more than 100 hostages in Moscow in November 2002.) According to the US Drug Enforcement Administration (DEA), the biological effects of fentanyls "are indistinguishable from those of heroin, with the exception that the fentanyls may be hundreds of times more potent." The report says that the drugs' profound effects may make it necessary

THE REPORT DRAWS ATTENTION TO AN "INTERESTING PHENOMENON" RELATED TO PRECEDEX USE—THE DRUG INCREASES PATIENTS' REACTION TO ELECTRICAL SHOCK.

to "check for the occasional person who may stop breathing (many medical reasons in the unhealthy, the elderly, and very young...)," as well as victims who "'go to sleep' in positions that obstruct their airway," both problems with so-called "non-lethal" chemical weapons that were horrifically demonstrated by the Russian Special Forces disastrous use of a fentanyl-based agent in the Moscow theater.

Club Drugs. Most of the JNLWD team's weapon candidates are controlled substances in most countries. Some are widely used legitimate pharmaceuticals that are also drugs of abuse, such as Valium and opiates. The Pentagon team advocates more research into the weapons potential of convulsants (which provoke seizures) and "club drugs," the generally illegal substances used by some at raves and dance clubs. Among those in the military spotlight are ketamine ("Special K"), GHB (Gamma-hydroxybutrate, "liquid ecstasy"), and rohypnol ("Roofies"). The latter two in particular are called "date-rape drugs" because of incidences of their use on victims of sexual and other crimes. Most are DEA Schedule I or II narcotics that provoke hallucinations and can carry a sentence of life imprisonment. For example, according to the DEA:

Use of ketamine as a general anesthetic for humans has been limited due to adverse effects including delirium and hallucinations.... Low doses produce vertigo, ataxia, slurred speech, slow reaction time, and euphoria. Intermediate doses produce disorganized thinking, altered body image, and a feeling of unreality with vivid visual hallucinations. High doses produce analgesia, amnesia, and coma.

Failed Drugs. The report also points out that pharmaceutical candidates that fail because of excessive side effects might be desirable for use as weapons:

Often, an unwanted side-effect...will terminate the development of a promising new pharmaceutical compound. However, in the variety of situations in which non-lethal techniques are used, there may be less need to be concerned with unattractive side-effects.... Perhaps, the ideal calmative has already been synthesized and is awaiting renewed interest from its manufacturer.

Chemical Cocktails. In 2002, the JNLWD team was researching a mix of pepper spray ("OC") and unidentified calmative agents. Pepper spray is the most powerful chemical crowd-control agent in use and has been associated with numerous deaths. Adding a pharmacological "calmative" to OC would create a hideous concoction. The report prioritizes Valium and Precedex (dexmeditomidine) for weaponization, and it is possible that these are the agents that could be mixed with OC. The researchers also suggest mixing ketamine with other drugs. The chemical cocktail proposals bear a resemblance to South Africa's apartheid-era weapons research, whose director claimed under oath to have attempted to develop a BZ and cocaine mixture for use on government enemies.

Torture. Precedex is a sedative approved for use in the US on patients hospitalized in intensive care units. The report draws attention to an "interesting phenomenon" related to Precedex use—the drug increases patients' reaction to electrical shock. The researchers suggest sensitizing people by using Precedex on them, followed by use of electromagnetic weapons to "address effects on the few individuals where an average dose of the pharmacological agent did not have the desired effect." Obviously, such a technique might be considered torture, and it certainly could be used to torture. To add to hypnotic and delusional properties, the researchers suggest that psychopharmaceutical agents could be designed to have physical effects including headache and nausea, adding to their torture potential.

The researchers suggest that transdermal patches and transmucosal (through mucous membranes) formulations of Buspar (buspirone), which are under development by Bristol-Myers Squibb and TheraTech, Inc., "may be effective in a prison setting where there may have been a recent anxiety-provoking incident or confrontation."

Use in the "War on Terrorism." Of course, uncooperative or rioting prisoners would be extraordinarily unlikely to accept being drugged with a transdermal patch or most conventional means. Any such application of a "calmative" would likely be on individuals in shackles or a straightjacket. The US has admitted that it forcibly sedates al Qaeda "detainees" held at the US base in Guantanamo, Cuba. Former JNLWD commander and retired Col. Andy Mazzara, who directs the Penn State team, says he has sent a "Science Advisor" to the US Navy to assist the "War on Terrorism." In October 2001, the JNLWD offered to equip US commercial aircraft with calmative-dispensing weapons.[1]

> THE ADVANCED STAGE OF THE CHEMICAL WEAPONS PROGRAM IS ALSO INDICATED BY THE FACT THAT A PENTAGON DOCUMENT RELEASED TO THE SUNSHINE PROJECT INDICATES THAT THE JNLWD-OPERATED PROGRAM IS PLANNING OR MAY HAVE ALREADY PERFORMED EXPERIMENTS ON HUMANS.

Modes of Delivery. A number of weaponization modes are discussed in the report. These include aerosol sprays, microencapsulation, and insidious methods such as introduction into potable water supplies and psychoactive chewing gum. JNLWD is investing in the development of microencapsulation technology, which involves creating granules of a minute quantity of agent coated with a hardened shell. Distributed on the ground, the shell breaks under foot and the agent is released. A new mortar round being developed could deliver thousands of the minute granules per round.

The team concludes that new delivery methods under development by the pharmaceutical industry will be of great weapons value. These include new transdermal, transmucosal, and aerosol delivery methods. The report cites the relevance of a lollipop containing fentanyl used to treat children in severe pain, and notes that "the development of new pain-relieving opiate drugs capable of being administered via several routes is at the forefront of drug discovery," concluding that new weapons could be developed from this pharmaceutical research.

Dart Guns. The researchers express specific interest in shooting humans with guns loaded with carfentanil darts. Carfentanil is a veterinary narcotic used to tranquilize large, dangerous animals such as bears and tigers. Anyone who has watched wildlife shows on tel-

evision is familiar with the procedure. In the US, carfentanil is not approved for any use on human beings. It is an abused drug and a controlled substance. Under US law, first-time offenders convicted of unlicensed possession of carfentanil can be punished by up to 20 years in prison and a $1-million fine.

Mortar Delivery. September 28, 2002, was a Pentagon contractor's deadline to deliver a test quantity of "non-lethal" 81mm mortar projectiles. This indicates that the program is more advanced than previously believed. Under a US$700,000 contract (DAAE-30-01-C-1077) signed on June 28, 2001, M2 Technologies of West Hyannisport, Massachusetts, must deliver three working examples of its final 81mm mortar round design. The projectiles are designed for firing from the US military's standard 81mm field mortar, to have a 2.5-kilometer range, and are suitable for delivery of chemical weapons. The contract indicates that they will contain a "generic payload for visual effect." JNLWD-funded experiments on a gas-generating payload canister (made by General Dynamics) have used colored water as a testing substitute for a chemical payload. A chemical mortar round with a 2.5-kilometer range has solely military applications and cannot possibly be justified for a US military domestic riot-control purpose.

Human Experiments. The advanced stage of the chemical weapons program is also indicated by the fact that a Pentagon document released to the Sunshine Project indicates that the JNLWD-operated program is planning or may have already performed experiments on humans. A contract between JNLWD and the Marine Corps Research University (at Pennsylvania State University), dated January 29, 2002, stipulates that the university is to perform an assessment of anti-personnel capabilities and seek expert advice "on the human effects testing planned, and/or executed" for a new military mortar round. The extent and nature of the experiments, which may be testing of mind-altering, sleep-inducing, or cramp-causing chemicals on human volunteers, and the institutional and legal framework for them, are not identified in the contract.

Secrecy. The JNLWD has made a systematic effort to hide its program from public view and to impede the Sunshine Project's investigation. JNLWD asked the US Navy Judge Advocate General (JAG) to perform a legal review of its "non-lethal" chemical weapons but then classified the JAG opinion, preventing its release.[2] JNLWD has placed export control restrictions on its 81mm "non-lethal" mortar specification.[3] In 2002, JNLWD officials trained US Marine Corps officers in its anti-personnel chemical weapons capabilities. It classified the training "secret."[4]

Interviewed by news media, JNLWD officials deny developing chemical weapons, but they are not reported to have denied seeking "calmative" chemical weapons. According to a story run by the Associated Press, a JNLWD spokesman said that the Directorate has decided to "step back and make sure the use of calmatives would not violate the Chemical Weapons Convention." If this statement is true, this small retreat is likely the result of a very recent decision provoked by international criticism of the chemical weapons program. It is not supported, however, by the overwhelming weight of written evidence: Ongoing JNLWD contracts with private companies and academic institutions, a cooperative chemical research program between JNLWD and the US Army, and other recent information all indicate that the program is not only active, it is moving forward quickly.

Furthermore, the JNLWD has informed the Sunshine Project in multiple telephone conversations that it will deny release of documents requested under the Freedom of Information Act because of "classified weapons development." With eighteen months elapsed since the Sunshine Project's first FOIA requests to JNLWD, almost two-thirds of the documents requested have not been released. In apparent violation of US law, the JNLWD has ordered the US National Academies of Science to halt release of documents it deposited in the public record at that institution,[5] despite the fact that the National Academies states that there are no security markings on the documents requested.[6]

Biochemicals and Treaties. Many of the proposed drugs can be considered both chemical and biological weapons banned by the Biological and Toxin Weapons Convention (BTWC) and the Chemical Weapons Convention (CWC). As a practical matter, biological and chemical "calmatives" must be addressed together. Because the agents are explicitly intended for military use and are intended to incapacitate their victims, they do not fall under the CWC's domestic riot-control agent exemption. Toxic products of living agents—such as the neurotoxin botulinum—are considered both chemical and biological agents. Any weapons use of neurotransmitters or substances mimicking their action is similarly covered by both arms control treaties. The researchers have developed a massive calmatives database and are following biomedical research on mechanisms of drug addiction, pain relief, and other areas of research on cognition-altering biochemicals. For example, the JNLWD team is tracking research on cholecystokinin, a neurotransmitter that causes panic attacks in healthy people and is linked to psychiatric disorders.

The JNLWD program runs afoul of the Chemical Weapons Convention (CWC), the global ban on the development and use of all chemical weapons. And JNLWD is well aware of this fact. JNLWD presentations in 2001 list the Chemical Weapons Convention as a major "challenge" to its calmatives program.[7] The previous year, JNLWD held a series of war games with British military officials. JNLWD's report of the war games concludes: "In all three game scenarios, players espoused calmatives as potentially the most useful anti-personnel non-lethal weapons," but "the principle concern was about the legality of the weapon and possible arms control violations..." Despite this, it continues: "The end result is that calmatives are considered the single most effective anti-personnel option in the non-lethal toolkit."[8]

At the end of the war games series, the JNLWD held a final, high-level meeting with UK officials. It included the participation of five active-duty US Marine Corps and Army generals. British officials objected to the US calmatives program, saying that it is illegal. The JNLWD replied by saying that it would proceed anyway (quoting from the report): "[A] research and development program with respect to...chemically based calmatives...[will] be continued as long as it is cost-productive to do so." In the same report, the JNLWD acknowledges that its research and development program violates Department of Defense regulations, declaring its intent to evade the law: "DOD is prohibited from pursuing [calmative] technology.... If there are promising technologies that DOD is prohibited from pursuing, set up MOA with DOJ or DOE." (DOD is the US Department of Defense; DOJ is the US Department of Justice; and DOE is the US Department of Energy. MOA is a Memorandum of Agreement.)[9]

Escalation Danger. The JNLWD's chemical weapons program not only violates international law, it presents an escalation threat. Any use of chemical weapons in a military situation—even if the agents are purported to be "non-lethal"—carries the inherent danger of escalation into an all-out chemical war and heightened violence. If attacked with a chemical of unknown nature with a fast incapacitating effect, victims may assume that lethal chemicals have been used, leading to heightened violence or even retaliation with actual lethal chemicals. This rapid escalation danger is one of the key reasons why the Chemical Weapons Convention prohibits the use of even tear gas or pepper spray as a method of warfare.

The Road to a Chemical Arms Race. In addition, the JNLWD's program might easily be used to disguise lethal chemical weapons development. Deadly chemicals are the former specialty of the JNLWD's partner in the program, the US Army's Aberdeen Proving Ground. Long-range delivery devices may easily be converted to use biological agents or other chemicals, including lethal nerve gas. Design and development of new delivery devices, production facilities or delivery experiments—all key parts of a lethal chemical weapons program—might easily be performed by the US or other countries if the buzzword "non-lethal" is used as a cover. If non-lethal chemical warfare programs are not banned, the basic principles of the CWC could fall apart, resulting in a new full-blown chemical arms race even before Cold War stocks are destroyed.

Action. The Sunshine Project is calling for immediate termination of this research and urges parties to both the Chemical Weapons Convention and the Biological and Toxin Weapons Convention to quickly condemn this research and to approve decisions reiterating the ban on these weapons. The Sunshine Project also calls upon the US Congress to investigate the JNLWD's arms control violations, to conduct public hearings, to hold the JNLWD and its superiors responsible for their actions, to freeze all JNLWD funding, and to immediately declassify all JNLWD documents. Finally, the Sunshine Project requests the Organization for the Prohibition of Chemical Weapons send a UN weapons inspection team to the US to investigate.

Endnotes

1. "Non-Lethal Weapons Suggested to Incapacitate Terrorists in Airliners." *Air Safety Week* 15.39 (15 Oct 2001). **2.** Response letter (3 Sept 2002) from US Department of the Navy, Office of the Judge Advocate General, International and Operational Law Division, to Sunshine Project Freedom of Information Request of 21 Aug 2002. **3.** Several JNLWD-funded contracts indicate this. See, for example, "81mm Frangible Case Cartridge." Contract DAAE-30-01-C-1077 (June 2001), US Army TACOM and M2 Technologies. **4.** "Non-Lethal Weapons: Acquisitions, Capabilities, Doctrine, &

Strategy: A Course of Instruction." Contract M67004-99-D-0037, purchase order M9545002RCR2BA7, between the US Marine Corps University (Pennsylvania State University Applied Research Laboratory) and the JNLWD, Dec 2001. **5.** Letter from Col. George Fenton to the National Academies of Science (NAS), 17 May 2002, text provided in an email from Mr. Kevin Hale, Director of the NAS National Security Office, to William Colglazier, Executive Officer, 17 May 2002. **6.** Letter from Kevin Hale (NAS) to Col. George Fenton (JNLWD), 17 May 2002. This letter and the email of note #5 were provided by the NAS Public Affairs office. **7.** Fenton, G. "To The Future: Non-Lethal Capabilities Technologies in the 21st Century." Presentation to the University of New Hampshire's Non-lethal Technology and Academic Research III symposium, November 2001. **8.** "US/UK Non-Lethal Weapons (NLW)/Urban Operations War Game Two Assessment." JNLWD, June 2000. The war game was held 13-16 June 2000 at the US Army War College, Carlisle Barracks, Pennsylvania. **9.** "Assessment Report: US/UK Non-Lethal Weapons (NLW)/Urban Operations Executive Seminar." JNLWD, November 2000.

TITLE OF SUBMISSION: ENHANCED DEGRADATION OF MILITARY MATERIEL

PROPOSED CONCEPT, CAPABILITY AND TECHNOLOGY INVESTMENT:

The proposed materials science research project will develop nonlethal systems specifically designed to degrade opposing forces' mobility, logistical support and equipment maintenance programs prior to or during military engagements, in a time frame of days to months. Such systems, patterned after microorganisms and their products, as well as "vaccinations" to protect materiel of friendly forces, will be directed exclusively at non-living targets such as highway and runway surfaces, metal parts and coatings of weapons, support equipment and vehicles, fuels and other supplies and replacement parts. Natural environmental microorganisms displaying relevant degradative capabilities will be identified, and their mechanisms(s) of degradation will be characterized. In addition, non-pathogenic laboratory strains will be genetically modified to express specific, focused degradative capabilities. These Genetically Modified Microorganisms (GEM) will be further modified to be self-limiting, either by incorporation of timed "suicide" genes, or other alterations that prevent their persistence in the environment beyond pre-determined limits of space or time. Ultimately these capabilities will be mimicked chemically, and transitioned into synthetic products that do not require living microorganisms. At the same time, chemical, physical and engineering modifications that can be applied to materiel of friendly forces to "vaccinate" and protect such targets will be investigated.

The proposed microbial-derived systems will be used to accelerate the corrosion, degradation or decomposition of roads and aircraft runways used by opposing forces. In addition, targeted deterioration of metal parts, coatings and lubricants of weapons, vehicles and support equipment, as well as fuels and other supplies, will significantly increase the cost and logistical burden to the enemy of sustaining military operations. An important focus area addressed by this proposal includes denial of land areas to vehicles and aircraft by reduction of terrain trafficability and vehicle operation. Another focus area is the ability to disable or neutralize equipment and facilities, by degrading fuels and other supplies, and increasing maintenance requirements.

POTENTIAL FOR JOINT APPLICATION:

All of the armed services in a joint military operation will benefit from technology that degrades the overall ability of the enemy to initiate and sustain combat operations. Degrading aircraft runway surfaces controlled by enemy forces gives an advantage to U.S. Air Forces in controlling the skies over target areas. Degrading road and highway surfaces in enemy territory reduces the mobility of opposition forces' troop and supply transport, reducing the threat to Army and Marine land forces. Degrading fuels, replacement parts and other supplies that support a war effort gives an advantage to all branches of our military by compromising the enemy's logistical support systems.

In addition, characterization of degradative mechanisms and development of "vaccination" strategies will have significant dual use applications in protecting military and commercial materials and materiel from naturally-occurring biodegradation problems, or offensive military and terrorist attacks of this nature. Scientific expertise capable of developing anti-materiel technology patterned after microbial systems unquestionably is already present in the laboratories of potential adversary states, and the likelihood of near-term development of such threats is great. Failure to counter this threat with a focused research program jeopardizes the warfighting capability of the U.S. and its allies.

TECHNICAL DESCRIPTION:

Nature has provided many examples of natural degradation by microorganisms of metals, fuels and a variety of synthetic products, as well as structures and systems that incorporate or depend on such products. An example of a military material that the proposed research would target is the synthetic high-strength polymer, Kevlar, or novel biomimetics of Kevlar based on spider silk. Asphalt is degraded by several strains of bacteria, leading to greatly reduced road surface lifetimes. Components of asphalt used for other construction purposes also suffer failure as a direct result of bacterial degradation. Cement is subject to rapid, component-specific attack by microbes. Most classes of paints and coatings are also vulnerable to degradation by microbial products. Virtually all petroleum, oil and lubricants (POL) of military relevance are vulnerable to degradation by microbial action. Many microorganisms also naturally produce minute granules called inclusion bodies that are made of salt crystals, metals or plastic-like compounds (polyhydroxyalkanates). These particles will quickly clog high efficiency filters, and convert critical lubricants of weapon systems into gums or abrasives. It is the purpose of the proposed research to capitalize on the degradative potential of these and other products from naturally-occurring microorganisms, and to engineer additional, focused degradative capabilities into GEM, to produce systems that will degrade the warfighting capabilities of potential adversaries. The out-years goal is to use the knowledge of natural microbial degradation pathways gained in this study to develop biomimetic chemical systems that are more robust, less expensive and easily deployed for field use in any warfighting environment. The genetic engineering techniques to be employed are standard laboratory practices, requiring no special isolation laboratories, and this proposed materials science research is not restricted in any way by the 1972 Geneva Convention on Biological Warfare or any other international agreement. Funding for this proposal will support scientific staff who will develop enhanced materiel-degrading technology for deployment to the field. Previous work by the P.I. (JRC) at the Naval Research Laboratory (NRL) identified and produced in the laboratory an enzyme from a naturally occurring fungus, which rapidly decomposes polyurethane, a common component of paint for ships and aircraft. This work was subsequently extended at NRL, to create a new GEM that overproduces the polyurethane degrading enzyme (U.S. Patent, Navy Case No.75461).

RISK AREAS:

The main risk area for this technology lies in the engineering of the GEM to produce or enhance the desired characteristics, and in the robustness of these strains for field deployment. In the hands of skilled molecular biologists these risks will be minimized, because a large selection of DNA vectors and host organisms already exists for engineering purposes, and the literature documents numerous successful techniques for designing and producing stable GEM. NRL and its scientists have an established track record in molecular biology, protein characterization and surface chemistry. Field robustness is a concern, because of the wide variety of environmental conditions that could be encountered by the microbial products when employed in different warfighting scenarios. However host microbes are available that grow readily, and synthesize degradative products that function well, under a range of conditions of temperature, pH, salinity and humidity, and NRL Code 6115 employs several microbial ecologists trained and experienced on these issues. Moreover, it is not the intention of this research to develop strains that will persist in the environment once they have delivered their effects to the target. On the contrary, microbial systems will be identified or engineered to produce the desired degradative effects within a matter of days to months, then die off and disappear. This technology will then be transitioned to chemically synthesized systems to improve and extend the desired characteristics.

TECHNICAL POC:

James R. Campbell, Ph.D., CAPT, MSC, USN
Naval Research Laboratory, Code 6106
4555 Overlook Ave, S.W.
Washington, D.C. 20375
(202) 767-0192, 404-7139 FAX
jcampbel@ccf.nrl.navy.mil

ANTI-MATERIEL BIOCATALYSTS & SENSORS

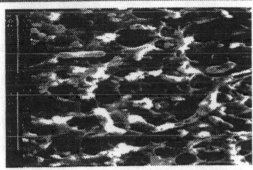

· Genetically engineered catalysts made by bacteria that detroy fuels, explosives, bio/chem weapons, etc (user defined)
· Can tolerate harsh delivery conditions

Potential Users: SOF, Peacekeeping forces, Counterdrug ops

Deliverables:
• Final report on effectiveness, health, safety, environmental impacts
• Proof of concept demonstration

Tasks:
· Engineer / demonstrate catalysts that destroy user defined substances
· Determine specific signature of catalyst to show it is working
· Determine reaction speeds and dose per amount target material
· Determine environmental impact

Cost/Schedule:
• $200K in FY98
  • Engineer biocatalysts specific for fuels
  • Lab demonstration
• $200K in FY99
  • Develop prototype for field demonstration
  • Conduct static field demonstrations

Dr Johnathan Kiel, AL/OER, DSN 240-3583

Title of Submission: Anti Materiel Biocatalysts

Proposed Technology Investment:
Focus area 3 describes the use of non-lethal technology to stop land and sea vehicles and to neutralize facilities and equipment. The common thread to all these is that they require fuel to power them or to generate power to operate them. If one could develop a rapidly acting, highly efficient, and environmentally safe substance to destroy the lubricants or seize the mechanical parts, then the vehicles or facilities could be "shut down" in a controlled fashion. Armstrong Laboratory at Brooks AFB is well on the way to doing just that.

Over the past couple of years, the Biotechnology Branch of the Radiofrequency Radiation Division has been pioneering research to understand the mechanisms of RFR interaction and to develop [a] quick, cheap, environmentally friendly way to clean up toxic substances. This work has led to the discovery of a patented process to genetically engineer catalysts specific to a particular substance (explosives, biological or chemical weapons, fuels, etc.). Heat, light, lasers, RFR activate the catalyst and initiate the reaction. The reaction creates enough heat to seize the engine or gunk the lubricants. The reaction has a unique luminescent signature so the destruction process can be remotely monitored (battle damage assessment) and does not produce any biohazards. The substance is exempt from biological warfare restrictions, can tolerate harsh delivery conditions, and is self amplifying (that is, a little goes a long way).

As an aside, this technology has application as a sensor. Intruders to restricted areas could be sprayed/painted and identified later (since the substance would luminesce under low RFR exposure). The technology could also be used to record cumulative exposure to RFR, something potentially useful for operators of high power RFR equipment or the soldier in an intense electromagnetic battlefield environment. The technology also has application in identifying friend or foe at long distances using the RFR sensitive substance on personnel or equipment insignia.

Potential for Joint Application: The application of this technology is limitless. Catalysts can be engineered to destroy whatever war materiel is desired. All Services would have an interest.

Technical Description: For the past 8 years Armstrong Laboratory has been conducting biotechnological research at the molecular level under AFOSR and, for the past 2 years, under SERDP support. These efforts led to the development of diazoluminomelanin (DALM), a biosynthesized catalyst, which interacts with a broad spectrum of optical and RFR, demonstrating enhanced reduction-oxidation (redox) activity including rapid breakdown of inorganic and organic hydrazines (rocket fuel) without fire or explosion. This controlled "burn" can destroy high energy materials as well as biological materials and plastics and other organic and bio-polymers [sic]. DALM has been biosynthesized on bacterial membranes in connection with existing imbedded [sic] enzymes. The work with DALM is a baseline. This baseline could be extended to attach other biocatalysts and conjugates to alter specificity and reactivity of the redox reactions. Altered spectral signatures (absorbance [sic] and emissions in the visible and infrared ranges) could provide an unusual catalyst that marks its own presence and activity for sensor and monitoring activities. This proposal is to adapt these biocatalysts to the internal combustion reaction to bring about the destruction of the engine parts or polymerization of the lubricants to render the vehicles/craft useless for military purposes.

Risk Areas: The risks are minimal since what has been learned for cleanup applications under the AFOSR and SERDP programs would be extended to NLT applications. The catalyst synthesis process is well known. The unknowns are how much is needed to stop and [sic] engine, how to deliver it, and determining any environmental impact.

Timeline/Cost:
> FY98: $200K
> engineer catalyst that destroys fuels/stops combustion engine (1st and 2nd qtr)
> determine specific signature of catalyst for monitoring (3rd qtr)
> determine reaction speeds and dose for effect (3rd and 4th qtr)
> conduct lab demonstration (4th qtr)

> FY99: $200K
> determine environmental impact of reactants and reaction products (1st-4th qtr)
> develop prototype for field demonstration (1st-3rd qtr)
> conduct static field demonstration (4th qtr)

Deliverables:
Final report on processes, effectiveness, environmental impacts, and results of demonstrations.

POC: Dr. Johnathan Kiel, GS-15
8308 Hawks Rd
Brooks, AFB, TX 78235
voice: DSN 240-3583, comm 210-536-3583
fax: DSN 240-3977, comm 210-536-3977
email: kiel@rfr.brooks.af.mil

CUBAN POLITICAL PRISONERS ... IN THE UNITED STATES

WILLIAM BLUM

The Florida Association of Criminal Defense Lawyers gave the defense team its "Against All Odds" award, given in honor of a deceased public defender who championed hopeless causes.[1]

Defending pro-Castro Cubans in Miami, in a criminal case utterly suffused with political overtones, with the US government wholly determined to nail a bunch of commies, is a task on a par with conducting a ground war with Russia in the wintertime.

Even in the absence of known anti-Castro Cuban exiles on the jury, the huge influence the exiles have on the rest of the community is an inescapable fact of life in Miami, a place where the sound of the word "pro-Castro" does what the word "bomb" does at an airport.

President Bush has assured the world repeatedly that he will not heed the many calls to lift the Cuban trade embargo unless Fidel Castro releases what Washington calls "political prisoners." Bush tells us this while ten Cubans sit in US prisons, guilty essentially of not being the kind of Cubans George W. loves. If a political prisoner can be defined as one kept in custody who, if not for his or her political beliefs and/or associations, would be a free person, then the ten Cubans can be regarded as political prisoners.

It all began in September 1998 when the Justice Department accused fourteen Cubans in southern Florida of "conspiracy to gather and deliver defense information to aid a foreign government, that is, the Republic of Cuba" and failing to register as agents of a foreign government.[2] Four of the accused were never apprehended and are believed to be living in Cuba. Five of the ten arrested, having less than true-believer faith in the American judicial system, copped plea bargains to avoid harsher penalties and were sentenced to between three and seven years in prison.

The US Attorney said the actions of the accused—who had been under surveillance since 1995—were an attempt "to strike at the very heart of our national security system and our very democratic process."[3] Their actions, added a judge, "place this nation and its inhabitants in great peril."[4]

Such language would appear more suitable for describing the attacks of September 11, 2001, than the wholly innocuous behavior of the accused. To add further to the level of melodrama: In the criminal complaint, in the indictment, in public statements, and in the courtroom, the federal government continuously squeezed as much mileage as it could from the fact that the Cubans had gone to meetings and taken part in activities of anti-Castro organizations— "duplicitous participation in and manipulation of" these organizations is how it was put.[5] But this was all for the benefit of media and jury, for there is obviously no law against taking part in an organization toward which you are unsympathetic; and in the end, after all the propaganda hoopla, the arrestees were never charged with any such offense.

The Cubans did not deny their activities. Their mission in the United States was to act as an early warning system for their homeland because over the years anti-Castro Cuban exiles in the US have carried out literally hundreds of terrorist actions against the island-nation, some as recent as 1997, when they planted bombs in Havana hotels. One of the exile groups, Omega 7, headquartered in Union City, New Jersey, was characterized by the FBI in 1980 as "the most dangerous terrorist organization in the United States."[6]

Some exiles were subpoenaed to testify at the trial, which began in December 2000, and defense attorneys threw questions at them about their activities. One witness told of attempts to assassinate Fidel Castro and of setting Cuban buses and vans on fire. Based on their answers, federal prosecutors threatened to bring organized crime charges against any group whose members gave incriminating testimony, and the Assistant US Attorney warned that if additional evidence emerged against members of Alpha 66, considered a paramilitary organization, the group would be prosecuted for a "long-standing pattern of attacks on the Cuban government."[7] (Cuba has complained for many years that US authorities ignore information Havana makes available about those in the US it claims are financing and plotting violence.)[8] None of the exiles who testified at the trial about terrorist actions or the groups they belonged to were in fact prosecuted.

> IF A POLITICAL PRISONER CAN BE DEFINED AS ONE KEPT IN CUSTODY WHO, IF NOT FOR HIS OR HER POLITICAL BELIEFS AND/OR ASSOCIATIONS, WOULD BE A FREE PERSON, THEN THE TEN CUBANS CAN BE REGARDED AS POLITICAL PRISONERS.

The arrested Cubans were involved in anti-terrorist activities—so cherished by the government of the United States in word—but were acting against the wrong kind of terrorists. Some of what they uncovered about possible terrorist and drug activities of Cuban exiles—including information concerning the 1997 hotel bombings— they actually passed to the FBI, usually via diplomats in Havana.

This presumably is what lay behind the statement in the criminal complaint that the defendants "attempted manipulation of United States political institutions and government entities through disinformation and pretended cooperation"[9]—i.e., putting every action of the Cuban defendants in the worst possible light.

THE FBI ADMITTED THAT THE CUBANS HAD NOT PENETRATED ANY MILITARY BASES AND THAT ACTIVITIES AT THE BASES WERE "NEVER COMPROMISED."

One of the Cubans, Antonio Guerrero, was employed as a manual laborer at the US Naval base in Boca Chica, Florida, near Key West. The prosecution stated that Guerrero had been ordered by Cuba to track the comings and goings of military aircraft in order to detect "unusual exercises, maneuvers, and other activity related to combat readiness."[10] Guerrero's attorney, to emphasize the non-secret nature of such information, pointed out that anyone sitting in a car on US-1 could easily see planes flying in and out of the base.[11]

This particular operation of the Cuban agents is difficult to comprehend, for it is hard to say which was the more improbable: that the US government would undertake another attack against Cuba, or that these Cubans could get timely wind of it in this manner.

The FBI admitted that the Cubans had not penetrated any military bases and that activities at the bases were "never compromised." "They had no successes," declared an FBI spokesperson. The Pentagon added that "there are no indications that they had access to classified information or access to sensitive areas."[12]

These statements, of course, did not rise from a desire to aid the Cubans' defense, but rather to assure one and all that the various security systems were impenetrable. But, in short, the government was admitting that nothing that could be termed "espionage" had been committed. Nevertheless, three of the defendants were charged with communicating to Cuba "information relating to the national defense of the United States...intending and having reason to believe that the same would be used to the injury of the United States."[13]

The FBI agents who closely surveilled the Cubans for several years did not seem worried about the reports that the "espionage agents" were sending to Havana and made no attempt to thwart their transmission. Indeed, the FBI reportedly arrested the Cubans only because they feared that the group would flee the country following the theft of a computer and disks used by one of them, which contained information about their activities, and that all the FBI surveillance would then have been for naught.[14]

Somewhat more plausibly, those arrested were each charged with "acting as an unregistered agent of a foreign government, Cuba." Yet, in at least the previous five years, no one in the United States had been charged with any such offense,[15] although, given the broad definition in the law of "foreign agent," the Justice Department could have undoubtedly done so with numerous individuals if it had had a political motivation as in this case.

In addition to the unregistered foreign agent charge, which was imposed against all five defendants, there was the ritual laundry list of other charges that is usually facile for a prosecutor to come up with: passport fraud, false passport application, fraudulent identification, conspiracy to defraud the United States, aiding and abetting one or more of the other defendants (sic), conspiracy to commit espionage, and furthermore tacked onto all five—conspiracy to act as an unregistered foreign agent.

There was one serious charge, which was levied eight months after the arrests against the alleged leader of the Cuban group, Gerardo Hernández: conspiring to commit murder, a reference to the February 24, 1996, shoot-down by a Cuban warplane of two planes (of a total of three), which took the lives of four Miami-based civilian pilots, members of Brothers to the Rescue (BTTR). In actuality, the Cuban government may have done no more than any other government in the world would have done under the same circumstances. The planes were determined to be within Cuban airspace, of serious hostile intent, and Cuban authorities gave the pilots explicit warning: "You are taking a risk." Indeed, both Cuban and US authorities had for some time been giving BTTR—which patrolled the sea between Florida and Cuba looking for refugees—similar warnings about intruding into Cuban airspace.[16]

Jose Basulto, the head of BTTR, and the pilot of the plane that got away, testified at the trial that he had received warnings that Cuba would shoot down planes violating its airspace.[17] In 1995, he had taken an NBC cameraman on a rooftop-level flight over downtown Havana and rained propaganda and religious medals on the streets below,[18] the medals capable of injuring people they struck. Basulto—a long-time CIA collaborator who once fired powerful cannonballs into a Cuban hotel filled with people[19]—described one BTTR flight over Havana as "an act of civil disobedience."[20] His organization's planes had gone into Cuban territory on nine occasions during the previous two years, with the pilots being warned repeatedly by Cuba not to return, that they would be shot down if they persisted in carrying out "provocative" flights. A former US federal aviation investigator testified at the trial that in the 1996 incident the planes had ignored warnings and entered an area that was activated as a "danger area."[21]

Also testifying was a retired US Air Force colonel and former regional commander of the North American Air Defense Command (NORAD), George Buchner. Citing National Security Agency transcripts of conversations between a Cuban battle commander on the ground and the Cuban MiG pilots in the air, he stated that the two planes were "well within Cuban airspace" and that a Cuban pilot "showed restraint" by breaking off his pursuit of the third plane as the chase headed toward international airspace.

Buchner's conclusion was at odds with earlier analyses conducted by the United States and the International Civil Aviation Organization (which relied heavily on intelligence data provided by the US). However, he added that the three planes were acting as one and that Cuba was within its sovereign rights to attack them—even in international airspace—because the plane that got away had entered Cuban airspace, a fact not disputed by the prosecution or other investigators.

"The trigger," said Buchner, "was when the first aircraft crossed the 12-mile territorial limit. That allowed the government of Cuba to exercise their sovereign right to protect its airspace." He stated, moreover, that the BTTR planes had given up their civilian status because they still carried the markings of the US Air Force and had been used to drop leaflets condemning the Cuban government.[22]

Two days after the incident, the *New York Times* reported that "United States intelligence officials said that at least one of the American aircraft—the lead plane, which returned safely to Florida—and perhaps all three had violated Cuban airspace." United States officials agreed with the Cuban government that "the pilots had ignored a direct warning from the air traffic control tower in Havana."[23]

Hernández was charged with murder for allegedly giving Cuban authorities the flight plan of the planes flown by Brothers to the Rescue.[24] Even if true, the claim appears to be rather meaningless, for the Federal Aviation Administration (FAA) stated after the incident that once BTTR had filed its flight plan with their agency, it was then transmitted electronically to the air tower in Havana.[25] In any event, on that fateful day in February, when the three planes crossed the 24th parallel—the beginning of the area before entering Cuba's 12-mile territorial limit, which the Cuban government, like other governments, defines as an air-defense identification zone—Basulto radioed his presence to the Havana Air Control Center and his intention to continue further south. Havana, which was already monitoring the planes' flight, replied: "We inform you that the area north of Havana is activated [air defense readied]. You are taking a risk by flying south of twenty-four."[26]

Hernández was also accused of informing Havana, in response to a request, that none of the Cuban agents would be aboard the BTTR planes during the time period in question; one of them had flown with BTTR earlier. This too was equated in the indictment with "knowingly...perpetrat[ing] murder, that is, the unlawful killing of human beings with malice aforethought."[27]

In the final analysis, the planes were shot down for entering Cuban airspace for hostile purposes after ignoring many warnings from two governments. After a January 13, 1996, BTTR overflight, Castro had issued orders to his Air Force to shoot down any plane that entered Cuban airspace illegally.[28] And just two weeks prior to the shootdown, a delegation of retired US officials had returned from Havana warning that Cuba seemed prepared to blow the Brothers' Cessnas out of the sky.[29] Gerardo Hernández was not responsible for any of this, and there was, moreover, a long history of planes departing from the United States for Cuba to carry out bombing, strafing, invasion, assassination, subversion, weapon-drops, agricultural and industrial sabotage, and other belligerent missions.[30] According to a former member of BTTR—who redefected to Cuba and may have been a Cuban agent all along—Basulto discussed with him ways to bring explosives into Cuba to blow up high-tension wires critical to the country's electrical system, and plans to smuggle weapons into Cuba to use in attacks against leaders, including Fidel Castro.[31] At the time of the shootdown, Cuba had been under a 37-year state of siege and could never be sure what such enemy pilots intended to do.

Yet Hernández was sentenced to spend the rest of his life in prison. Ramón Labañino and Antonio Guerrero, the manual worker at the US Naval base, were also sentenced to life terms; they and Hernández were all found guilty of conspiracy to commit espionage. Fernando González was put away for nineteen and a half years, and René González received fifteen years. All five were convicted of acting as an unregistered agent of a foreign government as well as *conspiracy*—that great tool of redundancy that is the lifeblood of American prosecutors—to do the same. All but one had the laundry list of identification frauds thrown at them.

For most of their detention since being arrested, the five men were kept in solitary confinement. After their convictions, they were placed in five different prisons spread around the country—Pennsylvania, California, Texas, Wisconsin, and Colorado—making it difficult for supporters and attorneys to visit more than one. The wife and 5-year-old daughter of René González were denied visas to enter the United States from Cuba to visit him. Hernández's wife was already at the Houston airport with all her papers in hand when she was turned back, although not before undergoing several hours of FBI humiliation.

The United States is currently engaged in a worldwide, open-ended, supra-legal campaign to destroy the rights of any individuals who—on the most questionable of evidence or literally none at

---

The prosecution of these Cubans, who are fighting terrorism, is even more ironic given that anti-Castro exiles have committed numerous terrorist acts *inside* the United States itself, including:

• attempts made on the lives of Castro's brother Raul and Che Guevara, the latter being the target of a bazooka fired at the United Nations building in New York in December 1964;[1]

• repeated bombings of the Soviet UN Mission, its Washington Embassy, its automobiles, a Soviet ship docked in New Jersey, the offices of the Soviet airline Aeroflot, with a number of American policemen and Russians injured in these attacks;[2]

• several bombings of the Cuban UN Mission and its Interests Section in Washington, plus many attacks upon Cuban diplomats, including at least one murder;[3]

• a bomb discovered at New York's Academy of Music in 1976 shortly before a celebration of the Cuban Revolution was to begin;[4]

• a bombing two years later of the Lincoln Center after the Cuban ballet had performed;[5]

• in 1979, the bombing of a New Jersey pharmacy that sent medical supplies to Cuba.[6]

Endnotes

1. *New York Times*, 12 December 1964: 1. **2.** Stein, Jeff. "Inside Omega 7." *Village Voice*, 10 March 1980. **3.** *San Francisco Chronicle*, 26 March 1979: 3; *San Francisco Chronicle*, 11 and 12 December 1979. **4.** *New York Times*, 13 September 1980: 24; *New York Times*, 3 March 1980: 1. **5.** Dinges, John, and Saul Landau. *Assassination on Embassy Row*. London: Writers and Readers Publishing, 1981: 251-2, footnote. (Originally published New York: Pantheon Books, 1980.) **6.** *CovertAction Information Bulletin* 6, (October 1979): 8-9.

CUBAN POLITICAL PRISONERS ... IN THE UNITED STATES
WILLIAM BLUM

all—might conceivably represent any kind of terrorist threat. But if the Cubans—with a much longer history of serious terrorist attacks against them by well-known perpetrators—take the most reasonable steps to protect themselves from further attacks, they find that Washington has forbidden them from taking part in the War Against Terrorism.

Endnotes

1. Associated Press, 11 May 2001. **2.** US District Court, Southern District of Florida, case #98-3493, Criminal Complaint, 14 September 1998, "Conclusion" paragraph. Hereafter, "Criminal Complaint." **3.** EFE News Service (based in Madrid, with branches in the US), 28 March 2001. **4.** *Miami Herald*, 18 September 1998. **5.** Criminal Complaint, paragraph 7. **6.** *New York Times*, 3 March 1980: 1. **7.** EFE News Service, 28 March 2001. **8.** See for example *Miami Herald*, 28 March 2001: 1B. **9.** Criminal Complaint, paragraph 7; see also paragraph 26. **10.** *Ibid.*, paragraph 19. **11.** *Miami Herald*, 23 September 1998. **12.** *Washington Post*, 15 September 1998; *Miami Herald*, 16 September 1998. **13.** US District Court, Southern District of Florida, Case No. 98-721, Second Superseding Indictment, 7 May 1999, Count 2, Section D. **14.** *Miami Herald*, 16 September 1998. **15.** Department of Justice, Bureau of Justice Statistics, reported to author by John Scalia, statistician at the Bureau. **16.** Associated Press, 8 May 2001. **17.** EFE News Service, 28 March 2001. **18.** Nagin, Carl. "Backfire." *The New Yorker*, 26 January 1998: 32. **19.** Morley, Jefferson. "Shootdown." *Washington Post Magazine*, 25 May 1997: 120. **20.** EFE News Service, 1 February 2001. **21.** EFE News Service, 1 March 2001. **22.** Associated Press, 21 March 2001; *Miami Herald*, 22 March 2001. **23.** *New York Times*, 26 February 1996: 1. **24.** Associated Press, 5 December 2000. **25.** *New York Times*, 26 February 1996: 1. It is not clear from the article whether the transmission was made by the FAA or by BTTR. **26.** *Op cit.*, Nagin: 34. **27.** *Op cit.*, Second Superseding Indictment, Count 3, Section A. **28.** *Op cit.*, Nagin: 33. **29.** *Newsweek*, 11 March 1996: 48. **30.** Franklin, Jane. *Cuba and the United States: A Chronological History*. North Melbourne, Australia: Ocean Press, 1997, see index under "Planes used against Cuba"; Blum, William. *Killing Hope: US Military and CIA Interventions Since World War II*. Monroe, Maine: Common Courage Press, 1995, Cuba chapter. **31.** *Washington Post*, 27 February 1996.

FOR MOST OF THEIR DETENTION SINCE BEING ARRESTED, THE FIVE MEN WERE KEPT IN SOLITARY CONFINEMENT.

In June 2002, Danish artist Jakob S. Boeskov, together with writer/editor Mads Brügger and designer Kristian von Bengtson, "founded" Empire North <www.empirenorth.dk>, a fake company that "creates" nonexistent weapons. One week later, Boeskov traveled alone to Beijing to infiltrate China Police 2002, an international weapons fair. With him he had 400 business cards, a digital camera, an expensive tie, some nasty stomach cramps, and a promotional poster for the ID Sniper rifle, a terrible weapon designed to shoot trackable GPS microchips into demonstrators "before they commit their crimes."

Below is some of what happened. This article is adapted from a much longer piece—"My Doomsday Weapon"—in the first issue of *BLACK BOX* magazine <www.blackboxmagazine.com>.

HOW I CRASHED A CHINESE ARMS BAZAAR WITH A RIFLE THAT DOESN'T EXIST

JAKOB S. BOESKOV

_INTRODUCTION

Basically, the idea was to come up with the most terrible weapon imaginable and to test it in a real environment. We had three days to "finish" the weapon. Our fake company, Empire North, already had a logo and a slogan ("The Logical Solution," aping the Nazi classic "The Final Solution"), but we had no weapon yet. Genius designer Von B and I worked overtime, and in two days we had the ID Sniper ready.

The day before I was leaving, *BLACK BOX* editor Mads Brügger called designer Von B and asked him to change the design, because "it was too far out and he couldn't be responsible for what happened, if I was found out."

Changing was not possible at this late stage. I guess he knew that. Maybe he was just, more or less elegantly, trying to shake off his share of the burden. I can understand it, because we were all becoming afraid. Afraid of what would happen if I was found out, and afraid of what might happen if the weapon were taken seriously. Would it be copied? Would we be responsible for the production of one of the most inhumane weapons in the history of man?

We justified our project by telling ourselves that right now a few people were walking around with so-called VeriChips implanted in their bodies, chips manufactured by the company Applied Digital Solutions. We kept reminding ourselves that right now prisoners in Sweden are doing time at home wearing GPS chip wristbands. It would merely be a question of time before the technology would be used pre-emptively on suspicious persons. As we repeatedly told ourselves, all new technology has been used for military purposes, and this technology would be, too, we concluded. Why not bring it out prematurely, so at least we could have a small part in getting a thorough discussion about this kind of technology? With this question, we basically came up with a brand new art concept. Let's for now, just call it "sci-fi conceptual art," defined like this: Take the essence of an imagined future, turn it into a concept, and present this concept in present-day reality. Report the reactions.

Would this new concept lead to a brave journey, searching for truth or would it just be a highly irresponsible prank? There was only one way to find out, and that was to do it.

GPS microchip-based identification rifle
Empire North is proud to present the preliminary showcase of the ID Sniper Rifle—a brand new tool in long-term riot control and anti-terror management. Please notice that some aspects of this cutting-edge technology are still in their outmost infancy, and more research is needed before the ID Sniper Rifle is a reality. Hence we are welcoming investors and business partners to join us in the important quest to develop the ID Sniper Rifle.

What is the ID Sniper Rifle?
To put it short, the idea is to implant a GPS microchip in the body of a human being, using a high-powered sniper rifle as the long distance injector. The microchip will enter the body and stay there, causing no internal damage, and only a very small amount of physical pain to the target. It will feel like a mosquito bite, lasting a fraction of a second.

At the same time, a digital camcorder with a zoom lens fitted within the scope will take a high-resolution picture of the target. This picture will be stored on a memory card for later image-analysis. GPS microchip technology is already being used for tracking millions of pets in various countries, and the logical solution is to use it on humans as well, when the situation demands it.

Why use the ID Sniper Rifle?
As the urban battlefield grows more complex and intense, new ways of managing and controlling crowds are needed. The attention of the media changes the rules of the game. Sometimes it is difficult to engage the enemy in the streets without causing damage to the all-important image of the state. Instead, Empire North suggests marking and identifying a suspicious subject from a safe distance, enabling the national law enforcement agency to keep track of the target through a satellite in the weeks to come.

What is Empire North?
Empire North is a young, progressive Danish Hi-Tech company committed to developing new tools for solving the problems of the 21st century.

We combine outstanding know-how, a network of gifted ad-hoc consultants, a flair for Danish design and creative thinking—and are always focused on discovering the logical solution.

The nonexistent ID Sniper rifle from Empire North.
Illustration by Kristian von Bengtson

Marching and Singing Teenage Policemen

I wake up early, before the hotel wake-up call. I look out the window. Is it already afternoon? I am suddenly confused; my sense of time is messed up from the jetlag. Did I oversleep? I feel another panic attack coming on, my heart racing as if I have had too much coffee. I still have terrible stomach cramps.

One hour later, I am at the National Agricultural Exhibition Hall of the People. It's the first public opening of Empire North, and I am late. Fuck. At the gates, it's total mayhem, an inferno of marching policemen, Chinese businessmen (all dressed in the traditional Chinese businessman uniform: white polo shirt, black polyester pants, silk socks, black loafers or pointy, shiny shoes, no tie), trucks unloading, Europeans getting out of cabs with sunglasses and briefcases, handing bills to drivers who whiff off, unbearable, blinding sunlight reflected in my eyes from shiny cars, helmets, mobile phones, and skyscrapers.

I wave my card and am allowed to pass the guards. A wide range of new police vehicles has been lined up since yesterday, police cars of all shapes and sizes, a few more helicopters, a couple of boats, and even a police tank in blue and white. It has some kind of auto-

> "TO PUT IT SHORT, THE IDEA IS TO IMPLANT A GPS MICROCHIP IN THE BODY OF A HUMAN BEING, USING A HIGH-POWERED SNIPER RIFLE AS THE LONG DISTANCE INJECTOR."

matic gun stuck to the roof. Jesus Christ! They are preparing for *war*! I am standing in the marble entrance of the hall waiting for my little bag to come through the X-ray machine, when a group of marching and singing policemen moves very quickly up the wide stairs, their just-out-of-puberty faces stern and determined.

I get my bag, go into the main hall, and am met by a cacophony of voices in all languages. I am trying to locate my booth, but I'm confused and also very afraid to go there. What should I say and what should I do and what will happen if they find me out? I shudder at the thought of getting involved with the Chinese police. I walk on the red carpets, going nowhere in particular.

Voice-over presentations are booming from sound systems; people shouting into mobiles; large groups of Chinese men shuffling about in units of seven or eight; French dealers of underwater equipment stand smiling at their booth, ready for business. A middle-aged European couple go through the metal detector. The woman, turquoise dress, heavy make-up, has an expression on her face like she is arriving at a suburban cocktail party.

I turn the corner and am about to collide with a six-wheeled robot that is driving towards me. It turns around, now facing me frontally, its heavy wheels spinning eagerly, like a huge mechanical insect. A hydraulic arm with a digital videocam mounted at the end lifts upwards, towards my face. A huge crowd of smiling and photographing Chinese men gather around the robot. I pass through them and the distracting flashlight and run into another group, fifteen or more plain-clothes policemen. They hover around a Chinese man selling Kevlar gloves, repeatedly cutting and stabbing at his gloved hand with a Stanley knife, shouting and laughing and gesturing, his head whirring like a happy animal. The policemen clearly like the glove, all of them grinning, some of them even clapping their hands.

Has Robocop arrived?
Photo by Jakob Boeskov

A Japanese girl is posing in front of a remote-controlled helicopter with a Sony camera mounted underneath it. Several people are drinking colas and Chinese soft drinks.

Bad Techno + Corporate Latex Teenagers From Japan

The heat and noise are unbearable.

I can't get myself together to go to my booth; I turn my card, so that nobody can see that I represent Empire North. A red-haired European man and two Asians are demonstrating voice-recognition software to a group of Chinese men; on their laptop, a 3-D landscape accompanies a Chinese word that's being repeated over and over.

In front of the Honda booth, four police motorcycles surround a large column, where massive Honda light-box logos are mounted next to three 40-inch Sony flatscreen monitors that show images of racing Honda police cars and off-road police motorcycles flying through the air. On screen, a clumsy white Honda robot appears, and a text reads "Honda—the power of dreams." Everything is cut fast, scratch-video style and accompanied by fast and bad Japanese techno.

Three teenage girls enter the elevated stage, dressed in shamelessly erotic militaristic clothes: miniscule white latex dresses and Honda-logoed red berets. They start posing in front of the motorcycles, then smilingly get on top of them, their tiny latex costumes radiant under the hard light. On the fringes of the stand are several male Honda people, older, all dressed in black pants and white Honda polo shirts, huge smiles on their faces, clearly enjoying the sight of their corporate whores flaunting themselves on top of their new technology.

I back away and find myself in yet another crowd. A caterpillar robot the size of an Icelandic pony rolls towards us, raising its huge robotic arm over the crowd, its mechanical fingers snapping high above people's heads. More pictures are taken.

It's very warm, and the heat is killing me. Young policemen in green uniforms, army-style, walk by in large groups.

The ID Sniper Goes Public

Turning a corner, I pass a Brazilian booth with a huge poster of a policeman opening his jacket, exhibitionist-style, revealing a wide array of grenades in many colors. Over it, huge white letters spell out: "Surrender to this concept!"

And there my booth is. I go into it, get behind the little table, put my bag in the space under it, and stand up, forcing a smile on my face. Here we go, now there's no turning back.

Fifteen seconds go by, and a balding Chinese man stops in front of the booth. While manically spewing out extremely bad English, he points to my poster and smiles and gestures wildly, and hands me his card. I introduce myself properly and start to explain to him the basic concept of the ID Sniper.

"First of all," I say, stuttering, making a gesture with my hands I have often seen made by politicians and people on American TV shows: palms facing outward, hands cupped as if I'm stroking an imaginary ball, "we are a very young company, this is a brand new concept." I point my finger at him, turning my head a bit sideways, in a Don Johnson kind of way. I continue with my presentation. He looks quite happy, but I am not sure if he understands what I am saying.

A CATERPILLAR ROBOT THE SIZE OF AN ICELANDIC PONY ROLLS TOWARDS US, RAISING ITS HUGE ROBOTIC ARM OVER THE CROWD, ITS MECHANICAL FINGERS SNAPPING HIGH ABOVE PEOPLE'S HEADS.

"What's so wonderful about this machinery is the general media friendliness of this weapon. Now, let's say we have a normal situation, a situation where the police want to control and identify a group of demonstrators. Normally, this would require quite solid methods, and the presence of cameras could mean that there might appear unwanted pictures on television; pictures of demonstrators bleeding, you know, that kind of stuff," I say and smile.

"Using the ID Sniper, you don't get unwanted media coverage. With the ID Sniper we can," I gesture as if I am holding an invisible ID Sniper, my right index finger pulling the trigger, pausing, "*mark* the subject with the GPS chip, and then," I raise my finger, "track down the demonstrator later on and then apply the necessary means."

The Chinese man smiles.

"CEO" Boeskov at Empire North's exhibition booth.
Courtesy of Jakob Boeskov

"I laik dis weapon!" he says, smiling and laughing, his head nodding, as if he were an eager, autistic kid.

"We can, uuh, do business together!" he says, handing me his card and saying something unintelligible in Chinese. I give him mine, we promise to stay in touch, and then he leaves. I am left at the booth, flabbergasted, feeling like Alice taking the first step through the looking glass.

Jason from Beijing Sen Qili Scientific Trade Centre

A tiny man, apparently no older than 25, with cheap glasses, pimples, and a body that looks like it belongs to a twelve-year old, suddenly appears. He's smiling and *very* energetic. He wears a blue polo shirt, and he gives me his card. His name is Jason Fong, and his company has the intriguing name of Beijing Sen Qili Scientific Trade Centre.

I give him my card and explain the concept to him: "So, generally speaking, it's a brand new concept, a brand new weapon! Now, it might not look like much," I say and gesture to the poster in my booth, "but we have the concept, we hold some patents, we have the software and the hardware and most important of all, we have the energy and the willingness to carry it out, so things are definitely looking very healthy for us!"

He looks very eager, smiling and nodding his head: "Yes, yes!"

"Our company," he says in his thick Chinese accent, manically gesturing to his small chest, "we make high-tech products, we make laser training gun equipment, high-tech, yes?" He hands me a pamphlet in Chinese about his company, and points to a postal address.

"This is only valid till first of August! We are moving office then," he says and points to a 3-D drawing of a skyscraper, about 50 stories high. "This is our new headquarter!"

So Denmark Makes Weapons Now?

A guy in a white suit starts to speak to me in French, then elegantly switches to English. He's from the French Embassy. He smiles and gestures towards my poster. "So Denmark is making weapons now, *oui*?"

"Yes, there are a few of us starting up now!" I say, not even lying. He then looks at the poster for quite a long time, eagerly scanning it.

"I have neeeever seen anything quiiiite like this before!" he says and smiles, crossing his arms over his chest. I break into a sweat.

The French diplomat looks at me intensely, with a sly smile on his face.

"So you fire off a GPS chip into the people, *oui*?"

"That's correct, we, err, mark them and then we locate them. We, uh, find them after the television cameras have gone away—"

He points his finger in the air. "But what caliber are you using?"

I feel blood rushing to my face. I know absolutely nothing about guns, a fact many people pointed out to me before I came here. I meant to research, but somehow I never found the time.

"That's optional!"

"Sorry?" He looks very confused; his face grimaced and tilted, mouth slightly open.

"Twenty-two," I say.

"Zero point 22 inches??" he asks. "But—"

"No, no, not inches, centimeters! Well 38, actually! We might use gas. We are not sure, really!" I realize how silly all of this must sound. I smile and check my pockets for cigarettes. The French diplomat has a slight frown.

"But, but, will you not have problems with causing damage to the intestines of the demonstrators? If you shoot it off, it doesn't stop,

"NORMALLY, THIS WOULD REQUIRE QUITE SOLID METHODS, AND THE PRESENCE OF CAMERAS COULD MEAN THAT THERE MIGHT APPEAR UNWANTED PICTURES ON TELEVISION; PICTURES OF DEMONSTRATORS BLEEDING, YOU KNOW, THAT KIND OF STUFF."

you know. It will enter into the body and then it will—*cause damage*." He looks at me.

"Well," I say, lowering my voice, "that's a really important issue you are raising there. It's a crucial issue. It's our weak point. It is an important problem we have to solve, but we are determined to solve it, and when we do, we will have a perfectly healthy market situation." I smile at him eagerly. He looks at me, a smile forming on his face.

"Well, *just shoot 'em in the butt*!" he says, grinning, hitting his own right buttock with a loud *slap*, and then he leaves, laughing, his head turning one last time, looking in my direction. I am left in my booth, bewildered.

More people arrive. I explain more, hand out a lot of business cards, receive a lot of business cards. I sweat and smile. This is exhausting.

After two hours, the crowd thins out a little. Some Arab- or Jewish-looking guys from across the aisle keep looking at me, smiling. I get out my laptop; my plan is to write down notes. I turn it on, and I'm suddenly terrified by my messy desktop.

I turn off the computer, putting it back underneath the table, and get out my paper notebook instead. But I feel so self-conscious, sitting there writing; nervous and sweating and still plagued by stomach

For the police department that has everything....
Photo by Jakob Boeskov

cramps. I can hardly keep the pen straight, so I leave my booth, go outside and buy some weird, cold Chinese food and a Chinese beer, sit in the shade under some bamboo, and start to scribble notes.

The Banquet

I am at the hotel. It's evening and time to get ready for the big banquet, hosted in honor of all international weapons dealers, including Empire North. In the package sent to me in Copenhagen was a gold-rimmed invitation printed on expensive paper, informing me that my presence was requested at the Great Wall Sheraton Plaza, on the 19th of June, at 1800 hours. That was about 45 minutes ago,

so I am in a hurry.

I put on an expensive tie I bought for this occasion, and to it I add a little something I got from a Chinese seller of shotguns today—a tiny golden tie clip, designed as a shotgun. I look quite spiffy.

I leave, get a cab, show the invitation to the driver, and off we go—zooming through the alien labyrinth of steel and concrete, neon lights, and ancient buildings, as the red sun sets. I look at my telephone to check the time: I am terribly late.

> **"WELL, JUST SHOOT 'EM IN THE BUTT!" HE SAYS, GRINNING, HITTING HIS OWN RIGHT BUTTOCK WITH A LOUD *SLAP*.**

Forty minutes later, I'm in front of the Great Wall Sheraton Plaza. A uniformed bellboy opens the door of the cab. Outside are the Chinese flag, the US flag, and a Motorola flag. I step out onto the red carpet, entering a gigantic temple of chrome, a futuristic monolith of old power and new wealth. A hostess in a black evening dress points me towards an escalator and up I go, towards the increasing noise of people partying. At the end of the second floor are two very tall doors, with yet another two hostesses standing by. As I approach, they open the doors, smile, and I enter.

The Rumpus Room of the Merchants of Death

I am in a stadium-sized room with no windows at all, lit from matted glass panels in the roof. It's filled to the brim with huge, round tables where people sit on high-backed chairs, eating and drinking. Everybody seems totally drunk now. Girls in low-cut silver Chivas Regal dresses pour generous portions of 20-year-old Chivas for everybody. Talk and drunken laughter fill the room. Much food has already been eaten; much alcohol has already been drunk.

I go to the Chivas-sponsored bar feeling mighty out of place. I make some nervous movements with my hand, and a boy pours me a glass full of amber liquid. After a few minutes, a loud Brazilian in his late thirties appears.

"Why are you not eating?" he shouts at me. "Come over here—we have some very nice snakes over here! *Haw haw*!"

"Oh no, I—I am really not hungry," I tell him, my stomach already revolting at his perverse suggestion. What does he want from me?

He gives me his card. His name is Federicio, and he is the director of a company called Welser Itage. His sidekick, a goofy hippie-character, also Brazilian, is doing the video presentations for the company. We start to chat, and I ask Federicio about the fair, not trying to hide that I am an upstart in this business.

"I see a great potential here!" Federicio tells me. "The Chinese police are building up a force of one million men. One million men!" He says this with much respect and gestures with his index finger.

"We're basically seeing all this because of the Olympics in 2008 and because China joined the WTO," Federicio says and lights up a

Cohiba cigar. More whisky is poured. The goofy video guy offers me a Chinese cigarette.

"Yes," I say, "but I am just worrying if they have the dedication to, uh, spend what it takes. They are used to old, cheap technology. I wonder if they are ready to go high-tech?"

"Oh, come on," Federicio says. "We are talking about a country with a growth rate of 9 percent, some places even 17 percent! Seventeen percent!"

He raises his Cohiba vertically, so it resembles a small chimney. "Money is clearly not a problem here. They have what it takes, no problem, no problem!"

"Yeah, you think so?"

"I know so!" he says loudly, before lowering his voice. "The only problem, as I see it, is to get in contact. They don't speak English. Email is a problem here and new to them. It's very difficult, very difficult! You have to have a personal contact; otherwise there is no business."

"THE CHINESE POLICE ARE BUILDING UP A FORCE OF ONE MILLION MEN. ONE MILLION MEN!"

Suddenly, a Chinese man appears on the platform. He introduces the next speaker as the Minister of Public Security. Another nondescript little man steps up and speaks into the microphone in a thick Chinese accent.

"Thankyou for ahrcomming. Goodnight!" The little man steps down.

Federicio and I laugh. "They are very fast speakers here, huh?" I say.

I tell Federicio and his goofy friend about the ID Sniper. After I am done, Federcio's face lights up a beaming smile and he yells: "That's *great*!! In Brazil, we have so many problems with prisoners escaping prisons. We put them there, but they just run away," he sighs, as if he is talking about little kids sneaking out of kindergarten.

"But with your technology, with the GPS, we can catch them again."

His face glows.

"You have my card, right? You see, we manufacture all kinds of nonlethal weapons, and if we get something going with these guys, we definitely need some new high-tech concepts to get them interested."

"Yeah! That sounds great!" I say, although I don't know exactly what it is he wants from me.

_EVIL DOES NOT EXIST

Then Federicio starts an endless, drunken ramble about the problems of Brazil, about how he is going to buy a bullet-proof car, and all the problems of the Landless Workers Movement who have connections with FARC in Colombia, and so on—paranoid thoughts of left-wing conspiracies against order and stability in the civilized world.

Back at the hotel room, I fall into a drunken sleep. And then suddenly a loud ring. The telephone wakes me. It's 1:30 AM. When I say "Hello?" somebody hangs up. This must clearly be a mistake. I light a cigarette. Fifteen minutes later the same thing happens. I get very nervous. I lie on the bed in a quiet panic, nasty stomach cramps.

Before I came here, I had some vague ideas about this world being sort of like a James Bond movie—filled with eccentric, cynical inventors, and colorful, ruthless traders. I couldn't have been more wrong: This is reality, not James Bond. And these people are *not* cynical, ruthless, evil people—they are basically nice people, who are absolutely, 100 percent convinced that they are doing the right thing. They believe that by pushing all their high-tech killing equipment, they are fighting for freedom and democracy and all that bullshit. And that's what makes them so fucking scary.

THE MYSTERIOUS DECLINE OF MEN ON CAMPUS

PHILIP W. COOK AND GLENN J. SACKS

_THE TREND IS CLEAR

Everybody wants to know where all the men have gone. The *Washington Post* calls their disappearance the "question that has grown too conspicuous to ignore,"[1] and *USA Today* notes "universities fret about how to attract males as women increasingly dominate campuses."[2]

Females now outnumber males by a four-to-three ratio in American colleges, a difference of almost two million students.[3] Men earn only 43 percent of all college degrees.[4] Among blacks, two women earn bachelor's degrees for every man. Among Hispanics, only 40 percent of college graduates are male.[5] Female high school graduates are 16 percent more likely to go to college than their male counterparts.[6]

"This is new. We have thrown the gender switch," says Christina Hoff Sommers, a resident scholar at the American Enterprise Institute and author of *The War Against Boys: How Misguided Feminism is Harming Our Young Men.* "What does it mean in the long run that we have females who are significantly more literate, significantly more educated than their male counterparts? It is likely to create a lot of social problems. This does not bode well for anyone."[7]

"As a nation, we simply can't afford to have half of our population not developing the skill sets that we are going to need to go into the future," says Susan L. Traiman, director of the Business Roundtable's education initiative.[8]

Researchers from Harvard University, the University of Michigan, and the United Negro College Fund have now agreed to study the issue.

"This is a powerful issue we need to stop talking about in generalities and really dig into," says Michael L. Lomax, president of Dillard University in New Orleans. "We just can't figure out how to get more male applicants, and we're not going to turn students down on the basis of gender. I don't understand what is happening in the male community that is making education seem less attractive and less compelling."[9]

The trend is unmistakable, and some fear it is irreversible. Men made up the majority of college graduates when the first national survey was conducted in 1870. Except during World War II, when slightly more females enrolled than men, males were in the majority until men's graduation rates began to decline in the late 1970s. By the early 1980s, women began to represent the majority of graduates.

In total, the US Department of Education estimates that 698,000 women received bachelor's degrees in 2002, compared to 529,000 men.[10]

Yet the loss in national productivity that this trend portends is not a concern to some. Jacqueline Woods, executive director of the American Association of University Women, denies that men's declining enrollment is a crisis or even a gender issue. She notes that those concerned about boys' sagging educational performance are "playing a zero-sum game" and says, "I refuse to play."[11] Columnist Ellen Goodman dismisses boy-friendly educational reformers as being motivated by the fact that "educated women have always made some people nervous."[12] She, Woods and writer Barbara Ehrenreich argue that the college gender gap is another example of the disadvantages faced by women! According to Ehrenreich, "[M]en...suspect they can make a living just as well without a college education, since they still have such an advantage over women in the non-professional workforce."[13]

Not only are the problems of college males being minimized in some quarters, but also much of the discussion about the lack of males in college surrounds the destructive impact it may have upon females. For example, an ABC.com report on the subject gloats: "No More Big Man on Campus?" while declaring that the "College Gender Gap Could Mean Women Lose Mating Game" and asking, "Must Women Go Slummin'?"[14] Canadian journalist Lysiane Gagnon laments in the *Globe and Mail* that "the next generation of Quebec women might face a difficult love life.... [I]n a few years the province will be filled with high-paid, ambitious, professional women. Across the dance floor will be a large group of losers—uneducated men stuck in small, low-paying jobs."[15]

_A HIDDEN ISSUE

Sophomore Adam Petkun and Senior Jesse Harding at the University of Oregon, who work at the Associated Students office, are typical of many male students on campuses across the country. They didn't know that women outnumber men on their campus. They were both surprised but not shocked by the information. Neither had any thoughts on why it was occurring or seemed concerned about the trend. Martin

FEMALES NOW OUTNUMBER MALES BY A FOUR-TO-THREE RATIO IN AMERICAN COLLEGES, A DIFFERENCE OF ALMOST TWO MILLION STUDENTS.

S., a junior at Portland State University, after giving it some thought didn't think the trend is ultimately a good thing. "I don't know why this is going on. It seems like blue-collar, physical jobs that usually go to men are on the decline, so you'd think there would be more men attending college, not less. I know some guys who have taken to going into high-tech and feel they don't need a degree, but even in quite a few of those jobs a degree is obviously a help. It's a mystery to me."[16]

It is also apparently a surprise and a mystery to most high-school counselors. "The few counselors I have talked with seem surprised by the trend," said Richard Wong, executive director of the American School Counselor Association, the nation's largest school counseling group. "I don't think there has been a conscious effort to exclude white males, because historically they have been able to take care of themselves. A lot more attention has been paid to other groups, minorities and women, but perhaps the pendulum has swung too far." Although the ASCA has conducted initiative programs for women and minorities, it does not plan any affirmative campaign to address the decline in male college attendance. "If it becomes a major issue, the board will likely consider a response," said Wong.[17]

> GIRLS GET BETTER GRADES THAN BOYS, AND BOYS ARE FAR MORE LIKELY THAN GIRLS TO DROP OUT OF SCHOOL OR TO BE DISCIPLINED, SUSPENDED, HELD BACK, OR EXPELLED.

According to Mark Kuranz, a former president of the ASCA and currently a high-school counselor in Racine, Wisconsin: "Certainly college is very accessible for girls, and there is more competition with boys for the available spots. You would think however, there would be a leveling off or the attendance and the graduation rate would be pretty level. Perhaps we have begun to expect less from boys."[18]

_AN EARLY START TO GIVING UP ON COLLEGE?

Boys have fallen seriously behind girls at all kindergarten through twelfth-grade levels. By high school, the typical boy is a year and a half behind the typical girl in reading and writing.[19] Girls get better grades than boys, and boys are far more likely than girls to drop out of school or to be disciplined, suspended, held back, or expelled.[20] Boys are four times as likely as girls to receive a diagnosis of attention deficit hyperactivity disorder (ADHD), and the vast majority of learning-disabled students are boys.[21]

The problem is a complex one, but a fundamental reason behind the phenomena is that modern K-12 education is not suited to boys' needs and learning styles. Success in school is tightly correlated with the ability to sit still, be quiet, and complete work that is presented in a dull, assembly-line fashion. There is little outlet for natural boyish energy and exuberance in schools, and as a result many boys—even those as young as five or six—end up being given Ritalin or other drugs so they can sit still. At every step of the way those whose natures are least accommodating to this type of education—boys—fall by the wayside.

Boys' educational problems often begin as soon as they go to kinder-

garten. Michelle Ventimiglia, director of a Los Angeles preschool, says:

Our schools simply aren't made for boys. I see this every September when my students go into elementary school. My boys do great here, but when they go on to elementary school all of a sudden some of them become "behavior problems" or "bad kids." How can a 6-year-old be "bad?"

Children need physically-connected activities, particularly boys. They learn best by doing. Too often teachers find it easier to simply give them worksheets instead. And now, with so much time being devoted to testing and preparing for testing, teachers' repertoires are even more limited, which is bad for children, particularly boys.[22]

When boys are unable to fit into a school environment that clearly is not suited to them, they are often diagnosed with ADHD and given Ritalin or other drugs. Nearly nine million prescriptions of Ritalin are written for American children each year, most of them for boys between the ages of six and twelve.[23] According to Stanford University's Thomas Sowell, author of *Inside American Education: The Decline, the Deception, the Dogmas*, the drugging of boys is "part of a growing tendency to treat boyhood as a pathological condition that requires a new three R's—repression, re-education and Ritalin."[24] He notes: "The motto used to be: 'Boys will be boys.' Today, the motto seems to be: 'Boys will be medicated.'"[25]

Kuranz says these issues are starting to be addressed in schools. "The conversation is beginning to be heard" regarding more active learning methods and the over-use of Ritalin.[26]

_LESS FOR MEN'S SPORTS

The decline of men's college sports has also contributed to the disappearance of men on college campuses. Title IX of the Education Amendments Act of 1972 bars sex discrimination in any educational program or activity that receives federal funding.[27] In the decades since, women's athletics have burgeoned in high schools and colleges. Title IX was and remains an important and laudable victory for the women's movement.

Some feminist groups, however, lobbied successfully to use an obscure bureaucratic action known as the 1979 Policy Interpretation to mandate that the number of athletes in college athletic programs reflect within a few percentage points the proportion of male and female students on campus. The problem is, as studies have shown, fewer women than men are interested in playing organized sports, even though the opportunity is available.[28] Even in all-female colleges, the number of women athletes falls considerably below that needed to satisfy Title IX requirements in coed colleges.[29]

In addition, the current Title IX equity calculations are misleading because they count college football's athletes and dollars without considering football's moneymaking ability. In fact, over 70 percent of Division I-A football programs turn a profit.[30]

Schools are caught in a vise. Because schools need football's revenue yet must also equalize gender numbers, they are forced to cut men's non-revenue sports. Todd R. Dickey, University of Southern California's general counsel, and many others argue that football should simply be taken out of the gender-equity equation because no other sport earns as much revenue, has such a large number of athletes or staff, and needs as much equipment. "You can't spend as much on women's sports as you can on men's, because there is no women's equivalent for football," Dickey says.[31]

Thus, women have gained a little, but men have lost a lot. According to the National Collegiate Athletic Association (NCAA), for every new women's athletics slot created between 1992 and 1997, 3.6 male athletes were dropped.[32] During the same period, colleges added 5,800 female athletes—and cut 20,000 male athletes.[33] More than 400 men's collegiate athletic teams have been eliminated nationwide since the advent of Title IX.[34] Kimberly Schuld, director of the Independent Women's Forum's Title IX Play Fair! Project, calls this "clear, government-sanctioned sex discrimination."[35]

The current situation in men's sports in college has prompted some recent reconsideration but no clear direction. The Commission on Opportunity in Athletics is looking at recommendations for Secretary of Education Rod Paige. In testimony before the commission, Deborah Zelechowski, a senior vice president at Robert Morris College in Chicago, said that she has a male student population of just 36 percent. "We need more males," she said, "yet we cannot offer more male athletic teams…. [T]he letter of the law of Title IX is interfering with the spirit of the law."[36]

_AN ANTI-MALE CAMPUS?

Nearly every large college campus and many smaller ones have a women's studies department. There are over 500 such departments and over 100 colleges that offer a degree program in women's studies.[37] There is not a single degree program or department in men's studies in the US. It is difficult to get exact numbers, but it appears that there are fewer than a dozen classes labeled men's studies being offered in colleges anywhere. Some that are labeled men's studies are in fact anti-male. Kenyon College, for example, has a men's studies program that, in the words of one professor, is in opposition to "the white, male, heterosexual, able-bodied, Christian, middle-class norm."[38]

Some academicians contend that the ascendancy of women's studies on campus was a mistake. They argue that such issues do not properly belong in a narrowly defined "feminist" approach to learning but in already established fields of study, such as sociology and history. In any case, there certainly has been little demonstrated movement among college administrators to offer men's studies departments or courses, and men's resource centers. Bret Burkholder, a professor at Pierce Community College in Puyallup, Washington, has set up a resource center on his campus. He says such efforts can

help: "We must learn and establish alternative ways of instruction and student services support that are more in step with the predominant ways that men learn and communicate. We have to respect men, their ways of learning and expression if we are to earn their respect and trust. No one stays where they aren't wanted or valued."[39]

The claim that an anti-male agenda exists in our universities is difficult to understand unless one is immersed in today's college culture.

Dinesh D'Souza, in his book *Illiberal Education: The Politics of Race and Sex on Campus*, argues that a system has emerged which has encouraged separatism: "By the time these students graduate, very few colleges have met their need for all-round development. Instead, by precept and example, the ideal of an educated person is largely a figment of bourgeois white male ideology, which should be cast aside." He charges that what the American students are getting is not a liberal education but "its diametrical opposite, an education in closed-mindedness and intolerance."[40]

> ACCORDING TO THE NATIONAL COLLEGIATE ATHLETIC ASSOCIATION (NCAA), FOR EVERY NEW WOMEN'S ATHLETICS SLOT CREATED BETWEEN 1992 AND 1997, 3.6 MALE ATHLETES WERE DROPPED.

D'Souza and others point to women's studies departments as a prime mover in this change. Thomas Sort, a professor of philosophy at Kenyon College, says, "Ideological dogmatism is the norm not the exception in women's studies. They practice the very exclusion that they claim to have suffered in the past."[41] It is not that men are not welcome just in women's studies programs. The programs may have fostered an environment in which the very presence of males on campus is a threat to a worldview that sees things only in terms of oppressors and the oppressed.

Deliberate misinformation about men and gender issues is an integral part of modern campus culture. Women's centers and women's studies departments publicize and promote discredited academic frauds like, "One in four college women has been the victim of rape or attempted rape," and, "Domestic violence is the leading cause of injury to women aged 15 to 44."[42] Sommers, who debunked many academic feminist claims in *Who Stole Feminism?*, calls these "Hate Statistics."[43] The statistics help to set up a campus mindset where it makes sense to be anti-male. If, for example, one believes the oft-stated feminist claim that on an average campus a woman is raped every 21 hours, who wouldn't be?[44] (In reality, there is an average of less than one reported rape per three American college campuses per year).[45]

Women's studies textbooks provide a view of the hostility towards men in our universities. According to an extensive study of women's studies textbooks released in 2002 by the IWF, a dissident women's group, the textbooks "ignore facts in favor of myths," "mistake ideology for scholarship," and encourage students to "embrace aggrievement, not knowledge."[46] The study, "Lying in a Room of One's Own: How Women's Studies Textbooks Miseducate Students," examined the five most popular women studies' textbooks in the United States and found relentless woman-as-victim/man-as-victimizer bias and hostility. According to the author, Christine Stolba, the textbooks construe or distort studies and statistics to infer that women are miserable and oppressed, and that men are privileged oppressors.[47]

Among the "truths" the textbooks tell students are: Women are under siege from virtually all sectors of society; little has changed for women in the past three decades; believing that women have achieved equality is "modern sexism"; and most women are not naturally sexually attracted to men but are the victims of "compulsory heterosexuality" maintained through male "social control."[48] Bad fathers are described as the rule rather than the exception; the prevalence of sexual abuse and molestation is wildly exaggerated; and students are told that in families fathers often represent a "foreign male element" that mothers and daughters must unite against.[49]

UCLA is one of the few universities in which a debate on the anti-male bias on campus has actually been allowed to take place, and this was only because of an ad in the campus newspaper. The IWF ran a full-page advertisement in UCLA's student newspaper, the *Daily Bruin*, which asked: "Are you tired of male-bashing and victimology?" The ad debunked what it called the "Ten Most Common Feminist Myths," including: "30 percent of emergency room visits by women each year are the result of injuries from domestic violence," "women have been shortchanged in medical research," "one in four women in college has been the victim of rape or attempted rape," and others.[50]

Feminists, led by Tina Oakland, director of the UCLA Center for Women and Men, and Christie Scott, executive co-chair of the UCLA Clothesline Project, launched campus demonstrations against what Scott called "a violent ad, a very hostile ad" which "breeds a very bad attitude toward campus women."[51] Oakland said that challenging the "one in four" rape statistic is like denying the Holocaust.[52] A feminist professor wrote to the *Daily Bruin* claiming that the IWF ad served to "ferment intolerant, anti-woman...sentiment and action on campus" and "incite hate."[53]

While the *Daily Bruin* refused to apologize for the ad, its viewpoint editor was cowed and expressed regret that the paper had "let something so anti-woman through."[54] Oakland, after being castigated by some in conservative magazines, backed off of her defense of the "one in four" rape figure, explaining that "the statistics don't really matter that much in the big picture."[55]

_CAN BALANCE BE ACHIEVED?

A serious national effort is needed to redress the gender imbalance in our universities, and the biggest solution to the absence of boys from our college campuses will be boy-friendly reforms at the K-12 level. Sommers notes that one of the greatest challenges reformers face is the fact that our society is largely unaware of or refuses to recognize the boy crisis in our schools. She contrasts this with England, which embarked upon boy-friendly educational reforms in the early 1990s and has met with some success.[56]

Part of this national effort will be a retooling of our schools to create boy-friendly classrooms and teaching strategies. Boys in particular need strong, charismatic teachers who mix firm discipline with a good-natured acceptance of boyish energy. Concomitantly, a sharp increase in the number of male teachers is also needed, particularly at the elementary level, where female teachers outnumber male teachers six to one. Same-sex classes can also be helpful, and schools should have the power to employ them when appropriate.[57]

Beyond reforms at the K-12 level, it is apparent that college campuses need to be places where males feel as welcome as females. Women's studies needs to be either abolished, converted to gender studies and its texts and studies put under strict peer review, or departments of equal stature and funding need to be created that are devoted to men's studies. It only seems fair and balanced. At the very least, many women's studies textbooks need to be replaced by texts which consider both male and female points of view on gender issues and which cite only academically credible research. Title IX needs to be brought back to its original intent, and viable men's athletic programs need to be restored.

The decline in male attendance and college achievement does not appear to be a statistical aberration, or one that will correct itself without attention being paid to the issue. Certainly society is not better off if a significant number of our best and brightest young men fail to seek or earn a college education. We need to take the first step by acknowledging that the decline of males on campus is a significant social and economic problem. This realization need not detract from the mission to provide equal educational opportunities for women. It may lead to recognizing that at least some real discriminatory lack of accommodation for males in education campus exists, and that reforms and different approaches are needed. If these steps are not taken, it seems clear that the decline of males on campus will continue at its present rapid rate.

Endnotes

1. Fletcher, Michael A. "Degrees of Separation: Gender Gap Among College Graduates Has Educators Wondering Where the Men Are." *Washington Post*, 25 June 2002. **2.** Sloan, Karen. "Hey, Where Are All the College Guys? Universities Fret About How to Attract Males as Women Increasingly Dominate Campuses." *USA Today*, 10 May 2001. **3.** Goodman, Ellen. "America's Women Are Advancing by Degrees." *Boston Globe*, 3 Sept 2002. **4.** Sealey, Geraldine. "College Gender Gap Could Mean Women Lose Mating Game." ABCNews.com, 18 July 2002. **5.** *Ibid.* **6.** "Statistical Abstract of the United States," 116th Edition, The National Data Book of the US Department of Commerce Statistics Administration. 1996. **7.** *Op cit.*, Fletcher. **8.** *Ibid.* **9.** *Ibid.* **10.** *Ibid.* **11.** *Op cit.*, Goodman. **12.** *Op cit.*, Goodman. **13.** Ehrenreich, Barbara, and Lionel Tiger. "Forum: Who Needs Men? Addressing the Prospect of a Matrilinear Millennium." *Harper's*, June 1999: 33. **14.** *Op cit.*, Sealey. **15.** Gagnon, Lysiane. "Here's a Shock for Women." *Globe and Mail* (Toronto), 14 Oct 2002. **16.** Interview with authors. **17.** Interview with authors. **18.** Interview with authors. **19.** Sommers, Christina Hoff. "The War Against Boys." *Atlantic Monthly*, May 2000. **20.** *Ibid.* **21.** Sommers, Christina Hoff. *The War Against Boys: How Misguided Feminism is Harming Our Young Men.* New York: Touchstone, 2000: 25-6. **22.** Interview with authors. **23.** Dunne, Diane Weaver. "Statistics Confirm Rise in Childhood ADHD and Medication Use." *Education World*, 12 Dec 2000. **24.** Sowell, Thomas. "The War Against Boys." *Capitalism Magazine*, 21 Oct 2001. **25.** *Ibid.* **26.** Interview with authors. **27.** Unsigned. "Women's Sports: Title IX Timeline." *Seattle Times*, 18 June 2002. **28.**

THERE ARE OVER 500 SUCH DEPARTMENTS AND OVER 100 COLLEGES THAT OFFER A DEGREE PROGRAM IN WOMEN'S STUDIES. THERE IS NOT A SINGLE DEGREE PROGRAM OR DEPARTMENT IN MEN'S STUDIES IN THE US.

Schuld, Kimberly. "Title IX Athletics: Background and Analysis of Government Policy Governing Sports in Schools." Independent Women's Forum White Paper, June 2000: 11-3. **29.** *Ibid.*: 17-8. **30.** Agthe, Donald E., and R. Bruce Billings. *Journal of Sport Management* 14.1 (Jan 2000). **31.** Boo, Joseph. "USC Athletics Accused of Title IX Non-compliance: Questions Raised About Conformity to Gender Equity Rules." *Daily Trojan*, 25 March 1999: 19. **32.** Schuld, Kimberly. "Look Who's Losing." *Women's Quarterly*, Winter 1998. **33.** Norris, Michele. "Leveled Playing Field? Title IX Opened Some Sports to Women, Closed Others to Men." ABCNews.com, 25 June 2002. **34.** Duff, Anna Bray. "Going to the Mat for Title IX." *Investor's Business Journal*, 9 Aug 1999. **35.** *Op cit.*, Schuld, "Title IX Athletics": 19. **36.** "High Schools, Junior Colleges Air Issues Unique to Their Situations." *USA Today*, 18 Sept 2002. **37.** "Report of the Committee on the Status of Women in the Academic Profession," American Association of University Professors. *Academe*, July-Aug: 35-9. **38.** D'Souza, Dinesh. *Illiberal Education The Politics of Race and Sex On Campus*. Free Press, 1991. **39.** Interview with authors. **40.** *Op cit.*, D'Souza: 229. **41.** *Ibid.*: 247. **42.** Sommers, Christina Hoff. *Who Stole Feminism? How Women Have Betrayed Women*. New York: Simon & Schuster, 1994: 212. **43.** Jalbert, Shana. "Differences Between Girls and Boys Subject of ProJo Lecture." *Brown Daily Herald*, 9 March 2001. **44.** V-Day's 2002 Press Kit: 5. <www.vday.org/post/vday_downloads/final2002presskit.doc>. **45.** Leo, John. "Miffing the Myth Makers: A Feisty Student Newspaper Ad Roils the College Feminists." *Jewish World Review.com*, 31 May 2001. **46.** Stolba, Christine. "Lying in a Room of One's Own: How Women's Studies Textbooks Miseducate Students." Independent Women's Forum White Paper, 2002: 31-2. **47.** *Ibid*. **48.** *Ibid.*: 19. **49.** *Ibid.*: 23. **50.** "Take Back the Campus." *Daily Bruin*, 18 April 2001. **51.** *Op cit.*, Leo. **52.** *Ibid.* **53.** Levy, Barrie. "Bruin Ad Misleading." *Daily Bruin*, 11 May 2001. **54.** Stockstill, Mason. "Students Protest Publication of Ad in Newspaper." *Daily Bruin*, 21 May 2001. **55.** *Op cit.*, Leo. **56.** *Op cit.*, Sommers, *War Against Boys*: 161-4. **57.** *Ibid.*: 162.

A SHARP INCREASE IN THE NUMBER OF MALE TEACHERS IS ALSO NEEDED, PARTICULARLY AT THE ELEMENTARY LEVEL, WHERE FEMALE TEACHERS OUTNUMBER MALE TEACHERS SIX TO ONE.

THE KWANGJU UPRISING AND THE US
WHEN IS AN INTERVENTION NOT AN INTERVENTION?
NICK MAMATAS

_KWANGJU?

A massacre of students. That sums up the 1980 uprising in the South Korean city of Kwangju and the eventual bloodshed that ended it, as far as the American media are concerned. Even in 1996, when the trials of former South Korean strongmen Roh Tae Woo and Chun Doo Hwan were worldwide front-page news, the incidents in Kwangju and the American involvement in the massacre were often boiled down to a brief mention along the lines of: "A revolt in Kwangju against the martial law order was put down by troops, who killed about 200 people."[1]

But the Kwangju Uprising was far more than that, and not the least of American obfuscation is the deliberate underselling of the casualties—Western witnesses reported seeing over 100 brutalized bodies stored in a single space even *before* the final massacre, and many bodies were removed by troops after the insurrection was crushed. Kwangju citizens claim that nearly 2,000 people were killed, and the missing certainly haven't come home yet.[2] But Kwangju is more than the story of a body count.

On May 18, 1980, nearly an entire city took to the streets and later took up arms to fight off martial law. In so doing, they had to face the practical realities of running a city with neither state nor capital: Who gets the guns captured from factory armories and police boxes? The vehicles liberated from factories? The gasoline? How do we get information out to the people of other cities, so that they may join us? Do we negotiate with the South Korean state, a state that has already demonstrated eagerness to kill its own citizens? How can we feed everyone? What do we do with the many, many dead? The answers were collective ones, a spontaneous socialism based initially on the pure need to survive and to continue to fight against the martial-law government, but ultimately on what can be called the "eros effect."

The eros effect is, in the words of social movement researcher George Katsiaficas, "the collective sublimation of the instinctual need for freedom."[3] When the eros effect emerges, the old dichotomy between individual sovereignty and collective endeavor collapses into a new form of consciousness that eliminates the old social categories that human beings are so carefully and completely placed in by their ruling classes.

The Kwangju Uprising was also a clear demonstration of the United States' insistence on Cold War hegemony over its own stated goals of increased democratization and support of human rights. Though the US and Carter-era State Department officials for two decades have tried to spin the massacre that ended the uprising as a slaughter that "represented neither American values nor American goals,"[4] the fact is that the South Korean Special Forces troops used to finally put down the uprising (after local police and soldiers joined it to defend their fellows) were under the Combined Forces Command (CFC), meaning that US approval was necessary to release troops from their posts so that they could go into the city and kill nearly 2,000 civilians.

The Carter Administration, eager to avoid "another Iran," treated the democratic rebels in Kwangju with contempt even as they made public noises about encouraging Chun Doo Hwan's coup government to embrace democratic reforms. The US approved the use of force to put down the very people making the same democratic demand the Administration supposedly was making.

ON MAY 18, 1980, NEARLY AN ENTIRE CITY TOOK TO THE STREETS AND LATER TOOK UP ARMS TO FIGHT OFF MARTIAL LAW.

Finally, though the Kwangju Uprising and the attendant massacre are virtually unknown in the United States, it is considered one of the most important events in South Korean history. Lee Jae-eui's definitive first-hand account of the uprising—translated and updated by Kap Su Seol and myself as *Kwangju Diary: Beyond Death, Beyond the Darkness of the Age* and published by the UCLA Asian Pacific Monograph Series in 1999—sold over one million copies in Asia, and copies were being circulated in Tiananmen Square during the 1989 uprising. A 1996 opinion poll of students attending Seoul National University showed that they believe the Kwangju Uprising to be the most important event in South Korean history, eclipsing the Korean War by a wide margin.[5] The "People's Power" movement of 1987, which finally ended gross dictatorship in South Korea, was directly inspired by Kwangju, and inspired millions of people to stand up to the government's brutal violence and take their country back.

_SOUTH KOREAN DEMOCRACY: AN OXYMORON, LIKE "MILITARY INTELLIGENCE"

South Korea was never a democracy. "Every Korean republic until the one elected in 1992, under Kim Young Sam, began or ended in massive uprisings or military coups."[6] And until this day, South Korea's National Security Law drastically limits the potential for parliamentary democracy; even a British-style Labour Party would smack too much of communism to be legal, and many books available in the US are banned in South Korea. The US State Department, which has been on record encouraging democratic reforms in South Korea for decades, called for the law to be revoked…in 1994.

The US spent much of the Cold War making sure South Korea remained a compliant client state, even intervening when dictators themselves broached the subject of democracy. Park Chung Hee, who took power in a 1961 coup and founded the Korean Central Intelligence Agency (KCIA) to eradicate domestic dissent, floated the idea of a referendum to see if his junta should remain in power, but Koreans never got to cast that vote, thanks to US opposition. By 1972, when Park declared himself President, he forgot all about referenda and redoubled his repression of the populace (including rewriting the Constitution to do away with direct presidential elections), all in order to protect them from the phantom menace of the North.

The coup of Chun Doo Hwan and Roh Tae Woo in 1979 began as just another, if weirder, chapter in the country's history of US-backed dictatorships. In August 1979, a sit-down strike was broken with deadly force by then-President Park. Huge protests erupted in the cities of Masan and Pusan, knocking the old order off balance.

On October 26, with the country still roiling and Park trying to determine whether another round of repression or some form of political decompression was more appropriate, he and his bodyguard met with Kim Chae-gyu, the director of the nation's all-pervasive Korean Central Intelligence Agency. During the meeting, Kim began to argue with Park's bodyguard and simply shot him. Then he turned to Park and shot him, as well.[7]

The military was, according to the oracular Pentagon at least, the only power center in South Korean society able to fill the vacuum of power left by Park's assassination. Generals Chun Doo Hwan and Roh Tae Woo took power by December, even arresting the country's Martial Law Commander and Defense Minister (Chun claimed they had plotted Park's assassination). Chun even removed troops under US-ROK joint command from the Demilitarized Zone (DMZ) to cement his power and by April of 1980, declared himself head of the KCIA.

This removal of troops is exceptionally important: These soldiers were not only under US command (General Richard Stilwell once referred to the US/SK joint command as "the most remarkable concession of sovereignty in the entire world"[8]), and not only were they moved without the knowledge or permission of the US, which deeply angered the Carter Administration, but these troops were the front line against North Korea. Containment of North Korea has been the excuse offered for the support of every South Korean dictator, every business break given to South Korean *chaebols* (huge corporate conglomerates), and ultimately, the excuse given for US support of the massacre of 2,000 civilians who wanted democracy. And to begin with, Chun weakened the force meant to stave off the North.

| WHEN STUDENT PROTESTERS AND SOME OTHER CITIZENS SPONTANEOUSLY CAME OUT TO FIGHT BACK WITH STONES AND STICKS, THE SOLDIERS AFFIXED BAYONETS TO THEIR RIFLES AND BEGAN KILLING.

_THE KWANGJU UPRISING

Student and worker protests erupted across the country, in spite of martial law, culminating in over a million people on the streets of Seoul on May 15, 1980, but the student leaders there hoped that the military government would reform itself and actually canceled actions scheduled for May 17 and 18. The student protesters in the city Kwangju were especially spirited and radical, taking the political lead away from their counterparts in Seoul, the capital, to press on into the week. Though most of the country was already under martial law, on May 17, Chun Doo Hwan extended martial law to Cheju Island, a signal that democratic reforms would not be forthcoming.

Instead, a clampdown came: Student leaders were arrested in Seoul and other cities; riot police and paratroopers under the Combined Forces Command (CFC) occupied provincial government office buildings; and the fight was on. In Kwangju, which has a history of rebellion dating back to the 1920s, military action was swift, but not quite swift enough—some student leaders had avoided arrest after being warned by their counterparts in Seoul.

On May 18, the coup government was spoiling for a fight: From the provincial hall in the heart of Kwangju, police and soldiers moved in with truncheons and CS gas and began beating and arresting anyone of college age, dragging some from buses and street-side cafes. When student protesters and some other citizens spontaneously came out to fight back with stones and sticks, the soldiers affixed bayonets to their rifles and began killing.

The revolt both deepened and spread. A dissident media in the form of hastily mimeographed or photocopied leaflets and underground newspapers published by college dissidents emerged by the afternoon of the 18th, offering up encouragement, tactical information, and appeals to support the students. Ordinary people—many of them parents, others workers tired of the massive exploitation that accompanies military dictatorships and client-state status—entered the fray, as well. By the next morning, the protests had become a full-fledged revolt. Here's the scene, from *Kwangju Diary*:

By 10:00 am [on May 19], nearly 4,000 people were crowded around [Kumnam] avenue, and their numbers were still increasing. Most watched silently as the soldiers set up cordons and checkpoints. They were victims of a crackdown they never expected and did not understand, but the crowd began to find a sense of unity. As the number of onlookers grew, their anger and sense of unity did as well. Students were a minority in the crowds; most of the people were street vendors, store clerks and housewives. Police manned their loudspeakers and ordered the people to disperse. Army helicopters flew overhead, making the same announcement. Nobody wanted to obey. People swore and shook their fists at the hovering aircraft.

At 10:40 am, police broke out the tear gas and attacked the crowd. People rushed to the side streets to escape the gas and threw rocks at the police, occasionally making small steps toward occupying Kumnam Avenue. They became increasingly violent. They threw broken flowerpots and bricks and barricaded the street with a guardrail and telephone boxes.

Some students began singing the national anthem, "Justice," and "Our Wish Is National Reunification," hoping to rally the people. Resistance became more militant. A nearby construction site provided steel pipes, small girders and wooden planks to fight the police with. A few people had Molotov cocktails. By that afternoon, protesters had made a huge number of them. Noktu Bookstore became an impromptu firebomb factory, as did some places in the residential areas.[9]

The revolt became generalized, as did the repression. Cabbies and bus drivers attempting to evacuate the wounded were pulled from their vehicles and beaten. The next day, hundreds of taxis and a dozen buses, driven by people sometimes still heavily bandaged, formed high-speed convoys that stormed the military cordons. In their homes, tens of thousands of people turned on their televisions, hoping to see some coverage, some explanation of the events. They were greeted with the usual evening soap operas and responded by attacking local television stations the next day. When the soldiers whipped out M-16s and began firing into the front ranks of the rebels, police stations and factory armories were looted of their guns so that Kwangju could defend itself.[10]

> THE NEXT DAY, HUNDREDS OF TAXIS AND A DOZEN BUSES, DRIVEN BY PEOPLE SOMETIMES STILL HEAVILY BANDAGED, FORMED HIGH-SPEED CONVOYS THAT STORMED THE MILITARY CORDONS.

The eros effect had emerged: "Apparently the long-held tradition, so valued in Korea, of never rising with arms against a Korean government was suddenly transcended by thousands of people."[11] Political identities shifted quickly as well: Tens of thousands of ordinary, apolitical people, unfamiliar with the peculiar etiquette of the riot, folks who hadn't spent their college years with their noses buried in Rosa Luxemburg's *The Mass Strike*, managed to spontaneously figure out what they needed to do, back-ended into solidarity by pure need.

As Katsiaficas explains, "The synchronicity of life in mass mediated societies, the immense influence of mass institutions, and the transformation of secondary groups into mass organizations are preconditions for the emergence of the eros effect..."[12] And indeed, these conditions were all present in Kwangju.

Most of their leaders gone, a second wave of students took up the fight and organizational responsibility.

Workers, stripped of their primary role in the reproduction of capital thanks to the disruptions of the protest, created a new collective identity informed by South Korean militarism, in order to fight the South Korean military.

Street vendors and housewives, normally used to acting either singularly or in competition with one another, were forged into instant

collectives for the production of everything from gas bombs to giant meals in parks to feed protesters.

Citizens who wanted to watch the drama unfold from the safety of their idiot boxes were betrayed by that modern opiate of the people and took to the streets themselves to put an end to the networks that fooled them for so long.

With assistance from coal miners from Hwasun, the Kwangju rebels obtained large quantities of dynamite and detonators. Seven busloads of women textile workers drove to Naju, where they captured hundreds of rifles. Changsong, Yonggwang, and Tamyang Counties also saw arms seizures. Armed demonstrators from Hwasun and Yonggwang Counties trying to reach Kwangju were gunned down by army helicopters. The main highways in and out of Kwangju were sealed tight, thanks to US-trained, US-funded troops under the joint command of the US and the military government. But, oh yes, the US was pressing for democracy.

In the end, it could be argued that the Kwangju Uprising failed not because of the spontaneity of the protests or the lack of long-term "revolutionary leadership"—to use the favorite slogan of those would-be Lenins who can be found on most campuses hawking their favorite "workers' newspapers" (no workers included)—but because the liberal leadership of the Seoul student movement feared spontaneity and reigned it in too well. Kwangju is a second-rank city; if the capital had exploded like this, the recriminations and decades of lies and mystification that surround the uprising would have been rendered moot as the social order would likely have been remade in its entirety.

_THE KWANGJU MASSACRE

But the Kwangju Uprising did not succeed. By May 21, a full-blown militia had emerged—retired military officers quickly gathered up rebels and formed combat cells—and, armed with obsolete reserve-army weaponry and commandeered vehicles, managed to push the national army out past the limits of Kwangju. The retreat was not orderly or simply tactical: "Senior police officials issued one hasty order: 'The situation is urgent. Escape at your discretion!'"[13]

For the next five days, Kwangju was on its own. Though depicted by the Korean government and US State Department as a rioting mob full of Communists, the city was at peace. The dead were counted as best they could be (over 600 were counted at this stage, prior to the final massacre),[14] medical care and collective pantries established, and a citizen's settlement committee was formed. Crime and individual looting (rather than collective confiscation of things like food, gasoline, and medical supplies for the good of the whole city) was unknown.

At the same time, agents provocateur, plains-clothed intelligence agents, and some soldiers began to sneak back into the city to plant rumors and sow chaos—one agent managed to destroy most of the detonators for the dynamite that the rebels had.[15] A split between younger radicals and older activists emerged; the former wished to fight, the latter wanted to surrender their weapons and wait for an apology from the Chun government. Even the more radical wing of the committee made a serious blunder: They believed that the

Carter Administration—given the choice between democratic rebels and the government of Chun, who had already betrayed America's trust by calling troops away from the DMZ during his December 1979 coup—would side with the dissidents, or at least act as a mediator to negotiate a peaceful settlement and gradual reforms.

Instead, on May 23, the US agreed "when asked to chop [i.e, mobilize] CFC forces to Korean command for use in Kwangju."[16] In a cable unearthed in 1996 by investigative reporter Tim Shorrock, US Ambassador William Gleysteen concluded: "If peaceful methods fail" (they were never actually tried), then the "government has 20th Infantry Division, plus airborne and special forces units, on alert in Cholla Namdo"[17] to deal with Kwangju. As far as "peaceful methods" go, Gleysteen wasn't interested in participating in any. Shorrock, who interviewed Gleysteen, explains:

When he received a last-minute request to mediate in Kwangju from a U.S. reporter on the scene in Kwangju, Mr. Gleysteen said the 20th Division was already rolling. In addition, Mr. Gleysteen said he had no idea of the authenticity of the group seeking the mediation and decided not to act. "I grant it was the controversial decision, but it was the correct one," he said. "Do I regret it? I don't think so."[18]

What's to regret after all? Paratroopers swarmed into the city and took it back, inflicting horrific casualties on the outgunned rebels. Truckloads of bodies, some of them rebels who had been shot after surrendering their arms, were carted away, and Chun Doo Hwan's ascendancy was finally complete. Between the first and second battle, most reasonable on-the-scene sources contend that as many as 2,000 civilians were killed. Only the US media and State Department hold to the number presented by the transparently unreasonable source of the Chun government itself, which claimed that only 191 civilians were killed but later agreed to compensate 288 families who lost members to the massacre.

_WHEN IS AN INTERVENTION NOT AN INTERVENTION?

I was first introduced to the Kwangju Uprising in 1995 by my co-translator Kap Su Seol, a Korean dissident and financial writer with whom I attended graduate school. Since then, through the translation and publication of *Kwangju Diary* (at the time of its release, the only book in print on Kwangju—several others have since been released, including apologia by both Gleysteen and fellow Carter Administration power brokers John Wickham and Richard Holbrooke), plus articles on the Disinformation and *Village Voice* Websites, I have attempted to bring both the hope and the horror of Kwangju to light. I have been repeatedly asked a single question:

"So, you wanted the US to intervene?"

This question boggles my mind every time I am asked it. The context is this: I am against US intervention generally. I opposed it during the first Gulf War, in Somalia, Haiti and the Balkans; I opposed the war against Afghanistan, and I oppose the Bush Administration's buildup in Iraq in late 2002 and early 2003. I also oppose the many interven-

tions in Latin America and Africa, the "quiet" ones. I've yet to see, with the possible exception of post-World War II Japan, any nation improved by either US war-making or "regime change." Indeed, repression—including the repression by the Saddam Husseins, the Noriegas, the Duvaliers, and the Chun Doo Hwans—often can be traced back directly to a previous intervention by the US.[19]

The question I'm asked over and over, by liberals, by conservatives, by Koreaphiles, even by self-proclaimed radicals, is absolutely nonsensical. The US did intervene. The US intervened when it threw its support behind Chun Doo Hwan after Park's assassination. The US intervened by saying nothing after this new military leader took troops away from the DMZ the first time. The US intervened when it gave explicit assent to Chun to send troops (again, troops under a *joint* command—the US decided whether they were to be released) who had been trained to infiltrate North Korea itself to put down the Kwangju Uprising.

> BETWEEN THE FIRST AND SECOND BATTLE, MOST REASONABLE ON-THE-SCENE SOURCES CONTEND THAT AS MANY AS 2,000 CIVILIANS WERE KILLED.

Nor were any of the troop movements, movements that had begun before the protests of mid-May, a surprise to the US government. The paper trail discovered by Shorrock is clear: The Carter Administration was closely monitoring the deployment of armed forces against South Korea's civilian population. In a cable from May 9, 1980, Gleysteen explains:

In none of our discussions, will we in any way suggest that the USG opposes ROKG contingency plans to maintain law and order, if absolutely necessary, by reinforcing the police with the army. If I were to suggest any complaint of this score I believe we would lose all our friends within the civilian and military leadership.[20]

Naturally, the State Department felt free to lie to both the US public and to the post-Chun/Roh South Korean government with a 1989 white paper that claimed "the Carter administration was alarmed by Mr. Chun's threats to use the military against the nationwide demonstrations in May 1980 and did not know in advance that Special Forces were being sent to Kwangju."[21] This is clearly false. Not only was the US aware of this, it gave explicit permission for troops under its command to be sent to Kwangju to put down the rebellion.

So, to answer the question simply, No. No, I did not want the US to support Chun Doo Hwan. I did not want the US to allow Special Forces troops to retake Kwangju at the cost of 2,000 lives (or 200, or even 20). I did not want the US to talk out of both sides of its mouth—specious verbiage about "democratic reform" for South Korea on one side, "Go right ahead, Dictator Chun, and use Special Forces troops against civilians," on the other side.

Oh ho, but what about North Korea? The North is the *bete noir* of the peninsula and has been used to justify every repressive statute, every smashed strike, and every violation of human rights on the peninsula, whether carried out by America's "friends" in the South Korean government or by the US itself. Challenging Chalmers

Johnson, who morally equates Kwangju with the actually less violent Tiananmen Square massacre and with Soviet repression in Czechoslovakia and Hungary, Richard Bernstein fumes, "In Korea the alternative to continued backing for General Chun would probably have been a collapse of order in South Korea, which might have induced North Korea to attact [sic]."[22]

Of course, the same could be said for any of the Communist interventions. A collapse of "order" in the Eastern Bloc in the 1950s or 1960s could have lead to massive upheaval; its actual collapse in 1989 sparked the decade-long Balkan Wars, wars in Georgia and Chechnya, and bombed-out economies from Siberia to Bulgaria that actually *increased* privation for many of the victims of Communist command economies. The "free market" was no panacea for these people. In the 1950s and 1960s, when Cold War tensions were much higher, the collapse of the Soviet Bloc could have ended with an ambitious local military leader getting his hands on a free nuke. That is no reason *not* to support democratic rebellions against repressive states.

If the Chinese student movement of 1989 had been generalized and had led to the collapse of Communist rule, perhaps a golden age of Jeffersonian democracy would have emerged; it is just as likely that a Warring States-style circumstance could have emerged as local bureaucrats, some enriched by China's experiments with export capitalism, others impoverished by the same, took individual initiative to set up their own fiefdoms.

We need not play guessing games about contingencies. Chun's use of troops that were stationed in the DMZ to cement his own power demonstrates a cavalier attitude about the possibility of invasion from Pyongyang, even as he claimed that massive repression was crucial to protect the South from…the possibility of massive repression from the North? And the Carter Administration's continued support of Chun months after he showed such disregard for the military integrity of the DMZ puts the lie to the claim that the US could only choose between Chun and the threat of Communist takeover. Chun's actions only increased anti-American sentiment throughout South Korea and increased calls for reunification between North and South.

CHUN'S USE OF TROOPS THAT WERE STATIONED IN THE DMZ TO CEMENT HIS OWN POWER DEMONSTRATES A CAVALIER ATTITUDE ABOUT THE POSSIBILITY OF INVASION FROM PYONGYANG.

What the US chose was order over freedom, the status quo over possibility, its own locus of control over the worry that South Korea would not only free itself from local dictatorship, but from its position as a compliant American client state and cash cow. Confronted with the future of the human condition as manifested in the general strike, in the eros effect itself, the United States—the world's leader in cementing and controlling the social, political, and economic pigeonholes that six billion people live under—decided to drown the potential transformation of human nature in blood.

Endnotes

1. Reuters. "World News Briefs; Korean Ex-President Denies Role in Massacre." *New York Times* (late edition). 7 May 1996: A11. **2.** Associated Press reporter Terry Anderson alone counted over 100 bodies in a single afternoon in Kwangju and recorded many accounts of truckloads of bodies being carted away by soldiers. He also states that "it was clear that more than 300 people (a conservative estimate) had died in that first burst of battle between the townspeople and the soldiers." See his "Remembering Kwangju" <168.131.50.85/kcs/book/reme.htm>. **3.** Katsiaficas, George. "The Eros Effect." Paper prepared for the American Sociological Association National Meetings, 1989: 8. <www.eroseffect.com/articles/eroseffectpaper.PDF> **4.** Bernstein, Richard. "Books of the Times; Another Evil Empire, This One in the Mirror." *New York Times*. 29 March 2000. **5.** WuDunn, Cheryl. "The People of Kwangju Recall 1980 Massacre." *New York Times*, 29 Aug 1996. Incidentally, this article, which is one of the longest the *Times* published about Kwangju since 1980, fails to make any mention of the claims of 2,000 murdered or of even the possibility that the US might have been complicit in the massacre. **6.** Cumings, Bruce. "Introduction." In *Kwangju Diary* by Lee Jai-eu. Los Angeles: UCLA Asian Pacific Monograph Series, 1999: 19. **7.** Was Kim working under orders from the CIA or the US? The KCIA and the CIA certainly have many close ties, but there is no proof of any collusion; Kim's actions remain inexplicable. He died the next day, resisting arrest. **8.** Op cit., Cumings: 19. **9.** Lee Jae-eui. *Kwangju Diary: Beyond Death, Beyond the Darkness of the Age.* Kap Su Seol and Nick Mamatas, trans. Los Angeles: UCLA Asian Pacific Monograph Series, 1999: 53-4. **10.** The heavily militarized economy of South Korea was nearly its undoing; mandatory conscription meant that every adult male had at least some knowledge of weapons and tactics, and the enormous reserve army meant that most large workplaces maintained stores of rifles and other weapons ripe for the taking. **11.** Katsiaficas, George. "Myth and Implications of the Kwangju People's Uprising." *The Defenestrator* (online edition). **12.** Op cit., Katsiaficas, "Eros Effect": 11. **13.** Op cit., Lee: 79. **14.** *Ibid*: 116. **15.** According to Lee, there was enough dynamite in the hands of the rebels to "wipe half of Kwangju off the map" (p 131). The rebels planned to use it as a bargaining chip to force legitimate negotiations and a peaceful settlement. **16.** Shorrock, Tim. "The U.S. Role In South Korea in 1979 and 1980.": Part E. <www.kimsoft.com/korea/kwangju3.htm#cherokee>. **17.** *Ibid*. **18.** *Ibid.* **19.** Long story, short. Read the following: Johnson, Chalmers. *Blowback: The Costs And Consequences of American Empire.* New York: Metropolitan Books/Henry Holt, 2001. **20.** Op cit., Shorrock. **21.** Op cit., Shorrock: Part B. The white paper issued by the Bush Sr. Administration was the official response to a request by the South Korean government for former Carter Administration officials to testify as to their involvement in the Kwangju incidents. **22.** Op cit., Bernstein. At least the online edition of this article contains the typo.

MYSTERY IN MEMPHIS
THE TROUBLING DEATH OF MICROBIOLOGIST DON WILEY

WAYNE MADSEN

Dr. Don C. Wiley was on the fast track to winning a future Nobel Prize for Medicine. In fact, the 57-year-old microbiologist had already been nominated on more than one occasion for the prestigious award. As Harvard University's John L. Loeb Professor of Biochemistry and Biophysics at the Department of Molecular and Cellular Biology and top investigator for the Howard Hughes Medical Institute (HHMI), he was world-renowned for finding new ways to help the human immune system battle such viral scourges as smallpox, influenza, AIDS, Ebola, and herpes simplex. Harvard called Wiley "one of the most influential biologists of his generation."

Wiley's work on the human immune system had already earned him and his Harvard colleague, Dr. Jack Strominger, the Japan Prize for discovering how the immune system protects humans from various infections. Wiley's pioneering work also secured him a seat on the Scientific Advisory Board of St. Jude Children's Hospital in Memphis. Wiley also served on the advisory boards of some leading-edge molecular pharmaceutical companies, including Vertex, Inc. of Cambridge, Massachusetts, and 3-Dimensional, Inc. of Exton, Pennsylvania.

Sometime during the night of November 15, 2001, Wiley disappeared in Memphis, Tennessee. Memphis police set about conducting one of the sloppiest high-profile investigations in that city since the assassination of Dr. Martin Luther King in 1968.

_THE PROFESSOR

Wiley's research lent great promise for the ability of people to fight off dangerous viruses. His research focused mainly on the molecular structure of viruses and proteins in the human immune system. In researching the molecular interplay that enables viruses to infect cells, Wiley sought to discover how antigens and defensive cells could be utilized to combat invading viruses.

Wiley was born October 21, 1944, in Akron, Ohio, and he grew up in Pennsylvania and New Jersey. After attaining a Bachelor of Science degree in Physics from Tufts University in 1966, Wiley received a doctorate in biophysics from Harvard. He became a full professor in Harvard's Department of Biochemistry and Molecular Biology in 1979.

In 1994, Wiley discovered that a protein known as a hemagglutinin permits viruses to enter a cell by fusing together the cell and the invading viral membranes. Wiley felt that if the fusion process could be stopped or reversed, there would be great hope for combating HIV, influenza, and measles. In 1994, Wiley, along with his colleague Dr. Pam Bjorkman of Cal Tech, were awarded Canada's Gairdner Foundation Award for successfully crystallizing cellular immune defensive structures and viral strands through a process known as X-ray crystallography, in order to better understand how cells fight off invading organisms, such as viruses. Earlier, in 1983, Wiley began using the crystallography process to research such virulent strains of influenza as the Hong Kong flu.

In 1997, when President Clinton and Secretary of Health and Human Services Donna Shalala announced new funding for AIDS research, Wiley was awarded a grant, through the Children's Hospital of Boston, for research of AIDS vaccines. Earlier that year, Wiley discovered that the AIDS virus uses a harpoon-like mechanism to penetrate uninfected cells.

Wiley's long-time research at Harvard's Structural Molecular Biology Laboratory actually resulted in the lab becoming known as simply "the Wiley lab." As top microbiologist at Harvard and an investigator for the HHMI, Wiley would have undoubtedly been aware of the groundbreaking results of HHMI's and Harvard's joint anthrax discovery announced on October 1, 2001. A team led by assistant professor William Dietrich isolated a mouse gene that made certain types of the rodent resistant to anthrax. The study's findings, published in the October 2001 issue of Current Biology, stated, "Since this biology is conserved across species, we believe that studying this mechanism in mice will tell us a lot about the infection process in other species, including humans." While his colleagues later said that Wiley's research did not involve anthrax bacteria defenses, the Harvard-HHMI results were quite similar to Wiley's own research into molecular and genetic structures to combat the smallpox and Ebola viruses. It is hard to believe that with Wiley's expertise, the anthrax research team would not have consulted him at some point during their research. In fact, the New York Times reported on August 11, 2002, that Wiley had been involved "in some work with anthrax."

Considering that the Harvard-HHMI joint research

HE WAS WORLD-RENOWNED FOR FINDING NEW WAYS TO HELP THE HUMAN IMMUNE SYSTEM BATTLE SUCH VIRAL SCOURGES AS SMALLPOX, INFLUENZA, AIDS, EBOLA, AND HERPES SIMPLEX.

team announced their research findings on October 1, Wiley must have been alarmed about the anthrax death of *The Sun* tabloid photojournalist Bob Stevens in Boca Raton, Florida, on October 5, 2001. According to a colleague of his, with the threat of bioterrorism suddenly looming, Wiley began examining ways to develop a safer smallpox vaccine (for people, like AIDS patients, with weak immune systems) by using the cross-immunity traits common in both the smallpox and cowpox viruses.

Wiley's work earned him a spot on the A-list for a number of prestigious international medical conferences and meetings. However, one meeting in Memphis in 2001 would prove to be the most fateful the professor had ever attended.

_THE LOBBY

On November 14, 2001, Wiley traveled to Memphis from Washington, DC, to attend a meeting of the St. Jude advisory board. The following evening, sometime after 7:00, Wiley arrived at the luxurious but slightly gaudy Peabody Hotel for St. Jude's perfunctory year-end annual banquet. He drank two glasses of wine with dinner. Between 9:30 and 10:00, the banquet concluded, and Wiley and a few of his colleagues strolled to the bar in the hotel's Italian Renaissance-style lobby. Built in 1869, the Peabody is well known for its rolling out the red carpet for a group of rooftop ducks that twice daily perform a "stupid pet trick" in which they are herded onto an elevator for a ride down to the lobby and a bath in the marble fountain.

Wiley ordered a glass of the "best port available" from the bartender. Receiving a glass of Sandeman, Wiley soon struck up conversations with two regular bar patrons. Wiley was curious about a flag pendant made from safety pins that the bartender was wearing. The bartender gave Wiley the pin and he pinned it on to the left side of his black suit jacket.

SOMETIME BETWEEN 11:45 AND MIDNIGHT, WILEY TOLD THE BARTENDER AND THE TWO PATRONS THAT HE HAD TO GET UP EARLY FRIDAY MORNING.

After his colleagues departed, Wiley ordered another Sandeman followed by three glasses of Perrier. Wiley then paid his $50.25 bill with his credit card and asked the bartender if the $20 tip was enough. That amused one of the regulars: "For a Nobel Peace Winner, you're not very smart when it comes to finances," he told the 6-foot-3-inch Harvard professor. Wiley responded by saying that he was in town for the St. Jude meeting and he was staying with family in Memphis. During the meetings at St. Jude, Wiley was staying with his father at his home in Bartlett, just northeast of Memphis. This was understandable since Wiley's mother had passed away the previous July. Sometime between 11:45 and midnight, Wiley told the bartender and the two patrons that he had to get up early Friday morning.

In fact, Wiley was expecting Katrin, his wife of 20 years, and their two children to arrive Friday in Memphis from Boston. From Memphis, the whole family planned to travel to Katrin's native

Iceland for a vacation.

The bartender and other banquet attendees did not think Wiley was intoxicated or otherwise impaired before he left the hotel. He was last seen heading past the check-in desk toward valet parking just outside the south lobby exit. Wiley would not be seen alive again.

_THE BRIDGE

Around 4:00 the next morning, a Memphis police officer responded to a trucker's report about an abandoned vehicle on the Interstate-40 Hernando DeSoto Bridge, which spans the Mississippi River between Tennessee and Arkansas. The officer discovered a white, four-door 2001 Mitsubishi Galant in the right-hand lane just before the "Welcome to Arkansas" sign on the westbound side of the bridge. No emergency lights were blinking, the doors were unlocked, and the key was still in the ignition. There was pale yellow paint scraped on the top and side of the left side of the front bumper. The hubcap on the front right wheel was missing, and the paint along the undercarriage of the passenger side was scraped, indicating that at some point the vehicle hit a curb or some other obstruction on the right side. A long-haul truck-driver who first reported the abandoned car to a 911 operator said the car was "in a position that [it] could have been struck by another vehicle."

The policeman discovered Avis rental car paperwork in the glove compartment, but strangely, no rental information, such as the driver's name and license number, was filled out. He then ran the car's vehicle identification number but received a negative response. After checking with Avis, the officer was informed the vehicle had been rented to a Dr. Wiley of Cambridge, Massachusetts.

Without taking any photos of the car on the bridge, police ordered it towed to an impound garage known as the "Crime Scene Tunnel." Only after being towed to the tunnel were photos taken of the vehicle. Police then noticed white residue on the right front tire and blackish scuff marks on the rear of the car. Police retrieved two partial fingerprints from the interior of the vehicle. Except for a map of the St. Jude medical complex, no personal items were found in the vehicle.

Between 11:45 PM on November 15 and 4:00 AM on the November 16, neither the Tennessee State Police, the Arkansas State Police, the Crittenden County, Arkansas Police, nor the West Memphis, Arkansas Police reported any calls to respond to any unusual incident on the DeSoto Bridge or the surrounding areas. Memphis police reported that when they checked the bridge at 3:00 AM, Wiley's rental car had not been there.

Sometime between 3:00 and 4:00, Wiley's car wound up on the bridge heading into Arkansas, the opposite direction from his father's house in Bartlett. The car could not have been stopped on the bridge very long. Since it was a traffic hazard, passing truckers would have been quick to alert police to the car's presence on the bridge long before 4:00. In addition, Wiley left the Peabody around midnight, and the bridge is mere minutes away from the hotel—not four entire hours. Moreover, the car's gas tank was full. Upon arriving at the scene of the abandoned rental car, police found no traces of Wiley either around the immediate vicinity or further along the bridge on the Arkansas side.

_THE FALL

From the outset, police believed Wiley had committed suicide. Memphis detective E.G. Wainscott notified the Coast Guard at 9:50 AM on Friday, November 16 that a "jumper" may have leapt from the bridge and that they should be on the lookout for a body. By midday Friday, Wiley's wife, father, brother, sister-in-law, and St. Jude's staff were all notified that Wiley's car was found on the bridge and that he was missing. Despite the Wiley family's insistence that Don, a tenured Harvard professor, did not have any mental or financial problems, police continued to treat his disappearance as a suicide. St. Jude security staff then made arrangements to pick up Wiley's wife at Memphis' airport.

The Memphis police reaction to Wiley's disappearance can only be described as lackadaisical. It was not until Saturday that Wiley's name was entered into the National Crime Information Center (NCIC) computer database as a missing person. Moreover, on Sunday, November 18, the Memphis police finally got around to "asking," not ordering, its aviation unit helicopter to begin searching for a body south of the bridge "when possible." On November 20, five days after Wiley's disappearance, the Memphis Harbor Patrol began searching the Mississippi south of the bridge

On Saturday, when police first began hearing reports that Wiley suffered from occasional seizures, their focus shifted from Wiley's mental state to his physical condition. In fact, the seizures Wiley suffered from are known as "night tremors," a mild sleep disorder that a number of people experience without the need for medication or other treatment. Wiley experienced no disorientation after such episodes. However, the police began wrongly referring to the seizures as an epileptic condition.

Even though the Peabody Hotel was notified Friday, November 16 about Wiley's disappearance, no effort was made by hotel security to secure the surveillance videotapes. On Tuesday, November 20, when police asked hotel security for copies of the surveillance tapes, the hotel staff informed them that because the taping equipment rewinds after 24 hours of recording, the tapes for the previous Thursday and Friday had already been taped over.

In addition, although Wiley was seen heading toward the Peabody's valet parking area, there is no record of his car ever being parked there. Peabody staff revealed that it is hotel policy not to give the keys to drivers who appear intoxicated. On the other hand, if someone else had obtained Wiley's valet parking stub, parking attendants do not require positive identification. Anyone with Wiley's stub would have been given the car. In addition, the turnover of the attendants, mostly high-school students trying to make some extra money, is very high.

When police later interviewed one of the valet attendants who worked the night of November 15, he said the photo of Wiley looked like a lot of people whose cars he had parked and that the Mitsubishi Galant looked like a lot of cars he parked and that he might have parked that one but could not be certain. Although parking valet stubs are retained by the Peabody for a substantial period of time, police were never able to locate a stub for Wiley's car.

_THE SEARCH

The position of the FBI in the search for Wiley is as baffling as its disregard for important evidence regarding the flight training by young Arab males prior to September 11, 2001. Although both St. Jude and the Howard Hughes Medical Institute in Chevy Chase, Maryland, posted a $26,000 reward for information leading to the "arrest and charge" of any individual responsible for Wiley's disappearance, the FBI said it would not get involved in the case, since there was no evidence linking Wiley's disappearance to terrorism. After Wiley was reported missing, Memphis FBI spokesman George Bolds told the media that the FBI had not opened a file on Wiley's case and was treating the entire matter as a missing persons case, deferring to the Memphis Police Department. He also implied that Wiley's profession as a microbiologist was only tantalizing to the media, not to the FBI.

> ON NOVEMBER 20, FIVE DAYS AFTER WILEY'S DISAPPEARANCE, THE MEMPHIS HARBOR PATROL BEGAN SEARCHING THE MISSISSIPPI SOUTH OF THE BRIDGE.

But the FBI was already aware that the two Memphis bridges spanning the Mississippi, the DeSoto Bridge and the I-55 Bridge (known as the "Old Bridge" by the locals) to the south, had recently been the subject of video surveillance by men of "Middle East appearance." According to the Arkansas State Police Department, which has been much more helpful in providing information than their Memphis counterparts, a few days after the September 11 attacks, it, the Memphis police and the FBI were alerted to two men of Middle Eastern appearance taking photographs of the bridges, including their undersides. They had seven cameras of different sizes and makes with them. Upon being detained by the FBI, the men claimed to have diplomatic immunity, and according to knowledgeable law enforcement officials, one man displayed a diplomatic passport. After the men were turned over to the Immigration and Naturalization Service (INS), the FBI dropped any further investigation.

The official record also shows that FBI Special Agent Bolds was not completely on the level about the Bureau's interest in the Wiley case. On November 20, an FBI Special Agent named Sturgis contacted Memphis police detective Robert "Bubba" Shemwell, who had taken over as chief investigator. Sturgis, who was assigned to the Safe Street Task Force, informed Shemwell that he had been contacted by his supervisor and was asked to offer the FBI's assistance if needed "due to the status of Dr. Wiley and his work with infectious diseases." It was Shemwell who advised Sturgis that foul play was not suspected. Nevertheless, Sturgis said he would check with Shemwell later for updates on the Wiley case.

A staff member of the Peabody Hotel also revealed that shortly after Wiley's disappearance, FBI agents in unmarked government cars descended on the hotel to talk to Peabody security personnel. In the meantime, the FBI was backing the Memphis police probe, which was putting suicide ahead of all other scenarios.

Adding to the confusion was the stance of the news media in covering Wiley's disappearance. Instead of launching any independent investigation, the news networks, which were still caught up in the post-9/11 terrorism hysteria, merely stated what Memphis and FBI officials were also stating: There was no evidence of foul play in Wiley's disappearance and it was a mere missing person incident.

According to a November 20 memo from the Memphis Police Special Investigation Division's Homicide Bureau, the only paper that seemed to be interested in going beyond the official press releases was the *Boston Globe*. Reporter Doug Bilkie called Memphis police lieutenant Joe Scott and asked if the department were handling the Wiley case differently in light of the events of September 11. According to the memo, Bilkie was particularly focused on Wiley's work on Ebola and "other biological factors."

In early December, in what can only be described as an astounding decision considering the fact that there were absolutely no clues as to Wiley's whereabouts, Memphis police director Walter Crews and deputy police chief Bob Wright chose to tell a crew from NBC's *Dateline* "as little information as possible" about the Wiley investigation. The two police officials merely told *Dateline* that the incident was being handled as a missing person case, disregarding the potential for television viewers who may have provided additional information if they had been given some more basic facts about the case.

But the lack of information about Wiley fueled all sorts of bizarre theories. People came forward to claim everything from Wiley's kidnapping by terrorists to his abduction by extraterrestrials. Meanwhile, the Memphis police came no closer to solving Wiley's disappearance.

The depth of the police investigation into Wiley's disappearance is also clouded by another important fact: Several witnesses, including Peabody Hotel employees later interviewed by the police, St. Jude's officials, and Arkansas police were under the impression that Wiley's car was originally discovered by police *not* on the DeSoto Bridge but on the I-55 Old Bridge. As one Peabody witness adamantly explained, "I was first told that his [Wiley's] car was found on the Old Bridge." If this were an honest misunderstanding by one or two persons not connected to the investigation, it could be easily explained as a mistake. But with a number of individuals, including police officers from the Arkansas side who had first-hand knowledge of the Wiley disappearance, believing his car was first found on the Old Bridge, and given the four hours that Wiley and his car were unaccounted for, the possibility that the car had been moved from the Old Bridge should have been investigated further.

By Wednesday, November 21, Sergeant Shemwell (who has since been promoted to lieutenant) went to inspect the rental car. He found a pink parking pass from St. Jude Hospital dated November 15. Oddly, there was some scribbling on the pass that looked like someone was attempting to get a pen to write. On the other side, written in a hurry, were letters that looked like "BYOB." Yet, when Wiley's car was first inspected, the only item found was a map of the St. Jude

complex. It is also odd that while the parking pass from St. Jude was found in the vehicle, no ticket from the Peabody's valet parking was discovered.

Shemwell also found in the glove compartment an Avis rental record showing Wiley's American Express card imprint. Yet, when the first police officer on the scene found the rental paper, the form was blank. Had it been filled out at that time, there would have been no need to contact Avis to determine who rented the vehicle found on the bridge. These were not the only discrepancies concerning the rental car, an important item of evidence that may have been tampered with after being towed from the bridge. And it was not until November 21, six days after the vehicle was first inspected, that Shemwell took photos of the car.

Shemwell also drove out to the bridge and noted that a concrete Jersey barrier separated the right westbound lane from the middle one. Nothing in the area was painted with the same type of yellow paint that was found scraped on Wiley's car.

Thursday, November 22 was Thanksgiving Day, and the entire police investigation into Wiley's disappearance ceased while investigators enjoyed turkey dinners and football games at home.

On November 23, Shemwell spoke to Memphis police officer S. Keane, the first policeman who inspected the abandoned vehicle a week before. He told Shemwell that he was the only bridge officer on duty that night and was to check the bridge every 30 minutes. The Memphis police had ordered the stepped-up surveillance of the bridge since the events of September 11. However, Keane only responded to the truck driver's alert about the abandoned vehicle at 4:00. If his schedule was to check the bridge every half hour and he failed to make the 3:30 check, thirty critical minutes elapsed between the required bridge check and the time Wiley's vehicle stopped on the bridge. More important, Keane told Shemwell that he did not find anything in the vehicle that indicated who the vehicle was driven by and that he did not recall seeing the right front hubcap missing or the scraping on the right side of the vehicle. The officer did call for a wrecker to tow the vehicle in order to avoid an accident.

The fact that the first officer on the scene did not notice two important clues, the missing hubcap and the right side paint scrapes, throws into question the entire conclusion on which the Shelby County Medical Examiner would later base his final determination of the cause of Wiley's death. Although yellow barriers close off traffic to touristy Beale Street and some of the on-ramps to the DeSoto Bridge, no test was made to determine if the yellow paint on the car was the same found on the barriers.

A STAFF MEMBER OF THE PEABODY HOTEL ALSO REVEALED THAT SHORTLY AFTER WILEY'S DISAPPEARANCE, FBI AGENTS IN UNMARKED GOVERNMENT CARS DESCENDED ON THE HOTEL TO TALK TO PEABODY SECURITY PERSONNEL.

In addition, Shemwell did not actually visit the bridge until November 21, six day after Wiley's car was found. It is clear from the police report that some of the construction barricades had already been moved from what may have been a crime scene. Shemwell states in the report, "At this time, without knowing the exact location of where the vehicle was towed from, [Shemwell] could not search for further evidence."

Meanwhile, some of Wiley's family members were getting upset about how the Memphis Police Department was handling the case. They were being told that Wiley was a typical "jumper" and that they would be notified when his body was fished from the river. Some of the family responded by stating that they were disappointed that the Memphis police were not being more aggressive, considering Wiley's international standing in the medical field.

The Memphis police wasted valuable time in bothering to follow up a number of ridiculous leads. On November 24, the manager of a Piggly Wiggly supermarket called police, saying he recognized Wiley in his store on the morning of November 15. He said the man in his store wanted to buy some butterbeans for his mother. The flannel-shirted man also told the manager that he was in town for a conference and that it was the first time he had been in Memphis. Before he left, the man asked the manager if there were a Mormon or Seventh Day Adventist Church in Memphis. Despite the facts that Wiley's mother had passed away in July, that Wiley was a Presbyterian, and that he would, under no circumstance, own or wear a plaid flannel shirt, the police decided to review a copy of the store's videotape anyway.

On Tuesday, November 27, Shemwell contacted the Coast Guard and asked them if they had recently located a "floater" in the Mississippi. The Memphis police were contacted by an East Precinct Neighborhood Watch Coordinator to report that a local busybody reported spotting Dr. Wiley at a yard sale asking to buy cat litter and chemicals. She became suspicious and obtained the tag number of the vehicle. Although the tip was obviously absurd, Shemwell made a couple of attempts to contact the woman, to no avail.

Shemwell was also notified that Peabody Hotel security had two surveillance tapes from November 15 and 16. The hotel had previously told police their recording system had recorded over the tapes from those two days. Hotel security informed Shemwell that when the tapes purported to be from November 15 and 16 were viewed, the date on which the monitors had been installed would be shown on the monitor. However, for some reason, the monitor was showing a default date of November 16, 2001. Police later viewed the tapes with particular focus on the time period between 11:00 PM on November 15 and 1:00 AM November 16. The tapes provided to the police did not show a white Mitsubishi.

ON NOVEMBER 28, A POLICE INFORMANT CALLED "SEVEN" WHO FREQUENTED THE STREETS AND BARS OF DOWNTOWN MEMPHIS TOLD POLICE THAT HE OVERHEARD A "PROSTITUTE" NAMED KATHY SMITH TALKING ABOUT "THE MISSING DOCTOR."

On November 30, police visited the Memphis Police Information System to obtain the video surveillance tapes from the downtown area on November 15 and 16, but the tapes were overwritten. The entire surveillance system rewrote itself after five days. Similarly, the police checked the tapes maintained by CDA, a security and surveillance company with offices on Beale Street. They were told that during the night of November 15, the system was programmed in a 24-hour mode and, thus, could not provide coverage of the early morning of November 16.

Not until the afternoon of November 27 did the Memphis police finally fill out the Violent Criminal Apprehension Program (VICAP) form to be entered into the FBI's NCIC system. According to the FBI, the VICAP database "contains reports submitted by participating law enforcement agencies concerning certain violent crimes, which can be used to analyze and link multiple cases." Yet, oddly, Memphis police were still looking at the Wiley case as a suicide, not a violent crime.

It is clear that by November 27, the FBI was monitoring the Wiley case more closely. FBI headquarters requested the Memphis police send the entire Wiley report. The day before, FBI Special Agent Sturgis called Shemwell and stated that he was instructed to closely monitor the Wiley case. Later, Sturgis assigned Sergeant Ryall from the Safe Streets Task Force as the FBI's official Memphis liaison officer on the case. In addition, the Boston FBI office assigned Special Agent Russell "Rusty" Chisholm as its own case officer for the Wiley matter. Boston FBI Special Agent William Woerner said the FBI was taking a special interest in the case, considering the post-911 events.

Chisholm and Harvard Police Department detective Robert Sweetland began examining Wiley's computer files and lab notebooks at his office at Harvard's Sherman Fairchild Biochemistry Building and his HHMI-funded laboratory at Children's Hospital. The theory that Wiley might have been kidnapped by bioterrorists in order to obtain viruses was dismissed when the FBI discovered that Wiley's lab was a Level 2 facility; no intact viruses were maintained in the lab.

On November 28, a police informant called "Seven" who frequented the streets and bars of downtown Memphis told police that he overheard a "prostitute" named Kathy Smith talking about "the missing doctor." Shemwell later concluded the prostitute in question was someone with whom the police were quite familiar. That Kathy Smith was a black female who had been arrested a number of times for prostitution and robbery. However, Seven was never sure who the Kathy Smith he had encountered was or in what area of downtown she worked. On December 5, Ryall told Shemwell he was trying to locate Seven to nail down Kathy Smith's identity. But Ryall had previously told Shemwell he was convinced that Kathy Smith was a local downtown prostitute. On December 6, Seven surfaced to tell Ryall that he overheard Kathy Smith talking about how "'they' took the doctor's car and put it on the bridge to make it look like a suicide."

Seven told Ryall that he knew of several locations where Kathy Smith might be found. On December 10, Ryall located a Kathy Smith at a house in Memphis where a number of prostitutes lived. The Kathy Smith that Ryall and another detective interviewed insisted that she had no first-hand knowledge about Wiley's disappearance and only knew about the case from the news reports. Ryall concluded that because the Kathy Smith he spoke to was a crack addict, he doubted she would be allowed to ply her trade in the downtown area. However, the name

"Kathy Smith" would soon resurface in another high-profile Memphis police investigation.

_THE "TRASHING"

On November 26, the Memphis police received a call from a Bill Willard who claimed he was a colleague of Dr. Wiley at Harvard. Almost a week before, St. Jude's Department of Pharmaceutical Sciences faxed the Memphis police a list of Wiley's close professional colleagues. Indeed, the list is a virtual "Who's Who" of top microbiologists from Harvard, Stanford, Princeton, Cal Tech, Northwestern, and Scripps. However, the name Bill Willard does not appear anywhere on the list. Nevertheless, Willard had quite a tale to tell police about his "friend" Dr. Wiley. He emphasized that he was probably the "closest" friend Wiley ever had at Harvard, a friendship he described as lasting some 20 years.

Although Willard told Shemwell that he didn't think Wiley would commit suicide, he said he "could see" Wiley getting drunk, stopping on the bridge, "playing around," and then falling over the side. When Shemwell asked Willard what he meant by Wiley getting drunk, he replied that Wiley used to drink quite a bit, even while working at his laboratory. Willard also said it was a "known fact" that Wiley, when out of town at conferences, would get drunk and become "loud." He also told Shemwell that Wiley would try to pick up women who were with other men.

Willard continued his eulogy of his "friend" by telling Shemwell that Wiley had been arrested for driving under the influence (DUI) before he began working with him. He said Wiley's driver's license had been suspended after the arrest, but he was not sure where the arrest took place. On the subject of Wiley's night tremors, Willard said he knew about two "blackouts" suffered by Wiley in the past 20 years, one at a conference in Atlanta.

Shemwell wisely decided to run an FBI Triple-I (Interstate Identification Index) check on Wiley to see if Wiley's fingerprints appeared in any arrest file. The Triple-I would contain fingerprints from arrests prior 1983. The check on Wiley came back negative. Shemwell was also informed that no arrest records were held on Wiley by either the Cambridge, Massachusetts police, the Massachusetts State Police, or any of the numerous smaller towns in the suburban Boston area.

Based on Willard's rather detailed dossier of his "friend's" life, Shemwell began focusing on the DUI arrest. The new "angle" on Wiley's "lifestyle" was adding credence to the suicide theory. Police director Crews reiterated in a national press release that Wiley's case was being handled as a suicide. After protests were made by members of the Wiley family, Crews and deputy police chief Wright were forced, in press conferences and statements, to backtrack on their "suicide" determination. Nevertheless, other senior Memphis police officers continued to tell the local press that Wiley was being handled as a suicide.

On November 29, Wiley's wife informed Shemwell that her husband had been involved in an auto accident in Concord, Massachusetts, in either 1971 or 1972. But still no proof emerged of a DUI, as alleged by Willard. On December 13, the Massachusetts State Police informed Shemwell that their files contained no fingerprints indicating any previous arrest of Wiley for DUI in Massachusetts.

> **WILLARD'S EFFECTIVE TRASHING OF WILEY'S REPUTATION IS EVEN MORE BIZARRE WHEN ONE READS THE ACCOLADES LATER BESTOWED UPON THE HARVARD PROFESSOR BY HIS ACTUAL FRIENDS AND COLLEAGUES.**

The effect of the "help" offered by Willard diverted Memphis police resources from the river to Beale Street, the famous "Home of the Blues," located just two blocks from the Peabody. Their reasoning was that if Wiley was a heavy drinker and womanizer, as suggested by Willard, he may have decided to party until the wee hours of the morning at such Beale Street watering holes as B.B. King's, W.C. Handy's, and King of the Blues. Police reasoned that if Wiley stayed on Beale Street until closing time, around 3:00 AM, he could have been heavily intoxicated when he began driving back to his father's house. Missing the correct turnoff on the interstate, he conceivably could have wound up on the westbound construction lane of the DeSoto Bridge. Striking a road obstruction or barricade with his car, Wiley might have stopped the vehicle in the middle of a traffic lane, got out to check out the damage, and either a gust of wind or a passing truck causing "road bounce" hurled Wiley over the side of the bridge. If Wiley were just another 50-something conventioneer in Memphis, the police theory might be plausible. But for a noted microbiologist and Nobel Prize nominee who was picking up his family the next day at the airport, the theory just did not fit the person.

Willard's biographical sketch of Wiley also prompted Shemwell to pursue another inconsequential angle. He asked the bartender at the Peabody if any females approached Wiley when he was at the bar. Indeed, the Peabody does attract its fair share of prostitutes that cater to the hotel's more moneyed clientele. They figure that if someone can afford a room at $250-$350 per night, there is a good possibility of making some handsome bucks from trolling the lobby bar. The bartender told Shemwell that a light-skinned African American woman named "Kimmie" had been in the bar on the evening of November 15. However, she decided to pursue one of the regular bar patrons, not Wiley or his colleagues. The bartender said Kimmie actually preferred to hang around the bar when basketball players such as Portland Trailblazer's star Scottie Pippin stayed at the hotel. Undeterred, Shemwell continued to pursue the prostitute theory. On December 3, he instructed his investigators to identify any prostitutes working at the Peabody the night of December 15 and to find out if there had been any vacancies at the hotel, just in case Wiley decided to check into a room that night.

Willard's effective trashing of Wiley's reputation is even more bizarre when one reads the accolades later bestowed upon the Harvard professor by his actual friends and colleagues. These appear on a Harvard online guest book later set up by Harvard's Molecular and Cellular Biology Department. A few samples follow:

"Don was a special scientist and a wonderful man. He radiated integrity and inspired all sorts of people. He

More praise for Wiley's work came in 1999 from the famed AIDS researcher and director of the National Institute of Allergy and Infectious Diseases, Dr. Anthony Fauci, upon the awarding of the Japan Prize to Wiley and Strominger for their work in isolating and characterizing the three-dimensional structures of certain key molecules, proteins, complexes, and interactions involving human immune response:

In their remarkable research careers, these outstanding scientists have greatly advanced our understanding of the induction and regulation of immune responses.... [B]y elucidating the structures and processes involved in antigen presentation, they have helped open the door to promising new therapeutic approaches to treating infectious diseases, immunologic conditions, and cancers.

_THE CONNECTION

While the Memphis Police and the FBI continued to handle the Wiley case as just another distraught "jumper" hurling himself 135 feet into the Mississippi River, other law enforcement agencies were not as sanguine. On November 30, Shemwell received a call from Detective Paul McKemmie of the National Security Investigation Unit of the Royal Canadian Mounted Police (RCMP) in Ottawa. McKemmie advised Shemwell that his unit was responsible for protecting scientists with Level-3 and Level-4 clearance at the Canadian Science Center for Human and Animal Health in Winnipeg, Manitoba.

The Canadian center houses the National Microbiology Laboratory, where scientists deal with the most dangerous and contagious animal pathogens and diseases, which are categorized as Level 4.

These include hantavirus, hepatitis, influenza, and haemorrhagic fevers such as the Ebola virus, Marburg virus, and Lassa Fever. In another highly protected laboratory, scientists work with Level-3 agents, which include bacteria such as anthrax that, although not contagious, can be transmitted through the air and can cause death or serious illness. The center's tight security is overseen by the RCMP and Canadian Security and Intelligence Service.

McKemmie told Shemwell that someone had posted an email suggesting that Dr. Wiley was not the target for a kidnapping to obtain anthrax but that a scientist working at the Winnipeg laboratory was a more likely target for a kidnapping by bioterrorists.

Nevertheless, the RCMP wanted to know if Memphis had any information that would indicate Wiley was the target of an abduction by terrorists. Shockingly, Shemwell fed the RCMP the same line he was feeding the Wiley family and the media: There was no evidence to support the theory that Wiley's disappearance was the result of foul play and that suggestions to the contrary were being mentioned only in the media.

Obviously not buying Shemwell's line, the Mountie indicated that the RCMP, like the FBI, also would continue to monitor Wiley's disappearance and check out any leads from Canada.

NEVERTHELESS, THE RCMP WANTED TO KNOW IF MEMPHIS HAD ANY INFORMATION THAT WOULD INDICATE WILEY WAS THE TARGET OF AN ABDUCTION BY TERRORISTS.

On December 10, John Kelly of a New Jersey-based criminal profiling organization known as S.T.A.L.K., Inc. (System to Apprehend Lethal Killers), a group that assists police in tracking down serial killers, contacted Memphis police and offered several theories on Wiley's disappearance. Kelly's main concern was the ongoing anthrax threat. Kelly later recalled Shemwell telling him that the FBI "wasn't interested" in the Wiley case and that the Memphis police immediately discounted terrorism as being behind the scientist's disappearance. But Shemwell, in departing from the suicide angle, admitted to Kelly that Memphis is, after all, "the murder capital of the world."

The RCMP, FBI, and S.T.A.L.K. had good reason to be suspicious. Although underplayed by the major media, the public was already coming to understand that Wiley's disappearance was not the only possible violence being visited upon microbiologists. On November 12, a week before Wiley disappeared, Dr. Benito Que, a microbiologist who, like Wiley, had worked on defenses against viruses like HIV, was found beaten to death with a baseball bat at his parked car outside the University of Miami's School of Medicine. Four men were said to have attacked Que as he approached his vehicle.

On November 23, Dr. Vladimir Pasechnik, who once worked for Biopreparat, the Soviet Union's biowarfare agency, and who defected to the West in 1989, was found dead from an apparent stroke in Wiltshire, not far from Britain's Center for Chemical and Biological Warfare Research at Porton Down, where Pasechnik was a consultant. His specialties included smallpox, tularemia, plague, and anthrax.

On December 10, Dr. Robert M. Schwartz, a well-known DNA researcher who received funding from HHMI, was found stabbed to death in his farmhouse outside of Leesburg in northern Virginia. Schwartz's daughter and three of her friends were later charged with murdering Schwartz using a sword in a bizarre, ritualistic occult sacrifice.

On December 14, Nguyen Van Set died at the Commonwealth Scientific and Industrial Research Organization in Geelong, Australia. He had gotten trapped in a storage room at his lab and died from being exposed to nitrogen. The scientific research agency studies animal diseases, including mousepox.

(In February 2002, three microbiologists would be violently murdered. The next month, two more prominent microbiologists would meet violent ends on consecutive days—David Wynn-Williams was run over by a car while jogging, and Steven Mostow was piloting a small plane that crashed.)

While the Memphis police were going down dead ends looking for prostitutes and Beale Street bartenders who might have seen Wiley during the night of November 12, the FBI, RCMP, and other law enforcement agencies suspected something much bigger.

The FBI in Boston had the wherewithal to check Wiley's HHMI laboratory appointment books, personal computer, and lab notes. His travels during 2001 took him to Iceland; Exton, Pennsylvania (the headquarters of 3-D Pharmaceuticals); Tel Aviv; New York City; Philadelphia; San Francisco; Seattle; Rome; Stockholm; Waterville Valley, New Hampshire; Memphis (in October, as well as November); Leuven, Belgium; Cranbury, New Jersey; and an HHMI conference in Chevy Chase, Maryland, just a week prior to his November meeting at St. Jude.

The subjects discussed at the seminars Wiley attended during 2001 are a clear indication of the cutting-edge research with which he was involved. In April 2001, Wiley participated in the New York symposium of the Aaron Diamond AIDS Research Center, part of Rockefeller University. Items discussed included "Diversity of HIV/SIV and Origin of the Epidemic," presented by Better Korber from Los Alamos National Laboratories, and "Fighting HIV/AIDS in Developing Countries," presented by Jeffrey Sachs, the noted Director of the Center for International Development at Harvard University. In May 2001, Wiley traveled to San Francisco to attend a Scientific Resource Board meeting at Genentech, a leading edge biopharmaceutical company.

But it was Wiley's attendance at the HHMI meeting in Chevy Chase near the National Institutes of Health (NIH) campus in Bethesda that is of particular interest. Discussion items on that meeting's agenda included "Bioethics and Research," certainly a hot topic considering the fact that anthrax-laden letters sent through the mail had already killed four people and infected thirteen others since the beginning of October.

Later, it was discovered that the finely-milled military-grade anthrax was the Ames Strain of the bacteria that was developed by the US Army's biological warfare program at Fort Detrick, Maryland. The Fort Detrick facility is officially known as the

United States Army Medical Research Institute for Infectious Diseases (USAMRIID), and it was known to be involved in secretive research activities at both HHMI and NIH. Considering HHMI's sponsorship of the conference, Wiley must have heard some interesting exchanges at the seminar on bioethics and research.

_THE BODY

On the morning of December 20 at around 9:41 AM, Lionel Whitmore—a supervisor for the Louisiana Hydroelectric Company in Vidalia, Louisiana, 320 miles to the south of Memphis—was informed by one of his crane operators that while removing trees and debris from the plant's in-flow channel leading from the Mississippi, he had spotted what looked like a body in the water. Whitmore called the Concordia Parish Sheriff's Office, which dispatched a unit to the scene. By the time the sheriff's department arrived, at about 10:48 AM, the body had floated back under the driftwood and was no longer visible. The crane operator began removing trees and debris in order to get the body to resurface. Thirty minutes later, the body reappeared amidst the debris.

A Louisiana Wildlife and Fisheries boat was sent to retrieve the body. A Wildlife and Fisheries agent found a wallet in the victim's trousers. The victim was then placed in a body bag before being put into a hearse and driven to the cold room of Young's, a funeral home in nearby Ferriday, Louisiana. Concordia Parish coroner Dr. Sarah Lee viewed the body as one of the sheriffs checked the contents of the wallet. The driver's license bore the name of Don Craig Wiley of Cambridge, Massachusetts. The wallet and its contents were then placed in an evidence bag and shipped along with the body.

The Concordia Sheriff immediately contacted the Cambridge Police Department, which, in turn, referred them to the Harvard police. Harvard then referred Concordia to the Memphis police. A number of questions can be raised about how effective the Memphis missing person alert was when the police down river in Louisiana were unaware of whom to contact if Wiley or his body were discovered.

When Dr. Lee and Concordia Parish Sheriff Randy Maxwell realized the body that had been fished out of the river was that of Wiley, they decided it would be best to get it to a qualified coroner's facility as soon as possible. As Dr. Lee later stated, "We're just a little podunk town down here in Louisiana. I'm a family practitioner, and I don't do autopsies." She said she conferred with Concordia Sheriff Randy Maxwell and quickly concluded that the discovery of Wiley's body was important because it might be "part of the missing scientists plot." Lee contacted Mississippi Mortuary Services of Jackson, Mississippi, and ordered the body to be sent there from Young's Funeral home. Young's confirmed that it is standard practice for bodies received from the Concordia coroner to be transported to Jackson. Yet, in sending the body to Mississippi, yet another jurisdiction became involved in the chain of custody for the most important evidence in the entire Wiley case: his body.

IN FEBRUARY 2002, THREE MICROBIOLOGISTS WOULD BE VIOLENTLY MURDERED.

Memphis police records indicate that Dr. Lee ordered Wiley's body be sent to Jackson to undergo an autopsy by Dr. Steven Haynes. However, Dr. O.C. Smith, the Shelby County coroner, requested the body be sent to the Shelby County Forensic Center for an autopsy. Smith later claimed Wiley's body was transported from Louisiana directly to Memphis. On the other hand, Dr. Lee, Young's Funeral Home, and Memphis police records indicate that the body was transported to Memphis via Jackson.

On December 21, Wiley's body arrived at the Memphis coroners' office where O.C. Smith conducted an autopsy. FBI Agent Bill Kay turned over Wiley's dental and medical records to Smith. At 6:00 PM, after Dr. Edgar Turner of the University of Tennessee Dental College had compared Wiley's dental records with the body, a positive identification was made.

The next morning, deputy police chief Wright told a press conference that the body found in Vidalia was positively that of Wiley. As far as the Memphis police were now concerned, pending O.C. Smith's ruling of cause of death, the Wiley case was closed. It was not.

A January 1, 2002, Memphis Crime Response Unit report states, "Crime Scene met forensics on the Hernando DeSoto bridge for photo's [sic] of area where victim possibly *jumped* [emphasis added]." After assuring the Wiley family and the media that the Wiley disappearance was being handled as a missing person case, the Memphis police were still convinced Wiley committed suicide, even before O.C. Smith's final determination of his cause of death.

_THE CORONER

The Shelby County Medical Examiner's Office is located in a nondescript red brick building in a seedy area of Memphis. Even for a medium-size city like Memphis, it is not unusual to see one body being wheeled on a gurney from an arriving ambulance and into the morgue's rear loading dock while another gurney passes it on its way out to an awaiting hearse.

O.C. Smith defies the stereotype attached to a medical examiner. Far from being the tall, gaunt figure often associated with morticians, Smith is a short and amicable man whose crew-style haircut makes one immediately think of the comedian George Gobel. A veteran of Desert Storm, Smith is a reserve Captain in the Naval Medical Corps and is often called upon to help with identification of bodies following Navy aircraft mishaps and crashes.

After conducting his autopsy, Smith issued a report on January 13, 2002. Contrary to the prevailing view within the Memphis police department, Smith ruled Wiley's death an accident resulting from a fall from the bridge. But on the official form "Report of Investigation by County Medical Examiner," Smith checked the box labeled "suspicious, unusual or unnatural" for the type of death. He later said that if there had been the slightest indication that foul play was involved in Wiley's fall, he would have ruled so without hesitation.

In his report Smith stated, "Dr. Wiley fell 135 feet from the Hernando

DeSoto Bridge into the 55-degree water of the Mississippi River. His fall time is calculated to be just under 3 seconds; he would impact at greater than 60 miles per hour. The force upon impact was responsible for fractures of the delicate facial sinuses, unstable neck fractures, crushing of the chest, and other fractures of the spine. The fracture pattern on the ribs and spine indicate he impacted on his right side." Smith continued, "From these injuries it is reasonable to conclude that Dr. Wiley was unconscious, paralyzed, and unable to breathe. He did not drown. There is no pattern of injury to suggest violence."

Smith also concluded that because there was significant damage to Wiley's rental car on both the driver and passenger sides, with yellow and rusty paint scrapings similar to those observed by Smith on the bridge's construction signs, Wiley must have had two mishaps with his vehicle, resulting in his abruptly stopping on the bridge. However, at no time had a laboratory analysis compared the yellow paint on the car and that on the construction signs. Smith's conclusions were based solely on a visual observation of the car and the signs.

BUT ON THE OFFICIAL FORM "REPORT OF INVESTIGATION BY COUNTY MEDICAL EXAMINER," SMITH CHECKED THE BOX LABELED "SUSPICIOUS, UNUSUAL OR UNNATURAL" FOR THE TYPE OF DEATH.

Dr. Lee in Vidalia had her own take on the feasibility of Wiley just suddenly stopping his car on the bridge. She said, "Nobody just stops on an interstate bridge." Her opinion is shared by a number of Wiley's family members and police officers outside of Memphis. One Tennessee State Police official commented that when it comes to Memphis, such random suppositions are no surprise. "We do things a lot differently here in Nashville," the official stated. The Tennessee State Police do not have jurisdiction over accidents or other mishaps on the Tennessee side of the DeSoto Bridge. Because Wiley's car was found one-tenth of a mile from the "Welcome to Arkansas" sign, a spokesman for the Arkansas State Police stated that they, likewise, were jurisdictionally barred from investigating the incident. Although some West Memphis, Arkansas, police also have their doubts as to the veracity of the Memphis police investigation, they too could not get involved, even though Wiley's car was heading toward their city. Such issues of jurisdictions and bungled police work currently plague law enforcement planning for handling future terrorist incidents, especially in a multi-jurisdictional metropolitan area like Memphis.

Shemwell later brushed off Smith's implication that the damage to Wiley's vehicle was "significant." In fact, photos of the car taken while it was in the Memphis police "tunnel" show the damage to the vehicle as so slight, it is barely visible.

Smith dropped another bombshell in his autopsy report: that Wiley's "seizures," coupled with his drinking alcohol earlier the night he disappeared, resulted in his "physical impairment." However, Smith seems to avoid coming right out an saying Wiley was driving drunk—a concept that had been advanced by Wiley's close "friend" Willard in his conversation with Shemwell. Smith states in his report: "It will never be known if this disorder [the so-called "seizures"] or drowsy driving due to the late hour and long day Dr. Wiley had put in, or the effects of alcohol he was seen to *imbibe* [emphasis added] earlier, contributed to the incident on the bridge. Toxicology studies are not yet complete but alcohol has been identified at levels suggesting impairment."

One microbiologist familiar with Wiley's work scoffed at the notion that after five weeks in the Mississippi, traces of the wine Wiley drank at the hotel would still be in his system. Smith, himself, seemed to counter his own conclusion by stating in the report, "However, interpretation of the levels [of alcohol] can never be clear-cut since alcohol fermentation after death coupled with diffusion from the stomach are real considerations *that can never be resolved*" [emphasis added].

There is another disturbing element in the coroner's findings. After stating that Wiley hit the river at 60 miles per hour, Smith later confided that none of the stitches had been torn on Wiley's clothing, which consisted of black trousers, a black shirt, underpants, and socks. Wiley's shoes and jacket were not listed on the medical examiner's receipt of evidence. Smith concluded that Wiley's fall must have been accidental because most suicide jumpers generally clear the 38-inch extended beam that runs the length of the bridge at twelve and a half feet below the guard rail and curb. The curb and railing together are a little over four feet high. Smith reasoned that because the third button on Wiley's shirt was missing and because the impact with the water was not forceful enough to cause the button to fracture, he must have hit his chest on the beam below the bridge rail. However, if Wiley's shirt had been laundered and pressed before his trip, there is the likelihood that the button could have been shattered and removed in that process, or it may have come off at any point in time and was never replaced.

Some law enforcement officials in the Memphis area, speaking on conditions of anonymity, believe that Wiley could have been slipped into the river elsewhere and that his car may have been later parked on the bridge to make it appear as a suicide. One such easy dumping place, according to one official, is the Army Corps of Engineers' boat ramp at the south end of Mud Island, which is adjacent to the Memphis side of the river and accessible by automobile.

Smith's final conclusion was that due to Wiley's height, the relatively low four-foot rail and curb, the possibility of road bounce or a gust of wind from a passing eighteen-wheeler, a collision with a construction sign, and Wiley's susceptibility to seizures, Wiley must have accidentally fallen over the side of the bridge while checking the car for damage. Case closed.

However, there are a number of problems with the finding of an accidental fall. Locals familiar with the Mississippi River have remarked that it is highly unlikely that after being in the river for five weeks, a combination of the strong river current, snapping turtles, and scavenging birds would not have resulted in some tearing of Wiley's clothing. And although Wiley's clothes remained intact and police recovered his watch, wedding band, belt, wallet, and a piece of candy, nevertheless, his jacket and shoes were never recovered, according to the police report.

Speaking on conditions of anonymity, one of the most experienced bridge engineers with the Federal Highway Works Administration in Langley, Virginia—the agency that oversees the interstate highway system, including the DeSoto Bridge—scoffed at O.C. Smith's conclusion that bridge bounce could have hurled Wiley over the bridge railing. "Any bridge bounce from a passing truck would be between one-half to one inch...not nearly enough to bounce a man off the bridge."

The Wiley case would not be the only event that would thrust O.C. Smith into the headlines. On February 10, 2002, Smith was called upon to identify the charred body of a woman found in a flaming car against a utility pole along Highway 72 in Fayette County, just east of Memphis. It turned out the body was that of Kathy Smith, a 49-year-old black woman and Tennessee Department of Motor Vehicles employee who was due to attend a hearing at the Memphis Federal Court on charges that she helped five Middle Eastern men from New York City obtain fake driver's licenses. She and the five men had been arrested on February 7, and Smith was released on her own recognizance. The five Middle Easterners, on the other hand, were held without bail. The FBI later concluded that Smith's death was no accident because gasoline had been found on her clothing.

The other interesting point is that "Kathy Smith" was the same name as the person that Memphis informant Seven spoke of—the woman who knew that a group of people had made Wiley's death look like a suicide. Police never identified the prostitute who went by the name Kathy Smith and supposedly made the statement about Wiley.

On the morning of March 13, 2002, O.C. Smith would have his own close brush with violence. A bomb and two smaller explosive devices were discovered outside Smith's office building. The devices were later taken to a Memphis police firing range, where they were safely detonated. But that would not be last incident that would plague the coroner.

On a quiet Saturday evening on June 1, Smith left his office building and was heading across the parking lot toward his car. An assailant suddenly threw acid in his face, wrapped him in barbed wire, strapped a bomb to his body, and left him outside the stairway to his building. Smith was not discovered until 12:30 AM by a passing security guard. Smith was then subjected to the same type of stonewalling that local and federal law enforcement had been practicing in the Wiley case. Just as with Dr. Wiley, police and federal agents, including those from the FBI, claimed they could not make any assumptions about why anyone would want to harm Smith, and they refused to disclose to the press any specifics about the case. Fortunately for Smith, he was relatively unharmed. But for the people of Memphis, it was like *déjà vu* all over again.

Today, Smith takes it all pretty much in stride. He explains the continuous presence of a bomb-sniffing German shepherd at his side as the idea of the Memphis Police Department because of "some

> AND ALTHOUGH WILEY'S CLOTHES REMAINED INTACT AND POLICE RECOVERED HIS WATCH, WEDDING BAND, BELT, WALLET, AND A PIECE OF CANDY, NEVERTHELESS, HIS JACKET AND SHOES WERE NEVER RECOVERED, ACCORDING TO THE POLICE REPORT.

recent unpleasantries" that have plagued his office.

The foul play naysayers like Shemwell and Smith now seem to have an influential ally: the *New York Times*. In an August 11, 2002, article titled, "The Odds of That," contributing *Times* writer Lisa Belkin suggests that conspiracy theorists are trying to link the Wiley death to that of other microbiologists, some of whom died before September 11. The article buttresses the finding of Smith that Wiley was under the influence of alcohol, disoriented by bridge construction, tired, and possibly having a seizure when he had an accident and checked out the damage to his vehicle. A passing truck causes a gust of wind equivalent to that generated by hurricanes or a bridge bounce. In any event, Wiley was hurled over the side of the bridge. The *Times*' conclusion: Any suggestion contrary to Wiley's death being an accident belongs in the same category as UFOs, crop circles, Grassy Knoll enthusiasts, and numerology.

In addition, the *Times* offers up the unsubstantiated theory that Dr. Que in Miami might have suffered a stroke at the same time he was being clubbed to death by four men with baseball bats. The reasoning: Que suffered from hypertension and high blood pressure, the same basic line of thinking used to explain away Wiley's fall—inebriation after a few glasses of wine over a period of some four hours coupled with "seizures."

The *Times* also questions Que's specialty in microbiology, claiming that Que was not "actually" a microbiologist but merely a cancer researcher at the University of Miami's Sylvester Cancer Center. A perusal of the Center's Website reveals that microbiology was as key to Que's research as it was to that of Wiley's. Cell biology and viral oncology research certainly involves the discipline of microbiology. And the Sylvester Center's research mirrored that of Wiley's lab in many other ways: Both labs were involved in cellular-level research of HIV and herpes, and both received funding from HHMI in Maryland.

_THE END?

For some family members and friends of Don Wiley, important lingering questions remain. Why were important clues overlooked, like the letter he received prior to going to Memphis from a failed Ph.D. candidate at the University College in Dublin, Ireland? In the letter, a female student warned Wiley about anthrax. Although the woman in question was later discovered by Wiley and his staff to have been dropped from the Ph.D. program in Dublin for "psychological problems," what specifically did she know about anthrax? Was she in any way credible?

IN THE LETTER, A FEMALE STUDENT WARNED WILEY ABOUT ANTHRAX.

What makes the letter all the more interesting is an October 2001 incident at the city's University College. A suspect letter thought to contain anthrax was found at the college. Irish Army experts were called in to handle the letter, which was later reported to have been a hoax. However, the suspicious powder from the University College letter, as well as eighteen other suspicious white powder samples, were transferred to Britain's Porton Down biowarfare facility. Why would potentially critical evidence be transferred internationally to a top-secret facility known to be involved with producing deadly anthrax and which is off-limits to non-cleared law enforcement personnel, especially those from Ireland?

Other questions beg the FBI to take another look at the Wiley case. Why was suicide the only theory seriously considered by the Memphis police? (In fact, Shemwell continues to believe that Wiley committed suicide, regardless of the coroner's report, the protestations of Wiley's family, and Wiley's own upbeat demeanor during the evening of November 15.) Where was Wiley for that four-hour period during the early morning of November 16? Why was the FBI in Memphis relatively disinterested in the matter, while FBI Headquarters and the FBI Boston office were actively monitoring the case? What information did the RCMP have that prompted them to inquire into the Wiley case? Why were no rips or tears found in Wiley's clothing after hitting the river at 60 miles per hour? What happened to his jacket and shoes? The Memphis police investigation resulted in more questions than answers.

In passing the Lorraine Motel in downtown Memphis, one can only think back on another Memphis police investigation involving another doctor that began on another fateful Thursday, this time in April 1968. To this day, family members of Dr. Martin Luther King remain unconvinced that the police investigation into his assassination was carried out effectively and professionally. It seems that in Memphis, some traditions never die—but people do.

Author's Note: I have made it a point in this article to respect the privacy of individuals who shared sensitive information and private thoughts with me. Most of the information on Dr. Wiley was obtained from the official police report and interviews with knowledgeable sources in Memphis and elsewhere. One final note about obtaining the 238-page police report, from which a number of details contained in this article were extracted. I requested a copy of the Wiley report from the Memphis Police Central Records Division on August 1, 2002. I was informed that because the computer was "down," I could not get the report. Repeated phone calls resulted in the same story. When I asked if the report was actually on the computer system, I was told that it was. The next day, Friday, August 2, the computer was still having problems in the morning. I was told that because of the backlog I should submit my request later in writing. I decided to show up at Central Records at 2:55 pm Friday afternoon, just five minutes prior to closing time. When I asked one of the few remaining staff for the report, she retrieved it from a filing cabinet, not from a computer terminal. I was told the report had nothing to do with the computer system.

THE WARREN REPORT: BELIEVE IT OR NOT
PRESIDENTS, SENATORS, AND OTHER HIGH OFFICIALS WHO DOUBT THE OFFICIAL VERSION OF THE JFK ASSASSINATION

WILLIAM W. TURNER

Robert Ripley's newspaper column "Believe It Or Not" was a theater of the absurd where it was left to the reader to accept or reject the facts portrayed. Left out of the column were the Warren Report's "magic bullet" theory that a single slug zig-zagged through President John F. Kennedy and Texas Governor John B. Connally (thus getting rid of the need for a second shooter), and the report's gullibility that mobster Jack Ruby rubbed out suspect Lee Harvey Oswald to spare Jacqueline Kennedy the ordeal of a trial. Most Americans have long rejected the Warren Report: A 2001 Gallup Poll found that 81 percent believe there was a conspiracy.[1]

What is even more surprising is the number of high officials who thought the Warren Report should take its place on the shelf with Aesop's Fables. Chief among them was the Chief Justice himself, Earl Warren, who was arm-wrestled into heading the Warren Commission by Lyndon Johnson. Warren was stymied from the start: The FBI was forced upon him as his investigative staff after its chief, J. Edgar Hoover, instantly jumped to the conclusion that Oswald and Ruby had each acted alone. After the Warren Report was published and controversy flared, Warren pointed out that it merely "found no evidence" of a conspiracy, leaving the door open should evidence be found in the future.

In 1967, Warren passed to the FBI information he received "regarding organized crime figure John Roselli's claim of personal knowledge relating to Cuban or underworld complicity," as a 1976 Senate Intelligence Committee report put it. Warren urged that the matter be probed, but Hoover "took repeated action to discredit the source." Recently the Chief Justice's grandson, Jeff Warren, confirmed that "Earl never closed the door on the possibility of a conspiracy."[2]

Even LBJ became skeptical of the report he commissioned. An internal FBI memorandum dated April 4, 1967, reported that a top aide, Marvin Watson, revealed the President "was now convinced" that the CIA was somehow involved in the assassination. This theme was repeated when, in November 1975, another ranking aide, Joseph Califano, told Dan Rather of CBS that Johnson "thought in time, when all the activities of the CIA were flushed out, then maybe the whole story of the Kennedy assassination would be known."[3]

It is interesting to note that Rather himself, who over the years had

adhered to the CBS editorial position that the Warren Report was valid, in 1993 remarked to deputy chief counsel Robert K. Tannenbaum of the House Select Committee on Assassinations: "We really blew it on the Kennedy assassination."

Senator Richard B. Russell was the first Warren Commission member to voice suspicions. A conservative Georgian who in the 1950s counseled staying out of Vietnam, Russell balked at signing off on the Warren Report because he was convinced that separate bullets had struck Kennedy and Connally. When his colleagues agreed to qualify the language, he signed for the sake of unaminity. But on January 19, 1970, in the *Washington Post*, the Senator broke silence by saying he now believed there had been a criminal conspiracy in Dallas. It was Oswald's recondite trip to Mexico City shortly before the murder, Russell said, that "caused me to doubt he planned it all by himself."

> RECENTLY THE CHIEF JUSTICE'S GRANDSON, JEFF WARREN, CONFIRMED THAT "EARL NEVER CLOSED THE DOOR ON THE POSSIBILITY OF A CONSPIRACY."

Congressman Hale Boggs of Louisiana also was an internal dissenter during deliberations, fending off FBI and CIA "shadings" of the probe. He contended that it would be a "disservice" not to dig deeper into Oswald's alleged relationships with the intelligence agencies, and expand the background check on Jack Ruby. But he was thwarted by the Commission's political deadline, dictated by the 1964 November elections. A Boggs staff member recalled, "Hale always returned to one thing: Hoover lied his eyes out to the Commission—on Oswald, on Ruby, on their friends, the bullets, the gun, you name it."[4] On April 5, 1971, Boggs took to the House floor to deliver a stinging indictment of Hoover, charging he "used the tactics of the Soviet Union and Hitler's Gestapo," and calling for his resignation. On October 17, 1972, Hale Boggs disappeared on a flight in Alaska.

Governor Connally and his wife, Nellie, who were riding in the Presidential limousine in jump seats in front of John and Jacqueline Kennedy, never wavered in their insistence that there were separate shots. The Connallys testified that to "a moral certainty" a bullet first hit Kennedy, then another bullet hit the governor a second later. It was physically impossible for Oswald to have squeezed off two shots in one second (in fact, the Zapruder film shows that Kennedy reacted to a shot three-quarters of a second before Connally). When Warren Report defenders pressured him, Connally held firm on

> SENATOR RICHARD B. RUSSELL WAS THE FIRST WARREN COMMISSION MEMBER TO VOICE SUSPICIONS.

A BOGGS STAFF MEMBER RECALLED, "HALE ALWAYS RETURNED TO ONE THING: HOOVER LIED HIS EYES OUT TO THE COMMISSION—ON OSWALD, ON RUBY, ON THEIR FRIENDS, THE BULLETS, THE GUN, YOU NAME IT."

his separate-bullets testimony but tossed them a bone by saying, absurdly, that he didn't believe there had been a conspiracy.

In a trailing limousine were presidential assistants Kenneth O'Donnell and David Powers, who, like other witnesses in Dealey Plaza, were interviewed by the FBI. It was not until 1989, when Thomas "Tip" O'Neill—former Speaker of the House who was close to the Kennedy family—published his memoir, *Man of the House*, that the nature of those interviews was revealed. In 1968, O'Neill was dining with O'Donnell and Powers at Jimmy's Harborside Restaurant in Boston when the subject turned to the assassination. "I was surprised to hear O'Donnell say that he was sure he had heard two shots that came from behind the fence [on the Grassy Knoll]," O'Neill wrote. "That's not what you told the Warren Commission," he braced O'Donnell. "You're right," O'Donnell said, "I told the FBI what I had heard, but they said it couldn't have happened that way and that I must have been imagining things." He explained that he let the FBI put words in his mouth because he "just didn't want to stir up more pain and trouble for the family." Powers echoed O'Donnell—two shots from behind the fence. Concluded O'Neill: "I used to think that the only people who doubted the conclusions of the Warren Commission were crackpots. Now, however, I'm not so sure."

So O'Donnell and Powers outed themselves as doubters, converting O'Neill in the process. But the larger context seems to have eluded the Speaker: The FBI suborned perjury on the part of JFK's two closest aides to perfect its cover-up of a conspiracy. It is not difficult to imagine the legendary disruption the pair would have caused the Warren Commission if they had raised their right hands and testified truthfully.

In the 1970s, Senator Richard Schweiker, a moderate Republican from Pennsylvania, and his Democratic colleague Gary Hart of Colorado became convinced by their probing of intelligence agencies' misdeeds that the Warren Report was, in Schweiker's words, "a house of cards." Their landmark Senate Intelligence Committee Report on the Kennedy assassination is widely credited with setting the stage for the House Select Committee on Assassinations with its finding of conspiracy. (A recommendation that the Justice Department take up where it left off went unheeded).

Senate Majority Leader Howard Baker of Tennessee, a centrist Republican, rose to the occasion by becoming a vocal critic of the Warren Report. In an interview on May 23, 1976, Baker pointed out that the Commission "did not know even of the 56 attempts by the CIA on Fidel Castro's life" which might have resulted in a blowback.[5]

Through all the controversy, Richard M. Nixon, preoccupied with his own 1974 forced resignation, did not publicly utter a word. But he did privately, as chronicled by White House tapes released in 2002. During his second term, in a conversation with John Connally in the Oval Office, he listens as Connally describes the fatal shot: "I was lying...down on Nellie's lap like this to shield her head on top of me and I had my eyes open and I heard that bullet hit his head.... I knew he was dead." This graphic detail may have influenced Nixon when, on a later occasion, he is heard on the tapes bluntly telling his aides that the Warren Report "was the greatest hoax that has ever been perpetuated."[6]

Nixon was not the only head of state to scoff at the Warren Report. When a reporter briefed him on its lone-nut verdict, French President Charles de Gaulle laughed, "*Vous me blaquez.* [You're kidding me.] Cowboys and Indians!"[7] De Gaulle intuitively rejected the idea that an assassination carried out with military precision could be the work of one unstable man. In August 1962, he had narrowly escaped a crossfire ambush on a Paris street when his driver accelerated out of danger. The police proved that it had been a conspiracy by military officers calling themselves the Secret Army Organization who were violently opposed to de Gaulle's pullout from Algeria.

De Gaulle remained so convinced that JFK, whom he admired, was the victim of a domestic conspiracy that in 1967 he assigned French intelligence to investigate. Their report was converted into a book, *Farewell America*, which defined the Cold War special interests they saw behind the assassination. Herve Lamarr, the French intelligence agent who came out of the cold to front for the project, let it be known that "through personal relationships" there was help from Kennedy insiders.

Intriguingly, Robert Kennedy himself sensed that there was more to his brother's death than the actions of a motiveless stranger. On the day after the assassination he called in one of the family's most trusted aides, Daniel P. Moynihan (later a Senator from New York), and instructed him to assemble a small staff to explore whether Teamster's boss Jimmy Hoffa played a role in the killing, and whether the Secret Service had been bought off. Moynihan was unable to implicate either.[8]

When it was in draft form, *Farewell America* was offered to New Orleans District Attorney Jim Garrison, who had initiated his own probe of the Kennedy assassination following a conversation in November 1966 with Louisiana Senator Russell B. Long. A populist Democrat, Long had held a press conference the week before in which he expressed doubt about the findings of the Warren Commission. He elaborated to Garrison that it was unlikely that a gunman of Oswald's "mediocre skills" could fire with pinpoint accuracy within a time constraint barely sufficient "for a man to get off two shots from a bolt-action rifle, much less three." Long saw Oswald as a "fall guy," a decoy to

GOVERNOR CONNALLY AND HIS WIFE, NELLIE, WHO WERE RIDING IN THE PRESIDENTIAL LIMOUSINE IN JUMP SEATS IN FRONT OF JOHN AND JACQUELINE KENNEDY, NEVER WAVERED IN THEIR INSISTENCE THAT THERE WERE SEPARATE SHOTS.

THE WARREN REPORT: BELIEVE IT OR NOT
WILLIAM W. TURNER

draw attention "while another man fired the fatal shot."

O'DONNELL SAID, "I TOLD THE FBI WHAT I HAD HEARD, BUT THEY SAID IT COULDN'T HAVE HAPPENED THAT WAY AND THAT I MUST HAVE BEEN IMAGINING THINGS."

Garrison cloistered himself, studied the Warren Report and its companion volumes, and emerged determined to produce a counterreport. His suspects had a common denominator: W. Guy Banister & Associates, 544 Camp St., New Orleans. Banister was a superannuated FBI executive whose detective agency provided cover for intelligence operations such as a diversionary strike timed with the CIA-sponsored Bay of Pigs invasion in 1961. Banister was already dead when the D.A. opened his investigation. David W. Ferrie, who committed suicide after being questioned, worked for Banister and was on the defense team of Mafia don Carlos Marcello, who had been summarily deported by RFK. Lee Harvey Oswald stamped the address on pro-Castro handbills he distributed in the summer of 1963. Banister's building housed Sergio Arcacha Smith, the local delegate of the Cuban Revolutionary Council, the Cuban exile coalition for the Bay of Pigs, which was angry at JFK for "withholding air cover" for the landing zone.

In interviewing a defector from the right-wing paramilitary Minutemen, I learned that Banister was closely associated in the Minutemen and intelligence activities with Maurice Gatlin, Sr. The defector, Jerry Milton Brooks, had been a kind of protege of Gatlin, who boasted, "Stick with me—I'll give you a license to kill." In Brooks' estimation, Gatlin was a "transporter" for the CIA. He vividly recalled Gatlin in 1962 displaying a thick wad of bills, saying it was $100,000 of CIA money consigned to a reactionary French clique planning to assassinate de Gaulle. Shortly after that Gatlin flew to Paris, and shortly after that came the Secret Army Organization's failed attempt to kill the President of France.

So it was not surprising that the *Farewell America* manuscript landed on Garrison's desk. What is surprising is what happened after Lamarr invited the D.A. to send an envoy to France to learn more. I was running for U.S. Congress and couldn't break away, so a young Garrison volunteer named Steve Jaffe went. Lamarr led him straight to the Elysee Palace to the open door of Andre Ducret, the chief of

when the Garrison probe started, RFK asked him to find out everything about it that he could. "I may need it in the future," he noted.[9] A month before the California primary election, campaign aide Richard Lubic tracked me down in Garrison's office. "After he's elected, Bobby's going to go," Lubic reported. "He's going to reopen the investigation."[10]

On June 5, 1968, RFK took to the podium in the Ambassador Hotel in Los Angeles to declare victory. "It's on to Chicago, and let's win there!" he buoyed the crowd, mindful that he was now the favorite to capture the nomination and beat Richard Nixon. Moments later, as he made his way through a pantry, shots rang out. A man named Sirhan Sirhan was caught with smoking gun in hand, and the Los Angeles authorities promptly announced he had acted alone. According to NBC correspondent Sander Vanocur, who flew back to New York on the plane carrying RFK's body, Teddy Kennedy didn't buy it. The youngest brother remonstrated bitterly about the "faceless men" charged in the slayings of RFK, JFK and Dr. Martin Luther King, Jr., who had been the victim of a sniper in Memphis two months before. "There has to be more to it," Kennedy said. He would never repeat those words in public.[11]

The unprecedented covert effort of a French President to influence an American presidential election wound up. A preface was added to *Farewell America* eulogizing RFK as "The Man of November 5" (the date to come of the general election), an obvious tribute from de Gaulle, who was known to his people as "The Man of June 18" (from the day in 1940 after the Germans overran France that he broadcast from London his stirring call to resist). But the books never were distributed in the United States—the French were closing shop.

Herve Lamarr, a Gitane cigarette dangling from his lips, made a farewell appearance. "You are professionals," he told me in arranging to deliver into my hands several boxes of the book and a canister. The book now contained an appendix revealing that the famed

NIXON IS HEARD ON THE TAPES BLUNTLY TELLING HIS AIDES THAT THE WARREN REPORT "WAS THE GREATEST HOAX THAT HAS EVER BEEN PERPETUATED."

the secret service, who announced how France appreciated Garrison's efforts. Ducret then excused himself and disappeared into de Gaulle's adjacent office for a few minutes. He emerged to hand Jaffe the President's calling card on which he had written, "*Je suis tres sensible a la confiance que vous m'exprimez.* [I am very moved at the confidence you have expressed in me.]" The book now had the imprimatur of the highest council of the French government.

Marketed without any hint as to its true genesis, *Farewell America* became a European bestseller. But its primary target was the United States, where Robert Kennedy was running for President on an anti-Vietnam War platform. While publicly accepting the Warren Report, RFK had a hidden agenda: Once in the White House, he would order the Justice Department to reinvestigate the assassination. His press secretary, Frank Mankiewicz, recently told author Gus Russo that

Zapruder film taken by a spectator at Dealey Plaza had somehow been liberated from its vault in the Time-Life offices in New York. The film would enable the general public, the appendix said, "to watch John Kennedy's head explode in a cloud of red blood lasting nearly a second, may see how the President was thrust violently backwards by a bullet fired at point-blank range by a gunman situated in front of the car."

It was the canister that held the surprise: the Zapruder film itself. The appendix had stated: "The Zapruder movie belongs to history and to men everywhere." I took that as an instruction and showed it on television and at lectures across the country until it fell into the public domain. I believe that the graphic footage of the Zapruder film is the single most compelling factor in America's overwhelming belief in a conspiracy.

As for the Presidents, Senators, and other powerful men who don't believe the Warren Report, they've surely seen even more powerful evidence.

| "THERE HAS TO BE MORE TO IT," TEDDY KENNEDY SAID.
| HE WOULD NEVER REPEAT THOSE WORDS IN PUBLIC.

Believe it or not.

Endnotes

1. *San Francisco Chronicle*, 14 April 2001. **2.** Author's interview with Jeffrey Earl Warren. *Marin Independent Journal* (Novato, California), 16 May 1997. **3.** Fensterwald, Bernard, Jr. *Coincidence or Conspiracy?* New York: Zebra Books, 1977: 125. **4.** *Ibid.*: 96. **5.** *Face the Nation* (TV show), CBS, 23 May 1976. **6.** Reuters, 28 Feb 2002; Anderson, Kevin. "Revelations and Gaps on Nixon Tapes," BBC News, 1 March 2002. **7.** Author's interview of French intelligence officer Herve Patrick Lamarre, San Francisco, 10 Sept 1968. **8.** Hinckle, Warren. *If You Have a Lemon, Make Lemonade.* G.P. Putnam's Sons, 1974. **9.** Russo, Guss. *Live by the Sword: The Secret War Against Castro and the Death of JFK.* Baltimore: Bancroft Press, 1998: 406. **10.** Author's phone interview with Richard Lubic, April 1968. **11.** Turner, William, and Jonn Christian. *The Assassination of Robert F. Kennedy.* New York: Thunder's Mouth Press, 1993: xxxiii.

FOOD-DROP FIASCO
HUMANITARIAN AID FOR AFGHANISTAN DOOMED FROM START TO FINISH

RUSS KICK

Shortly after the US attacked Afghanistan for supposedly sheltering Osama bin Laden and al Qaeda, our TV screens were filled with images of planes dropping food rations into the bombarded country. The little packets were shoved out of cargo holds by the thousands. You could almost hear the government patting itself on the back as it said, "See, we're actually helping the starving people of Afghanistan."

Trouble is, those food drops were a complete disaster. News reports mentioned some of the problems with the humanitarian effort, but there's a lot they either didn't tell us or got wrong. A nonprofit aid organization called Partners International Foundation decided to see what was going on. These guys aren't granola-crunching flower children—they used to be in Special Forces units of the US military. And they didn't content themselves to sit in an office interviewing people by phone. They went into Afghanistan during the heaviest part of the war to find out what was happening for themselves.

Their "Assessment Report: United States Humanitarian Food Drops in Afghanistan" was released November 25, 2001, when over 1.2 million rations had already been dropped. Here's what it uncovered:

• You know those little packets in vitamin bottles and clothes that are supposed to keep them fresh? Well, many of the little meal packs dropped on Afghanistan contained at least one of those packets (called a desiccant) to keep the food fresh. Unfortunately, the Afghans aren't familiar with desiccants, so they tore them open and ate the powder. Some thought it was medicine, so they noshed it straight. Others figured it was a funky American spice, so they sprinkled it on their beans, rice, or pasta. Lots of Afghans got sick, though we don't know if any deaths occurred. In fact, it's hard to say whether people got sick from chowing down on desiccant or because the food in the packets was usually spoiled.

> IN ALL, THE TEAM FOUND THAT OVER 90 PERCENT OF THE MEAL PACKETS HAD BEEN DAMAGED AND WERE CONTAMINATED BY FUNGUS OR BACTERIA.

• You see, these plastic-wrapped meals weren't made to be dropped from 25,000 to 40,000 feet. During freefall, the air pressure caused them to expand like balloons, and the cold at those altitudes made the outer plastic brittle. If they hadn't already split during their plummet, they probably did when they hit the ground. Some burst wide open, while others got small tears, letting in water, dirt, and debris. Even in meals where the outer wrapping didn't split, the wrapping of individual pieces of food inside the meal packet was often torn.

In all, the team found that over 90 percent of the meal packets had been damaged and were contaminated by fungus or bacteria. "They emitted a gaseous odor and foul smell," according to the report. But because the Afghans were so hungry, or because they thought that's how American kibble is supposed to smell, they wolfed down the food anyway. When large numbers of people got sick, the Taliban said that the US was poisoning them. The American government countered that the Taliban must've been tainting the food packs to frame the US. Neither side was apparently right.

• Even if the food hadn't gone rotten, it wasn't appropriate for the

Afghan culture. The locals eat rice, bread, and a little meat. Who knows what they made of the pasta, peanut butter, and pastries in the packets? It was kind of like serving goat meat, fried crickets, and unidentifiable glop to Americans. While any food is welcome in an emergency, that strange foreign grub wasn't suitable for "sustained feeding as currently applied," according to the report.

• Another problem was that the food was distributed haphazardly. Sometimes the packets wouldn't be noticed for days or weeks, giving them plenty of time to go rotten. When dropped in remote locations, they were often hoarded or sold by the few people who happened to find them.

• Remember that urban legend about dropping a penny from the Empire State Building and killing someone on the sidewalk below? Same principle for the food packets. Each plane would dump 35,000 of these little projectiles, which reached speeds of up to 100 miles per hour. The team didn't report on anyone hurt by plummeting packets, but they did see several huts with holes in their roofs caused by falling food.

EACH PLANE WOULD DUMP 35,000 OF THESE LITTLE PROJECTILES, WHICH REACHED SPEEDS OF UP TO 100 MILES PER HOUR.

• But even if no Afghans got conked on the head, they still had to be careful of packets on the ground. Why? Thanks to its war with the Soviet Union, Afghanistan is littered with unexploded mines and bombs. Go after a food packet in a field, and it may be the last thing you ever do. To make matters worse, some geniuses chose yellow plastic to wrap some of the meals. It just so happens that the bomblets from the US's cluster bombs are the same shade of yellow. Meal packets and unexploded bomblets look unbelievably similar. Thus, Afghanis were introduced to a new form of Russian roulette.

• As lame as the attempts were, they must have had something going for them, right? At the very least, they must've been a cheap way to feed people. Wrong again. A bag of rice that can feed a family for a month costs $50, including delivery by land into Afghanistan. Using food drops, it cost over $145 to feed a family for a month.

That is, assuming the food packets didn't give them a concussion, ptomaine, or send them into a minefield.

BELGIUM: THE PEDOPHILIA FILES
SANDRA BISIN

On August 13, 1996, Belgian child-rapist Marc Dutroux was arrested. Four days later, the bodies of 8-year-olds Mélissa Russo and Julie Lejeune were discovered in his garden: They had been starved to death. For the Belgian people, that was the beginning of a nightmarish series of discoveries that will haunt their psyche for years to come.

Six years after these events, in August 2002, Judge Jacques Langlois ended the investigation of the most traumatic criminal case Belgium has dealt with in decades. The actual trial will not start before the end of 2003. Marc Dutroux is accused of having kidnapped and raped six young girls and murdered four of them.[1]

Today, the question remains: Did Dutroux act alone or was he part of a very well-organized child-sex organization? The country is divided in two groups: those who believe that pedophile networks exist, which would mean that many cases could be linked together, and those who don't. Among the latter we find most of the Belgian judicial officials and elite.

The Belgian people who support the idea of a pedophile network point at the blatant dysfunction of the justice system in the handling of the case. Many questions remain unanswered. Why doesn't the justice system follow the right tracks? Why does it omit convincing evidence? Why are officials who investigate evidence of an organized ring pulled off the case? These are the questions being asked by Jean Nicolas—an independent investigative journalist who has reported for the respected German newsweekly *Der Spiegel*, among others—in his book *Dossier Pédophilie* (*The Pedophilia Files*).[2] The journalist nicknames Belgium "the Nigeria of Europe," in reference to both countries' well-known corruption.

Marc Dutroux had already been sentenced to thirteen years of imprisonment for numerous rapes of underage girls, and released in 1992, against psychiatrists' advice, when he had served only one-third of his sentence. In 1995, when Julie and Mélissa went missing, the police had suspected Dutroux of being responsible but kept silent in order to investigate on their own. Police *twice* searched one of Dutroux's homes, yet both times they failed to find two girls being kept prisoner in a secret chamber in the basement. What is more, in 1998, Dutroux managed to momentarily escape the police. He was then taken back into custody. But that additional example of a lack of efficiency completely discredited the police.

There was more to come. The first judge appointed to the case, Jean-Marc Connerotte—who became a national hero after he managed to rescue Laetitia and Sabine, two girls that had been ensnared by Dutroux, on August 15, 1996—was suddenly taken off the case. He had made the mistake of agreeing to take part in a "spaghetti dinner" organized by the grateful families of the girls.

In October that same year, 300,000 outraged citizens took to the streets of Brussels in the "White March" in order to denounce the dysfunction of the Belgian justice system. Many citizens' associations—among them the Coordination of the White Committees, the Julie and Mélissa Committee, and *Pour la Vérité* (For the Truth), led by psychiatrist Marc Reisinger—were founded at the same time. Their aim is to fight for the protection of the children's rights and reveal the existence of pedophile organizations to their fellow people.

Connerotte was replaced on the spot by Judge Langlois, who dismissed many pieces of evidence that allegedly could have sped up the investigation. In 1997, the financial department of the police force discovered movements of money into Dutroux's bank accounts after each kidnapping. This evidence was removed from the file.

What is more, Jean Nicolas mentions in his book the fact that this man, who allegedly got money solely from a disability pension, which would have amounted to US$900 per month, was able to buy, in a span of four years, six old houses in the region of Brussels. "And they are trying to make us believe [Dutroux] acted on his own?" writes Nicolas.[3]

Even the testimonies of some of the witnesses were not admitted as evidence by the court. These witnesses were accused of distorting the truth. The most striking example of this surprising phenomenon is the story of Regina Louf, which she relates in an overwhelming book: *Silence, On Tue des Enfants!* (*Hush, They're Killing Children!*).[4] In September 1996, following Judge Connerotte's call for witnesses, 27-year-old Regina Louf decided to contact the judicial authorities. She met crime inspector Patrick De Baets and told him about the sexual abuses, molestation, and sadomasochist tortures she endured from a very early age until she was sixteen. She also was able to give a minute description of the places in which those scenes had taken place. She named as orchestrators Marc Dutroux and Michel Nihoul, a Brussels businessman charged numerous times for financial fraud, as well as many Belgian businessmen and

> IN OCTOBER THAT SAME YEAR, 300,000 OUTRAGED CITIZENS TOOK TO THE STREETS OF BRUSSELS IN THE "WHITE MARCH" IN ORDER TO DENOUNCE THE DYSFUNCTION OF THE BELGIAN JUSTICE SYSTEM.

politicians. According to Regina Louf, they were taking part in a large-scale pedophile organization. That led to seventeen filmed hearings attended by numerous judicial officials.

Louf was given a code name, "X1," in order to protect her from any kind of threat from her torturers. Thanks to her testimony, the police officers were able to reopen many judicial files. For example, during one of those hearings, Louf spoke about the "mushroom bed" case, which included the murder of a 16-year-old girl, Christine Van Hees, whose burnt corpse was found in a basement in 1984. She had been severely sexually abused. Nobody had been able at the time to determine the circumstances that led to her death. Twelve years later, Louf was able to give a very precise description of the building (it had since been demolished), which was corroborated by the owner of the place.

As she affirmed that she had attended the murder and had been forced to take part in it, she also provided the investigators with a lot of details concerning the injuries inflicted on the girl. Some of those details (for example, Regina said that a nail had been driven into the victim's wrist) were not even mentioned in Van Hees' post-mortem examination report. The investigation file, as well as many press articles, mentioned that the girl's hands and legs had been tied with barbed wire. X1 asserted that an electric wire whose envelope had melted had actually been used. The investigators checked the information and were able to confirm Louf's testimony.

Regina also told crime inspector Patrick De Baets that the victim had been raped with a knife, and her blood sponged up by a Tampax. When De Baets and his team checked the file related to Van Hees, they found out that a Tampax soaked with blood had effectively been collected on the scene of the crime. These elements had not been released to the press.

What is more, X1 described very precisely the private life of the victims of the "mushroom bed" and of their alleged torturers (among them Marc Dutroux, his wife Michèle Martin, and Michel Nihoul). X1 also disclosed the secret addresses of some upper-class people, which turned out to be correct. And she described the interior decoration of their houses, which also was right.

After an analysis of the investigation file, X1's version of the facts was eventually acknowledged. During the new investigation that was started on January 27, 1997, 300 witnesses were interviewed. Many corroborated Regina Louf's testimonies on crucial aspects of the case. The other X-witnesses, one of whom worked for the police, gave similar details of childhood abuse.

In January 1997, Brussels Judge Jean-Claude Van Espen, who formerly had been in charge of the case, was back in office. A few months later, he cast doubt on the trustworthiness of crime officer Patrick De Baets and his team's investigation. (It was later proved that Judge Van Espen himself had not "realized" that at the time the Van Hees murder occurred, he had been the lawyer of one of the people incriminated by Regina Louf in the "mushroom bed" investigation: Annie Bouty, Michel Nihoul's companion at that time.) De Baets had come to believe Louf's testimony, after checking out her statements about the murders.

A re-reading of Regina Louf's hearings was organized, led by French officers who had no understanding of the Flemish language and were given ill-translated documents. Following the re-reading, Patrick De Baets was dismissed from the investigation, accused of having tried to influence the witness through his questioning and manipulating the entire process of the investigation. In June 2000, De Baets was cleared. Two journalists from *Le Soir Illustre* were brought to court for slandering him and his team: They were ordered to pay the investigators 2.2 million Belgian francs (US$55,000), plus costs. Although De Baets has been exonerated, his assignments have been completely moved away from the pedophile files. He has now become an investigation instructor.

One of De Baets' colleagues, Aime Bille, has further verified that Louf's testimony matched the facts in several cases.

THE INVESTIGATORS CHECKED THE INFORMATION AND WERE ABLE TO CONFIRM LOUF'S TESTIMONY.

At a press conference that was held in Paris on November 19, 2002, Marc Reisinger, one of the psychoanalysts who support Regina Louf's testimony, said that the authorities were altering the evidence to discredit Louf. He even went so far as to say that "a few parts of the re-reading had been modified so that the meaning of Louf's answers to certain questions was changed." Reisinger also mentioned this during a Belgian television program in which he took part; the following day, the police searched his house.

At the Paris press conference, Louf asserted that although she had given all the information and details she could, "none of the murders [she had alluded to] had been solved." She declared, "This is unbearable for a so-called democracy like Belgium. It is a frustration that I have to deal with every day."

Jean Nicolas reports that "thirteen searches aimed at checking the veracity of certain elements in Regina Louf's testimony, and eventually supposed to help charging the murderers with the death of Christine Van Hees, were canceled at the last moment by the police chief."[5]

In the meantime, the media took hold of Louf's story and launched a severe assault against her, ridiculing her testimony in a kind of reversed witch hunt. Many assumed that the woman was "totally nuts," although she had been declared perfectly sound of mind by a college of psychoanalysts. Today, the "X files" are closed, although Louf's alleged major tormentor, Antoine Vanden Bogaert, alias Tony, acknowledged having sexually abused the girl as soon as she turned twelve, having possessed her house key (given to him by her mother), hiring the girl for parties, and forcing her girlfriends into sexual games.

Very few journalists supported Louf, among them two reporters from *De Morgen*, Annemie Bulté and Douglas de Coninck, and one from *Journal du Mardi*, Marie-Jeanne Van Heeswyck. In a courageous book, *The X Files: What Belgium Was Not Supposed to Know About the Dutroux Affair*,[6] they describe how the judicial processes in the Dutroux case were thwarted by economically and politically influential people. The assertions of the book are emphasized by passages drawn from police files and transcriptions of the X-witnesses' testimonies. Heeswyck has been fined 500,000 francs (approximately

From the Parliamentary Report

These extracts are from the Belgian parliamentary report on the Dutroux affair, specifically the portion about Mélissa and Julie. Translated by Sandra Bisin.

This file [about Mélissa and Julie] is no doubt the most complex of all, in time and in space. It takes place in three locations: Charleroi, Liège and Brussels. It lasts from 1993 to 1996. The conclusion is tragic. If the information had been dealt with seriously in 1993, the kidnappings may have been avoided. If good decisions had been taken in 1995, the girls could have been found alive.

....

The searches dated November 8, 1993, were not followed up. Three transmitter-receivers that made it possible to pick up the police frequencies were found. A .22 long rifle was also found, which carried no registration number. That information was never exploited due to committing magistrate Lorent's ambiguous methods of working, which consisted in leading an unofficial investigation under cover of the official investigation.

....

The commission must state that committing magistrate Lorent, who was in charge of that criminal investigation, did not exploit the results of the searches done in 1994 (among them, the discovery of Slovak currency and of a Czech national staying illegally in our country).

....

[On September 4, 1995, Dutroux's mother sent authorities a letter expressing her suspicions that her son was involved in the disappearance of the girls.] The commission believes that the information contained in Dutroux's mother's letter and its importance were not considered with the necessary attention by committing magistrate Lorent within the context of the missing children files.

....

The technical examination of the place [Mélissa and Julie's neighborhood], as well as of the route on which the kidnappings occurred, was led in a very superficial way and without the punctiliousness it deserved. The investigation concerning the neighbors should have been initiated sooner and was not led with enough precision. The same criticism is to be made concerning the investigation carried out concerning the passers-by. The wanted notice was not transmitted in the appropriate way, either, and the investigation concerning the parents and families was not done with the necessary tact, information, and caution. The responsibility is due to warrant officer Gilot, who was in charge of the operational leadership of the investigation, but also to committing magistrate Doutrève, who was in charge of the effective leadership of the investigation. The commission believes that committing magistrate Doutrève should have gone to the scene immediately or at least in the first days following the disappearances. Her first visit was on August 3, 1995. [The girls had been abducted on June 24.]

US$79,000) for revealing prosecution secrets, which certainly indicates that she revealed *bona fide* insider information about the case.

In an article about this book, the *International Herald Tribune* states:

Judicial authorities are not allowed to comment publicly on the case, but a retired prosecutor, Judge Guy Poncelet, called the thesis of the book "brilliant and convincing." He said that "certain political and judicial authorities," with the help of the state radio and television and much of the press, had deliberately played down disturbing evidence uncovered in the Dutroux investigation.[7]

Jean Nicolas also acknowledges the importance of Louf's testimony: "[F]rom that moment on, Judge Connerotte understood that he was facing an exceptional...criminal network behind Dutroux and his accomplice Michel Nihoul."[8] In his book, the journalist mentions the report of a parliamentary commission of inquiry (headed by Belgium's Minister of Justice), which, in Nicolas' words, hints at the fact that "the deputy-investigators were forced to stop their investigations because of the protection that Dutroux and his accomplices were supposed to have enjoyed." He adds that "the press focused a lot on that aspect at the time, especially because of the indignation of Green party deputy Vincent Decroly."[9] The report indeed says:

[T]he commission notes that concerning the investigation led in the city of Liège, a certain number of fundamental questions remain unanswered. Such is the case for the way the investigation was organized and the fact that it was limited to sex offenders around the Liège judicial district. Moreover, the commission remains convinced that certain leads were not examined thoroughly enough. Such is the case for the F. lead: someone Julie and Mélissa knew; as well as the lead of a convict who asserted having information concerning Mélissa, which happened after the Julie and Mélissa kidnappings.[10]

Nicolas also asserts that Judge Connerotte was becoming too dangerous; by uncovering the networks, he would have uncovered other "unpleasant" stories involving political officials, and to some extent King Albert II of Belgium. In *The Pedophile File*, Nicolas explains how the Dutroux file would have ramifications with the "Pinon file," named after a Brussels psychoanalyst who emigrated to Portugal. Many people and places mentioned by witnesses in the Dutroux file are similar to those mentioned in the Pinon file. This file dates back to the 1980s, when Doctor André Pinon found himself at the foundation of a judicial case concerning pedophile networks involving officials from the government.

According to Nicolas, a few elements from the file indicate

> **"[T]HE COMMISSION NOTES THAT CONCERNING THE INVESTIGATION LED IN THE CITY OF LIÈGE, A CERTAIN NUMBER OF FUNDAMENTAL QUESTIONS REMAIN UNANSWERED."**

that King Albert II himself, who was at the time Prince Albert, had taken part in and even organized orgies that included children. That was a severe blow to the Belgian authorities; in September 2001, the Belgian government decided to bring the French publishing house Flammarion to court for libel. On October 11, 2001, the Paris county court did not suppress *The Pedophile File*. Rather, it simply ordered Flammarion to insert the following note within the book: "The Paris county court president advised us to state the Belgian King's protest against the attacks on his reputation contained in this book."

In France, the Dutroux scandal has had a direct impact on the handling of some cases, among them the "Yonne Missing Girls" file, involving the disappearance, at the end of the 1970s, of seven mentally-disabled young girls in the French region of Yonne. All of them were driven to school by bus-driver Emile Louis.

Authorities knew of the connection of Louis to all the missing girls in June 1984. But it was only in *1997*, more than 20 years after the disappearances began, that an investigation was launched by the Paris court of appeal. In December 2000, Louis was arrested. He admitted to the murders but retracted his statement two days later. Today, Louis is in prison, and the investigation is still being processed.

To many observers, it seems that the man had not acted alone and had been protected by others higher up. Besides the fact that local law enforcement sat on their information about Louis for thirteen years (until a court forced the issue), the most striking clue is the disappearance of *all* files related to unexplained cases of missing girls and young women in the Yonne region between 1958 and 1982.

Disappearing evidence. Allegations of altered evidence. Blatant failures to investigate. Bungled searches. The people of Belgium and beyond are demanding answers.

Endnotes

1. The murdered victims are Mélissa Russo (8), Julie Lejeune (8), An Marchal (17), and Eefje Lambrechts (19). The two who escaped after being kidnapped, drugged, repeatedly raped, and imprisoned are Laetitia Delhez (14) and Sabine Dardenne (12). **2.** Nicolas, Jean. *Dossier Pédophilie*. Paris: Flammarion Publications, 2001. **3.** *Ibid.*: 38. **4.** *Hush, They're Killing Children!* by Regina Louf came out in Flemish in 1998. The French translation came out in 2002 from Mols Publications, Belgium. **5.** *Op cit.*, Nicolas: 75. **6.** Bulté, Annemie, Douglas de Coninck, Marie-Jeanne Van Heeswyck. *The X Files: What Belgium Was Not Supposed to Know About the Dutroux Affair*. Belgium: EPO Publications, 1999. **7.** James, Barry. "Book Revives Fear of Grand Conspiracy: Belgium Pedophilia Scandal / Did Authorities Cover Up Its Scope?" *International Herald Tribune*, 16 Dec 1999. **8.** *Op cit.*, Nicolas: 72. **9.** *Ibid.*: 103. **10.** *Ibid.*: 102.

SUITABLE FOR FRAMING
WAYNE WILLIAMS AND THE ATLANTA CHILD MURDERS
MICHAEL NEWTON

The kidnap-murder of a child is every parent's most horrifying nightmare. The specter of a psychopath at large and killing children by the dozens goes beyond that primal fear, to traumatize entire communities. It is the kind of panic that turns peaceful neighbors into vigilantes, searching for a monster to eradicate.

Atlanta, Georgia, lived with that oppressive fear for two long years, between July 1979 and June 1981. The nightmare was exacerbated by issues of race and politics that threatened to set "the South's most liberal city" on fire. When a solution was finally offered, weary citizens and career-minded politicians embraced it with near-hysterical relief. There was only one problem.

The "solution" solved nothing.

The nightmare endures.

Officially, the Atlanta "child murders" case began on July 28, 1979. That afternoon, a woman hunting for empty bottles and cans along Niskey Lake Road, in southwest Atlanta, stumbled upon a pair of corpses carelessly concealed in roadside undergrowth. One victim, shot with a .22-caliber weapon, was identified as 14-year-old Edward Smith, reported missing on July 21. The other was 13-year-old Alfred Evans, last seen alive on July 25. Pathologists attributed his death to "probable" asphyxiation. Both dead boys, like all of those to come, were African American.

On September 4, 1979, 14-year-old Milton Harvey vanished during a neighborhood bike ride. His body was recovered three weeks later, but the cause of death remains undetermined.

Nine-year-old Yusef Bell was last seen alive when his mother sent him on a shopping errand on October 21. He was found dead in an abandoned schoolhouse on November 8, 1979, manually strangled by a powerful assailant.

Twelve-year-old Angel Lenair was the first recognized victim in 1980. Reported missing on March 4, she was found six days later, tied to a tree with her hands bound behind her. The first female victim, Lenair had been sexually assaulted and strangled; pathologists found a pair of panties, not her own, lodged in the girl's throat.

One day after Lenair's body was recovered, Jeffrey Mathis vanished on an errand to the store. Eleven months would pass before his skeletal remains were found, advanced decomposition ruling out a declaration on the cause of death.

Fourteen-year-old Eric Middlebrooks left home on May 18, 1980, after receiving a telephone call from persons unknown. He was found the next day, bludgeoned to death with a blunt instrument.

The terror escalated in summer 1980. On June 9, 12-year-old Christopher Richardson vanished en route to a neighborhood swimming pool. LaTonya Wilson was kidnapped from her home on June 22, the night before her seventh birthday, thus bringing FBI agents into the case under the Lindbergh Law, which makes kidnapping a federal crime if the victim is taken out of state. (The FBI acts on a "presumption" of interstate abduction after a fixed period of time, but they're much more likely to move in on a case if (a) it's a child and (b) an abduction from home makes it a clear-cut kidnapping.)

Ten-year-old Aaron Wyche was reported missing by his family on June 23. Searchers found his body the next afternoon, lying beside a railroad trestle, his neck broken. Originally classified as an accident, Wyche's death was subsequently added to Atlanta's list of murdered and missing black children.

The killer's pace slowed in July, but he did not abandon the hunt. Nine-year-old Anthony Carter disappeared while playing near his home on July 6; found the next day, he was dead from multiple stab wounds. Earl Terrell joined the list on July 30, when he disappeared from a public swimming pool. His skeletal remains, recovered on January 9, 1981, would yield no clues about the cause of death.

Next on the list was 12-year-old Clifford Jones, sodomized and strangled on August 20, 1980. Eyewitness Freddie Crosby told Atlanta police that he saw a white man, Jamie Brooks, rape and strangle Jones in the backroom of a laundromat Brooks managed. Four other witnesses confirmed Crosby's account of watching Brooks carry a corpse to the trash dumpster behind his laundromat. Under police questioning, Brooks admitted various sexual encounters with young boys, some in the laundromat's backroom. He denied killing Jones, but failed several polygraph tests. Nonetheless, Atlanta detectives ignored the five eyewitness statements, listing Jones with other victims of the "unknown" murderer. (In 1981, Jamie Brooks was convicted and imprisoned for aggravated assault and sodomy on a young boy, in an unrelated case.)

> BOTH DEAD BOYS, LIKE ALL OF THOSE TO COME, WERE AFRICAN AMERICAN.

Eleven-year-old Darren Glass vanished near his Atlanta home on September 14, 1980. He was never found, and joined the growing list primarily because authorities could do nothing else with his case.

Charles Stephens was reported missing on October 9 and was found the next day, his life extinguished by asphyxiation; two Caucasian hairs were reportedly found on the body.

Authorities found the skeletal remains of LaTonya Wilson on October 18, 1980, but they never could determine how she died. Two weeks later, on November 1, Aaron Jackson's frantic parents reported him missing; he was found one day later, another victim of asphyxiation.

Fifteen-year-old Patrick Rogers disappeared on November 10, 1980. His pitiful remains, with his skull crushed by heavy blows, were not recovered until February of the following year.

Two days after New Year 1981, the elusive slayer picked off Lubie Geter, strangling the 14-year-old and dumping his corpse where it would not be found until February 5. Witness Ruth Warren told police that she had seen Geter enter a car driven by a scar-faced white man on the day he vanished, but she had not noted the license number.

Fifteen-year-old Terry Pue disappeared on January 22 and was found the next day, a victim of ligature strangulation. This time, police told the press that special chemicals enabled them to lift a suspect's fingerprints from the corpse. Unfortunately, they were not on file with any law enforcement agency in the United States.

Twelve-year-old Patrick Baltazar vanished the day after Lubie Geter's body was recovered. Another victim of ligature strangulation, Baltazar was found a week later, along with the skeletal remains of Jeffrey Mathis. Thirteen-year-old Curtis Walker was strangled on February 19 and found the same day.

The case took another strange turn on March 2, 1981, when 16-year-old Joseph ("Jo Jo") Bell dropped out of sight. The next evening, Bell telephoned the Atlanta restaurant where he worked part-time and told the assistant manager: "This is Jo Jo. They're about to kill me. I'm about dead. They are about to kill me. Jerry, they're about to kill me." With that, the line went dead.

A friend of Bell's, Timothy Hill, disappeared on March 14, and the same restaurant received another call the following night. This time, the caller was an anonymous woman whose voice "sounded white." She told the café manager "her man" was dangerous—a killer, in fact. She said Jo Jo Bell was "different from the other murdered kids," a friend of hers, and she was trying to negotiate his safe release. Before hanging up, the woman warned that "they" would kill Bell if police were informed of her call. Both Bell and Hill were subsequently pulled from local rivers, their deaths ascribed respectively to asphyxiation and drowning.

On March 30, 1981, Atlanta police added the first adult victim to their list of murdered and missing children. He was 20-year-old Larry

Rogers, linked to several younger victims solely by the fact that he had been asphyxiated.

No cause of death was determined for 21-year-old Eddie Duncan, but he made the list anyway, when his corpse was discovered on March 21. Michael McIntosh, a 23-year-old ex-convict, was added to the list on April Fool's Day, another victim of asphyxiation.

EX-COP AND AUTHOR DAVE DETTLINGER, EXAMINING POLICE MALFEASANCE IN THE CASE, SUGGESTS THAT 63 POTENTIAL "PATTERN" VICTIMS WERE CAPRICIOUSLY OMITTED FROM THE OFFICIAL ROSTER, 25 OF THEM OCCURRING *AFTER* A SUSPECT'S ARREST SUPPOSEDLY ENDED THE KILLING.

■ ■ ■ ■ ■ ■ ■ ■ ■ ■

By April 1981, it seemed apparent that the Atlanta "child murders" case was getting out of hand. Community critics denounced the official victims list as incomplete and arbitrary, citing cases like the January 1981 murder of Faye Yerby to prove their point. Yerby, like "official" victim Angel Lenair, had been bound to a tree by her killer, hands behind her back; she had been stabbed to death, like four acknowledged victims on the list. Despite those similarities, police rejected Yerby's case on grounds that she was a female (as were victims Wilson and Lenair) and that she was "too old" at age 22 (although the latest victim listed had been 23).

Ex-cop and author Dave Dettlinger, examining police malfeasance in the case, suggests that 63 potential "pattern" victims were capriciously omitted from the official roster, 25 of them occurring *after* a suspect's arrest supposedly ended the killing.

In April 1981, FBI spokesmen declared that several of the Atlanta crimes were "substantially solved," outraging the black community with suggestions that some of the victims (left unnamed) had been slain by their own parents. While that storm was raging, Roy Innis, head of the Congress of Racial Equality, went public with the story of a female witness who described the murders as sacrifices committed by a cult involved with drugs, pornography, and Satanism. (The woman, unlike murder suspect Jamie Brooks, passed two polygraph tests.) Innis led reporters to an apparent ritual site, complete with large inverted crosses, but police by that time had focused their attention on another suspect, narrowing their scrutiny to the exclusion of all other possibilities.

On April 21, 1981, 21-year-old ex-convict Jimmy Payne was reported missing from Atlanta. Six days later, when his body was recovered, death was publicly attributed to suffocation, and Payne's name was added to the list of murdered "children." Seventeen-year-old William Barrett disappeared on May 11; he was found the next day, another victim of asphyxiation.

Several bodies had by now been pulled from local rivers, and police were staking out the waterways by night. In the predawn hours of May 22, 1981, a rookie officer stationed under a bridge on the

Chattahoochee reported hearing a "splash" in the river nearby. Above him, a car rumbled past, and officers manning the bridge were alerted. Police and FBI agents halted a vehicle driven by Wayne Bertram Williams, searching his car and grilling him for two hours before they released him. Two days later, the corpse of Nathaniel Cater, a 27-year-old ex-convict, was pulled from the river downstream. Authorities connected the dots and thereafter focused their probe exclusively on Wayne Williams.

From day one, he made a most unlikely suspect. The only child of two Atlanta schoolteachers, Williams still lived with his parents at age 23. A college dropout, he cherished ambitions of earning fame and fortune as a music promoter. In younger days he had constructed a functional radio station in the basement of the family home. Still, he was young and black, as predicted in the FBI's profile of the "Atlanta child killer," and a black suspect was required to cool simmering racial tension in Atlanta.

AUTHORITIES FORMALLY INDICTED WILLIAMS FOR TWO MURDERS, OF ADULT VICTIMS CATER AND PAYNE, ON JULY 17, WHILE NEWSPAPERS TRUMPETED THE CAPTURE OF ATLANTA'S "CHILD KILLER."

Williams was arrested on June 21, 1981, charged with killing Nathaniel Cater—this despite testimony from two witnesses, known to police, who recalled seeing Cater alive on May 22 and 23, *after* the infamous Chattahoochee "splash." Authorities formally indicted Williams for two murders, of adult victims Cater and Payne, on July 17, while newspapers trumpeted the capture of Atlanta's "child killer."

At his trial, convened on December 28, 1981, the prosecution painted Williams as a violent homosexual and bigot, so disgusted with his own race that he hatched a hare-brained plot to wipe out future generations by killing black children before they could breed. Direct evidence was as flimsy as the alleged motive. Witness Robert Henry, himself once imprisoned for sexual assault, claimed he had seen Nathaniel Cater "holding hands" with Williams a few hours before Williams was stopped on the Chattahoochee bridge, but he later recanted that testimony in a sworn affidavit. A 15-year-old witness told the court that Williams had once paid him two dollars for the privilege of fondling his genitals. Meanwhile, police added a final victim, 28-year-old John Porter, to the official list of Atlanta's dead and missing "children."

Defense attorneys tried to balance the scales with testimony from a woman who admitted having "normal sex" with Williams, but the prosecution won a crucial victory when Judge Clarence Cooper (a longtime friend of District Attorney Lewis Slaton) permitted introduction of evidence concerning ten "pattern" murders, though Williams was charged with none of those crimes. The additional victims included Alfred Evans, Eric Middlebrooks, Charles Stephens, William Barrett, Terry Pue, John Porter, Lubie Geter, Joseph Bell, Patrick Baltazar, and Larry Rogers. The "pattern," as described in court, included fifteen separate elements:

1. All victims were black males.
2. All came from poor families.
3. All were raised in broken homes.
4. None of the victims owned a car.
5. All were deemed "street hustlers" by the state.
6. None showed evidence of forcible abduction.
7. All died by strangulation or asphyxiation.
8. All were transported after death.
9. All were dumped near "major arteries" of travel.
10. Bodies were disposed of in "unusual" fashions.
11. Clothing was absent from the murder scenes.
12. No valuables were found with any of the bodies.
13. Similar fibers were found on several victims.
14. No motive was apparent for any of the crimes.
15. Williams denied contact with any of the victims.

Discounting the last two points (which are equally consistent with Williams' claim of innocence) and number twelve (with its contradictory suggestion of robbery as a motive in the slayings), prosecutors still had glaring problems with their "pattern." Seven of the ten were too young to drive, so their lack of cars was superfluous, and victims Middlebrooks and Harvey vanished while riding bicycles. Victims Rogers and Middlebrooks were beaten to death, not strangled or asphyxiated. Edward Smith, a gunshot victim, was excluded from the "pattern" list although his corpse was found with that of Alfred Evans.

Prosecutors likewise ignored the strange phone calls that followed Joseph Bell's abduction (referring to multiple abductors) and their own reported discovery of unidentified fingerprints on Terry Pue's corpse. A witness who described glancing out the window of his workplace, seeing Williams and Lubie Geter together on the day Geter disappeared, was found to be lying; his manager testified that the "witness" had not worked on the day in question. A second witness, Ruth Warren, changed her original story of seeing Geter with a scar-faced white man the day he vanished; in court she described an African American suspect "resembling" Wayne Williams.

The most impressive evidence of guilt was offered by a team of scientific experts, dealing with assorted hairs and fibers found on certain "pattern" victims. Testimony indicated that some fibers from a brand of carpet found inside the Williams home (and countless other homes, as well) had been identified on several bodies. Furthermore, victims Middlebrooks, Wyche, Carter, Terrell, and Stephens all supposedly bore fibers from the trunk liner of a 1979 Ford automobile owned by the Williams family. The clothes of victim Stephens also allegedly yielded fibers from a second car—a 1970 Chevrolet—owned by Wayne's parents.

Curiously, jurors were not advised of a critical gap in the state's fiber case: Wayne Williams had no access to the vehicles in question at the times when three of the five "fiber" victims were killed. Wayne's father took the Ford in for repairs at 9:00 AM on July 30, 1980, some five hours before Earl Terrell vanished that afternoon. Terrell was long dead before Williams got the car back on August 7, 1980, and it was returned to the shop the next day, still refusing to start. A new estimate on repair costs was so expensive that Wayne's father refused to pay, and the family never again had access to the vehicle. As for Charles Stephens, kidnapped on October 9, 1980, Wayne's family did not purchase the 1970 Chevrolet until October 21, twelve days after Stephens' death. At trial, no mention was made of the two Caucasian hairs recovered from Stephens' body.

Wayne Williams was convicted of two murder counts in January 1982 and received a double life sentence on February 27. Two days later, the Atlanta "child murders" task force disbanded, announcing that 23 of 30 official "list" cases were considered closed with Williams' conviction, although he had never been charged. (One of the cases thus "solved" was that of Clifford Jones, excluded from trial testimony to avoid introduction of eyewitness statements blaming another suspect for his death.) The remaining seven cases, still open, reverted to Atlanta's normal homicide detail and remain unsolved today.

In December 1982, the families of twelve Atlanta victims filed suit in federal court, demanding either that Wayne Williams be charged and tried for the deaths of their children, or that the cases be officially reopened. The lawsuit was dismissed, Lew Slaton telling reporters that he would not waste his time or Fulton County's money on another Williams trial.

Georgia's Supreme Court reviewed the Williams case in 1983, with Justice Richard Bell assigned to draft the court's opinion. Bell, a former prosecutor, criticized Judge Cooper for admitting prosecution "pattern" evidence, specifically in regard to victims Baltazar, Evans, Middlebrooks, Porter, and Stephens. As Bell explained in his draft:

> There was no evidence placing Williams with those five victims before their murders, and as in all the murders linked to Williams, there were no eyewitnesses, no confession, no murder weapons and no established motive. Also, the five deaths, while somewhat similar to each other in technique, were unlike the two for which Williams was tried.

After a review of Bell's draft, as detailed in the *Washington Post* two years later, Bell was pressured to change his opinion and finally lent his name to a majority ruling *upholding* the Williams verdict.

Ex-cop Chet Dettlinger and journalist Jeff Prugh published a critique of the Atlanta prosecution in 1983, snaring themselves a Pulitzer Prize nomination in the process. Their book, *The List*, challenged the official myth that "pattern" murders in Atlanta ended with Williams' 1981 arrest. In fact, the authors noted, at least 25 "profile" victims had been slain between the date when Williams was jailed and mid-1983. The dead included sixteen males and nine females, ranging in age from 13 to 28 years. Prugh and Dettlinger named only five, one of them being 21-year-old Stanley Murray, an uncle of "List" victim Curtis Walker. Murray had been gunned down in 1981 near the spot where Walker vanished in February of the same year. The others named included 16-year-old Clarence Davis, 17-year-old Kenneth Johnson, and 23-year-old Roderick Williams (all shot in 1981), plus 13-year-old Lucretia Bell, strangled in her own home in 1983. Prugh and Dettlinger noted: "The List—not the murders—stopped in 1981."

In November 1985, a new team of defense lawyers uncovered once-classified documents concerning an investigation of the Ku Klux Klan, conducted during 1980 and 1981 by the Georgia Bureau of Investigation. A spy inside the Klan told GBI agents that Klansmen were "killing the children" in Atlanta, hoping to ignite a race war that would turn into a statewide purge of blacks. One Klansman in particular, 30-year-old Charles Sanders, allegedly boasted of murdering "List" victim Lubie Geter following a personal altercation. Geter reportedly struck Sanders' car with a go-cart, prompting Sanders to tell the GBI informant, "I'm gonna kill him. I'm gonna choke that black bastard to death." Geter was in fact strangled, some three months after the incident in question. Carlton Sanders, father of Charles and subject of 35 arrests since 1951 (including one for molestation, case dismissed), matched Ruth Warren's original description of the scar-faced white man seen with Geter on the day he vanished.

Another "List victim," Charles Stephens (found with Caucasian hairs on his underclothes), was dumped near a trailer park frequented by brothers Charles, Don, and Terry Sanders.

Based on reports from their informant, GBI agents obtained warrants for wiretaps on the various Sanders telephones. On April 1, 1981, the taps recorded a conversation between brothers Don and Terry Sanders (themselves both Klansmen). The transcript read in part:

> *Don*: Is Ricky around?
> *Terry*: Well, he just left with Kenneth.
> *Don*: Did he?
> *Terry*: Yeah.
> *Don*: Where's he headed?
> *Terry*: To his apartment or something.
> *Don*: Do you think he'll be back?
> *Terry*: Oh yeah.
> *Don*: After a while.
> *Terry*: Yeah.
> *Don*: I'll just give a buzz back, and I might get out and ride around a little bit, and I might come by there.
> *Terry*: Go find you another little kid, another little kid?
> *Don*: Yeah, scope out some places. We'll see you later.

The GBI informant also recounted another conversation with one of the Sanders brothers from early 1981, warning authorities that "after 20 black-child killings they, the Klan, were going to start killing black women." Perhaps coincidentally, police records document the unsolved murders of several black women in Atlanta in 1980-82, with most of the victims strangled.

Armed with new information, Williams and his attorneys continued their battle in court. On July 10, 1998, Butts County Superior Court Judge Hal Craig rejected an appeal based on charges of prosecutorial misconduct (specifically, suppression of exculpatory evidence by D.A. Lewis Slaton) and claims of ineffective representation at trial. A year later, on July 8, 1999, the state Supreme Court reversed that decision on a 4-to-3 vote and sent the case back to Judge Craig for further study. A further eleven months passed before Craig reject-

"THERE WAS NO EVIDENCE PLACING WILLIAMS WITH THOSE FIVE VICTIMS BEFORE THEIR MURDERS, AND AS IN ALL THE MURDERS LINKED TO WILLIAMS, THERE WERE NO EYEWITNESSES, NO CONFESSION, NO MURDER WEAPONS AND NO ESTABLISHED MOTIVE."

ed the new-trial motion a second time, on June 15, 2000. Four years and counting since defense attorney Lynn Whatley called for DNA testing of the state's forensic evidence—vowing to "show there is no linkage in Wayne Williams"—no apparent progress has been made toward scientific resolution of the case.

■ ■ ■ ■ ■ ■ ■ ■ ■ ■

Was Williams framed?

There is no doubt that certain evidence—the Pue fingerprint, eyewitnesses to the Jones murder, apparent Klan links to the Geter case, etc.—were withheld from the defense and from the jury in 1981. Whether or not suppression of that evidence qualifies as criminal misconduct, its introduction at trial would have shattered the state's "pattern" case and might have provided sufficient reasonable doubt for an acquittal.

▌A RACE WAR IN ATLANTA WAS A PERVASIVE FEAR DURING THE "CHILD KILLER'S" REIGN OF TERROR.

Is the Klan conspiracy plausible? We know that Klansmen have committed thousands of atrocities since their organization was founded in 1866. Collusion with racist police to obstruct prosecution has been documented since the days of Reconstruction, and Atlanta has been the Klan's national Mecca since defrocked preacher William Simmons revived the order in 1915. The KKK's "grand dragon," one Samuel Roper, led the Georgia Bureau of Investigation in the 1940s, and Klan membership was a virtual prerequisite for Atlanta police recruits through the early 1950s.

As far as plotting "race war" goes, the theme has recurred among Klansmen and affiliated neo-Nazi groups since the mid-1960s, when long hot summers of ghetto rebellion produced the first echoes of "white backlash" against the civil rights movement. One fascist cult, the World Church of the Creator (WCC), uses RAHOWA!—Racial Holy War —as its motto, while other cliques have progressed from fighting words to action. The most recent example, reported from straitlaced Boston in July 2002, involves the alleged plot by white supremacist (and alleged WCC associate) Leo Felton to bomb prominent black and Jewish targets (Jesse Jackson, Al Sharpton, Steven Spielberg, the Holocaust Museum) to ignite a wave of ethnic cleansing in America, driving Jews and nonwhite "mud people" from the nation.

Preposterous? Of course. But to extremists of the Klan-Creator sort, absurd conspiracies are day-to-day reality, and none the less deadly to innocent victims simply because they spring from addled minds.

More to the point, a race war in Atlanta was a pervasive fear during the "child killer's" reign of terror. One month to the day before Edward Smith and Alfred Evans were found dead in Atlanta, on June 28, 1979, a young white physician was killed by black muggers while attending a medical convention. Four months later, a white legal secretary was killed on her birthday by a mentally unbalanced black assailant. Atlanta's black mayor and police commissioner heard the calls for a crackdown on street crime, along with rumors that a white conspiracy lay behind the murders of young blacks. Indictment of a white suspect, much less an outspoken racist with ties to militant terrorist groups, risked igniting the powder keg. Official Atlanta *needed* a black "child killer," both to defuse the conspiracy talk and to demonstrate for the record that black officials were doing their job without fear or favor.

Would the FBI collaborate to frame an innocent man? The question seems ludicrous today, after exposure of the Bureau's collusion with New England mobsters to convict various patsies for murders committed by active-duty FBI informers. Peter Limone and John Salvati were sentenced to die in Massachusetts for a 1965 gangland slaying they did not commit; their sentences were later commuted to life in prison and both served 30-plus years before they were finally exonerated. Today, one of the FBI agents responsible is himself imprisoned for accepting Mafia bribes, while the man behind the slayings—gangster James ("Whitey") Bulger—is a fugitive on the Bureau's Ten Most Wanted list.

Sadly, the case is not unique. In another Massachusetts frame-up, the Sacco-Vanzetti case of 1920, G-men suppressed exculpatory evidence, infiltrated the defense team, and stole vital money from its coffers. In 1933, FBI agents framed bootlegger Roger Touhy for a kidnapping in St. Paul, Minnesota (actually committed by "Ma" Barker's gang); when jurors acquitted Touhy of that charge, the feds collaborated with rival Chicago mobsters to convict Touhy of a second kidnapping that never occurred. (Touhy was exonerated by a federal court in 1946, murdered by former bootleg competitors soon after his release from prison.) Another case from 1933 saw G-men frame the wife of George ("Machine Gun") Kelly for an Oklahoma kidnapping; 26 years later a federal court exonerated Kathryn Kelly, when the FBI refused to disclose exculpatory evidence suppressed for over a quarter-century. Elmer ("Geronimo") Pratt, a one-time member of the Black Panther Party, spent nearly three decades in a California prison after FBI agents and local police conspired to frame him for murder in the early 1970s.

Those cases, and the belated exoneration of their innocent defendants, are a matter of public record. Others, including the highly suspicious convictions of alleged cop-killers Leonard Peltier and Mumia Abu-Jamal, invite closer scrutiny in light of the FBI's demonstrated propensity for fabricated evidence and perjured testimony. To be sure, Wayne Williams was neither a notorious "public enemy" nor a "radical" minority activist at the time of his arrest, but he was what the doctor ordered for Atlanta in its time of racial crisis.

As for the FBI, its current spokesmen have forgotten the April 1981 statements of their predecessors, blaming black parents for the murder of their own children in Atlanta. Today, retired agents (John Douglas, Robert Ressler, Roy Hazelwood, *et al*.) tout the Williams case in their memoirs as a marvel of psychological profiling, one more instance where G-men worked their magic and inexorably ran their prey to ground.

If only it were true.

Sources

Baldwin, James. *The Evidence of Things Not Seen*. New York: Holt, Rinehart and Winston, 1985.

Dettlinger, Chet, and Jeff Prugh. *The List*. Atlanta: Philmay Enterprises, 1983.

Douglas, John, and Mark Olshaker. *Mind Hunter*. New York: Pocket Books, 1995.

Fischer, Mary. "Was Wayne Williams Framed?" *GQ* (April 1991): 228-35, 264-6.

G. Kelly Associates. *Atlanta Child Murders: Interim Report*. Submitted to the Congress of Racial Equality, December 1981.

Jenkins, James. *Murder in Atlanta*. Atlanta: Cherokee Publishing, 1981.

Newton, Michael. *The Encyclopedia of Serial Killers*. New York: Facts on File, 2000.

Siegel, Micki. "Atlanta Postscript." *US* (30 March 1982): 14-7.

AS FOR THE FBI, ITS CURRENT SPOKESMEN HAVE FORGOTTEN THE APRIL 1981 STATEMENTS OF THEIR PREDECESSORS, BLAMING BLACK PARENTS FOR THE MURDER OF THEIR OWN CHILDREN IN ATLANTA.

SUITABLE FOR FRAMING
MICHAEL NEWTON

The following is an unpublished outtake from my latest book, *Secrets: A Memoir of Vietnam and the Pentagon Papers* (Viking Press, 2002). It was to appear between Parts III and IV of the book but had to be taken out due to space constraints. This passage starts on June 28, 1971, as the *New York Times* and other newspapers continued publishing portions of the Pentagon Papers. For thirteen days, I had been avoiding arrest for leaking the documents on the United States' role in Vietnam. [Part of this outtake is adapted from my earlier book, *Papers on the War* (Simon & Schuster, 1972).]

SPEER
WHAT ALBERT SPEER CAN TEACH GOVERNMENT OFFICIALS ABOUT ACCEPTING RESPONSIBILITY

DANIEL ELLSBERG

After entering the Post Office Building, attorneys Charlie Nesson and Leonard Boudin, my wife Patricia, and I took the elevator to the eleventh-floor offices of the US Attorney, Herbert F. Travers, Jr. Apparently, I wasn't even under arrest yet. They were going along with the script that I was surrendering to the US Attorney, right on the schedule my lawyers had promised. (We had arrived at the Square at almost exactly 10 o'clock.) I introduced myself to Travers and said that I was appearing in response to the arrest warrant. FBI agents in the office placed me under arrest and took me to the US Marshals office for photographs and fingerprinting. Patricia and my lawyers went off to the courtroom where I would be appearing for arraignment.

It was the first time I'd ever been arrested. (The next time, for an action of civil disobedience, was five years later at the Pentagon. Since then I've gone through this process between 60 and 70 times.) It was also the first time I'd stood for a mug shot, but I was an old hand at being fingerprinted. I'd given my prints in the Marine Corps and every time I got a new clearance at RAND, the Defense Department, the State Department.[1]

When I'd cleaned off my fingers, we went up a flight to the courtroom on the twelfth floor, with two Federal Marshals holding my arms tightly (in lieu of handcuffs).[2] With Patricia in the spectator section, I sat behind a brass rail while Leonard Boudin debated Assistant US Attorney Lawrence P. Cohen over bail. Cohen said that the "severity of the crime as measured by the punishment"—a possible ten years in prison and a $10,000 fine—justified setting bail at $100,000. He argued that this was further required because I had eluded the FBI over the weekend instead of turning myself in immediately upon issuance of the warrant. "This suggests the defendant has the resources to remain in hiding and frustrate this court."

Boudin asked in contrast that I be released on my own recognizance. Magistrate Princi expressed a concern that if the defendant were proved guilty of being insensitive to laws protecting secret documents, then "might he not be also insensitive to his obligation to appear if he found things were not going as he anticipated?" Boudin's answer was to read a long list of my accomplishments and former positions, including special assistant to the Assistant Secretary of Defense and special assistant to the United States Ambassador to Vietnam, as evidence of my reliability. Of course, that recital seemed to cut two ways. Recent events leading to my seat at the moment behind the brass rail might suggest that my reliability, from some points of view, was not what it had once been. Furthermore, my lawyer was not entirely candid when he went on to say that the reason I had waited until today to surrender was to avoid the "Roman holiday" atmosphere that sometimes surrounded major FBI arrests. If that had been my objective, it would not have seemed very successful in view of the scene in the Square below. But the magistrate seemed, after all, to be searching for a reason not to have to set bail for me. He asked my lawyers if they would be responsible for my later appearances.

That wasn't the kind of stance I wanted to take. I didn't want to hide behind lawyers. And in explaining my actions or talking about the war or the contents of the Papers, I didn't want my public statements from now on to be framed by lawyers, or to have that appearance. From the beginning, I had Boudin's agreement that I would be my own spokesperson on all matters that weren't legal technicalities. Other lawyers, less in tune with our politics and unconcerned about political objectives in the trial, would have wanted to clamp a lid on me and might have demanded to be the sole channel for communications to the press. I could never have accepted that. But the issue never arose with Boudin and Nesson, or the others who joined our defense team.

My lawyers understood that from my point of view this was a continuous political action, with political objectives. That was true not only of the initial actions and my public statements but of key aspects of the conduct of my legal defense in the trial. I had to be free to talk to the press and the public and to be the judge of what I wanted to communicate. This was one of those moments. One of my main themes was to encourage officials and former officials to acknowledge their personal responsibility for their actions, even in the face of superior orders. And on this day, I was trying to ram home at every possible opportunity that I bore sole responsibility for the actions that had brought me here, not shared with any former colleagues. Before my lawyers could respond to the magistrate's suggestion that they might be responsible for me, I stood up and asked permission to address the court. I said, "Your honor, no one here can take responsibility for me. I am responsible for myself, for my own actions. I ask that my own responsibility for my appearance be accepted."

selves and repeated my hope that the disclosures would help free us from the war. Someone asked if I had any regrets. I said certainly not, that I was very pleased with the way the newspapers had defended the First Amendment. "As a matter of fact, it's been a long time since I had as much hope for the institutions of this country. When I see how the press and the courts have responded to their responsibilities to defend these rights, I am very happy about that as an American citizen."

As I finished speaking to the crowd of press outside the Post Office Building, a *New York Times* reporter identified himself and asked if he could speak to me separately. I had a moment's hesitation, remembering Lloyd Shearer's warning about giving exclusives, that seeming to favor one outlet over another would make other journalists angry. But the *Times* did seem to have a special claim in my case, even though many of the nineteen papers that had followed its lead were also represented in this throng. The reporter ended his story about Monday's events:

After having consented somewhat reluctantly to the interview, [Ellsberg] discussed his motives for publicizing the documents. "I have wanted for about two years to try to raise the issue of personal responsibility and accountability of officials," he said, "not to punish but to make current officials conscious of their responsibility." He took pains to dispute press reports that he was racked by guilt over his role in Vietnam, where he was connected with the pacification program.

"The simple fact is that I never felt tortured by guilt by anything I did in Vietnam," he asserted. "The kind of thing I do blame myself for is not informing myself earlier than I did about the origins of the conflict." He went on to say that his knowledge of the contents of the study was what drove him because it gave him a responsibility.

> "I HAVE WANTED FOR ABOUT TWO YEARS TO TRY TO RAISE THE ISSUE OF PERSONAL RESPONSIBILITY AND ACCOUNTABILITY OF OFFICIALS, NOT TO PUNISH BUT TO MAKE CURRENT OFFICIALS CONSCIOUS OF THEIR RESPONSIBILITY."

I was just trying to make the point. I didn't expect it to be accepted. I had already assumed I would have to spend time in jail while bail was being arranged, and I suspected that my intervention now to reject the magistrate's alternative made that even more likely. But Princi said, "I am going to take you at your word. I am going to put you on $50,000 bail without surety." Releasing me on this "personal recognizance bond" meant I didn't have to put up any cash or bond, though I would be liable for the full amount if I missed any court appearances. He also ordered that my passport be turned over to the court. He said, "You're going to walk out and be free." It was a nice beginning to our two years of court proceedings. Princi set July 15 for a hearing on my removal to Los Angeles, where the case was expected to be tried.

Patricia and I left the courtroom and went down to face a bank of cameras and reporters in the midst of the crowd still filling Post Office Square. I urged everyone to read the documents for them-

Of course, it was more than my reading of the Papers that had given me a sense of responsibility. It was my whole association with the war. In these, my first public comments on my motives after the release of the Papers, I was trying to send a message to my former colleagues, former officials, and researchers and consultants on the war, some still serving as insiders. It was a message about responsibility that I hoped might encourage some of them to do something like what I had done, to go beyond what they might otherwise have thought of doing, ideally to tell the public what they might know, with documents, about current policy.

I must say that my hopes of inspiring some insiders to follow my example didn't seem to meet with much success, so far as I knew. I suspect that failure reflected less the shortcomings of my own efforts than on the success of the Administration's efforts—precisely by putting me on trial facing heavy criminal penalties—to warn them against imitating me. Still, I could have been much more explicit in urging current and former insiders to do just that and in seeking out individuals and addressing groups with that appeal, and in retrospect I wish I had done that. I feared then and later that it would seem self-serving and invidious for me to make that point— "You should consider doing what I did"—and so it would, no doubt. But they needed to hear it from someone, and regrettably, no one else was telling them that.

The Administration's aims in this area were exactly opposite to mine. Its decision to bring an unprecedented criminal prosecution was in large part motivated by its need to dampen the encouragement to potential imitators of my open and unapologetic challenge to the norms of the secrecy system. No doubt Nixon and Kissinger failed to perceive that their secret Vietnam policy was foolish, reckless, and hopeless, but they did understand that many others would see it that way if, by virtue of new leaks, it ceased to be secret from the American public. In this respect of discouraging revelations by others, my prosecution may have been a success, even though some Administration officials may have foreseen that they might not win or sustain a conviction.

In these very first public comments on June 28, my focus on feelings of personal responsibility as a spur to action and revelations reflected a "sermon" I had given just over a month earlier. I had been invited to address the congregation of the Community Church in Boston, which had a long history of speakers on civil rights and antiwar issues. On Sunday, May 23, I chose the topic, "The Responsibility of Officials in a Criminal War."

> **SPEER WAS THE ONLY ONE OF THE DEFENDANTS AT THE NUREMBERG TRIAL WHO ACCEPTED FULL RESPONSIBILITY FOR HIS ACTIONS AND FOR THOSE OF THE REGIME.**

That focus, in turn, had been stimulated just the previous week by reading an interview with Albert Speer—third man in the wartime Nazi hierarchy—in, of all places, the current June issue of *Playboy*. That interview had sent me back to his memoir *Inside the Third Reich*, published that year, 1971. I ended my talk that Sunday by reading aloud a number of excerpts from that book and the interview. It was unusual to be reading from *Playboy* in a church sermon, but this was an unusual interview; in fact, I've never seen one comparable to it. Certainly no American Cabinet officer has ever given an interview like it.

■■■■■■■■■

Speer had spent 20 years in Spandau Prison for his service in charge of war production in Hitler's Third Reich. He had put the time to good use by reflecting on his experience and how he had come to persist so long in so mad and wrongful an enterprise. None of my former superiors or colleagues had had such an opportunity (though Nixon did his best to provide it for me; I was the only American civilian official put on trial for activities related to the Vietnam War). We all could benefit a great deal, it seemed to me, from his reflections, despite the great and obvious differences in the two historical episodes.

Speer was the only one of the defendants at the Nuremberg trial who accepted full responsibility for his actions and for those of the regime. He included those acts in which he had taken no part, even those of which he said he had been ignorant at the time. His fellow defendants were amazed by this position, and his own lawyer urged

him not to take it.

Ever since that trial there have been some observers who felt that by claiming ignorance about the Holocaust yet acknowledging culpability for it nevertheless and showing remorse, Speer was simply following a clever and cynical strategy to minimize his guilt and evade hanging. But that's not at all the conclusion I reach from his writings or the *Playboy* interview. These made a very strong impression on me when I read them in mid-May 1971, at a time when I was still working and hoping imminently to bring the Pentagon Papers to the public, either through the *Times* or Representative Pete McCloskey or Senator Mike Gravel. They were much in my mind, not only when I spoke to the audience at the Community Church— a surprising number of whom, it turned out, were refugees from Hitler's Germany—but a month later when I first faced the press outside the courthouse.

It seemed to me that Speer was setting for himself, and implicitly for others, an unfamiliar and very high standard of accountability. Nevertheless, once you thought about it, it was hard to reject. Taken seriously, it had very challenging implications for myself and for my former colleagues.

Speer was saying that his (claimed) ignorance of certain criminal operations of the regime in which he had been a high official was not a defense, that it did not even attenuate his own responsibility for these crimes. How could that be? He said it was because he had been in a position to know about them, that he could and should have known, and that in effect he chose not to know. And he said that such willed ignorance, far from being an excuse for inaction against such evils, conveyed full responsibility for them (just as if he had fully known, and had failed to do all he could to expose and prevent them). Few Americans have been willing to take that standard seriously; many, both inside and outside government during the Vietnam War, including myself, would stand condemned by it.

Speer writes:

> **[N]ot to have tried to see through the whole apparatus of mystification was already criminal. At this initial stage my guilt was as grave as, at the end, my work for Hitler. For being in a position to know and nevertheless shunning knowledge creates direct responsibility for the consequences from the very beginning....**
>
> **In the final analysis I myself determined the degree of my isolation, the extremity of my evasions, and the extent of my ignorance.... Whether I knew or did not know, or how much or how little I knew, is totally unimportant when I consider what horrors I ought to have known about and what conclusions would have been natural ones to draw from the little I did know. Those who ask me are fundamentally expecting me to offer justifications. But I have none. No apologies are possible."**[3]

"Could it be," John McNaughton once asked me in 1964, as he copied cables about the US-encouraged military coup against the elected president of Brazil, "that our foreign policy is nothing but counter-revolution?"

"If what you say is true," he had said six months later to RAND researchers briefing him on the motivation and morale of Viet Cong guerrillas in Vietnam, "we're fighting on the wrong side." Might it be true? Six months after that I asked McNaughton: "Could Victor Bator be right, in his description of the '54 Geneva Accords? Could we be the ones in greatest violation of that agreement?"

"If we're willing to use B-52s in Vietnam," I had asked myself that spring when they were first employed, "where would we draw the line? What will we end up doing?" All of these were questions that, if pursued, might have led at the least to troubled consciences for us, and trouble for our careers if we had acted on that conscience. It was no accident that we didn't pursue them. It was after these questions were raised—and for that matter, six months after the onset of the Rolling Thunder bombing campaign against North Vietnam, whose hopelessness and wrongfulness was not for me a question at all but a near-certainty—that I volunteered to serve in Vietnam.

Speer, too, acknowledges vague but urgent warnings, evidence for suspicion: Precisely enough, he reflects later in his prison cell, to warn him away from following them up. An old friend, Hanke, came expressly to tell him, in a faltering voice:

[N]ever to accept an invitation to inspect a concentration camp in Upper Silesia. Never, under any circumstances. He had seen something there, which he was not permitted to describe and moreover could not describe. I did not query him. I did not query Himmler, I did not query Hitler, I did not speak with personal friends. I did not investigate—for I did not want to know what was happening there. Hanke must have been speaking of Auschwitz. During those few seconds, while Hanke was warning me, the whole responsibility had become a reality again. Those seconds were uppermost in my mind when I stated to the International Court at the Nuremberg Trial that as an important member of the leadership of the Reich, I had to share the total responsibility for all that had happened. For from that moment on, I was inescapably contaminated morally; from fear of discovering something that might have made me turn from my course, I had closed my eyes. This deliberate blindness outweighs whatever good I may have done or tried to do in the last period of the way. [He had disobeyed and even sabotaged Hitler's direct orders to him to execute a scorched-earth policy in Germany.] Those activities shrink to nothing in the face of it. Because I failed at that time, I still feel, to this day, responsible for Auschwitz in a wholly personal sense.[4]

From 1965 to 1968, and perhaps to this day, Robert McNamara managed to believe that the strict monitoring of targets and Rules of Engagement that he and the President were exerting at their Tuesday Luncheons were reflected on the ground in North Vietnam in a virtual absence of damage to civilians. When Pulitzer Prize-winning *New York Times* reporter and editor Harrison Salisbury came back from Hanoi with the contrary evidence of his own eyes, he was accused by the Defense Department of peddling Communist propaganda.

In our study of Roles and Missions relating to pacification for the Embassy in 1966, one of the 81 recommendations to Ambassador Lodge and General Westmoreland that we singled out as especially important was that an urgent study be made of the actual impact of current practices of bombing and artillery, both the physical consequences in terms of VC and civilians killed and injured and the effects on rural attitudes. Nearly everyone in our study group already believed from his own personal observations that the great majority of our bombing and artillery—aside from close support of ground combat operations—was "counterproductive" in both its human and political effects and should be terminated. But we knew that there would be strong military opposition to any reduction in bombardment. If we had simply proposed to eliminate most of it immediately, we knew our recommendations would be dismissed as subjective and unfounded, even though our group included some of the most experienced Americans in Vietnam, among them John Vann and our leader, Colonel George Jacobson. We thought it would be harder for the various agencies to reject a proposal for a study, which, after all, had never been undertaken.

But it turned out not to be that hard. That was almost surely because those agencies included people who knew as well as we did that such a study would support our personal opinions, that we should stop what amounted to indiscriminate bombing and shelling of the rural population. That was, of course, why such a study had never been done—and was never to be done. But they didn't say that. The Mission Council simply rejected our cautious proposal (along with most of our others), saying that it was "unnecessary." Even the civilian Public Affairs Office opposed it, obviously fearing that any leak to the press of official statistics on civilian damage would have bad effects on public opinion at home. It was for the same reason that no agency collected any data whatsoever on civilian injuries and deaths or projected any estimates of these. It was the institutional counterpart of Speer's (and, I would guess, then-Defense Secretary Robert McNamara's) personal "need not to know."

Two and a half years later, under a new Administration, one of the questions I drafted as part of National Security Study Memorandum-1 (NSSM-1) was: "How adequate is our information on the overall scale and incidence of damage to civilians by air and artillery, and looting and misbehavior by RVNAF [Republic of Vietnam Armed Forces]?" In the spring of 1969, I reviewed for President Nixon the answers from all relevant agencies to this question, which made clear, as I expected, that such information remained inadequate or nonexistent. I reported this to the President, and I drafted a presidential directive on the subject of "Reporting and Compensation of Civilian Damage in South Vietnam."

I proposed that the Secretary of Defense, with the assistance of the Secretary of State and the Director of Central Intelligence, establish procedures assuring comprehensive regular reporting of damage to

IT WAS FOR THE SAME REASON THAT NO AGENCY COLLECTED ANY DATA WHATSOEVER ON CIVILIAN INJURIES AND DEATHS OR PROJECTED ANY ESTIMATES OF THESE.

civilian lives and property caused by US and allied operations. As a base point for this reporting, a study should establish as realistically as possible the magnitude of past and current damage and the nature of current gaps in our knowledge and reporting. The two Secretaries should evaluate the adequacy in scale and promptness of current programs for compensating civilian victims, providing medical aid for civilian injured, and handling refugees, and recommending needed improvements, including US support costs.

A week after I sent this draft memorandum, along with others, to Henry Kissinger for his approval on March 1, 1969, I was told that all the proposals looked worthwhile but that the agencies "had been asked enough questions [by me, in NSSM-1] for the moment." That seemed reasonable, for the moment. But two years later, when the list of studies directed had reached over a hundred, this particular one had still not been included (as Winston Lord had confirmed for me in January 1971, the night I questioned Kissinger at the MIT Runnymede Conference). There were some things Executive officials well knew that they didn't want to know.

I could try to comfort myself by telling myself that I had used opportunities that had come my way to urge my superiors to inform themselves about the human consequences of their policies. The effort had failed, but I had been on the right side of that issue. And yet, as I read Speer's interview, I was forced to remember that the first recommendation was in the middle of my two years in Vietnam. It was followed by another year in which, though I did make other such recommendations, I did not by any means do everything I could have done to inform myself of the dimensions of the burden imposed on the people of Indochina by US firepower, let alone to inform anyone else. And the same was true of my effort in early 1969.

Thus, on that first day "up from underground" when I was asked what I regretted or felt guilty about, what first came to mind was my own long persistence in ignorance—of the full impact of the American way of war upon the people of Indochina and of the history of the conflict bearing on the nature and legitimacy of our involvement. Willful ignorance was not the only thing to blame, in me or in many other people inside and outside government; but it was a fault for which the release of the Pentagon Papers offered a partial cure. On that day and in the days that followed, I was inviting my former colleagues and the rest of the public to take advantage of the Pentagon Papers now and to go beyond them in reducing their own ignorance.

But speaking a month earlier at the Community Church, before the Papers were available to my audience, I focused only on my own experience and what was to be learned from Speer's. In his words, in the interview published that month:

If I was isolated, I determined the degree of my own isolation. If I was ignorant, I ensured my own ignorance. If I did not see, it was because I did not want to see.... In my own case, there is no way I can avoid responsibility for the extermination of the Jews. I was as much their executioner as Himmler, because they were carried past me to their deaths and I did not see. It is surprisingly easy to blind your moral eyes. I was like a man following a trail of bloodstained footprints through the snow without realizing someone has been injured.[5]

What dominated Speer's impressions of the past was the Nuremberg trial itself, with its testimony and photographs that presented, inescapably, not abstract "enemies" but individual human beings, victims, who had become, at last, real to the criminal defendants. As real, one might say, as their own hands. Speer recalled in particular "one photograph of a Jewish family going to its death, a husband with his wife and children being led to the gas chamber. I couldn't rid my mind of that photograph; I would see it in my cell at night. I see it still. It has made a desert of my life."[6]

When I started reading these passages by Speer aloud to the audience at the Community Church, my private mood was detached. I was, in fact, imagining that Robert McNamara, National Security Advisor McGeorge Bundy, Secretary of State Dean Rusk, or the Presidents they served were listening. I was reading to them. But as I reached the stunning image of the trail of bloodstained footsteps, I heard my voice grow low and halting. I paused, and said to my hearers, "I am finding this difficult to read." After a moment, I went on, but I brought the talk to an end. I knew that I was one of the listeners I had imagined. It was my own eyes filling in response, my voice gone husky speaking these indictments.

"IF I WAS ISOLATED, I DETERMINED THE DEGREE OF MY OWN ISOLATION. IF I WAS IGNORANT, I ENSURED MY OWN IGNORANCE. IF I DID NOT SEE, IT WAS BECAUSE I DID NOT WANT TO SEE." — ALBERT SPEER

I was there, too, however minor and "innocuous" and skeptical my role. "How can you be part of this?" Patricia had asked me in Saigon in 1966 (in the very week of our abortive recommendations in the Roles and Missions study), shortly before I drew back from our engagement. Years later, hearing me say once again, truthfully—as I told the Times reporter the day of my surrender in Boston—that I felt no guilt for anything I had personally done in Vietnam, she said: "You know, I always hear you say that. But somehow, you should feel more guilty than you do." It was a while, even then, before I realized that she was right. Yet that knowledge was already implicit in my response to my readings at the Community Church in May.

"My moral failure," Speer says, "is not a matter of this item and that; it resides in my active association with the whole course of events." That accusation—and the more specific ones of willful, irresponsible ignorance and neglect of human consequences, and prolonged blinding of conscience—are truths I must live with.

Endnotes

1. Patricia wasn't with me having the same experience, since for some reason she hadn't been arrested and indicted—as Tony Russo later was—or even named as an "unindicted co-conspirator" like Vu Van Thai, whose prints were found on one volume. After all, since our copying that spring, her fingerprints were all over those documents, probably more even than Tony's. We could never figure out why she wasn't indicted. My own guess had been that the prosecutor didn't want to put her in front of a jury, because she was too sympathetic a figure. We never really knew until ten years later, when we got arrested together, along with Dan Berrigan, protesting the University of California's ties with the Nuclear Weapons Labs. She remarked, as we were all being fingerprinted, that this was the first time she had ever been fingerprinted. I could hardly believe it. I was only seven years older than she was, and I'd given my prints a dozen times before I'd ever been arrested. But our careers had been different. That finally answered why she hadn't been indicted. They had her prints on the Papers, all right, but they didn't have her matching prints on file. Now they did, so she couldn't get away with that again. It made a difference only for her first act of civil disobedience, copying the Pentagon Papers. But that first step was a tall one. **2.** These details and subsequent quotes from the arraignment are from Robert Reinhold's story in the *New York Times*, 29 June 1971, datelined 28 June from Boston. **3.** Speer, Albert. *Inside the Third Reich*. New York: Avon, 1971: 19, 113. Emphasis added. **4.** *Ibid*.: 113. **5.** Albert Speer interview. *Playboy*, June 1971: 72. **6.** *Ibid*.: 74.

THE UNDERSIDE OF DE BEERS DIAMONDS

JANINE ROBERTS

The glitter of a diamond is hard. "It sparkles but is brittle," said William Goldberg, Fifth Avenue diamond merchant. He specializes in the cutting and marketing of million-dollar diamonds. These he purchases from De Beers, the powerful diamond company, which has ruled most of the diamond world for over a hundred years. Goldberg stood with his legs apart to show me a fine diamond, one foot on the sidewalk and the other on the road. He carefully held the diamond over the road and explained, "If I drop it now, it will not break. But if I dropped it over the harder concrete of the sidewalk, it might shatter."

Many dreams were shattered for me as I investigated the diamond world. Any illusion I had that I was examining a world of glamour was to splinter into a thousand shards when I went to see the operational headquarters of De Beers in Kimberley, South Africa.

I drove into the city as it grew dark. I first went to see De Beers' long, elegant, veranda-sided two-story headquarters. A uniformed attendant like that of an elegant hotel greeted me at the entrance. But it was not the officials in this office that I first wanted to see. I asked him for directions to the mining union headquarters.

As I drove into the suburbs where the mining workers lived, dust started to swirl around the car. Children darted from the darkness to vanish from the flickering light of my headlights as I hesitatingly drove on unpaved, unlit roads through the dust storm that enveloped a seemingly endless shantytown. The dust had a peculiar gritty feel. It crusted my lips, irritated them. It reminded me that I was in Kimberley, the town that gave birth to De Beers and the modern diamond trade, for the dust on my lips was kimberlite, the ore from which diamonds are extracted.

It swirled unhindered through razor wire from acres of gray waste tips, from mines dug into Kimberley's heart, clouding the air as it had for a century. But I hoped there would be a change, to see elation in the steps of the black Africans whom the dust enshrouded. Apartheid had been ended. For the first time they were living in a democracy. Much had now changed. A former diamond mineworker was now the Premier in Kimberley.

The miners took me to a meeting with workers in a De Beers hostel by a diamond mine. It was redbrick and marked with a sign forbidding visits after working hours, and stood amid barbed wire-protected wastelands. That night I was taken to the township home of a mineworker where I was to stay, across the road from a diamond mine waste treatment plant. On the way, my host showed me the squatter camps where thousands lived in tiny shanties of corrugated iron. I thus met the people who had won De Beers its fortune.

I should have been better prepared given the length of time I had been engaged in this investigation. But nothing I had read had prepared me for this sea of squatter camps and townships that stretched to the horizon. The city of diamonds on which the De Beers fortune was founded, the city that gave Cecil Rhodes the funds needed to expand the British Empire throughout East Africa, was surrounded by poverty. The sheer scale of destitution overwhelmed me.

> **ON THE WAY, MY HOST SHOWED ME THE SQUATTER CAMPS WHERE THOUSANDS LIVED IN TINY SHANTIES OF CORRUGATED IRON. I THUS MET THE PEOPLE WHO HAD WON DE BEERS ITS FORTUNE.**

Near a diamond waste reprocessing plant within these "suburbs," I came across a vast graveyard that was evidently for blacks only. Many graves were marked by heaps of rough rocks. Many were freshly dug. Sometimes these heaps were covered by the signs of grief of the extremely poor: a cracked jug, an old teapot, broken cups. From the graves' sizes, many were of children. Some had black tombstones. Others had the name of the dead scratched on a piece of metal. Many were nameless. The wall around the graveyard was cheaply erected of rough rocks without municipal help. Not far away, on the city side of the blacks' township, was the large white graveyard, its graves spaced in wide, neat lawns. The fence around it was high and robust. Thus apartheid seemingly survived even in the world of the dead.

■ ■ ■ ■ ■ ■ ■ ■ ■ ■

I had come to see how De Beers was doing in post-apartheid Africa. When I arrived in Johannesburg, the National Union of Mineworkers, by a fortunate coincidence, was about to hold a conference for shop stewards from De Beers' diamond mines. As part of this, they had planned to show our film, *The Diamond Empire*. They were surprised and delighted when I turned up, and they asked me to talk to the miners about what we had discovered while making the film for the BBC.

I did this—and was then enthusiastically invited to all of the mines.

Three days later I hired a car and set out to Kimberley, some five hours drive from Johannesburg. Every town I passed had a sister town of hovels. A constant stream of black servants walked back and forth along dirt paths, some in cleanly pressed uniforms, some in gardening or garage overalls. They were servicing the homes of the white folk.

> **A DE BEERS TRUCK DRIVER IN 1994 TOLD ME HIS TAKE-HOME PAY FOR A 50-HOUR WEEK WAS 96 RAND—ABOUT US$28 OR £18, NOW ABOUT £10.**

Around Kimberley the townships are divided by large, overgrown heaps of blue rock, the remains of diamond mines. Excavators and bulldozers moved through the haze, busily reprocessing the waste rock to check for diamonds that might have been missed earlier. De Beers sold the waste at so much a truckload to licensed contractors who had to sell any diamonds they found back to De Beers—the only permitted buyer. I stopped by a gate to talk to some black women. They told me they were waiting to make sure their men did not waste their pay. A De Beers truck driver in 1994 told me his take-home pay for a 50-hour week was 96 rand—about US$28 or £18, now about £10.

A senior government official said they had asked De Beers to contract unemployed black workers to search these waste tips for missed diamonds. The answer was, No way! The reason given was that blacks would gather like "vultures" (De Beers' word) to search for diamonds, and this would encourage "illicit diamond buying" (IDB). Instead, De Beers was selling these waste tips to Canadian diamond enthusiasts.

In South Africa the law prohibiting IDB stipulated that any rough, uncut diamond found on public land must be sold to the government, which then resells it to De Beers. Africans gasped with amazement when I told them I had seen diamonds being openly traded on the street in Bombay and New York. For them to do this would mean jail. Despite this, I learned that there was a highly secretive local black market in diamonds run by men who hated De Beers for its low wages and mean treatment of workers.

The miners over the next days drove me along countless miles of potholed and rock-strewn dirt roads lined with shacks, showing me the more substantial yet tiny, overcrowded homes and not showing me the poorer for fear of shaming their owners. Despite their poverty, residents were house-proud. The owners of even the poorest homes took care every day to remove the dust from their steps and windowsills.

The bare earth surrounding the hovels was raked daily and attempts were made at gardens. In the evening their windows were lit by weak electric lights or by flickering flames, as many could not afford electricity. Power bills could easily amount to R300 a month per household, the entire income of a worker on the diamond dumps. Two-thirds of South Africans had no electricity in their homes.

In the Kimberley Mines Division of De Beers, there were between 1,200 and 1,400 workers, of which 1,100 were black. Most lived in the townships and squatter camps. A senior government official in Kimberley told me that when they had approached De Beers for financial help to rebuild these homes in the name of the Reconstruction and Development Program (RDP) of the ANC government of National Reconciliation, De Beers replied that they had given their annual R120,000 from their Chairman's Fund and could give no more.

I also visited the suburbs constructed for white miners and managers. These had names such as "De Beers" and "Ernestville," after diamond magnate Ernest Oppenheimer. The homes were spacious, green with lawns, well garaged; the only inadequacy was in the "maids' quarters." These were not large enough to house the numbers of servants employed. Thus, early every morning I saw crowds of black women servants walking to work over dusty paths from the townships and taxi stands.

The major tourist attraction in Kimberley is the "Big Hole," a vast crater of terraced sides descending to cliffs above an extremely deep lake— a diamond mine abandoned not because it had run out of diamonds but because it was endangering the stability of the town center. The dusty tips it created are scattered throughout the town. The miners took me to another big hole on the outskirts of the city, disused and dangerously ill protected. The debris of diamond mining surrounds Kimberley. The museum at the official "Big Hole" told of the exploits of the white prospectors, of the first miners, of Cecil Rhodes and the siege of Kimberley when guns, ammunition, and an armored train were manufactured in De Beers' workshops as Boers and English fought for the diamond mines. But I saw no mention of the thousands of black miners whose labor built the mines or of the important role played by Kimberley's diamond bosses in developing apartheid.

■ ■ ■ ■ ■ ■ ■ ■ ■ ■

Up until the discovery of diamonds in South Africa in the 1870s, most Southern African nations or "tribes" were economically independent of the white settlers. They supplied the first miners with meat from their cattle herds and farming products. These black nations at first controlled the alluvial diamond fields by the Orange River, traded in diamonds, and restricted the white prospectors' use of mining equipment. When large diamond deposits in Kimberley were found on the dry plateau to the east of the river, the Africans at first worked these deposits for white prospectors in order to earn the funds they needed to purchase such goods as guns. When they had what they needed, they quit the mines and returned to their farms.

As the diamond diggings got deeper, the small mine companies became increasingly dependent on black labor to remove the ore, break it up, and repair the roads that constantly collapsed into the diggings. The wages paid to the black miners made up three-quarters of the costs of the white owners. So in July 1876, the owners formed a combine to try to slash black wages in half. The result was devastating. Four thousand black miners stopped work and went home. They did not return until wages were restored to their former level. As the Africans traditionally lived by barter, they did not require cash to survive. This gave the mine bosses little control over them.

Then taxes were imposed that had to be paid in cash, which could only be obtained by working for whites. This forced the Africans to leave their farms for the mines. Soon touts were auctioning black workers in the Market Square in Kimberley as if they were slaves.

The touts took a fee equal to four months of a miner's wages. The employers got their workers but regretted having to pay the touts.

The mine owners also worried about workers supplementing their meager wages by retaining diamonds. Many workers, both white and black, saw little wrong in keeping a portion of the finds. Owners estimated that 30 to 40 percent of the stones found went into this secret distribution system. In 1883, the mine owners passed a law allowing them daily to search all employees, white and black. Black employees (but not whites) were in the future forced to wear shapeless mealie flour sacks at work so they had no pockets in which to hide diamonds. In April 1884, white workers who refused to be searched were sacked by the Kimberley mines. Black workers then went on strike in sympathy. The strike was put down by force, killing six white miners. Shortly after this, the daily searching of white employees ceased.[1]

In 1879, a Cornish mine engineer, T.C. Kitto, advocated the mining companies adopt the methods used with black slaves in Brazilian diamond mines. He wrote: "The blacks are housed in barracks built in the form of a square,... an overseer locks them in every night.... I believe the natives of South Africa, under European supervision, are capable of being made almost—if not quite—as good as the blacks of Brazil, providing they are dealt with in the same manner."[2] The mine owners thought this an excellent suggestion that would keep down wages and stop theft. In 1882, Cecil Rhodes advocated that all De Beers' black workers (but not white) should be confined to barracks when not at work. He calculated that the profits that could be made from selling food to the captive workers would pay half of De Beers' labor costs. In July 1886, De Beers confined its 1,500-strong black workforce in barracks. By 1889, all the 10,000 black miners in Kimberley lived in these locked compounds.

BLACK EMPLOYEES (BUT NOT WHITES) WERE IN THE FUTURE FORCED TO WEAR SHAPELESS MEALIE FLOUR SACKS AT WORK SO THEY HAD NO POCKETS IN WHICH TO HIDE DIAMONDS.

These were in fact real prisons, for De Beers mixed convicts with blacks to further minimize labor costs. From 1884 to 1932, De Beers used hundreds of convicts as workers, paying a minimal fee to the government instead of paying wages. Ironically, or perhaps deliberately, many of these convicts had only been imprisoned for not having travel passes. They had been forced by the taxes to come to the diamond mines to seek paid work despite not having these hard-to-get passes.

Families were excluded from the compounds. When the miners wanted to leave a compound, they were usually dosed with mild laxatives, stripped, and locked into cells for five to ten days with their hands fastened into leather bags. Every part of their bodies and even their excrement was then inspected for diamonds. De Beers was determined that not a single diamond would escape its grip. Eventually they used a newly invented machine to more dependably search human stools for secreted diamonds.

These diamond mine practices became enshrined in legislation, and thus helped shape the new apartheid system. In 1889, it was decreed: "No native shall work or be allowed to work in any mine, whether in open or underground mining, excepting under the responsible charge of some particular white man as his master or 'baas.'"

The richest of all the diamond mines, the Oppenheimer, controlled CDM in South West Africa (now Namibia), initially importing cheap black labor from Botswana. The author Colin Newberry reported: "By 1923 over half the labor force of 5,000 consisted of outside recruits from northern Botswana who suffered a high mortality rate...with scurvy or tuberculosis."[3] Some also died from dehydration and exhaustion while searching the desert sands for diamonds. Laurie Flynn, who has extensively written on southern Africa and was a researcher on *The Diamond Empire*, reported seeing one of the houses provided. It was like "a telephone box set on its side."[4] Strict company regulations governed the lives of the miners. These regulations had in practice the force of law, as the company paid the local police wages and expenses.

Soon the Oppenheimers were running their Namibian mine under the same apartheid system they had helped develop in South Africa. The company town they built, Oranjemund, had all the usual conveniences, including married quarters for the white workers and only single-sex hostels for black workers. The workforce became Ovambo tribesmen recruited en masse in northern Namibia. They were only allowed to travel south to the mines if they had a contract. They could not bring their wives or families. They were not allowed into retail stores, cinemas, or clubs, all of which were owned by the company. Everything was segregated. There were separate counters for whites and blacks in the post office. Blacks had to wait to be served at the back of the store. The blacks got on average less than a tenth of the pay for whites. An internal CDM report on mine costs said that they were paying African workers an average of R61 a month, while paying white workers an average of R767.[5]

In 1969, the United Nations revoked South Africa's authority over Namibia. Two years later, the World Court upheld this decision. In 1971 and 1972, the Ovambo contract workers withdrew their labor en masse from the diamond mine, protesting that their contracts were unjust, and, risking arrest, they returned home. On January 10, 1972, after a large protest meeting at Oluno, Ondongwa, an agent reported to De Beers that the workers were furious about the "kontrak" and the "Draad" (the latter meant the "fence" or "prison," meaning their quarters at the mine).[6] They complained that they were not allowed to change jobs and could be rounded up, jailed, or forcibly returned if they left their workplace. They could not go home for family sickness or family emergencies. They were frequently humiliated by being publicly stripped naked for medical examinations. It was a form of slavery. One speaker said:

Every person is perfectly created by God, but the contract system leads to complete indifference to human value, which was created by God himself.... The contract system has changed the so-called homelands into a slave labor market.... This slavery has resulted in Ovambo compounds in the form of a prison, with one entrance and sharp pieces of glass cemented on the top of walls, and hard beds made out of concrete which cripples the people.[7]

Such concrete beds were also the rule in Kimberley hostels near the De Beers headquarters until very recent years (they were shown to me in 1994).

An internal De Beers managers' report of October 1972 reported that the miners complained of poor pay and food and the lack of privacy in hostels, where ten men shared a prison-like room with closed windows at ceiling height. They could not stay up at night, for the lights were switched on and off at fixed times from the administration block. There were no dining halls. There were no partitions, cubicles, or doors in the lavatories, so people had to defecate in public. (I found similar conditions continued throughout the 1990s in South African diamond mines.)

But these conditions were not just in the diamond mines. There was appalling accommodation also in Oppenheimer's gold mines. An internal March 1976 report by Anglo American staff of the Western Holdings mine reported the black miners as saying: "We live like animals in the compounds without our wives.... The life we lead here is worse than slavery or the life of a beast of burden." (Again, it was the same in 1994 at De Beers mines.) When Anglo asked the Chamber of Mines' Human Resources Laboratory to analyze working conditions, they found "poor pay, inferior living conditions, severe food shortages, dirt." It was calculated that bringing black accommodation up to full white worker standards would cost a quarter of a year's profits. This deterred change.

Oppenheimer argued that his companies could not use their strength and dominance of South African industry to pressure the South African government to adopt more liberal policies. "We have to co-operate with the government on many occasions. It would be quite wrong to use Anglo to pressure the government." But former South African Prime Minister H.F. Verwoerd disagreed. He said Oppenheimer "can pull strings. With all that monetary power and with his powerful machine, which is spread over the whole of the country, he can, if he so chooses, exercise an enormous influence against the Government and the State."

The National Union of Mineworkers was set up in Kimberley only in the 1980s, although there had been many earlier attempts to organize workers. The 1987 strike involved 340,000 workers in 44 mines and was the largest in South African history. During this, the police raided the union offices and arrested the entire regional leadership. The mine compounds were forcibly entered with armored vehicles. Fifty thousand workers were dismissed, and union organization was forced underground. In early 1994, bomb blasts shattered union offices. But after the ANC election victory that year, the threat sharply diminished. By late 1994, NUM was one of the strongest of the South African unions, although somewhat weakened by losing many officials who were elected to Parliament.

■ ■ ■ ■ ■ ■ ■ ■ ■ ■

In Kimberley in 1995, the union asked permission of De Beers for me to go into two diamond mines, Koffiefontein and Finsch. The union branch secretary, Joseph Leburu, told me such requests were always granted, and indeed the signs were good. But a few days later, Leburu called me into his office: "The branch officers of the union were called in by De Beers yesterday for what it called an 'urgent divisional meeting.' We were simply told the General Manager, John Vassey, wanted to see us. When we entered, we were told they had instructions from Head Office that you were not to be allowed in because of your association with *The Diamond Empire* film. It was a two-minute meeting." Leburu said he could not remember anyone else getting banned—at least since the 1985-6 State of Emergency.

The ban made De Beers mineworkers even more interested in the film—and in talking to me. They quietly arranged to watch it on De Beers' premises and afterwards commented that they thought it very accurate. If the company had let me come to the mines, no doubt I would have had a sanitized and bowdlerized tour of all the cleanest areas of the mines. Instead, I now learned about conditions in the more dangerous parts of the mines from the viewpoint of the miners.

> THEY COMPLAINED THAT THEY WERE NOT ALLOWED TO CHANGE JOBS AND COULD BE ROUNDED UP, JAILED, OR FORCIBLY RETURNED IF THEY LEFT THEIR WORKPLACE.

At Koffiefontein, a 90-minute drive south from Kimberley in the Orange Free State, a shop steward took me to view the mine pit, a vast circle of cliffs surrounding what looked like rotting gray cheese. This center was the diamond-rich core, made up of a blue-gray kimberlite that decays when exposed, powdering into fine dust. The mine was now too deep for the use of the terraced roads that still spiraled down into the pit. Instead, shafts had been sunk, lifts installed, and tunnels driven horizontally into the pipe. The holes I saw in the decaying kimberlite were the tunnels through which diamond ore was now extracted and the pits ventilated. Rock falls were frequent, as were dust storms.

Sometimes mudflows closed down a mine, as at Wesselton in 1992. The Kimberley mine by 1992 was 995 meters (3,264 feet) deep, the Finsch 680 meters (2,231 feet), and the Koffiefontein 370 meters (1,214 feet).

The diamond mine was surrounded by razor wire. The entrance gate was more appropriate to that of a prison, a fortress constructed to stop diamonds escaping. The mine was about to start reprocessing the vast waste hills nearby, looking for any diamonds it had earlier missed. These hills were secluded behind more barbed-wire fences patrolled by trail bikes and four-wheel-drives driven by people from outside Koffiefontein, since the mine did not trust local people.

I spoke at a mass meeting of the miners of Koffiefontein about my research and the effort by De Beers to ban me. They told me what life underground was like. Explosive methane gas was a constant danger. Dust blew in thick clouds from the holes in the crater floor to obscure vision throughout the mine. Sometimes they could not see more than three yards. They said: "Dust is thick everywhere, on every level. It blocks our noses with black stuff despite our flimsy nosebags [dust masks]. It is especially bad when mixed with the fumes from the blasting." They said that the mine management took scant care for their welfare. Ventilation and dust control measures were appallingly bad on all levels. A worker told me that when they had showers after work, "We even have to bring our own soap."

I asked about health problems from the dust.

"Yes, many of us have lung and breathing problems. When the mine inspector comes, he just visits what the mine manager shows him."

"What about medical records?"

"De Beers controls all health matters. Medical certificates from doctors that do not work for De Beers may not be accepted. We are told we must get a certificate from one of the two De Beers doctors. These doctors do not listen to us. If the doctor sees you can't breathe properly, they retrench you, certifying you are healthy, then, when you are offered work, perhaps two months later, they then discover you are too sick to be employed! The mine chases you out so it won't have to pay [sick pay or compensation]."

I asked: "Are many miners laid off as sick?"

"De Beers hires workers as temporary in the first place—and if they fall sick they say the 'lungs are wet' and so cannot make them permanent. It is hard for us to get compensation even if permanent. White workers with damaged lungs get R49,000 to R51,000. Colored workers get over R30,000. But R2,800 is the maximum for black workers."

When I gained entry into Finsch, despite being banned from it, I soon found out how very dangerous was the dust in the diamond mines. I learned that the rock within the diamond pipe sometimes contains a dangerous form of serpentine, more commonly called asbestos. The union's Health and Safety Officer told me that mine staff had privately confided to him that asbestos made up 30 percent of the dust contaminating most levels of the Finsch mine—although the management had denied this, admitting to only 1.5 percent asbestos. Since asbestos is so dangerous that a building in which it is found in England would be immediately sealed until fully protected workers could remove it, even the level admitted by management is a cause for much alarm. At Finsch, remote-controlled trucks extracted dangerously decayed diamond-rich rocks directly from the bottom of the 423-meter deep open pit, but this created still more dust clouds.

> "MEDICAL CERTIFICATES FROM DOCTORS THAT DO NOT WORK FOR DE BEERS MAY NOT BE ACCEPTED. WE ARE TOLD WE MUST GET A CERTIFICATE FROM ONE OF THE TWO DE BEERS DOCTORS."

The Health and Safety Officer told me: "Some levels of the mine are more filled with asbestos than others. Sometimes the diamonds lie in asbestos. The dust is often so thick one can only see a meter ahead. We sometimes get nosebags to wear, but we are told the mine hasn't that many, and we must make one nosebag last at least a year. In 20 minutes a new mask gets filled with dust and stops working properly. Our noses are always getting plugged up, filled with black muck. The smell of the chemicals used in explosions also gives us heavy headaches, affects our sinuses." The hills near Finsch are officially called "the Asbestos Hills" because they are full of this dangerous mineral. Prospectors looking for asbestos, not diamonds, had discovered Finsch.

As for ventilation, another miner alleged: "Many of the fans in the underground mine have not been working for over two years." The union safety officer added: "They say electricity is so expensive that they have to turn off the fans and dust extractors for whole days at a time." He emphasized, "The whole mine is full of dust." If these accounts of dangerous cost-saving measures are true, it is no wonder that the mining superintendent at Finsch, Mark Button, could boast in 1994: "Our costs compare with the best in the De Beers group."[8] I do not imagine they pay out much for funeral expenses of blacks.

I researched the asbestos allegations. A Kimberley doctor told me he never saw the miners most affected by the dust. Only miners paid at C-band or higher had the needed health insurance. "The A- and B-band miners [the black miners], who are the most exposed, have no health insurance. De Beers' doctors instead give them free medical aid—and keep their health records secret. Only these doctors have the relevant health records." The De Beers doctors had asked De Beers for a modern X-ray machine, but they were still using a model that belonged in a museum. I checked with a senior nurse at a Kimberley hospital. She said that she had many patients with inflamed lung disorders that were similar to asbestosis. She did not know of any relevant independent research.

At the suggestion of a Kimberley doctor, I asked staff at the De Beers geology department if they knew of any studies of asbestos content in mine dust. They did not. But I discovered reports by Russians saying that asbestos dust was a grave problem in Russian diamond mines, so the lack of published information on this in South Africa was remarkable. I found myself asking, How dangerous was the dust that blew from the mines over the townships and the children's playing grounds? What price were black South Africans paying for De Beers' negligent management of its diamond mines?

Another health danger was the X-rays used in diamond mines to detect diamond theft. I was told at Koffiefontein: "The washing plant and sorting house workers go everyday to the X-ray." At a De Beers mine on the coast, a De Beers security guard who operated the X-ray machines explained: "Many black miners are X-rayed daily as they leave the premises, but they do not know it. My boss sets the rates for X-raying. It can vary, but I am told it should not be done generally more than three to four times a week. But I have a manual override, and when I am suspicious I can do it more often. I have to do it more often to protect myself if a miner is suspected, as I am responsible if a miner is found to have smuggled out a diamond. On the forms we only mark up three X-rays per person a week. If there are more X-rays a week for any miner, these are recorded on the forms under 'S' for 'Search' or 'O' for 'Other.' Management knows what is happening."

The "General Rules for X-Raying," signed by Judy Alexander, the Senior Security Officer at the De Beers mine at Kleinzee, on November 19, 1992, stated: "The maximum permissible dose may not be exceeded i.e. 350 mr per year (about 3-4 shots per week, 12 -15 per month or 150 per year)." The X-ray operating security officer said when I showed this document to him: "There is no way the health authorities can discover how often a man is X-rayed. He can be X-rayed several times a day. De Beers is using a new pelvic area X-ray. It is supposed to be safe, but pregnant women are barred from working in the mine's security areas, as they are not to be X-rayed. We don't know what effect these X-rays have on our own fertility." He added that the operators have a film badge for their own protection but no protective clothing.

At the Kimberley mines the X-rays for the "red," high-security area are not pelvic sensitive but head-to-toe—and can mistake a swallowed peanut for a diamond. One such unfortunate man was rushed to the hospital for a high-powered X-ray before they discovered the error.

At Koffiefontein I was taken to inspect the accommodation provided for miners. De Beers had provided some black families with round metal homes, like water tanks with roofs. They were bitingly cold in winter and blisteringly hot in summer. The National Party, prior to the 1994 elections, decided it could not leave the provision of housing for blacks solely to the ANC. They obtained land by the mine and put one water tap in each housing block. That was that. These were "serviced blocks" without sewerage or electricity. Desperately poor families, some trying to live on De Beers' wages, some unemployed, had to build their own homes on the blocks. All they could afford were tin shacks. But they were allowed to name each block—so they named their apartheid housing after the heroes of the resistance.

But even these shacks were threatened when a diamond was found nearby. De Beers, like a miser who wants no one else to be rich, surrounded the area of the discovery with barbed wire and covered it deeply with heavy waste so that no one else might find a diamond there. Shop Steward Joseph Botile took me there and told me: "It was very beautiful here. Our children used to play here under the trees."

Nearby, more land had recently been locked up behind high razor-wire fences solely because three white children found a diamond there. This area had been used by the black community to graze the donkeys that pulled carts which served them as taxis into town. Behind the new fences I saw strips of bare earth raked so any footprint could be detected. De Beers seemed to have ultimate control over all land used by blacks.

I was also taken to the town dump. The refuse was thrown into a disused diamond digging where blue kimberlite rock could still be seen. As I drove up to it, I passed children walking back to the slums carrying boxes with their scanty finds on their heads. When I arrived at the dump, I found mothers gathering food scraps into plastic bags while four-year-old children played in the refuse. Old people tottering on walking sticks were also looking for food. One shouted at children, telling them not to take some firewood, as he needed it. The children dropped the wood and gathered more. One child inspected soft-drink bottles for any remaining liquid. A little girl in a brown dress, hair neatly braided, left the tip carrying a plastic bag and dragging a large piece of firewood. A ten-year-old followed her with an old Tupperware box and firewood. The children were not playing, as I first thought, but working.

It took me some time to discover the subcontracted or "migrant" labor hidden inside De Beers property. Without announcing my presence to management, I went to meet the miners living on De Beers mining leases, driving somewhat nervously up a road that bypassed the main gate. They took me first to see the accommodation provided by De Beers. There were no longer concrete beds, as

were provided earlier at Bultfontein mine. They were now in school-like dormitories or two to rooms about eight feet wide. Some rooms had no doors. The toilets were dilapidated. Cooking equipment was of the camping sort and minimal.

But I was astonished to be told by the miners that most of them were no longer officially working for De Beers—even though they lived in De Beers buildings on De Beers land and were working underground in a De Beers mine. They were formally working for contractors, former white employees of De Beers who were paid by De Beers to recruit and run teams of black workers.

There were approximately ten such teams of between eight and 50 members at Koffiefontein. Some members were paid only R180 a month (US$53 or £35). The average was between R300 and R400 a month. If directly employed by De Beers, their minimum union-negotiated pay would have been R1,070 a month (US$295 or £194). They were not allowed to join the union. The highest paid subcontracted man I met told me he made R600—but this was for working seven days a week, nine hours a day.

The subcontracted workers were accommodated in much worse conditions than the regular De Beers workers. They told me that they also worked in much more dangerous conditions than did the mineworkers directly employed by De Beers. A shop steward explained that as they were not working directly for De Beers, the company allegedly claimed to have no responsibility for their safety. "Some subcontracted teams have no safety gear. They have no protection. No medical or unemployment provision protects them." They told me they wanted to find a way to join the union. "But if our boss should find out, we would be sacked. The boss would throw us out and drive to Lesotho to get replacements."

When I gained entry to Finsch without De Beers' permission, I found it was a more modern mine than Koffiefontein, with newer facilities, even with its own church, where I thought things would be better. But they were far worse. The hostels were hidden deep inside De Beers property, accessed by private roads and invisible to the public. Again the hostels were single-sex. Those for De Beers' directly-employed workers were fine outside, surrounded with lawns with neat edges, but inside, again there was no privacy. The miners shared small rooms with enough space for a single bedside table between their beds. The showers had no curtains or doors, were dirty and ill maintained. The floors both inside and outside the toilets were cracked, broken, filthy, and stank.

"THEY SAY ELECTRICITY IS SO EXPENSIVE THAT THEY HAVE TO TURN OFF THE FANS AND DUST EXTRACTORS FOR WHOLE DAYS AT A TIME."

But down the side of a hill below the mine, still on De Beers property, I found the hostels for subcontracted labor. Here about 500 men were accommodated, one half of the subcontracted labor force at Finsch, according to an ANC Member of Parliament, Godfrey Oliphant, a former mineworker. (He told me that half the 2,000-strong workforce at Finsch was subcontracted.) The union took me on a tour. In one building the floor had rotted away, leaving large holes covered with dustbin and saucepan lids. In one building they could not use bedsteads because the bed legs went through the rotten floor timbers—so they slept on the floor. Some rooms slept up to fourteen in crowded bunks. Cooking facilities were primitive. The shower had no roof and doubled as a refuse dump. Their tiny store had the barest essentials, like white sugar and tea. Rubble and waste covered the ground around the hostels. All of this was on De Beers property in one of their newest mines.

As for the wages, a worker in this camp told me he received only R310 a month. This was one-quarter of union minimum rates. Another reported that he received far less, R165 (US$48 or £30) for a whole month's work. There were nine contractor gangs at Finsch, all white-controlled. A union organizer told me that when workers were laid off temporarily because De Beers requirements for diamonds had dropped (500 were thus laid off in August 1992), they were replaced by cheaper, non-unionized contract labor when production rose again. The black workers bitterly told me that the "white contractors are living in splendor on the basis of slave labor."

I was also smuggled in to meet the miners in the sparsely furnished older hostels in the Dutoitspan mine, close to Kimberley's town center. They said that De Beers had also introduced contract labor into their mine and that these workers stayed in the same hostel as them—but received less than a third of union rates and were sacked if they joined the union. They feared this practice was spreading. They told me, "We cannot help a contractee if they are wounded. They have no health protection. De Beers says it is not us, it is the contractor who is responsible." This system was being expanded with new contractor teams while I was there.

> IN ONE BUILDING THE FLOOR HAD ROTTED AWAY, LEAVING LARGE HOLES COVERED WITH DUSTBIN AND SAUCEPAN LIDS.... THE SHOWER HAD NO ROOF AND DOUBLED AS A REFUSE DUMP.

De Beers allegedly denied any responsibility for these low-paid workers, despite a provision in the Mines legislation making a mining company responsible for the well-being for all on their mine's land. De Beers took responsibility only for the workers it directly employed, but even then paid them at a minimal rate—R1,060 to R1,500 a month, scarcely enough to support a family. Apartheid is officially abolished in South Africa, but literate and intelligent black miners told me how De Beers still appointed "unqualified, illiterate whites over us, even when we are much more qualified. They are stupid. Some cannot even write reports. One could not even spell 'weekend.' De Beers bends over backwards to help them, but it is very hard for us to get promotion or further training." No white gets employed below the C2-band wage, while nearly all blacks are in the low-paid A- and B-bands.

When the unionized mineworkers of Kimberley asked De Beers for more pay, De Beers' General Manager complained: "Ordinary people were keeping diamonds in Angola. We have no control over these people. They are giving diamonds into the wrong hands. We have to pay them market prices, so we cannot afford to pay you more." They were referring to buying diamonds mined by UNITA, which would eventually get banned as "blood" or "conflict" diamonds because they were helping to fund a murderous war.

De Beers today says the diamonds it mines are free from any such taint. But you, my reader, must judge for yourself. For me, the diamonds that De Beers mines in South Africa and Namibia are deeply steeped in blood and exploitation. There is no need to mine diamonds this way. The profits are vast. International attention should move from ending the trade in conflict diamonds to reforming this cancer at the heart of the diamond world. Only when diamonds are mined with care for the health and well-being of all concerned, and cut with care, without exploitation, only then should anyone dare to sell diamonds as symbols of human love.

Endnotes

1. NUM Mining Handbook, Vol.1: 122. **2.** *Ibid*.: 123. **3.** Newbury, Colin. *The Diamond Ring: Business, Politics and Precious Stones in South Africa, 1867-1890*. Oxford: Clarendon Press, 1989: 243. **4.** Flynn, Laurie. "*Studded with Diamonds and Paved with Gold*." London: Bloomsbury Press, 1992: 40. **5.** Included in Appendages to the Eighth Interim Thirion Report; *Commission of Inquiry into Alleged Irregularities and Misapplication of property. S.W. Africa*. **6.** Memorandum on Ovambo meeting from Chief Security Superintendent, CDM, Oranjemund, 28 Feb 1972. **7.** *Op cit*., Flynn: 42. From the above memorandum by the Chief Security Officer. **8.** *Financial Times*, 6 Sept 1994.

CORPORATIONS CLAIM THE "RIGHT TO LIE"
BUT THE BIG LIE IS THAT CORPORATIONS ARE PEOPLE

THOM HARTMANN

While Nike was conducting a huge and expensive PR blitz to tell people that it had cleaned up its subcontractors' sweatshop labor practices, an alert consumer advocate and activist in California named Marc Kasky caught them in what he alleges are a number of specific deceptions. Citing a California law that forbids corporations from intentionally deceiving people in their commercial statements, Kasky sued the multibillion-dollar corporation.

Instead of refuting Kasky's charge by proving in court that it didn't lie, however, Nike instead chose to argue that corporations should enjoy the same "free speech" right to deceive that individual human citizens have in their personal lives. If people have the constitutionally protected right to say, "The check is in the mail," or, "That looks great on you," then, Nike's reasoning goes, a corporation should have the same right to say whatever they want in their corporate PR campaigns.

Nike took this argument all the way to the California Supreme Court, where it lost. The next stop may be the US Supreme Court, and the battle lines are already forming.

For example, in a column in the *New York Times* supporting Nike's position, Bob Herbert wrote, "In a real democracy, even the people you disagree with get to have their say."

True enough.

But Nike isn't a person—it's a corporation. And it's not their "say" they're asking for: It's the right to deceive people.

Corporations are created by humans to further the goal of making money. As Buckminster Fuller said in his brilliant essay *The Grunch of Giants*, "Corporations are neither physical nor metaphysical phenomena. They are socioeconomic ploys—legally enacted game-playing..."

> **INSTEAD OF REFUTING KASKY'S CHARGE BY PROVING IN COURT THAT IT DIDN'T LIE, HOWEVER, NIKE INSTEAD CHOSE TO ARGUE THAT CORPORATIONS SHOULD ENJOY THE SAME "FREE SPEECH" RIGHT TO DECEIVE THAT INDIVIDUAL HUMAN CITIZENS HAVE IN THEIR PERSONAL LIVES.**

Corporations are non-living, non-breathing, legal fictions. They feel no pain. They don't need clean water to drink, fresh air to breathe, or healthy food to consume. They can live forever. They can't be put in prison. They can change their identity or appearance in a day, change their citizenship in an hour, rip off parts of themselves and create entirely new entities. Some have compared corporations with robots, in that they are human creations that can outlive individual humans, performing their assigned tasks forever.

Isaac Asimov, when considering a world where robots had become as functional, intelligent, and more powerful than their human creators, posited three fundamental laws that would determine the behavior of such potentially dangerous human-made creations. His Three Laws of Robotics stipulate that non-living human creations must obey humans yet never behave in a way that would harm humans.

Asimov's thinking wasn't altogether original: Thomas Jefferson and James Madison beat him to it by about 200 years.

Jefferson and Madison proposed an Eleventh Amendment to the Constitution that would "ban monopolies in commerce," making it illegal for corporations to own other corporations, banning them from giving money to politicians or trying to influence elections in any way, restricting corporations to a single business purpose, limiting the lifetime of a corporation to something roughly similar to that of productive humans (20 to 40 years back then), and requiring that the first purpose for which all corporations were created be "to serve the public good."

The amendment didn't pass because many argued it was unnecessary: Virtually all states already had such laws on the books from the founding of the US until the Age of the Robber Barons.

Wisconsin, for example, had a law that stated:

No corporation doing business in this state shall pay or contribute, or offer consent or agree to pay or contribute, directly or indirectly, any money, property, free service of its officers or employees or thing of value to any political party, organization, committee or individual for any political purpose whatsoever, or for the purpose of influencing legislation of any kind, or to promote or defeat the candidacy of any person for nomination, appointment or election to any political office.

The penalty for any corporate official violating that law and getting cozy with politicians on behalf of a corporation was five years in prison and a substantial fine.

Like Asimov's Three Laws of Robotics, these laws prevented corporations from harming humans, while still allowing people to create their robots (corporations) and use them to make money. Everybody won. Prior to 1886, corporations were referred to in US law as "artificial persons," similar to the way Star Trek portrays the human-looking robot named Data.

NOWHERE IN THE DECISION ITSELF DOES THE COURT SAY CORPORATIONS ARE PERSONS.

But after the Civil War, things began to change. In the last year of the war, on November 21, 1864, President Abraham Lincoln looked back on the growing power of the war-enriched corporations, and wrote the following thoughtful letter to his friend Colonel William F. Elkins:

We may congratulate ourselves that this cruel war is nearing its end. It has cost a vast amount of treasure and blood. The best blood of the flower of American youth has been freely offered upon our country's altar that the nation might live. It has indeed been a trying hour for the Republic; but I see in the near future a crisis approaching that unnerves me and causes me to tremble for the safety of my country.

As a result of the war, corporations have been enthroned and an era of corruption in high places will follow, and the money power of the country will endeavor to prolong its reign by working upon the prejudices of the people until all wealth is aggregated in a few hands and the Republic is destroyed. I feel at this moment more anxiety than ever before, even in the midst of war. God grant that my suspicions may prove groundless.

Lincoln's suspicions were prescient. In the 1886 *Santa Clara County v. Southern Pacific Railroad* case, the Supreme Court ruled that the state tax assessor, not the county assessor, had the right to determine the taxable value of fenceposts along the railroad's right-of-way.

However, in writing up the case's headnote—a commentary that has no precedential status—the Court's reporter, a former railroad president named J.C. Bancroft Davis, opened the headnote with the sentence:

The defendant Corporations are persons within the intent of the clause in section 1 of the Fourteenth Amendment to the Constitution of the United States, which forbids a State to deny to any person within its jurisdiction the equal protection of the laws.

Oddly, the Court had ruled no such thing. As a handwritten note from Chief Justice Waite to reporter Davis that now is held in the National Archives said: "[W]e avoided meeting the Constitutional question in the decision." And nowhere in the decision itself does the Court say corporations are persons.

Nonetheless, corporate attorneys picked up the language of Davis' headnote and began to quote it like a mantra. Soon the Supreme Court itself, in a stunning display of either laziness (not reading the actual case) or deception (rewriting the Constitution without issuing an opinion or having open debate on the issue), was quoting Davis' headnote in subsequent cases. While Davis' *Santa Clara* headnote didn't have the force of law, once the Court quoted it as the basis for later decisions, its new doctrine of corporate personhood became the law.

Prior to 1886, the Bill of Rights and the Fourteenth Amendment defined human rights, and individuals—representing themselves and their own opinions—were free to say and do what they wanted. Corporations, being artificial creations of the states, didn't have rights, but instead had privileges. The state in which a corporation was incorporated determined those privileges and how they could be used. And the same, of course, was true for other forms of "legally enacted game-playing," such as unions, churches, unincorporated businesses, partnerships, and even governments, all of which have only privileges.

But with the stroke of his pen, Court Reporter Davis moved corporations out of that "privileges" category—leaving behind all the others (unions, governments, and small unincorporated businesses still don't have "rights")—and moved them into the "rights" category with humans, citing the Fourteenth Amendment, which was passed at the end of the Civil War to grant the human right of equal protection under the law to newly-freed slaves.

On December 3, 1888, President Grover Cleveland delivered his annual address to Congress. Apparently, the President had taken notice of the *Santa Clara County* Supreme Court headnote, its politics, and its consequences, for he said in his speech to the nation, delivered before a joint session of Congress:

As we view the achievements of aggregated capital, we discover the existence of trusts, combinations, and monopolies, while the citizen is struggling far in the rear or is trampled to death beneath an iron heel. Corporations, which should be the carefully restrained creatures of the law and the servants of the people, are fast becoming the people's masters.

Which brings us to today.

The US Supreme Court will decide whether or not to hear Nike's appeal of the California Supreme Court's decision that Nike was engaging in commercial speech, which the state can regulate under truth-in-advertising and other laws. And lawyers for Nike are preparing to claim before the Supreme Court that, as a "person," this multinational corporation has a constitutional free-speech right to deceive.

The US Chamber of Commerce, Exxon/Mobil, Monsanto, Microsoft, Pfizer, and Bank of America have already filed amicus briefs supporting Nike. Additionally, virtually all of the nation's largest corporate-owned newspapers have recently editorialized in favor of Nike and given virtually no coverage or even printed letters to the editor asserting the humans' side of the case.

On the side of "only humans have human rights" is the lone human activist in California—Marc Kasky—who brought the original complaint against Nike.

People of all political persuasions who are concerned about democracy and human rights are encouraging other humans to contact the American Civil Liberties Union (125 Broad Street, 18th Floor, New York, NY 10004) and ask them to join Kasky in asserting that only living, breathing humans have human rights. Organizations like ReclaimDemocracy.org are documenting the case in detail on the Web with a sign-on letter, in an effort to bring the ACLU and other groups in on behalf of Kasky.

CORPORATE AMERICA IS RISING UP, AND, UNLIKE YOU AND ME, WHEN LARGE CORPORATIONS "SPEAK," THEY CAN USE A BILLION-DOLLAR BULLHORN.

Corporate America is rising up, and, unlike you and me, when large corporations "speak," they can use a billion-dollar bullhorn. At this moment, the only thing standing between their complete takeover of public opinion or their being brought back under the rule of law is the US Supreme Court.

And, interestingly, the Chief Justice of the current Court may side with humans, proving that this is an issue that is neither conservative nor progressive, but rather one that has to do with democracy versus corporate plutocracy.

In the 1978 *Boston v. Bellotti* decision, the Court agreed, by a one-vote majority, that corporations were "persons" and thus entitled to the free-speech right to give huge quantities of money to political causes. Chief Justice William Rehnquist, believing this to be an error, argued that corporations should be restrained from political activity and wrote the dissent.

He started out his dissent by pointing to the 1886 *Santa Clara* headnote and implicitly criticizing its interpretation over the years, saying, "This Court decided at an early date, with neither argument nor discussion, that a business corporation is a 'person' entitled to the protection of the Equal Protection Clause of the Fourteenth Amendment. *Santa Clara County v. Southern Pacific R. Co., 118 U.S. 394, 396 (1886)*."

Then he went all the way back to the time of James Monroe's presidency to re-describe how the Founders and the Supreme Court's then-Chief Justice John Marshall, a strong Federalist appointed by outgoing President John Adams in 1800, viewed corporations. Rehnquist wrote:

Early in our history, Mr. Chief Justice Marshall described the status of a corporation in the eyes of federal law:

"A corporation is an artificial being, invisible, intangible, and existing only in contemplation of law. Being the mere creature of law, it possesses only those properties which the charter of creation confers upon it, either expressly, or as incidental to its very existence. These are such as are supposed best calculated to effect the object for which it was created."

Rehnquist concluded his dissent by asserting that it was entirely correct that states have the power to limit a corporation's ability to spend money to influence elections (after all, they can't vote—what are they doing in politics?), saying:

The free flow of information is in no way diminished by the [Massachusetts] Commonwealth's decision to permit the operation of business corporations with limited rights of political expression. All natural persons, who owe their existence to a higher sovereign than the Commonwealth, remain as free as before to engage in political activity.

Justices true to the Constitution and the Founders' intent may wake up to the havoc wrought on the American political landscape by the *Bellotti* case and its reliance on the flawed *Santa Clara* headnote. If the Court chooses to hear the *Kasky v. Nike* case, it will open an opportunity for them to rule that corporations don't have the free-speech right to knowingly deceive the public. It's even possible that this case could cause the Court to revisit the error of Davis' 1886 headnote and begin the process of dismantling the flawed and unconstitutional doctrine of corporate personhood.

As humans concerned with the future of human rights in a democratic republic, it's vital that we now speak up, spread the word, and encourage the ACLU and other pro-democracy groups to help Marc Kasky in his battle on our species' collective behalf.

Thom Hartmann is the author of Unequal Protection: The Rise of Corporate Dominance and the Theft of Human Rights *(Rodale Press, 2002) <www.unequalprotection.com>. This article is copyright by Thom Hartmann, but permission is granted for reprint in print, email, or Web media so long as this credit is attached.*

DIRTY PLAYERS OF WORLD FINANCE

LUCY KOMISAR

_HOW ENRON USED THE OFFSHORE SYSTEM—WITH THE HELP OF BIG BANKS

• "The smell of offshore is all over Enron," says an attorney from a firm suing the disgraced energy corporation.

• Enron officials used shell companies to hide their involvement in insider deals.

• Citicorp and JP Morgan Chase banks set up their *own* shell companies to disguise loans to Enron as income.

Enron is being investigated by Congress, the Justice Department, bankruptcy officials, and lawyers for class-action plaintiffs. The latter are mostly state and trade union pension funds that, at the direction of the Houston judge, have combined their cases.

The investigators agree that the role of the offshore system was central to the massive Ponzi scheme Enron created that cheated thousands of investors and left employees without jobs and pensions. Their discoveries about the use of offshore has implications for investors and employees in other American companies.

Of the company's 3,000 subsidiaries and partnerships, a fourth of them were registered in Grand Cayman or Turks and Caicos.

The offshore corporations were used by Enron officials who structured deals for the company. The lawyer, who asked not to be named, explained:

Enron was an entrepreneurial culture. People inside would propose deals. Someone would say, "Let's build this pipeline from Texas to Florida." They would have to line up financing and contractors and formal ownership. The deal would be "structured," meaning setting up the various corporations that would invest and own.

There were people who witnesses described to us as *mystery men*—people who were supposedly investors. An Enron executive would be proposing a deal. He would say, "We will create a new corporation to hold the assets, and Mr. Wood will be a 40-percent equity holder." A guy would ask, "Who is Mr. Wood?"

These mystery men would have to be paid $100,000 here, $100,000 there, with no reason. "He's bringing financing," was the reason given. The financing would be via offshore corporations you couldn't penetrate to find the owners. In many cases, I've heard that Fastow [i.e, Andrew Fastow, Enron's Chief Financial Officer] or other people inside Enron were signatories on these bank accounts.

We asked for but haven't gotten discovery on the signatories on the offshore companies' bank accounts. That's the key.

In discovery, a plaintiff can demand a defendant's internal records.

The attorney says lawyers taking depositions from officials of the audit firm Arthur Andersen are asking them whether they moved money offshore or if they were participants in offshore operations.

Enron chief Kenneth Lay says that he had $100 million in cash, and now it's gone. The lawyers want to know if Lay bought anything of value offshore or is the owner of a beneficial trust outside the US. And the same for the other top Enron officials.

They have a lot of questions for Enron's biggest bankers, Citicorp and JP Morgan Chase, who are key defendants in the fraud lawsuit, because they have the most money.

"THERE WERE PEOPLE WHO WITNESSES DESCRIBED TO US AS *MYSTERY MEN*—PEOPLE WHO WERE SUPPOSEDLY INVESTORS."

Citigroup and JP Morgan Chase set up phony offshore companies that they controlled as sham trading partners for the purpose of allowing Enron to disguise its multimillion-dollar loans as trades. JP Morgan had used this system before with a Sumitomo trader and had to pay a $125-million settlement.

There's a big difference in the financial world between cash that comes from business activity and cash that comes from a loan. The first can boost and the second can lower a company's credit rating and stock value.

Analysts and credit-rating agencies already thought the cash flow that Enron was bringing in wasn't sufficient to support its level of debt.

So the offshore companies were used to book "trades" with Enron that were really loans. They used "prepays"—arrangements in which a company is paid in advance to deliver a service or a product at a later date. To be legitimate prepays, there had to be independent parties and price risk. But they were phony prepays. No product was intended to be delivered, or the payments were hedged, cancelled by parallel trades.

This is how the banks set them up.

■■■■■■■■■

JP Morgan Chase. (Chase acquired JP Morgan in 2000.) Chase hired Mourant and Company, a corporate services firm in Jersey (in the Channel Islands), to set up a shell company call Mahonia which was beneficially "owned" by a charitable trust, with officers and directors supplied by Mourant. Chase officials called to testify in July 2002 before the Subcommittee on Investigations of the Senate Governmental Affairs Committee repeatedly denied that Chase owned or controlled it.

An exasperated Democratic Senator Carl Levin, Chair of the Subcommittee, pulled out a sheaf of papers and said, "Okay, let's look at Mahonia now just to see how independent Mahonia was." He showed a letter Mourant sent to the registrar of corporations and trusts in Jersey. "Our clients, Chase Bank and Trust Company Limited are considering promoting from time to time special purpose vehicles for use in particular banking transactions. The possible areas in which the SPVs could be used are numerous, but at this stage it could be foreseen that the likely use for them would be..."—and the letter says one of the reasons is when a company wishes to raise finance via a transaction, and not by borrowing.

The letter says, "For obvious reasons it is important that the SPVs, special purpose vehicles, are controlled by Chase. But for accounting and other requirements it's not desirable that they are wholly owned by Chase. Accordingly, Chase is considering establishing a charitable trust which would own all the shares of a holding company which, in turn, would wholly own the various SPVs." Mourant wrote later letters informing officials that it was Chase's agent for the shell companies Eastmoss Ltd. and Mahonia. It also set up Stoneville Aegean Ltd. in Jersey to use in the phony trades.

Levin declared: "It's a shell, and it's a shell game, and Chase should own up to it, be honest about it, and it's not." He said, "You use an offshore jurisdiction, a secrecy jurisdiction. Mahonia was created for Chase, created by Chase, paid for by Chase, controlled by Chase, run by Chase's agent, fees paid for by Chase. And yet you sit here and just repeat the mantra that you believed it was independent. That does not satisfy the responsibility of a major bank."

Morgan set up parallel opposite transactions that cancelled each other out. For example, on September 28, 2001, JP Morgan Chase transferred about $350 million to Mahonia, which sent that same amount to Enron, which would pay back $356 million six months later. On the surface this transaction appears to be a series of arm's-length trades among independent entities, and the advance of cash from Mahonia to Enron is booked as a trading activity by Enron rather than a loan. However, it's really a set of integrated, pre-

arranged trades that wash each other out.

In an email that the Subcommittee obtained, a bank official wrote: "Enron loves these deals as they are able to hide funded debt from their equity analysts." The bank's Texas lawyers, Vinson & Elkins, who got over $100 million in legal fees, gave a false legal opinion that these loans were trades. The firm is also being sued.

A JP Morgan Chase official who testified said the bank used the same system with other companies and that, "The use of entities like Mahonia is standard activity in structured finance."

Citicorp. The use of shell companies to disguise financial operations was also standard for Citicorp. A Citicorp official admitted at the hearing that Citicorp's lawyers, Milbank Tweed, had worked with the Cayman Islands agent Maples and Calder to set up the Delta Corp in 1993 to do commodity swap transactions. But no commodities ever changed hands between Enron and Delta.

> IN AN EMAIL THAT THE SUBCOMMITTEE OBTAINED, A BANK OFFICIAL WROTE: "ENRON LOVES THESE DEALS AS THEY ARE ABLE TO HIDE FUNDED DEBT FROM THEIR EQUITY ANALYSTS." ·

Delta was owned by a charitable trust, Grand Cayman Commodities Corporation. The Citicorp official, Richard Caplan, explained, "Citibank forms special-purpose entities to do lots of structured finance transactions, much as other institutions in the market form special-purpose entities." He said, "We do this all the time. This is standard operating procedure in the structured finance industry."

Levin asked, "You're forming an entity. The operations of that entity are hidden. There's linkage between the transactions. Why are you forming this kind of entity in the Cayman Islands, a secrecy jurisdiction? Why do you hesitate to say that you'll give us authority to try to pierce that secrecy to find out who owns that trust which holds the stock in Delta? That's troubling, and I want to know your answers. Why do you do this in secrecy jurisdictions? Why not open, do it in daylight?"

Caplan replied, "I think if you would examine other special-purpose entities used by Citibank and other banks and other corporations in receivables financings or mortgage financings, you will find that they have very similar characteristics to Delta." He added, "Andersen knew fully well about Delta and requested certain representations be made by Delta saying—effectively certifying its status as a special-purpose entity that was separate from Citibank." Citigroup's own accountant then and now is KPMG.

■■■■■■■■■

The deals by Citigroup and Chase enabled Enron to keep at least $8 billion of debt off its balance sheet for six years from 1992, including $3.7 billion from twelve transactions with Chase and $4.8 billion from fourteen transactions with Citigroup.

The financial statements showed that Enron had total debt in 2000 of about $10 billion and fund flows from operations in the range of

$3.2 billion. If Enron had properly accounted for these transactions, its total debt would have increased by about 40 percent to $14 billion, and its fund flows from operation would have dropped by almost 50 percent to $1.7 billion. The true debt-to-equity ratio was 65 percent, instead of an alleged 49 percent. If the loans had been known, Enron would have lost its investment-grade rating.

When Enron collapsed and declared bankruptcy in December of 2001, it had about $5 billion in outstanding prepays that were unknown to the company's creditors and investors.

DOCUMENTS SUPPLIED TO THE SEC PURPORT TO SHOW THAT THE FUNDS WERE MOVED TO LIECHTENSTEIN FOUNDATIONS CONTROLLED BY KPMG AND CREDIT SUISSE, BOTH IN ZURICH.

Levin, who has been leading the US Congress' fight against offshore, said the system was "just a little bit like the *Wizard of Oz* when Toto pulls back the curtain to show the great Oz; he's no more than just an old man rapidly manipulating pyrotechnic devices. When you pull back the curtain of the offshore shell companies, it reveals that the banks were calling the shots and pulling the strings."

He said, "I don't believe that Enron could have done what it did in hiding debt and disguising it as cash flow from operations without the assistance and participation of the banks." And, "Chase and Citicorp knew what Enron was doing, assisted Enron in those deceptions, and profited from their actions." Enron paid interest of 6.5 to 7 percent on these loans, instead of the 3.75 to 4.25 percent it would have paid borrowing openly.

An investigator for the committee called the system "fraud on the market"—the company's stock price is supported in the marketplace by false and misleading information. When it becomes known, the market price drops, so people who buy stock during that time period have been defrauded.

Levin said, "All of the documents, the records here are going to be referred, as I indicated, to the SEC and the Department of Justice."

Citibank lent $1.5 billion to Enron and then sold securities to the public to hedge their own position. Morgan Chase, instead of selling securities, got surety contracts for over $900 million. Now the insurers won't pay, because they say the trades were frauds. Morgan Chase sued, and, ironically, one of the defendants is Travelers Insurance, which is owned by Citigroup. A New York federal judge ruled that the evidence supports the insurers' claims that the arrangements were "a disguised loan."

Both Chase and Citicorp have marketed the prepay structures to other firms. Citicorp boasts in its sales pitch that the structure expands capability to raise non-debt financing and eliminates the need for capital market disclosure. Chase entered into Enron-style prepays with seven companies in addition to Enron. Citigroup sold its prepay structure to two other companies. The two banks made more than $200 million in fees on these transactions.

At a hearing on Enron in February 2002, soon after Enron's fraud

was exposed, Democratic Senator John Kerry, whose committee headed the investigation into BCCI a decade ago, said:

I just want to direct my colleagues to one particular component of this that I've been harping on for a number of years, because as we fight a war on terrorism, and as we talk about holding other systems accountable, so we can follow the flow of money, we have all of us in this Congress allowed to stand for too long a system that undermines our capacity to do that, and that's offshore subsidiaries and tax havens.

_THE SEC AND JUSTICE DEPARTMENT INVESTIGATE EVIDENCE THAT KPMG AND CREDIT SUISSE HID MARCOS' MILLIONS

At a time when the integrity of global accounting firms is being questioned, the Securities and Exchange Commission and the Justice Department are looking into charges that KPMG Zurich, a division of the international audit company, helped Credit Suisse hide hundreds of millions of dollars looted by Philippine dictator Ferdinand Marcos. A KPMG spokesperson confirmed the investigation.

Representative Dan Burton, a conservative Republican from Indianapolis, wrote the SEC that he had been informed that the agency has been "presented with evidence against KMPG concerning money laundering and subversion of a joint Philippine and Swiss freeze order for a series of accounts containing millions of US dollars." Burton, a member of the House International Relations Committee, requested "prompt action" by the SEC "in seeking out the truth." The SEC passed on its information to the Justice Department.

The freeze order had been issued by the Swiss Banking Commission in March 1986, after Marcos was ousted. Documents supplied to the SEC purport to show that the funds were moved to Liechtenstein foundations controlled by KPMG and Credit Suisse, both in Zurich. KPMG—then known as Fides—had been a Credit Suisse subsidiary till a few years before.

KPMG Zurich is a member of KPMG International, headquartered in Amsterdam, which includes the giant US audit firm of the same name. Credit Suisse is part of the Zurich-based Credit Suisse Group, the world's third-largest private banking group, which owns the US investment bank Credit Suisse First Boston. Credit Suisse spokespersons in Zurich and New York declined to speak about the investigation. KPMG spokesperson Kate Maybank in London said, "We are aware of it, but it isn't something we would make any comment on."

The key documents in possession of the SEC and Justice Department include:

• records found in Malacañang Palace after Marcos fled that detail transactions involving his "foundations" and accounts in Switzerland and Liechtenstein;

• an affidavit from a Philippine banker who said that in March 1986 he was given power of attorney by Marcos to move his money out

DAN BURTON
6TH DISTRICT, INDIANA

COMMITTEES:
GOVERNMENT REFORM AND OVERSIGHT
CHAIRMAN

INTERNATIONAL RELATIONS

SUBCOMMITTEES:
INTERNATIONAL OPERATIONS
AND HUMAN RIGHTS
WESTERN HEMISPHERE

Congress of the United States
House of Representatives
Washington, DC 20515-1406

WASHINGTON OFFICE:
2185 RAYBURN BUILDING
WASHINGTON, DC 20515-1406
TELEPHONE: (202) 225-2276

DISTRICT OFFICES:
8900 KEYSTONE AT THE CROSSING
SUITE 1050
INDIANAPOLIS, IN 46240
TELEPHONE: (317) 848-0201
TOLL-FREE: (800) 382-6020

435 EAST MAIN STREET
SUITE J-3
GREENWOOD, IN 46142
TELEPHONE: (317) 882-3640
TOLL-FREE: (800) 678-3642

WORLDWIDE WEB PAGE:
http://www.house.gov/burton/

August 23, 2002

Ms. Karen Pennington
Assistant Regional Director
Securities and Exchange Commission
233 Broadway
New York, New York 10279

Dear Ms. Pennington:

Mr. Brett Pauszek, a constituent of mine, has brought to the attention of my staff a possible investigation by your office into the activities of KPMG International, a U.S. accounting firm. Mr. Pauszek and I are requesting prompt action by the Securities and Exchange Commission (SEC) in seeking out the truth in this matter.

My office has been informed that the SEC has been presented with evidence against KMPG concerning money laundering and subversion of a joint Philippine and Swiss freeze order for a series of accounts containing millions of U.S. dollars. In addition, Mr. Pauszek informed my staff that the Philippine government will formally request that the SEC take civil/administrative action against KPMG to return these accounts. I'm aware that the SEC cannot comment about ongoing investigations, however, I would appreciate your office keeping me updated as to a resolution of this important matter.

Thank you for your prompt attention to this matter. Please direct any questions to Ms. Brenda Summers of my legislative staff at (317) 848-0201.

Sincerely,

Dan Burton
Member of Congress

DB/bcs

of Switzerland. The banker, Michael de Guzman, said a Credit Suisse official in Zurich told him the transfer order was unnecessary because Marcos' foundations and account names had been changed to ensure that neither the Philippine government nor Swiss authorities would get the Marcos deposits and investments;

• the testimony of Marie-Gabrielle Koller, a former lawyer for KPMG in Zurich, who told a French parliamentary committee and attempted to interest the US Justice Department in her account of how officials of Fides (the antecedent of KPMG) moved the Marcos money. She said she learned from colleagues in 1997 how their predecessors had worked to hide the accounts to beat an expected freeze order.

During his 20 years in power, Ferdinand Marcos routinely siphoned off cash from the Treasury, pocketed bribes, and stole money from IMF and World Bank loans and from US foreign aid. When I was in the Philippines in 1986 to cover the political turbulence that ended with Marcos' overthrow, US Embassy officials told me that the CIA calculated the dictator had stashed $5 billion outside the country. His favorite bankers were the Swiss, and among them, Credit Suisse.

From 1928, Credit Suisse had an accounting subsidiary called Fides Trust. Fides would split several times, yielding the present Credit Suisse Trust (Vaduz) and KPMG Fides (Zurich). KPMG Fides continued to provide audit and tax advice to Credit Suisse. In its annual report, KPMG lists as an affiliate Limag AG, which happens to be located in the same building as Credit Suisse Trust in Vaduz. Credit Suisse, KPMG Fides, and Limag Management AG maintain a tight relationship, with easy communication, as the cities are just 72 miles apart.

Limag is a fiduciary, or asset manager. Documents found at the Philippines' Malacañang Palace showed Limag had set up Marcos foundations on whose boards Limag president Ivo Beck and vice president Ulrich Siegfried served. Liechtenstein foundations, or "Anstalts," are not required to keep books, present balances to tax authorities, or undergo any state supervision. They are shells notoriously used by money launderers. Malacañang documents showed that Fides Trust and Credit Suisse officials sat on Marcos foundation boards.

After Marcos flew to Hawaii aboard a US military plane on February 28, 1986, Philippine banker Michael de Guzman, then 38, thought he could pick up some easy cash. He knew the son of Marcos' security chief, and so he visited the dictator in Honolulu and, as he later described in a 1986 affidavit, offered to move Marcos' money to his Export-Finanzierungsbank GmbH, Vienna, which had impenetrable bank secrecy. Marcos gave him a power of attorney and had his son "Bong Bong" alert Ernest Scheller, a senior vice president and principal contact for Marcos at Credit Suisse.

Credit Suisse officials informed the Swiss government of the transfer attempt. According to De Guzman, when he arrived March 24, he was informed by Scheller that the Banking Commissioner had decreed that "all Swiss banks must monitor movements of accounts directly related or even indirectly related to Ferdinand E. Marcos and his family." He said Scheller told him that two weeks earlier, he'd gotten instructions from a Marcos aide to hide accounts—that funds and assets had been transferred to Fides Trust. De Guzman said that when he asked for account statements, Scheller replied that they weren't available, because Fides

people were in the process of moving the accounts and foundations.

That evening, the Swiss Federal Council (the Swiss cabinet) issued an emergency order freezing assets of Marcos, his family, his corporate entities, and his cronies. It was the first time the Swiss froze a dictator's accounts.

De Guzman returned in the morning and learned of the freeze. Gustave-Adolphe Rychner, a senior Credit Suisse officer, told him that foundations and account names had already been changed, that neither the Philippine government nor Swiss authorities would be able to freeze Marcos' deposits and investments.

The Malacañang documents revealed that the Marcoses and their cronies had 60 accounts under the names of seventeen foundations at six Swiss banks, including Credit Suisse in Zurich, and in New York, where securities and gold were kept in a Marcos sub-account of the Credit Suisse account at Swiss American Securities Inc. (SASI).

Weeks after the dictator's escape, Philippine authorities had opened a criminal action against "Marcos and consorts," and on April 7, 1986, lawyers officially asked Bern for legal assistance. The request cited documents indicating where stolen money had gone—to Credit Suisse Zurich; Societe de Banques Suisse in Fribourg and Geneva; Banque Paribas, Geneva; Bankers Trust, Geneva and Zurich; Banque Hoffman & Cie, Zurich; Banque de Paris et des Pays Bas, Geneva. The Philippines also sought information from Swiss banks relating to securities deposited in foreign countries, "in particular in Liechtenstein (Limag AG and the foundations certainly) or in New York (SASI New York through Credit Suisse)." And the request named fifteen individuals, including the Credit Suisse and Fides officials who had worked with Marcos accounts.

But the Swiss investigative magistrates and prosecutors refused to act. There would follow years of efforts by the Philippines to recover the Marcos money and years of stonewalling by Swiss banks, helped by their government. The only person the Swiss district attorney ever interviewed was Geel, Credit Suisse general counsel.

Not until the Philippines gave Swiss authorities documents about specific accounts did Bern announce that those and only those were the ones it had frozen, valued at $356 million in Credit Suisse and Swiss Bank Corporation. It wasn't until December 1990 that the Swiss Supreme Court authorized the transfer of the Swiss bank documents to Manila authorities. The banks denied records on 51 other accounts identified by the Philippine government.

DURING HIS 20 YEARS IN POWER, FERDINAND MARCOS ROUTINELY SIPHONED OFF CASH FROM THE TREASURY, POCKETED BRIBES, AND STOLE MONEY FROM IMF AND WORLD BANK LOANS AND FROM US FOREIGN AID.

A chance event in 1997 would lead to another revelation about the events of 1986. Fides, once a subsidiary of Credit Suisse, had gone through various splits and spawned KPMG, Zurich. Marie-Gabrielle Koller, a Canadian lawyer, had started work there in 1996 and was assigned the Credit Suisse account.

She'd left her previous job in Liechtenstein after she discovered that her boss was involved in a scheme to sell improperly tested blood. She told Liechtenstein authorities about the blood scheme, and after a Swiss inquiry, a prosecutor called her to testify. Her ex-boss' accounts were in Credit Suisse, and he was a good friend of a director of Credit Suisse Trust. Koller says KPMG fired her that same day at the behest of Credit Suisse, the firm's principal Swiss bank client.

In May 2000, Koller told a French National Assembly parliamentary commission investigating money-laundering in Switzerland, that KPMG/Fides had moved the Marcos money. She had learned about the transfers to Liechtenstein from officials of Limag AG and KPMG Fides who allegedly bragged about how clever the firms had been in not being caught by legal actions after Marcos fled the Philippines. She recounted how staff had worked through the night to "redocument" accounts holding $400 million and that Limag resolved Liechtenstein officials' nervousness by giving a well-paid board chairmanship to Prince Constantin, the 70-year-old cousin of the ruling Prince Franz-Josef II. Officials of the companies denied the charges.

The money with interest now would approach $1 billion.

Last year Koller approached the US Justice Department via Virginia lawyer David Smith, a former associate director of the Department's Asset Forfeiture Office, who also served as associate independent counsel in the 1995 investigation of Clinton Administration Agriculture Secretary Mike Espy. On June 28, 2001, Smith sent New York FBI Agent Mark Lauer a fax that said:

I hope you find the attached e-mail letter from Koller useful. Have you had a chance to read the write-up I previously sent you? Have you circulated it to others at the Bureau or in the US Attorney's Office? Is there any interest? It's very frustrating to us, because we believe the information is extremely valuable. As far as we know, the government hasn't followed up on any of it, even the Marcos stuff that Asset Forfeiture & Money Laundering said it was interested in. I may send a copy to Mr. Freeh [i.e., Louis Freeh, FBI Director from 1993 to 2001].

Smith and Lauer said they could not discuss the matter. Justice Department and FBI spokespersons also declined to comment.

Did Marcos money end up in Liechtenstein? The German Intelligence Agency (BND), in a classified February 2000 paper, cited several Vaduz asset managers that it said handled Marcos money and were also launderers for drug traffickers. Asked to authenticate the document, a BND press spokesperson replied by email, "We certainly regret that the report you mentioned has been leaked. Yet, we do not wish to comment [on] this issue any further and hope you will understand."

Zurich district attorney Peter Cosandey and his successor, Dieter Jann, have never interviewed any of the bankers or fiduciaries who dealt with Marcos accounts. Cosandey said, "As far as I remember, I interviewed a guy from Credit Suisse, Markus Geel of the legal department of the bank." No others? "The Philippines didn't ask for it." That is contradicted by the Philippines' legal assistance request. When, in 1998, Cosandey quit as the official Swiss searcher after the Marcos plunder, he was appointed partner and director of Forensic and Litigation Services at KPMG Switzerland.

_EXPLOSIVE REVELATION$

In the tax haven of Luxembourg, a little-known outfit called Clearstream handles billions of dollars a year in stock and bond transfers for banks, investment companies, and multinational corporations. But a former top official of this clearinghouse says Clearstream operates a secret bookkeeping system that allows its clients to hide the money that moves through their accounts.

In these days of global markets, individuals and companies may be buying stocks, bonds, or derivatives from a seller who is halfway across the world. Clearinghouses like Clearstream keep track of the paperwork for the transactions. Banks with accounts in the clearinghouse use a debit and credit system and, at the end of the day, the accounts (minus handling fees, of course) are totaled up. The clearinghouse doesn't actually send money anywhere; it just debits and credits its members' accounts. It's all very efficient. But the money involved is massive. Clearstream handles more than 80 million transactions a year, and claims to have securities on deposit valued at $6.5 trillion.

> **CLEARSTREAM HANDLES MORE THAN 80 MILLION TRANSACTIONS A YEAR, AND CLAIMS TO HAVE SECURITIES ON DEPOSIT VALUED AT $6.5 TRILLION.**

It's also an excellent mechanism for laundering drug money or hiding income from the tax collector. Banks are supposed to be subject to local government oversight. But many of Clearstream's members have real or virtual subsidiaries in offshore tax havens, where records are secret and investigators can't trace transactions. And Clearstream, which keeps the central records of financial trades, doesn't get even the cursory regulation that applies to offshore banks. On top of that, it deliberately has put in place a system to hide many of its clients' transactions from any authorities who might come looking.

According to former insiders:

• Clearstream has a double system of accounting, with secret, non-published accounts that banks and big corporations use to make transfers they don't want listed on the official books;

• though it is legally limited to dealing with financial institutions, Clearstream gives secret accounts to multinational corporations so they can move stocks and money free from outside scrutiny;

• Clearstream carried an account for a notoriously criminal Russian bank for several years after the bank had officially collapsed, and clearinghouse accounts camouflaged the destinations of transfers to Colombian banks;

• Clearstream operates a computer program that erases the traces of trades on request from its members;

• Clearstream was used to try to hide a dubious arms deal between French authorities and the Taiwanese military.

Many of these charges were first made in a controversial book called *Révélation$*, written by Denis Robert, a French journalist, and Ernest Backes, a former top official at the clearinghouse who helped design and install the computer system that facilitated the undisclosed accounts.

The book's impact was explosive. Six European judges called it the black box of illicit international financial flows. Top Clearstream officials were fired. The scandal made headlines in big European newspapers; TV networks broadcast specials; the French National Assembly's financial crimes committee held a hearing. Luxembourg authorities ordered an investigation, and then they effected a cover-up. Yet *Révélation$* remains unpublished and relatively unknown in the United States.

■■■■■■■■■■

A bearded, heavyset man in his mid-50s, Backes spoke with me in Neuchâtel, Switzerland, where he'd gone to attend a conference on international crime, and explained how he'd started fighting organized crime in banking.

Ernest Backes was born in 1946 in Trier, Germany. (As he likes to joke, there were two important people born in Trier; the other is Karl Marx.) His father was a Luxembourg metal worker, his mother a German nurse. From fourteen, he worked on an assembly line to pay for school and joined the Young Catholic Workers. After a job in the Luxembourg civil service, he was hired in 1971 by Clearstream's predecessor, Cedel (short for central delivery office), set up the year before by a consortium of 66 international banks. Backes helped design and install Cedel's computerized accounting system in the 1970s.

Cedel and its main competitor, Brussels-based Euroclear, were starting to manage transfers of eurodollars, US currency kept in banks outside the United States. According to Barbara Garson's book *Money Makes the World Go Around*, eurodollars were invented in the 1950s by the Chinese and the Soviets so they would not have to put their assets in banks where the US government could seize them. But others saw value in eurodollars, and they began to be traded for other currencies. Some banks attracted eurodollars with higher interest than was being paid in America, and US corporations and individuals began using the accounts to avoid laws on domestic banks. The euromoney market was born. (By the 1990s, the Federal Reserve estimated that about two-thirds of US currency was held abroad as eurodollars.)

Cedel and Euroclear eventually expanded into handling transfers of stock titles and other financial instruments. Their clients needed a system that would guarantee the creditworthiness of their trading partners and keep records of the trades. The clearinghouses provided speed, discretion, and a system that didn't make the records of their deals and profits readily accessible to outsiders. Every few months, a list of members' codes was distributed. For transfers, members just entered the codes, and Clearstream handled the deals with no further inquiries.

In 1975, several big Italian and German banks wanted to centralize their accounting and didn't want other members of Cedel to send transfers through their numerous individual branches. The Cedel council of administration, its board of directors, authorized banks with multiple subsidiaries not to put all their accounts on the lists. Backes and Gerard Soisson, then Cedel's general manager, set up a system of non-published accounts. A bank would send a transfer to the code of the headquarters bank, which would send it on to the non-published account of its subsidiary. The bank would regulate this operation internally.

Ernest Backes
photo by Lucy Komisar

Soisson authorized each non-published account, which would be known only by some insiders, including the auditors and members of the council of administration. As Cedel's literature to clients explained: "As a general rule, the principal account of each client is published: the existence of the account, as well as its name and number, are published.... On demand, and at the discretion of Cedel Bank, the client can open a non-published account. The non-pub-

THE BANK LAUNDERED DRUG- AND ARMS-TRAFFICKING MONEY FOR THE ITALIAN AND AMERICAN MAFIAS AND, IN THE 1980s, CHANNELED VATICAN MONEY TO THE CONTRAS IN NICARAGUA AND SOLIDARITY IN POLAND.

lished accounts don't figure in any printed document and their name is not mentioned in any report."

Requests for non-published accounts came from some banks that weren't eligible, but Soisson turned them down.

■■■■■■■■■■

By 1980, Backes had become Cedel's number-three official, in charge of relations with clients. But he was fired in May 1983. Backes says the reason given for his sacking was an argument with an English banker, a friend of the CEO. "I think I was fired was because I knew too much about the Ambrosiano scandal," Backes says.

Banco Ambrosiano was once the second most important private bank in Italy, with the Vatican as a principal shareholder and loan recipient. The bank laundered drug- and arms-trafficking money for the Italian and American mafias and, in the 1980s, channeled Vatican money to the Contras in Nicaragua and Solidarity in Poland. The corrupt managers also siphoned off funds via fictitious banks to personal shell company accounts in Switzerland, the Bahamas, Panama, and other offshore havens. Banco Ambrosiano collapsed in 1982, with a deficit of more than $1 billion. (Unknown to many moviegoers, Banco Ambrosiano inspired a subplot of *The Godfather, Part III*.)

Several of those behind the swindle have met untimely ends. Bank chairman Roberto Calvi was found hanged under Blackfriars Bridge in London. Michele Sindona, convicted in 1980 on 65 counts of fraud in the United States, was extradited to Italy in 1984 and sentenced to life in prison; in 1986, he was found dead in his cell, poisoned by cyanide-laced coffee. (Another suspect, Archbishop Paul Marcinkus, the head of the Vatican Bank, now lives in Sun City, Arizona, with a Vatican passport; US authorities have ignored a Milan arrest warrant for him.)

Just two months after Backes' dismissal in 1983, Soisson, 48 and healthy, was found dead in Corsica, where he'd gone on vacation. Top Cedel officials had the body returned immediately and buried, with no autopsy, announcing that he had died of a heart attack. His family now suspects he was murdered. "If Soisson was murdered, it was also related to what he knew about Ambrosiano," Backes says. "When Soisson died, the Ambrosiano affair wasn't yet known as a scandal. [After it was revealed,] I realized that Soisson and I had been at the crossroads. We moved all those transactions known later in the scandal to Lima and other branches. Nobody even knew there was a Banco Ambrosiano branch in Lima and other South American countries."

After leaving Cedel, Backes got a job in the Luxembourg stock market, and later became manager of a butchers' cooperative. But he kept friends inside the clearinghouse and began to collect information and records about Cedel's operations.

With Soisson out of the way, there was nothing to stop the abuse of the system. Whereas Soisson had refused numerous requests to open non-published accounts (from such institutions as Chase Manhattan in New York, Chemical Bank of London, and numerous subsidiaries of Citibank), Cedel opened hundreds of non-published accounts in total irregularity, especially after the arrival of CEO André Lussi in 1990. No longer were they just sub-accounts of officially listed accounts, Backes charges. Some were for banks that weren't subsidiaries or even official members of Cedel. At the start of 1995, Cedel had more than 2,200 published accounts. But in reality, according to documents obtained by Backes, Cedel that year managed more than 4,200 accounts, for more than 2,000 clients from 73 countries.

Clearstream was formed in 1999 out of the merger of Cedel and the compensa-

October Surprises

In November 1979, the US Embassy in Iran was seized, and 52 Americans were held hostage. Their capture, and the Carter Administration's failure to win their release, became a major issue in the 1980 presidential campaign.

Carter had frozen billions in Iranian assets in US banks, money that was being claimed by American firms and individuals who had lost property in the Islamic revolution. American and Iranian officials were negotiating the amount of funds to be released in return for freeing the hostages. The Iranians also wanted Carter to release arms that had been ordered and paid for by the deposed Shah.

Reagan campaign officials allegedly met with Iranian representatives several times during the 1980 campaign, promising arms and money if Iran delayed release of the hostages until after the November election. This scandal would become known as the "October Surprise."

Reagan won the election, but Carter officials continued to negotiate with the Iranians. Finally, around the turn of the year, an accord was reached under which the United States would release $4 billion but no arms. However, the Iranians did not release the hostages immediately.

A few days before Reagan's inauguration, Ernest Backes recalls, Cedel got an urgent joint instruction from the US Federal Reserve Bank and the Bank of England to transfer $7 million in bearer bonds—$5 million from an account of Chase Manhattan Bank and $2 million from an account of Citibank—both in offshore secrecy havens. The money was to go to the National Bank of Algeria, and from there to an Iranian bank in Teheran. Backes was informed that the $7 million was a small fraction of sums being sent from around the world and concentrated in the Algerian bank. He was told the transfers were linked to the fate of the hostages.

The Fed and the Bank of England were not members of Cedel, and by its rules had no right to order the transfers. Backes' two superiors were absent. He informed the president of the Cedel administrative council, Edmond Israel, then acted to execute the order. (Israel, now honorary chairman, did not respond to phone and email messages.)

On Banking with Bin Laden

Following the September 11 attacks on the World Trade Center and the Pentagon, the United States started focusing its investigation on the financial trail of Osama bin Laden and the al-Qaeda network.

Like any other large, global operation, international terrorists need to move large sums of money across borders clandestinely. In November 2001, US authorities named some banks that had bin Laden accounts, and it put them on a blacklist.

One was Al Taqwa ("Fear of God"), registered in the Bahamas with offices in Lugano, Switzerland. Al Taqwa had access to the Clearstream system through its correspondent account with the Banca del Gottardo in Lugano, which has a published Clearstream account (No. 74381).

But bin Laden may have other access to the non-published system. In what he calls a "spectacular discovery," Ernest Backes reports that in the weeks before CEO André Lussi was forced to leave Clearstream in May 2002, a series of sixteen non-published accounts were opened under the name of the Saudi Investment Company, or SICO, the Geneva holding of the Saudi Binladen Group, which is run by Osama's brother, Yeslam Binladen (some family members spell the name differently).

Yeslam Binladen insists that he has nothing to do with his brother, but evidence suggests SICO is tied into Osama's financial network. SICO is associated with Dar Al-Maal-Al-Islami (DMI), an Islamic financial institution also based in Geneva and presided over by Prince Muhammed Al Faisal Al Saoud, a cousin of Saudi King Fahd, that directs millions a year to fundamentalist movements. DMI holds a share of the Al Shamal Islamic Bank of Sudan, which was set up in 1991 and partly financed by $50 million from Osama bin Laden.

Furthermore, one of SICO's administrators, Geneva attorney Baudoin Dunand, is a partner in a law firm, Magnin Dunand & Partners, that set up the Swiss financial services company SBA—a subsidiary of the SBA Bank in Paris. SBA Bank director-shareholder Mahfouz Salem bin Mahfouz was president until 1993 of the Saudi-Sudanese Bank in Khartoum which, at the time was 60-percent owned by the National Commercial Bank run by Khaled bin Mahfouz. Closing the circle, Khaled bin Mahfouz's younger sister is married to Osama bin Laden.

tion company of Deustche Börse (the German stock exchange). "No accounts are secret," insists spokesman Graham Cope. "We are controlled by the local authorities...who have access to information on all accounts. The term 'secret' is misused again and again. Our customers choose to have unpublished accounts, which simply means like a telephone number they choose not to display the name and number in our publications. Customers often have many unpublished accounts, which they use for their own internal management purposes to ensure there is no confusion between their accounts."

But Backes thinks otherwise. "I discovered an increasing number of unpublished accounts," he says. "There were more unpublished than published accounts, and a [large] proportion were not sub-accounts of a principal account, which is what the system was supposedly for. The owners of these accounts were not inscribed on the official list of the clients of the firm."

How does the system work? Backes explains, for example, that a bank with a published account could open a non-published account for a branch in the Cayman Islands, an offshore tax haven. A drug trafficker easily could have the Cayman branch debit cash from his personal account to buy stocks on Wall Street. The transaction would be handled by Clearstream, which would transfer the money electronically to a New York bank that had its own clearinghouse account. Soon the shares could be sold to buy real estate in Chicago with "clean" money. But regulators or investigators, depending only on published accounts, would find it nearly impossible to trace the money. Backes says Clearstream employees joke that the company name means "the river that washes."

While clearinghouse clients may want to keep transactions secret, detailed information on every transfer, including those via non-published accounts, is listed on "daily security statements"—records to prove that the stock or cash has been sent. These statements are stored on microfiche and, under Luxembourg law, must be kept ten years for commercial enterprises and fifteen years for banks. A Clearstream insider gave Backes ten years' worth of these records. "The documents are a mine of information for any financial inquiry," Backes says. "The archives of the clearinghouses can contribute to retracing where funds have gone. The knowledge of the list and the codes relative to non-published accounts, until now guarded secrets, offer immense possibilities."

> BACKES SAYS CLEARSTREAM EMPLOYEES JOKE THAT THE COMPANY NAME MEANS "THE RIVER THAT WASHES."

Backes notes that similar records exist for the other big clearinghouses, Euroclear and Swift, also based in Brussels. "It is possible," he explains, "when one knows the date of an operation and the bank of entry, to reconstitute inside the clearing companies the voyage of the money and stocks or bonds—to follow the tracks."

Révélation$ charges that Cedel/Clearstream further violated its own statutes by setting up non-published accounts for industrial and commercial companies. With accounts in their own names, companies could avoid passing through banks or exchange agents to use the clearinghouse. They thus skirted mandated due diligence and record-keeping. When Siemens was proposed for membership, Backes says, some Cedel employees protested that this violated Luxembourg law. However, management told them that Siemens' admission had been negotiated at the highest level.

Among the major companies with secret accounts, Backes discovered the Shell Petroleum Group and the Dutch agricultural multinational Unilever, one of whose accounts was associated with Goldman Sachs. On the French TV broadcast *Les Dissimulateurs* (*The Deceivers*) in March 2000, Clearstream President Lussi simply denied the accounts existed. "Only banks and brokers are eligible for membership," he said, "as it has always been the case. No private company accounts, no commercial or industrial companies."

But his own spokesman contradicts this claim. "Customers of Clearstream can be banks or, exceptionally, corporate clients who have their own treasury departments the size of banks," Cope wrote in an email to me. "We cannot accept CEOs of multinationals or terrorists and have strict account-opening procedures to prevent such problems."

■■■■■■■■■

By 2000, according to Backes, Clearstream managed about 15,000 accounts (of which half were non-published) for 2,500 clients in 105 countries; most of the investment companies, banks, and their subsidiaries are from Western Europe and the United States. Most of the new non-published accounts were in offshore tax havens. The banks with the most non-published accounts are Banque Internationale de Luxembourg (309), Citibank (271), and Barclays (200).

Backes found numerous discrepancies in the lists he obtained of the secret accounts. For example, code No. 70287 on the published list belongs to Citibank NA-Colombia AC in Nassau, and code No. 70292 is that of the Banco Internacional de Colombia Nassau Ltd. But on the non-published list, the numbers both belong to Banco Internacional de Colombia in Bogota. There's no mention of Citibank. Based on the published list, members may think they are dealing with two banks in the Bahamas, one of which is a subsidiary of Citibank, but anything sent to these establishments goes directly to the country of cocaine cartels. On the April 2000 Clearstream list, there are 37 Colombian accounts, of which only three are published. (Richard Howe, spokesman for Citicorp in New York, declined repeated requests for comment. Cope declined to talk about any individual customers or accounts, citing Luxembourg banking secrecy laws.)

Clearstream's dealings with Russian banks are another area of concern. Menatep Bank, which had been bought in a rigged auction of Soviet assets and has been linked to numerous international scams, opened its Cedel account (No. 81738) on May 15, 1997, after Lussi visited the bank's president in Moscow and invited him to use the system. It was a non-published account that didn't correspond to any published account, a breach of Clearstream's rules. Menatep further violated the rules because many transfers were of cash, not for settlement of securities. "For the three months in 1997 for which I hold microfiches," Backes says, "only cash transfers were channeled through the Menatep account."

"There were a lot of transfers between Menatep and the Bank of New York," Backes adds. Natasha Gurfinkel Kagalovsky, a former Bank of New York official and the wife of a Menatep vice president, stands accused of helping launder at least $7 billion from Russia. US investigators have attempted to find out if some of the laundered money originated with Menatep, which they believed had looted Russian assets. (The Justice Department declined to comment on the investigation.)

Even though Menatep officially failed in 1998, it oddly remained on the non-published list of accounts for 2000. (Clearstream also lists 36 other Russian accounts, more non-published than published.) Kathleen Hawk, a US spokeswoman for Clearstream, says that was "a mistake." But Cope contradicts her: "Closed accounts remain on our files and systems even though they're non-active because we don't reuse numbers. We keep the records for many years so there is no future confusion from reused numbers."

But Backes explains that there's no systematic rule about delisting canceled accounts. He found that "some that didn't exist any longer were on the list. Others were delisted when they didn't exist. And still other accounts were delisted, when we knew they existed, though the numbers no longer appeared."

Régis Hempel, a computer programmer who worked for Clearstream, says that some dormant accounts were activated for special transactions. "Such an account can be opened in the morning, used for a transaction, and closed to appear as delisted in the evening," Backes explains. "Only the guy who gave the order to open it in the morning knows about the transaction. An investigator or auditor would not look at such an account because it doesn't appear on the accounts list."

Hempel also claims that Clearstream erased the records of some transfers. In testimony before the French National Assembly's financial crimes committee last year, he explained that a computer system had been developed to wipe out the traces of transactions in non-published accounts. When a bank wanted to carry out such a transaction, Hempel testified, it simply contacted a Cedel staff person. "We made a 'hard coding' in the program and corrected the instruction that was going to come," he explained. "[An instruction could be] a purchase, a sale, a movement of funds or a security. We made it disappear, or we put it on another account. Then, when all was finished, we put back the old program and removed the exception. It was not seen or known."

He said such requests came every two or three days.

■■■■■■■■■

Hempel volunteered to help Luxembourg prosecutor Carlos Zeyen investigate Clearstream. But Hempel says local authorities seem more interested in blocking an investigation than in exercising oversight. Zeyen responded that the inquiry into Hempel's charges hadn't produced any evidence and dismissed claims that Hempel had been prevented from seeing relevant files as "rubbish." In a July 2001 public statement, Zeyen said the investigation would continue.

Luxembourg sources say Zeyen was looking into how Menatep

"SUCH AN ACCOUNT CAN BE OPENED IN THE MORNING, USED FOR A TRANSACTION, AND CLOSED TO APPEAR AS DELISTED IN THE EVENING," BACKES EXPLAINS.

used the system and also into improper ways André Lussi might have gained personally. In January 2002, a French judge took depositions about Menatep corruption. According to Luxembourg journalist Marc Gerges, writing in the local newspaper *Land,* the FBI and the German BKA are also interested in what might be revealed about the role of Menatep in the diversion of IMF funds. Gerges says investigators are also looking to implicate Lussi in suspected financial swindles conducted through holding companies and trusts in the offshore financial havens of Guernsey or Jersey. (Lussi could not be located; his attorney did not respond to phone and email requests for comment.)

The publication of *Révélation$* brought forward others with stories about how Cedel/Clearstream had facilitated corruption. Joël Bûcher, former deputy general director of the Taiwan branch of the bank Société Générale, wrote Zeyen volunteering to testify that SG used the clearinghouse to hide bribes and to launder money. In his deposition for Zeyen—which is cited in Denis Robert's new book on the Clearstream saga, *The Black Box*—Bûcher said he had worked for the bank for 20 years, but quit in 1995 out of disgust at its rampant money-laundering. He said much of that occurred though a Luxembourg affiliate working through non-published accounts at Cedel. "Cedel didn't ask any questions about the origin of funds that would have appeared suspect to any beginner," he told Robert. "[As a result] we directed our clientele with funds of doubtful origin to Luxembourg."

In the early 1990s, Bûcher contends, Cedel was used to launder $350 million in illegal "commissions" on a contract for the sale by Thomson-CSF, a French government arms company, of six French frigates to Taiwan. He said that the money, handled by an SG subsidiary, was paid as a registered securities transfer to a "nominee"—a stand-in for the real beneficiary—and that Thomson (now known as Thales) didn't appear in the transaction except in the Cedel archives.

The kickbacks, which totaled over $760 million, were exposed after the 1993 murder of a naval captain named Yin Ching-feng, who had written a critical report on the purchase and its inflated $2.8-billion price. Bûcher told Taipei authorities that a third of the kickbacks went to Taiwanese generals and politicians, while the rest was pocketed by French officials. Taiwan courts sentenced thirteen military officers and fifteen arms dealers to between eight months and life in prison for bribery and leaking military secrets.

UNLIKE BANKS, CLEARSTREAM HAS NO EFFECTIVE OUTSIDE SURVEILLANCE.

"SG is very much implicated," Bûcher told me. "Taipei police searches found many records of transfers of commissions" relating to the frigates and also to the sale of French Mirage fighter planes. In New York, SG spokesman Jim Galvin denies that the bank had any involvement in the arms deal.

There has been no legal action by the Luxembourg prosecutor based on any of his investigations. However, Clearstream Banking, Lussi, and others have filed ten lawsuits for libel in Luxembourg, France, Belgium, and Switzerland against Backes, Robert, and their publisher, Les Arenes. The first case, *Clearstream v. Backes*, went

to court in March 2002 in Luxembourg. Another case began its first hearings in Paris a few days later. With no sense of irony, the liquidator of Russia's notorious Menatep Bank is also suing the authors and publishers for damage to its reputation. (Mikhail Khodorkovsky, the Russian oligarch who controlled Menatep, did not respond to a request for comment.)

■ ■ ■ ■ ■ ■ ■ ■ ■ ■

Backes' knowledge and records make him a valuable investigative partner, and he cooperates with numerous authorities, though he prefers not to say in which countries. But his agenda is larger than that. Backes is lobbying for oversight by an international public body. Unlike banks, Clearstream has no effective outside surveillance. It is audited by KPMG, one of the "big five" international accounting firms, which either has been ignorant of or has overlooked the non-published accounts system. KPMG announced last year that it found "no evidence" to support the allegations made in *Révélation$*, though its report was not made public.

Local officials' attempts to defend financial secrecy are not surprising. Luxembourg's multibillion-dollar financial sector brings in 35 percent of the GNP and gives the inhabitants a per capita income of more than $44,000, the highest in the world. (Next on the list are Liechtenstein, Switzerland, and Bermuda, all money-laundering centers, with the United States fifth.) For years, local officials have refused to provide bank information to other countries.

But Luxembourg authorities have turned their sights on Backes. Using a March 2001 judicial order based on a complaint made by Lussi before he was fired, police raided Backes' house on September 19, 2001, in search of records. He says they seized unimportant documents and diskettes; he keeps the microfiches outside the country as "life insurance." "The raid was organized to impress [others] not to repeat what this dangerous guy Ernest Backes has done," he says. "Those who know me well know I am not at all impressed by such a raid."

THE ENEMY WITHIN
RAPE AND SEXUAL HARASSMENT IN THE US MILITARY
TERRI SPAHR NELSON

There are four misconceptions (lies) that some people want you to believe about rape and sexual harassment in the US military:

1. The problems of rape and sexual harassment in the US military are not that bad.
2. The situation has significantly improved over the past decade.
3. Many of the women or men who do report ("cry") rape or sexual harassment are lying, crazy, or seeking revenge.
4. The men who are often accused of sexual misconduct are generally "good soldiers."

Consider the following facts to decide for yourself what is right and what is wrong.

_MISCONCEPTION #1: THE PROBLEMS OF RAPE AND SEXUAL HARASSMENT IN THE US MILITARY ARE NOT THAT BAD

The truth: Over three-fourths of female service members and over one-third of male service members reported experiencing some type of sexually abusive behavior on active duty in one year alone.[1]

There is ample documentation and testimony to verify the pervasive, highly underreported (often discarded) accounts of uncontrolled sexual violence and harassment by military personnel. Tellingly, the sources that best substantiate the extent of the problem are actually the military's own studies and findings. Ever since the exposure of the embarrassing Tailhook convention in 1991, numerous studies and committees have looked at the issue of sexual victimization in the military services. Here's a peek at what the US armed forces discovered about this pervasive problem that has invaded its rank and file.

One of the largest and most cited military studies on the topic was commissioned by the Department of Defense (DoD) and completed in 1995.[2] The service-wide study served as a follow-up to a 1988 sexual harassment assessment in which the DoD obtained its first baseline data on the extensiveness of the problem. The 1995 surveys were sent to over 90,000 male and female active-duty members representing all service branches. The findings of this extensive study speak for themselves.

• One of every two active-duty women (55 percent) and one in seven men (14 percent) (in all of the services combined) reported unwanted, uninvited sexual attention at work in the year prior to the survey.

• The likelihood of experiencing sexual harassment or sexual abuse was significantly higher for women in the Marines and the Army. Two-thirds of the women (64 percent of Marines and 61 percent of Army women) reported at least one sexually harassing incident in the year prior to the survey.

The incidence of sexually abusive experiences jumped when the list of behaviors included a wider range of harassing actions occurring on or off duty by military personnel (e.g., crude/offensive behaviors, unwanted sexual touching, sexual coercion, and sexual assault).

• More than three-fourths (78 percent) of women and over a third of men (38 percent) reported experiencing some form of sexually abusive behavior while on active duty. Yet, on the 1995 DoD survey (titled "Gender Issues") many of the women and men did not identify some of these behaviors as sexual harassment.

The facts are even more appalling when looking at the intensity of sexual violence and the criminal acts of rape within the armed forces.

• *In just one year prior to the survey*, one in every 25 women on active duty (4 percent) reported experiencing a rape or attempted rape.

If 4 percent of all military women were raped in one year, the numbers of women who are sexually assaulted during the course of their entire service are significantly higher. Unfortunately, these data were not collected in the DoD study, since the focus was only on the year prior to the survey and not on lifetime military experiences. However, other studies have found the incidence of rape among female veterans to be significantly high. Most of these studies involve women who have sought care at a Veterans Affairs facility (which could indicate a higher likelihood of past victimization, since women with sexual trauma histories are more likely to seek additional medical care). Some of these studies reported rates of sexual assault among female veterans at 23 percent,[3] 30 percent,[4] and 43 percent.[5] In another study, researchers found the rate of attempted and completed rape among women who were in the service to be 20 times higher than among civilian government workers.[6] Clearly, the likelihood of being a victim of sexual assault increases for women when they are in the military.

> OVER THREE-FOURTHS OF FEMALE SERVICE MEMBERS AND OVER ONE-THIRD OF MALE SERVICE MEMBERS REPORTED EXPERIENCING SOME TYPE OF SEXUALLY ABUSIVE BEHAVIOR ON ACTIVE DUTY IN ONE YEAR ALONE.

With regard to men as victims of rape, the data are even more elusive. The DoD survey discovered that sexual assault among male service members was not reported at a level high enough for inclusion in the study (less than 0.5 percent responding).

There are numerous documented cases of men being raped by their fellow service members. The lack of documentation or lack of acknowledgment of sexual assault of men in the DoD study does not verify the absence of this problem. In fact, it further validates that sexual violence against men and women in the military often goes undetected. Acknowledging and reporting a sexual offense in the military can be a formidable task. It should be noted, as well, that the incidence of men being raped in general is drastically underreported, even more so than for women. There are several reasons for this, mainly having to do with the fact that men experience added layers of shame and humiliation since they often feel that they should have been able to fend off their attackers and that the violation somehow undermines their heterosexuality.[7]

In just two years after the DoD study, the vastness of the problem resurfaced with reports of widespread abuses at military training installations, most notably at Aberdeen Proving Ground and Fort Leonard Wood. Ironically, in the calm before the storm of Aberdeen, one journalist found over 200 examples of sexually abusive misconduct by military personnel recorded in the *Army-Navy Times* over a nineteen-month period just prior to the Aberdeen exposure.[8] More than ever before, victims of sexual abuse by military personnel were coming forward about what happened to them.

Consequently, the Army may have gotten more than it expected when the Secretary of the Army sent a task force on sexual harassment to speak with service members at installations across the US and abroad. The findings of the task force were undoubtedly a harsh wake-up call for the Army:

In September of 1997 the Army issued a scathing critique of itself, saying [that the] reporting [of] sexual harassment and discrimination charges is woefully inadequate and that Army leaders have allowed the problem to persist.... Sexual harassment is so commonplace that "soldiers seem to accept such behaviors as a normal part of Army life."[9]

The problem was of such magnitude that members of Congress were compelled to speak out, as did Senator Olympia Snowe in her public remarks:

It isn't just sexual harassment. It is sexual abuse and misconduct. It's rape. It's sodomy. It's assault. These are very serious charges.[10]

In less than a decade after the Tailhook scandal hit the news, there have been countless other reports of violent crimes against servicemen and servicewomen, as well as against civilians. The list of uncontrolled violence perpetrated by members of the US armed forces is as overwhelming as it is horrific: It includes the rape and murder of a young Albanian girl in Kosovo by a member of the US peacekeeping force; the gang-rape of a teen in Alaska by military

personnel; numerous accounts of servicewomen raped by drill sergeants, recruiters, and other military leaders; and the murders of women by their military spouses.

Some military leaders have suggested that the problem is due to a "few bad apples" and is not endemic to the culture within the military.[11] Many have argued that the military is just a microcosm of society, so the military is not that much different when it comes to these issues.

Are the military's problems with sexual harassment and sexual victimization truly comparable to that of the civilian workforce? There are many complexities about active-duty military life that make it entirely different from working in the civilian sector. Without going into all the reasons why sexual victimization and its aftermath are indeed more complicated in the military, let's look at the basic facts. Consider a comparison of two similar studies on sexual harassment conducted at about the same time by the DoD[12] and by the US Merit System Protection Board (USMPB)[13] on their respective workforces.

> THERE ARE NUMEROUS DOCUMENTED CASES OF MEN BEING RAPED BY THEIR FELLOW SERVICE MEMBERS.

Civilian vs. military comparison of sexual harassment. USMPB 1987 findings: 35 percent of all female respondents and 12 percent of all male respondents experienced unwanted sexual attention on the job. DoD 1988 findings: 64 percent of women and 17 percent of men reported unwanted sexual attention on active duty.

Civilian vs. military comparison of rape. USMPB 1987 findings: 0.8 percent of all female respondents and 0.3 percent of all male respondents experienced actual or attempted rape. DoD 1988 findings: 5 percent of women and less than 0.5 percent of men reported experiencing rape or attempted rape on active duty.

The facts speak for themselves: Sexual harassment and rape are indeed considerable problems in the US military.

_MISCONCEPTION #2: THE SITUATION HAS SIGNIFICANTLY IMPROVED OVER THE PAST DECADE

The Truth: There have been some improvements in all services over the past decade, but there is still a long way to go in order to effectively address and reduce this pervasive problem within the military.

One might speculate that if Tailhook had been the tip of the iceberg in 1991, shouldn't the outcome be different now if the military truly investigated what was under the surface for all those years? The armed services knew about this problem long before Tailhook emerged, yet abuses perpetrated by military personnel continue to grow more alarming every year.

Consider what would happen if three-fourths of the men in the military were affected by an illness or a problem which originated on active duty. One would expect at the very least a stand-down, a call to action, immediate attention to the problem with devotion of resources, finances, and manpower to determine the cause of the problem and to make immediate corrections. We could not afford to risk our national defense and the health and welfare of so many service members to any single problem. Why, then, has it taken so long for the Department of Defense to respond accordingly to this threat to the health and welfare of so many troops? The armed forces are losing countless numbers due to sexual victimization and subsequent complications of post-traumatic stress disorder, job reprisals, lost promotions, ruined careers, and lost lives. Has the progress and commitment to this issue thus far been truly sufficient considering the implications?

One only needs to look as far as the actual conviction rates of sexual offenders in the military to know how seriously this issue has been addressed over the past decade.

Once again, the military's own numbers and systemic responses are evidence enough to validate the pervasiveness of this problem.

DEPENDING ON THE COMMANDER, A RAPE OR SEXUAL HARASSMENT ALLEGATION MAY NEVER GO BEYOND THE COMMANDER'S OFFICE AND THEREFORE WILL NEVER BE OFFICIALLY DOCUMENTED IN ANY REPORT.

The actual numbers of reported rapes and resulting convictions come directly from the military, though this information was not readily available. The military services generally do not keep records on all reported sexual assaults. It's a complicated system, and there are some (not so good) reasons for the barriers to compiling accurate data within the military. Here are a few of the reasons:

Many rapes are reported by the victim directly to the chain of command instead of the military police and are therefore never "officially" recorded. Service members are strongly encouraged to report their concerns through their chain of command. In turn, the commanders have the authority to receive such complaints, assess their merit, and make dispositions as they see fit. In many cases, commanders do not refer complaints that are a violation of the Uniform Code of Military Justice (military law) to the military criminal investigation organization. In fact, the complaints are often dropped at command level with minimal, if any, intervention. Servicewomen and servicemen have repeatedly indicated their dissatisfaction with the manner in which their reports were mishandled by their commanders.

These problems and barriers in the system have been documented in numerous studies, including the DoD service-wide survey and an international study on rape and sexual harassment in the military.[14] Depending on the commander, a rape or sexual harassment allegation may never go beyond the commander's office and therefore will never be officially documented in any report.

Despite a 1996 directive by the Department of Defense for all services, ships, and installations to begin systematically reporting violent crimes, including rape, the designated Defense Incident-Based Reporting System (DIBRS) was still not in operation or implemented years later.[15] The potential exists for compiling this important information, but it has not been a priority for funding or implementation. If the services admit there's a problem, they will have to do something about it. Hence, the mandate for the reporting and accountability system was put on the far back burner. Until DIBRS becomes fully operational and all levels are held accountable for complying with the reporting mandates, the problem of unreported and discarded rape allegations will persist. It will remain a crime that can be easily minimized or covered up within the ranks of the military.

Another barrier is the difficulty for the victims to come forward; therefore, most rapes are never reported at all. The reasons why victims often do not make an official report are numerous and often comparable to the civilian sector: concerns about repercussions, fears about the rapist, shame, not wanting others to know, not wanting to go through a demanding criminal justice process, concerns about confidentiality in counseling, and so on. However, there are some issues that are unique to military victims. These are addressed in more detail in the next section. As long as the psychosocial and systemic barriers to reporting are perpetuated in the military, the problem of underreporting will continue.

Given that reported rapes are just a small percentage of those that have actually occurred, the following data on reported sexual offenses and convictions are even more startling. In the aftermath of the sexual abuse scandals at military training installations in 1997, the Pentagon compiled data on reported rapes in each of the services over the preceding five-year period (1992-1996) at the specific request of a member of Congress. The data represents only sexual offenses that were officially reported to a military criminal investigative authority. Therefore, the numbers do not include sexual assaults that were informally reported through the chain of command or rapes that were never reported at all. The data were provided directly to me as an unpublished document from the Office of the Undersecretary of Defense at the Pentagon. It was reportedly the most recent compilation of this information available at the time.[16] The following is a summary comparison of the first and the last years reported, 1992 and 1996.

In 1996:

• The Army reported 440 sexual assaults, of which 33 resulted in convictions (8 percent).

• The Air Force reported 164 sexual assaults, with 19 convictions (12 percent).

• The Navy/Marines reported 412 sexual assaults, leading to 32 convictions (8 percent).

In comparison, in 1992 (just after the national attention to the Tailhook scandal):

• Of 422 reported sexual assaults in the Navy and the Marines, 80 percent (341) of the alleged rapists never faced a court-martial.

• Of those 422 reported sexual assaults, only 4.5 percent ended in a conviction; over 95 percent (403 service members) formally accused of a sexual assault were free to go on with their lives (or stay in the Navy or Marines if they so desired).

Based on these criterion of reported rapes and conviction rates, has there been improvement over time? The answer depends on how you look at the data. The conviction rates did increase from 4.5 percent to 8 percent in the Navy/Marines, suggesting a more proactive application of the "zero tolerance" policy, such as it is.

However, the numbers of reported sexual assaults did not change significantly over the five-year period. This strongly suggests that the systemic barriers to reporting persist, as does the underlying cultural climate that contributes to the problem. In fact, low reporting rates continued despite a congressional mandate requiring a review of these issues by the Department of Defense Task Force on Discrimination and Sexual Harassment. Specifically, the review assessed whether or not additional data collection and reporting policies on sexual misconduct should be enacted with a potential for disciplinary action for those who did not comply.[17] The recommendations for more stringent data collection and reporting efforts were made in 1994, and the DIBRS directive was issued in 1996. We are still waiting for the full implementation of and compliance with these mandates.

_MISCONCEPTION #3: MANY OF THE WOMEN AND MEN WHO REPORT ("CRY") RAPE OR SEXUAL HARASSMENT ARE LYING, CRAZY, OR SEEKING REVENGE

The truth: Women and men who have been raped or sexually harassed are often *told* they are lying, crazy or just seeking revenge. As an amendment to the National Defense Authorization Act for fiscal year 1995 admitted:

Despite yearly assurances of reform, women who are victims of sexual abuse by military members are still discouraged from pursuing charges. Instead of receiving help, they are treated like criminals.[18]

If you want to know if things have really improved, just ask any service member who was raped or sexually harassed. There are reasons why victims of sexual assault and harassment are reluctant to come forward to report their abuse in the military. Many of them know that they will be ridiculed, degraded, sent for a psychiatric consult, ordered for an early discharge, or face other reprisals if they try to report abuse. They do not think they will be believed, and for the most part, they believe it would do more harm than good to report the abuse. Consider the case against former Sergeant Major of the Army Gene McKinney. Despite the fact that six women (all unknown to each other) independently accused McKinney of sexual harassment, his attorney publicly scorned the women at the court-martial, saying that some of them were seeking revenge and that all of them were liars.[19]

> "I WAS INTERROGATED AND TOLD 'WHAT DID YOU EXPECT IN THIS MAN'S ARMY?' THEY SAID IT WAS MY FAULT."

Numerous studies and victim's reports have recorded this problem within the military culture for some time now.[20, 21, 22] Even the DoD's own extensive study in 1995 acknowledged fear of reprisals and not being believed as key reasons for not reporting abuse. Similar concerns were reiterated by numerous victims in a five-year (1997-2002) international study on rape and sexual harassment in the US military.[23] The following comments are from male and female military victims speaking about their experiences in trying to report the sexual offenses. Their own words speak volumes:

"When I reported the assault to Colonel [name deleted], she looked at me over her glasses and told me sodomy was against the law.... She was accusing and disgusted. I feared she would report that I (willingly) engaged in sodomy.... All I can say is that the Air Force creates an environment where it is unsafe to report assaults."

"The rape caused me to lose out on promotions.... I could not get a top-secret clearance. I could not 'be all I could be.'"

"It makes me incredibly sad to see/know that so many women have suffered this kind of abuse.... The worst thing I experienced wasn't the assault.... It was how I was treated by my command after the investigation was dropped."

After the rape was reported, "I was sent away to another base where I had no family or friends."

"Lt. Colonel [name deleted] called me a liar and gave me an article 15 [i.e., nonjudicial punishment]."

"I wasn't believed and I became the target of the investigation—temporarily lost my clearance."

"I was interrogated and told 'What did you expect in this man's Army?' They said it was my fault."

"No action was taken since I didn't act enough like a 'victim.' (Someone asked me) 'was his cock big?'"

"The commander stood in front of the unit and announced that a woman in the unit said she was raped by another Marine.... I was the only female in the unit."

"My commanding officer filed false charges against me to punish me.... They tried to ruin my reputation, take away my medical retirement and give me an 'other than honorable discharge.'"

"My career was brought to an early end."

"I was sent to psych after I reported the rape and was discharged against my will due to an 'inability to adapt to military life.' I wanted the military to be my career. I didn't want to leave."

"I worked for a commanding (two star general). His aide-de-camp called me at home and asked if I was gay.... He heard at drill that I was a dike [sic] because I reported an attempted sexual assault by the command sergeant major."

"The colonel called me into his office and said he

would discharge me if I didn't stop crying on the job. I was told to 'keep it under wraps' since he (the man who raped me) was an officer and no one would believe me."

"I was told to forget about it, according to a Catholic priest with 20 years active duty experience."

"My commander belittled me. He threatened to kick me out of the military because I was a liar.... I attempted suicide."

Fortunately, not all military men and women are ridiculed, humiliated, or become the target of reprisals when they try to report rape or sexual harassment. In fact, some service members indicated that they were treated with great compassion, sensitivity, and respect in the aftermath of their abuse. Yet the fact that so many are maliciously hurt when trying to report abuse is evidence of another weak link in a system in need of immediate attention. No one should be further traumatized or harassed when trying to get help, including those serving in the military.

_MISCONCEPTION #4: THE MEN WHO ARE OFTEN ACCUSED OF SEXUAL MISCONDUCT ARE GENERALLY "GOOD SOLDIERS"

The truth: Anyone who would sexually victimize or rape another person is not a "good soldier" and is a dishonor to the military.

"I will never forget that I am an American, fighting for freedom, responsible for my actions, and dedicated to the principles which made my country free."
—Article VIII, Military Code of Conduct

There is no way to get around it. Sexual offenders are not adhering to the military code of justice, nor are they respecting the values inherent in the military. Anyone who supports the misconception that rapists can be good soldiers should reexamine what it means to demonstrate integrity, honor, valor, and *esprit de corps*. Being a good soldier is more than doing a good job. It reflects how you live your life and the choices you make in order to serve your country with honor. Rape and sexual harassment dishonors the values of the military and those who truly are good soldiers.

ANYONE WHO SUPPORTS THE MISCONCEPTION THAT RAPISTS CAN BE GOOD SOLDIERS SHOULD REEXAMINE WHAT IT MEANS TO DEMONSTRATE INTEGRITY, HONOR, VALOR, AND *ESPRIT DE CORPS*.

These issues have been a problem for many years, yet the military services have not been successful in effectively addressing rape and sexual harassment within the ranks. The problems persist at unacceptable levels and, for the most part, the offenders continue to get by with a nod and a wink. This is neither indicative of significant improvement nor a serious commitment to zero tolerance.

It is time to stop minimizing the problem and ignoring the facts. These criminal acts should be exposed—not to bring discredit to the

military, but to strengthen the conviction to confront the problem. When rape and sexual harassment are tolerated or minimized, then honor, unity, and integrity will suffer. There is no honor without truth. We owe this much to those who sacrifice and endure so much in service to our country. The time is now to challenge the misconceptions about rape and sexual harassment in the US military and to move forward, together.

As one rape victim and veteran asked, *"Hasn't this gone on long enough?"*

Endnotes

1. Bastian, L. D., A. R. Lancaster, & H.E. Reyst. "Department of Defense 1995 Sexual Harassment Survey." (Report No. 96-104). Arlington, VA: Defense Manpower Data Center, 1996. **2.** *Ibid.* **3.** Hankin, C.S., K.M. Skinner, L.M. Sullivan, D.R. Miller, S. Frayne, & T.J. Tripp. "Prevalence of Depressive and Alcohol Abuse Symptoms Among Women VA Outpatients who Report Experiencing Sexual Assault While in the Military." *Journal of Traumatic Stress* 12.4 (Oct 1999): 601-12. **4.** Sadler, A.G., B.M. Booth, D. Nielson, & B.N. Doebbeling. "Health-related Consequences of Physical and Sexual Violence: Women in the Military." *Obstetrics and Gynecology* 96.3 (Sept 2000): 473-80. **5.** Fontana, A., & R. Rosenheck. "Duty-related and Sexual Stress in the Etiology of PTSD Among Women Veterans Who Seek Treatment." *Psychiatric Service* 49.5 (1998): 658-62. **6.** Murdoch, Maureen, & Kristin Nichol. "Women Veterans' Experiences with Domestic Violence and Sexual Harassment While in the Military." *Archives of Family Medicine* 5 (4 May 1995): 411-8. **7.** Scarce, Michael. *Male on Male Rape: The Hidden Toll of Stigma and Shame.* Insight Books (Plenum Press), 1997. **8.** Lombardi, Chris. "Violence From One's Own Comrades Is a Fact of Life For Military Women." Knight-Ridder/Tribune News Service, 19 Sept 1996. **9.** Schafer, Suzanne. "Study: Army Riddled with Harassment: Misconduct Crosses All Ranks, Lines." Associated Press, 12 Sept 1997. **10.** Warner, Margaret. (1997) "Conduct Unbecoming: Harassment in the Military." *Newshour.* Public Broadcasting System, 4 Feb 1997. <www.pbs.org/newshour/bb/military/jan-june97/harassment2-4.html> **11.** Feminist Daily News (1997) "Sexual Harassment in Army Not Only Result of 'a Few Bad Apples.'" Feminist Daily News Wire, 10 Feb 1997. **12.** *Op cit.*, Bastian. **13.** US Merit System Protection Board. "Sexual Harassment in the Federal Government: An Update." Washington, DC, 1988. **14.** Nelson, Terri Spahr. *For Love of Country: Confronting Rape and Sexual Harassment in the US Military.* New York: Haworth Press, 2002. **15.** Department of Defense "Defense Incident-Based Reporting System (DIBRS)," Directive 7730.47, 15 Oct 1996; Department of Defense (1998) Manual for Defense Incident-Based Reporting System, DoD 7730.47M. Washington, DC, 1998. Under Secretary for Defense for Personnel and Readiness. **16.** Five-year summary of sexual offenses as reported to military criminal investigative authorities. These data were provided by the Pentagon, Office of the Undersecretary of Defense for Personnel and Readiness (1997) as an unpublished summary report. **17.** Defense Authorization: DoD Investigation of Sexual Misconduct (1994) National Defense Authorization Act for fiscal year 1995, S. 2182. Nunn/Moseley-Braun/Murray second-degree substitute amendment No. 2147 to the DeConcini amendment No. 2146. 103d Congress, 1 July 1994, page S-8171. **18.** *Ibid.* **19.** Gearan, Anne. (1998) "Former Top Army Officer Denies Harassment—Accusers Seeking Revenge, He Says." *Cincinnati Enquirer,* 4 March 1998: A2. **20.** *Op cit.,* Bastian, *et. al.* **21.** *Op cit.,* Nelson. **22.** National Academy of Public Administration. *Adapting Military Sex Crime Investigations to Changing Times.* Washington, DC: NAPA, 1999. **23.** *Op cit.,* Nelson.

OPERATION PIPELINE
PULLING OVER MINORITY MOTORISTS AS AN EXCUSE TO SEARCH THEIR CARS
GARY WEBB

Let me apologize in advance for some of the stilted language and bureaucratese you will find in the following report. While I tried to make it as entertaining as possible, some of my best turns-of-phrase and my more acidic observations were deleted as being inappropriate for a government-issued report. Apparently the idea is to make them so dull no one will read them.

How this report, written for the California Legislature's Joint Task Force on Government Oversight, came to be made public is a story worth relating. After it was completed and turned in, someone—I was never told who—decided that it was best not to release it publicly. By then, though, many people were aware of its existence, and, after months of waiting for its release, the American Civil Liberties Union filed an Open Records Act request with the Legislature demanding a copy.

Eventually my report was released with an official cover letter disavowing it, claiming that it was an unscientific draft based on nothing but anecdotal information; that the Task Force which had produced it had been disbanded, and that no disrespect was intended to the fine men and women of the California Highway Patrol.

The letter was given to a reporter for the *Los Angeles Times*, who dutifully wrote a story saying the Legislature had disavowed the study and that its author was a former journalist who'd written a "widely discredited" series about CIA involvement in drug trafficking ("Dark Alliance"), meanwhile giving only the briefest mention of what the report actually contained. Shortly after that he left the *LA Times* and was hired by the Governor's Office as a PR man.

Ultimately, a class-action suit was filed against the Highway Patrol alleging illegal racial profiling, and my report was cited as evidence of it. The suit was settled out of court in early 2002, in exchange for the Governor's Office releasing $3 million to fund the data collection system that I had recommended in the study.

_SUMMARY

In spring 1998, California's Joint Legislative Staff Task Force on Government Oversight received information from a law enforcement source alleging that a little-known California Highway Patrol (CHP) program known as Operation Pipeline was being used to detain and search Latino motorists to determine if they were transporting guns and drugs.

Under Operation Pipeline, CHP attempts to find illegal drugs through "intensified enforcement" of traffic laws. According to the CHP, "intensified enforcement" involves generating "a very high volume of legal traffic enforcement stops to screen for criminal activity, which may include drug trafficking." By blanketing motorists on certain routes with traffic tickets or warnings, Pipeline teams are able to pull over a great many cars to find drivers who fit established "profiles" of what drug couriers reportedly look like and act like. If the motorist "fits" the profile, then the officer's goal becomes to conduct a warrantless search of the car and its occupants, in the hope of finding drugs, cash, and/or guns.

The CHP, while denying it permitted racial or cultural profiling, agreed to allow a Task Force consultant to attend training sessions and review hundreds of internal activity reports and documents. After an extensive review of this program—both in California and in other states conducting similar drug interdiction operations—the evidence strongly suggests that the program's effectiveness is not only being greatly overstated, but that the brunt of Operation Pipeline is, in fact, falling upon Latino motorists specifically and minority drivers in general. According to the CHP's own figures, 80 to 90 percent of all motorists arrested by Pipeline units since 1997 have been members of minority groups. Only 10 percent have been white.

CHP records revealed that thousands of innocent motorists whose race/ethnicity is not yet known have been subjected to roadside interrogations and warrantless searches of their cars and their luggage. Sworn testimony from CHP officers indicates that two-thirds or more of those motorists were Latino, a percentage far out of proportion to the number of Latino drivers in this state.

This program has been conducted with the support of CHP management. Individual officers involved in these operations and training programs have been carrying out what they perceived to be the policy of the CHP, the Department of Justice, and the administrations of former California Governors George Deukmejian and Pete Wilson. Thus, we are not faced with a situation involving "rogue" officers or individual, isolated instances of wrongdoing. The officers involved in these operations have been repeatedly commended by their supervisors for the jobs they are doing.

While CHP has a strong official policy against racial profiling and unwarranted traffic stops, it appears that some of these activities were unofficially tolerated and, at lower supervisory levels, even encouraged. Upper-level CHP managers did not generally concern themselves with the means the troopers were using to achieve the program's goals, except when troopers failed to meet their monthly expected numbers of stops, searches, and finds.

Key to the program is the use of "verbal warnings" to pull over suspicious-looking motorists in order to question and, if need be, search them. Verbal warnings are regarded by drug interdiction troopers as a tool of the trade, and by their superiors as a measure of the trooper's productivity and aggressiveness in the search for drugs. Since Pipeline officers are not expected to write many traffic tickets, and occasionally are discouraged from doing so, there can be no legitimate reason why they would stop and detain thousands of motorists simply to warn them against insignificant vehicle code infractions. There can be little doubt that verbal warnings have been used by CHP drug interdiction teams as pretexts to investigate motorists for drug crimes.

As a result, many motorists have been subjected to intense, invasive, and extremely protracted roadside interrogations. A Task Force consultant watched approximately 30 hours of videotaped stops done in the Needles, California, area in 1998. It was not uncommon to see travelers spending 30 minutes or more standing on the side of the road, fielding repeated questions about their family members, their occupations, their marital status, their immigration status, their criminal histories, and their recreational use of drugs and alcohol. Motorists who were taking prescription drugs or herbal remedies were interrogated about why they needed them and whether they were carrying prescriptions. If an actual search of the car ensued, stops sometimes lasted more than an hour. Many of these motorists were given field sobriety tests or had their pulses taken to detect signs of nervousness, which was then cited as grounds for requesting a "consent" search of the car. CHP figures show that in nine of ten cases, the searches turn up nothing incriminating.

Troopers are under considerable pressure by their supervisors to pull over as many motorists as possible and to conduct as many warrantless searches as possible. They are commended when they find drugs or cash, and are chastised if too much time passes between finds. In at least one case, an unproductive trooper was advised in writing to "be more selective" in determining which motorists to stop for investigation.

THE OFFICERS INVOLVED IN THESE OPERATIONS HAVE BEEN REPEATEDLY COMMENDED BY THEIR SUPERVISORS FOR THE JOBS THEY ARE DOING.

The Task Force questions the efficiency of using highway interdiction as a method of detecting illegal drugs and contraband. Based upon the CHP's records and a viewing of the videotaped traffic stops, it is clear that thousands of man-hours have been spent on unwarranted and intimidating searches of innocent motorists, most of whom are minorities. In terms of its potential impact on the civil rights of drivers, this program has been virtually unmonitored for nearly a decade. While that may allow the CHP to accurately say it has no evidence of racial profiling or civil rights violations, CHP officials also recognize that this lack of information makes it virtually impossible for the agency to defend itself against such charges. There is evidence the state may be on the verge of an explosion of litigation regarding this issue.

After the Task Force brought these issues to the attention of CHP Commissioner D.O. Helmick, policy changes were ordered—mainly in the area of internal oversight—that might correct some of the situations that allowed these activities to occur. The Task Force, however, makes a number of additional recommendations regarding changes in law or policy that will permit a closer monitoring of this program, both by the CHP and the citizens of California. Among them:

• The installation of video cameras in drug interdiction cars and routine audits of those tapes.

• A more comprehensive reporting process that will permit CHP to track the activities of drug interdiction officers more closely.

• Quarterly and annual reporting of this information to the public, preferably via the Internet, to allow citizens' groups to independently survey the activities of the drug interdiction units.

• Motorists should be given more information by troopers about their rights regarding warrantless searches and roadside interrogations about their personal lives.

_BACKGROUND

In spring 1998, the Joint Legislative Task Force on Government Oversight received information that California Highway Patrol officers assigned to special highway interdiction units were routinely pulling over non-white drivers for minor or nonexistent traffic infractions and pressuring these drivers into allowing searches of their cars and luggage—in the hopes of finding guns, drugs, and cash.

It was alleged that these CHP units were using "profiles" to single out motorists they suspected might be involved in criminal activity, that most of these motorists were Latino, and that the vast majority of them were doing nothing illegal.

In an attempt to corroborate this information, the Task Force located numerous small newspaper articles that had appeared over the past few years, mostly in the *Bee* newspapers in Sacramento, Modesto, and Fresno. These brief stories told of CHP units finding drugs in vehicles traveling on Interstate-5 during "routine traffic stops." In nearly every case, the stories revealed, drivers were Latino.

Shortly afterwards, Associated Press reporter Steve Geissinger wrote a story ("CHP Teams on Trail of I-5 Drug Smugglers." *Sacramento Bee*, 13 April 1998) which provided some corroboration of the allegations received by the Task Force—particularly the allegation regarding the searches of many innocent motorists. Geissinger witnessed a stop made by a CHP drug interdiction team assigned to "Operation Pipeline," which was described as a program using special units which "move up and down the highway teeming with truckers and travelers, trying to spot and stop the smugglers."

The final paragraph quoted the CHP sergeant who supervised the search: "It's sheer numbers. Our guys make a lot of stops. You kiss a lot of frogs before you find a prince."

_SCOPE OF INQUIRY

The Task Force attempted to determine whom the CHP's Operation Pipeline units were stopping, their ethnic and/or racial makeup, the reasons they were being stopped, the reasons they were being searched, and what these searches revealed. We hoped to learn how many innocent motorists were impacted by this program. We tried to determine how and upon what basis CHP officers were selecting motorists for searches, and whether these criteria were influenced by racial considerations. We also looked at other states that have instituted this program to see what their experiences have been.

With the Highway Patrol's permission, in August 1998 a Task Force consultant attended a two-day Operation Pipeline training session in Susanville, California, during which approximately a dozen Northern California police officers were given intermediate-level training. CHP officials also made themselves available for interviews. Following the training session, the consultant requested from CHP specific factual and statistical information concerning the field operations of the drug interdiction units. The Task Force also filed a Public Records Act request with the Governor's Office of Criminal Justice Planning for documents pertaining to its funding of the Pipeline program.

The OCJP conducted an extensive document search and provided considerable information. After initially refusing to cooperate, the CHP agreed to provide the Task Force with all of its field-level records and some management-level records regarding Operation Pipeline's canine units, its field-level activity reports for individual Pipeline officers, management reports to the federal Drug Enforcement Administration, and more than 100 hours of videotape made by one Pipeline officer in the Needles, California, area. The CHP also agreed to run specific statistical analyses for the Task Force and answer additional questions in writing. In exchange for this access, the Task Force agreed not to identify individual Pipeline officers by name in this report or reveal confidential law enforcement techniques.

The consultant also interviewed public and private attorneys, private investigators, DEA officials, and current and former Pipeline officers, performed a review of legal and popular literature, reviewed criminal and civil court cases and trial transcripts, and obtained considerable documentary information from both public and private sources.

However, the most useful information in understanding how this program works came from the CHP's own files. Once CHP Commissioner D.O. Helmick made the decision to assist the Task Force's inquiry, the agency provided complete access to thousands of pages of internal records. CHP also provided the Task Force with temporary office space and audio-video equipment, and was generous with the time of its Special Representative to the Legislature, Assistant Chief Joseph A. Farrow, who provided useful insights into the CHP and this program. Commissioner Helmick's willingness to provide this information to the Task Force was of great assistance in assessing the scope of the problem and in the preparation of this report. Helmick's efforts to date towards making the policy changes necessary to prevent recurrences have been notable.

> "IT'S SHEER NUMBERS. OUR GUYS MAKE A LOT OF STOPS. YOU KISS A LOT OF FROGS BEFORE YOU FIND A PRINCE."

_WHAT OPERATION PIPELINE IS

Operation Pipeline is a national effort sponsored by the US Drug Enforcement Administration (DEA) to find and remove drugs and weapons from the nation's highways. The DEA provides training and instructors for state and local police agencies, teaching them how to profile highway travelers to spot potential drug couriers. The California Highway Patrol first became involved, to a limited degree, in the Pipeline program in 1988-89. But in the wake of favorable court rulings, the CHP, the California Attorney General's Bureau of Narcotics Enforcement (BNE), and the Governor's Office of Criminal Justice Planning (OCJP) increased their involvement considerably.

In 1992, the CHP acquired a large complement of drug-sniffing dogs. The following year, with the help of a $100,000 OCJP grant, it put eleven canine units on the road. Today, there are more than 40, and Pipeline teams are running formal operations on all of California's major highways. CHP officers and BNE agents also conduct regular Pipeline training classes for local police agencies. California has become one of the states most actively involved in the Pipeline program and is consistently in the top ten nationwide in terms of seizures of US currency, methamphetamine, heroin, cocaine, and marijuana.

"AS FAR AS [ISSUING] CITATIONS ARE CONCERNED, DO NOT BE CONCERNED," ONE SUPERVISOR REASSURED A CANINE OFFICER IN NOVEMBER 1996.

In a grant application submitted to the OCJP in 1992, Highway Patrol officials offered this description of Operation Pipeline:

The Operation Pipeline Program consists of specialized training which focuses on indicators of narcotics trafficking, enabling Officers to develop probable cause to further investigate and search vehicles after a legitimate traffic stop.

Similarly, an operational plan for a 1996 Pipeline sweep called "Operation Northcoast," which was conducted in the areas of Garberville, Humboldt, and Ukiah, defined its "primary objective" as "highway drug interdiction and narcotic enforcement. Specifically, the Operation seeks to apprehend drug traffickers and confiscate illegal drugs."

The Task Force reviewed all monthly activity reports by canine officers between 1996 and late 1998. Those reports make clear that Pipeline units exist for one reason only—narcotics interdiction—and that traffic safety, which is the primary function of the CHP, is only a minor part of their jobs.

"As far as [issuing] citations are concerned, do not be concerned," one supervisor reassured a canine officer in November 1996. "I would like you to concentrate the major portion of your energies toward drug enforcement." The next month, the same supervisor told the same officer: "Continue to concentrate on drug enforcement duties and let the field officers handle the traffic problems."

_HOW OPERATION PIPELINE WORKS

The CHP attempts to find illegal drugs through "intensified enforcement" of traffic laws. According to CHP briefing materials supplied to the Task Force, "intensified enforcement" means generating "a very high volume of legal traffic enforcement stops to screen for criminal activity, which may include drug trafficking." By blanketing motorists on certain routes with traffic tickets or warnings, Pipeline teams are able to pull over a great many cars to find drivers who fit established "profiles" of how drug couriers are supposed to look and act. Once a profile fits, then the officer's goal becomes to search the car and the occupants.

"One would logically expect that a profile-minded trooper would be strongly inclined to conduct searches, since a search is the means by which the trooper would ultimately accomplish his or her drug interdiction objective," the New Jersey Attorney General's State Police Review Team wrote in a recent study of racial profiling in that state.

Sometimes, squads of Pipeline teams are deployed for days or weeks along highways the police believe are being used by drug couriers. Among these are nearly all of the state's major traffic arteries: I-5 north of Chico, I-8 in Imperial County, I-10 in Southern California, I-40 near Needles, I-15 in San Bernardino County, US-101 in Santa Clara and Mendocino Counties, and CA-58 in Kern County, for example. More typically, though, Pipeline officers are assigned to local drug interdiction duties, and they patrol their section of the highway on a regular basis.

At the outset, it should be emphasized that this program has been conducted with the support of CHP management. Individual officers involved in these operations and training programs have been carrying out what they perceived to be the policy of the CHP, the Department of Justice, and former California Governors. Thus, we are not faced with a situation involving "rogue" officers or individual, isolated instances of wrongdoing. The officers involved in these operations have been told repeatedly by their supervisors that they were doing their jobs exactly right.

The following excerpts from CHP troopers' supervisory reports are illustrative of the kinds of activities Pipeline officers are encouraged to perform. They also show the pressure that officers are under to generate a large number of traffic stops—called "enforcement contacts"—in order to conduct drug profile screenings and, hopefully, searches. Troopers whose enforcement contact numbers fall below certain levels can expect to be questioned by their superiors.

Officer P.

"You need to make more stops and be on the road more." (Oct 1998)
"Remember, keep the number of stops up." (June 1998)
"You are bringing up the number of stops made per day, but you're not there yet. A full day on the road should yield 8-10 stops per day, if you do not get a load. Work on it." (July 1998)
"Keep patrol time and stops up. No [drug] loads this month." (Aug 98)
"Contacts are up but there is still room for improvement. Six grams of grass is not what is expected. Keep trying!" (Sept 1998)

"Contacts are up. I would still like to see 10 stops a day. Searches are up also but without results. Keep trying." (Oct 1998) (It should be noted that Officer P. stopped at least 81 cars and conducted 30 searches that month.)

"You and your partner are going to need to step up your enforcement efforts." (Nov 1998)

Officer H.

"Keep your enforcement contacts up and increase the odds of a find." (Sept 1996)

"Keep banging away and keep the total contacts up.... [T]ry to keep those contacts up to increase your seizure opportunities." (Oct 1996)

"REMEMBER TO STOP ANYTHING THAT COMES YOUR WAY."

"Keep the stops up." (Sept 1997)
"Keep the pressure on and the big one will happen." (June 1997)
"Keep the pressure on and keep the contacts up." (May 1997)
"Generate as many stops as possible." (July 1998)

Officer J.

"Continue to make copious amounts of stops." (Aug 1996)
"Keep stopping lots of cars." (Sept 1998)

Officer K.

"Overall activity looks a little light. Just simply playing the odds it seems reasonable to assume that the more stops you make the higher the probability of encountering drugs. Would like to see more stops made." (Oct 1998)

Officer S.

"Remember to stop anything that comes your way." (Sept 1998)

Conversely, officers who make large numbers of stops and searches can expect praise from their superiors, and they are held up to other officers as examples of what drug interdiction officers should be doing.

Officer R.

"You take seriously your primary function of stopping the transportation of drugs on our highways. You are aggressive and conduct quite a few searches." (Sept 1996)

Officer B.

"Your numbers indicated you were out there looking hard." (Sept 1997)

Officer P.

"It appears you are beating the bushes for drugs and money." (June 1997)

"Your (numbers) indicate you are certainly looking for dope. Out of your 122 enforcement contacts, you searched 34 vehicles." (April 1998)

"You...searched 30 vehicles this month, equaling about 1/2 of those stopped. I know you are a hardworking diligent officer and it is only a matter of time until you hit the big one again." (June 1998)

Officer N.

"During the month you had 104 enforcement contacts...this shows that you were stopping vehicles and looking for dope." (Nov 1996)

Officer W.

"Your overall enforcement activity is a strong indicator that you are out there stopping people that display drug indicators." (Feb 1997)

_HOW "ENFORCEMENT CONTACTS" OCCUR

The key to Operation Pipeline is the use of a minor traffic infraction to launch a roadside narcotics investigation. Under current case law, the police cannot stop motorists simply because they look like they may be drug couriers or because they seem suspicious. Such actions have been ruled unconstitutional. But since the Supreme Court decision in *Whren v. U.S.*, 116 S. Ct. 1769 (1996), it is permissible for any police officer to stop suspicious-looking motorists for any reason, so long as a traffic offense occurs first.

As has been the practice in other states—namely Oregon, Florida, Maryland, and New Jersey—Pipeline teams operate by pulling over suspects for trivial reasons. The most common reasons used by CHP officers, according to documents reviewed by the Task Force, are:

• Mechanical violations, such as excessively tinted windows, windshield cracks, items hanging from rearview mirrors, burned-out taillights, and absent license-plate lights. Cases are pending in which rosary beads hanging from a rearview mirror were cited as grounds for the stop. More than one-third (38 percent) of the Pipeline arrests from spring 1998 to fall 1999 resulted from these kinds of minor offenses. Out-of-state motorists whose home states allow dark tinting of the front side windows are particularly vulnerable to being pulled over by a Pipeline unit on the grounds that California law doesn't permit any tinting on those windows.

• Obscured license plates, out-of-date registrations, and missing front plates account for nearly one in ten stops. Vehicles with trailer hitch balls on their bumpers are stopped for having "obscured" plates. Out-of-state motorists are routinely stopped for not having front plates, irrespective of whether their home states even issue one. Currently, 21 states do not.

OUT-OF-STATE MOTORISTS ARE ROUTINELY STOPPED FOR NOT HAVING FRONT PLATES, IRRESPECTIVE OF WHETHER THEIR HOME STATES EVEN ISSUE ONE.

• Unsafe lane changes, weaving, lane straddling, and following too closely. These are popular reasons for making Pipeline stops because these infractions are judgment calls by the officer. Motorists pulled over for following too closely, for example, are told that state law requires them to maintain a three-second distance between the car in front of them. Cases were found where motorists were pulled over for driving below the speed limit and warned against obstructing traffic. The interstate highway involved was in the middle of the desert.

• Driver or passenger failure to wear a seat belt. When the California legislature passed the mandatory seatbelt laws, one of the compromises reached was that this would not be an infraction that, by itself, police could use to pull over a motorist. A more serious violation needed to occur first. That prohibition was lifted recently, and seat belt violations are routinely used by Pipeline units to justify their stops and searches.

• "Immigration status checks," a practice that appears confined to an adjunct CHP program called the Imperial Valley Project. Judging from reports, this involves stops where an officer's curiosity about a motorists' immigration status is a reason for pulling over the car. The CHP described the Imperial Valley Project as "an ongoing narcotics interdiction program funded by the California Border Alliance Group, which in turn is funded by the High Intensity Drug Trafficking Area federal program." It is administered by the San Diego Police Department, and the CHP provides the officers and vehicles. The CHP "assign[s] CHP personnel from El Centro and neighboring Areas to patrol specific corridors with the intent of interdicting narcotic traffickers. Deployment of personnel is based on drug trafficking intelligence. Personnel assigned to this project are required to have received Operation Pipeline training and/or be a member of a Canine Narcotic Enforcement Team [CNET]."

The Task Force did not learn of the existence of this special program until just prior to this report's release. Further investigation of the Imperial Valley Project and its use of "immigration status checks" may be warranted.

The official policy of the CHP is that no traffic stop can be made without proper legal justification, and students in Operation Pipeline training courses are repeatedly reminded that they must first observe a violation of the motor vehicle code before they can initiate a stop. It is also the CHP's policy that racial considerations are to play no part in a trooper's decision to stop a motorist.

"Uniformed employees shall not look for characteristics associated with drug trafficking until the officer has a valid reason to contact the occupants within the vehicle," CHP officials wrote in their OCJP grant proposal.

But a review of CHP records indicates that thousands of drivers have been pulled over merely to be given a "verbal warning" by Pipeline officers, indicating that the alleged traffic infraction wasn't serious enough to justify even a written warning, much less a traffic ticket. CHP supervisors often commend their officers for the high number of "verbals" they pass out each month, viewing them as evidence of aggressive drug-seeking activity:

"Your verbals indicate that you are putting forth an excellent effort to hunt down the individuals who are moving drugs on the freeways. Remember, you are only as good as your last find and that better not have been too long ago."

"Your verbal warnings and total contacts are high. Indicates you're making the contacts to increase the odds of drug interdiction."

"Keep the stops up — lots of verbals, etc."

"Your number of verbals indicated you were out there looking hard."

"Looks like you did a lot of looking — 85 verbals."

"Your 40 verbal warnings indicates you were busy in your efforts with interdiction."

"You issued 53 verbal warnings, which is another good indicator that you were looking for drug loads..."

According to a 1997 CHP report regarding a Pipeline sweep called "Operation Northcoast '96"—conducted from October 4 to December 13, 1996, in Humboldt, Mendocino, and Lake Counties—CHP officers issued 1,764 verbal warnings and 245 citations and made 150 drug arrests. These figures strongly suggest that the overwhelming majority of motorists who were detained during Operation Northcoast '96 were innocent travelers who had not even committed a serious motor vehicle violation.

The difference between the number of tickets a Pipeline officer writes and the number of "verbals" he gives out is often significant. The Task Force examined the monthly reports (CHP100N) of several officers who patrolled an area in Southern California from 1996-98. We found:

Officer M.

1996: 51 tickets, 824 verbals
1997: 24 tickets, 823 verbals
1998: 11 tickets, 776 verbals (does not include Nov-Dec)

Officer C.

1996-97: 82 tickets, 1,692 verbals
1998: 6 tickets, 1,239 verbals (does not include Dec)

Not every Pipeline officer displayed such one-sided enforcement patterns, but it is fair to say that in the majority of cases, the numbers of verbal warnings far exceeded the numbers of written warnings or citations. In fact, as we will see below, there is some evidence to suggest that the only reason Pipeline troopers are told to write citations is to lull defense attorneys and judges into believing that they are ordinary traffic officers, not narcotics investigators who are looking for people who fit drug courier profiles.

This reliance on verbal warnings as a way of pulling over motorists for a drug investigation has occasionally caused concern among some CHP supervisors. Their concerns, however, were not that the practice was occurring but that it was occurring so blatantly. Officers were told, in writing and by their supervisors, to start writing more traffic tickets (215's) and written warnings (281's) to counter suspicions that drivers were being stopped for no legitimate reason. Examples:

"Good effort with enforcement stop totals of 93. Remember to write a few 281's just in case you ever get challenged in court regarding pretext stops."

"Would like to see a little more effort in the way of documented enforcement contacts. I understand the purpose and goals of the CNET program and don't want to distract you from your efforts. What I am suggesting is that when you have a violator stopped, turn some of those verbals into enforcement documents."

"I really need to see some more paper production from you. Start a new book of 281's and try to finish it off this month. The 281 is a great tool and they all go toward the total enforcement count. Strive to use every conceivable violation observed to make stops. Whenever you get the opportunity, have the violator leave with some paper."

"Remember on all your contacts that you should be issuing some type of enforcement document occasionally, so as to establish enforcement patterns. The 281 would work just fine for minor mechanical violations."

"I also encourage you to keep issuing cites. Two for the first half won't go far to establishing your credibility in court when you have to testify on PC [probable cause] searches. KEEP AT THOSE SEARCHES!"

"Write some 281's and 215's to cover your PC stops."

"Write cites or 281's for the PC violations for which you make your stops."

"Good job with all the verbals, searches and enforcement contacts. How's about throwing in a few more 215's—you know, just for the fun of it?"

The CHP keeps few records of these stops for verbal warnings. At most, the officer jots down the license plate number of the stopped car on the back of a CHP Form 415, his daily activity log. No information about the race of the driver is kept, and the reasons for the stop are kept only sporadically. At the Task Force's request, the CHP conducted a license plate search in an attempt to determine the race of those stopped for verbal warnings in all seven CHP Divisions. The CHP provided the Task Force with a chart showing the percentage of verbal warnings given by canine officers to drivers with Hispanic surnames in each division between December 1996 and January 1997. The percentages ranged from nearly 39 percent in the Central and Border Divisions, to 10 percent in the Northern Division. Currently, Hispanics make up about 27 percent of the state's population. The CHP stressed that the percentages are derived from incomplete data.

"REMEMBER TO WRITE A FEW 281's JUST IN CASE YOU EVER GET CHALLENGED IN COURT REGARDING PRETEXT STOPS."

It is clear that verbal warnings are regarded by drug interdiction troopers as a tool of the trade and by their superiors as a measure of the trooper's aggressiveness in searching for drugs. Since Pipeline officers are not expected or even encouraged to promote traffic safety, there can be no legitimate reason why they would be pulling over thousands of motorists to warn them about insignificant vehicle code infractions. Obviously, verbal warnings are being used by CHP drug interdiction teams as a pretext to investigate motorists for drug crimes.

_THE USE OF PROFILES

Once a stop has been made, motorists are compared against a well-established set of "indicators" to see if they fit the profile of a drug courier. The use of profiles, while controversial, has been upheld by the courts, but not for the purpose of detaining motorists in order to conduct drug searches. That is why CHP trainers stress to Pipeline students that they cannot use the profile as the sole basis for pulling over a suspicious person. They must first find some traffic violation, however minor.

CHP training officers advise students that the indicators are not widely known outside law enforcement circles, so they should seek judicial protection against being forced to disclose them in open court, in order to keep defense attorneys and defendants from learning them. The CHP's unofficial Pipeline training manual, *Drugs on Wheels,* offers the same advice.

But the CHP's belief in the confidentiality of its drug profile is unwarranted. The Task Force easily obtained a complete list of all the indicators used by the CHP from a variety of public sources—including the Lexis-Nexis database, which most defense lawyers have access to. The indicators are virtually identical in every state involved in the Pipeline program (they are public record there, also), and they have remained largely unchanged since they were first compiled in the early 1980s.

In California, the profile became a matter of public record within months of the CHP instituting the Pipeline program. The following testimony was delivered by one of the CHP's most decorated

Pipeline officers and trainers in a 1989 trial in Siskiyou County.

Q. Okay, officer, you stated that for ten or eleven months, you had the drug courier profile committed to memory, correct?

A. Yes.

Q. Could I test your memory? Could I approach the witness and ask you what the profile is, without looking at the list?

A. Sure...it is characteristic that the vehicle doesn't belong to them. Quite often, well, almost every time, they are extremely nervous. Also find that the passengers, if there are some in the vehicle, are extremely nervous and want to keep an eye on, and if possible, hear what's transpiring. Generally they don't have much luggage with 'em. If any. They usually use fast foods. They don't stop and go into restaurants and have full dinners. Usually stop at Quick Marts and things like this where they can gas and get fast food items. They generally don't stop to sleep. And quite often they carry pillows and blankets. They also, at times, you'll find that they have lots of different various types of communications equipment, such as CB radios, police scanners, radar detectors, this type of thing. Also, cellular phones are very popular, as are phone pagers. You also occasionally find odor-masking materials, such as powdered soap, scattered around inside the car. Coffee grounds is another one. You can also find—they will go into the service stations and they buy these little plastic odor—not masking, but perfume type scents that you—

Q. Uh-huh.

A. And you find that quite often a lot of those are scattered around the vehicle. Usually they have got road maps with 'em, up in—very readily available that they are using...

Other indicators the officer cited in his testimony included "excessive jewelry" and "certain types of clothing."

Q. And what types of clothing is that?

A. Some of the gang members wear certain types of clothing that are readily identifiable.

Q. You mean Blood and Crip type clothing?

A. Right.

These "indicators" are tallied up by the Pipeline officer. If there are few or none, either a traffic citation or a warning is given and the motorist is sent on his or her way. If the officer finds some of the physical and behavioral "indicators" of drug trafficking mentioned above, he is trained to continue the traffic stop and "ask questions designed to reveal the indicia of drug trafficking," *Drugs on Wheels* advises. "The officer should use this free time to develop his reasonable suspicion that the defendant is a drug courier."

_THE INTERROGATION

This is the second phase of a Pipeline stop: the interrogation of the motorist and any passengers. The officer is trained to subtly ask questions about their registration papers, their destination, their itinerary, the purpose of their visit, the names and addresses of whomever they are going to see, etc. Officers are trained to make this conversation appear a natural and routine part of the collection of information during the issuing of a citation or warning. They are advised to interrogate the passengers separately, so their stories can be compared. The officer will apply more "indicators" at this point, including how long it took them to answer the questions, how they acted, how consistent their stories were, and what kind of eye contact they made.

"The second thing in nervousness is avoiding eye contact, like when you have a little kid or child lying, thinking up stories. Adults do the same thing," a CHP officer testified in federal court in 1998. "They look away from you. They will kick the ground. They will just act like a bigger child when they are lying to you. It's pretty easy to recognize."

A Task Force consultant watched approximately 30 hours of videotaped stops done in the Needles, California, area in 1998 and was therefore able to observe the interrogations of many motorists. The questioning that was done was intense, very invasive, and extremely protracted. It was not uncommon to see travelers spending 30 minutes or more standing on the side of the road, fielding repeated questions about their family members, their occupations, their marital status, their immigration status, their criminal histories, and their recreational use of drugs and alcohol. Motorists who were taking prescription drugs or herbal remedies were interrogated about why they needed them and whether they were carrying their prescription with them. If an actual search of the car was involved, stops often lasted more than an hour.

During the training session the consultant attended, officers were advised to take the motorist's pulse during the interrogation, to see if the motorist's heart is beating rapidly. During the videotaped Pipeline stops, the officer was repeatedly seen taking motorists' pulses, pronouncing them "way up there," and then demanding to know why the motorist was so nervous. Pulse-taking was also used in conjunction with questions regarding the motorist's possible use of intoxicating drugs, particularly methamphetamines, and a high pulse rate was cited on several occasions as the officer's reasons for requiring a field sobriety test.

> **IT WAS NOT UNCOMMON TO SEE TRAVELERS SPENDING 30 MINUTES OR MORE STANDING ON THE SIDE OF THE ROAD, FIELDING REPEATED QUESTIONS ABOUT THEIR FAMILY MEMBERS, THEIR OCCUPATIONS, THEIR MARITAL STATUS, THEIR IMMIGRATION STATUS, THEIR CRIMINAL HISTORIES, AND THEIR RECREATIONAL USE OF DRUGS AND ALCOHOL.**

_THE SEARCH

If the officer is unsatisfied with the answers or the motorist's demeanor or his pulse rate, the stop enters its third phase. The motorist's license and registration will be returned. Legally, at this point, the traffic stop is over and the motorist is free to walk away from the officer, though few motorists realize they have this right. As a result, anything that is said from that point forward is presumed by the courts to be the result of a voluntary "consensual" conversation between the police officer and the motorist. As such, the officer can legally ask any question for any, or no, reason.

Pipeline officers are trained to strike up a conversation with the motorist, with the objective being to eventually get their permission to search the car. Unless the officer sees drugs or guns or cash with his own eyes, he has little probable cause to conduct a warrantless search, so most motorists are asked to "consent" to a search of the car. CHP instructs its officers to obtain written consent whenever possible, and consent forms are available in English and Spanish.

Typically, the motorist will be told that the CHP is trying to keep the highways free of guns and drugs and is looking to enlist the public's support for these efforts. The motorist will then be asked if there are any guns or drugs in the car and, if the answer is negative, the officer will ask permission to search the car and its contents.

SOME PIPELINE OFFICERS KEPT NO RECORDS OF THEIR SEARCHES.

CHP officials say that the vast majority of motorists agree to be searched, and they sign written consent forms allowing it. Judging solely from the videotaped stops, that is true. Very few motorists were seen refusing to let the police search them. But it must be remembered that when the drivers finally consented, most of them had undergone intense questioning for at least ten minutes, had seen their family members interrogated, and had their criminal history and driving records checked. On top of that, some had been given pulse tests, eye exams, and sobriety tests. Usually the officer expressed suspicion of the motorist's explanations.

If the motorist refuses to consent, the officer has the option of calling for a K-9 unit to do a sniff test around the exterior of the vehicle. If the dog alerts on something, then the officer can conduct a warrantless search, using the drug dog's reaction as his probable cause.

The CHP has never formally collected data on how many consent searches its drug interdiction teams have performed. The only field level-reporting is done on the back of the CHP Form 415, the officer's daily activity log. Whenever an officer pulls over a car, he writes down the license plate number of the car being stopped, the infraction involved (sometimes), and the duration of the stop. The Task Force reviewed several hundred Form 415's for drug interdiction officers from 1996 to 1998.

Some Pipeline officers kept no records of their searches. Many would write the letters "VS" or "CS" next to the license plate number to denote that a consent search or vehicle search was conducted. If nothing illegal was found, the CHP says, no further records exist,

including the name and race of the driver and the reason for the search. CHP says it has not collected or analyzed the consent forms motorists sign, which usually remain in the officer's possession for two years.

It is possible, however, to roughly determine the frequency with which these "consent" searches occur, at least insofar as CHP canine units are concerned. Nearly all canine officers report their monthly activities to their supervisors on CHP's Form 100N. That report usually contains a raw number of searches conducted by that officer during the previous month. Again, no racial data is reported, since the information in the 100N form is compiled from the officer's daily activity logs, the Form 415s.

Unfortunately, those reports are filed only by canine officers. Officers without dogs are not required to file them. Without those numbers it is impossible to get a completely accurate idea of how many road-side searches are taking place. Still, according to the 100N forms, it is clear that Pipeline officers conduct many hundreds of "consent" searches every month. Some canine units have conducted as many as nine searches per day, and officers are encouraged by their supervisors to search as many cars as possible, for any reason.

"Keep in mind, use consent searches even when you don't think drugs/money may or may not be involved. Who knows? You might get something unexpected," an officer in the Golden Gate Division was advised by his supervisor in September 1996.

Once a search begins, the interdiction officer faces additional pressures to find something, which is why Pipeline stops can take so long. Troopers are trained to look into natural cavities of the vehicle's body, and those are usually accessible only by removing interior panels, seats, gas tanks, spare tires, luggage, dashboards, heater ducts, and air bags. In addition, many searches involve walking a drug-sniffing dog inside and outside of the car several times.

"A trooper who is bent on finding drugs will be more likely to rely on the consent-to-search doctrine," the New Jersey Attorney General's State Police Review Team concluded in its April 1999 report. "Furthermore it is reasonable to expect than any such officer would engage in comparatively protracted patrol stops, since his or her objective would not be simply to issue a summons or a warning but rather to undertake a full-blown criminal investigation."

A string of unsuccessful searches is regarded with skepticism and concern by CHP supervisors. Trooper S.'s experience is demonstrative of this.

_THE CASE OF TROOPER S.

Trooper S. was assigned to the Central Division of the CHP in 1996, which covers an area stretching from Bakersfield to Modesto. In late 1996, his 100N forms show, he began receiving pressure from his supervisor to step up his searches in the hopes that he would soon find some drugs. He was instructed to concentrate all of his efforts on drug interdiction and not to concern himself with traffic issues.

"I know you're discouraged by not making any drug busts. Remain patient and continue to work at it. Something will turn up," the trooper's supervisor wrote. That month, the trooper conducted 27 searches and stopped 115 motorists to give them "verbal warnings."

The next month, December 1996, he found nothing. "It's only a matter of time before you start hitting," his supervisor wrote.

By February 1997 the supervisor was beginning to show signs of frustration. The trooper's monthly activity report showed he had stopped 115 vehicles and searched 43 of them, to no avail. "And the search continues. Someday we have to hit," the sergeant wrote. "Changing hours and working different shifts will be tried to see if we can come up with some drugs."

Throughout the spring and summer of 1997, the trooper's unlucky streak continued, despite his increased efforts to search more cars. Between February and August 1997, he searched 169 cars, while making only four arrests, mostly for minor personal-use quantities of drugs.

"It has been several months since you and [your dog] found any drugs. I know that finding drugs is not an exact science but you do need to find drugs on a regular basis," Trooper S.'s supervisor wrote in August 1997. "If what you are doing now doesn't work, we need to find something that will work. The drugs are on the highways. We just need to find tactics that will make this operation successful." That month, Trooper S. reported stopping 130 cars for verbal warnings and searching 36 of them. Before the year was out, the trooper would search another 45 cars but make only one arrest.

By April 1998 the supervisor was becoming impatient. Despite searching 23 cars that month, Trooper S. had made no arrests. Once again, he was advised to be more creative in his approach to drug interdiction.

NOT ONCE DURING THE ENTIRE 30 HOURS OF VIDEOTAPE DID THE CONSULTANT SEE THE OFFICER MAKE A DRUG-RELATED ARREST, DESPITE DOING MANY SEARCHES.

"Sometimes we have to step back and evaluate our tactics. I know you are on the highway every day. Maybe we need to look for other/additional indicators of drug trafficking to increase your effectiveness in doing your assigned duties," the sergeant wrote.

Trooper S. pulled over 123 cars for verbal warnings the next month and searched 30 of them. Once again, he found nothing.

"You are in quite a drought," the supervisor wrote in May 1998. "This is the second month without a seizure. When times like this occur you need to step back and reevaluate your procedures. Your present tactics are not effective. Let's try something different. I know you are on your beat working. I also know that sometimes we push too hard to try to make something happen. This month, try to relax and let's try something different."

Trooper S. redoubled his efforts, pulling over 163 cars for verbal warnings that month and searching 31 of them. He made no arrests.

"I don't expect an arrest a week but one arrest/seizure a month is a

reasonable expectation," his supervisor complained. "Maybe riding with a partner and changing hours will aid you in accomplishing what I know you can do."

The trooper's luck improved in July 1998, and he made two arrests on eight searches, but by August—despite pulling over 109 cars and doing 30 searches—he was back to zero. "In the past five months you have seized five pounds of marijuana," his supervisor reminded the trooper. "As you know, this is not acceptable. I also know that you are putting a lot of pressure on yourself. We have to do something to get you up to speed. Relax, quit pushing, *be more selective in your stops* [emphasis added]. After making a stop, let's speed the search up.... [W]hatever you have been doing is not working. Let's turn this program around get back to business."

The next month, Trooper S. pulled over 128 cars, did six searches, and made no arrests. It was the final straw.

"Beginning next month you are being assigned to assist the Pipeline interdiction units in Los Banos and Kern County," Trooper S.'s supervisor informed him on his monthly activity report. "Maybe with more exposure we can get you back on track...perhaps you are spending too much time training your canine."

_THE TALE OF THE TAPES

Trooper S.'s experience, while arguably unique, is nonetheless useful in understanding not only the day-to-day expectations that Pipeline officers must meet but in recognizing how difficult and inefficient this method of drug interdiction can be. But the trooper's case is by no means the only way to judge the efficiency of the program.

Using federal grant money, CHP installed a dash-mounted video camera inside the patrol car of one of its most highly regarded Pipeline troopers in June 1998 and began regularly taping all of his traffic stops in the Needles area along I-40. When the Task Force consultant discovered this in late 1998, the CHP produced 51 videocassettes, and CHP officials said they did not believe anyone within the agency had yet reviewed them. The consultant selected fifteen tapes to view from the box of 51. The selection process was not entirely random as the CHP numbered the tapes in chronological order, so, in order to get a fair sampling, the tapes were separated into three time periods—early, middle, and late—and five tapes were randomly selected from each group.

Not once during the entire 30 hours of videotape did the consultant see the officer make a drug-related arrest, despite doing many searches. The only arrest captured on the tapes was that of an African-American man from Brooklyn, New York, who refused to sign his ticket for having tinted windows, claiming that he was always being pulled for insignificant traffic violations and wasn't going to put up with it any longer. He was arrested, and his car was impounded and searched.

Only two seizures were observed. In one case, a loaded .25-caliber pistol was seized from under the seat of a car driven by a young, married African-American couple. They said they had purchased it legally for their protection while on the road. The pistol was confiscated, and the driver was ticketed for having a loaded gun in the car. The second seizure involved a partly smoked marijuana cigarette taken from the shirt pocket of a white motorist. The motorist was released with a warning that "you shouldn't have this." The remainder of the videotapes showed the officer stopping and searching dozens of motorists and finding nothing illegal.

_HOW OFTEN ARE DRUGS FOUND?

Again, because the CHP keeps no record of the number of consent searches its troopers do and because reporting requirements are not uniform, it is difficult to absolutely assess the frequency of fruitless searches. But it is possible to draw some conclusions from the canine officers' monthly activity reports, which show that they can go weeks between "finds." Their supervisors are frequently reminding them not to get discouraged by their lack of success.

Trooper P.

"Remain patient. I'm sure as often as you search and the volume of vehicles you stop the load is going to turn up." (Dec 1996)
"I know you are a hardworking and diligent officer and it is only a matter of time until you hit the big one again. You did locate some personal use marijuana." (June 1998)
"As usual, you did another great job this month. Despite your 43 searches, no drugs were found." (July 1998)

Trooper S.

"Keep up your level of enthusiasm. I know that it seems seizures can be few and far between." (Jan 1997). The trooper's reports for the first nine months of 1998 show that he issued 1,264 verbal warnings, conducted 163 searches, and had 18 finds, about 1 percent of all the stops he made.

> **STATISTICAL ANALYSES DONE IN OTHER STATES SHOW IT IS COMMON FOR BETWEEN 70 PERCENT AND 95 PERCENT OF ALL PIPELINE STOPS TO PRODUCE NO ARRESTS OR CONTRABAND SEIZURES.**

Trooper C.

"When you are out there you are making many stops/searches. Sooner or later you will hit." (Oct 1998)

Trooper W.

"You had high volume stops but no hits. Keep at it. It'll happen." (May 1997)

Another way to judge the effectiveness of the Pipeline program is

through the use of the monthly Departmental Canine Program Reports filed by K-9 officers with the CHP's Investigative Services Section. Each month, the officer lists the number of searches his canine conducted, how often it made finds, and what was detected.

When the Task Force asked the CHP for records of its consent searches, these reports were not included. A Task Force consultant discovered them late in the inquiry and then only because some had inadvertently been included among other documents the CHP did make available. As a result, the Task Force has not had a chance to fully analyze and tabulate the search results.

However, the reports that were found show that a great many of the canine searches were unproductive. For example, in April 1998, one officer reported performing 57 searches and making only four "finds," a success rate of 7 percent. His "find" percentages for other months ranged between 7 percent and 17 percent. Even when the searches were successful, most of the time they turned up only small amounts of drugs.

Statistical analyses done in other states show it is common for between 70 percent and 95 percent of all Pipeline stops to produce no arrests or contraband seizures. After examining the consent searches done by New Jersey State Police troopers, the New Jersey Attorney General's Office wrote that "most of the consent searches that we considered did not result in a positive finding, meaning that they failed to reveal evidence of a crime…. [M]ajor seizures of significant drug shipments are correspondingly rare." Only 19 percent of the searches in New Jersey produced an arrest or a seizure.

Data obtained by the Task Force regarding several Pipeline sweeps in 1993 suggest that those low percentages are reflective of the CHP's experience, as well. As part of the OCJP grant agreement providing partial funding for Operation Pipeline, the CHP was required to file quarterly progress reports, which the Task Force obtained through the California Public Records Act. From August 20-27, 1993, under the code name Operation Central Sweep, eight Pipeline officers conducted traffic stops on CA-99 and CA-41 near Fresno. From August 30 to September 24, 1993, eight Pipeline officers and two K-9 teams worked CA-99 and I-5 through the San Joaquin Valley. Collectively, they issued 532 tickets and searched 482 vehicles. They made 44 drug arrests—which means that at least nine out of every ten searches they conducted produced nothing. It also suggests that if the officers are applying the drug courier profile correctly, its worth as a predictor of criminal activity is highly questionable.

According to the same report, a similar CHP operation conducted in the so-called Emerald Triangle area of northern California—the marijuana-growing regions of Humboldt and Mendocino Counties—was even less successful. There, Pipeline officers spent a week in late September 1993 on Operation Harvest Sweep, issuing 206 citations and conducting 216 searches. Officers seized less than two kilos of marijuana, approximately two kilos of methamphetamine, several sheets of LSD, and a small amount of heroin.

An earlier progress report for the period of April to September 1993 showed similar results. The report stated that nine Pipeline teams had been funded by the grant and two of them had found no narcotics. The teams issued 83 citations, conducted 95 searches, and arrested five people on drug charges. Again, this means nine out of every ten searches were fruitless. Slightly over one kilo of cocaine, a small quantity of marijuana, and a miniscule amount of methamphetamine were found.

The CHP says that these teams, on occasion, discover large quantities of drugs and cash, which is certainly true. Six-figure and seven-figure cash seizures have occurred, and there have been cases where hundreds of kilograms of cocaine and marijuana have been found secreted inside cars and motor homes. But since we do not know how many innocent motorists were searched and questioned to achieve these occasional finds, it is misleading to draw a conclusion about the program's effectiveness solely from what is found. The experience in other states, and the available evidence in California, shows Pipeline units find contraband in a very small percentage of the stops they make. The vast majority of their detainees, therefore, are innocent citizens.

> ## SLIGHTLY OVER ONE KILO OF COCAINE, A SMALL QUANTITY OF MARIJUANA, AND A MINISCULE AMOUNT OF METHAMPHETAMINE WERE FOUND.

In April 1999, the New Jersey Attorney General recommended that the State Police conduct "an evaluation of the effectiveness of the use of consent searches…to determine whether these searches represent an appropriate and efficient deployment of State Police Resources." The Task Force makes the same recommendation to the CHP.

_WHO IS BEING STOPPED AND SEARCHED?

From the earliest days of the Pipeline program in California, there have been troubling indications that many of the drivers being subjected to this "intensive enforcement" of highway traffic laws are Latino. During the 1989 Siskiyou County criminal trial cited earlier, a CHP trooper gave the following testimony:

Q. When you were taught at the DEA these factors, did they explain to you what the scientific basis was or the statistical basis of the factors of the drug courier profile?

A. If I am understanding you right, they gave us no actual, you know, numbers. They just said that with this encounter, these are very, very prevalent characteristics that you encounter. They didn't say like, 99 percent of the time or something like this. They have just said, you know, that it is very common. It is very likely that this is what you are going to see.

Q. Well, with your arrests yourself, how come Hispanic isn't on this list [of indicators]?

A. What does Hispanic have to do with it?

Q. Isn't it true, in your arrests, far and away the majority of them included Hispanics or Mexicans?

A. The majority, yes.

Q. As a matter of fact, well over 50 percent, isn't that correct?

A. That's correct.

Q. How come that is not written down here?

A. That has nothing to do with characteristics.

Q. Perhaps I don't understand. I don't want to belabor it. I thought the characteristic was if something comes up the majority of the time and you find this common thread in all of these cases, then it becomes a characteristic. That's how you added road maps, rights?

A. No. Right. I have arrested quite a few Caucasians for the same thing.

Q. Isn't it true that the majority of your arrests over the past two years--

A. Yes. The majority. Probably 65 percent.

CHP does not keep racial data on those drivers who are stopped for verbal warnings, but at the Task Force's request, it began collecting that data for all verbals issued by its canine units during January and February 1999. Of 2,870 verbals issued, 36.8 percent of the drivers had Hispanic surnames. That compares to 28.1 percent of the 3,357 verbal warnings issued for the two-month period of December 1996 and January 1997, which the Task Force selected as a comparison period. CHP officials attributed the increase in warnings to Latinos to its statisticians' ability to more accurately determine the motorists' race, and not because more Latinos were being stopped.

The New Jersey Attorney General's recent review showed that, at least in New Jersey, "minority motorists were much more likely to be searched than non-minority motorists…. [R]ace and ethnicity may have influenced the exercise of discretion by some officers during the course of some traffic stops."

It is significant to note that many of the CHP's drug interdiction officers received their training from the New Jersey State Police, which was recently found by that state's Attorney General to have engaged in discriminatory tactics against minority motorists.

Unlike those drivers who are searched and released, CHP *does* maintain fairly complete records of the race of motorists who are arrested after a successful search. Those details are routinely reported to the Drug Enforcement Administration's El Paso Intelligence Center (EPIC) and other law enforcement databases on special computer forms known as Mask Menu Item #50.

The Task Force obtained copies of all MMI #50 reports that the CHP had filed with the DEA in 1996-1997 and analyzed them to determine the racial makeup of drivers arrested under Operation Pipeline. In 1996, of 476 arrests, 320 (67 percent) were of Latinos. Whites made up 22 percent of arrestees, and African-Americans were arrested in 10 percent of the cases.

Those figures were largely the same for 1997. Of 546 traffic stops that resulted in arrests, 409 (74.9 percent) of the drivers were Latino or African-American. All other racial groups, including white, accounted for the remaining 137 arrests.

The Task Force interviewed a former highway drug interdiction officer in Florida who told of routinely stopping African-American drivers for lane violations such as weaving or following too closely. The Task Force examined the racial makeup of arrested drivers who in 1997 had been initially stopped for weaving, following too closely, or making an unsafe lane change. Out of 156 such drivers, 121 of them (77.5 percent) were Latino, 24 of them (15.3 percent) were white, ten were African American (6.4 percent), and one was unknown. These percentages mean one of two things: Either minorities have special difficulties driving safely at interstate speeds, or they are being singled out for stops on grounds of their race.

Defense lawyers in *U.S. v. Barajas* (CR-S-93-495, US District Court, Eastern District of California) analyzed the racial makeup of motorists ticketed by a specific CHP Pipeline officer, one of the few times such an analysis has been performed. CHP agreed to provide a list of drivers ticketed by the Pipeline officer, along with a list of drivers ticketed by other CHP officers who patrolled the same area, but who were *not* involved in Operation Pipeline. The Pipeline officer ticketed Latinos 46.2 percent of the time, while the traffic officers stopped them 12.9 percent of the time. This is consistent with the results of a study done by the Federal Public Defender's office in New Jersey, which revealed that the more discretion an officer was given in his job, the more likely it was that he/she would ticket minority drivers. New Jersey state police units assigned to catch speeders, for example, ticketed African-American motorists only 18 percent of the time, while troopers who were assigned to general law enforcement duties ticketed them 43.8 percent of the time.

The following testimony, which emerged during a 1989 federal case (*U.S. v. Jose Luis Solis*, CR-S-88-346, Eastern District of California), suggests that the percentage of Latinos searched by CHP is even higher than their arrest rates. Again, the witness was one of the CHP's Pipeline instructors:

Q. So you don't know how many cars that you have stopped and done this search routine, didn't have contraband? You don't know how many that number is?

A. No.

Q. How many—do you have any idea how many were of Mexican descent and how many were of some other race?

A. I would imagine that probably 60 percent, maybe 65 percent, are Hispanic.

Q. Does that match how many Hispanics are on the highway? Sixty-five percent of the drivers are Hispanic?

A. No. It seems to match the number of people that I stopped that the car doesn't belong to them and...the other characteristics [which are] very high in Hispanic groups.

Q. You are saying it is more true with Hispanics?

A. No. What I am saying is that it has been my experience that I have run into more Hispanics in the last year that fit the profile, and that I probably asked them for searches, probably the majority of, 60 and 65 percent of the time, that I asked for consent to search.

During Operation Pipeline training classes, students were told repeatedly by instructors that racial profiling was illegal and was against CHP policy, and they were discouraged from pulling over motorists because of their race. However, unless one is willing to accept the idea that Latinos are worse drivers overall than other ethnic groups and more heavily involved with narcotics transportation, such disparate racial percentages cannot be legitimately explained if the traffic laws are indeed being applied in a race-neutral fashion. And in the opinion of at least one California judge, they are not.

OF 546 TRAFFIC STOPS THAT RESULTED IN ARRESTS, 409 (74.9 PERCENT) OF THE DRIVERS WERE LATINO OR AFRICAN-AMERICAN.

In February 1998, a drug case in Needles was thrown out by the court on the grounds that the stop was racially motivated. "I do not believe that Officer G. stopped this van because it had a cracked windshield, because it was following too closely, or because he saw a foot sticking out a window," Superior Court Judge Joseph R. Brisco said in a ruling from the bench. "I think his motivation was he saw a green van with three African-American males in it and I think that's why he stopped it.... I don't think Officer G. was completely candid with this court and that's the basis of my ruling."

In an earlier drug case, the same Pipeline officer admitted under oath that he had "probably arrested or searched more minorities than Caucasians."

Since the dismissal of the February 1998 case, the local district attorney has moved to disqualify Judge Brisco from hearing any more drug cases involving that officer, on the grounds that the judge is prejudiced against him. Approximately 62 cases involving Pipeline stops have been transferred from Brisco's court to a court in Barstow since then.

_WHISPER STOPS

Another aspect of Operation Pipeline that raises troubling legal and ethical questions is the use of so-called "whisper stops" or "wall cases." These are cases in which the CHP receives a tip from another law enforcement agency that a suspected drug courier is on the road, and a CHP officer is assigned to follow the suspect and look for a traffic violation in order to pull him over and search the vehicle.

Key to this stop, according to both the CHP's official manual and the training given to officers, is that the suspect is not to know that the traffic stop is anything other than routine. This is presented in the manual and in training class as a way in which to protect confidential informants. CHP officers are instructed not to divulge this information in their reports. According to the CHP manual:

Whisper enforcement stops shall be conducted as though involved Officers had not received information regarding drug trafficking. Officers are not to disclose the information provided by the allied agency requesting the whisper stop to vehicle occupants.... [I]f probable cause is developed and an arrest is made, in-custody reports shall not contain information regarding the whisper stop details provided by allied agencies. This information is confidential and should not be disclosed in the report. Officers should begin their report at the point of establishing independent probable cause.

While it may be true that release of such information would tip off a suspect that he was under investigation by another agency, another reason police officials might want this information concealed is because it would raise questions about whether the traffic stop was indeed "routine" and whether the officer assigned to follow the defendant pulled the vehicle over as a pretext to search for drugs. Such information would likely encourage defense counsel to probe the mechanics of the stop itself, in order to see if a traffic violation really occurred or if one was invented in order to conduct an illegal search.

IN FEBRUARY 1998, A DRUG CASE IN NEEDLES WAS THROWN OUT BY THE COURT ON THE GROUNDS THAT THE STOP WAS RACIALLY MOTIVATED.

An additional problem is that CHP officers who are under instructions to keep this information confidential may feel compelled to commit perjury in order to do so. In a recently publicized case in federal court in Sacramento, the Federal Defender's Office suggested that both a CHP officer and an Assistant US Attorney suborned perjury in order to conceal the existence of a "whisper stop" from defense counsel. In that case, a CHP Pipeline officer testified that the "only reason" he stopped a particular suspect was because he saw rosary beads hanging from the suspect's rearview mirror, which the officer claimed were obstructing the driver's vision. The Federal Defender's office discovered that the CHP officer had been an active participant in an attempted "sting" of the same motorist three weeks earlier, something neither the prosecutor nor the officer disclosed during an evidentiary hearing. Earlier grand jury testimony did, in fact, state that the CHP had received a tip to be on the lookout for the suspect. The case, which involved a major drug seizure and the possibility of a life sentence for the defendant, was dismissed by the federal prosecutor's office, and a state prosecutor also declined to press charges. The incident is under investigation by the Justice Department's Office of Professional Responsibility.

_WHO OVERSEES THIS PROGRAM?

CHP officials believe that any problems that may have arisen over the years with the Pipeline program can be traced to a lack of central supervision. When the program was getting underway in the mid-1980s, they said, it was directly administered and overseen from CHP headquarters by the Investigative Services Section (ISS), which is part of the policy branch of the CHP. ISS, which an internal CHP newsletter likened to the Central Intelligence Agency, concentrates on auto theft and narcotics crimes. ISS still retains some policy-setting control over the Pipeline program and receives intelligence information gathered during arrests. It also monitors the performance of the CHP's canine units. But it appears to have done little to monitor the program for potential abuses.

As one trooper was informed in August 1997: "Remember, ISS is focused on dope out of vehicles. Continue to lean in that direction."

After the Pipeline program expanded, CHP made a policy decision in 1990-91 to shift immediate oversight responsibility from ISS to the Divisional level, where the Pipeline teams are monitored by local CHP officers and where primary oversight remains.

As made clear by the records the Task Force has reviewed, supervision has been poor. The main line of supervision has been the trooper's immediate superior, usually a sergeant, and has been geared largely towards making sure the officer is pulling over and searching as many motorists as possible. Though the officers' monthly activity reports are routinely sent up the chain of command—ending up with the Area commander—in many cases, the commanders did not initial the reports or give any other indication that they had read them. In other cases, the commander simply added his compliments to the sergeant's and encouraged the officer to make more stops. The activity reports did not appear to receive much more than a cursory glance once they left the trooper's supervisor. Also, different CHP divisions have required different kinds of reports and collected different kinds of information from its Pipeline officers over the years.

Basically, it appears that as long as the drug interdiction officers continued to find drugs or cash, the CHP did not concern itself much with the means its troopers used to achieve that end. Though there was some indication before the Task Force began its inquiry that some managers within CHP were interested in monitoring the program—witness the decision to install video cameras in one trooper's car—the fact that no one had yet reviewed the videotapes suggests that this has not been a priority.

_POLICY CONCERNS

In terms of its potential impact on minorities or on the civil rights of drivers, this program has been virtually unmonitored for nearly a decade. While that may permit the CHP to accurately say that it has no evidence of racial profiling or civil rights violations, CHP officials also recognize that this lack of information makes it virtually impossible for the agency to defend itself against such charges if they are untrue.

Operation Pipeline is a program with a very real potential for significant abuse. In state after state, the use of profiling to conduct high-way drug interdiction has caused divisive public controversies, not to mention class-action suits by minority groups, at least one of which resulted in a six-figure settlement. The Eagle County (Colorado) sheriff paid $800,000 to settle a class-action suit after a federal judge ruled that the county's Pipeline team was making "racist assumptions" about interstate drivers who were being pulled over and searched for drugs. Maryland State Police have already lost or settled two civil rights suits stemming from this program. New Jersey judges have dismissed upwards of 600 cases in recent years because of concerns over racial stereotyping, and the New Jersey Attorney General's office just concluded—very publicly—that the New Jersey State Police were engaged in racial discrimination.

Because of the CHP's stepped-up use of this program, defense attorneys in California are gradually becoming aware of it and are beginning to challenge the stops in court. The Task Force is aware of at least one civil suit that is pending as the result of a Pipeline stop in the Needles area in 1996, during which two truckers hauling a load of horses were handcuffed in a CHP station for up to eleven hours while a Pipeline officer conducted a warrantless search of their tractor-trailer. The search revealed no contraband. Additionally, the truckers were charged $660 by the mother-in-law of the CHP trooper who made the stop for "horse storage" while their tractor-trailer was being searched. An arbitrator awarded the truckers $15,385, which the CHP rejected, and the case is proceeding to trial.

BASICALLY, IT APPEARS THAT AS LONG AS THE DRUG INTERDICTION OFFICERS CONTINUED TO FIND DRUGS OR CASH, THE CHP DID NOT CONCERN ITSELF MUCH WITH THE MEANS ITS TROOPERS USED TO ACHIEVE THAT END.

The American Civil Liberties Union recently announced a campaign to encourage motorists to report instances in which they were stopped and questioned after a minor traffic violation. During the course of its investigation, the Task Force discovered that the Federal Defender's Office in Sacramento was putting together its own task force to take on so-called "Pipeline cases" made along I-5, and is gathering evidence suggestive of racial profiling, as is the Federal Defender's Office in San Jose. Thus, it is likely that we are on the verge of an explosion of litigation regarding these practices. To believe the CHP and the state can avoid liability if civil rights violations are found to be occurring is unwarranted.

There is another, even more troubling, development in this program: Local police agencies are now instituting it and are setting up drug interdiction units on the interstate highways, sometimes in competition with the CHP. The Pipeline training session attended by the Task Force consultant was comprised mostly of local law enforcement officers from Northern California. Thus, it is not unreasonable to assume that the problems CHP is experiencing with this program will now be filtering down to the local level, probably with even less supervision than the CHP provided its troopers.

Another potential problem area is the extraordinary increase in the amount of cash being seized from motorists, which has soared in the past few years, coincident with the CHP's increased activities. In 1995, cash seizures amounted to $2.1 million. In the first six months of 1998 alone, the figure stood at $13.1 million. Forfeiture laws allow the police to keep most of this money, often without requiring the filing of criminal charges, and CHP documents show that CHP officials have anticipated offsetting the costs of some Pipeline operations with money forfeited from motorists. Because of documented problems in another state, namely Florida, where drug interdiction teams were found to be taking cash from minorities who were not charged with any crime, these highway cash seizures should be closely monitored.

Whether or not the State of California should continue participating in Operation Pipeline is obviously a policy question that ultimately is up to the CHP and the legislature. While the program sometimes results in large drug or cash seizures, it also consumes hundreds of man-hours in fruitless and intimidating searches of motorists who, for the most part, are Latino and are guilty of nothing more than a minor traffic infraction, if that. The program also falls heavily upon tourists and vacationers. CHP routinely exploits differences in state motor vehicle laws regarding window tinting and license plates to stop out-of-state vehicles and interrogate the passengers.

The bigger question, obviously, is whether traffic safety officers should be involved in narcotics investigations at all. If Pipeline training was being used simply to make traffic officers more aware and alert to signs of criminal activity that they may encounter during their routine duties—which was the intent of the training in its early days—it is doubtful CHP would be facing these kinds of problems. But that is not what many law enforcement agencies are doing with this program. Officers are being trained and assigned specifically to perform drug interdiction duties. Therefore, they no longer are traffic officers. They are narcotics investigators, and, as such, their motivations and attitudes become different than those of a traffic officer. Pipeline troopers get special cars, work in special units, get heightened and mostly favorable attention from the media, and earn praise and acclaim for finding drugs and cash. Their supervisors pressure them to pull over as many vehicles as they can and conduct as many warrantless searches as possible, in order to increase the "odds" of making a drug arrest. Their job performance evaluations depend upon their success in beating these rather formidable odds. When all of these pressures and motivations are combined, it creates a situation that invites abuses.

Unlike ordinary patrolmen who are looking for unsafe drivers and vehicles, Pipeline officers are expected to find contraband. It is only natural that they would concentrate their efforts on people who, to them, seem likely to be transporting it. Thus, these troopers do not randomly select motorists from the hundreds of vehicles committing traffic offenses on the road. They focus their efforts upon those who appear to be the most promising drug suspects, based on their training and experience. As Trooper S.'s supervisor advised him when he was having difficulty locating drugs, they must "be more selective" in their stops. In and of itself, this raises the specter of unfair and unequal treatment, racial profiling, and cultural stereotyping.

INVASION OF THE CHILD-SNATCHERS
HOW "CHILD PROTECTION AGENCIES" DESTROY FAMILIES AND TRAUMATIZE KIDS
DIANE PETRYK-BLOOM

After nineteen months in foster care, tiny Taler Corbin Barnes, who began life as a premature but healthy infant, was returned to his mother broken, brain-damaged, and blinded.

He was taken by the State of Kansas shortly after his birth in 1997, when the hospital reported his mother for refusing to apply for Medicaid. Never mind that the family had good, in-force medical insurance, or that the application form required the mother to lie and say she had been a resident of Kansas for six months when, in fact, she lived in Missouri. Social worker Grace Thompson filed a "Child in Need of Care" petition.

Once in foster care, Thompson and her colleagues ignored repeated bruises on Taler and evidence of what ophthalmologist Michael Varenhorst would later term "non-accidental trauma" to both eyes. Taler's left eye showed six crescent-shaped retinal ruptures that led Varenhorst to believe someone was repeatedly gouging his eyes with a fingernail. The baby's right eye was so destroyed that it collapsed. Doctors had to operate to replace missing vitreous fluid with silicone.

Taler's injuries, including multiple fractures and trauma-caused intracranial hemorrhage, happened during the six weeks he was in the foster care of Joel and Linda Hoffman of Salina Street in Wichita, where they have an unlisted phone number.

TALER'S LEFT EYE SHOWED SIX CRESCENT-SHAPED RETINAL RUPTURES THAT LED VARENHORST TO BELIEVE SOMEONE WAS REPEATEDLY GOUGING HIS EYES WITH A FINGERNAIL.

After authorities finally acknowledged the abuse and found complaints against Taler's parents, Cheryl and Eugene Barnes, to be baseless, they still had to go to court to get him back. Meanwhile, Taler was in another foster home for nearly a year and a half, finally to be returned home at nineteen months old weighing only sixteen pounds. He gained three pounds in his first week home, his mom said.

No one has ever been criminally charged for his injuries. The Hoffmans and Thompson and the birth hospital, Columbia Wesley Medical Center in Wichita, all declined to comment.

■ ■ ■ ■ ■ ■ ■ ■ ■ ■

Two-year-old Dominic James was in bed asleep June 18, 2002, when his parents were reported for yelling at each other. His mom was intoxicated. His dad was fine, though, and so were his grandparents, but the State of Missouri took the Greene County toddler into protective custody and placed him in the home of John and Jennifer Dilley of Willard. The boy's parents were allowed only supervised visits.

After each visit they found new bruises to report—on the back of their son's head, on his spine, around his eye.

Social workers told them they were "overreacting."

If authorities had looked, they would have discovered that the local county courthouse had a file on John W. Dilley, Jr. His former wife had asked for an order of protection after "repeated physical and emotional abuse" and described Dilley as having an uncontrollable temper.

Even after the tot had been airlifted to a hospital with mysterious seizures, a local fire station worker had reported bruises on him, and Dominic's juvenile officer and guardian *ad litem* had raised concerns, the child-protectors returned the boy to the same foster home.

But it wasn't to be for long. After another rush to the hospital in late August, little Dominic James died. Details of his apparent tortures were "kind of unbearable," said a family friend. John Dilley's foster-fathering days may be over. He's been charged with Dominic's murder-by-shaking.

■ ■ ■ ■ ■ ■ ■ ■ ■ ■

There are no Amber Alerts for the 3,000 children kidnapped each day by state governments in the name of child protection, but these kids are often left with maniacal strangers on deadly par with the abductor who creeps through a bedroom window at night.

Of children taken by the states, about 30 are killed by abuse each year. According to the US Department of Health and Human Services, there were 32 such deaths in 2000. Countless others are "protected" into non-fatal beatings, shakings, scaldings, maimings, deprivations, and sexual abuse.

Incredibly, almost 70 percent of the 3,000 children removed from their homes each day—more than a million a year—have parents who have not abused or neglected them in any way. That's by official tallies. On top of that, "substantiated" abuse is often such a stretch of credulity that no reasonable person could believe it.

Some children are taken from their parents when all the family needs is a little financial help with rent or utility bills. So why would states prefer the costlier alternative of foster care? Because the federal government now pays a bounty on kids taken from their homes—anywhere from $25,000 to $250,000 per year for each child, according to Utah attorney Michael Humiston. The feds pay $3 for every dollar a state can show it spent on child protective services.

The feds pay nothing for efforts to keep a child home or a family together.

Mackinac County, Michigan, attorney Stuart Spencer said child protective services is not about helping kids—it's about job security for the social service workers, family court officers, and the therapists, doctors, and lawyers on the payroll.

It's a growth industry, too, a monster out of control, said Humiston.

"Utah's juvenile courts eliminate all but a thin façade of due process. By law, parents can be accused and never get to face their accusers. There's no right to a jury, no right to remain silent, and no presumption of innocence. Worst of all, proceedings are conducted in secret. The state regularly terminates parental rights without ever showing that the parents are unfit."

Utah is not the worst, or even an anomaly. The other states differ in very slim degrees.

"Child abuse is serious, but we have ample means to cope with this problem without abandoning all our constitutional rights," Humiston says.

Once trapped in the web of a state child-welfare bureaucracy, parents can spend years and life savings trying to get their kids back. They lose their homes and their health. At some point, a child protective worker may agree that you're innocent, but sorry: The kids are in the court system now. Go ask a judge to give them back. See if you can get on the docket this year. Meanwhile, the children may be in torment.

Regarding state care, one woman who works in the system told the *San Diego Union*, "You'd rather die than have your own children in it."

Taler's mom died a thousand deaths while watching evidence of her tiny son's torture and not being able to do anything to protect him. Pleadings for his transfer to another home and for normal medical detective work went unheeded until the permanent damage was done.

Evidence shows errors in Thompson's report that led to Taler's plight. Joel Stephens was the Columbia Wesley hospital social worker who wanted that Medicaid application or else. He refused to comment for this article. Even if there were a real problem with insurance, there should have been no reason to block his family's bonding opportunity and his mother's breastfeeding. No one had ever suggested she was a danger to her child. Yet supervised visitation would not accommodate breastfeeding. A few steps away from her baby in the hospital nursery, Barnes had to pump her breasts for milk if he was to get any of it.

"I had to go to the pumping station at the nursery every hour, and I walked a few feet from where Taler was but I could not go see him," she says. "I knew he was on the other side of that wall, just a few steps away. It was heartbreaking…. [O]nly a mother would understand."

■ ■ ■ ■ ■ ■ ■ ■ ■ ■

There is no shortage of case histories showing social workers devoid of compassion for parents and so blind to foster care abuses that foster care credentials are almost a license to kill.

Statistics published by the US Department of Health and Human Services' Administration for Children and Families (ACF) describe a rosier picture. Citing a federally-mandated report, "Child Maltreatment 1999," the agency says that 1.5 percent of victims of abuse were maltreated by substitute care providers, while parents abused at a whopping rate of 87 percent!

Here's how this statistic is lying:

Almost all children live with one or both parents; less than 1 percent are in substitute care. Of course there is more abuse by parents in *absolute* numbers. But when you look at abuse per thousand, kids are at least two to three times more likely to be abused while in state care. For instance, Missouri, in 1998, had 11,000 "substantiated" reports of abuse by parents and 242 of abuse in state care. That's eight out of 1,000 for parents, and nineteen out of 1,000 for the state/foster care system.

The Department of Health and Human Services' report "Child Maltreatment 2000" shows an even worse situation for the nation as a whole. Despite the fact that approximately 0.8 percent of children are in foster care, they comprise 2.7 percent of all child-abuse fatalities. That's almost 3.5 times the rate we would expect to find if the situation in substitute homes were equitable with the situation in all other homes.

WHEN YOU LOOK AT ABUSE PER THOUSAND, KIDS ARE AT LEAST TWO TO THREE TIMES MORE LIKELY TO BE ABUSED WHILE IN STATE CARE.

Not all foster care fatalities are making it into the statistics, either. Barnes, who founded the monitoring group CPSWatch, says news clippings of foster care atrocities often outnumber official totals for several states.

But, when analyzed, the official reports paint a grim enough picture. The ACF offers a state-by-state breakdown of child abuse victims and non-victims removed from their homes in 2000. Nothing I am reporting should be construed as defending actual abuse or leaving children unprotected from abuse. But the number of children removed from their non-abusing families, abuse in itself, is staggering—66,203 in 2000. And that was with only 36 states reporting.

ABUSE YOUR ILLUSIONS

Populous states had big numbers—California, 11,406; Missouri, 8,583; New York, 5,004; Michigan, 4,406; Florida (the state that can't even locate many of its foster kids), 3,499; and Ohio, 2,918. But, again, percentages tell the real story.

In fatalities in foster care, California continues to lead: It had 30 child abuse deaths in 2000, with twelve of those (40 percent) in foster care.

Other states excessively prone that year to kidnap the kids of non-abusing parents include Nebraska, Hawaii, Missouri, and Arizona, all with double-digit percentages for ripping innocent homes apart. Again, with 2000 figures the latest available, Nebraska took 18.1 percent of its "non-victims" of reported child abuse, or 1,132 children, from their homes. Hawaii took 13.2 percent, or 349 kids; Arizona 12.3 percent, or 5,459 children.

"THEY WILL CANCEL YOUR VISITATION THEN TELL YOUR CHILDREN THAT YOU CANCELED BECAUSE YOU DON'T LOVE THEM."

Missouri, second-highest in numbers and third in percentages, took 12.9 percent—8,583 youngsters from homes.

Barnes estimates that any child in America has a one-in-25 chance of being the subject of a child abuse investigation these days. Humiston says the system feeds on itself. Whenever there is a scandal—like in Florida when authorities had no clue where some of their foster kids were—a politician gets up and says the system is over-burdened and underfunded. When they throw more money at it, more cases are manufactured, more federal bounty money arrives.

Poverty increases your chances of being targeted, of course. Social workers like to apply their own middle-class standards to how people should live. And they can more easily manipulate the impecunious and less articulate among us.

■ ■ ■ ■ ■ ■ ■ ■ ■ ■

But this is *not* a story about what terrible things happen to an underclass, just to the socioeconomic group at the bottom of the heap. It's about what one writer calls a "hydra-headed monster," one that might appear frothing at any of our doors, regardless of our degree of wealth, our occupation, race, or any other status.

"Child Protective Services Is capable of reaching into and destroying any home in America," contends author Brenda Scott in *Out of Control* (1994), one of the earliest books to expose the burgeoning child protection debacle. "No matter how innocent and happy your family may be," she wrote, "you are one accusation away from disaster."

Once child-protectors come, she said, they will have you believe that if you just cooperate and talk, it will all get straightened out. You have nothing to hide, so why not? Stop. This is guaranteed: Anything you say will only make it worse. The system works on information. Never mind that you are a good parent who hasn't done anything wrong and that there is no legal reason to take your child.

"It doesn't matter," Humiston informs on his Website, Nationaloutrage .org. "This is because once they have your child *they* have a monopoly on the flow of information. They can program your child to say anything and you can't disprove it. They can get their doctors to accuse you of anything and you can't stop it. And you can't get any more information from your child. You can't tell your children you love them. They will cancel your visitation then tell your children that you canceled because you don't love them."

Don't tell anyone you're depressed about it, either. "They'll use it as an excuse to put you on drugs and keep your kids away from you. This system is designed to play on your fear and anxiety."

Many people are not aware of social workers' extraordinary police powers. If they can get to your children without a warrant (at school, or if you let them in your home), they can whisk them away. They often force medical exams before parents are informed, although the Ninth Circuit Court of Appeals recently said that's impermissible. The attorney for Dominic James' parents, Shawn Akinosie, put it this way:

These people wield power unparalleled with any other government agency. The reality is, it's over our most prized possession—our children. I'm not sure of the words to describe the kind of distrust and fear this should cause people. Dominic might be alive today.

Their power is strengthened by nearly complete immunity from prosecution for malfeasance and misfeasance on the job—a power that has corrupted mightily. It has been shown that child protective services workers will connive and lie to prevail if they want to grab and adopt out your kids.

The *Springfield News-Leader* showed that the Greene County Division of Family Services that took Dominic James lied when it said it had only an anonymous report of his bruises. The call was made by a Willard Fire Department worker who gave her name, and witnesses attest to that. Even so, when DFS said no mandated follow-up could occur because the call was made anonymously, it was a tragically comedic remark coming from a system that takes major impetus from anonymous calls.

In 1992, a San Diego Grand Jury reported that it had:

• seen evidence of social workers' perjury in court records and testimony;

• heard testimonies by attorneys and court-appointed therapists that social workers have threatened to have them removed from court-appointed lists if they failed to adhere to the social workers' recommendations;

• heard testimonies that social workers have threatened to remove additional children from families who fail to exactly follow the social workers' recommendations (these can include great indignities, such as repeated urine-testing, regardless of any indication of drug use, and penile plethysmography—more on this later) when there is no issue regarding the other children;

• heard testimonies that even repeated adverse reports by professionals about individual social workers have failed to result in discipline;

• heard testimonies by attorneys that when faced with the most blatant abuses of power, there are still no remedies for their clients;

• heard therapists testify that social workers threatened to ruin their careers with a report that they have "accommodated the denial" of a client, or questioned a "true finding";

• saw evidence of social workers conspiring to place children for adoption with their own (social workers') family members, even while reunification with the natural family was in process;

• saw evidence of social workers placing children in particular foster homes which would render the opportunity to reunify the family non-existent;

• read numerous social study reports filled with innuendo, half-truths, and lies;

• saw evidence of social workers so obsessed with molestation scenarios that they were unable to maintain even a semblance of objectivity.

If your children are taken, you will get a court hearing later, but it is often before a judge who barely glances up from the social worker's report. The courts don't like you to talk or compile evidence. Barnes was forbidden from videotaping her visits with Taler. Jack Stratton in Charlotte, North Carolina, was jailed after disobeying District Court Judge Libby Miller's order that he not talk to the press about his child neglect case.

You can find your child "disappeared" (apologies to Argentina) if he or she got bruised playing baseball, if your little girl scratched her crotch, if a neighbor made up a story because she doesn't like the way you park your car, if someone reports a spanking—even one that doesn't leave a mark—at your house, if you argue loudly with your spouse or partner, if the drugstore photo developer reports those cute baby-in-the-bathtub pictures, if you homeschool, if your toddler accidentally saw you step out of the shower, if your kids get scratched or sunburned, or when any of countless other possible parenting decisions you may make conflict with a social worker's personal prejudices. And heaven help you if your little daughter blurts out, "Daddy and I have a secret."

■ ■ ■ ■ ■ ■ ■ ■ ■ ■

A phrase you often hear invoked—"Err on the side of the child"—if there is any doubt that a child is at-risk—is used to justify removing him from his home. Why not? If nothing is amiss, no problem, the child will be returned. Tell that to Dominic James' parents, Taler Barnes' parents, or the mother of Constance Porter, age two.

Shavia Porter lost her job, and consequently her apartment, in early 2001. She needed a little time to get another job and get straightened out, so she voluntarily gave Constance to the child-protectors in Jackson County, Kansas. The little girl was placed in the foster home of Tina Clayton, which had already been the subject of a call from a child abuse hotline, according to the *Kansas City Star*. Clayton was soon charged with Constance's shaking and beating death. The other foster children she had were removed, but her biological children were allowed to stay with relatives.

In another case, one mentally retarded 15-year-old was saved from foster abuse only after his horrific flogging was surreptitiously videotaped by neighbors.

Foster mom drags child with car (the child is returned to the same home); foster dad impregnates two foster girls; 2-year-old foster child drowned in bathtub; 5-year-old killed by foster family's Rottweiler.... If you can take it, there's plenty more of these news stories at www.donttakeourkids.com

Parents kill and abuse their children, too. But social workers are so busy running down anonymous tips about trivialities that they miss the children who really need their protection, says *Wounded Innocents* author Richard Wexler, a journalist turned crusader for child protection reform.

Those parents who get their kids back basically intact from foster care know it usually isn't until they have been dragged through awesome emotional terrors and financial burdens. There are kindly, well-meaning foster caregivers. But even children treated compassionately in foster care suffer traumatic separation from their parents, repetitive interrogations, and horribly intrusive physical exams.

IN ANOTHER CASE, ONE MENTALLY RETARDED 15-YEAR-OLD WAS SAVED FROM FOSTER ABUSE ONLY AFTER HIS HORRIFIC FLOGGING WAS SURREPTITIOUSLY VIDEOTAPED BY NEIGHBORS.

Rachel Nixon, 24, of Colorado, told me she was treated well by social workers and foster caregivers and had a nice adoptive home. But she and her sister weren't taken from her father (at ages 7 and 9) for anything substantive. She's just beginning to realize how he spent years in court trying to get them back. She's understanding that when her fondness toward the father she remembered ended, it was because of the false things adults were telling her. They told her masturbation was evidence of sexual abuse, for one thing. In short, she's beginning to realize her father was unjustly taken from *her*. How much it hurt him, she has yet to grasp.

In a case Brenda Scott detailed in her book, a child protective unit kidnapped a 6-year-old girl from her kindergarten class because she rubbed herself between her legs. "The child was forced to strip, pose for photographs and submit to a vaginal exam. She had a yeast infection." Without a trial, the child-protectors demanded that the father leave home unless he admitted guilt. Frequently it doesn't matter how heinous your crime. As long as you admit your guilt, you're no longer a danger to your kids. But pleading guilty opens up a host of other problems.

Sometimes the accused are children, who, in normal acts of exploring their bodies, find themselves charged as sexual offenders. At Arizona's Phoenix Memorial Hospital, as well as 168 junvenile offender programs across the country, according to Scott, boys as young as eleven are ordered to undergo penile plethysmography. With the plethysmograph collar around their penises, the boys are shown pictures of naked children in bondage poses. Supposedly, increases in their penile tumescence at the sight of these pictures determines their tendency toward pedophilia. If it seems they are aroused by these pictures, they are then told to look at them some more and inhale ammonia! This is widely accepted aversion therapy for "sexual perversion." Penile plethysmography, which is questionable at best even for adults males, is totally unethical for prepubescent children, says clinical psychologist Toni Cavanaugh Johnson, who works with child sex offenders. As quoted by Scott, she says no one understands arousal in young boys. "These kids get erections when they're scared, they get erections when they're angry."

When her book came out eight years ago, Scott estimated that over one million people are falsely accused of child abuse in the United States each year. At that time my colleagues at the *Times-News*, a *New York Times*' regional newspaper in Hendersonville, North Carolina, decided to do a series on child sexual abuse, and false accusations became my topic. I was put in touch with accused persons claiming their innocence by Gail Searcy, a Hendersonville leader of VOCAL, Victims of Child Abuse Laws.

The first man I interviewed told me his story with the requisite claim of innocence. One starts out assuming, sure, everyone charged with a crime *claims* to be innocent. But by the fourth or fifth case study, the similarities became too clear to ignore. Often there was a divorce or family dispute predating the accusation. Social workers moved in without evidence and removed the kids. They insist on an admission of guilt, and other family members must say they believe in the guilt or they will never get to see the child again, either. No character witnesses for the accused are ever allowed. Bizarre, impossible scenarios go unquestioned. Children are questioned incessantly until their stories flip-flop the desired way.

If it isn't a family dispute, it's often a medical misdiagnosis. Attorney Spencer says that if he didn't have to make a living, he would like to spend all of his time defending unjustly accused parents of children with brittle bone disease, osteogenesis imperfecta. Often their infants turn up with broken bones, and often it is assumed that the parents have done something to them. Some children have their first injury soon after birth, others when they try to walk for the first time, according to the Brittle Bone Society, based in Scotland.

The plight of several families plagued by both brittle bones in their kids and pig-headed social workers was described by writer Ivan Helfman in *Michigan Monthly* in 1996. Helfman wrote of "a small contingent of rogue social workers" who snatched these babies and had them wrongfully adopted. "Once adopted out, their biological parents are history. Afterwards, wronged parents could expose social workers' errors under a 1,000-watt spotlight and Michigan courts won't see a thing."

Spencer says US doctors are afraid to testify about brittle bone disease because it is politically incorrect, so he relies on a Scottish expert. "But if a child is taken away from his parents because of broken bones and the child continues to have broken bones in foster care, what could be clearer?"

During my look at false accusations, I saw how interrogation can turn a child's first statements 180 degrees. I heard from parents who were criticized by social workers for behaviors during supervised visitations, which included peeling an apple for the child, pulling a little girl's dress down for modesty, and holding a 2-year-old girl with hand under her diapered bottom (this criticism was directed at a male).

From former Massachusetts Department of Social Services attorney Diane Webster-Brady I heard that this was considered damning criticism: "Takes baby for walks but didn't have a destination in mind."

Barnes said a mother called her to say she's under the gun for a 3-year-old still sleeping in a crib. "And if the baby fell out of bed and hit his head, they'd ask her why he wasn't still in a crib," she says.

In North Carolina I was a single mother with a 4-year-old myself at the time and was starting to be concerned that if I wrote all that I had found I might hear a knock at the door. Never more so than when Brevard attorney Ladsen Hart told me about a sex abuse set-up.

Social workers in Transylvania County were working diligently to keep a dad from obtaining custody of his little girl. The mom had taken off, and, although they weren't married, the father wanted to bring up his child, and his mother, the girl's grandmother, was there to help.

Through the months, while social workers asked the dad to go to this parenting class to learn to bathe a baby and to that class to learn to feed a baby, the grandmother contacted Searcy at VOCAL for moral support. Her son was jumping through all the hoops, but word got out that his cute little girl was being sought for adoption by a friend of the social worker involved, and they were tenaciously holding the father at bay. Just before the social worker was going to allow the dad's first overnight visitation with his child, Searcy had a concern, or maybe it was a premonition. At least she offered this warning: "Don't let him be alone with the child."

Family and friends posted a 24-hour vigil with father and daughter during the visitation over Christmas. So thorough was the watch, that when the child was brought back to social services custody and within a few hours the father was threatened with a sex abuse charge, Hart was able to say: "You'd better think of something else, because we've got that one covered."

CHILDREN ARE QUESTIONED INCESSANTLY UNTIL THEIR STORIES FLIP-FLOP THE DESIRED WAY.

Soon after, the father won custody. The story didn't get included in the piece I wrote for the *Times-News* because after such a long battle the family didn't want to rock the boat, and I became less concerned about my byline on the piece putting my own child in jeopardy.

■ ■ ■ ■ ■ ■ ■ ■ ■ ■

I put the false accusations topic behind me for a while and eventually moved on to edit a weekly newspaper in a resort town in Michigan's Upper Peninsula. One day, Misti Laverty came to my office. A judge was threatening to take her 9-year-old daughter away forever. Publicity was her last hope.

Misti wasn't accused of doing a thing. Her crime was that she didn't think her husband had, either.

But Mackinac County Probate Court Judge Thomas North ordered her to say she believed Kenneth Laverty molested their daughter or he would terminate her parental rights, too. Misti didn't want to lie, and even if she went along with a lie, it would put her husband in criminal jeopardy. Here's how events unfolded:

When she was age nine, around Thanksgiving 1994, Rachelle Laverty told her mother that her father (Kenneth Laverty) made her perform sexual acts. Mrs. Laverty immediately took Rachelle to a physician, who could not confirm the girl had been sexually abused.

Rachelle's persistence in the accusation, using the term "sexual abuse," came to the attention of social workers who promptly took the girl into custody. A social services' physician, seven days after Rachelle was sequestered in foster care, found indications of possible sexual abuse.

Mrs. Laverty believed that if Rachelle had been abused, it happened after she was in foster care. For one thing, Kenneth Laverty, a truck driver, was out of the state on the one specific date Rachelle claimed abuse had taken place.

A polygraph test administered by Michigan State Police showed Laverty answered honestly when he said he did not molest Rachelle. And, powerfully persuasive to Misti, her sons, ages ten and twelve, said their father didn't do what Rachelle claimed.

Charges were made, and Laverty steadfastly maintained his innocence. State Police investigator Robin Sexton investigated the original charges and interviewed Rachelle. "I'm certain I have statements from her inconsistent with the truth," he told me. "A competent attorney could tear her story apart in ten minutes." In 1995, because of Sexton's doubts and lack of evidence, the Mackinac County Prosecutor's Office decided not to pursue charges against Laverty.

But the rules are different with social services and family courts. The Lavertys hired Stuart Spencer, and he explained that in criminal court a jury must find guilt "beyond a reasonable doubt." But in a civil matter, in family court, the criteria is "more likely than not."

Even so, it was hard to see how the Lavertys could lose. Spencer said Rachelle's statements were full of contradictions and impossibilities. For instance, she once told of being taken into a back bedroom by her father when she had been playing with Barbie dolls with a friend. That friend later testified that Kenneth Laverty wasn't even home at the time she had been visiting.

All the jury has to find in such a case, Spencer said, is that some part of the claim is true. The jury is likely to lean that way, because, after all, they're not depriving anyone of their freedom, they're just giving jurisdiction to the court. Or, practically speaking, to social workers.

After the court took jurisdiction over Rachelle in 1995, the Lavertys struggled for two years to maintain visitation, please counselors and psychotherapists, and juggle court appearances. They lived apart to increase Misti's chances of keeping Rachelle. But in the end the demand to Misti was the same: Believe your daughter or lose her.

She suspected that putting her husband in criminal jeopardy would be futile anyway. Linda DeKeyser, on the staff of Michigan's Family Independence Agency, submitted the petition to terminate the Lavertys' parental rights three and a half months early. "Family reunification was never on her agenda," Mrs. Laverty said.

In preparing to write the Lavertys' story, I interviewed Judge North. He said little because, as is always the case in matters involving children, *everything* is confidential. He scowled at my wanting to look into the matter. His written opinion said the most: "Even if there is some possibility Mr. Laverty did not abuse Rachelle, her belief that he did creates a certainty of harm to her mental well-being if returned home."

Spencer said Rachelle had motivation to lie. Her father had just gone out on the road as a truck driver and was beginning to spend time away from home. She was jealous of that, he said. Then there's the continual reinforcement of the social workers and therapists. They treat her like a queen, he said. Then she sees all the material things she can have in the economically advantaged foster family.

MISTI WASN'T ACCUSED OF DOING A THING. HER CRIME WAS THAT SHE DIDN'T THINK HER HUSBAND HAD, EITHER.

I had the Lavertys' story written shortly before the date scheduled for their final hearing on parental rights. It was set in column form and pasted up on the page to be part of the *St. Ignace News* the next day. But just before it was to go to print, the newspaper's publisher, Wesley Maurer, Jr., got a call from Judge North. Maurer, who originally liked the story, caved in to the claim that secrecy was in the best interest of the child and ripped the story from the page. I have come to believe that it is all the secrecy we allow child protective services that permits the unjust destruction of families.

The Lavertys may get a glimpse of their daughter around Mackinac County once in awhile, Spencer said. She would be about sixteen now. He hopes the truth will someday be known.

■ ■ ■ ■ ■ ■ ■ ■ ■

While the Lavertys were blue collar and a little "rough around the edges," Danica Cordell-Reeh's case proved that upper crust is no protection from the child-savers.

For the Upper West Side Manhattan mom, social services' "knock on the door" came in the form of a buzz from her doorman in October 2001.

It was out of the blue, as it often is. Cordell-Reeh was bathing her 4-year-old twins when the two social workers from the Administration for Children's Services arrived. After an hour-long interview she found out that she was accused of depriving her children of food and forcing her daughter into acts of oral sex.

It soon became clear that the accuser was the nanny she had fired the day before. All of a sudden, her children were allowed to spend only two or three nights a week in her home, always with a court-appointed watcher present.

Cordell-Reeh's description of the experience, as quoted in *New York Magazine*, points out the Catch-22 of supervised visitation. The parent needs to prove he or she is affectionate and loving while being suspected of sex abuse, so "you're being told not to even touch your kids. You can't hug them; they're used to you helping them after their bath and you're told not to even help change their clothes. If you walk into the bathroom with one of the children, somebody follows you there. How do you explain who these strangers are? They're watching whatever you say, whatever you do, whatever you don't do. Heaven forbid the kid decides to let go of your hand while you're crossing the street. You've just endangered a child. So you freeze. Your movements become wooden."

Many attorneys prefer to defend someone on a murder charge rather than child abuse. At least with murder, there's a presumption of innocence until guilt is proven.

THAT DIDN'T FAZE CPS, EITHER. THEY KEPT THE CHILD AND FILED NEW CHARGES IN FRONT OF A NEW JUDGE THE NEXT DAY.

Despite her substantial financial resources, Cordell-Reeh almost couldn't find the type of legal help she needed. She lucked out when friends told her of Bernard Clair, known for tackling lost causes. And even he hesitated. But he went on to discover that the nanny had made uncannily similar charges about another former employer after she had been fired and that she had accused her own brother of sexual abuse. Without that, Cordell-Reeh might have lost her kids.

■ ■ ■ ■ ■ ■ ■ ■ ■ ■

Even a simple and obvious case of injustice can wind on for weeks, months, and years. Recall the breastfeeding mom who lost her toddler for a year for asking about sexual arousal? Syracuse, New York, mother Denise Perrigo's biggest mistake was not looking up the number for the La Leche League herself. When she called a local community center to find out how to contact the breastfeeding advocacy and support group in January 1991, she explained she wanted to find out if it was normal to become sexually aroused while nursing. Well, it is perfectly normal. But Perrigo was referred to a rape crisis center instead of the La Leche League. A volunteer there put together her question, and the fact that she was nursing a 2-year-old, and came up with a conclusion of sex abuse, which she reported to the child abuse hotline. Perrigo found herself spending the night in jail and her daughter taken into "protective" custody.

It would be a year of court nightmares before she would get her daughter back. Criminal charges were dropped immediately. Undaunted, child-savers pursued charges of sexual abuse and neg-

lect in family court. The family court judge ruled that no abuse had occurred and ordered the child be returned to her mother.

That didn't faze CPS, either. They kept the child and filed new charges in front of a new judge the next day. They managed to twist the little girl's description of having her temperature taken rectally into sex abuse. By November, eleven months after the absurdity began, another judge ruled that no abuse had taken place but that Perrigo was neglectful for failure to wean the child earlier and for exposing the child to CPS investigations by calling about breastfeeding in the first place. (We must watch what questions we ask and of whom.)

If the judge had bothered to learn anything about breastfeeding, he would have found that toddler breastfeeding is actually a wise choice. Dr. Jack Newman explains this clearly on thebestfedbaby.com. UNICEF encourages mothers to breastfeed at least a year and thereafter as long as both mother and child like. Breastfeeding to three and four years of age is common in much of the world.

■ ■ ■ ■ ■ ■ ■ ■ ■ ■

On February 6, 2000, 65-year-old New Jersey grandmother Marian Rubin was arrested at her neighborhood MotoPhoto when she arrived to pick up a roll of film she had taken of her granddaughters, ages three and eight, frolicking naked after their bath on an overnight visit with her. Despite the fact that the parents' children had no problems with the pictures, it cost $30,000 in legal fees to see the matter resolved. She writes on her Website:

It is now 18 months since I was arrested: finger-printed, "mugged" and released on $50,000 bail (usually reserved for murderers), $4000 non-refundable. For several weeks I was denied any contact with my granddaughters, while my family was "investigated" and my granddaughter questioned by the Division of Youth and Family Services. My home was searched twice (once when I wasn't there) where police seized photographs, my computers, my printer, scanner, every CD-Rom and every floppy disk.

A social worker in a public school system for 32 years, I was suspended from my job until the case was finally dismissed in Feb.2001, after completing a Pre-Trial Intervention Program and given one year of Probation! This is a program designed to keep "first-time offenders" out of the criminal justice system!

■ ■ ■ ■ ■ ■ ■ ■ ■ ■

If you still think these are isolated cases, aberrations, get over it. You can't protect yourself and your children from the child welfare system, unless you can overcome some basic misconceptions, Humiston warns. "The hardest part is not understanding the details. It is simply believing this is happening."

He continues, "We all suffer from some mental blocks that blind us…. The illusion is this: We think that caseworkers, police, and judges want to know the truth, want to do what's fair, and want to protect the best interest of children.

"They do not."

Because of the money, he said, "their sole intent and purpose is to remove every child, any child that they can without encountering serious resistance. Unless you understand this principle, the child welfare system will always have power over you."

If you have children in foster care, Barnes advises that you check for them on Internet adoption sites. While you may think you are making progress toward family reunification, you may find the state planned to adopt out your children from day one.

Here's a description of a sibling group, two boys and one girl, once advertised for adoption: "They are not legally free and regular visits with the birth family continue. Termination of parental rights is expected in June 1999."

So, the children were in regular contact with their parents, proving they aren't monsters, Barnes said. "The parents may have believed they were working to get their children home while the state was advertising them for sale on the Internet."

Knowledge is your best defense. The first thing to know is that you do not have to let social workers in when they come to the door, unless they have a warrant. They may say otherwise, but they are bluffing.

In Plattsburgh, New York, my colleagues at the *Press Republican* covered the Barbara Rivers story, but later I had an opportunity to sit down for a long philosophical talk with her attorney, Diane Webster-Brady, who once worked for social services in Massachusetts. She saw social workers often as young people who, without kids of their own, haven't walked in the shoes of those they criticize.

> ## WHILE YOU MAY THINK YOU ARE MAKING PROGRESS TOWARD FAMILY REUNIFICATION, YOU MAY FIND THE STATE PLANNED TO ADOPT OUT YOUR CHILDREN FROM DAY ONE.

Rivers lost her daughter after a verbal argument with her boyfriend. The girl, Shiann, was not harmed in any way, but social workers thought they could provide a better home for her. And why not? She was a darling little 2-year-old. Rivers also had an son with a learning disability. How curious that social workers never thought they could or should find a better home for him!

Rivers' ordeal began when her daughter was just shy of her second birthday. Social workers called her negligent for the discord with her boyfriend. Reduced to just supervised visitation, Rivers fought back. So social services moved to strip her parental rights entirely, and Clinton County Family Court Judge Timothy Lawliss went along with it.

No effort was made to reunite the mother and daughter. To the contrary, Webster-Brady said, they moved the little girl too far away for that. The State Supreme Court Appellate Division agreed that social services was remiss.

Social services' response was not to attempt the reunification they failed earlier, but to try to have Rivers declared cuckoo. Failing that—psychologists wouldn't go along—they finally had to bring the girl home to her mother. By this time, Rivers had missed four years of her daughter's life. That's most of your life when you're about six, but the mother-child bond remained. Little Shiann ran up and hugged her mom when she first saw her after the separation.

■ ■ ■ ■ ■ ■ ■ ■ ■ ■

The same bunch of rights-trampling social workers invaded my privacy and my child's in 2000. Nothing remotely tragic happened, but I want to mention it because I think it shows that if it can happen to me, it can happen to anyone. It came as a total surprise. It wasn't because of anything I had written. I let my then 9-year-old visit his grandmother in an elder-care home for a couple of hours while I was at work. That was called in as neglect and lack of guardianship.

My 86-year-old mother had lived with us, but her health was in rapid decline with heart disease and worsening senile dementia. She needed supervision I couldn't provide because I work. I found accommodation for her at the Samuel P. Vilas Home in the city, near where we lived and where I worked. It was an attractive place, but lonely. My mother's daytimes were often monotonous while I was at work and her grandson was at school. Once, at about 6 PM, when I had to work late, I dropped my son off at the home and asked him to "take granny to the piano lounge and play your songs for her." She enjoyed listening to him practice the piano, and it was about the only social diversion she got. I said I would pick him up at 9 PM, which I did.

The next day I got an angry call from the home's supervisor, saying my mother was not capable of babysitting. Never mind that my son often watched after her, not vice versa. Later I asked my son if anything had happened to get anyone's attention while he was there. I wondered if there had been a commotion or something. He said no. In fact, he didn't even play the piano because when they got to the lounge, he observed a man sleeping in his room next door. "The door was open, mom," he said, "so I decided we'd better just go back to the room." They quietly watched TV until I arrived. My son showed the good judgment I knew he would and was in no way in any danger at an old folks' home with feeble elderly residents, nurses watching the elderly, and a door security system.

But thanks to that visit to grandma and a caller whom social services wouldn't identify, for the next three months I was mentally held hostage by the child-protectors. My son was pulled from his fourth-grade classroom and interrogated. I hadn't trained my son enough on not talking to social workers, so they got information that was not their business. If I could do it over I would have given him activist Charles Schulze's "reverse Miranda" on a card:

NOTICE TO GOVERNMENT AGENTS

You are hereby informed that I have a right to have my parents present prior to answering any questions. I am now exercising that right and request that you contact my parents immediately at: [fill in contact number].

In her useful book, *Profane Justice*, Suzanne Shell highly recommends that all kids carry the reverse Miranda. Shell went through loss of her 13-year-old over a spanking.

Humiston elaborates on warning children: Teach your child the sanctity of the family, because the schools are teaching your children to rat on you. Teach your children the other side, the danger to which they expose your whole family by saying something that could be misconstrued or simply disapproved of by someone with other opinions. "Teach your children that dozens of children have committed suicide while in foster care. Hundreds have died. Teach them they have the right to remain silent, and if they chose not to remain silent, each and every word they say will be used against their mommy and daddy. Love them, love them, love them."

TEACH YOUR CHILD THE SANCTITY OF THE FAMILY, BECAUSE THE SCHOOLS ARE TEACHING YOUR CHILDREN TO RAT ON YOU.

I don't disagree that tips on possible abuse should be checked out. But dragging it out for three months damaged our quality of life. I always had a good feeling at my son's school. That was ruined. I never went in there again without thinking that I was being thought an abuser. And, although "unsubstantiated," the report will always be on file with the state's Central Register to possibly rear up later for some reason. Social worker Rich Holcombe wanted to come to my house and give me some "helpful suggestions." What that means is, he wanted to look for something to use against me.

■ ■ ■ ■ ■ ■ ■ ■ ■ ■

If you think I'm exaggerating the risk, read Richard Wexler's story of the Humlen family in *Wounded Innocents*. They were sent through hell because their 8-year-old got hit with a baseball. No one would listen to reason. Their uninvolved 16-month-old daughter was taken to an orphanage where she was abused and starved. A sensible judge, who had had baseball bruises herself as a child, eventually ended the tragedy, but the children's personalities have been forever changed and the family scarred.

"We have effectively repealed the Fourth Amendment, which protects both parents and children from unreasonable searches and seizures," Humiston says. "[W]e have severely eroded the Fourteenth amendment which guarantees parents and children they will not be deprived of their liberty without due process of law."

Brian and Ruth Christine, a college-educated couple, were traveling across the US with their daughters in the summer of 2000 when an anonymous caller told Oregon social services that one of the kids looked dehydrated. The story is involved, but it the end, a vindictive Oregon moved to terminate the Christines' parental rights. In a desperate move, Brian, a former Eagle Scout, and Ruth, a former missionary who worked under Mother Teresa, kidnapped their children back from the state. But they were eventually caught, tried, found guilty, and sent to Orgeon's state prisons. Brian must serve fourteen years because he brandished a gun. Ruth must serve seven and a half years.

Where will this all end? Shell predicts in violence.

Humiston is wondering why some parent hasn't already just lost it and come out shooting.

If you aren't paranoid yet, think about this. The one-in-25 chance Barnes cites means a child's chance of being the subject of a child abuse or neglect investigation is more likely than having a flat tire on your car. "Be prepared," she warns. "The idea that you don't have to worry about CPS until they come to your door is about as ridiculous as thinking you don't need a spare tire until you have a flat."

THE AGENCY AND THE ATOM
THE CIA'S RADIATION WEAPONS PROGRAMS AND EXPERIMENTS ON HUMANS
JOHN KELLY

Forget assassinations. Try mass destruction. Since its inception, the CIA feverishly sought to create radiological weapons of mass destruction, according to the CIA itself.[1] Having admitted this, the CIA would have us believe that nothing came of this effort and that no human subjects were exposed to radiation. But this denial flies in the face of its own documents, the few it did not destroy. The Agency's explaining away of these documents and ignoring of others is totally implausible. At times, ludicrous.

For instance, on March 30, 1965—long after the CIA supposedly stopped its radiation R&D—CIA researcher Dr. James Alexander Hamilton reported to the CIA: "We are now conducting a new series of experiments on 100 prisoner-subjects, in which radio-active iodine uptake of the thyroid and T-4 uptake of red cells, and several other measures which we have developed are being related to previously-studied variables." In a preceding report, Hamilton recommended that the "'thyroid function' should be investigated through another parameter, radio-iodine uptake.... [I]t is possible that its inclusion in the experimental test battery may help to clarify some of the relationships which have been observed."[2]

Dr. Sidney Gottlieb told the author that he was very familiar with Hamilton, who worked with George White under MKULTRA, and that he did carry out this experiment. (Gottlieb was in charge of MKULTRA.) Dr. T. Lawrence Clanon, former superintendent of the Vacaville Medical Center, where Hamilton experimented, also confirmed that he conducted thyroid experiments for the CIA on 124 prisoners between 1962 and 1966.[3] Hamilton himself said that the CIA provided the funds to set up his lab to do thyroid research on prisoners.

However, referring specifically to the March 30, 1965, report, the CIA claimed this was a "cover story for the underlying psychological research that the CIA was really interested in, and that it did not fund the radiation work." Even if this were true, it doesn't make any sense. A researcher's legitimate, innocuous experiments serve as his cover for unethical research, not the other way around, as the CIA is claiming here. Moreover, this was a highly classified report to the CIA. Cover stories are for the public, and it's just not credible for the CIA to contend that Hamilton was providing them with a false report or one in which they were not interested. If they weren't interested, why was it in their files some 30 years later?[4]

The CIA also explained away the radiation warfare work of Dr. Charles Geschickter in the same way. Geschickter was specifically funded by the CIA to do radiation warfare R&D under MKULTRA at the Georgetown University Medical Center. Yet the CIA claimed it "funded radiation research as a cover for other activities, when in the 1950s it provided funds for the construction of a wing of Georgetown University Hospital through Dr. Charles F. Geschickter, who used the wing for his own radiation research."[5] This denial makes less sense than the one for Hamilton. Why would they fund research and expect no return? Geschickter was already a working doctor at the hospital, and thus had a ready-made cover. As another CIA report at the same time noted: "CIA hoped to use the legitimate research in this wing as a cover for later research work under MKULTRA." Similarly, the CIA document establishing this subproject states that it was to serve as a cover "for highly sensitive projects in certain fields, including covert biological, chemical and radiological warfare."

In fact, this wing of the hospital was so involved in CIA work that the CIA referred to it as its "hospital safehouse." Geschickter himself contradicted the CIA when he testified before Congress that he studied the effects of radar, a form of radiation, for the CIA. Geschickter did this work in conjunction with the National Institutes of Health (NIH), which was also collaborating with the CIA. A key objective of this MKULTRA subproject was to develop a means to knock out someone with invisible rays. It was not without its obvious dangers. "If you got in too deep," testified Geschickter, "you injured the heat center of the brain the way you cook meat, and there was a borderline there that made it dangerous."[6]

> SIMILARLY, THE CIA DOCUMENT ESTABLISHING THIS SUBPROJECT STATES THAT IT WAS TO SERVE AS A COVER "FOR HIGHLY SENSITIVE PROJECTS IN CERTAIN FIELDS, INCLUDING COVERT BIOLOGICAL, CHEMICAL AND RADIOLOGICAL WARFARE."

This danger did not deter the CIA or Geschickter, who continued radiating monkeys, as well as patients. He also testified that the CIA provided him with $375,000 worth of radioisotope labs and isotope equipment and that the unit containing this equipment was the "only place I was interested in." Yet the CIA claimed it had no interest in this research. The CIA even went so far as to report that an unnamed CIA researcher and "Dr. Geschickter may well have performed human radiation experiments during the time they were doing unrelated work for CIA."[7] With Nazi-like bravado, Geschickter defended this work by telling Congress: "All I can say is any understanding of the way the body works and how chemicals work or pharmologicals or drugs work is important for any agency in the Government to know."[8]

The CIA's denials came after a four-month investigation which left much to be desired, including the fact that there were deletions in its report. As part of its investigation, the CIA interviewed former CIA officers who were involved, yet no one "remembered" any radiation experiments. Of course, these are people sworn to secrecy and lying, so their remarks hardly qualify as evidence, and their mention reflects poorly on the CIA. Sidney Gottlieb was interviewed by the CIA, and we don't know what he told the Agency, but what he told this author contradicted what the CIA reported. He said that James Hamilton definitely exposed human subjects to ionizing radiation, and other CIA researchers possibly did.

Furthermore, the CIA ignored other researchers, such as Dr. Wallace Chan, who was funded by the CIA to inject human subjects with radioisotopes as an attempt to develop covert markers. This experiment could have had a second purpose of studying the use of radioisotopes as a weapon. In its oblique reference to this, which did not name Chan, the CIA said it "does not seem to have been further explored."[9] Again, Gottlieb told us that Wally Chan worked under him, and it was his remembrance that Chan did inject radioisotopes in humans. Asked whether radioisotopes were used in operations, Gottlieb said: "It's one of the few things I would feel constrained not to talk to you about."

The CIA's remarks about Chan's work related only to MKULTRA's subproject 86. The Agency did not mention the related subproject 78, which also investigated personnel marking systems using radioactive "tagging," as well as "radioactive resistant" mechanisms.

One of the CIA's most important radiation consultants at the time was Dr. Robley Evans, who was associated with MIT and the Massachusetts General Hospital. In an early experiment, funded in part by a CIA conduit, the Josiah Macy Jr. Foundation, Evans and his colleagues injected radiosodium into ten burn patients at the Massachusetts General Hospital, followed by excisional biopsies. These patients included a 54-year-old epileptic woman and a 5-year-old boy who received his injection of radiosodium upon his arrival at the hospital. Two of these patients died within ten days of their injections, so their excisional biopsies were taken postmortem. The stated purpose of this experiment was "to investigate the histochemical changes in burned skin." This was typical of radiation experiments at the time, which had dual offensive and defensive objectives. There was no medical benefit to the patients. On the contrary, the radiosodium may have exacerbated their conditions.[10]

Around the time of his radiosodium experiment, Evans wrote a classified manuscript for the Symposium of Certain Aspects of Atomic Warfare, which was held under the auspices of the Commandant First Naval District at the Harvard Medical School on October 15, 1948. In preparing his paper, Evans was assisted by the Office of Naval Intelligence, the Atomic Energy Commission (AEC), and the NIH, all of whom collaborated with the CIA's radiation warfare R&D. Indeed, Evans conducted human radiation experiments for the Navy and the AEC.

Evans also studied more than 450 cases of humans who had carried skeletal deposits of radium and mesothorium for years. These included the well-known radium dial-painters, or luminizers, who licked self-luminous radium compounds from the fine brushes with which they painted numerals on watches and clocks, as well as radium chemists and individuals who ingested or were injected with radium for medical reasons. As part of this study, eight human subjects were fed a mock dial paint containing a mixture of radioactive radium and thorium to compare the percentage of each that reached the bloodstream. There was no medical need or benefit from this experiment.[11]

During World War II, Evans had sought to feed radium to conscientious objectors. In a classified letter to Lieutenant Joseph W. Holland, he wrote: "Confirming our conversation last week, I would like to propose that conscientious objectors or other volunteer human subjects be sought through your channels for use in an experimental study of the rate of elimination of radium." As usual, there would have been no medical need or benefit from this proposed experiment.[12]

HE PERSONALLY APPROVED THE FEEDING OF RADIOACTIVE MATERIALS TO RETARDED CHILDREN AT THE WALTER FERNALD SCHOOL IN WALTHAM, MASSACHUSETTS.

Shortly after the war, Evans found an even more vulnerable radiation target: retarded children. He personally approved the feeding of radioactive materials to retarded children at the Walter Fernald School in Waltham, Massachusetts. Evans denied that this was done for the CIA, but at least one of the experiments was classified for national security reasons. Like Sidney Gottlieb, he defended this type of experiment by claiming that the amounts of radioactivity were "trivial," so small that parents did not have to be notified about the radioactivity—which they were not. Evans went so far as to deny that these were radiation experiments because they were only "tracer experiments." "It's absolutely much ado about nothing," he told the press.[13]

Charles Vest, president of MIT, which administered the experiments, thought differently. "I was sorry," he wrote, "to hear that at least some of the young people who participated in this research and their parents apparently were unaware that the study involved radioactive tracers. People should not unknowingly become the subjects of research studies of this type." A state-appointed commission found that the experiments were in violation of the Nuremberg Code of Medical Ethics.[14]

It was also reported that Fernald children who ate seven meals containing a radioactive iron supplement in 1949 could have received between 544 and 1,024 millirems of radiation to their spleens, where radioactive iron can do the most damage.[15]

Between 1943-48, Evans and his colleagues also gave radioactive iodine (142 microcuries) to 130 hyperthyroid patients as part of an experiment. Initially, the patients suffered nausea, slight fever, and swelling and tenderness of the thyroid for a few days. They also gave radioiodine to pregnant women in the second and fifth months of pregnancy, while writing that "we advise against use of the isotope in pregnancy beyond the third month." Myxedema (i.e., underproduction of thyroid hormone) was produced in four cases, and there was no medical follow-up.

Later, in the 1950s, Evans injected radioiodine into 23 pregnant women at the Boston-Lying-In Hospital, now known as the Brigham and Women's Hospital, in order "to discover how long iron transfused from the mother's blood persists in her baby after it is born." Commenting on this experiment, Dr. David Rush, professor of nutrition and community health at Tufts University, told the *Boston Globe*: "Even the diagnostic X-ray during pregnancy has been associated with leukemia in the offspring."[16]

The CIA claimed Evans did no radiation warfare R&D for them and only worked on radiation safety, radiation detection, and radiation communication. If this were so, why did he work only for the Technical Services Staff and the Technical Services Division, which were conducting radiation warfare R&D for MKULTRA and developing weapons for operational use? Why didn't he work for the Office of Scientific Intelligence and its successors? Evans himself admitted doing human radiation experimentation for the AEC, Department of Defense (DoD), and other agencies while under contract to the CIA, but none of this was for the CIA? It's hard to believe he could compartmentalize himself like this, but even if it were true, the CIA had total access to his AEC and DoD work. So we have a distinction without a difference. Evans also participated in the Pentagon's Joint Panel on the Medical Aspects of Atomic Warfare, as did the CIA.[17]

Dr. Linwood Murray, who was Evans' principal point of contact at the CIA, made a rather peculiar statement to the Agency. "Dr. Murray fully recalls the radiation safety and detection projects on which he and Dr. Evans collaborated," reported the CIA. "He is unaware of any human effects radiation tests and is sceptical of their existence for exactly the reasons Mr. Boston stated—these are slow-acting 'poisons' and entirely unsuitable for the type of experiments MKULTRA supported."

Another CIA contractor overlooked by the CIA investigators is Dr. Albert M. Kligman of the University of Pennsylvania in Philadelphia. Little wonder. His research track record is enough to stand your hair on end. Kligman worked for the MKULTRA-related Project Often, which experimented on humans at the US Army's Edgewood Arsenal. He also applied radioactive materials to prisoners. In one such experiment for the Army, he applied a poisonous compound tagged with radioisotopes to the skin of prisoners. "This is a program for national defense," Kligman told the *Philadelphia Inquirer*, "for once such vapors get through the skin, they can destroy the nervous system and the central function of the brain. We shall see how heat and cold affect this penetration. What exercise does. The objective is to prevent the vapors from getting into the system. Do we need to coat the skin in advance? Treat it immediately after the vapor hits?"

IN ONE SUCH EXPERIMENT FOR THE ARMY, HE APPLIED A POISONOUS COMPOUND TAGGED WITH RADIOISOTOPES TO THE SKIN OF PRISONERS.

The CIA and the Army were also studying the offensive use of poisonous chemicals and radioisotopes. As Kligman himself added, "the Army not only wants to know what will prevent vapors from penetrating it (skin) but what will permit them to get through."[18] Apparently Kligman never published the results from this particular experiment, but based on his other publications and declassified reports, it's fair to assume that the prisoners were harmed, at least temporarily, if not permanently, from the poisonous vapors and radioisotopes which could have exacerbated the effects of the vapors.

Years later, Kligman wrote in reference to this experiment: "I cannot recall publishing anything on radioisotopes. These were preliminary studies using methods that were not very sophisticated by today's standards."[19] In a follow-up letter, Kligman wrote: "To my recollection, we did not apply radioactive materials to the skin of volunteers.... Christophers [Kligman's student] applied radio-labeled testosterone, I think and measured its disappearance with a Geiger counter."[20]

In fact, shortly after his interview with the *Philadelphia Inquirer* about the poisonous vapor experiment, Kligman, along with Christophers, published findings of an experiment at Holmesburg Prison wherein they applied radio-labeled testosterone, as well as radiosodium, on the back skin of 20 prisoners. In the first phase, the testosterone was applied to the backs of ten young (20 to 30 years) and ten aged (71 to 82 years) healthy males and sealed with Saran Wrap for 24 hours. Later the radiosodium was injected into the upper backs of the prisoners. In both cases, the radioactive material entered the bloodstream, and the prisoners received no medical benefit nor was there any medical follow-up.[21]

Kligman continued to inject radiosodium into prisoners in further experiments as a means of measuring the permeability of skin hardened by exposure to irritating chemicals. In one classified report submitted to the Army, Kligman described the procedure as follows:

> It is only in the smallest vessels that an exchange of gases and nutrients occurs across vascular walls. This may be measured by determining the rate of removal of a freely diffusable ion such as 22Na. The radioactive ion is injected intradermally and the site monitored by a gas-flow chamber. The plot of radio-activity against time is linear on semi-og paper enabling the determination of the "half-clearance time."

Kligman also continued applying radioactive testosterone to the skin of prisoner-subjects. In one such experiment, the backs of 20 prisoners were daubed with radioactive testosterone to measure the percutaneous absorption of dimethyl sulfoxide, which was then being touted as a "miracle drug." As Kligman described it: "Malkinson's method (a gas-flow chamber to follow the disappearance of topically applied substances tagged radioactively) was used to compare (1) alcohol, (2) alcohol solutions of various concentrations of dimethyl sulfoxide, and (3) EGME as vehicles for testosterone propionate 1 4C penetration." He added that "the method is unfortunately lacking in exactitude."[22]

Following his exposure for misconduct in this experiment by the Federal Drug Administration, Kligman wrote that his article about dimethyl sulfoxide contained "a regrettable inaccuracy," and that one prisoner "experienced giant hives in the trunk at night [and] I failed to note that happening.... Since 20 subjects were not treated for the full period, the laboratory data as given cannot be accepted as properly validated."[23] Kligman also revealed that some subjects withdrew from the experiment for unknown reasons.

In addition to sodium, Kligman injected other radioactive materials into prisoners. In one such experiment, he injected radioactive tritiated histidine into prisoners after they had been exposed to long ultraviolet ray

(LUV) irradiation. It is well known that radioisotopes exacerbate any burns. At the time, the Army and the CIA were studying the use of radiation to do exactly that. As a result of this study, Kligman concluded that "LUV can no longer be considered harmless in the production of sunburn and its sequalae (solar degeneration and cancer)."

Here we see a perfect example of the dual application of medical research by CIA experimenters. From his publication, the medical community learns that LUV can cause cancer. This can lead to positive awareness. At the same time, the CIA was seeking methods to induce cancer, and Kligman's finding was obviously of use to them. Despite his conclusion, there was no medical follow-up to check for skin cancer.[24]

In another report that cautions the reader to "destroy this report when no longer needed," Kligman summarized three years of research wherein he injected radioactive thymidine, radioactive sodium, and radioactive saline into scores of prisoners at Holmesburg. This work was done for the Medical Research Laboratory at Edgewood, Maryland. At the time Kligman was also working for the CIA, which had access to the data. According to a published article based on declassified documents: "In June 1968, Kligman set up the Ivy Research Laboratory, Inc., and received an additional two CIA contracts totaling $127,000. The contracts with the CIA were by way of the Army Medical Corps Medical Research Laboratory, Edgewood Arsenal, according to the records of an eight-year study by the US Inspector General."[25]

| "FOR EXAMPLE, TURPENTINE WOULD BE VERY SUITABLE WERE IT NOT FOR THE DEVELOPMENT OF CONTACT SENSITIZATION IN ABOUT HALF THE SUBJECTS. THESE REACTIONS MAY BE QUITE SEVERE WHEN AN ENTIRE FOREARM IS INVOLVED."

The following excerpts from the report deserve quoting at length, for they underscore the sheer horror of CIA research and why it was ordered that the report be destroyed. Basically, radioactive materials were injected and toxic chemicals were applied to the skin with no concern for the subjects' well-being:

Substances which have been studied by patch tests on the back include phenol, salicylic acid, coal tar, octylamine, cationic detergents (Hyamines), anionic detergents (sodium lauryl sulfate and soaps), fatty acids (capric and propionic), hydrochloric acid, sodium hydroxide, croton oil, zinc chloride, benzene, ethylene glycol monomethyl ether, hexane, DMSO, and mercuric chloride. Some degree of hardening [of the skin] is obtainable with all of these but the circumstances are vastly different and for some, quite limited. For example, when destructive chemicals such as hydrochloric acid and sodium hydroxide are applied in concentrations that induce intense inflammation on the first exposure, no hardening is achieved.[26]

...

With these, a severe inflammatory reaction is pro-

voked which reaches a peak in about 10 days, accompanied by a rather frightening amount of crusting.[27]

...

For example, with pure-undiluted ethylene glycol monoethyl ether, three of three subjects exhibited psychotic reactions (hallucinations, disorientation, stupor, etc.) within 2 weeks and had to be hospitalized. With pure-undiluted dimethylacetamide, headaches and febrile reactions caused termination.[28]

...

Another complication is contact allergy. For example, turpentine would be very suitable were it not for the development of contact sensitization in about half the subjects. These reactions may be quite severe when an entire forearm is involved.[29]

...

We have kept perhaps a dozen subjects "hardened" for a year to both SLS and a chlorinated phenol.[30]

...

Clearly, the intensity of the inflammatory process is concentration dependent. High concentrations provoke a swift, violent dermatitis...[31]

...

Attempts were made to accomodate skin to allergens to which subjects were experimentally sensitized, notably nickel and neomycin. One hour daily immersions utilized as with irritants. This project turned out to be unfeasible. The subjects complained bitterly. After weeks of apparently peak inflammation, the skin exhibited no willingness to become hardened and the willingness of the subjects to go on diminished to zero. The study was terminated.[32]

...

We selected potent irritants which produce distinctive reactions by exposures of a few hours.[33]

...

The radioactive ion (sodium) is injected intradermally and the site monitored by a gas flow chamber.... The half-clearance time was almost always less for the hardened (irritated) area...[34]

...

Cantharidin blisters are produced with greater difficulty on hardened skin.[35]

...

Hardened skin is more susceptible to experimental Candida albicans infection. (We plan to study staphylococcal infection.)[36]

Kligman told the *Philadelphia Bulletin* that when he first visited Holmesburg Prison: "All I saw before me were acres of skin. I was like a farmer seeing a fertile field...an anthropoid colony, mainly healthy, which wasn't going anywhere."

"We had an ethical problem," added Kligman. "How much right do you have to cause risk in a prisoner in medical tests from which he has no direct benefit? The tradition has been, from ethical or moral considerations, to test only those people who could draw some direct benefit from the testing."

Kligman chose to contravene that tradition. "All the prisoner taking part in a test has is money," said Kligman. "We pay him to lend us his body for some time. But we pre-determine whether a test is dangerous, and the prisoner has to depend on our judgement."

"I feel almost like a scoundrel—like Machiavelli," concluded Kligman.[37] When the Prison Board of Trustees shut down Kligman's research program at Holmesburg, board chairman Angelo Galeone stated: "There were some violations, and the program was being run even this week. But the doors are shut now and the situation is shut. It's shut down in every respect. There is no phasing out, no completing any cycles. We're rid of it." Earlier, Galeone had described the testing as "demeaning and dehumanizing."[38]

Kligman, however, continued his dehumanizing experiments. In one such experiment, he injected radioactive chemicals into the cheeks of healthy subjects ranging in age from 20 to 74 simply to study the effect of aging on the sebaceous glands.[39] In another experiment, Kligman radiated the faces of 20 retarded inmates with "destructive (of the serbaceous glands) doses of x-rays" (75r to 1,500r) which inflamed their acne lesions. At the beginning of his published article about this experiment, Kligman admitted: "The modern trend is one of increasing conservatism in the use of x-rays for benign skin conditions, not only because of the risks, but also because of the mounting skepticism regarding benefits." Yet he used 1,500r at a time when 100r was the norm.

Kligman was also fully aware that X-ray treatment of acne provided only a temporary clearing and often produced radiodermatitis and malignant tumors. He himself later reported that the X-ray treatment caused "an increased risk of malignant tumors of thyroid or parotid gland in patients irradiated.... Thirty-five percent of about 400 patients in one series developed malignant tumors, but none occurred in control subjects." Again, Kligman could have also been studying the use of X-rays as a weapon, which had been recom-

mended by a CIA consultant as early as 1949.[40]

In its investigatory report, the CIA did admit to an early consideration of using radiation "to harm or control selected individuals."[41] In January 1950, Boris Pash, then-chief of PB VII of the Office of Policy Coordination (OPC), volunteered to undertake biological, chemical, and radiological warfare operations and sought permission to select targets and determine suitable agents and methods.[42] A few months later, a memorandum was prepared for Frank Wisner to send to Marshall Chadwell, the CIA's Assistant Director for Scientific Intelligence, seeking the development of new unconventional—read "illegal"—warfare weapons in the fields of biological, chemical, and radiological warfare. Information was sought on "methods which will enable small resistance groups to overcome the present greater superiority of the security forces."[43]

"These proposals moved a step closer to implementation," wrote the CIA, "when CIA officials subsequently tried to interest the military and Atomic Energy Commission in developing nuclear and radiation weapons suitable for use by guerrillas or saboteurs."[44] The Pentagon was not interested in the clandestine employment of radiation weapons, at least not on behalf of the CIA, but the AEC was. So Allen Dulles asked AEC Chairman Gordon Dean to meet with Joseph A. Frank, OPC's Special Assistant for Research, about the possibility of "research, development or adaptation of atomic weapons and radiological warfare materials that would be suitable and appropriate for employment by clandestine means."[45] Dulles, who was an exponent of brain warfare, sought the creation of a portable ray gun ominously tabbed "The Thing," which the CIA's Deputy Director of Plans, Richard Bissell, later spent years trying to create.

Dean met with Frank, and in March 1952, the AEC told Wisner that a nuclear weapon could be built to hypothetical CIA specifications. Wisner informed CIA Director Walter B. Smith, who promised Wisner that he would raise the matter at the proper levels if Wisner specified "in the clearest and most convincing terms the strategic or tactical value of our proposed use of The Thing."[46]

Smith was skeptical about The Thing, and if one is to believe the CIA, the creation of it, as well as radiation warfare, ended right here. But as we saw, Wisner was his own master, and two years later, the CIA's Christian Freer had developed a full-scale plan for a radiation weapon with a recommendation that it be provided to the French for use against the Vietnamese. Freer's plan had the approval of the CIA's Nuclear Energy Division, and Wisner sent the proposal to the Technical Services Staff (TSS). TSS rejected the plan, but shortly thereafter Dulles approved a large TSS project for the research and development of "covert biological, chemical and radiological warfare" at the Georgetown University Medical Center under Dr. Charles Geschickter, who conducted human radiation experiments on his patients under the guise of medical treatment.[47]

The Georgetown Project had the full support of the AEC, in particu-

> "THESE PROPOSALS MOVED A STEP CLOSER TO IMPLEMENTATION," WROTE THE CIA, "WHEN CIA OFFICIALS SUBSEQUENTLY TRIED TO INTEREST THE MILITARY AND ATOMIC ENERGY COMMISSION IN DEVELOPING NUCLEAR AND RADIATION WEAPONS SUITABLE FOR USE BY GUERRILLAS OR SABOTEURS."

lar its chairman, Lewis Strauss, a personal friend of Geschickter and Dulles. Strauss originally promised $500,000 in 1950 dollars, and wrote to Dulles that the AEC had a "very active interest in the utilization of radioisotopes in the chemotherapy of chronic diseases." "The knowledge of your special interest in this program," concluded Strauss, "will naturally serve to guide us in our judgement relative to the form and amount of [redacted] support to this commendable program." Since the CIA had no interest in chemotherapy, the program was clearly to create radiation weapons, and this was obvious to Strauss, as well.

While radioisotopes in tracer amounts were being used in medical research, they were also being studied and developed as radiation warfare agents and were not harmless, as the CIA and AEC claimed. As early as 1946, Dr. Joseph G. Hamilton, the godfather of radiation warfare, reported that radioisotopes, including the widely-used radioiodines, "produce internal radiation of the very sensitive bone marrow and even rather trivial amounts can produce lethal effects."[48]

> DR. JOSEPH HAMILTON REVEALED IN A MEMO ENTITLED "RADIOACTIVE WARFARE" THAT RADIOISOTOPES OR TRACERS WERE STUDIED SIMULTANEOUSLY FOR THEIR MEDICAL AND WARFARE USES.

Originally, plutonium was considered the prime possibility for a radiation weapon agent because dispersion of radioactive plutonium dust could wipe out a population, along with animals and vegetation, without damage to property or land. But the problem with plutonium was that it rendered the affected area unsafe for years, if not decades, thus precluding occupation by the aggressor. The solution was radioisotopes of much lighter elements with specific, shorter half-lives, which would allow occupation by the aggressor after a set period of time.

Dr. Joseph Hamilton revealed in a memo entitled "Radioactive Warfare" that radioisotopes or tracers were studied simultaneously for their medical and warfare uses. He wrote: "As a result of tracer studies at Berkeley, and subsequent experiments including an investigation of radiation effects which were accomplished elsewhere on the Project, the following cursory picture has been compiled. The inhalation of 10 millicuries of the unseparated fission product mixture described above is estimated to be a minimum lethal dose for the average adult human."

The "Project" was the Plutonium Project at the University of Rochester Medical Center. One participant was the late Dr. Harold C. Hodge, a covert CIA contractor who studied radioisotopes and their effects on humans for MKULTRA. Other participants in the Project went on to become members of an AEC's radiation warfare panel, designed to assist in creating radiation warfare techniques. In 1946, the AEC, which worked hand-in-glove with the CIA, decreed that a "program in radiological warfare was essential."

"It is presumed," continued Hamilton, "that lethal injury will arise in the main through pulmonary damage rather than bone marrow destruction. The oral ingestion of at least 10 millicuries of such a mixture would be required to produce lethal injury which in this case would arise primarily from bone marrow damage produced from the strontium and barium absorbed from the digestive tract and subsequently deposited in the skeleton."

Obviously, he was not talking about radiotherapy. The particular radiation warfare application he was envisioning was "area denial," wherein you spray an area with a radioactive aerosol, and the target can no longer use that area for a period of time. At the same time, all or most living things are destroyed. A significant number of individuals would experience "some degree of irreversible radiation damage," concluded Hamilton. This was exactly the type of radiation warfare proposed for operational use by the CIA's Christian Freer in 1954.

Hamilton added that radiation warfare techniques could also produce crop damage and the sterilization of agricultural lands. He further revealed that methods for dispersing radioactive materials were developed at Berkeley for the purposes of studying the behavior of fission product aerosols and that these aerosols could be used "to subject urban populations to fission product poisoning by inhalation." The CIA was intensely interested in crop warfare and had an entire project devoted to the research and development of aerosol delivery systems.

Although Sidney Gottlieb confirmed that Hamilton gave radioiodine to prisoners and Hamilton filed his report with the CIA, the Agency claims that his radiation research "was a cover story for the underlying psychological research that the CIA was interested in, and that it did not fund the radiation work." This statement is right out of the Mad Hatter and 1984 Doublespeak. It alone deprives the CIA of any credibility to its denials of research and development of radiation weapons. As mentioned before, a cover story is for the public, not for the CIA itself. It's absurd to contend that Hamilton was providing a false story to the CIA. Moreover, Hamilton was a psychiatrist, so conducting radiation research would not have been a very good cover for him. In 1994, Hamilton admitted doing radiation research for the CIA but claimed he never conducted the reported experiment.

The way a cover works was seen in the document creating MKULTRA subproject 35 under Geschickter at the Georgetown University Hospital. This document stated that Geschickter's normal hospital research and treatment would serve as a "cover" for his covert chemical, biological, and radiation warfare research for the CIA. But even here the CIA claimed that the radiation research was "a cover for other activities."[49] This time the Agency was even less credible because it said it funded the radiation research but was not interested in the findings, even though one purpose of the projects was radiation research and development.

Geschickter's project contradicts the CIA's claim that its radiation warfare endeavors ended with TSS's rejection of Freer's proposal. In fact, the document establishing TSS states that TSS's Chemical Branch would "assume primary responsibility for the research and development of items in the chemical field including BW, CW, RW, and other branches of chemistry applicable to the activities of the R&D Division."[50] This was in 1951. In 1954, a CIA document stated that the mission of MKULTRA, under TSS, included the development of "covert biological, chemical and radiological warfare."[51] On July 26, 1963, CIA Inspector General John S. Earman reported:

The MKULTRA activity is concerned with the research and development of chemical, biological, and radiological materials capable of employment in clandestine operations.... Over the ten-year life of the program many additional avenues to the control of human behavior have been designated by the TSD [Technical Services Division, the successor to the TSS] management as appropriate to investigation under the MKULTRA charter, including radiation, electro-shock.... [A]ctive projects [include] projects in offensive/defensive BW, CW, and radiation.

Earman then recommended that Richard Helms assign Sidney Gottlieb "to operate MKULTRA as a program for research and development of chemical, biological, and radioactive materials, and of techniques for the employment of electro-shock, capable of producing human behavioral or physiological change." Helms did continue MKULTRA, which was renamed MKSEARCH, the mission of which was "to develop, test, and evaluate capabilities in the biological, chemical, and radioactive material systems."[52] In 1975, the CIA again reported that MKULTRA "considered various possible means for controlling human behavior of which drugs were only one aspect, others being radiation, electro-shock, psychology, psychiatry, sociology, anthropology, harrassment [sic] substances, and paramilitary devices and materials."

> "THE MKULTRA ACTIVITY IS CONCERNED WITH THE RESEARCH AND DEVELOPMENT OF CHEMICAL, BIOLOGICAL, AND RADIOLOGICAL MATERIALS CAPABLE OF EMPLOYMENT IN CLANDESTINE OPERATIONS." —CIA INSPECTOR GENERAL JOHN S. EARMAN, 1963

In its denials of doing radiation warfare R&D, the CIA failed to mention that at the time this R&D began, Frank Wisner wrote to the CIA's Assistant Director of Scientific Intelligence that "OPC is at present engaged in covert unconventional activity on a limited scale," and for that reason it "wanted to make use of the latest scientific and technological advances to modernize the field of clandestine unconventional warfare.... We are particularly interested in the possibilities of BW, CW and RW," including the application of "nuclear energy." The CIA has released no information on this possible R&D by the Office of Scientific Intelligence.

The CIA began working on zapping peoples' brains even before MKULTRA. One researcher for Project ARTICHOKE, which preceded MKULTRA, proposed radiating specific areas of the brain, such as the amygdaloid nucleus:

At present this brain center can be specifically stimulated by a current passed through wires inserted through the brain by operation. Such a procedure is obviously useless to this project; but ultrasonics or other means of radiant energy may yet be improved or modified so that a "cross-fire" (as with X-rays) arrangement could be focussed on a selected small region in the brain without affecting the surrounding areas.... Temporary inhibition of this region (possibly of others), should tame humans.

Such procedures could obviously be lethal, and the CIA has admitted that the objective of these techniques was "to harm or control selected individuals."[53] There was follow-through on this proposal, and the CIA met with Dr. Webb Haymaker, then with the Armed Forces Institute of Pathology, concerning the use of radiation to affect "emotional centers in the brain or elsewhere in the nervous system." Haymaker was apparently unnerved by the CIA's proposal, for a CIA memo of the meeting noted "that Dr. Haymaker was uncomfortable. Certainly he would not care to be consulted again in this matter." However, Drs. Turner, Overholser, and Hyslop "were respectively encouraging and interested."

Despite his discomfort, Haymaker, who coauthored a book with the Nazi scientist Hubertus Stronghold, subsequently conducted human radiation experiments of the worst kind. In one such experiment, a 43-year-old comatose man received eight injections to the brain of radioactive tritiated thymidine over a six-month period, with the last injection being given four hours before he died. It is not known if Haymaker did this for the CIA, but it was exactly the type of testing the Agency was seeking, and it was sponsored by the AEC, which supported the CIA's development of radiation warfare techniques and provided the results of its research to the CIA.[54]

The author of the radiant energy proposal also wrote that radioactive tracers could produce a "chemical lobotomy": "A non-toxic drug may be found, by radioactive-tracer techniques, that will be attracted to such an area (of the brain), and so produce a taming that can last for some time." The author advised enrolling researchers at Harvard and the Massachusetts General Hospital in Boston because "several of our most important consultants have constantly urged exploration of the tracer techniques as a method of advancing ARTICHOKE studies."

More evidence that the CIA undertook the research and development of radiation weapons, as well as biological and chemical ones, comes from the Secretary of Defense's Ad Hoc Committee on Chemical, Biological, and Radiological Warfare (CEBAR). This was a secret, powerful group that included the CIA. CEBAR called for the creation of chemical, biological, and radiological weapons, which it decreed were neither immoral nor weapons of mass destruction. CEBAR also declared that the US policy of "use in retaliation only" should simply be ignored. "Radiological warfare seems to possess unique military characteristics," wrote the committee, "and further study of its potential military worth should be undertaken."

CEBAR found many advantages to radiation warfare including the fact "that RW acts in a silent manner against living targets, with its presence and the bodily damage it causes being initially undetectable by the human senses." In addition, "RW agents are compact, with pounds rather than tons being necessary to secure contamination ranging from harassing to major casualty producing [and] RW, as a new weapon about which most people are poorly informed, is potentially valuable for harassment through rumor."

Exactly what the CIA wanted.

The CIA had extensive participation in CEBAR, including the presence of Willis A. Gibbons, then-associate director of research and development for the US Rubber Company, who went on to become chief of the CIA's TSS, which researched and developed radiation weapons. Other CIA personnel who prepared reports for CEBAR include: Dr. Willard Machle, Dr. Malcolm Pratt, Lt. Colonel W.K. Benson, and Dr. Frank L. Campbell. CIA Director Sidney Souers and CIA consultant Caryl P. Haskins provided information to the committee, while Dr. Sidney Gottlieb served as a consultant.

CEBAR FOUND MANY ADVANTAGES TO RADIATION WARFARE INCLUDING THE FACT "THAT RW ACTS IN A SILENT MANNER AGAINST LIVING TARGETS, WITH ITS PRESENCE AND THE BODILY DAMAGE IT CAUSES BEING INITIALLY UNDETECTABLE BY THE HUMAN SENSES."

CEBAR's proposals went into effect almost immediately, and at this time H. Marshall Chadwell left the AEC to join the CIA, where he helped create Project BLUEBIRD and then directed its successor, Project ARTICHOKE, both of which investigated the operational uses of radiation. So there was a major push and investment in radiation warfare by the US government, the CIA in particular, and it was not simply an isolated, harebrained idea here and there by an individual agent which was rejected. This is what the published CIA report would have us believe, the same CIA report that does not even mention CEBAR or many other relevant, historical facts.[55]

As early as 1947, CIA official Robert Amory urged a series of nuclear bombings to cut off Soviet supply routes from Russia to Eastern Europe.[56] Shortly thereafter, the CIA began developing its own arsenal of biological, chemical, and radiation weapons. Planning for the R&D began at least as early as 1949 and was assumed under Project BLUEBIRD, and its successors, ARTICHOKE, MKULTRA, and MKSEARCH.

Endnotes

1. Warner, Michael. Memorandum for the Record, 14 Feb 1995. Subject: "The Central Intelligence Agency and Human Radiation Experiments: An Analysis of the Findings." Central Intelligence Agency: 9. **2.** James A. Hamilton to the Geschickter Fund for Medical Research, 30 March 1965, S-1-16. **3.** Bathen, Sigrid. "Drug Experiments: Vacaville Facility Was Site of CIA-financed Mind Control Research." *Sacramento Bee*, 13 October 1977. **4.** Memorandum. To: Members of the Advisory Committee on Human Radiation Experiments. From: Advisory Committee Staff. Re: CIA Documents Describing Human Radiation Experiments, 8 Feb 1995: Tab 1-3; *op cit.*, Hamilton. **5.** *Ibid.* **6.** Senator Edward Kennedy's Hearings on MKULTRA, 1977: 90. **7.** *Op cit.*, Warner: 4. **8.** *Op cit.*, Kennedy Hearings: 86. **9.** *Op cit.*, Warner: 3. **10.** Moore, Francis D., Robley D. Evans, and Margaret H. Ball. "The Biochemistry of Burned Skin." *Annals of Surgery* 128.2 (Aug 1949). **11.** Evans, Robley D., *et al.* "The Effect of Skeletally Deposited Alpha-Kay Emitters In Man." *British Journal of Radiology* 39.468 (Dec 1966). **12.** RHTG #82/549/2, Box #161, 28 Oct 1944. **13.** "CIA: Humans Weren't Used in Its N-tests." *Houston Chronicle*, 8 Jan 1994: 6; *Toronto Star*, 8 Jan 1994: A10. **14.** Wilson, Charles. "MIT Researchers Say Radiation Doses Were 'Trivial.'" Reuters, 7 Jan 1994. **15.** *Boston Globe*, 30 Dec 1993. **16.** "MIT Records Show Wider Radioactivity Testing at Fernald." *Boston Globe*, 31 Dec 1994: 1. **17.** *Op cit.*, Warner, 8. **18.** *Philadelphia Inquirer*, 22 Sept 1963. **19.** Letter to John Kelly, 23 Nov 1994. **20.** Letter to John Kelly, 22 Dec 1994. **21.** Christophers and Kligman. "Percutaneous Absorption in Aged Skin." *Advances in the Biology of Skin, Volume VI, Aging.* (Proceedings of the Symposium held at the University of Oregon Medical School, 1964). Pergamon Press, 1965. **22.** *Journal of the American Medical Association*, 193.10: 797. **23.** Letter to the editor. *Journal of the American Medical Association*, 197.13 (26 Sept 1966). **24.** *J. Invest. Derm.* 59.6 (Dec 1972): 416. **25.** Jamison, Harold. "CIA Linked to Prison Tests." *Philadelphia Tribune*, 20 Feb 1981: 3. **26.** DA-18-035-AMC-126 (A), Annual Report by Albert M. Kligman and Herbert W. Copeland, May 1967, ADE472009: 3. **27.** *Ibid.* **28.** *Ibid.* **29.** *Ibid.*: 4. **30.** *Ibid.*: 5. **31.** *Ibid.*: 8. **32.** *Ibid.*: 10. **33.** *Ibid.*: 11. **34.** *Ibid.*: 12. **35.** *Ibid.*: 13. **36.** *Ibid.* **37.** Katz, Adolph."Holmesburg Inmates Test Medicines, Serve as Aides in Laboratory Work." *Philadelphia Evening Bulletin*, 27 Feb 1967: 1,6. **38.** Antosh, Lou. "Medical Testing Lab Closed at Holmesburg." *Philadelphia Evening Bulletin*, 29 Jan 1974. **39.** Plewig, Gerd, and Albert Kligman. "Proliferative Activity of the Serbaceous Glands of the Aged." *J. Invest. Derma.* 70.6 (June 1978): 324. **40.** Plewig, Gerd, and Albert Kligman. *Acne and Rosacea, 2nd Completely Revised and Enlarged Edition*. Springer-Verlag, 1993. **41.** *Op cit.*, Warner: 6. **42.** Memorandum for: CS-III, Subject: [redacted], Boris T. Pash/Chief PB VII, 23 Jan 1950, with attached functional statement. **43.** Frank Wisner, Assistant Director for Policy Coordination. To: Marshall Chadwell, Assistant Director for Scientific Intelligence. "Scientific Intelligence of Interest to OPC." 20 June 1950 [redacted]. **44.** *Op cit.*, Warner: 9. **45.** *Op cit.*, Warner: 9.; Allen W. Dulles to Gordon Dean, Chairman, Atomic Energy Commission, 4 Oct 1951 [redacted]. **46.** Frank G. Wisner, Deputy Director for Plans. To: Joseph A. Frank, Special Assistant for Research, Office of Policy Coordination. "AEC Offer of Assistance in Development of Special Device." 21 March 1952 [redacted]. **47.** Christian M. Freer, Deputy Deputy Director for Plans. "Suggestion for New Radiological Warfare Development." 28 October 1954, [redacted]; [redacted], Chief, Technical Services Staff. To: Allen Dulles, Director of Central Intelligence. "Project MKULTRA, Subproject 35" 15 Nov 1954; *op cit.*, Warner: 4. **48.** From: Joseph G. Hamilton, M.D. To: Colonel K. C. Nichols. Subject: Radiological Warfare. 31 Dec 1946. **49.** *Op cit*, #4. **50.** *Op cit.*, Warner: 5. **51.** *Ibid.*: 4. **52.** *Ibid.*: 7. **53.** *Ibid.*: 6. **54.** Johnson, H.A., W.E. Haymaker, J.R. Rubini, T.M. Fliedner, V.P. Bond, E.P. Cronkite, W.L. Hughes. "A Radioautographic Study of a Human Brain and Glioblastoma Multiforme after the In Vivo Uptake of Tritiated Thymidine." *Cancer* 13.3 (May-June 1960): 636-42. **55.** Report of the Secretary of Defense's Ad Hoc Committee on Chemical, Biological and Radiological Warfare, 30 June 1950. **56.** O'Toole, George. *Honorable Treachery*. Atlantic Monthly Press, 1991: 462.

THE AGENCY AND THE ATOM
JOHN KELLY

THE WHITE HOUSE CAMPAIGN AGAINST DRUG REFORM INITIATIVES
ANTI-DRUG ADS SWAY THE VOTE OF THOSE WHO PAY FOR THEM
DANIEL FORBES

Drug reform proponents in states and cities nationwide appealed directly to the people at the ballot box again in 2002, seeking, as they have now for years, to outflank recalcitrant government officials. The most prominent measures, which sought the liberalization of marijuana laws in Arizona and Nevada, as well as treatment rather than prison for nonviolent drug offenders in Ohio, lost by convincing margins. A host of factors, including a post-9/11 turn from liberal social policies and—on the brink of war—the campaigning of a popular Republican President, contributed to reformers' unaccustomed electoral defeats. Reformers of all stripes had previously triumphed in seventeen of nineteen ballot measures, including thirteen of fourteen sponsored by billionaires George Soros and Peter Lewis and multimillionaire John Sperling.

Another apparent and effective boost to the status quo was the White House's taxpayer-funded social marketing, a campaign geared to sway the votes of those who pay for it. Valued at a staggering some $96 million for just the last months of the year, the White House Office of National Drug Control Policy's (ONDCP) television-based advertising campaign helped poison the well for voter-initiated drug reform. But that's precisely what the anti-drug media campaign was designed to do at its conception at a meeting convened by Clinton Drug Czar Barry McCaffrey a scant nine days following the passage of the first two medical marijuana initiatives in 1996. And ONDCP's pre-election effort, with its focus on marijuana—that is, buy some pot and either help slaughter a family of innocents, cripple an innocent bystander, or bomb a restaurant (yes), or directly run over a kid on a bicycle or mistakenly shoot a friend—was launched in September 2002 to help defeat reform initiatives.

That, anyway, is the sole conclusion to be drawn from an address by ONDCP Deputy Director Mary Ann Solberg to an anti-initiative strategy session attended by some 50 judges, sheriffs, prosecutors, state police, private anti-drug coalition members, federal Drug Enforcement Administration officials, and the "Drug Czar" of Michigan held August 26, 2002, at the DEA office in Detroit. They gathered a week before Labor Day's quickening of the electoral pulse to ponder how to defeat reform initiatives at the behest of DEA Special Agent in Charge Michael A. Braun, who runs federal anti-drug efforts in Michigan, Ohio, and Kentucky. The meeting was held in Detroit, since Michigan's own treatment-not-prison measure had not yet been disqualified due to its backers' dazzlingly boneheaded error in drafting it: They assigned it the same number as an unrelated part of the state constitution, meaning it would have replaced the existing language.

According to a formal invitation printed on DEA/US Department of Justice letterhead (date-stamped 8/2/02 and signed by Braun, it was sent to James Halushka, an Oakland County, Michigan, Deputy Prosecutor), the meeting would both "provide insight on successful strategies to combat legalization" and "provide presentations on how the DEA can assist state leaders in this battle." Participants would discuss how to "share their ideas and strategies and possibly combine resouces in combating" what Braun referred to as "drug legalization [sic] proposals." (No matter the reform initiative in question, drug warriors invariably call it "legalization," their proponents, "legalizers." The Ohio and Michigan treatment measures were far from legalization.)

One meeting participant, Judge Brian W. MacKenzie, District Judge in Michigan's 52nd District, told me that Solberg "talked of the federal government's new initiative with regard to marijuana." He stated that she described it as a new nationwide ad campaign designed to educate the public about pot's dangers, including the discounted notion that it serves as a gateway drug to abuse of more pernicious substances. (The gateway theory was exploded for the umpteenth time, though quite safely after the election, by the decidedly establishment RAND Corporation.)

The upcoming ad campaign was pretty much Solberg's entire focus in Detroit, MacKenzie said. Underscoring the ads' political utility, he added that a fellow attendee asked Solberg about the possibility of the campaign targeting or emphasizing Michigan and Ohio. She replied that that wasn't possible. The two states would instead settle, as would Nevada and Arizona, for their standard share of the huge White

> **VALUED AT A STAGGERING SOME $96 MILLION FOR JUST THE LAST MONTHS OF THE YEAR, THE WHITE HOUSE OFFICE OF NATIONAL DRUG CONTROL POLICY'S (ONDCP) TELEVISION-BASED ADVERTISING CAMPAIGN HELPED POISON THE WELL FOR VOTER-INITIATED DRUG REFORM.**

House ad buy, including the national spots that air in every state.

With November's election looming, dozens of high-powered, state-control types and private drug warriors from Michigan, Ohio, Kentucky, Georgia, and Washington, D.C., women and men with stressful jobs—people with guns, some of them, who face down, prosecute, or judge criminals—didn't travel to Detroit that August Monday to hear a lecture on the White House media campaign just for their abstract edification. The gathering entirely proactive,

Solberg's disquisition on the government's new anti-drug ad campaign makes sense only if you meld her discussion of the ads with the meeting's intent as stated by Braun and quoted above. Clearly, Solberg felt the ad campaign would contribute to the anti-initiative effort. Otherwise, why would this senior White House official (her post required Senate confirmation) head north to waste these no-nonsense folks' time discussing it?

A contemporaneous ONDCP "Talking Points" memo on marijuana stated that: "TV, print, radio, and interactive advertising deliver[ing] powerful messages to dispel the myths [will involve] spending nearly $48 million in advertising just through December '02...." Since Congress requires that all ONDCP ad buys are on a 50-cents-on-the-dollar, take-it-or-leave-it basis, that $48 million is matched dollar for dollar by the media. So, a whopping $96 million in vicious anti-drug advertising flooded the country during and just after the election season.

Vicious? Consider the marijuana scare-ads that were foisted on the voting public starting in mid-September, a couple of weeks after Solberg's promise to the initiative foes gathered in Detroit. In one, the American protagonist buys some pot. As events inevitably unfold in the ONDCP worldview, the ad describes the chain of distribution, ending with: "And this is the family that was lined up by Dan's cartel and shot for getting in the way." In a second, an innocent bystander was crippled for life. Another has a young kid intoning mindlessly, "I kill mothers, I kill fathers," etc., down through children and grandparents and then the current *ne plus ultra*: his killing of policemen and *firemen*. That's a direct reference to the World Trade Center. In yet another ad, "Sophie" discusses her weekend activities, including that she "helped bomb a crowded restaurant." This one ends with the tagline: "Drug money supports terror. If you buy drugs you might too." Any name will do, so why "Sophie" in particular for that—Mideast?—restaurant bombing? Money from the Humboldt County, California, crop is apparently funneled to Hezbollah.

On October 7, more ads came into "heavy rotation," ONDCP boasted, the populace being blanketed through "television, radio, youth magazines, online banners, and in theaters, arcades and schools." Marijuana-fueled date rape—or molestation, at least, of a hopped-up young vic, the *denouement* is unclear—is featured in one. A bunch of kids in a car, who unrealistically puff up clouds of smoke in a very public fast-food drive-thru lane, barrel over a little kid on a bicycle. In a third, two feckless teen stoners with a spewing bong are goofing around at home. One expresses admiration for the other's sister who replies with an oblique threat. The annoyed brother then picks up a pistol lying out unsecured. Of course it goes off just as he points it at his friend. Guess whether there's any mention of proper gun safety. The several new ads expressly promoting membership in community anti-drug coalitions will be discussed below.

The pre-election advertising focused specifically on marijuana and its supposed link to terrorism and mindless death, either foreign or domestic. But with no marijuana initiatives on the immediate horizon, ONDCP retreated from that contortion in a post-election print ad that referred, rather than to marijuana, to "drugs" and "drug money" funding "intimidation, bribery, torture and murder." No mention, of course, of prohibition's central role in those pathologies.

Interestingly, in November 2002, the Federal Communications Commission ruled, despite protest from the government and its partners, that the White House must actually follow the law and identify itself when buying TV advertising. Lloyd D. Johnston, a University of Michigan psychologist who has run annual national teen drug-use surveys for the feds since 1975, testified at both House and Senate hearings on the ad campaign's lack of efficacy in June 2002. He addressed the fact "that the more recent ads have somehow had less salience" than did prior ads, particularly among older teens. For tenth- and twelfth-graders, the ads' "judged impact has not risen very much even though their rate of recalled exposure has."

In other words, the government is throwing hundreds of millions of dollars down a rat-hole with its barrage of ads. That is borne out by Johnston's own taxpayer-funded, $5-million-a-year survey, called, oddly enough, "Monitoring the Future," though it measures the past. In 2002, lifetime drug use for tenth-graders was almost 45 percent, down just slightly from 1997's historical peak of around 47 percent. Statistically speaking, over that time frame, that's a random fluctuation. For twelfth-graders in 2002, the lifetime figure was 53 percent, down also randomly just a bit from 1999's historical peak of under 55 percent. Yet, articles from such big-league papers as the *Washington Post* obligingly quoted White House Drug Czar John P. Walters' hollow assertion: "This survey confirms that our drug prevention efforts are working, and that when we work together and push back, the drug problem gets smaller."

> ANOTHER AD HAS A YOUNG KID INTONING MINDLESSLY, "I KILL MOTHERS, I KILL FATHERS," ETC., DOWN THROUGH CHILDREN AND GRANDPARENTS AND THEN THE CURRENT *NE PLUS ULTRA*: HIS KILLING OF POLICEMEN AND *FIREMEN*.

Pondering why the ads were a bust, Lloyd Johnston told Congress:

> My own hypothesis for some time has been that placing the name Office of [National] Drug Control Policy as a tag line at the end of each ad causes many young people to dismiss the message content immediately upon viewing. After all, the credibility of the message is judged in large part by the identity of the message giver, and an "office" involved in "control" and "policy" is not likely to be a source from whom adolescents would welcome a communication.

Never mind some "office"—it's the White House, dude, beaming out from your TV set, telling you how to live your life.

Johnston was correct to the degree that the ONDCP did in fact identify itself, but he also created a straw man for the ads' lack of effect since the ONDCP identified itself rarely. That is, it soon started tagging the ads with something called "the anti-drug." This imaginary, stealth sponsor—which was ostensibly behind the ads for years—was far less offensive to teens worried about autonomy issues than admitting this social marketing came from the White House. The ONDCP is well aware of that; that's why it created the silly brand in the first place and why, hiding behind the fig leaf of the Ad Council,

THE WHITE HOUSE CAMPAIGN AGAINST DRUG REFORM INITIATIVES
DANIEL FORBES

it fought the surprisingly forthright FCC ruling and is appealing it as of this writing.

Despite the FCC ruling, the sponsoring organization featured prominently at the bottom of the national print ad mentioned above—an ad not subject to FCC dictates—was that amorphous entity: "the antidrug.com."

To be able to defend against the charge of running deceptive advertising, the phrase "Office of National Drug Control Policy" actually does appear in the ad, though in a way guaranteed to compound the dissembling. The phrase appears not at the bottom of the page, the normal placement for such sponsor identification, but rather in the far upper-lefthand corner, in tiny six-point type, printed *vertically* up against the ad's vertical dark border. I guess they ran out of invisible ink. Given its placement and barely visible type, folks who even saw it and then bothered to peer and squint would probably assume, given its placement on the page, it was just a photo credit for the picture of the mopey-looking teen—presumably a funder of "intimidation, bribery, torture and murder"—at the top of the ad. Nothing like being proud of your work.

Boston University School of Public Health professor William De Jong consulted with a White House contractor on the media campaign's initial design. I quoted him in a pre-election article on AlterNet.org ("Drug Warriors Crusade Against Reform Initiatives," October 24, 2002). Interpreting Solberg's remarks in Detroit, De Jong said, "Their true motivation is being revealed: to influence referenda, though they will claim otherwise." He added, "They're trying to use the media campaign to present information that might influence the outcome of voter referenda." Dr. David Duncan, an associate professor of medicine at Brown University, helped design a study of the ads' efficacy for an ONDCP consultant. His pre-election interpretation: "It's pretty obvious they are hoping the ads will shade people's opinions on drugs in general, and that that will spill over to their views on the initiatives." Kevin Zeese, president of Common Sense for Drug Policy, said, "No doubt these sorts of ads lay a foundation of fear that can be used by the initiative's opponents. Ads that seek to create fear about marijuana lead to the sort of fear and ignorance that drive the drug laws and work against reform, work for just sending people to jail."

Though the ONDCP's Mary Ann Solberg is one of the nation's main proponents of anti-drug coalitions, she apparently failed to address such topics as coalition-building or drug courts or how the officials attending the Detroit meeting might voice their opposition to the two treatment initiatives. Indeed, someone unacquainted with the history of the White House media campaign might wonder why her presentation was even considered on-topic. As has been its custom under Bush, the ONDCP failed to respond to numerous phone calls from this reporter to defend her discourse at this anti-initiative confab. Given the Administration's silence, it's useful to note the entire media campaign's political genesis and intent.

As I disclosed July 2000 in a *Salon* article entitled, "Fighting 'Cheech & Chong' Medicine"—the phrase is McCaffrey's—the White House

media campaign (now in its second five-year appropriation) was engendered at a meeting McCaffrey convened in Washington nine days after medical marijuana initiatives passed in Arizona and California in 1996.

Minutes of this meeting reveal that some 40 officials and private-sector executives met to discuss the need for taxpayer-funded messages to thwart any potential medical marijuana initiatives in the other 48 states and perhaps even roll back the two that had just passed. They included two policy advisors from the Clinton White House, the head of the DEA, and representatives of the FBI, Departments of Justice, Health and Human Services, Treasury, and Education, along with state law enforcement personnel. One private-sector participant was quoted in the meeting's minutes as saying, "We'll work with Arizona and California to undo it and stop the spread of legalization to [the] other 48 states."

The ONDCP anti-marijuana ads Solberg touted are part of a second five-year ad campaign that press reports indicate Congress decided to reauthorize at $762 million over five years, starting in fiscal year

> MINUTES OF THIS MEETING REVEAL THAT SOME 40 OFFICIALS AND PRIVATE-SECTOR EXECUTIVES MET TO DISCUSS THE NEED FOR TAXPAYER-FUNDED MESSAGES TO THWART ANY POTENTIAL MEDICAL MARIJUANA INITIATIVES IN THE OTHER 48 STATES AND PERHAPS EVEN ROLL BACK THE TWO THAT HAD JUST PASSED.

2003. This media boondoggle was approved despite the fact that, according to an early July 2002 Associated Press story, Drug Czar Walters "has repeatedly criticized the ad campaign, saying teenagers were ignoring the ads. In May, he said [the ONDCP] would cancel the campaign if it was not effective." The AP cited a survey released that May that "found no evidence the ads were discouraging drug use."

According to *USA Today* (also in July 2002), of the $762 million that federal taxpayers will pony up over the next five years, some $130 million annually—or approximately $650 million total—will go to buy advertising, along with a very small amount for media planning. (The remaining $112 million over five years is a heck of a chunk for expenses, ancillary or otherwise, one reason the second five-year contract was bitterly contested on Madison Avenue.)

Should the subsequent five years mirror the campaign's strategy during the first five, then half the ad budget will go to ad-buys targeting adults—that is, voters. And, if past similarly remains prologue, that $650 million is only the half of it since, as mentioned, Congress requires the media to sell its ad time and space to ONDCP for half-price. That is, broadcasters, publishers, and other media cough up two ad slots for the price of one.

So, minus those relatively tiny media planning fees, approximately $1.3 billion over five years will be available for anti-drug advertising. Half will be directed at adult voters, and all of it will tend, however indirectly, to poison the drug-reform well. Never mind that, according to a National Institute on Drug Abuse evaluation of the media campaign released in June 2002, "There is little evidence of direct favorable [ad] Campaign effects on youth…and no tendency for those reporting more exposure to Campaign messages to hold more desirable beliefs." In fact, for many kids, including girls as a group, NIDA found that more exposure to the ads was correlated with greater rates of marijuana initiation! As to the ads directed at adults, NIDA concluded: "[T]he evidence does not as yet support an effect of parent exposure on youth behavior." That is, "There was no cross-sectional associational evidence for any group that parent exposure was associated with lower marijuna consumption among youth."

Such statements by the Bush Administration as to the ads' negligible or even negative effects on youth drug use lend credence to the assertion here that the ads—half of them directed, however ineffectually, at adult potential voters—are a political construct. This despite the fact that, as was stated to me back in 2000 by Clinton deputy press secretary Jake Siewert: "The ONDCP is prohibited from involving itself in political causes in its advertising."

_PARSING CLUES ON PARTICIPANTS

Though the DEA raised the drawbridge around that Detroit meeting, it's still possible to glean some notion of its participants, including the "state leaders from Michigan, Kentucky and Ohio" that Braun's invite promised. Just who were the 50 or so federal, state, and local officials—and did any take a personal vacation day to attend? Noting the participants gives some indication of the vast scope of the official, multi-state anti-initiative campaign.

Along with confirming his own particpation, Oakland County Deputy Prosecutor James Halushka told me the DEA's public affairs and congressional liaison dirctor, Christopher Battle, attended, as did "some CADCA people too, a couple of representatives from Lansing and Battle Creek who continue to spread the word." CADCA refers to the Community Anti-Drug Coalitions of America, whose board of directors Solberg graced prior to joining ONDCP.

(In December, 2001, Bush announced his intention to reauthorize a Department of Justice program which, if fully funded, would distribute $450 million over five years to community anti-drug groups. Approximately one-fifth of that money is available for what is termed "voter education.")

Judge Brian MacKenzie, who attended only part of what he called a 9-to-3 meeting, was particularly interested in the presentation by Judge Harvey Hoffman, the president of a Michigan drug court advocacy group, the Michigan Association of Drug Court Professionals. He said Hoffman discussed the impact of California's Prop. 36, which was the Michigan and Ohio initiatives' template.

MacKenzie also noted the presence of Oakland County Sheriff Michael Bouchard. Charles List, a coordinator for the Committee to Protect Our Kids, declared Sheriff Bouchard and Saginaw County Prosecuting Attorney Michael Thomas this committee's co-chairs and directed all inquiries to them. Bouchard confirmed his attendance to me but said little else, and Thomas declined comment. In any event, this "registered ballot question committee formed to

oppose" the treatment initiative was represented at the meeting. That was its description in an August 9, 2002, letter sent to Michigan's Bureau of Elections by its counsel, the powerhouse Michigan law firm of Dykema Gossett.

Dykema Gossett partner and head of its Government Policy and Practice Group, Richard McLellan, is a hand-in-glove ally of Michigan Governor John Engler, himself a rabid initiative foe. (As an expression of his opposition to the treatment measure, as well as two other initiatives, Engler vetoed $845 million in state revenue for local municipal services such as fire and police departments, a veto that was soon overridden by a combined vote of 141-to-2.) McLellan spearheaded the successful September 2002 effort to disqualify the Michigan treatment initiative on the purely technical—albeit damning—grounds of the drafters' mistake in numbering it. In 1990, McLellan served as director of Governor-elect Engler's transition team, and he subsequently chaired a committee helping Engler and President George W. Bush pick federal appeals court judges. He has also served as Michigan's Drug Czar and as an advisor to President Gerald Ford. According to a filing with the Michigan Secretary of State, the Committee to Protect Our Kids' treasurer is Richard M. Gabrys, an executive with the accounting and consulting firm Deloitte & Touche. He and McLellan both refused comment.

Referring to Protect Our Kids and other initiative opponents, prior to the measure's disqualification, Deputy Prosecutor Halushka said they would hope to mount a "massive public education campaign...to expose [proponents'] myths in a sound-bite world." Though decrying the impossibility of matching the rich backers' potential ad budget, he added, "We are raising money, going [nationally] to big-name donors."

Additional DEA meeting participants, said Judge MacKenzie, included members of the state police; one or more representatives of Detroit anti-drug coalitions (to complement the Lansing and Battle Creek activists Halushka mentioned as attending); both a "police

> SO, MINUS THOSE RELATIVELY TINY MEDIA PLANNING FEES, APPROXIMATELY $1.3 BILLION OVER FIVE YEARS WILL BE AVAILABLE FOR ANTI-DRUG ADVERTISING.

commander" and a prosecutor from Ohio; as well as someone from Kentucky. Altogether, MacKenzie estimated the crowd at "50 or 60 people in a big conference room."

More clues regarding attendance come from the fact that prior to the meeting, the office of Representative John Conyers (Democrat-Michigan), ranking minority member of the House Judiciary Committee, obtained a copy of Braun's invitation, according to Deanna Maher, a special projects coordinator on Conyers' staff. Wearing two hats, Maher works part-time for Conyers and part-time for the initiative's sponsor, the Michigan Campaign for New Drug Policies, the national CNDP's state affiliate. CNDP's Fratello stated that Maher segregates her time religiously—a common practice, he said, of congressional staffers with outside political pursuits.

With Braun's invitation in hand, the week before the meeting Maher called both Braun and DEA Special Agent Rich Isaacson (whose name and number were also on the invite) to inquire about the meeting. Isaacson extended an invitation to Maher, who declined. Isaacson told her that Craig Yaldoo, the Director of Michigan's Office of Drug Control Policy, four judges, representatives from the anti-initiative Committee to Protect Our Kids, and "regional" officials would be among those assembling at the Detroit DEA office.

Along with Solberg, another featured speaker was Sue Rusche, executive director of Atlanta-based National Families in Action. She fired up the troops with visions of the perfidy they faced. Describing her as "a nationally recognized expert on the history of the drug legalization effort in the United States," Braun promised Rusche's "insight[s] on successful strategies to combat legalization." Rusche's Website is indeed a comprehensive distillation of drug reformers' either stark truth-telling or public *faux pas*—depending on your point of view.

It's worth noting that, according to Philanthropic Research, Inc., Rusche's National Families in Action had total 1999 revenues of $487,376; of this, a whopping $429,503 was from the government. Figures for the prior two years are similar: 1998 total revenue, $542,762, of which $490,913 was from the government. In 1997, the total was $507,291; the government's portion, $451,123.

Describing Rusche as the "keynote" speaker, Halushka said, "She basically talked of the arguments that needed to be made, talked of the myths and the [proponents'] true agenda. She proved it with a statistic-filled" presentation.

Braun had also promised potential attendees that "DEA's Demand Reduction and Congressional and Public Affairs Sections will provide presentations on how the DEA can assist state leaders in this battle." The reference was presumably to Christopher Battle, who runs the DEA's PR and congressional affairs operations from its Washington headquarters. Halushka said Battle attended and "talked of the need for a grassroots [effort], of working with community groups." (As mentioned, such community coalitions get massive federal funding to spread the Drug-War creed, Bush calling for $450 million over five years in late 2001. That's in addition to millions of dollars in government advertising promoting coalition membership.) Thus, according to Halushka, Battle, a senior DEA official, sent the gathering forth to proselytize to the public about the upcoming election. Halushka also said the meeting focused, in part, "in terms of getting the word out."

> IT'S WORTH NOTING THAT, ACCORDING TO PHILANTHROPIC RESEARCH, INC., RUSCHE'S NATIONAL FAMILIES IN ACTION HAD TOTAL 1999 REVENUES OF $487,376; OF THIS, A WHOPPING $429,503 WAS FROM THE GOVERNMENT.

To that end, Halushka added that he, Judge MacKenzie, and a Michigan county sheriff visited the editorial board of a local paper to voice their opposition to the initiative. He also gave "some speeches during the day to community coalitions and prevention groups." But, he said, "That's part of my job: public education regarding public safety." It seems voters might have endangered their safety with the wrong vote had the measure remained on the ballot in Michigan.

Detroit's own Rep. John Conyers first disclosed the Detroit DEA event. Obtaining Braun's invitation the week before the strategy session, Conyers wrote DEA Director Asa Hutchinson demanding an investigation and then issued a press release the next day, Friday, August 23, 2002. Conyers' letter and subsequent statement called on Hutchinson to investigate the DEA's "possible misuse of federal funds without proper authorization by Congress and in contravention of existing law." Conyers stated: "It appears that the DEA has been actively engaged across the country in collaboration with groups who are opposed to ballot proposals involving reform of our drug laws."

Referring to political campaigning "on federal property and on government time," Conyers charged that the meeting undoubtedly violated a 2001 federal law "which clearly states that no part of any appropriation for DEA can be used for 'publicity or propaganda purposes' not authorized by Congress." He wondered whether the upcoming meeting would run "afoul of federal laws prohibiting unauthorized lobbying activities by federal agencies." Conyers also castigated the judges who participated in violation of their Canon of Ethics and implied that the DEA's activities have compromised "the integrity of our national government."

Referencing Braun's "invitation to a forum 'to discuss drug legalization efforts,'" Conyers concluded, "I am concerned that this meeting, with its specific purpose of devising a lobbying and public campaign against Michigan drug reform proposals, is...an unauthorized use of funds." MacKenzie said that one notable speaker was a DEA lawyer who parsed Conyers' advance criticism of the meeting. He added that the lawyer discussed at some length how "it was not a violation."

Had he ended up chairing the House Judiciary Committee following the 2002 election, Conyers would have undoubtedly held a hearing geared to limiting such inappropriate official politicking in future. One question he would've want answered is, Who paid for all these people to make their way to Detroit? Someone from Kentucky was there, along with at least two from Ohio, according to Judge MacKenzie. Private citizen Sue Rusche came up from Georgia. Reaching her by phone, she voiced nothing but her intention to hang up—and did so as I blurted a question on whether the DEA had paid for her trip.

Then there's the question, as Conyers pointed out, of all these government officials taking this time while on the clock, ostensibly serving the public in non-partisan fashion. It's quite a stretch to think they all took personal days and traveled at their own expense. As discussed below, the DEA's Rich Isaacson said his overnight lodging was paid for by the taxpayers of Ohio, his time and travel by federal taxpayers, when he attended a similar anti-initiative meeting at the Governor of Ohio's mansion in October 2001.

Curiously, the same day that Conyers publicly blasted the DEA (August 23), it responded by sending Detroit-area Democratic Representative Carolyn Cheeks Kilpatrick an anti-initiative ten-point memo that Halushka told me he helped write. While the memo does artfully and often disingenuously critique the initiative, it doesn't excuse or even address the issues raised by partisan electioneering by dozens of officials at a federal office in Detroit.

According to Conyers' staffer, Deanna Maher, Rep. Kilpatrick received a call the Friday before the Monday meeting from Asa Hutchinson denouncing the initiative. He then faxed her Halushka's effort: "10 Reasons that 'The Michigan Drug Reform Initiative' is **BAD FOR MICHIGAN**." (Upper case and bold in original.)

(The memo's second point stands out as egregiously false: "It effectively legalizes use of all dangerous drugs, including cocaine, ecstasy and heroin, for anyone who merely states that they seek treatment, regardless of whether they even attend treatment sessions.")

REFERRING TO POLITICAL CAMPAIGNING "ON FEDERAL PROPERTY AND ON GOVERNMENT TIME," REP. CONYERS CHARGED THAT THE MEETING UNDOUBTEDLY VIOLATED A 2001 FEDERAL LAW "WHICH CLEARLY STATES THAT NO PART OF ANY APPROPRIATION FOR DEA CAN BE USED FOR 'PUBLICITY OR PROPAGANDA PURPOSES' NOT AUTHORIZED BY CONGRESS."

Perhaps the state and local officials took their cue on overt politicking from the top, since Hutchinson himself did not shrink from the fray. A DEA release noted the boss's address in October 2001 to an Ohio drug court graduation ceremony. He thanked the defendants for their success and "for the example you've set." And he warned of "a growing challenge to drug courts": that is, the Ohio ballot initiative. The measure lacks accountability, Hutchinson asserted, and was thus "a program that is doomed to failure." Then in May 2002, Hutchinson blasted the Ohio initiative in an op-ed published by the *Columbus Dispatch*.

_SOLBERG THE MASTER

Aside from her dangling the promise of new anti-marijuana advertising, there's more to be said of ONDCP Deputy Director Mary Ann Solberg. Asked the genesis of the anti-initiative Committee To Protect our Kids, Halushka said, "The godmother is Mary Ann Solberg." Replying to a question, he added, "The spark came from Mary Ann—no question." That spark flared months after President Bush publicly nominated her to her ONDCP post in July 2001. He did so based on her experiences running a string of anti-drug coalitions north of Detroit.

Halushka noted that back in 2000 Solberg had enlisted prosecutors in Detroit and in Oakland and McComb Counties to fight the threat of a potential marijuana legalization initiative. Then, in November and December of 2001—months after her nomination—Halushka said Solberg "alerted" him and "wanted to galvanize people" regarding the threat of the proposed new treatment initiative. Consequently, he examined its "frightening" language and "brought it to my boss," David Gorcyca, Oakland County Prosecuting Attorney.

Along with her own efforts, Halushka said that Solberg spurred on both himself and Gorcyca to make a stand. Halushka also spoke of

getting Michigan Drug Czar "Craig [Yaldoo] organized to get the state organized." He added, "Craig is working more on a statewide level." Aiding that effort, Gorcyca enlisted the Prosecuting Attorneys Association of Michigan to get all 83 counties involved. One wonders if Yaldoo and Gorcyca's outreach to their colleagues occurred entirely during off-hours.

Oakland County Sheriff Michael Bouchard then signed on, said Halushka, and Halushka's own January 2002 address to the Troy coalition Solberg had run for years "started the ball rolling." Halushka added, "We've been proactive in Oakland County…. David Gorcyca, myself and Solberg have worked in Oakland." Though it's certainly more racially integrated than it once was, Oakland can be fairly described as the white-flight county north of Detroit.

As to Solberg's current involvement, Halushka said, "She has continued to be of help—she has continued to help with connections to people and data. She does come to town. She was in town Monday [8/26/02] at DEA headquarters in Detroit." Indeed she was, lecturing the meeting about the ad campaign. Speaking of the initiative in general, he reiterated: "She was responsible for alerting us."

Informed of Solberg's participation (which I had disclosed), initiative campaigner Dave Fratello stated: "I always knew Mary Ann Solberg would take the White House too far. She's a zealot, hired to be on the far right on the drug-abuse issue. She's not cautious and she's not being restrained. I always thought her zeal would get the better of her, and now she's taken the White House over a cliff." In a pre-election reference to the initiatives' active opponents sprinkled throughout the highest levels of Michigan and Ohio officialdom, reformer Kevin Zeese added, "They fear these millionaires and activists who are getting their message out."

Such fear had White House Drug Czar John Walters barnstorming the country at taxpayer expense, railing against the initiatives at appearances in Arizona, Ohio, Michigan, Pennsylvania, Nevada (in both July and October), and other states. Walters typically appeared before carefully screened audiences—in one case before just the typically uncritical very young and very old—for fire-and-brimstone denunciations that were then parroted in the local press. In Arizona in October for instance, he stated, according to the *Arizona Republic*: "I don't believe voters in Arizona are going to buy a stupid, insulting con like this proposition." In Ohio a week later, according to the *Toledo Blade*, Walters "blasted" that state's measure with a startling bit of rhetoric: It "would weaken the ability of society to use 'compassionate coercion….'"

In early September in the *San Francisco Chronicle*, he declared that today's pot is up to 30 times more powerful than that of "the Woodstock era." And that it produces, at high doses, "paranoia or even violence." I dissected some of his prevarications in *Slate* ("The Myth of Potent Pot," November 19, 2002). For instance, his "30 times" figure (up from the "10 to 20 times stronger" claim he made in May 2002—before the Nevada initiative surfaced) refers to the fiercest sinsemilla. While one or three extreme samples seized by the government might be that strong, what most people, especially most kids, smoke is only a couple of times stronger than yesterday's pot—which Walters categorized as far weaker than it was so as to further boost his claims. He also cited sky-rocketing adolescent marijuana treatment admissions without mentioning that some two-thirds of these kids were forced admissions, either at the hands of the criminal justice system or their school.

Walters' overt thumping of the bully pulpit was of a piece with the more secretive efforts carried out by numerous public officials. In fact, a string of covert strategy sessions, dating back to July 2001, was convened by state and federal officials—typically while on the clock, ostensibly serving the public—to plan proactive campaigns to defeat Ohio's and Michigan's drug reform initiatives. Particularly striking was the strident, eighteen-month anti-initiative campaign led by Ohio Governor Bob Taft, a Republican, First Lady Hope Taft, and the highest reaches of his administration—a campaign grounded in political malfeasance, the misuse of public funds, and the inappropriate use of state and federal government resources.

Such charges are supported by my analysis of the first six months of the Taft-led campaign to usurp the voters' franchise that was published in May 2002 by the venerable Washington, DC, think tank, the Institute for Policy Studies. Entitled *The Governor's Sub-rosa Plot to Subvert an Election in Ohio*, it's at <www.ips-dc.org/projects/drugpolicy/ohio.htm>.

One highlight (and notice the long lead time) was the July 2001 anti-initiative strategy session hosted in the US Capitol building itself by a senior Senate Republican staffer, William Olson. This skull session was for Hope Taft's benefit, along with the State of Ohio's directors of criminal justice and substance abuse policy, who both report to the Governor. Also gathered under the Capitol dome was Betty Sembler, the founder of a prominent Drug-War lobby—and wife of the former finance chair of the Republican National Committee and current ambassador to Italy—as well as four senior executives from the supposedly apolitical Partnership for a Drug-Free America.

The Partnership for a Drug-Free America, which has foisted ineffective (so the government's own research declares) anti-drug ads on the country since the late 1980s, has been overshadowed the last couple of years, its leading role assumed by its partner since 1997, the big-bucks ONDCP. So it was perhaps willing to violate its presumed scruples by getting involved in partisan politics—not that it hasn't, in effect, done so since the first two medical marijuana measures passed in 1996. Though it ended up producing no ads to aid the Taft effort, internal Taft administration memos prove its evident willingness to do so, starting with the July 2001 planning session, which the Partnership's Director of Operations, Michael Y. Townsend, termed a "counter-legalization brainstorm session." Other Taft allies included Solberg and the Drug Czars of the two other potential treatment initiative states, Florida and Michigan.

Readers can find a dense tale of offical misconduct at the IPS site; not a word has been challenged.

_SOLBERG TO OHIO'S FIRST LADY: TV IS KEY

As discussed in the IPS report, upon Solberg's July 2001 nomination to the ONDCP, she received a congratulatory email from Ohio First Lady Hope Taft. Referring to the Ohio and Michigan initiatives, Taft wrote, "We are interested in sharing info and ideas with both states and wondered who in Michigan will be in charge. Could you let me know what you know or think?"

Taft assumed as a matter of course that someone in Michigan would be in charge of opposing the ballot measure.

In her reply, Solberg immediately referred—not to some private individual more suited to run a political campaign—but to Michigan's new Drug Czar, Craig Yaldoo, who attended the DEA-hosted Detroit meeting. She wrote: "I met with Craig last week, and he is very interested in taking up the fight and appears to be on top of the Soros people and their movements in Michigan. I suggested he form a partnership with you to fight the prop[osition]."

Quite telling in a brief email, Solberg then told Taft: "It would be very effective if we could pool resources to produce TV spots. I have some funding commitments, and I believe we could raise even more as a team. I would love to meet with an Ohio/Michigan team before I leave Troy [Michigan] to begin planning."

Solberg was not referring at that point to the combined $1.3-billion worth of ads over five years that taxpayers will buy and the media will be bludgeoned into collectively providing. Nonetheless, note her immediate emphasis on TV ads and the money to air them in what she told Taft would be "a very hard fight." (An April 2001 Pew Research Center for People and the Press study found, according to the *Wall Street Journal*, "that a 52% to 35% majority of adults believe drug use should be treated as a 'disease,' not a crime." Similarly, a Soros-funded poll released in February 2002 found that 63 percent of "Americans describe drug abuse as a medical problem that should be handled mainly through counseling and treatment," while 31 percent believe it "a serious crime that should be handled mainly by the courts and prison system.")

As it turned out, given Governor Taft's fund-raising clout (plus help from his gubernatorial fund-raiser), especially with companies that do business with the State of Ohio, the anti-initiative campaign raised $775,000, according to the preliminary campaign finance report available as of this writing. As in any campaign, the money went primarily for television. Along with companies and individuals doing business with the state, CNDP asserts that nearly a third of the donors, oddly enough, were wine and liquor wholesalers—interested for some unfathomable reason in keeping drug penalties harsh.

The IPS report details a session similar to the DEA meeting, a "Multi-State Drug Policy Forum" held at the Tafts'

> IN FACT, A STRING OF COVERT STRATEGY SESSIONS, DATING BACK TO JULY 2001, WAS CONVENED BY STATE AND FEDERAL OFFICIALS—TYPICALLY WHILE ON THE CLOCK, OSTENSIBLY SERVING THE PUBLIC—TO PLAN PROACTIVE CAMPAIGNS TO DEFEAT OHIO'S AND MICHIGAN'S DRUG REFORM INITIATIVES.

official residence in Columbus, Ohio, on October 12, 2001. Solberg, DEA Agent Rich Isaacson, Michigan Drug Czar Craig Yaldoo, and Florida Drug Czar James McDonough all attended. The State of Ohio offered to pay for meals and lodging for out-of-state attendees and did in fact pay $2,000 to a local "meeting facilitator." As mentioned, Isaacson's lodging was paid for by the taxpayers of Ohio, his time and travel by federal taxpayers.

In early 2002, I questioned DEA spokesperson Thomas Hinojosa about the potential impropriety of Isaacson's government-paid trip. The DEA was then responding to my queries, and Hinojosa told me, "[Isaacson's] job is drug investigations and stopping the flow of narcotics." Asked how attending a strategy session on defeating initiatives fit that brief, Hinojosa said, "That initiative deals with illegal drugs, which come under the Controlled Substances Act. So there's nothing wrong with that."

"THEY HAVE PEOPLE [APPEAR] ON THE LOCAL NEWS OR THEY FEED THEM DIFFERENT STORIES."

Isaacson himself told me (also in early 2002) that the Ohio meeting in October 2001 was "merely to determine what is happening in these states regarding possible legalization efforts." Evaluate his statement in light of a five-page "outcomes" memo summarizing the day's conclusions. Among the numerous political tactics the twenty-odd participants agreed were necessary, it featured such overt exhortations as: "Have a seamless, collaborative effort of organizations involved, mobilized and working hard to oppose the Initiative." To quote a second "outcome," one of many: "Beat the Initiative back in the entire country, not just in each state." At meeting's end, the Ohio, Michigan, and Florida officials pledged to work together and stay in touch through email, conference calls, and possible future meetings.

_PUBLIC MONEY FUELS PRIVATE JUGGERNAUT

Solberg's activities in Michigan prior to her April 2002 Senate confirmation shed light on the state- and federally-funded private apparatus that defends the Drug-War status quo. Her base was the Troy Community Coalition for the Prevention of Drug and Alcohol Abuse, which, according to the US Department of Justice, was formed with federal money in 1991. (Philanthropic Research, Inc. notes that for the fiscal year ending in June 1999, the Troy Coalition had total revenues of $254,000, with government grants providing $163,000.)

The next calendar year, in September 2000, it received a $100,000 Justice Department grant, the money to be spent in part, according to the DoJ, for the group to act "as a catalyst for collaboration among all segments of the community, thereby building...awareness that will lead to an increase in the perception of the health risks involved [with drugs] and *growing social disapproval* within the community." [Emphasis added.] Not incidentally, the DoJ requires that grantees include "at least one" media representative in their effort.

The year before, in 1999, the Coalition of Healthy Communities (CHC), an umbrella group for seven community coalitions located north of Detroit that Solberg also directed, received $99,209 in Justice Department money. According to the DoJ Website, CHC

used some of that money to "implement a public awareness campaign." Referring to this social marketing, Mary Louise Embrey of the DoJ Office of Congressional and Public Affairs told me, "The way they were going about it is multi-faceted: They've hooked in with the Ad Council and the national ONDCP anti-drug media campaign—they use print materials from ONDCP. And they used the local media to make connections. They have people [appear] on the local news or they feed them different stories."

My series of *Salon* articles (archived at <www.mapinc.org>) proved that the White House used taxpayer funds to reward broadcasters and publishers who inserted White House-approved and even White House-dictated anti-drug content into their shows and articles. But, in addition, according to Embrey of the Justice Department, public funds were also used to help local coalitions influence voters through local media north of Detroit.

Such local coalitions, many of which are affiliated with the national umbrella group, the Community Anti-Drug Coalitions of America, serve as a taxpayer-funded infrastructure to help maintain current interdict-and-incarcerate policies. Recall Halushka's and MacKenzie's statements regarding Michigan coalition members' attendance at the DEA meeting. Part of such coalitions' government funding is a Department of Justice program that was authorized at $144 million for its first five years. As mentioned, in December 2001, the White House proposed—President Bush himself attending CADCA's annual convention to make the announcement—to reauthorize it for another five years at $450 million, or more than triple the cost. (Approximately two-thirds of the first $144 million's 464 total grants went to CADCA member coalitions; the rest went to other local groups.)

Since ONDCP ultimately determines these DoJ grants' distribution, depending on John Walters' degree of micromanagement, Solberg may have more say than anyone in the country as to this proposed $450 million's ultimate destination and purpose.

It's a role she'll find familiar, since she was a 1998 Clinton appointee, along with Ohio First Lady Hope Taft, to the Advisory Commission on the Drug-Free Communities Program. As detailed in my Institute for Policy Studies report, Solberg was actually co-chair of this eleven-member body that advises both the DoJ and ONDCP on, says the White House, the "distribution of grants to community organizations." Solberg's tenure on the presidential commission influencing the then $144-million program's disbursements was fraught with conflict of interest since (along with the Partnership for a Drug-Free America's Steve Pasierb) she also served on CADCA's board. Not surprisingly, two Detroit-area coalitions she ran before heading to Washington both received the standard, approximately $100,000 grant, one in FY 1999, the other in FY 2000. A real go-getter, Solberg has also served on a panel advising a US Department of Health and Human Services agency: the Center for Substance Abuse Prevention—another ready, steady source of federal funds.

And, prior to her ascension to the ONDCP deputy directorship, Solberg also helped advise the Ad Council's Community Anti-Drug Campaign. The Ad Council is the private nonprofit responsible for a host of public service announcements, some more palatable than others. Though it didn't receive much notice that I'm aware of, during 2000 and 2001 the effort, said the White House, "received more than $120 million in donated [sic] media support through the Ad Council's media outreach and ONDCP's" 50-cents-on-the-dollar deals with the media. That's a very quiet $120 million of social marketing that supports, among other causes, the Drug-War status quo.

In addition, in mid-August 2002, the ONDCP indicated its intent to team with the Ad Council to "launch new ads next month to promote awareness of—and involvement with—community drug-prevention coalitions..." This new campaign, distinct from the ONDCP anti-marijuana ads, would feature, said the White House, a Website and toll-free number and "TV, radio, print, outdoor and Web banner ads" designed to help people "get involved with or start a coalition and locate a coalition in their community." And the ONDCP did start showing several television ads expressly pumping community anti-drug coalitions. They directed viewers to a Website, <www.helpyourcommunity.org>, replete with CADCA material, including invitations to join an existing chapter or start a new one, and messages from its director. Yes, indeed, your tax dollars at work promoting private groups that spend up to a fifth of their government-swollen budgets seeking to influence your vote on fiercely contested social issues.

head of the National Organization for the Reform of Marijuana Laws, said, "Her presence gives enormous empowerment to the local partisans—to know that the federal government, the White House in particular, is supporting their efforts. Sitting in Detroit, when the White House shows up, it may not be illegal, but it sure as hell is improper."

Numerous phone calls to the ONDCP and the DEA, including to ONDCP PR chief Thomas Riley and to DEA Special Agents Battle (its PR boss) and Braun, were not returned. Reaching Solberg's personal voicemail and hoping to prompt a response, I outlined my imminent article on her Detroit discourse on the ads. But without much of a leg to stand on, the White House and the DEA refused to teeter on the precipice of actually discussing their active opposition to state ballot measures—conservatives' rhetoric about devolution of power to the states, indeed the entire concept of states' rights, be blowed.

> "HER PRESENCE GIVES ENORMOUS EMPOWERMENT TO THE LOCAL PARTISANS—TO KNOW THAT THE FEDERAL GOVERNMENT, THE WHITE HOUSE IN PARTICULAR, IS SUPPORTING THEIR EFFORTS. SITTING IN DETROIT, WHEN THE WHITE HOUSE SHOWS UP, IT MAY NOT BE ILLEGAL, BUT IT SURE AS HELL IS IMPROPER."

In January 2002, CADCA spokeswoman Betsy Glick told the *Detroit Free Press*, "Under federal law, the nonprofit coalitions generally can spend up to 20 percent of their budgets 'to educate voters.'" According to the article: "Solberg said she is determined to see more coalitions spawned and strengthened. And...she is expected to help them play a key role in opposing any easing of drug laws" (i.e., any initiatives). The *Free Press* added, quoting one of Solberg's Michigan coalition colleagues: "Behind the scenes, Solberg is 'spearheading the campaign against this [treatment] initiative.'"

With December 2001's planned huge reauthorization, 20 percent of $450 million (or up to $90 million) would be available over five years for publicly-funded voter education to influence elections. Such pedagogical influence might fall unabashedly on a state initiative question, or more indirectly on a race for county sheriff between a Drug War hard-liner and a potential reformer—or even, perhaps, on a presidential contest.

As to any "spawning," on September 9, 2002, Solberg was slated to address the annual Michigan Substance Abuse Conference, speaking on "Successful Strategies for Coalition Building." Sponsored by state and federal health agencies, attendees' expenses were tax-deductible at the sold-out, two-day seminar, a meeting substantial enough to qualify for professional continuing education credits.

In August 2002, with the Michigan treatment initiative still headed for the ballot along with its companion measure in Ohio, the federal, state, and local officials gathered in Detroit no doubt welcomed the presence of Solberg, the ex-school teacher whose deft politics helped her find her way to the White House, in an advisory capacity under Clinton and as a deputy director under Bush. Keith Stroup,

THE MAN WHO INVENTED NORMAL

LUCY GWIN

_EVERYTHING IT AIN'T

The single most powerful illusion at large in our universe may be the illusion of Normal. Sit still a minute and here it comes: searching, stalking, measuring, rank-rank-ranking. Normal is all about your rank, your place in the power structure. Michel Foucault—and he was no slouch—called it "a principle of coercion," a means to bring us to heel. Normal operates in your life and mine, whirring away like a nanny-cam, as invisibly vigilant as the crack troops of Homeland Security. Normal never sleeps.

In all your struggles to live up to that thing, surpass it, or just wiggle out from under it, did you ever actually clap eyes on it? I capitalize *Normal* today to wrench it into visibility, and even then it's hard to bring up on the view screen. Like Masculinity, Normal makes only a few appearances in library card catalogs. I think that means it's not available for inspection. No, it's only the air we breathe, the power-that-be, concealed in a fog of our unquestioned assumptions.

We assume that Normal is science or at least partakes of scientific pragmatism, moral neutrality. Normal is none of that. We assume that the Norm is at least mathematically real, like median, like mean, somewhere in the neighborhood of average. Not that, either. Just the way that the disease of alcoholism can't be cultured in a petri dish, the Norm is not to be found in math.

We do get Normal confused with Average. Normal is more powerful than that, and you know it. Here's my current formula for their relationship: Normal exceeds Average by degree of Superiority.

Francis Galton, the man who invented Normal, believed that superiority was a heritable quality, transmitted through the germ plasm. At the high end of one chart, he drew in superiority, with subhumanity at the low end. The midpoint he labeled "M." "M = Mediocrity," the chart's legend informs us. Normal ain't that.

In *Statistics on the Table*, ace science historian Stephen W. Stigler pegs Normal as "a one-word oxymoron," representing both the unremarkable middle and the peak of superiority. George Carlin put it another way: "Everyone driving slower than you is an idiot. Anyone driving faster than you is a maniac."

So Normal is you. It just has a little more history.

_THE NORMAL POLICE

One time Normal gave me the blues so bad, I went looking for the factory to send it back to. I thought I'd be tunneling through to pre-history, but when I got to 1877 A.D., there it was at the right hand of its inventor, Sir Francis Galton. And he wasn't alone. Behind him, stretching as far as the eye could see, stood regiments of the Normal Police, all of them pumped up with a missionary spirit so ferocious it could crack a whip. Cue the rebel yell for race hygiene. Enter the crusade for eugenics.

Eugenics, the science of human improvement. Normal, its measuring stick. Galton invented them to effect the salvation of the race. He used that *race* word a lot. The race must take its heredity, its evolution, into its own hands. Urgent duty to the race required the generation of the racially best specimens, in quantity. Meanwhile, "gradually and gently" he asked this excellent race, his own, to make the lesser races extinct. Literally, extinct. And don't get him started on class; you'd get the same spiel. Race and class were everything, or nearly. Not surprising that this message should come from a well-heeled white guy from a well-educated family of doctors, bankers, munitions manufacturers, people whose homes had given names.

Cousin to Charles Darwin, Galton was an immediate convert to that revolutionary 1859 dictum, survival of the fittest. Come to find out that

> AT THE HIGH END OF ONE CHART, HE DREW IN SUPERIORITY, WITH SUBHUMANITY AT THE LOW END.

Darwin arrived on the scene after Herbert Spencer, and others, had already theorized evolution. (Spencer, by the way, was Galton's mentor and pal. They shared day trips to the racetrack, nights on the town.) What Darwin did was set forth natural selection as the operating principle of evolution. Dog eat dog, every man for himself, and devil take the hindmost—the time-tested universal operating principle.

Now that the civilizing influence has made sure that natural selection could no longer rule through raw competition for resources, the law of the jungle, eugenics would do the selecting in and selecting out. Normal would be the measure of eugenic fitness. And we'd all live happily ever after, the race and the realm safe at last. Yeah, it sounds like some queer kind of Dungeons and Dragons, but once you get situated in the nineteenth century you'll see why eugenics, with Normal enforcing it, came to be one of the largest and most successful social movements in history. And why it's still pumped up, still policing us 150 years later.

_BIOLOGY AND DESTINY

"Biology is destiny"—remember that? "Destiny" was code for "empire," the British empire in this case. Biology was empire's justification, proving that just as privilege and entitlement are inherited, so are criminality, pauperism, the predisposition to slothfulness. People got what they deserved, see. Those who started out with a lot? They got more, and this was nature's way.

Darwin's 1859 book, *Origin of Species*, sold more than a half a million copies and may have caused some churchmen to grumble, but it made evolution and inheritance the talk of the town. A remarkable event: that God Almighty should be dethroned by an amateur naturalist and a handful of apes, with barely a squawk from the Archbishop of Canterbury. The real powers-that-be—rulers of coal mines, shipyards, and breweries, the dogs who ate the dogs—actually took a liking to Darwin's idea. John D. Rockefeller explains why: "The growth of a large business is merely a survival of the fittest.... This is not an evil tendency. It is merely the working out of a law of nature." That's not wealth grinding poverty under its heel but nature at work, culling out the weaklings. Agitating for a six-day work week violates natural law. Do try one of these cigars....

Revolution, in the air since 1770, was likely to topple industrial-grade lords from their stewardship, not to mention the cash registers of empire. Evolution, that was different. Evolution may mean change, but change at a pace where whole millennia passed before a whisker underwent relocation. That must have been a comfort to the lords of creation.

As evolution took the stage, a hue and cry over the "differential birth rate" was already in progress. The filthy poor, breeding like rabbits, would soon outnumber the excellent rich and drag all of civilization down with them. Can't have that. As Galton put it, "Those whose race we especially want to have leave few descendants, while those whose race we especially want to be quit of crowd the vacant space with their progeny." Not to be left in the dust by his cousin, Galton seized the moment to publish his own heresy, the 1865 article "Hereditary Talent and Character." "The subject of human heredity," it said, "has never been squarely faced." Here was the man to face it. This public debut of his big idea, though, fell flat.

_A SUCK-UP MASTERPIECE

The shower of ridicule that greeted Galton's eugenical ideal would have made a permanent joke of a lesser man. He said later that "even the word *heredity* was considered fanciful and unusual." Editorial writers howled. Did Galton expect to breed humans from a stud stable? Would he force marriages between the fittest? Did he imagine that parents would allow him to test their newborns, culling the unfit?

Making a manful comeback, Galton next published a best-seller that took what he called "public sentiment" into account. It's fair to call his book, *Hereditary Genius*, the suck-up masterpiece of the century, if

not of all time. It was a scientific and statistical study of well-placed British families, his own included. He'd researched their pedigrees in the pages of *Burke's Peerage*, *Who's Who*, and other compendiums of celebrity biographies. His findings proved to the reading public's satisfaction that genius did indeed issue from pedigree. Even better, the lords of industry embraced him. There wasn't a dry checkbook in the house. Galton's moment had come.

THE REAL POWERS-THAT-BE—RULERS OF COAL MINES, SHIPYARDS, AND BREWERIES, THE DOGS WHO ATE THE DOGS—ACTUALLY TOOK A LIKING TO DARWIN'S IDEA.

His eugenics would be called upon to save what he called "the superior stock" (that's him) from "the battered figures who slouch through the street" (that's you, on a bad hair day). It's common sense: If the differential birth rate didn't get turned around, our betters would soon be awash in charity cases, taxed into bankruptcy. Foreclosure of the empire itself was a possibility. With the supply of superiority diminishing, and mankind no longer subject to the law of the jungle, man must now take the role of natural selector. Since Galton and his followers believed mankind had just about peaked out physically, mental evolution was key. The feeble-minded, the insane, the lower races, and criminal types, all noted for combining unbridled lust with low mentality, emerged as natural targets for social intervention.

_YOUR TYPICAL GENIUS

It's fair to call Galton the Thomas Edison of the social sciences. He formulated the first research questionnaire, coined the terminology for the debate of his century and the next (nature versus nurture), punched the first punch card, conducted the first opinion polls, attempted the first tests of intelligence. Back before Sigmund Freud formulated the existence of the subconscious, Galton wrote of investigating his own through the technique of word association, another Galtonian invention.

He was the first to note the individuality of fingerprints and imagine how that might be useful in law enforcement. Naturally, he took his findings straight to Scotland Yard. He had a reputation by then, so the Yard didn't blow him off but called him a genius. Me, I'd call him a genius of the jack-of-all-trades phenotype. This is the same Francis Galton who invented the weather map and conjured up the theory of isobars. He had a keen and restless mind and would try just about anything in the way of what he called thought experiments.

Galton tested the operation of free will and found that even an excellent specimen such as himself exercised it fully no more than six times per week. He published a study of "The Efficacy of Prayer," which compared the longevity of noted theologians and presumably godless playwrights and scientists. He found a negative correlation between prayerfulness and life span. Of more than 100 scientific books and papers he authored from 1850 to 1909, only a couple were straight out of the crackpot. Example: "Arithmetic by Smell." He founded the science of biometry, the whole-body successor to phrenology that's still going strong.

But in 1877, on the day he invented Normal, he'd found his true calling, breeding the perfect beast. And this beast came from a box.

_THE BOX TO SORT US ALL OUT

What today we call the bell curve was known for a while as "Galton's curve." He noted that a few excellent fellows before him had inferred its existence. Left unsaid was the fact that he'd done them all one better when he made the sketch shown here and hired a skilled carpenter to do an extraordinary thing: build from it a model of the hereditary sort system. Sounds farfetched, but then so was Edison's device, built that same year, to etch the human voice in wax.

Galton couldn't take a walk in the park without ranking female passersby on his prototype punch card. He kept it hidden in his pocket, where he could punch it discreetly with a device he called "the pricker." Women, and he judged himself to be a fair judge of them, ranked as either Attractive (three pricks), Indifferent (two), or Repellent (one).

A guy like that, I see him supervising the carpenter who built this millennial box of Normal. Galton meant it to demonstrate that a large number of small accidents produces a distribution of hereditary deviations—from idiocy to genius, from ugliness to beauty, madness to clarity, criminal degeneracy to moral excellence. And it worked.

Glass-fronted, the wooden box had a funnel at the top into which Galton released lead shot. Falling through a succession of offset rows of precisely-placed pins, the shot sorted itself into vertical compartments at the bottom, distributing itself in the same curve each time. M for Mediocre piled up in the middle, with a scattering of sub-humans to the left, a few leading supermen to the right. Now what name would he give to this breakthrough of a curve?

For two thousand years before Galton, "norm" had been the word for the carpenter's square, a tool for creating the perpendicular line and the right angle. Calligraphers used a similar tool, also called the norm, now known as the T-square. A century earlier, colleges where teachers learned to educate children in the duties of upright citizenship had borrowed the same word for their own use—Normal schools.

Inspired, I believe, by the exactitude of the carpenter's norm, Galton named it the Normal curve. Like his research questionnaire and the punch card, Normal and its curve soon moved out of his lab and set up shop in our lives. Normal meant not "average" but "up to specifications," in this case the specs for who's fully human, who's nearly human, and who's not.

Later, as he'd hoped, nations and their bureaucracies commandeered his curve to select out the dangerous or incompetent, the not-human, from throngs of faceless draftees, immigrants, schoolchildren.

_A LITTLE REMINDER

Social Darwinism is bad enough. Hereditary-biological determinism

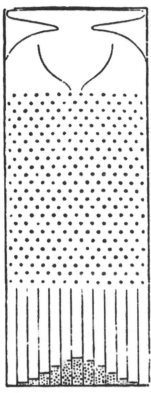
Galton's sketch for a box that demonstrates heredity.
Courtesy Lucy Gwin

measured on the Normal curve? Watch out. By now we ought to have learned its consequences, but they seem to be slipping our minds. Here's that wake-up call you asked for. Heinrich Himmler, fresh from a railway siding where he'd pitched in to get a few Jews sorted out, remarked to Adolf Eichmann that he'd developed a fascinating new hobby. And what was that?

"Natural selection," he said.

_MANY STRANGE BEDFELLOWS

Tracking Darwin and Galton, I've discovered some very strange bedfellows. Karl Marx was a big fan of Darwin and asked his permission to dedicate the first issue of *Das Kapital* to him. (Darwin could not read German and declined the honor.)

One English eugenist, on a visit to the USSR, asked a Kremlin insider to convey the eugenic ideal—that's what they called it—to Stalin on his behalf. Stalin sent back orders that the eugenist was to be seized and shot. The visitor fled the country, tiptoeing over the border on snowshoes just ahead of his pursuers. I'm no fan of Stalin, but I do like his thinking on the subject of racial hygiene: *Nyet!*

Adolf Hitler, on the other hand, could be counted as Francis Galton's best-known and most effective fan. You've probably heard enough about him, but in 1937, by the time he had ordered more than

> OLIVER WENDELL HOLMES, IN THE SUPREME COURT'S *BUCK V. BELL* DECISION (1927), AUTHORIZED THE FORCIBLE STERILIZATION OF CARRIE BUCK, CONCLUDING THAT "THREE GENERATIONS OF IMBECILES ARE ENOUGH."

100,000 sterilizations of defectives, *Fortune Magazine* polled its US readers and found that 66 percent were in favor of the compulsory sterilization of mental defectives. Slightly fewer, 63 percent, favored the sterilization of habitual criminals.

Teddy Roosevelt rallied to eugenics when it came under attack, calling any other course "race suicide." Alexander Graham Bell calculated how many children a eugenically-sound mother should bear. (Ten.) Oliver Wendell Holmes, in the Supreme Court's *Buck v. Bell* decision (1927), authorized the forcible sterilization of Carrie Buck, concluding that "three generations of imbeciles are enough." Andrew Carnegie, Henry Ford, the Harriman family, the Russell Sage Foundation, all could see which side race betterment was buttered on.

THE MAN WHO INVENTED NORMAL
LUCY GWIN

Other notable supporters of the eugenic ideal included Margaret Sanger, Luther Burbank, Helen Keller, George Bernard Shaw, the respected physician and Talmudic scholar Maurice Fishberg, and the Roman Catholic Cardinal of Baltimore. Eugenics itself had become something of a religion; Clarence Darrow, at first a true believer, in 1926 called it a cult.

Mark Twain was one of the few who poked fun at the nature-nurture debate, theorizing that boys might be raised in barrels and fed through the bung-hole until the age of fourteen. As he spoke, hundreds of thousands of American boys and girls were in fact being herded into barrel-bunghole arrangements—the Kansas State Asylum for Imbecile and Lunatic Youth for one lurid name, Louisville's Home for the Incurables for another—so as to prevent their propagation. There was and probably still is one near you, renamed many times over by now but largely intact. Some, with improvements in care, have been converted to prisons.

FYI: The term "segregation" was coined by early eugenists, in the interests of preventing crossbreeding. For the most part, monsters are still segregated—I would call it ensqualidated—in those formerly magnificent brick buildings with the major-league smokestacks at what in the nineteenth century were the outskirts of town. Even where monsters have been moved to what are called community placements, they are carefully monitored.

A more recent development in placement science, nursing homes, didn't flower until the 1960s when Lyndon Johnson opened a taxpayer vein for that purpose. What with an unforeseeable rise in the cost of carelessness, that vein remains open to the tune of you-don't-want-to-know-how-many hundreds of billions of your dollars. Even when they're past breeding age, we don't want the monsters around.

_RANKING REEKING HUMANITY

Normal was born to a rule, the rule of exclusion. Like London's Athenaeum, the gentleman's club to which its inventor belonged, Normal excludes the lower races; the weaker sex; non-English-speaking foreign visitors of sub-ambassadorial rank; immigrants; perverts; criminals and miscreants; the doddering old; paupers; artisans, tradesmen, the lower classes generally; actors, artists, and a wide spectrum of borderline cases. Find your own category on this list. Check one or check many, it doesn't matter. Either way, you won't be recommended for membership.

Did they ever wonder who would be left to do their laundry?

Anyway. Let's be clear about this. Normal was invented so the members of the club could maintain a numerical advantage. They gotta have their *lebensraum*.

Galton, who coined the term *eugenics*, translated it as "well-born." He even had a name for members in good standing in Club Wellborn. He called them "Eugenes." I am not—repeat, not—making this up.

Freaks, monsters, and maniacs, then as now, were of course excluded from the club's deliberations on how best to remove their ill-born "gemmules" from hereditary circulation, how finally to make

them extinct. Galton reserved a special loathing for epileptics and often referred to their "excess of vices." A careful premarital examination of pedigrees would of course limit many degenerative influences on the human gemmule pool. In time, he predicted, all the major dysgenic influences would be identified. Eugenics would then become a hereditary science, genetics.

FYI: THE TERM "SEGREGATION" WAS COINED BY EARLY EUGENISTS, IN THE INTERESTS OF PREVENTING CROSSBREEDING.

For the time being, he urged unspecified "curbs on their fertility" but believed that such curbs should be "applied mercifully." "There exists a sentiment," he said, "for the most part quite unreasonable, against the gradual extinction of an inferior race." I don't know about you, but I hear sci-fi sound effects behind that little speech. Oooo-eeee-oooo...

Women, since necessary, could not be slated for extinction. Still, "it is better," he said, "to use the best mares as breeders rather than workers." Note: Women's and paupers' right to vote was another hot topic in his time. Galton disapproved of democracy on principle, calling it "that utterance of a mob of nobodies." He believed we would not be worthy of it until we bred out the "hereditary taint due to the primeval barbarism of our race." If then.

I've been reading too much nineteenth-century science, and lots of it is like I turned on the movie just when they start explaining the weird science. But if Galton's prediction about the role of genetics is weird science, it was prescient, too. Catch your morning paper where some prestigious institute you never heard of announces that it's found the gene predisposing its unlucky owner to homosexuality, Tay-Sachs Syndrome, shyness, to random Friday-night violence, or some newly identified "behavior disorder" acronym. Here we are, back to the future, where biology is destiny and predisposition = predestination. Reading the stuff I do, after a while I can't tell a keynote address at a March of Dimes conference from a passage in Galton's *Essays* from the Wagnerian eugenics of *Mein Kampf* from news releases out of the National Institutes on Health. All of them love that Normal thing.

"Evolution is a bloody business," eugenic crusader Albert Wiggam wrote in 1926, "but civilization tries to make it a pink tea." Today the pink tea is served with chorionic-villus sampling, amniocentesis, alpha-fetoprotein tests, and of course skilled analysis of prenatal ultrasounds. In some European countries, one or more of these tests are compulsory, and your O.B. is sure to raise the subject. The wonders of hereditary determination may never cease, and the name of its progress is Normal. It's the perfect beast, under construction.

_THE BETTER TO SORT YOU WITH, MY DEAR

You've heard the statistical term "regression to the mean"? That's how Galton accounted for the decay wrought by civilization. He coined the term when he confronted the puzzle that great men, even when mated with witty women, could so often produce merely mediocre children. This was, he said, "regression," "reversion to type." That same widely-held idea—racial reversion, atavism—caused J. Langdon Down to denominate "mongolian idiocy." (Note that we've renamed it Down Syndrome in his honor.) Folks found in possession of it were unfortunate throwbacks to an evolutionary dead end, the yellow races. Do I smell a missing link around here somewhere?

Now Galton had to explain how a great man could sire a deviant criminal or lunatic. It was, he believed, an example of "deviation from the norm." Galton's number-one disciple, his biographer Karl Pearson, coined another familiar statistical term, "standard deviation."

And looky here. Statistics—Galton is considered one of its founding fathers—originated not in the hard sciences but in the soft social ones. It didn't separate itself from eugenics to become a math-department specialty until 1933, and this was a hotly contested divorce. The word *statistics* originated in the German *statistiks*, "state arithmetic." Galton himself called it "statesmanship." No surprise it's become the bureaucrat's primary tool, measuring us all off.

My friend Kathleen, a recovering social worker, wants me to point out that the Normal curve, regression to the mean, and deviation from the norm are boons to science and medicine. How else would the lab know whether your cholesterol is high or low? Dear Kathleen, I say, I have no quarrel with the curve itself, or with those uses for it. But when it measures fitness, as in hereditary fitness to rule, or unfitness to live, we start dancing down the road to the final solution.

Normal's inventor, Francis Galton
Courtesy Lucy Gwin

The apology I just made there, though, suddenly has the ring to me of, "Guns don't shoot people. People shoot people." Well, yeah, but not if they don't have guns. Not if they don't have the Norm.

_A BLOODY BUSINESS

That twentieth century's master race imported its ideological gunpowder from Galton and his fans, some of whom wrote glowing reports of events in Indianapolis and at Hadamar. In case you came in late, Harry C. Sharp, a physician at the Indiana State Reformatory, performed the world's first vasectomy in 1899, on a "moral imbecile," during his search for methods of eugenic sterilization. Before that little fad ran itself out, tens of thousands of America's freaks, monsters, and maniacs had been summarily sterilized. Governors currently are stampeding to apologize for that thing. No one has yet apologized for the smoking gun, Normal.

> **THE WORD *STATISTICS* ORIGINATED IN THE GERMAN *STATISTIKS*, "STATE ARITHMETIC." GALTON HIMSELF CALLED IT "STATESMANSHIP."**

Hadamar, now, that was one of a number of German segregation centers—loony bins, imbecile lock-ups, old folks' dumps—where Deutschland's own "lives unworthy of life" were sterilized. Soon, lives answering that description were starved, shot, injected, even frozen in order to relieve them of their inferiority. That's where Zyclon B (hydrogen cyanide gas) was developed, to make this euthanasia more efficient. The method of incineration for corpse disposal was developed and mechanized at some of those same facilities. Later, these efficiencies were employed to eliminate another menace to racial hygiene, Europe's Jews.

Uh-oh. Only very lame writers have to haul out Hitler to get a point across. Guess I feel defensive. So listen here. What we call Nazi atrocities? They were just eugenics in uniform. Plus, yes, a few bogus and nasty research projects...but come to think of it, they weren't much different from our own postwar testing of plutonium isotopes on Illinois lunatics, our more recent delivery of radioactive Quaker Oats to retards in Rochester. The other atrocities were only war, and we all do that, right? Right? I mean, hey, I'm talking about progress here, for godsakes.

_THE LINE WE WALK

Of course, yes, you're right, every society must have its Normal or at least its norms, its experts and authorities, improvements, efficiencies, cults. When Normal presses us, though, the straight and narrow line we walk in life gets narrower. When those who can't—or won't, or don't—walk the line get kicked screaming over the edge, or implanted with isotopes, or terminated for the crime of polydactyly (more than ten fingers or toes), it's time to send the norms out for enlargement. Don't you think? I mean, come on, get real. This stuff is dangerous.

We'll exit the Holocaust in just a minute, but here's something peculiar. Even Holocaust museums resist mentioning, let alone memorializing, the lost monsters—those crazies, idiots, cripples, old folks, disabled veterans, sexual perverts. For the record: They numbered one quarter of a million souls, some say more than a million. Even so, monsters are barred from all the clubs, even the victim clubs. Political biology marches on, arm in arm with Normal. Jews are Normal, for now. Seen any kids under age ten with Down Syndrome lately? I didn't think so. You may have to explain to your grandchildren what Down Syndrome was.

THE MAN WHO INVENTED NORMAL
LUCY GWIN

_NATURAL SELECTION SELECTS YOU IN ____ OUT ____.
CHECK ONE

Normal, the illusion that will not die, deserves large-scale public abuse. I am not hopeful. Headlines and even front-page photos of Nazi atrocities put a kink in anti-Semitism but didn't get in the way of eugenics. Years after Hadamar came to light, eugenist Edward East was urging compulsory sterilization for ten million unfit Americans. True, the Eugenics Society moderated its acclaim for German methods and quickly morphed into the Genetics Society.

Jack Kevorkian, a latter-day natural selection buff, has been jailed for his hobby, but a clinical brand of Kevorkian's compassion goes on sale in state referenda every election year. Health care rationing is official in only one state so far, Oregon, the same state that finances euthanasia for the poor. (The drug that gets the job done costs $140.) I don't think it's rash to infer a connection between managed care efficiencies and death by compassion. Fact is, way many of us are cheaper dead than alive. I hear all about the so-called safeguards against non-voluntary euthanasia, but as soon as your medical bills exceed your tax-paying productivity by $140—I wonder if that's annualized—you, too, can qualify for better-off-dead status. Just so you know.

> **EVEN HOLOCAUST MUSEUMS RESIST MENTIONING, LET ALONE MEMORIALIZING, THE LOST MONSTERS—THOSE CRAZIES, IDIOTS, CRIPPLES, OLD FOLKS, DISABLED VETERANS, SEXUAL PERVERTS.**

And before you go signing a Do Not Resuscitate order, or one of those living wills, look hard into the eyes of the person you delegate to decide exactly when you're better off dead. Do not, repeat, *not*, pick a social scientist or even a social worker to play that part. Yeah, I know, you want to be spared the indignity of diapers. Note, though, that Walgreen's sells more Depends than aspirins. All that indignity out there on the hoof. Interesting.

One more note on dignity: When we segregate, sterilize, kill, and deport what eugenics called "the inefficients," we're likely to do it in the name of their dignity. Insert moment of silence here, then take this metaphorical tangent. Down through the ages, as we closed the eyes of our dearly departed, were we preserving their dignity? Or preserving ourselves from their vacant stares? Check one.

_ARE YOU ABOVE AVERAGE YET?

You probably won't like this part, either. But we've really and truly left the Holocaust era, so it won't be long. Tracking Normal's missionaries through the generations, I find their successors still pumped, still glory-bound, as high on the social ladder as ever, and all of their children scoring near the top of the Normal curve. Now go to the nearest college library and check out *Dilemmas of the Genetic Counselor*. It might come in handy if you ever need to needle prospective parents into doing the right thing, the eugenic-genetic-perfectly-planned-parenthood thing—the prevention-or-termination-of-monstrous-offspring thing—without stepping into that naughty ethical gray area where the genetic counselor becomes "overly directive." It can be done, and usually within the time-limited consult. It says so right here.

Remember how I started on this quest with a case of the blues? I came back with the heebie-jeebies. A friend tells me I'm about as much fun now as a deathwatch. Gee, I hope he's wrong about that.

We have made drastic cuts in the monster supply, yes, and also in what medical ethicists call "human suffering," most of it through painless prevention. No one in his right mind could object to prevention. Since you put it that way, here's where I shake out. Remember that line we walk, the straight and narrow line of Normal? That thing keeps on getting straighter, narrower, more precarious, and hey, way duller, too, as our conformation and behavior become more typical, more standardized. I call that process slicing the curve, the Normal curve. Next thing you know, we'll all be in uniform. Uniformity, the ticket to Normal.

_SURVIVAL: THE ELIMINATION ROUNDS

Until we arrive at perfect uniformity, it is good to keep in mind that the law of Normal is not just enforced against incipient monsters. Nobody gets off easy. I do try to keep up with Normal's development and find that every 141st day, on average, brings a whole new professional field under the wing of what we used to call social work. Every 98th day brings the announcement of one or more newly-discovered expressions of mental illness, none of which can be cultured in a petri dish. Genetic markers for previously unidentified disorders are harder to track because not all of them make the newspapers. When they do, they disappear real quick into our fog of illusions about that amazing RNA-DNA deal. We hope, in the distracted way most of us hope now, that its products will soon arrive on pharmacy shelves.

In case you missed Barry Commoner's 2002 article in *Harper's*, the much-ballyhooed Human Genome Project was a bust. It's not about chromosomes, they find out. It's about "spliceosomes" and "variant protein molecules." Who knew? A bigger and better Human Genome Project is on the drawing board. And in case you missed the one-inch article in the previous year's *New York Times*, the first and much-celebrated recipient of a miracle cure via gene therapy seems to have developed something like leukemia—genetically-modified leukemia, maybe.

Speaking of genetic miracles, this one cracks me up. I caught it on the Learning Channel in 2001 in a program entitled, *Superhuman Body: The Future of Medicine*. My kind of show. The scientist in charge showed a naked lab rat with a human ear growing out of its back. The actual ear form, constructed of biodegradable fibers, had been dipped in and then injected with some gooey pink stuff, a gene cocktail that grows human flesh. Eventually the "cartilage" biodegrades and, presto, you got yourself a perfect human ear.

Then there are those cryogenic sperm banks swarming with Nobel-prize-winning gametes. Makes me laugh when I think about Alfred Nobel himself, how he was born too soon to impart his dynamite gemmules thisaway. We might not be too late to clone him, though. You never know.

Go on, call me a genetic Luddite, a Cassandra of progress. I'm here to haunt you with visions of Normal marching into your life, your bedroom, your body, making a beeline for that secret place not even your first spouse knew about, where you thought your own genetic marker for monstrosity was hidden.

Normal, now, it can't promise a miracle cure, but it's sure got your number. And I don't know how to get that bad thing back in the box. Do you? Maybe if the President appointed a commission? Meantime, I picture that guy in the white lab coat after a hard day of conducting Normal's elimination rounds. All of a sudden he notices that things got awfully quiet. So he looks up from his clipboard, and you guessed it: He's all alone in the universe. The species did need improvement. And who could resist?

_LORD OF CREATION

Although I began this piece with perfectly good intentions, they didn't exactly pan out. Honest, I didn't want to demonize Normal's inventor or even his invention. I came down here to shine a light on the coercive, even totalitarian, nature of the thing. In the course of laying it out, I've lost hope that my mission can be accomplished without armies of Anti-Normal Police armed to the teeth with alarmist headlines about the epidemic at hand.

So I'll leave you with Sir Francis Galton. He's right here at my elbow and yours, quietly exuding Normal, that glow of dominion. Cue the spook movie music. "It is now ordering our acts more intimately than we are apt to suspect," he said, "because the dictates of public opinion become so thoroughly assimilated that they seem to be original and individual to those who are guided by them."

He got that right, didn't he? Working as invisibly as he predicted, Normal may outlive us all. Enthroned in our common-sense lobe, it is the lord of creation, the perfect beast, holding in its steady, well-bred hands the future of our race. A race of perfect beasts may or may not have room for you and yours. It's purely scientific, though, and certainly an improvement over natural selection. If you should find yourself falling off the edge, remember me on your way down. I did try to warn you.

THE FIRST AND MUCH-CELEBRATED RECIPIENT OF A MIRACLE CURE VIA GENE THERAPY SEEMS TO HAVE DEVELOPED SOMETHING LIKE LEUKEMIA—GENETICALLY-MODIFIED LEUKEMIA, MAYBE.

THE MAN WHO INVENTED NORMAL
LUCY GWIN

ARE SECRECY OATHS A LICENSE TO LIE?

DANIEL ELLSBERG

Between 1968 and 1971, I repeatedly broke a solemn, formal promise that I had earlier made in good faith: not to reveal to any "unauthorized persons" any information that I received through certain channels, and under certain safeguards, collectively known as the "classification" system.

I have never doubted that—in revealing the contents of the top-secret Pentagon Papers on the Vietnam War to the Senate and the press—I did the right thing under the circumstances confronting me, even though it involved breaking these promises on secrets-keeping I had made earlier to various government agencies and to the RAND Corporation.

It was the only way—I had considered many others and tried most of them—to inform Congress and the American public of information that was still being wrongfully withheld from them. It was information that was vital to Constitutional processes of decision-making on an ongoing war in which tens of thousands of Americans, and many more Vietnamese, had been, in effect, lied to death.

> **BY 1971 IT WAS CLEAR TO ME THAT IT WAS MY EARLIER BEHAVIOR, KEEPING MY PROMISE TO KEEP SECRETS FROM CONGRESS AND THE PUBLIC, THAT HAD BEEN MISTAKEN AND CENSURABLE, NOT MY LATER CHOICE TO TELL THE TRUTH.**

That had occurred with the complicity of a generation of officials—myself among them—who had put fidelity to their secrecy oaths (and their bosses, and their careers) above their loyalty to the Constitution and to their opportunity, by exposing lies and telling the truth, to avert or end an unnecessary, wrongful, hopeless, and vastly destructive war. By 1971 it was clear to me that it was my earlier behavior, keeping my promise to keep secrets from Congress and the public, that had been mistaken and censurable, not my later choice to tell the truth.

The formal promise I violated was one I should never have given, in the form it was presented and in the spirit in which it was meant to be understood. Nor should I have been asked to do so.

I signed secrecy "oaths" (or contractual agreements, or undertakings) in many capacities over the years: as a US Marine officer, on being employed by or renewing my contract with RAND, as a consultant to the Office of Secretary of Defense, the State Department, and the White House, and later as an employee of the Defense Department and the State Department. All of these were blanket promises never to reveal any information I received in those capacities that was marked or identified as safeguarded, "secret, classified," to any person who had not been authorized to receive it by the person or agency giving me the information.

What was *implicit* in my promise was this: I will not reveal such information to such "unauthorized" persons *no matter what this information might be or reveal*; no matter whether it reveals evidence of official lies, crimes, planning for wars in violation of ratified treaties or the Constitution, plans to violate or past violations of laws of Congress; no matter if the persons or agencies not authorized to receive it are officials of Congress or courts, who vitally need this information to discharge their Constitutional functions, or who are legitimately asking me to tell them the truth about it under oath; no matter if an election or a congressional investigation or vote deciding issues of war and peace might turn on whether voters or representatives are deceived by my silence or obedient lies about what their government has done or is contemplating; no matter how many people have died and how many others might yet die because this information is still being wrongfully withheld, by my colleagues and superiors, under a policy of secrecy and deception.

That is how I was *meant* to understand those promises. And for many years, that is how I acted, in keeping my promises of secrecy. Of course, these emphatic warnings were not spelled out explicitly in the papers I signed or in the accompanying briefings. If they had been, they would have given me a good deal of pause, to say the least. (That is why they are not spelled out, for prospective employees).

Would I have signed anyway? Probably so, in the beginning, which was in the mid- and late-1950s. Government secrets had been so well kept, by so many people before me, that as a young citizen I was unaware that I was ever likely to see such problematic information in the service of the US Government. I would not have believed that the circumstances or conflicts suggested above were ever likely to arise.

On the other hand, I knew better within a year after I first signed such an agreement in 1958: a decade before I first copied secret information that had been wrongfully withheld and gave it to Congress and the press. Over that decade, it would have been harder and less likely for me to keep repeating such promises as I took new jobs, renewed contracts, or was offered new, higher clearances, if the obligation to keep silence about knowledge of crimes and lies had been formalized and explicit.

It would have been harder for me to conceal from myself that what I was being asked to sign was an agreement to *participate* and accept complicity—at least by keeping silent, and perhaps by actively misleading or lying, even committing perjury under oath—in major governmental conspiracies or grave obstructions of justice. It would have been obvious that an oath so stated or interpreted was in flagrant violation of my oath to uphold the Constitution and the laws of the United States, which was obviously superseding.

I should never have been asked to make such a promise; nor should any official, or representative, or citizen in a democracy be encouraged or obliged to make such a promise in this form or under this interpretation. Nor, of course, should they agree to make such a promise, if it is proposed.

Yet the fact is that millions of patriotic Americans do believe, in perfectly good conscience, that they have made just such a pledge (though usually without realizing at first all that it might entail). They see no Constitutional problem in their being asked to give such an assurance, so understood, as a condition of federal employment, or in their agreeing to give it. Yet true popular sovereignty, in particular democratic control of foreign and military policy, is simply impossible to achieve if official behavior reflecting this understanding is widespread—as it is—and is not challenged as unacceptable.

The solution is not to make such an obligation-to-lie explicit in secrecy agreements (which may themselves be secret), but the opposite: to forbid agreements that encourage or permit such an interpretation. Every American should be made aware that an agreement or oath so interpreted is not only *not* legally or morally binding but that it in fact is wholly improper. Nothing Americans can sign can give them a *right* to lie to Congress or courts, or for that matter, to the electorate.

That does not mean that there cannot be obligations of discretion or even formal secrecy agreements in a wide variety of settings in a democratic republic. But if democratic government is to survive and to function in a meaningful sense—and like many other Americans, I have long felt it was worth giving my life, if necessary, to preserve that—those secrecy agreements must be understood to be provisional, subordinate to higher loyalties, laws, and obligations, and limited by our existing Constitution and Bill of Rights.

Very simply, every secrecy agreement that anyone is asked to sign as a condition of employment or access to information in the setting of a democratic government with a rule of law should state *explicitly*: "I understand that nothing in this agreement obliges me or permits me to give false testimony to Congress or a court, or in particular to commit perjury under oath."

Such a clause would not in itself bestow a "right to disclose" but rather, simply, a "right not to lie to Congress," a right not to be forced to commit perjury, or to promise to do so, as a condition of employment or of access to a security clearance or to classified information. It would deny that a security clearance or a non-disclosure agreement conveys a right to lie under oath to Congress or courts, or constitutes legal protection against prosecution for perjury, or negates

the right and duty of every citizen to tell the truth in sworn testimony.

The Executive could not oppose such legislation with precisely the same constitutional and practical arguments it musters against congressional efforts to promote and protect disclosure. In fact, it would have a hard time opposing it at all—though it would do its best—since it is considerably less easy to openly defend lying to Congress than to defend the possible withholding of information, even though secrecy managers may feel with great conviction that one requires the other.

NO MATTER WHETHER IT REVEALS EVIDENCE OF OFFICIAL LIES, CRIMES, PLANNING FOR WARS IN VIOLATION OF RATIFIED TREATIES OR THE CONSTITUTION, PLANS TO VIOLATE OR PAST VIOLATIONS OF LAWS OF CONGRESS.

If enacted (over a probable presidential veto), this legislation would have several benefits:

1. It would alert officials newly entering into the secrecy system to the possibility (probability) that at some point they might be asked or expected by their superiors to give deceptive testimony or even to lie under oath, and alert them to the likelihood that this will be presented to them as justified and even required by the need for secrecy and the obligations they have accepted by signing this non-disclosure agreement. This clause should at the least prepare them to question that representation.

2. Reading and signing this clause will not end all perjury or deceptive testimony to Congress and courts. Superiors will be able to suggest very strong bureaucratic incentives and persuasive rationales for giving misleading or false reports to those outside their own agency, including congressional committees. But obliging employees to read and sign this clause will force them to recognize that in that situation they face a personal *choice*, with personal responsibility and accountability if they choose to comply with their superiors or to comply with their own inclinations to give deceptive or false testimony.

It will act to deprive them of the belief—otherwise widely held and strongly encouraged by the secrecy bureaucracy—that in such a situation they "have no choice" but to deceive or to withhold the truth, simply by virtue of their having signed this agreement and by the bureaucracy's decision to classify certain data. And it will warn them that this agreement, in itself, will not protect them from the possible consequences of committing perjury.

In reality, at present such consequences are pretty mild or hypothetical, compared to the likely career consequences of defying one's superiors and telling Congress truths that one's agency doesn't want told. Probably no official has ever spent a day in jail for lying to Congress on a matter that can be claimed to involve "national security." (It would be very helpful if that record could be changed.)

Still, quite apart from fear of prosecution or punishment, many officials have undoubtedly been influenced in their willingness to lie to Congress, to courts or to the public by their belief that they have in good faith *promised to lie*, if necessary, to keep officially designated secrets. Making the contrary clause proposed above an explicit part of their non-disclosure agreement would, on its face, deprive them of this belief.

In practice, it would at best weaken that belief, which would still be instilled by verbal warnings and advice from their bureaucratic colleagues and by observing their actual behavior, in a way that could not be prevented by any legislation. But at a minimum this legislation would warn them that they could not cite this belief as a compelling justification if they were actually caught lying to Congress or a court, as, for example, Richard Helms and Elliott Abrams claimed, perhaps with some sincerity, when their lies were exposed.

3. Thus, if this legislation were enacted and implemented, the effect should be somewhat more truth-telling, less lying and deception, in testimony to Congress and perhaps even to the public. There might even be marginally less adoption of policies whose attractiveness depends on non-accountability, on secrecy from Congress, courts, and voters because of their criminal nature, their violation of laws, treaties, or declarations, or their excessive costs or dangers. For this reason, this legislation would almost surely be opposed fanatically by "national security" agencies and by the Executive branch.

But the very process of proposing and pressing for this legislation, to the extent it can force this opposition into the open, can be politically educational on the nature, the implications, and the dangers of the secrecy system. Forcing representatives of the "secrecy community" to defend explicitly in political debate their need and their right to demand that their employees be ready to lie to Congress would be enlightening to many. It could contribute to a willingness by Congress and the public to reexamine the need for the entitlements of the secrecy system in the post-Cold War era, and its dangers for policy and for democracy.

If such a paragraph had been in plain print on the secrecy agreements that had been offered for signature to millions of Americans every year of the Cold War, I believe that there would be over 50,000 fewer names on the Vietnam Memorial. Tens of thousands fewer nuclear warheads would have been produced (including in the Soviet Union, despite the secrecy which was indeed central to *its* form of government), even if the actual arsenals on both sides were still dangerously excessive. Over 100,000 lives might have been saved in Guatemala and the rest of Central America. And the US would be far more secure today than it is from prospects of nuclear proliferation and terrorism.

This is not because no official would ever have lied to Congress or a court or the public, under orders or voluntarily, after signing an agreement with this explicit reservation. But they would not have lied or concealed the truth under the sincere impression that they were obliged to do so, by a promise they had made, or by loyalty to a boss or agency that outweighed loyalty to laws and the Constitution, or by their agency's interpretation of the requirements of "national security."

Under these circumstances I believe many officials—enough of them to have made a crucial difference—would have chosen *not* to mislead, conceal from, or lie to Congress or courts, or the public, in these cases. And these catastrophic follies—whose preparation and persistence depended crucially, in a democracy, on deception—would have been averted. That would be reason to praise democracy, and to struggle to preserve the openness and accountability for truth-telling on which it depends.

One further addition to the secrecy oaths—to be mandated by legislation—would also serve these vital ends. Since these oaths are signed so frequently and taken so seriously, there is no better place to remind government employees of their obligations as stated in the Code of Ethics for Government Service, passed by Congress on July 11, 1958: "Any person in government service should put loyalty to the highest moral principles and to the Country above loyalty to persons, party, or Government department."

WHAT IS A TERRORIST?
JEFF COHEN

ter·ror·ist (ter'er-ist), *noun.*

1: One who engages in acts or an act of terrorism.

2: One who leads an armed group that kills civilians as a means of political intimidation—*unless he terrorizes Haitians while on the CIA payroll, as did 1990s death squad leader Emmanuel Constant, in which case the US refuses to extradite him to Haiti, even after September 11, 2001.*

3: One who targets civilian airliners and ships—*unless he blows up a Cuban civilian airliner, killing 73 people, and fires at a Polish freighter, like Orlando Bosch, in which case he is coddled and paroled by the Bush Justice Department in 1990, and his extradition is blocked.*

4: One who leads a group that engages in kidnapping and murder—*unless the victims are Hondurans attacked by CIA-backed death squad Battalion 316, in which case Battalion architect Gustavo Alvarez becomes a Pentagon consultant, while the then-Ambassador to Honduras who downplayed the terror, John Negroponte, is appointed US Ambassador to the United Nations days after 9/11.*

5: One who uses rape and murder for political purposes—*unless the victims are four US churchwomen sexually assaulted and killed in 1980 by members of El Salvador's US-backed military, in which case excuses and distortions pour forth from then-UN Ambassador Jeane Kirkpatrick ("these nuns were not just nuns; they were also political activists") and Secretary of State Al Haig (the nuns "may have tried to run a roadblock").*

6: One who designates civilians as "soft targets" to be attacked in the cause of political transformation—*unless the targets are Nicaraguans killed by Contra guerrillas armed and directed by the US who, according to Human Rights Watch, "systematically engage in violent abuses…so prevalent that these may be said to be their principal means of waging war."*

7: One who facilitates a massacre of civilians—*unless the victims are 900 Palestinians shot and hacked to death in the Sabra and Shatila camps by Lebanese Christian militia as Israeli soldiers stood guard in 1982, in which case Israel's then-Defense Minister (now Prime Minister) Ariel Sharon remains a US "War on Terrorism" ally after being censured as indirectly responsible for the massacre by an* Israeli *commission of inquiry.*

PIECES OF THE 9/11 PUZZLE
RUSS KICK

"The American people must know the full story has yet to be told."
—Senator Richard Shelby, referring to 9/11, as quoted in the *New York Times*, November 12, 2002[1]

Although the events of September 11, 2001, have been compartmentalized in the mass mind as "Islamic terrorists hijack four planes, crash them into big targets and a field," 9/11 actually remains a huge cipher. Scratch just below the surface, and you'll be inundated by impossibilities, contradictions, lies, vagueness, and more questions than answers.

Almost no aspect of the attacks stands up to scrutiny. And I'm not talking about believing in conspiracy theories that often have very little, if any, hard evidence to support them. All you have to do is look at the official record—mainstream media reporting, statements from government officials, oral histories of people who were there, interviews with rescue workers, military personnel, etc. to see that it just doesn't add up.

In this article I will look at some of the most intriguing and troubling aspects of 9/11. This is *not* intended to be a comprehensive survey about all we know, don't know, and don't know that we don't know about that momentous day. Many aspects will remain unmentioned, simply because of limitations of time and space. Entire books could be and should be written to look beyond the Official Version of Events. (Some have already started to appear.) Let this article, then, be seen as a look at some of the pieces of the puzzle, rather than an attempt to construct the entire puzzle.

_SENATOR ADMITS AT LEAST ONE FOREIGN COUNTRY WAS BEHIND 9/11

Let's start with one of the most startling revelations to be cold-shouldered by the media. On December 11, 2002, the Senate and House Intelligence Committees released portions of their joint report on intelligence failures regarding the September 11 attacks. *NewsHour with Jim Lehrer*, on PBS, reported on the release that day. After asking her guests a bunch of predictable questions, and receiving predictable answers, guest host Gwen Ifill asked Senator Bob Graham, Chairman of the Senate Select Committee on Intelligence, a good question and got an amazing answer. What follows is their complete exchange, copied directly from the transcript at the PBS Website:

GWEN IFILL: Senator Graham, are there elements in this report, which are classified that Americans should know about but can't?

SEN. BOB GRAHAM: Yes, going back to your question about what was the greatest surprise. I agree with what Senator Shelby said the degree to which agencies were not communicating was certainly a surprise but also I was surprised at the evidence that there were foreign governments involved in facilitating the activities of at least some of the terrorists in the United States.

I am stunned that we have not done a better job of pursuing that to determine if other terrorists received similar support and, even more important, if the infrastructure of a foreign government assisting terrorists still exists for the current generation of terrorists who are here planning the next plots.

To me that is an extremely significant issue and most of that information is classified, I think overly-classified. I believe the American people should know the extent of the challenge that we face in terms of foreign government involvement. That would motivate the government to take action.

GWEN IFILL: Are you suggesting that you are convinced that there was a state sponsor behind 9/11?

SEN. BOB GRAHAM: I think there is very compelling evidence that at least some of the terrorists were assisted not just in financing—although that was part of it—by a sovereign foreign government and that we have been derelict in our duty to track that down, make the further case, or find the evidence that would indicate that that is not true and we can look for other reasons why the terrorists were able to function so effectively in the United States.

GWEN IFILL: Do you think that will ever become public, which countries you're talking about?

SEN. BOB GRAHAM: It will become public at some

point when it's turned over to the archives, but that's 20 or 30 years from now. And, we need to have this information now because it's relevant to the threat that the people of the United States are facing today.[2]

Here we have a powerful US Senator—the Chairman of the committee that oversees intelligence operations, the very committee that co-issued the report—saying that some country (or countries) actively aided the worst terrorist attack against the US. Yet none of the media followed up on it. Not one pursued this bombshell revelation spoken by Senator Graham on a national news program.

> "I WAS SURPRISED AT THE EVIDENCE THAT THERE WERE FOREIGN GOVERNMENTS INVOLVED IN FACILITATING THE ACTIVITIES OF AT LEAST SOME OF THE TERRORISTS IN THE UNITED STATES." —SENATOR BOB GRAHAM

So which nation(s) was it? We mere mortals don't know, but we can make an educated guess about which countries it *wasn't*. It obviously wasn't any nation that the US government hates and would love to demonize. If it had been Iraq, for example, the report would *not* have been classified; it would've been personally faxed by Defense Secretary Donald Rumsfeld to every reporter in the nation. No, the one or more facilitators of 9/11 were obviously allies, "friendly" countries, nations that the US doesn't want to alienate.

_REPORTERS DESCRIBE EXPLOSIONS JUST AS THE SOUTH TOWER COLLAPSES

Beth Fertig—a WNYC radio reporter and contributor to NPR—was on the scene in Manhattan and wrote of the South Tower:

The building came down so orderly, floor by floor, that I presumed it was a controlled demolition. I hoped that it was. *Maybe they got all the people out and now they're bringing the building down to prevent mass casualties.*[3]

Interestingly, many reporters *did* mention explosions coming from the South Tower. John Bussey, foreign editor for the *Wall Street Journal*, described the scene:

I heard this metallic roar, looked up and saw what I thought was just a very peculiar site of individual floors, one after the other exploding outward. I thought to myself, "My God, they're going to bring the building down." And they, whoever they are, had set charges. In fact, the building was imploding down.

I saw the explosions, and I thought, "This is not a good place to be, because we're too close to the building, and it's too easy for the building to topple over."[4]

Carol Marin, a contributing reporter to CBS News, recalls:

I was frantically punching my cell phone number and one of the things I hit was my Chicago producer's number. I told them I was on my way to the World Trade Center. As I said that, the first collapse of the tower happened. I was on the line and said, "Oh my God, there's been an explosion."[5]

A photojournalist for the *New York Post*, Bolívar Arellano, says: "The building was in front of me, but I turned my back. Then I hear the explosion. I saw the top of the building coming down."[6]

Marty Glembotzy is a cameraman for WABC-TV. He recreates the scene that morning:

[WABC-TV reporter N.J. Burkett] said he wanted to do a stand-up. He motioned, "Me, the firefighters and tilt up to the building." I asked for another one [a second take], as I always do, because you never know, there could be a crease in the tape or whatever. As I tilted up, the density of the sound in the area changed. It became thick. As I tilted up, I could feel it, but I could really tell you that I knew what I was seeing. I was seeing the building blow up.

I kept tilting and heard him [Burkett] say that the building was exploding.[7]

And we must consider the words of Louie Cacchioli, a firefighter with Engine 47. The 20-year veteran of the NYFD told *People* magazine:

We were the first ones in the second tower after the plane struck. I was taking firefighters up in the elevator to the 24th floor to get in position to evacuate workers. On the last trip up a bomb went off. We think there was bombs set in the building.[8]

When the North Tower collapsed, there weren't nearly as many witnesses, since most people had either been killed by, incapacitated by, or had gotten far away from the first collapse.

CBS News contributor Carol Marin was very near the North Tower when it collapsed: "I hear simultaneously this roar and see what appears to be a gigantic fireball rising up at ground level." As she's running, a fireman pushes her against the wall, covering her with his body. Once the collapse is finished, Marin is led by a policeman. "I remember thinking that the fire and explosion didn't get us but the smoke will if we don't get out of here soon."[9]

She reiterates: "I remember seeing this giant ball of fire come out of the earth as I heard this roar and thinking, 'Who's going to explain to my kids that I needed to be at the World Trade Center on this day?'"[10]

Later that day, WNYC Radio reporter Beth Fertig was at Mayor Rudolph Giuliani's command center.

The reporters were trying to figure out what had happened. We were thinking that bombs had brought the buildings down. The mayor talked to us and said he had no evidence of bombs.[11]

Well, that settles that.

_THE EXPLOSION IN BUILDING 6

During CNN's coverage of the attacks, viewers were treated to a bizarre site: a huge explosion in Building 6, an eight-story structure known as the US Customs building. This amazing scene went totally uncommented upon by CNN and the rest of media. Below is a still-frame from the broadcast. To the left of the Twin Towers is a huge plume of smoke, dust, and debris. It's coming from Building 6, which is behind the taller Building 7. Since WTC 7 had 47 floors, we see that this plume went much higher into the air than 47 stories. For an eight-story building to give off that much smoke and dust, the explosion must've been quite powerful.

Screen shot of CNN airing the explosion in WTC 6 (to the left of the Twin Towers and behind the much taller WTC 7). The contrast in this picture has been enhanced to bring out the details for publication in grayscale.
CREDIT: CNN

Reporter Christopher Bollyn, writing for *American Free Press*, contacted CNN about the footage. It wasn't broadcast live on the network but, rather, was shown later. The CNN archivist confirmed that the explosion took place around 9:04 AM, just after the South Tower was hit. When asked by Bollyn what he thought caused the explosion, the archivist replied: "We can't figure it out."

> DURING CNN'S COVERAGE OF THE ATTACKS, VIEWERS WERE TREATED TO A BIZARRE SITE: A HUGE EXPLOSION IN BUILDING 6, AN EIGHT-STORY STRUCTURE KNOWN AS THE US CUSTOMS BUILDING.

Besides US Customs, several federal departments and agencies had offices in the building. Bollyn asked them all for comment, but only one replied:

A spokesman for the Export-Import Bank of the United States, which had an office with four employees on the sixth floor of the Customs House, confirmed the time of the explosion and told AFP that the employees had survived and been relocated.[12]

Authorities claim that WTC 6 collapsed under the weight of debris from the towers, but this footage shows that the building was dev-astated by a huge explosion. Furthermore, in post-disaster photos, WTC 6 doesn't look like it has "collapsed," but, instead, the center of the building looks like it was blown out.

The remains of the "collapsed" WTC 6. It looks more like an explosion tore out the center of the building.
CREDIT: US Customs Service Website

_FOOTAGE OF THE PENTAGON CRASH

The image of Flight 175 plowing into the South Tower of the World Trade Center is probably etched on the minds of everyone who was alive at the time. The footage of Flight 11 hitting the North Tower is less ingrained, probably because only one known piece of footage exists. Still, most of us have seen the images captured by a documentary crew who happened to film the first impact of the day. Obviously, there's no footage of Flight 96 hitting a field in rural Pennsylvania.

But what about the crash of Flight 77 into the Pentagon? Why have we never seen any footage of this? We know for a fact that one video camera—and possibly three others—captured the impact.

For almost six months, the public saw absolutely *no* images of the actual Pentagon collision. It was only on March 7, 2002, that NBC News "obtained" five images of the crash. NBC didn't explain how they got the images, but Pentagon officials quickly pronounced them authentic.[13]

The images are stills of video taken from a Defense Department video camera. Not only are they so grainy as to be almost useless, but only one of the images even shows the plane (an extremely blurry image on the right side). The other four still-frames show an orange fireball erupting.

This obviously begs the questions: Why haven't we seen the actual video from which these stills are taken? Why are we allowed to see only a mere five frames?

But the questions don't stop there. We have strong indications that at least three other video cameras recorded the ramming of the Pentagon. Ten days after the attacks, the *Washington Times*' "Inside the Ring" column ran the following segment:

These pictures don't look so great printed in grayscale, but the problem is that the full-size color images don't look much better.
CREDIT: MSNBC

Video of attack

The electronic news media have broadcast repeatedly the attack on the World Trade Center. They are perhaps the most dramatic news images since the explosion of the first atomic bomb over Hiroshima.

Now word has reached us that federal investigators may have video footage of the deadly terrorist attack on the Pentagon.

A security camera atop a hotel close to the Pentagon may have captured dramatic footage of the hijacked Boeing 757 airliner as it slammed into the western wall of the Pentagon. Hotel employees sat watching the film in shock and horror several times before the FBI confiscated the video as part of its investigation.

It may be the only available video of the attack. The Pentagon has told broadcast news reporters that its security cameras did not capture the crash.

> WHY HAVE WE NEVER SEEN ANY FOOTAGE OF THIS? WE KNOW FOR A FACT THAT ONE VIDEO CAMERA—AND POSSIBLY THREE OTHERS—CAPTURED THE IMPACT.

The attack occurred close to the Pentagon's heliport, an area that normally would be under 24-hour security surveillance, including video monitoring.[14]

That December, the *Times-Dispatch* of Richmond, Virginia, ran a story which included the following segment:

Three months ago, on September 11 at 9:38 a.m., a Tuesday, Jose Velasquez heard the rumble of imminent death overhead. "I knew something was wrong. The planes come more from the north and west [to land at Reagan National Airport] not from the south. And not so low."

He was talking on the telephone that morning to a friend who was feeding him gauzy reports about airplane crashes at the World Trade Center in New York. But Velasquez slammed down the receiver and raced outside when he felt the gas station he supervises suddenly begin to tremble from a too-close airplane.

"It was like an earthquake," the Costa Rican native said last week. What Velasquez felt above him almost within touching distance was American Airlines Flight 77 just seconds before impact.

His gas station, open only to Department of Defense personnel, is the last structure between the Pentagon and the hillside that, hours later, would become a wailing knoll. "By the time I got outside all I could see was a giant cloud of smoke, first white then black, coming from the Pentagon," he said. "It was just a terrible, terrible thing to be so close to."

Today, Velasquez still trembles when he talks about the incident that has forever changed the military, government, and technology polyglot that is Northern Virginia. "Even today," said Velasquez, "people who come here tell me they are frightened to come to work. You can see it in their eyes."

Velasquez says the gas station's security cameras are close enough to the Pentagon to have recorded the moment of impact. "I've never seen what the pictures looked like," he said. "The FBI was here within minutes and took the film."[15]

Sandra Jontz, a reporter for the military newspaper *Stars and Stripes*, was in her office when Flight 77 hit. Rather than evacuate, she stayed to help the wounded. In telling her story in the book *At Ground Zero*, she says:

Outside the Pentagon we saw light poles strewn across the field. The plane had clipped them. We could visualize its path. It must have been so low that people who had been in the cars on Route 27, a major roadway passing next to the Pentagon, could have almost reached up and touched it as it passed. I saw a Department of Transportation camera that monitors traffic backups pointed toward the crash site. But I haven't seen any video from it yet.[16]

To sum up, we know of the following cameras:

• A Pentagon camera, which definitely caught the crash (still-frames have been leaked)

• A hotel camera, which reportedly caught the crash (employees watched it)

• A gas station camera, which should have caught the crash (it was filming in the right direction)

• A Transportation Department camera, which should have caught the crash (it was pointed in the right direction)

Yet none of these videos has been released. The two from private businesses were confiscated by the FBI, and—according to the *Washington Times* article—the Pentagon lied by saying that its cameras didn't record the crash. Why? What possible legitimate reason could exist for withholding video of the Pentagon being struck?

_THE FINAL 911 CALL FROM FLIGHT 93

Rick Earle, the Westmoreland County Bureau Chief for WPXI-TV, was on his way to the site of Flight 93's crash near Shanksville, Pennsylvania, when he phoned 911 to see what was happening. He talked to an emergency dispatcher who told him about a call that the 911 center had received at 9:50 that morning. The caller—later identified as Edward Felt—told the 911 worker that he was on a flight that was being hijacked, giving the correct flight number and model number of the plane. Based on this information, Earle phoned in his breaking report, which concluded:

He said that he was at this point being walked back to the bathroom of the plane. 911 was talking to him, trying to get more information at that time. The gentleman who had made the call from the airplane said there was just an explosion, then there was a cloud of white smoke, and then seconds later they lost the caller.[17]

Reporter Todd Spangler of the Associated Press talked to Glenn Cramer, the dispatch supervisor, who confirmed the account:

"We are being hijacked, we are being hijacked!" Cramer quoted the man from a transcript of the call.

The man told dispatchers the plane "was going down. He heard some sort of explosion and saw white smoke coming from the plane and we lost contact with him," Cramer said.[18]

Was the plane hit by a missile from a pursuing military jet? Other callers from the plane reported that one of the terrorists had a bomb strapped to him. For example, Lisa Jefferson—a customer service supervisor with Verizon Airfone—took a call from Todd Beamer, a passenger on the plane: "He said that two of them had locked themselves into the cockpit, and one had a bomb strapped around his waist with a red belt."[19] It's been said that this must've been a fake bomb made to scare the passengers into compliance. Maybe it was real.

Soon, though, the authorities and the media locked onto the story of the "heroes of Flight 77," who tried to wrest control of the plane from the terrorists. The first-hand report of an explosion and smoke didn't jibe with this preferred version, so it has been conveniently forgotten—but never explained.

_THE UNMARKED WHITE PLANE AND FLIGHT 93

The *Daily Mirror* of London writes:

The unmarked military-style jet swooped down at high speed through the valley, twice circled the smouldering black scar where Flight 93 had careered into the ground just seconds earlier and then hurtled off over the horizon.

At least six eyewitnesses saw the mysterious aircraft on the morning of September 11 last year.[20]

The paper's US editor interviewed several eyewitnesses, including a woman who takes care of special-needs children:

Susan Mcelwain, 51, who lives two miles from the site, knows what she saw—the white plane rocketed directly over her head.

"It came right over me, I reckon just 40 or 50ft above my mini-van," she recalled. "It was so low I ducked instinctively. It was travelling real fast, but hardly made any sound.

"Then it disappeared behind some trees. A few seconds later I heard this great explosion and saw this fireball rise up over the trees, so I figured the jet had crashed. The ground really shook. So I dialled 911 and told them what happened.

"I'd heard nothing about the other attacks and it was only when I got home and saw the TV that I realised it wasn't the white jet, but Flight 93.

"I KNOW OF TWO PEOPLE—I WILL NOT MENTION NAMES—THAT HEARD A MISSILE." —MAYOR OF SHANKSVILLE, PENNSYLVANIA

"I didn't think much more about it until the authorities started to say there had been no other plane. The plane I saw was heading right to the point where Flight 93 crashed and must have been there at the very moment it came down.

"There's no way I imagined this plane—it was so low it was virtually on top of me. It was white with no markings but it was definitely military, it just had that look.

"It had two rear engines, a big fin on the back like a spoiler on the back of a car and with two upright fins at the side. I haven't found one like it on the internet. It definitely wasn't one of those executive jets. The FBI came and talked to me and said there was no plane around.

"Then they changed their story and tried to say it was a plane taking pictures of the crash 3,000ft up.

"But I saw it and it was there before the crash and it was 40ft above my head. They did not want my story—nobody here did."[21]

A further boost to the shootdown scenario comes from none other than the mayor of Shanksville, Ernie Stuhl. He told a reporter for the

Philadelphia Daily News:

"I know of two people—I will not mention names—that heard a missile," Stuhl said. "They both live very close, within a couple of hundred yards. . .This one fellow's served in Vietnam and he says he's heard them, and he heard one that day." The mayor adds that based on what he knows about that morning, military F-16 fighter jets were "very, very close."[22]

_THE SCATTERED DEBRIS OF FLIGHT 93

Jon Meyer, a reporter for WJAC-TV, was one of the very few journalists to make it to the site of the crater before authorities forced the press to stay a mile away. He walked right up to the edge:

There was just a big hole in the ground. All I saw was a crater filled with small, charred plane parts. Nothing that would even tell you that it was a plane. I could tell something very large had crashed, and the smell of jet fuel was strong. You just can't believe that a whole plane went into this crater. First thought I had was, "I've gotta write down what I'm seeing." I could see some charred trees and smoke off in the woods. It was only a matter of minutes before police said, "You've got to get out." There were no suitcases, no recognizable plane parts, no body parts. The crater was about 30 to 35 feet deep.[23]

As it turns out, the wreckage of the plane was strewn over *eight miles*. The *Washington Post* reported on September 14: "Investigators also found small pieces of wreckage yesterday as far as eight miles from the crash site in southwestern Pennsylvania—much farther than previously discovered. An explosion has not been ruled out, [FBI Special Agent Bill] Crowley said."[24]

> "THE PASSENGER KILLED WAS DANIEL LEWIN, SHOT BY PASSENGER SATAM AL SUQAMI. ONE BULLET WAS REPORTED TO HAVE BEEN FIRED." —FAA MEMO

CNN reported: "A *second* debris field was around Indian Lake about 3 miles from the crash scene. Some debris was in the lake and some was adjacent to the lake."[25]

The *Pittsburgh Post-Gazette* chimed in:

Finding the flight data recorder had been the focus of investigators as they widened their search area today following the discoveries of more debris, including what appeared to be human remains, miles from the point of impact at a reclaimed coal mine.

Residents and workers at businesses outside Shanksville, Somerset County, reported discovering clothing, books, papers and what appeared to be human remains. Some residents said they collected bags-full of items to be turned over to investigators.[26]

To top it off, a 1,000-pound chunk of one of the plane's engines was found over *one mile* from the crater.[27]

This widely scattered wreckage lends strong credence to the theory that Flight 93 exploded in midair, either from a missile or an onboard bomb.

_WAS THERE A GUN ON ANY OF THE FLIGHTS?

Deena Burnett's husband, Tom Burnett, was a passenger on Flight 93. He called Deena from his cellphone. She relates:

And he told me what was going on. "They've already knifed a guy. I think one of them has a gun." I started asking questions, and he said, "Deena, just listen." He went over the information again and said, "Please call the authorities," and he hung up.[28]

When relating this conversation to the author of the book *Among the Heroes*, she recounts what her husband said:

We are in the air. The plane has been hijacked. They already knifed a guy. One of them has a gun. They're saying there is a bomb onboard. Please call the authorities.[29]

A Federal Aviation Administration memo from that day says that not only did a hijacker on a different plane, Flight 11, have a gun, a passenger was actually shot. The memo—stamped September 11 at 5:30 PM—was posted at WorldNetDaily. It reads, in part:

The American Airlines FAA Principle Security Inspector (PSI) was notified by Suzanne Clark of American Airlines Corporate Headquarters, that an on board flight attendant contacted American Airlines Operation Center and informed that a passenger located in seat 10B shot and killed a passenger in seat 9B at 9:20 a.m. The passenger killed was Daniel Lewin, shot by passenger Satam Al Suqami. One bullet was reported to have been fired.

A spokeswoman for the FAA told WorldNetDaily that the memo was an early draft of the executive summary for that day. The reference to a shooting was "a mistake." She said, "It was a miscommunication between American Airlines dispatch people and our people."[30]

American Airlines, though, denies giving any information of this type to the FAA. An AA spokesman further says that he listened to the tape of flight attendant Betty Ong's call, and that she never mentioned a gun.[31]

WorldNetDaily reports: "Even some American Airlines officials, speaking on the condition of anonymity, admit they are puzzled as to how such a detailed account, if indeed false, could have wended its way into a critical memo to FAA chief Jane Garvey."[32]

The FAA spokeswoman refused to release the final draft of the executive summary to WorldNetDaily. Indeed, in June 2002, I filed a

Freedom of Information Act request for the FAA's Daily Alert Bulletins for the days of September 10, 11, and 12, 2001. The FAA flatly refused.

_THE EXTRAORDINARILY SLOW MILITARY RESPONSE

Libertarian commentator Joseph R. Stromberg has dubbed 9/11: "The Day the Defense Department Stood Still."

At 8:13 AM Eastern time, Flight 11's transponder is shut off. An air traffic manager said: "We considered it at that time to be a possible hijacking." By 8:20, Boston ground control is convinced the plane has been hijacked. At 8:21, flight attendant Betty Ong, who's on the plane, calls American Airlines reservations department, confirming that the plane has been hijacked. At 8:46, Flight 11 hits the North Tower.

At 9:03—seventeen minutes later—Flight 175 slams into the South Tower. At 9:41, Flight 77 nails the Pentagon. This is almost one hour after the first crash, and almost an hour and a half after Flight 11 is considered "a possible hijacking."

> LIBERTARIAN COMMENTATOR JOSEPH R. STROMBERG HAS DUBBED 9/11: "THE DAY THE DEFENSE DEPARTMENT STOOD STILL."

At 10:06 AM, Flight 93 goes down in rural Pennsylvania. It's now going on two hours since Flight 11 aroused suspicion.[33]

Yet during all this time, no military planes were able to intercept any of the flights? This seems hard to believe, and when you put together all the accounts of that day, it's nearly impossible to believe. Detailing the staggering inaction of the military would take up at least a very long article. For a minutely detailed examination of the military's non-response that day—drawn completely from mainstream and official accounts—I recommend articles by Jared Israel and others on the Emperors' New Clothes Website,[34] as well as "The Complete 9/11 Timeline" by Paul Thompson.[35] Here are just three representative excerpts from Thompson's colossal work:

(After 9:03 A.M.) Shortly after the second WTC crash, calls from fighter units start "pouring into NORAD and sector operations centers, asking, 'What can we do to help?' At Syracuse, New York, an ANG commander [tells Northeast Air Defense Sector (NEADS) commander Robert] Marr, 'Give me 10 min. and I can give you hot guns [plane-mounted machine guns]. Give me 30 min. and I'll have heat-seeker [missiles]. Give me an hour and I can give you slammers [air-to-air missiles known as Amraams].'" Marr replies, "I want it all." [Aviation Week and Space Technology, 3 June 2002] Yet supposedly, the first fighters don't take off from Syracuse until 10:44 - over an hour and a half later. These are supposedly the first fighters scrambled from the ground aside from three at Langley, two at Otis, and two fighters that took off from Toledo at 10:16. [Toledo Blade, 9 December 2001] What happened to all these volunteer fighters? Armed fighters could have

been in the air from Syracuse by 9:20 or so, yet supposedly, when NORAD needed fighters to go after Flight 93 at least 20 minutes after that, the only ones they sent were two completely unarmed fighters on a training mission near Detroit! [ABC News, 30 August 2002] The only likely explanation is that these fighters were prohibited from taking off. Aircraft cannon (the "hot guns" mentioned) would have been all that was needed in such a situation, since any fighter would presumably follow procedure and intercept visually first, tip their wings from a very short distance away, fire a warning shot, and so on, before firing on the plane.

....

(9:27 A.M.) NORAD orders 3 F-16 fighters scrambled from Langley Air Force Base in Virginia to intercept Flight 77. Langley is 129 miles from Washington. Ready aircraft at Andrews Air Force Base, 15 miles away, are not scrambled. [Newsday, 23 September 2001] [9:24, NORAD, 18 September 2001; 9:27, CNN, 17 September 2001; 9:25, Washington Post, 12 September 2001; 9:35, CNN, 17 Sept 2001; 9:35, Washington Post, 15 September 2001] Note that according to the official NORAD timeline, they ordered the F-16's scrambled the same minute they were told about the hijacking. A rare example of competence. But earlier, according to their own timeline, they waited 6 minutes before scrambling fighters after Flight 11. Why? Flight 77 had supposedly been missing from the radar screen since 8:56. Why wait 31 minutes to send a plane and find out where it is?

....

9:30 A.M. The F-16's scrambled towards Flight 77 get airborne. [9:30, NORAD, 18 September 2001; 9:35, Washington Post, 12 September 2001] If the NORAD departure time is correct, the F-16's would have to travel slightly over 700 mph to reach Washington before Flight 77 does. The maximum speed of an F-16 is 1500 mph. [AP, 6/16/00] Even traveling at 1300 mph, these planes could have reached Washington in 6 minutes - well before any claim of when Flight 77 crashed. Yet they obviously don't.

_BUSH TWICE SAYS HE SAW THE FIRST CRASH LIVE ON TV THAT MORNING

No one saw a live shot of the first plane hitting the WTC. The only known footage of that crash happened to be captured because a film crew from Gamma Press was working on a documentary about the New York Fire Department. They were filming firefighters responding to a possible gas leak a few blocks from the Trade Center. Hearing the loud roar of jet engines, the camera operator panned up and caught Flight 11 hitting the North Tower. (This fact in and of itself has struck some people as too coincidental to be believed.)

Naturally, lots of video cameras (and still cameras) were trained on the Twin Towers, filming the resultant fire, when the second plane hit. This image was transmitted live across the world. But it wasn't until later that we saw the footage of the first plane hitting.

Yet President Bush has said that he saw the first plane hit as it happened. He said this not once but twice. On December 4, 2001, Bush was at a "town hall meeting" in Orlando, Florida, when a third-grader named Jordan asked him: "One thing, Mr. President, is that you have no idea how much you've done for this country. And another thing is that, how did you feel when you heard about the terrorist attack?" Taken from the White House's transcript of the event, Bush replied:

Thank you, Jordan. Well, Jordan, you're not going to believe what state I was in when I heard about the terrorist attack. I was in Florida. And my Chief of Staff, Andy Card—actually, I was in a classroom talking about a reading program that works. I was sitting outside the classroom waiting to go in, and I saw an airplane hit the tower—the TV was obviously on. And I used to fly, myself, and I said, well, there's one terrible pilot. I said, it must have been a horrible accident.

But I was whisked off there, I didn't have much time to think about it. And I was sitting in the classroom, and Andy Card, my Chief of Staff, who is sitting over here, walked in and said, "A second plane has hit the tower, America is under attack."[36]

In this response, Bush clearly says that he was watching a television outside the classroom when he saw the first plane hit the tower. It was later, after he had gone into the classroom to hear the children read, that Card told him that "a second plane" had hit.

"WHEN WE WALKED INTO THE CLASSROOM, I HAD SEEN THIS PLANE FLY INTO THE FIRST BUILDING." —PRESIDENT BUSH

Bush repeated this impossible scenario a month later. The scene was another "town hall meeting," this one in Ontario, California, on January 5, 2002. An unidentified man tells Bush, "First of all, I'm very impressed in how you handled the situation on September 11th." After the requisite applause, he asks: "What was the first thing that went through your head when you heard that a plane crashed into the first building?"

Again taking this straight from the official White House transcript of the event, Bush replies:

Yes. Well, I was sitting in a schoolhouse in Florida. I had gone down to tell my little brother what to do, and—just kidding, Jeb. (Laughter.) And—it's the mother in me. (Laughter.) Anyway, I was in the midst of learning about a reading program that works. I'm a big believer in basic education, and it starts with making sure every child learns to read. And therefore, we need to focus on the science of reading, not what may feel good or sound good when it comes to teaching children to read. (Applause.) I'm just getting a plug in for my reading initiative.

Anyway, I was sitting there, and my Chief of Staff—well, first of all, when we walked into the classroom, I had seen this plane fly into the first building. There was a TV set on. And you know, I thought it was pilot error and I was amazed that anybody could make such a terrible mistake. And something was wrong with the plane, or—anyway, I'm sitting there, listening to the briefing, and Andy Card came and said, "America is under attack."

And in the meantime, this teacher was going on about the curriculum, and I was thinking about what it meant for America to be under attack. It was an amazing thought. But I made up my mind that if America was under attack, we'd get them. (Applause.) I wasn't interested in lawyers, I wasn't interested in a bunch of debate. I was interested in finding out who did it and bringing them to justice. I also knew that they would try to hide, and anybody who provided haven, help, food, would be held accountable by the United States of America. (Applause.)

Anyway, it was an interesting day.[37]

Again, Bush is specific: Watching TV before he entered the classroom, he saw the first plane crash into the towers.

To repeat, this simply is not possible. The first plane crash was not televised live. Your first reaction may be, Well, he's just a little confused. He saw the second plane hit, and he's remembering it as the first. But this explanation doesn't hold water. Both times, Bush specifically says that he saw the first hit. Both times, he says he didn't think much of it, just that a pilot (presumably of a small private plane) accidentally flew into the tower. Both times, he says that Andrew Card came in and told him that the *second* plane had hit and, thus, that the US was under attack.

So imagine that Bush really was confusing the first and second planes. Go through it in your head. Watching a TV in the hall, he sees the second plane hit the towers. Then he goes into the classroom for the reading lesson. But he says that Card told him about the second plane. And the party line on that morning's events, repeated *ad infinitum*, is that Card whispered in his ear about the second hit. Plus, based on the timeline of that morning, we know that Bush was indeed in the classroom when the second plane hit. Thus, he *couldn't* have seen the second plane hit. He was in the classroom at the time. This is what a simple reading of the facts tells us, and this is what the Official Version of Events also tells us. And even if he was somehow watching the live shots of the second plane hit, he obviously wouldn't have thought it was just pilot error at that point.

Bush couldn't have seen the first plane hit, and we know he didn't see the second plane hit. Yet twice, a month apart, he repeated the same impossible story about when he saw and learned about the attack on the Twin Towers. What was it he saw on the TV? Why can't we get a straight answer out of him?

_WHEN DID HE KNOW?

This leads us into the general issue of when, where, and how Bush was made aware of the terrorist attacks. Trying to sort out the tangled web that's been woven around this issue isn't easy, and it deserves an article of its own. The best two examinations of this aspect are "The Complete 9/11 Timeline" by Paul Thompson[38] and several articles by Jared Israel and others on the Emperor's New Clothes Website.[39] Both resources rely completely on mainstream media reports and official statements.

To give you just a taste of what these articles have put together, here is a short excerpt from "Bush in the Open" by Illarion Bykov and Jared Israel:

ABC journalist John Cochran was traveling with the President. He reported on ABC TV on Tuesday morning:

> **Peter, as you know, the president's down in Florida talking about education. He got out of his hotel suite this morning, was about to leave, reporters saw the White House chief of staff, Andy Card, whisper into his ear. The reporter said to the president, "Do you know what's going on in New York?" He said he did, and he said he will have something about it later. His first event is about half an hour at an elementary school in Sarasota, Florida.**

> <u>**'ABC News'**</u> **Special Report**

So Bush knew about the first WTC incident before leaving his hotel.

Of course, this completely contradicts Bush's insistence that he learned of the attacks by seeing the first crash on TV and by being told about the second one by Chief of Staff Andrew Card. And that's just the start of the convoluted tale. For much more, check out the resources I've recommended.

_WHAT DID BUSH DO?

Bush received a lot of flak for his actions on September 11. To begin with, when he was in the Florida classroom and Andrew Card whispered to him "America is under attack" (Bush's own words), Bush didn't react at all. He sat there, listening to the schoolkids reading a story. And he sat some more. And he told the children what good readers they are. Then he sat even more. Finally, he left the classroom.

The videotape of the President's visit that morning shows that he sat for at least two minutes after being told that New York City was being attacked by terrorists. However, the tape, created by the elementary school where he was appearing, is edited. It shows Card whisper to Bush, then it shows Bush sitting for two minutes. The video then jumps to the outside of the school as it's being evacuated, and it

cuts to the President giving his initial speech. We can't be sure how long he stayed in the classroom. The edited version shows two minutes elapsing, so we know it was at least that long. Card whispered in the President's ear at 9:05 AM; Bush didn't make his speech until 9:30 AM (some sources put it a minute or two earlier). Just before his speech, he briefly consulted by phone with Vice President Cheney and National Security Adviser Condoleezza Rice. If we allow five minutes for this, that puts Bush leaving the classroom around 9:25. Thus, for no less than two minutes and no more than 20 minutes, the leader of the free world did nothing while his country was being attacked.

Bush has never explained his inaction, and, in fact, his Administration has tried to cover it up. On the first anniversary of 9/11, various high-level officials and staff members made the rounds on the TV news. They showed the tape, which had been severely edited. On September 11, 2002, millions of viewers saw Card whispering to Bush, then a jump cut to Bush leaving the classroom. The intervening two to 20 minutes were cut out, and no one—not the officials or their interviewers—said anything about the doctoring of the tape.

The fact that Bush sat listening to the children isn't the only strange aspect of what can be seen on the video. When Card leans over to tell Bush that the country is being attacked, the Chief of Staff doesn't wait for a reply. He gives Bush the message, lasting about three seconds; without waiting for a reply from the Commander in Chief, Card immediately walks away. The President, looking distinctly unconcerned, turns his attention back to the children.

Adding to the inexplicable lack of action, the Secret Service doesn't swoop in to whisk away the President. Bear in mind that at this point no one knows how many more attacks are going to occur, what form(s) they will take, or when they will end. Many planes are still in the air, including two that are hijacked. Bush is making a scheduled, previously announced public appearance. Yet the Secret Service, the Chief of Staff, and the President himself see no reason to be concerned, no need to hustle out of there and take command of the situation. It's bizarre beyond belief.

But the hijinks don't end there. Instead of immediately returning to Washington to lead the country in a time of "war" (the word that Bush and other officials have used since that day), the President shuttled to secured Air Force bases in Louisiana and Nebraska, before getting back to DC late that afternoon.

Bush didn't publicly speak about his actions that day for more than eight months. When he finally did break his silence, it was to a television station in *Germany*. He said that he had been trying to "get out of harm's way."

"I MEAN, I WAS TRYING TO GET OUT OF HARM'S WAY." —PRESIDENT BUSH

This stunning admission went completely unreported in the US, except for the *Los Angeles Times*. Here we have the President of the United States speaking for the first time about what he did on that monumental day, and only one news outlet saw fit to report it. One can only guess that they wanted to save the President—and the US in general—from embarrassment.

The Administration certainly knew that the remark was humiliating. A few months later, when the first anniversary of the attacks rolled around, Bush's actions that day were heroic, according to various officials, including Bush himself.

For the record, the President told ARD German Television:

I mean, I was trying to get out of harm's way. We were concerned about threats on the president. We were worried about future attacks, and there's a lot of belief that Flight 93 was headed to the White House.[40]

And what was Bush worried about? "I was concerned about things like, is my wife safe? You know, I was worried about that. I was worried about things such as my parents. I was worried about my girls." He called Laura and his parents, who were stranded in Wisconsin. But, he added, "At the same time, you need to know about me that I was also thinking clearly about how to respond."

_WERE THERE PLANS TO HIJACK OTHER FLIGHTS?

The horror of September 11 is overwhelming, but what if it had been only a part of the planned day of destruction? Other prominent buildings would've been hit and destroyed, and hundreds or thousands more people would've died. A convincing amount of evidence, now forgotten, indicates that this was the plan.

On September 22, 2001, *Time* reported: "US officials are compiling what one called 'growing' evidence that other hijackings may have been planned for September 11."[41]

Three days prior, the *Guardian* of London had said: "The FBI is increasingly certain that up to six planes were intended to take part in last week's terrorist attacks on New York and Washington."[42]

> "US OFFICIALS ARE COMPILING WHAT ONE CALLED 'GROWING' EVIDENCE THAT OTHER HIJACKINGS MAY HAVE BEEN PLANNED FOR SEPTEMBER 11." —*TIME*

One week after the attacks, a *Chicago Tribune* article stated:

The FBI is investigating the possibility that suicide hijackers were on board a fifth transcontinental airline flight last Tuesday, one that was cancelled just minutes before its scheduled 8:10 a.m. departure from Boston due to a mechanical problem, according to sources familiar with the investigation.

Federal agents are searching for an undetermined number of passengers who were on board American Airlines Flight 43, according to one source familiar with the passenger manifest. The flight was to have departed Boston 25 minutes after American Flight 11, which struck New York's World Trade Center, this source said.

In addition, one of the sources said that the FBI was "very interested" in passengers whose names appeared on the manifests of "several" other American flights that were in the air when the first attacks occurred. Those planes landed prematurely when air traffic controllers, responding to the attacks on the World Trade Center and the Pentagon, ordered all flights in the U.S. to touch down as soon as possible.

None of the passengers in whom the FBI has expressed interest reappeared to continue their journeys after commercial flights resumed late last week, one of the sources said.[43]

Unfortunately, the article gives no indication why the passengers of these flights were under suspicion. We do get more details about suspicious incidents from other articles, though. *Time* reported:

Officials from both the government and the airline industry tell TIME Magazine that a knife-like weapon was found on each of two separate Delta Airlines aircraft later that day [i.e., 9/11], although neither plane took off due to the nationwide grounding after the World Trade Center and Pentagon attacks on hijacked United and American airlines planes.[44]

From the *Independent* of London:

Investigative sources tapped by various US media, said two Delta planes—one leaving Atlanta for Brussels and the other leaving from Boston—were found to have small knives and box-cutters on board in the passenger areas....

The Justice Department has made no official comment on the discovery, other than to say that box-cutters were found on an unspecified number of other aircraft.[45]

The *Boston Globe* reported that a knife was found on a Northwest Airlines plane on September 11. According to the same article, on September 22, "Massachusetts Port Authority officials" confirmed that a knife had been found on that plane and a Delta plane in Boston. Other officials, though, denied that a third plane in Boston had been targeted.[46]

And there's this from the London *Guardian*:

An intelligence source in the US said another plane due to have been hijacked was a Continental Airlines flight from Newark on the morning of September 11. Retractable knives (similar to Stanley knives) of the same type used in the four successful hijackings were found taped to the backs of fold-down trays.

The source did not give details of the sixth plane. However, similar knives were found stashed in the seats on a plane which had been due to leave Logan airport in Boston the same morning, and which was delayed and then cancelled.[47]

On September 14, a passenger onboard an Air Canada flight found several box-cutters "concealed" in an overhead compartment. The plane had been due to fly from Toronto to New York on 9/11, but was grounded. It sat unused on the runway until the 14th.[48]

The finding of all these box-cutters/knives aboard planes on 9/11 raises the possibility that the hijackers on the four known flights didn't bring their weapons aboard; instead, the weapons may have been placed their by inside accomplices. Of course, this line of thinking leads to the possibility of a wider conspiracy, something that only a loon would believe. Except that the *Independent* of London reported that the finding of knives aboard the Delta planes "has raised suspicions [among investigators] that staff at US airports may have played an active role in the conspiracy and helped the hijackers to circumvent airport security."[49] The New York *Daily News* noted: "Federal investigators are increasingly leaning toward a theory that the suicide hijackers got inside help from airport employees."[50]

And *Time* said:

Investigators are not yet certain how these weapons came to be on board the aircraft. But they increasingly believe that the weapons may have been prepositioned by accomplices for use by others. As one US official told TIME, "These look like inside jobs."

The new evidence is causing officials to broaden their investigative and security efforts to encompass not only the carry-on bag screening system but the entire aviation security apparatus at US airports. The new evidence raises the worrisome possibility that the hijackers may have had accomplices deep within the 'secure' areas of airports—that may include the shops and restaurants in the terminal behind the metal detectors, or amongst the thousands of people who work in catering, fueling or cleaning aircraft; or anyone who might have access to the airplane before takeoff.[51]

Besides finding box-cutters/knives in other planes due to fly on 9/11, we have reports of some unusual incidents that day. The *Globe and Mail* of Toronto reported:

The FBI is investigating whether a fifth cell of suicide hijackers, on board a Boeing 767 about to take off from New York for Los Angeles, was thwarted when the flight was cancelled at about the time another Boeing 767 slammed into the World Trade Center.

"We're looking for them [to see] whether they are involved in the larger plot," Joseph Valiquette, an FBI spokesman in New York, confirmed yesterday.

United Airlines flight 23 to Los Angeles was scheduled to leave New York's John F. Kennedy airport at 9 a.m. on Tuesday. Shortly before its scheduled departure, passengers were told the flight was cancelled.

"AUTHORITIES DETAINED TWO ARMED GROUPS AT NEW YORK AIRPORTS YESTERDAY [SEPT. 13], FEARING THEY INTENDED TO HIJACK A PAIR OF JETLINERS AND MOUNT ANOTHER SUICIDAL TERRORIST STRIKE ON A U.S. TARGET, GOVERNMENT OFFICIALS SAID."

Three men angrily protested and demanded that the flight proceed. They argued so vehemently that UA personnel called police from the Port Authority of New York and New Jersey, which runs the airport, but the three disappeared.

"They got pretty belligerent," Port Authority spokesman Dave Jamieson said yesterday.

UA Flight 23 closely matches the profile of the four aircraft that were hijacked.

"They do seem to be of interest," Mr. Valiquette said of the still-missing UA Flight 23 passengers.[52]

The *Times* of London also covered this incident:

United Airlines Flight 23 was standing on the runway at John F. Kennedy airport, waiting to take off for Los Angeles, when news broke of the attacks on the World Trade Centre.

The airport was immediately closed and the pilot announced that the aircraft was returning to the terminal. At that point four male passengers of Middle Eastern appearance stood up in the cabin and began urgently consulting each other, sources told The *New York Times*. Flight attendants asked them to return to their seats but they refused and "as soon as the door opened these guys bolted", an official said.[53]

On September 23, the *Boston Globe* summarized an article that it had run four days earlier:

The same day, the Globe, citing a "well-placed law enforcement official" as its source, reported that when grounded planes taxied back to terminals on Sept. 11, an "Arab-looking" passenger on one unidentified flight stood up, became agitated, and complained that the flight would not be leaving. After the plane reached the gate, the report said, the man disappeared.[54]

Another suspicious occurrence was reported by the *Washington Times*:

A Middle Eastern man arrested when he tried to fly into Chicago on Sept. 11 with false passports and two airline uniforms was traveling with at least four accomplices who still may be at large, say other passengers on the flight.

FBI agents in Chicago have been questioning passengers this week from Lufthansa Flight 430, from Frankfurt, Germany, which was diverted to Toronto in the wake of terrorist attacks on the United States. Agents reportedly are seeking a laptop computer shared among at least five men aboard the flight....

Witnesses aboard the aircraft have told the FBI that when the pilot announced that the flight would be forced to land in Toronto because of an unspecified "catastrophic event" in the United States, Nageeb Abdul Jabar Mohamed Al-Hadi and others apparently traveling with him produced a bottle of wine from carry-on luggage and shared celebratory sips with each other as they huddled near a midcabin restroom.....

Al-Hadi is jailed in Toronto, awaiting extradition to the United States. Neither the FBI nor the Royal Canadian Mounted Police would comment on whether other passengers have been detained or are being sought.[55]

Then we have the possibility that the hijackings that were frustrated on 9/11 were to be attempted the first day that air travel resumed, September 13. In a front-page story dated the 14th, the *Washington Post* reported:

Authorities detained two armed groups at New York airports yesterday, fearing they intended to hijack a pair of jetliners and mount another suicidal terrorist strike on a U.S. target, government officials said.

Both groups carried knives, false identification and open tickets to U.S. destinations dated Tuesday—the day of the attacks on the World Trade Center and the Pentagon, sources said. They also, had certificates from a Florida flight training school attended by some members of the previous hijacking teams, who were similarly armed when they commandeered four aircraft.

Jim Hunter, a passenger on an American Airlines flight scheduled to leave John F. Kennedy International Airport for Los Angeles yesterday, said officers with guns drawn stormed the flight from the front and rear at about 8 p.m. They handcuffed and removed three people after ordering all passengers to the floor. The flight was canceled."...

In foiling what they feared was a second wave of attacks yesterday, authorities said they took into custody five people at John F. Kennedy International Airport, and five men at LaGuardia International Airport. Both airports, which had reopened yesterday, were immediately shut again.[56]

In another page-one story on the same day, the *Post* reported:

The three New York area airports, after opening for a few hours, were shut down

again after nine men and one woman were detained at John F. Kennedy International and La Guardia airports. Police officials said at least one of the men used a forged pilot's identification to bypass a security checkpoint.[57]

In addition to giving us a fascinating, terrifying glimpse of what could have been, these incidents are important for understanding what happened that day. What did these investigations of possible insider-accomplices yield? What have we learned about Al-Hadi, the man arrested with false passports and pilots' uniforms? What about the ten people arrested at New York airports on September 13? In this last case, at least, it would seem that some hijackers from the 9/11 gang were apprehended. Where are they now? Have they revealed anything?

Some people will say that these incidents must not have yielded anything significant; otherwise, we would've heard about it. This is untrue. The government's fondness for secrecy, which has always been strong, has become overwhelming since 9/11. This is especially true when it comes to people arrested or "detained" on suspicions of terrorist activity. They are held in secret locations; they aren't allowed to contact family; they are sometimes denied access to lawyers. The media are rebuffed at every turn when trying to find out anything about them, even something as basic as a name. My Freedom of Information Act requests concerning 9/11 are routinely turned down because releasing such material could supposedly jeopardize ongoing investigations and prosecutions.

Could there be any innocuous reason why two groups of five people—carrying knives, false I.D., and tickets dated 9/11—were boarding planes on 9/13?

_WHO WERE THE HIJACKERS?

The day after the attacks, ABC News reported that "federal officials" were claiming to have already identified the hijackers.[58] A mere three days after 9/11, the US government announced their supposed identities. Their names, photos, and personal details (such as birthdays) were released, five on each of the planes, except Flight 93, which had four. Just one problem, though. As reported primarily by the London press, many of the alleged hijackers were alive.

Waleed Al Shehri, supposedly on Flight 11, protested that he was still alive and a pilot for Saudi Arabian airlines. Abdulaziz Al Omari, also supposedly a Flight 11 hijacker, is actually an engineer at Saudi Telecoms. He says he lost his passport while living in Denver in 1995; he returned permanently to Riyadh in 2000. Saeed Alghamdi, who was purported to have been on Flight 93, was interviewed by *Asharq Al Awsat*, an Arabic-language newspaper published in London. Another alleged Flight 93 hijacker, Ahmed Al-Nami, is a supervisor at Saudi Arabian Airlines, still quite alive. A reported Flight 77 hijacker, Salem Al-Hamzi, is actually a worker at a Saudi Arabian chemical plant. He's never been to the US, and his passport

HOW DID THE FBI DECIDE THAT THESE NAMES, PHOTOS, AND PERSONAL DETAILS BELONGED TO THE MEN WHO CARRIED OUT 9/11? AND IN JUST ONE DAY?

had been stolen in Cairo in 1998. The BBC further notes: "And there are suggestions that another suspect, Khalid Al Midhar, may also be alive."[59] The *Daily Telegraph* of London interviewed several of these men, who were reportedly "furious" about being identified as the perpetrators of 9/11.[60]

When the list first came out, FBI Director Robert Mueller said he was "fairly confident" that the identities were genuine. But when informed of the "hijackers" who were still alive and well on the other side of the world, an FBI spokesman admitted: "The identification process has been complicated by the fact that many Arabic family names are similar. It is also possible that the hijackers used false identities.... If we have made mistakes then obviously that would be regrettable but this is a big and complicated investigation."[61] Yet, to this day, the official list of 9/11 hijackers on the FBI's Website contains the original nineteen names and other data, including those of the men whose identities were stolen.

This obviously presents huge problem for the official version of 9/11. With this many men mistakenly pegged as the hijackers, how we can have any confidence that the remaining people on the FBI's list are correct? And if we don't know the identities of some, or perhaps all, of the hijackers, then we have no clue as to who they were, where they came from, what their motives were, etc.

We're also led to another, more general question: How did the FBI decide that these names, photos, and personal details belonged to the men who carried out 9/11? And in just one day? We've been told that some of the passengers and crew who called from the hijacked flights gave the seat numbers of the hijackers. There are several flaws in this claim.

First, did someone on every single flight call in and give all five seat numbers (four in the case of Flight 93)? We know that two flight attendants on Flight 11 called the ground, two passengers and one flight attendant on Flight 175 phoned, Flight 77 had one passenger (Barbara Olson) who called, and over 30 people onboard Flight 93 used phones. Media reports say that one of the attendants on Flight 11 gave the hijackers' seat numbers, and it's certainly possible that at least one of the many callers from Flight 93 did so, as well. But according to published reports, none of the three callers from Flight 175 did, and Barbara Olson's two brief calls to her husband, by all accounts, didn't contain this information, either. So how could anyone have identified the hijackers on these two flights by their seat numbers (or anything else)?

Second, there's a problem with the story about Flight 11. Flight attendant Madeline Amy Sweeney called American Airlines ground manager Michael Woodward during the hijacking, talking to him for 25 minutes. ABC News reported:

She gave him the seat numbers for four of the five hijackers, allowing airline staff to pull up their names, phone numbers, addresses—and even credit card numbers—on the reservations computer. One of the names that came up was Mohamed Atta, the man the FBI would later identify as the leader of all 19 of the Sept. 11 hijackers.[62]

The Associated Press even provided specifics: "Mohamed Atta, who piloted the plane, was assigned seat 8D, according to the documents released in U.S. District Court. Another hijacker, Abdulaziz Alomari, was in 8G."[63]

> **THUS, BY AN AMAZING STROKE OF LUCK, THE LEAD TERRORIST'S BAGGAGE WAS STILL SITTING IN BOSTON, WAITING TO REVEAL ITS INCRIMINATING CONTENTS.**

But an article from the BBC throws a spanner in the works. Titled "The Last Moments of Flight 11," it ends: "Also, the seat numbers she gave were different from those registered in the hijackers' names."[64]

Similarly, the *LA Times* reports: "Investigators noted that Sweeney even had the presence of mind to relay the exact seat numbers of the four suspects in the ninth and 10th rows, although a few of those seats do not match up with the seats assigned to the hijackers on the tickets they purchased."[65] (This leads to yet another point: Sweeney told Woodward that there were four hijackers, but the official story says there were five.)

So how did the FBI come up with the identities of the hijackers?

Then we come to the strange issue of the passenger lists. The hijackers' names (or aliases) are not on them. This is odd because, according to what we've been told, all of the hijackers were ticket-carrying passengers who got past security with box-cutters (which weren't forbidden at the time) and ceramic knives. To have gone through security and have boarded the planes, they would've had to present their tickets and photo identification. Thus, their names (whether real or phony) would have been in the airlines' computers.

Indeed, this is the reason we've been given regarding why the airlines and authorities were able to identify the hijackers so quickly. People onboard the planes supposedly gave seat numbers of the passengers who took over the plane. Yet none of these names—or even any Arabic names at all—shows up on the passenger lists as provided by the airlines and published by CNN, AP, and the *Boston Globe*.

Well, maybe the airlines purposely didn't include them. This explanation doesn't jibe because, for one thing, there would be no reason to do this. Plus, the number of people on each plane, as reported by the airlines and the media, is a little more than the number of people on the lists. For example, we've been told since day one that 92 people (passengers and crew) were onboard Flight 11. The list for Flight 11 contains 90 people. As stated, none of these names matches the hijackers' names/aliases given by the FBI. None is Arabic. Even if the missing two people are hijackers, what about the other three?

All of which makes me wonder: Who the hell were these guys?

_ATTA'S LUGGAGE

Mohamed Atta's route on September 11 was to fly from Portland, Maine, to Boston's Logan International Airport. There, he boarded Flight 11 to Los Angeles, which ended up crashing into the WTC's North Tower. In Portland, he checked two bags through all the way to LA.

These bags were found to contain "a hand-held electronic flight computer; a simulator procedures manual for Boeing 757 and 767 aircraft; two videotapes relating to 'air tours' of the Boeing 757 and 747 aircraft; a slide-rule flight calculator; and a copy of the Quran,"[66] "a Saudi passport, an international driver's licence, a religious cassette tape,"[67] "airline uniforms,"[68] Atta's will, and the strange note discussed below.[69]

But how do we know what they contained? Weren't they utterly destroyed when Flight 11 slammed into the WTC? Nope. For reasons never explained, Atta's luggage was not transferred from the first leg of his flight (Portland-Boston) to the second leg (Boston-LA). Thus, by an amazing stroke of luck, the lead terrorist's baggage was still sitting in Boston, waiting to reveal its incriminating contents. No media report even attempts to explain how or why this happened, instead vaguely stating that Atta's bags "didn't make" the connection.

As for why he would bring bags with him on a suicide fight, there is a logical explanation. Perhaps he figured that not having any luggage for a two-leg, cross-country trip would seem suspicious. Fair enough. But the contents of those bags can't be explained as easily when you bear in mind that Atta knew his luggage would be destroyed along with him.

For instance, why would he have brought his will? Wouldn't he have left that where it wouldn't be destroyed?

And why bring two pilot uniforms? He obviously wasn't using them. Shouldn't such useful, hard-to-obtain aids in committing air terror have been saved for other hijackers to use in the future? Same thing goes for the videotapes, passport, and flight computer. Why bring them along to be destroyed when they could aid other terrorists?

"THE PROBLEM IS THAT NO MUSLIM—HOWEVER ILL-TAUGHT— WOULD INCLUDE HIS FAMILY IN SUCH A PRAYER."

We should also wonder why he would put these items in bags he was checking through (which means that they were placed in the cargo hold of the plane, where he couldn't get to them). It's conceivable that the procedures manual and the flight computer could've been useful during the hijacking. So why didn't he put these items in a piece of carry-on luggage, so he would have had access to them?

Nothing about this makes sense. And neither does the note found in one of the bags. The London *Independent* pointed out some of the problems with its contents:

"The time of Fun and waste is gone," Atta, or one of his associates, is reported to have written in the note. "Be optimistic ... Check all your items—your bag, your clothes, your knives, your will, your IDs, your passport ... In the morning, try to pray the morning prayer with an open heart."

Part theological, part mission statement, the document—extracts from which were published in *The Washington Post* yesterday—raises more questions than it answers.

Under the heading of "Last Night"—presumably the night of 10 September—the writer tells his fellow hijackers to "remind yourself that in this night you will face many challenges. But you have to face them and understand it 100 per cent ... Obey God, his messenger, and don't fight among yourself [sic] where [sic] you become weak ... Everybody hates death, fears death ..."

The document begins with the words: "In the name of God, the most merciful, the most compassionate ... In the name of God, of myself, and of my family."

The problem is that no Muslim—however ill-taught—would include his family in such a prayer. Indeed, he would mention the Prophet Mohamed immediately after he mentioned God in the first line. Lebanese and Palestinian suicide bombers have never been known to refer to "the time of fun and waste"—because a true Muslim would not have "wasted" his time and would regard pleasure as a reward of the after-life.

And what Muslim would urge his fellow believers to recite the morning prayer—and then go on to quote from it? A devout Muslim would not need to be reminded of his duty to say the first of the five prayers of the day—and would certainly not need to be reminded of the text. It is as if a Christian, urging his followers to recite the Lord's Prayer, felt it necessary to read the whole prayer in case they didn't remember it.

American scholars have already raised questions about the use of "100 per cent"—hardly a theological term to be found in a religious exhortation—and the use of the word "optimistic" with reference to the Prophet is a decidedly modern word.

However, the full and original Arabic text has not been released by the FBI. The translation, as it stands, suggests an almost Christian view of what the hijackers might have felt—asking to be forgiven their sins, explaining that fear of death is natural, that "a believer is always plagued with problems".

A Muslim is encouraged not to fear death—it is, after all, the moment when he or she believes they will start a new life—and a believer in the Islamic world is one who is certain of his path, not "plagued with problems".[70]

_NO EVIDENCE

In April 2002, FBI Director Robert Mueller made an astonishing comment when he spoke at the Commonwealth Club of California in San Francisco:

In our investigation, we have not uncovered a single piece of paper—either here in the US or in the treasure trove of information that has turned up in Afghanistan and elsewhere—that mentioned any aspect of the September 11th plot.[71]

Excuse me? There's no paper trail? Mueller makes it clear in his speech that "paper" refers to *any* sort of documentation, including emails, computer files, phone calls, fund transfers, etc. He blamed the lack of evidence on the terrorists' cunning ability to plan without leaving any evidence behind. The implication being that there's no way the FBI could've picked up on the plot. Hey, we can't even pick up on the plot *afterward*, never mind in advance! Whaddya want from us?

Too bad this statement flies in the face of everything that had been reported up to that time. Yes, we had been told the hijackers and their accomplices were pretty crafty about using public computers and face-to-face meetings.

Just over a week after the attacks, the *New York Times* reported:

A senior F.B.I. official said today that the authorities were examining hundreds of e-mail messages to and from the suspected hijackers and their known associates.

The messages were mainly in English and Arabic, said the official, who would not describe the content aside from saying that the messages were provided by large Internet service providers.[72]

At the beginning of November, the *Times* elaborated on more evidence:

With all the suspects dead and no conclusive evidence, as yet, of any accomplices, investigators have been left to recreate the architecture and orchestration of the plot largely from the recorded minutiae of the hijackers' brief American lives: their cellphone calls, credit card charges, Internet communications and automated teller machine withdrawals.

What has emerged, nearly two months into the investigation, is a picture in which the roles of the 19 hijackers are so well defined as to be almost corporate in their organization and coordination....

> "A SENIOR F.B.I. OFFICIAL SAID TODAY THAT THE AUTHORITIES WERE EXAMINING HUNDREDS OF E-MAIL MESSAGES TO AND FROM THE SUSPECTED HIJACKERS AND THEIR KNOWN ASSOCIATES."

The coordination was so thorough that each of the four hijacking teams had its own bank account, and each team's A.T.M. cards used a single PIN....

Most of the 19 obtained Social Security numbers, which allowed them to open bank accounts and obtain credit cards.[73]

About a month after Mueller's remarks, the London *Times* provided some details:

Credit card records of the suicide hijacker Muhammad Atta show that he was in Manhattan the day before he crashed an aircraft into the World Trade Centre.

The FBI believes that Atta, the leader of the 19 hijackers, was in New York to check the co-ordinates of the twin towers, which he then fed into a handheld electronic navigation device. It was used so that the hijackers did not have to rely on the complex navigation systems on board the hijacked jets, which they probably could not understand.

Widely available Global Positioning System (GPS) devices use satellite signals to allow drivers to pinpoint places easily and follow suggested routes. Reliance on these devices explains the unusual flight paths taken by the aircraft.

Through the records of 27 credit cards, the FBI has learnt that the four GPS devices probably used were bought from Sporty's Pilot Shop in Ohio. Atta also bought a number of flight simulator video games at the shop.

Prosecutors of Zacarias Moussaoui, who is on trial in Virginia for his alleged part in the hijackings, say that on June 25, 2000, he too visited the shop and bought a GPS receiver and flight simulation software for two types of Boeing 747s.[74]

Since this was reported after Mueller's claim of no paper trail, perhaps we should forgive him. Maybe this was the one and only piece of evidence to surface. Or maybe not, as we see in this *Washington Post* article from October 4, 2001, entitled "Agents Follow Suspects' Lengthy E-Trail":

They booked airline tickets online. They used the Internet to learn about the aerial application of pesticides. They exchanged scores of e-mails.

The tech-savvy hijackers and alleged associates who orchestrated the attacks on New York and Washington appeared to use a web of electronic connections to plan and communicate in relative anonymity.

But their computer habits also left a lengthy electronic trail. A small army of law enforcement agents using subpoenas and at least one warrant under the Foreign Intelligence Surveillance Act (FISA) is working to chart the conspirators' path through the online clues they left behind—and, possibly, to head off future acts of terrorism.

During the past three weeks, federal officials have visited libraries from Florida to Virginia, culling log-in sheets and seizing computer equipment where suspected hijackers and associates may have logged time. In searches across the United States, they have seized computers the suspects and alleged accomplices may have used.

Agents have handed out subpoenas and search warrants to just about every major Internet company, including America Online, Microsoft, Earthlink, Yahoo, Google, NetZero, Travelocity and many smaller providers.

One warrant issued under the FISA allows authorities to monitor e-mail, chat rooms and Web sites of an Earthlink user, said Dan Greenfield, vice president of communications for the Internet provider.

The orders have yielded hundreds of e-mails linked to the hijackers in English, Arabic and Urdu, according to a source. *Some messages have included "operational details" of the attack, FBI sources said.*

> ## "SOME MESSAGES HAVE INCLUDED 'OPERATIONAL DETAILS' OF THE ATTACK, FBI SOURCES SAID."

Authorities also have asked banks and credit card companies to scour their databases for information about the suspected hijackers and their associates.

Prosecutors in South Florida have subpoenaed records from ChoicePoint, one of the nation's largest information providers, sources said. Law enforcement officials want former addresses, job histories, property records and an array of other information about the alleged conspirators.

The number of digital leads for investigators to run down is "astounding," a source said. There is so much to sift through that the core FBI computer forensics team working on the 11th floor of the agency's headquarters on Pennsylvania Avenue has been augmented by more than 50 other specialists, most from other government agencies, spokeswoman Debbie Weirman said.[75]

_GOVERNMENT REFUSES TO RELEASE COMMUNICATIONS FROM 9/11 PLANES

The *Village Voice*'s James Ridgeway and I teamed up to make Freedom of Information Act requests regarding communications from the four doomed flights of 9/11. We were completely rebuffed. Our request letter stated:

I request a copy of all documents relating to communications emanating from the four hijacked flights of September 11, 2001: American Airlines Flight 11, American Airlines Flight 77, United Airlines Flight 93, and United Airlines Flight 175. This includes:

1) Recordings of communications from any parties on any of the above-mentioned planes during their flights on September 11, 2001. (This would include pilots radioing air traffic control, the widely-reported 911 calls made by passengers, etc.)

1.1) Transcripts of any of these communications.

1.2) Any documents relating to the existence (or nonexistence) of these communications and/or the recordings of these communications.

2) Records relating to any signals, alarms, or any other form of nonverbal communication emanating from any of the above-mentioned planes during their flights on September 11, 2001.

3) Any other documents—whether in written or recorded form—having to do with communications from any of the above-mentioned planes during their flights on September 11, 2001.

The Federal Aviation Administration's response to the first part of the request:

1) The recordings of communications, transcripts and any documents relating to your request are part of an ongoing, sensitive investigation. Therefore, the contents of the investigative file are protected from mandatory disclosure under Exemption 7 of the FOIA, 5 U.S.C. 552(b) (7). Exemption 7(A) protects information to the extent that if disclosed it could reasonably be expected to interfere with enforcement proceedings. Accordingly, your request for recordings of communications and any documents contained in the investigative file is denied.

Extremely frustrating but not unexpected. At least we have confirmation that the recordings of these communications exist.

Regarding the second part of the request, the FAA responds:

2) There are no records or other correspondence relating to any signals, alarms, or any other form of nonverbal communications emanating from the four hijacked flights.

This would seem to indicate that no form of nonverbal communication came from the planes. This claim conflicts with a transcript published by the *New York Times* of radio communications between the New York Air Route Traffic Control Center and several planes on the morning of 9/11. At 8:44 AM, US Air 583 tells the Control Center it received a signal from Flight 11: "I just picked up an ELT [emergency locator transmitter] on 121.5 it was brief but it went off." The Control Center acknowledges: "O.K. they said it's confirmed..." A minute later, another plane confirms the signal: "DAL2433 at 290 we picked up that ELT, too, but it's very faint."[76] No records of alarms or signals, indeed.

As for the final part of our request:

3) There are no documents in written or recorded form having to do with communications from any of the four hijacked flights.

This is the real puzzler: There are no documents of any kind having to do with the communications. The recordings of the communications exist; we were told this in #1. Yet there are no documents *regarding* these recordings? No transcripts? No translations of portions in Arabic? No reports on the meaning or ramifications of what was said in these communications? No notes on technical matters (frequencies used, etc.)? No documents regarding follow-ups with relatives who received phone calls from passengers on the flights? This strikes me as inconceivable.

Ridgeway and I also sent the same request to the FBI. They refused, citing the FOIA exemption for "records or information compiled for law enforcement purposes, but only to the extent that the production of such law enforcement records or information (A) could reasonably be expected to interfere with enforcement proceedings..."

The CIA simply passed the buck, saying: "The information you seek falls under the jurisdiction of the Federal Bureau of Investigation and/or the Federal Aviation Administration." We never heard back from the National Security Agency (NSA).

> "SUCH DESTRUCTION OF EVIDENCE SHOWS THE ASTOUNDING IGNORANCE OF GOVERNMENT OFFICIALS TO THE VALUE OF A THOROUGH, SCIENTIFIC INVESTIGATION OF THE LARGEST FIRE-INDUCED COLLAPSE IN WORLD HISTORY."
> —*FIRE ENGINEERING* MAGAZINE

I find it hard to think of a legitimate reason why such vital documents concerning a national nightmare should be withheld. If we've already been told the complete truth about what happened onboard those flights, how would the release of these recordings jeopardize investigations into 9/11? The only answer that makes any sense is that the communications from the planes reveal things about which we haven't been told.

_FIREFIGHTING MAGAZINE DENOUNCES GOVERNMENT'S "DESTRUCTION OF EVIDENCE"

Fire Engineering magazine was started in 1877 and is the premier publication on the nitty-gritty, technical aspects of firefighting. In the January 2002 issue, Bill Manning, *Fire Engineering*'s editor-in-chief, went ballistic about the authorities' decision to get rid of the Twin Towers' remains. It is nothing less than "destruction of evidence," he says.

This is true in more than just an informal sense—the area encompassing the remains of the WTC towers was declared to be a literal crime scene during the day of September 11. If I'm not mistaken, removing and destroying evidence from a crime scene is a felony.

Manning wrote:

Did they throw away the locked doors from the Triangle Shirtwaist Fire? Did they throw away the gas can used at the Happyland Social Club Fire? Did they cast aside the pressure-regulating valves at the Meridian Plaza Fire? Of course not. But essentially, that's what they're doing at the World Trade Center.

For more than three months, structural steel from the World Trade Center has been and continues to be cut up and sold for scrap. Crucial evidence that could answer many questions about high-rise building design practices and performance under fire conditions is on the slow boat to China, perhaps never to be seen again in America until you buy your next car.

Such destruction of evidence shows the astounding ignorance of government officials to the value of a thorough, scientific investigation of the largest fire-induced collapse in world history. I have combed through our national standard for fire investigation, NFPA 921, but nowhere in it does one find an exemption allowing the destruction of evidence for buildings over 10 stories tall....

Fire Engineering has good reason to believe that the "official investigation" [of the towers' collapse] blessed by FEMA and run by the American Society of Civil Engineers is a half-baked farce that may already have been commandeered by political forces whose primary interests, to put it mildly, lie far afield of full disclosure. Except for the marginal benefit obtained from a three-day, visual walk-through of evidence sites conducted by ASCE investigation committee members—described by one close source as a "tourist trip"—no one's checking the evidence for anything....

The destruction and removal of evidence must stop immediately.

The federal government must scrap the current setup and commission a fully resourced blue ribbon panel to conduct a clean and thorough investigation of the fire and collapse, leaving no stones unturned.[77]

_THE CONGRESSIONAL INQUIRY INTO 9/11

The government may want you to forget it, but it's a fact that the President and Vice President both pressured the Senate Majority Leader to hobble the congressional investigation into 9/11. This was widely reported in the media and is best summed up by CNN:

President Bush personally asked Senate Majority Leader Tom Daschle Tuesday to limit the congressional investigation into the events of September 11, congressional and White House sources told CNN.

The request was made at a private meeting with congressional leaders Tuesday morning. Sources said Bush initiated the conversation.

He asked that only the House and Senate intelligence committees look into the potential breakdowns among federal agencies that could have allowed the terrorist attacks to occur, rather than a broader inquiry that some lawmakers have proposed, the sources said.

Tuesday's discussion followed a rare call to Daschle from Vice President Dick Cheney last Friday to make the same request.

"The vice president expressed the concern that a review of what happened on September 11 would take resources and personnel away from the effort in the war on terrorism," Daschle told reporters.[78]

When the congressional hearing—a joint investigation by the Senate and House Intelligence Committees—opened, the first to testify was Joint Staff leader Eleanor Hill. Before giving her opening statement, she noted that there were two types of information she was forbidden from divulging. The first was anything relating to a "key" al Qaeda operative whose identity the CIA wouldn't declassify "despite an enormous volume of media reporting on this individual."[79]

The second issue the CIA refused to declassify was this:

Any references to the intelligence Community providing information to the President or White House...

According to the DCI [Director of Central Intelligence], the President's knowledge of intelligence information relevant to this Inquiry remains classified *even when the substance of that intelligence information was declassified*.[80]

In other words, even if we know the information that was given to the President, we still can't know *when* or *if* that information was given to the President.

ELEANOR HILL'S OPENING STATEMENT TO THE JOINT PANEL

When the Intelligence Committees of the House and Senate formed a Joint Inquiry on the attacks, the head of the Joint Inquiry Staff, Eleanor Hill, shocked everybody (and enraged the intelligence community) by presenting some hard-hitting information gleaned from the staff's access to reams of unseen documents and its interviews with officials, agents, and workers at the FBI, CIA, NSA, Defense Department, and elsewhere.

As you read these excerpts from Hill's opening statement, keep in mind the lie we were told repeatedly by officials from the Administration, the FAA, intelligence agencies, and elsewhere: that no one had any inkling that terrorists would hijack passenger planes and use them to ram targets. Such a thing was inconceivable, we were told again and again. It was totally unprecedented and the possibility never occurred to anybody whose job is to protect the United States. Here are a few of the things Hill had to say regarding that:

In January 1996, the Intelligence Community obtained information concerning a planned suicide attack by individuals associated with Shaykh Omar Adb al-Rahman and a key al-Qa'ida operative. The plan was to fly to the United States from Afghanistan and attack the White House;...[81]

In June 1998, the Intelligence Community obtained information from several sources that Usama Bin Ladin was considering attacks in the U.S., including Washington, DC and New York. This information was provided to senior U.S. Government officials in July 1998;...[82]

> "PRESIDENT BUSH PERSONALLY ASKED SENATE MAJORITY LEADER TOM DASCHLE TUESDAY TO LIMIT THE CONGRESSIONAL INVESTIGATION INTO THE EVENTS OF SEPTEMBER 11."

In August 1998, the Intelligence Community obtained information that a group of unidentified Arabs planned to fly an explosive-laden plane from a foreign country into the World Trade Center. The information was passed to the FBI and the FAA. The FAA found the plot highly unlikely given the state of that foreign country's aviation program. Moreover, they believed that a flight originating outside the United States would be detected before it reached its intended target inside the United States. The FBI's New York office took no action on the information, filing the communication in the office's bombing repository file. The Intelligence Community has acquired additional information since then indicating there may be links between this group and other terrorist groups, including al-Qa'ida;...[83]

In the fall of 1998, the Intelligence Community received information concerning a Bin Ladin plot involving aircraft in the New York and Washington, DC areas;...[84]

In November 1998, the Intelligence Community obtained information that a Bin Ladin terrorist cell was attempting to recruit a group of five to seven young men from the United States to travel to the Middle East for training. This was in conjunction with planning to strike U.S. domestic targets;...[85]

A classified document signed by a senior U.S. Government official in December 1998 read in part: "The intelligence community has strong indications that Bin Ladin intends to conduct or sponsor attacks inside the United States";...[86]

In late 1999, the Intelligence Community obtained

information regarding the Bin Ladin network's possible plans to attack targets in Washington, DC and New York City during the New Year's Millennium celebrations;...[87]

In March 2000, the Intelligence Community obtained information regarding the types of targets that operatives in Bin Ladin's network might strike. The Statue of Liberty was specifically mentioned, as were *skyscrapers*, ports, airports, and nuclear power plants;...[88]

A briefing prepared for senior government officials at the beginning of July 2001 contained the following language: "Based on a review of all-source reporting over the last five months, we believe that UBL will launch a significant terrorist attack against U.S. and/or Israeli interests in the coming weeks. The attack will be spectacular and designed to inflict mass casualties against U.S. facilities or interests. Attack preparations have been made. Attack will occur with little or no warning";...[89]

Hill also quoted part of the 1995 National Intelligence Estimate on terrorism. The portion on threats to civil aviation was created with the help of the FAA. This portion of the NIE mentioned Project Bojinka, a plot by radical Muslims (led by the mastermind of the 1993 WTC bombing) to, among other things, blow up twelve US airliners in midflight and use hijacked passenger planes to ram US targets, including CIA headquarters, the White House, the Pentagon, and the World Trade Center. Philippine officials uncovered the plot in 1995 and have always claimed that they warned American authorities. Of course, US officials have never acknowledged receiving the warning of this proto-9/11 plot, so Hill's testimony is proof-positive that the FAA and intelligence agencies were fully aware way back in 1995.

Furthermore, Hill quotes a section of the 1995 NIE:

Our review of the evidence...suggests the conspirators were guided in their selection of the method and venue of attack by carefully studying security procedures in place in the region. If terrorists operating in this country [the United States] are similarly methodical, they will identify serious vulnerabilities in the security system for domestic flights.[90]

She then quotes a section of the 1997 update to the 1995 NIE:

Civil aviation remains a particularly attractive target in light of the fear and publicity the downing of an airliner would evoke and the revelations last summer of the U.S. air transport sectors' vulnerabilities.[91]

Allowing yet another portion of a still-classified document to escape the shadowy confines of the intelligence world, Hill quotes from "The 11 September Attacks: A Preliminary Assessment," dated November 19, 2001. This analysis was written by the CIA:

We do not know the process by which Bin Ladin and his

lieutenants decided to hijack planes with the idea of flying them into buildings in the United States, but *the idea of hijacking planes for suicide attacks had long been current in jihadist circles.*[92]

Having read these revelations (and there's plenty more in Hill's testimony and elsewhere), reacquaint yourself with these claims from two administration bigwigs.

National Security Adviser Condoleezza Rice: "I don't think anybody could have predicted that these people...would try to use an airplane as a missile, a hijacked airplane as a missile."[93]

> "IN THE FALL OF 1998, THE INTELLIGENCE COMMUNITY RECEIVED INFORMATION CONCERNING A BIN LADIN PLOT INVOLVING AIRCRAFT IN THE NEW YORK AND WASHINGTON, DC AREAS."

White House Spokesman Ari Fleischer: "There was...an awareness by the government, including the president, of Osama bin Laden and the threat he posed in the United States and around the world. That included long-standing speculation about hijacking in the traditional sense, but not involving suicide bombers using airplanes as missiles."[94]

_THE JOINT INQUIRY'S FINAL REPORT

In early December 2002, the Joint Inquiry released its final report. Or, more accurately, it released a sliver of its final report. The public got to see nine pages of findings and fifteen pages of recommendations—24 pages of a 450-page report. The rest is classified, and no one holds much hope for seeing it released.

Still, the 5 percent that was released contains a few revealing nuggets, including:

4. <u>Finding</u>: From at least 1994, and continuing into the summer of 2001, the Intelligence Community received information indicating that terrorists were contemplating, among other means of attack, the use of aircraft as weapons. This information did not stimulate any specific Intelligence Community assessment of, or collective U.S. Government reaction to, this form of threat.

....

5.g. The Joint Inquiry confirmed that at least some of the hijackers were not as isolated during their time in the United States as has been previously suggested. Rather, they maintained a number of contacts both in the United States and abroad during this time period. Some of those contacts were with individuals who were known to the FBI, through either past or, at the time, ongoing FBI inquiries and investigations. Although it is not known to what extent any of these contacts in the United States were aware of the plot, it is now clear that they did provide at least some of the hijackers with substantial assistance while they were living in this country.

....

5.i. Prior to September 11, the Intelligence Community had information linking Khalid Shaykh Mohammed (KSM), now recognized by the Intelligence Community as the mastermind of the attacks, to Bin Ladin, to terrorist plans to use aircraft as weapons, and to terrorist activity in the United States.

....

17. Finding: Despite intelligence reporting from 1998 through the summer of 2001 indicating that Usama Bin Ladin's terrorist network intended to strike inside the United States, the United States Government did not undertake a comprehensive effort to implement defensive measures in the United States.[95]

_MORE WARNINGS

In my article "September 11, 2001: No Surprise,"[96] I detail many warnings that the 9/11 attacks were going to occur. This includes alerts from several other countries, including Russia, Israel, and Germany. Since I wrote that article, further foreign warnings have been revealed.

> "FROM AT LEAST 1994, AND CONTINUING INTO THE SUMMER OF 2001, THE INTELLIGENCE COMMUNITY RECEIVED INFORMATION INDICATING THAT TERRORISTS WERE CONTEMPLATING, AMONG OTHER MEANS OF ATTACK, THE USE OF AIRCRAFT AS WEAPONS."

The International Herald Tribune reported that Jordan's intelligence service, the GID, had sent such a warning:

Sometime in the summer of 2001 GID headquarters in Amman, Jordan, made a communications intercept deemed so important that King Abdullah's men relayed its contents to Washington, probably through the CIA station at the U.S. Embassy in Amman.

To be doubly sure that the message got through, it was passed through an Arab intermediary to an Iranian-born German intelligence agent who was visiting Amman at the time.

The text stated clearly that a major attack was planned inside the continental United States. It said aircraft would be used. But neither hijacking, nor, apparently, precise timing nor targets were named. The code name of the operation was mentioned: in Arabic, Al Ourush al Kabir, "The Big Wedding."[97]

The author of that article directly confirmed this with "senior Jordanian officials." In the same article, the Tribune relates news reports of a warning from Morocco:

As for the Moroccan case, last November a French magazine and a Moroccan newspaper simultaneously reported a story that has since met a wall of silence.

The reports said that a Moroccan secret agent named Hassan Dabou succeeded in infiltrating Al Qaeda. Several weeks before Sept. 11, the story ran, he informed his chiefs in King Mohammed VI's royal intelligence service that Osama bin Laden's men were preparing "large-scale operations in New York in the summer or autumn of 2001." The warning was said to have been passed on to Washington.[98]

The New York Times adds Egypt to the list:

Egyptian intelligence warned American officials about a week before Sept. 11 that Osama bin Laden's network was in the advance stages of executing a significant operation against an American target, President Hosni Mubarak said in an interview on Sunday.

Using a secret agent they had recruited who was in close contact with the bin Laden organization, Mr. Mubarak said, his intelligence chiefs tried unsuccessfully to halt the operation.[99]

But you haven't heard anything yet. The US was warned by the Taliban. The Independent of London broke the story:

Weeks before the terrorist attacks on 11 September, the United States and the United Nations ignored warnings from a secret Taliban emissary that Osama bin Laden was planning a huge attack on American soil.

The warnings were delivered by an aide of Wakil Ahmed Muttawakil, the Taliban Foreign Minister at the time, who was known to be deeply unhappy with the foreign militants in Afghanistan, including Arabs.

Mr Muttawakil, now in American custody, believed the Taliban's protection of Mr bin Laden and the other al-Qa'ida militants would lead to nothing less than the destruction of Afghanistan by the US military. He told his aide: "The guests are going to destroy the guesthouse."

The minister then ordered him to alert the US and the UN about what was going to happen. But in a massive failure of intelligence, the message was disregarded because of what sources describe as "warning fatigue".[100]

Former Colorado Sen. Gary Hart said in an interview on WABC Radio that he warned National Security Adviser Condoleezza Rice of an attack days before 9/11:

After giving a speech on the terrorist threat in Montreal on Sept. 5, Hart said he requested an urgent meeting with Dr. Rice in Washington.

"I said to her, 'You must move more quickly on homeland security. An attack is going to happen.'

"That was Sept. 6, 2001," Hart told WABC, without characterizing Dr. Rice's reaction.[101]

In the days and weeks after the attacks, how many times were we told that US intelligence had failed to penetrate the shadowy, amorphous al Qaeda? That's why it was pretty surprising to read this in the *Boston Globe* on the opening day of congressional hearings into the attacks:

American agents had infiltrated Al Qaeda and had raw information prior to Sept. 11 that the terrorist group was planning a large-scale attack, according to a US intelligence official.

The disclosures are contained in some 400,000 pages of documents the CIA has made available to the House and Senate intelligence committees, which together are investigating national security breakdowns that may have kept authorities from anticipating the attacks.[102]

However, according to this official and an article in *USA Today*, these agents didn't know specifically about 9/11.[103]

Then there's the infamous August 6 briefing memo, which was widely covered by the mainstream media in May 2002. The *Washington Post* reported:

The top-secret briefing memo presented to President Bush on Aug. 6 [2001] carried the headline, "Bin Laden Determined to Strike in U.S.," and was primarily focused on recounting al Qaeda's past efforts to attack and infiltrate the United States, senior administration officials said.

The document, known as the President's Daily Briefing, underscored that Osama bin Laden and his followers hoped to "bring the fight to America," in part as retaliation for U.S. missile strikes on al Qaeda camps in Afghanistan in 1998, according to knowledgeable sources.[104]

The next day, the *Post* additionally revealed: "White House officials acknowledged last week that President Bush was provided a written briefing on Aug. 6 stating that bin Laden and his followers had discussed the possibility of hijacking U.S. airplanes."[105]

Newsweek put it in perspective:

Because Bush has long insisted he had no inkling of the attacks, the disclosures touched off a media stampede in a capital long deprived of scandal. The fact that the nation's popular war president might have been warned a little over a month before September 11—and that the supposedly straight-talking Bushies hadn't told anyone about it—opened up a serious credibility gap for the first time in the war on terror.[106]

It would appear that all of these warnings didn't go completely unnoticed by those whose job is to protect the US. Again, we read in *Newsweek*:

[Condoleezza] Rice also disclosed that during the course of last summer, the Federal Aviation Administration issued several "information circulars" warning the aviation industry of possible terror attacks. NEWSWEEK has learned that as many as 10 to 12 such warnings were issued to all U.S. airlines and major airports in the period between June 2001 and September 11. According to sources who have read them, more than two of the warnings specifically mentioned the possibility of hijackings.[107]

And the *New York Times* disclosed this stunning revelation:

The Central Intelligence Agency warned its stations around the world in August 2001 that Zacarias Moussaoui had been arrested in Minnesota after raising suspicion at a flight school there and that he was a *"suspect airline suicide hijacker"*...[108]

And we're still supposed to believe that the authorities didn't have the foggiest notion of what was brewing?

_TOP OFFICIALS ADMIT 9/11 WAS PREVENTABLE

After reading about all of these warnings, if you're thinking that 9/11 could've been prevented, you're not alone. A lot of top US officials feel the same way. Unfortunately, their remarks appear in isolated instances, quickly surfacing and fading away. They're gathered here for the first time.

> "WEEKS BEFORE THE TERRORIST ATTACKS ON 11 SEPTEMBER, THE UNITED STATES AND THE UNITED NATIONS IGNORED WARNINGS FROM A SECRET TALIBAN EMISSARY THAT OSAMA BIN LADEN WAS PLANNING A HUGE ATTACK ON AMERICAN SOIL."

As noted in my article "September 11, 2001: No Surprise," when *Parade* magazine asked Defense Secretary Donald Rumsfeld why the US was caught so flat-footed, without any warnings, he amazingly replied: "There were lots of warnings."[109]

It took Robert Mueller eight months to admit it—and then he said it in a confusing way—but even the head G-man had to come clean. The *New York Times* informs us:

The director of the F.B.I., Robert S. Mueller III, acknowledged today for the first time that the attacks of Sept. 11 might have been preventable if officials in his agency had responded differently to all the pieces of information that were available.

"I cannot say for sure that there wasn't a possibility we could have come across some lead that would have led us to the hijackers," Mr. Mueller told reporters after listing several missed opportunities by officials to discern a pattern of terrorist planning before Sept. 11.

He also said that while there was no specific warning, "that doesn't mean that there weren't red flags out there, that there weren't dots that should have been connected to the extent possible."[110]

At a commencement speech at Seton Hall Law School, Assistant Attorney General Michael Chertoff—described by the Associated Press as "the Bush administration's top anti-terrorism prosecutor"—said: "As of Sept. 10th, each of us knew everything we needed to know to tell us there was a possibility of what happened on Sept. 11th."[111]

> "I DON'T BELIEVE ANY LONGER THAT IT'S A MATTER OF CONNECTING THE DOTS. I THINK THEY HAD A VERITABLE BLUEPRINT, AND WE WANT TO KNOW WHY THEY DIDN'T ACT ON IT."
> —SENATOR ARLEN SPECTER

Then we have this choice quote from Senator Bob Graham, who at the time was the Chairman of the Senate Select Committee on Intelligence, as well as the co-chairman of the joint panel investigating 9/11:

Had one human being or a common group of human beings sat down with all that information, we could have gotten to the hijackers before they flew those four airplanes either into the World Trade Center, the Pentagon or the ground of Pennsylvania.[112]

But Graham is a Democrat, so this must be a politically-motivated statement to make the Bush Administration look bad, right? Then how to explain the remarks of the *Republican* co-chairman of the joint panel, Representative Porter J. Goss? The Congressman is also Chairman of the House Permanent Select Committee on Intelligence. He said:

Should we have known? Yes, we should have. Could we have known? Yes, I believe we could have because of the hard targets [CIA operatives were tracking].[113]

For another similar opinion, we turn to Senator Richard Shelby, who was the ranking Republican on the Senate Intelligence Committee: "They don't have any excuse because the information was in their lap and they didn't do anything to prevent it."[114]

Senator Arlen Specter was another Republican on the joint committee. After it had held one of its numerous closed-door sessions, Specter told CBS News:

I don't believe any longer that it's a matter of connect-

ing the dots. I think they had a veritable blueprint, and we want to know why they didn't act on it.[115]

Even Vice President Dick Cheney got in on the act, telling interviewer Larry King: "If you put all those pieces together, I don't say you could have prevented September 11th, but there might have been some warning, had it been handled properly."[116]

Of course, this Clintonian mincing of words begs the question: If there could've been "some warning," why *couldn't* the attacks have been "prevented"? But we can forgive Cheney for this *non sequitur*; he undoubtedly admitted more than he meant to during the live interview.

So if anyone gives you a hard time for believing that the government knew enough to have prevented the attacks, just tell them that you're in powerful company. The Secretary of Defense, the Director of the FBI, the Assistant Attorney General, one Democratic Senator, two Republican Senators, one Republican Representative, and the Vice President feel that way, too.

_MOST THINK BUSH HIDING KNOWLEDGE OF 9/11

In May 2002—amid a surprising flurry of mainstream news reports about how much the government knew in advance—CBS News polled 681 adults at random across the US. Asked the question, "Is [the] Administration telling the public all it knew before 9/11?," 65 percent of the respondents said the Administration is "hiding something," and 8 percent said the Administration is "lying." Just 21 percent of respondents thought the Administration was "telling the entire truth." When you add up the people who said "hiding" or "lying," 73 percent—almost three-fourths—believe we're being kept in the dark about the government's foreknowledge.[117]

_SAVING THEIR OWN SKINS

Scattered throughout the mainstream media, we find mentions of concrete steps that authorities took, mainly to save their own skins, in the hours, days, and months before September 11, 2001.

Attorney General John Ashcroft stopped flying on commercial aircraft the summer before the attacks. Attorneys General fly in commercial airplanes. Janet Reno did. John Ashcroft did. That is, he did up until July 2001. When CBS News asked why Ashcroft suddenly had started flying in leased private jets, an FBI spokesman said, "There was a threat assessment and there are guidelines. He is acting under the guidelines." The FBI, the Justice Department, and Ashcroft himself all refused to say what the threat was.[118]

The FAA refused to let author Salman Rushdie fly in North America starting the week before 9/11. From the *Times* of London: "On September 3 the Federal Aviation Authority made an emergency ruling to prevent Mr Rushdie from flying unless airlines complied with strict and costly security measures. Mr Rushdie told *The Times* that the airlines would not upgrade their security." The FAA confirmed that it had banned Rushdie from flying in the US and Canada but refused to say why. The author himself—who is famously hated by Muslims for his novel *The Satanic Verses*—says he believes the authorities knew the attack was coming.[119]

"ON SEPT. 10, *NEWSWEEK* HAS LEARNED, A GROUP OF TOP PENTAGON OFFICIALS SUDDENLY CANCELED TRAVEL PLANS FOR THE NEXT MORNING, APPARENTLY BECAUSE OF SECURITY CONCERNS."

Four days before the attacks, Florida Governor Jeb Bush activated the National Guard, citing "terrorism." On September 7, 2001, President Bush's brother called up Florida's National Guard in order to help in the event of "civil disturbance" and/or "acts of terrorism." This executive order was published on the official Website for the Florida Governor's Office.[120]

From the first issue of *Newsweek* published after the attacks: "On Sept. 10, *Newsweek* has learned, a group of top Pentagon officials suddenly canceled travel plans for the next morning, apparently because of security concerns."[121]

On September 10, 2001, San Francisco's mayor was warned against flying to New York the next morning. Around 10:00 PM on the day before the attacks—not exactly business hours—Mayor Willie Brown was advised to use extreme caution if flying the next morning to New York City. Brown refused to tell the *San Francisco Chronicle* exactly who gave him the prescient warning, citing only "my security people at the airport."[122]

CIA Director George Tenet warned at least some members of Congress of "an imminent attack on the United States of this nature." From National Public Radio's on-the-scene reporting during the attacks:

I spoke with Congressman Ike Skelton—a Democrat from Missouri and a member of the Armed Services Committee—who said that just recently the Director of the CIA warned that there could be an attack—an *imminent* attack—on the United States of this nature. So this is not entirely unexpected."[123]

_FBI AGENTS BLOCKED

Robert Wright and John Vincent, FBI special agents and partners, were told by their superiors to quit tracking a Chicago-based terrorist cell involved with those who bombed two US embassies in Africa. (The official US position, of course, is that al Qaeda was the primary group behind the embassy bombings *and* 9/11.) Wright told ABC News: "September the 11th is a direct result of the incompetence of the FBI's International Terrorism Unit. No doubt about that. Absolutely no doubt about that. You can't know the things I know and not go public."

He says that when he wanted to follow the money trail of the Chicago cell, his supervisor told him, "I think it's just better to let sleeping dogs lie." At one point, a supervisor from FBI headquarters literally yelled: "You will not open criminal investigations. I forbid any of you. You will not open criminal investigations against any of these intelligence subjects."

Mark Flessner, the federal prosecutor based in Chicago, was outraged at the shutting down of such a ripe investigation, telling ABC News: "There were powers bigger than I was in the Justice Department and within the FBI that simply were not going to let it [the building of a criminal case] happen. And it didn't happen."

ABC concludes: "One month after the [9/11] attacks, the U.S. government officially identified al-Kadi—the same man the FBI had ordered Wright and Vincent to leave alone years earlier—as one of bin Laden's important financiers."[124]

_THE ROWLEY MEMO

This leads us to the famous memo sent by 21-year FBI Agent Coleen Rowley to Director Mueller.[125] Published almost in full by *Time*, reported on by every major news outlet, and the subject of televised congressional hearings, this memo doesn't need too much explanation here. One May 21, 2002, Rowley, based in Minneapolis, wrote that her office desperately tried to get FBI headquarters to put through a warrant to search Moussaui's belongings, including his computer. The field agents were consistently rejected and, feeling that Moussaui represented an imminent danger, they completely broke with protocol and warned the CIA directly.

What *does* need further elaboration are the exact charges in Rowley's thirteen-page memo. A lot of the media coverage mischaracterized her accusations. In fact, this slanting even took place during the congressional inquiry. The Senators asking the questions, as well as Rowley herself, consistently focused on the bureaucratic culture of the FBI—its aversion to risk, its timidity. The Senators also wailed about the lack of info-sharing and the outdated computers used by the FBI. What they studiously avoided was the actual language Rowley used in her memo.

In it, she says that the "Supervisory Special Agent (SSA) who was the one most involved in the Moussaoui matter...seemed to have been consistently, almost deliberately thwarting the Minneapolis FBI agents' efforts."

Further, she wrote: "Even after the attacks had begun, the SSA in question was still attempting to block the search of Moussaoui's computer..."

Here are some more excerpts:

The fact is that key FBIHQ personnel whose job it was to assist and coordinate with field division agents on terrorism investigations and the obtaining and use of FISA searches (and who theoretically were privy to many more sources of intelligence information than field division agents), continued to, almost inexplicably, throw up roadblocks and undermine Minneapolis' by-now desperate efforts to obtain a FISA search warrant, long after the French intelligence service provided its information and probable cause became clear. HQ personnel brought up almost ridiculous questions in their apparent efforts to undermine the probable cause....

When, in a desperate 11th hour measure to bypass the FBIHQ roadblock, the Minneapolis Division undertook to directly notify the CIA's Counter Terrorist Center (CTC), FBIHQ personnel actually chastised the Minneapolis agents for making the direct notification without their approval!...

My only comment is that the process of allowing the FBI supervisors to make changes in affidavits is itself fundamentally wrong...

I understand that the failures of the FBIHQ personnel involved in the Moussaoui matter are also being officially excused because they were too busy with other investigations, the Cole bombing and other important terrorism matters, but the Supervisor's taking of the time to read each word of the information submitted by Minneapolis and then substitute his own choice of wording belies to some extent the notion that he was too busy....

We just wanted to make sure the information got to the proper prosecutive authorities and was not further suppressed!...

We were prevented from even attempting to question Moussaoui on the day of the attacks when, in theory, he could have possessed further information about other co-conspirators....

> "JOKES WERE ACTUALLY MADE THAT THE KEY FBIHQ PERSONNEL HAD TO BE SPIES OR MOLES, LIKE ROBERT HANSEN, WHO WERE ACTUALLY WORKING FOR OSAMA BIN LADEN TO HAVE SO UNDERCUT MINNEAPOLIS' EFFORT." —FBI AGENT COLEEN ROWLEY

During the early aftermath of September 11th, when I happened to be recounting the pre-September 11th events concerning the Moussaoui Investigation to other FBI personnel in other divisions or in FBIHQ, almost everyone's first question was "Why?—Why would an FBI agent(s) deliberately sabotage a case? (I know I shouldn't be flippant about this, but jokes were actually made that the key FBIHQ personnel had to be spies or moles, like Robert Hansen, who were actually working for Osama Bin Laden to have so undercut Minneapolis' effort.)...

Although the last thing the FBI or the country needs now is a witch hunt, I do find it odd that (to my knowledge) no inquiry whatsoever was launched of the relevant FBIHQ personnel's actions a long time ago. Despite FBI leaders' full knowledge of all the items mentioned herein (and probably more that I'm unaware of), the SSA, his unit chief, and other involved HQ personnel were allowed to stay in their positions and, what's worse, occupy critical positions in the FBI's SIOC Command Center post September 11th. (The SSA in question actually received a promotion some months afterward!)...

In the day or two following September 11th, you, Director Mueller, made the statement to the effect that if the FBI had only had any advance warning of the attacks, we (meaning the FBI), may have been able to take some action to prevent the tragedy. Fearing that this statement could easily come back to haunt the FBI upon revelation of the information that had been developed pre-September 11th about Moussaoui, I and others in the Minneapolis Office, immediately sought to reach your office through an assortment of higher level FBIHQ contacts, in order to quickly make you aware of the background of the Moussaoui investigation and forewarn you so that your public statements could be accordingly modified. When such statements from you and other FBI officials continued, we thought that somehow you had not received the message and we made further efforts. Finally when similar comments were made weeks later, in Assistant Director Caruso's congressional testimony in response to the first public leaks about Moussaoui we faced the sad realization that the remarks indicated someone, possibly with your approval, had decided to circle the wagons at FBIHQ in an apparent effort to protect the FBI from embarrassment and the relevant FBI officials from scrutiny. Everything I have seen and heard about the FBI's official stance and the FBI's internal preparations in anticipation of further congressional inquiry, had, unfortunately, confirmed my worst suspicions in this regard. After the details began to emerge concerning the pre-September 11th investigation of Moussaoui, and subsequently with the recent release of the information about the Phoenix EC, your statement has changed. The official statement is now to the effect that even if the FBI had followed up on the Phoenix lead to conduct checks of flight schools and the Minneapolis request to search Moussaoui's personal effects and laptop, nothing would have changed and such actions certainly could not have prevented the terrorist attacks and resulting loss of life. With all due respect, this statement is as bad as the first! It is also quite at odds with the earlier statement (which I'm surprised has not already been pointed out by those in the media!) I don't know how you or anyone at FBI Headquarters, no matter how much genius or prescience you may possess, could so blithely make this affirmation without anything to back the opinion up than your stature as FBI Director....

You do have some good ideas for change in the FBI but I think you have also not been completely honest about some of the true reasons for the FBI's pre-September 11th failures.

Regarding "a series of e-mails between Minneapolis and FBIHQ," Rowley wrote that they "suggest that the FBIHQ SSA deliberately further undercut the FISA effort..." In the same paragraph, she mentions that "these events [were] characterized in one Minneapolis agent's e-mail as FBIHQ is 'setting this up for failure.'" In a footnote, she says "the SSA continued to find new reasons to stall."

During the congressional hearings on this matter (and in a lot of the related media coverage), we were given the impression that the reasons for failing to act on Moussaui were passive in nature. The FBI had a blindspot that caused it to benignly overlook the information from Minneapolis.

But by reading Rowley's actual memo, we see that this was not a passive nonaction but, instead, was a series of repeated, deliberate actions. Just look at the language she uses: "consistently, almost deliberately thwarting," "attempting to block," "throw up roadblocks and undermine," "apparent efforts to undermine," "substitute his own choice of wording," "suppressed," "prevented," "undercut," "stall," "protect...the relevant FBI officials from scrutiny," "deliberately further undercut," "setting this up for failure," and "deliberately sabotage."

(For more on how and why the FBI and intelligence agencies were actively forbidden to investigate Islamic terrorist networks, see the work of Greg Palast: his article in this anthology, "Exile on Mainstream"; his book, *The Best Democracy Money Can Buy* (Penguin, 2003); and his Website <www.gregpalast.com>.)

_REWARDING A JOB WELL DONE

Much has been made of the fact that no one has been held accountable for 9/11. No heads have rolled; no one has been fired or even been given a public tongue-lashing. The buck apparently doesn't stop anywhere anymore.

But there are a couple of known instances where those responsible have been *rewarded*. As Rowley mentions in her memo, the unnamed Supervisory Special Agent at FBI headquarters who played the lead role in "undermining" and "undercutting" the investigation of Moussaoui received a promotion.

> NO HEADS HAVE ROLLED; NO ONE HAS BEEN FIRED OR EVEN BEEN GIVEN A PUBLIC TONGUE-LASHING. THE BUCK APPARENTLY DOESN'T STOP ANYWHERE ANYMORE.

Also, Marion "Spike" Bowman is the head of the FBI's National Security Law Unit, which refused to seek a warrant to search Moussaui's computer and other belongings. On December 4, 2002, he was given an FBI award for "exceptional performance," which includes "cash bonuses of 20 percent or 35 percent of each recipi-ent's base salary and a framed certificate signed by the president." In an internal announcement, FBI Director Mueller said that the recipients "are strongly linked to our counter-terrorism efforts."[126]

_THE 9/11 COMMISSION

Bush and Cheney both opposed an independent commission. They wanted the matter to be handled solely by Congress' intelligence committees.[127]

Once public pressure became too great (including pressure from families who lost loved ones in the attacks), the Administration suddenly said that it supported such a probe, pretending that it had always felt this way.

The National Commission on Terrorist Attacks, as it's officially called, was hobbled from its creation. It was given a year and a half to do its job, starting in late November 2002. The first meeting didn't take place until the last week of January, meaning that it had squandered two precious months.

The total budget allotted to it is a paltry $3 million. As the Associated Press cuttingly observed: "By comparison, a federal commission created in 1996 got two years and $5 million to study legalized gambling."[128]

When the commission was formed, Bush appointed master cover-up artist Henry Kissinger—wanted in several countries for questioning about war crimes and assassinations—to lead it. As one commentator noted, Kissinger should be the *subject* of a probe, not the head of one. (Kissinger soon stepped down, citing conflicts of interest with clients of his consulting firm.)

Finally, the big day was drawing near. The first meeting of the probe. But the week before, the panel announced that its maiden meeting was closed to the public. Then it announced that its second meeting would be off-limits. (The law creating the commission states that it should hold public hearings "to the extent appropriate.") Surely this is a harbinger of things to come.[129]

_BLOCKING INFORMATION RELEASE

The federal government has done its best to prevent the release of information about 9/11. Bush and Cheney personally interceded by asking Senator Daschle to kneecap Congress' inquiries into the matter. They originally opposed the formation of an independent commission to investigate the attacks. When the probe was formed, officials made sure it was hobbled by a piddling budget, a short timeframe, and a compromised leader.

The FAA, FBI, CIA, and NSA have all refused to comply with my Freedom of Information Act request for any material having to do with communications from the four flights. Likewise, the Air Force has deep-sixed my FOIA request for the procedures for intercepting hijacked planes that were in place on the morning of 9/11.

But the blockade efforts don't end there. The *New York Times* sued the administration of New York City Mayor Michael Bloomsberg for access to documents, including "audiotapes of the Fire Department dispatchers, hundreds of individual accounts of firefighters or transcripts of radio communications from that day."[130] The city refused to release the material, using the excuses that it would somehow interfere with the proceedings against Moussaui and that it would violate the privacy of the individuals involved and/or their families. Later, the Port Authority of New York and New Jersey released the firefighters' tapes to the *Times* (which published a few snippets from them), and at least some of the tapes of 911 calls were given to the media. Eventually, State Supreme Court Justice Richard Braun ruled that the city had to turn over almost all of the requested documents. The city filed an appeal.[131]

In another, more far-reaching effort to prevent release of material about the attacks, the *New York Post* reports:

Families of victims killed in the Sept. 11 terror attacks who are suing the airlines are facing a government attempt to stymie their cases, The Post has learned.

A letter from the U.S. attorney's office asks a federal judge to temporarily stop the families' lawyers from seeking any documents in the suits filed in Manhattan federal court against United Air Lines and American Airlines.

The letter, obtained by The Post, argues that the discovery of documents raises "grave national security concerns" and warns that the federal government will "intervene in these cases," even though it is not a party.[132]

About two weeks later, the federal judge overseeing the lawsuits "granted the Justice Department a role in reviewing—and potentially withholding—information requested in Sept. 11 injury and death lawsuits against airlines," the Associated Press reported. "The judge asked the parties to set up a committee structure to review information to determine what could be released as part of pretrial discovery. Hellerstein did not specify the composition of the committees."[133]

_US REFUSES TO HELP IN FIRST 9/11 TRIAL

To date, there has been only one trial of a person suspected of taking part in the 9/11 attacks. Mounir El Motassadeq, from Morocco, went on trial in Germany in October 2002. He was charged with 3,000 counts of aiding and abetting murder, related to his alleged role as paymaster for the Hamburg terrorist cell, supposedly led by Mohamed Atta. (As of January 2003, the trial is still in progress.)

Now, if you think that the US would be eager to help prosecute the first suspected 9/11 terrorist facing trial, you're in for a rude awakening. Cooperation has not been forthcoming.

Twice the Hamburg court asked FBI Director Mueller to testify in the case. Twice the Department of Justice flatly refused.

More than once, the court requested that alleged conspirator Ramzi bin al-Shaibah, currently "detained" at an undisclosed facility in the US, be allowed to testify. Each time, the US has refused. [134]

So much for the widespread promises of justice for the victims and their loved ones.

_SO MANY QUESTIONS, SUCH LITTLE TIME

There's so much more that needs to be addressed, but limitations prevent it. Here, briefly, are a few of the more crucial issues that need further investigation.

Who bought a huge number of puts on airlines (particularly United and American), cruise lines, insurance companies, and big businesses headquartered in the Twin Towers (including Morgan Stanley and Bank of America) in the two weeks before 9/11?

What is the exact nature of Osama bin Laden's relationship with the CIA? The Agency trained him as part of the Muslim resistance to the Soviet invasion of Afghanistan. Did this relationship ever end?

We've been led to believe that the US was unprepared, unable, and incapable of scrambling jets in anything resembling a competent manner on 9/11. Then how did the military manage to scramble "fighter jets to chase suspicious aircraft" *67 times* in the period from September 2000 to June 2001?[135] That's an average of one scramble per week.

The South Tower was hit second, yet it collapsed first. From the time the South Tower was struck to the time it fell, 56 minutes passed. Yet one hour and 42 minutes elapsed from strike to collapse of the North Tower. Why such a huge difference? The discrepancy is even more peculiar when you realize that the North Tower endured a straight-on hit that plowed deep into the heart of the building, while Flight 175 struck the South Tower at an angle, just hitting a corner. This caused most of the jet fuel to flood out of the building, resulting in the spectacular fireball we saw so many times.

> "FAMILIES OF VICTIMS KILLED IN THE SEPT. 11 TERROR ATTACKS WHO ARE SUING THE AIRLINES ARE FACING A GOVERNMENT ATTEMPT TO STYMIE THEIR CASES."

Why Were Vice President Cheney and White House staff given cipro—the antidote to anthrax—on 9/11, three weeks before the first victim of the anthrax mailings came to light?[136]

Had agents of Israel's intelligence service, Mossad, been tailing the hijackers and, thus, did they know of the planned attacks? Convincing evidence of this scenario has been presented by Fox News, *Jane's Defense*, Salon, the BBC, *Forward* (a Jewish magazine), and several highly-respected non-English publications, including *Die Zeit*, *Der Spiegel*, and *Le Monde*. A leaked DEA report confirmed that dozens of Israelis—some with military and intelligence backgrounds—had been posing as "art students" and conniving their way into unmarked, non-public offices of federal agencies. Many them were clustered in the small town of Hollywood, Florida, blocks away from a cell of the 9/11 terrorists, including Mohamed Atta. These "students" were questioned and quietly deported.[137]

What was that strange, cylindrical object that arced past the WTC right as Flight 175 hit the South Tower? It's clearly visible in at least two videos of the impact. One angle, taken by Gamma Press and broadcast on Fox News, shows the object appearing from behind the buildings.

Gamma Press—which caught the only footage of the first plane strike—also filmed the second hit. When broadcast on Fox News, a cylindrical object could be seen moving past the towers as Flight 175 hit the South Tower.
CREDIT: Gamma Press USA and Fox News

The other angle, broadcast in Japan (and perhaps elsewhere), gives a more panoramic view from the other side of the towers. It is beyond doubt that the object is not part of the plane or part of the building. In this long shot, the plane has almost hit the South Tower when the object appears on the far right of the screen. It forms a gentle arc, passing the Twin Towers right as Flight 175 hits its target. The object passes alongside the buildings, reaches its apex, then begins to slowly descend as it disappears off the left side of the screen.

In this still-frame from video broadcast in Japan, we see Flight 175 (above white arrow) about to hit the South Tower.

As the plane moves even closer to the tower, the object appears on the far right of the screen (above white arrow).

THEN HOW DID THE MILITARY MANAGE TO SCRAMBLE "FIGHTER JETS TO CHASE SUSPICIOUS AIRCRAFT" *67 TIMES* IN THE PERIOD FROM SEPTEMBER 2000 TO JUNE 2001?

The object (above white arrow) is a little further along.

Flight 175 is impacting the tower as object (above white arrow) moves closer.

Object (above white arrow) has now passed the Twin Towers.

Object (above white arrow) continues.

Object (above white arrow) continues as explosion from Flight 175's impact barely becomes visible.

Explosion in South Tower is now clearly visible as object has left screen.

How could anyone have found the intact passport of hijacker Satam al Suqami among the millions and millions of pieces of paper and other debris from the WTC site? This is exactly what the government claims happened three days after the attacks.

Why is it that the black boxes of the two WTC flights were never recovered and considered destroyed? They're built to withstand even more punishment than they received.

The current head of the independent probe of 9/11, Thomas Kean, has been involved in business deals that also involve a brother-in-law of Osama bin Laden. This man, Khalid bin Mahfouz, is suspected by authorities of financing al Qaeda.[138]

"THEY KNEW THIS BUILDING WAS A TARGET. OVER THE PAST FEW WEEKS WE'D BEEN EVACUATED A NUMBER OF TIMES, WHICH IS UNUSUAL."

Let's hear more about what Ben Fountain—"a financial analyst with Fireman's Fund" who worked in the South Tower—told *People* magazine: "How could they let this happen? They knew this building was a target. Over the past few weeks we'd been evacuated a number of times, which is unusual. I think they had an inkling something was going on."[139]

What caused the collapse of the 47-story World Trade Center Building 7? The *New York Times* wrote: "The 2 million-square-foot building, 7 World Trade Center, had suffered mightily from the fire, and had been wounded by beams falling off the towers. But experts said no building like it, a modern, steel-reinforced high-rise, had ever collapsed because of an uncontrolled fire."[140]

The Unanswered Questions Website[141] raises another crucial concern: "According to published and confirmed mainstream reports Mohammed Atta was wired $100,000 by the Pakistani intelligence agency, the ISI, just prior to the attacks. The man who approved this wire, General Mahmud was meeting with top officials of the US government, including Intelligence Committee Chairmen Representative Porter Goss (R-FL) and Senator Bob Graham (D-FL) on the morning of the attacks."

Independent 9/11 researcher Nico Haupt has written a list of 500 questions that deserve to be answered. Among them:

When was it decided to cancel building a pipeline from

Turkmenistan through Afghanistan to Pakistan?

Why did FEMA spokesman Tom Kenney tell Dan Rather he was in New York on Sept. 10?

Why did Clinton abort an attack on Bin Laden in October 1999?

Why did they not let the media or any reporters take video or photos of the [Flight 93] crash site?

Despite the length of this article, there are still plenty more contradictions, impossibilities, unbelievable coincidences, withheld information, inexplicable behavior, ignored anomalies, and—above all—unanswered questions regarding that epochal day. I say we don't rest until we know exactly what happened on 9/11, the days leading up to it, and the days that followed. If it takes our lifetimes or more, so be it.

_POSTSCRIPT: 7 ASTRONAUTS VS. 3,000 PEOPLE

As this book was about to go to press, the space shuttle *Columbia* exploded/disintegrated upon reentry on February 1, 2003.

Amazingly, *two* official investigations were announced *that same day*. NASA and the House of Representatives' Science Committee each said that they would conduct their own investigations.

But it gets even better. On the very day of the disaster, an independent panel was formed and started its investigation.[142]

The *Columbia* debris hadn't even cooled off, and already three official investigations had been formed. And one of them—an independent probe—went to work.

Why wasn't this kind of quick action taken in the case of 9/11? Certainly, it's important to find out what went wrong with the Shuttle so that it doesn't happen again, but isn't it more important to find out what happened on September 11 to make sure nothing like *that* ever happens again?

The loss of seven astronauts is definitely a tragedy. But what about the loss of 3,000 people? Those killed on 9/11 include 319 firefighters, 50 law enforcement personnel, 89 military personnel, and five civilian pilots. If seven astronauts rate three separate investigations on the day they're killed, don't all these people?

Yet it took *five months* before the Senate and House Intelligence Committees announced the formation of their joint inquiry into the attacks. It was almost another four months until the inquiry held hearings.[143]

Even worse, an independent panel was established to investigate 9/11 over *one year and two months* after the attacks. It would be an additional two months before the panel would hold its first meeting. (The head of the panel, Thomas Kean, told the Associated Press that these first meetings would be concerned with "logistics," such as finding office space.)[144]

IT TOOK CONGRESS FIVE MONTHS TO SET UP ITS ONE AND ONLY PROBE, AND IT TOOK OVER A YEAR FOR AN INDEPENDENT COMMISSION TO BE AUTHORIZED. YET THESE THINGS HAPPENED WITHIN MERE HOURS OF THE *COLUMBIA* DISASTER.

Some people might try to argue that the investigations of 9/11 couldn't be set up as fast as those for the *Columbia* because the attacks were so disruptive. We were too worried about whether more attacks were coming to set up probes that day. True, but it was soon clear that the country was out of immediate danger. After all, commercial air traffic was fully functional on September 13, just two days after the attacks.

Still, it took Congress five months to set up its one and only probe, and it took over a year for an independent commission to be authorized. Yet these things happened within mere hours of the *Columbia* disaster.

Add to this the various ways the nation's highest officials have hamstrung these inquiries, and it couldn't be more obvious that the authorities don't really want us to know what happened on September 11, 2001.

Endnotes

1. Dwyer, Jim. "In Rescuers' Voices, 9/11 Tape Reveals a Gripping History." *New York Times*, 12 Nov 2002. **2.** Public Broadcasting System. Transcript of *NewsHour with Jim Lehrer*, 11 Dec 2002. **3.** Bull, Chris, and Sam Erman. *At Ground Zero: 25 Stories From Young Reporters Who Were There.* New York: Thunder's Mouth Press, 2002: 184. **4.** The Newseum with Cathy Trost and Alicia C. Shepard. *Running Toward Danger: Stories Behind the Breaking News of 9/11.* Lanham, MD: Rowman & Littlefield Publishers, 2002: 87. **5.** *Ibid.*: 91. **6.** *Ibid.*: 92. **7.** *Ibid.*: 93. **8.** Unsigned. "Our Heroes." People.com, 12 Sept 2001. **9.** *Op cit.*, Newseum: 119. **10.** *Ibid.*: 239. **11.** *Ibid.*: 203. **12.** Bollyn, Christopher. "Unexplained 9-11 Explosion at WTC Complex." *American Free Press*, 14 July 2002. **13.** Unsigned. "Moment of Impact at Pentagon." MSNBC, 7 March 2002. **14.** Gertz, Bill, and Rowan Scarborough. "Inside the Ring" (column). *Washington Times*, 21 Sept 2001. **15.** McKelway, Bill. "Three Months On, Tension Lingers Near the Pentagon Bill." *Richmond Times-Dispatch*, 11 Dec 2001. **16.** *Op cit.*, Bull: 281. **17.** *Op cit.*, Newseum: 150. **18.** Spangler, Todd. "United Jet Crashes in Pa.; Passenger Reported Hijacking." Associated Press, 11 Sept 2001. **19.** Fink, Mitchell, and Lois Mathias. *Never Forget: An Oral History of September 11, 2001.* HarperCollins, 2002: 196. **20.** Wallace, Richard. "What Did Happen to Flight 93?" *Daily Mirror* (London), 23 Jan 2003. **21.** *Ibid.* **22.** Bunch, William. "We Know It Crashed, but Not Why." *Philadelphia Daily News*, 15 Nov 2001. **23.** *Op cit.*, Newseum: 148. **24.** Eggen, Dan, and Peter Slevin. "Armed Groups Caught Boarding N.Y. Flights; U.S. Readies for War." *Washington Post*, 14 Sept 2001: A01. **25.** Unsigned. "'Black Box' From Pennsylvania Crash Found." CNN, 13 Sept 2001. **26.** Gibb, Tom, James O'Toole, and Cindi Lash. "Investigators Locate 'Black Box' From Flight 93; Widen Search Area in Somerset Crash." *Pittsburgh Post-Gazette*, 13 Sept 2001. **27.** *Op cit.*, Wallace. **28.** *Op cit.*, Fink: 192. **29.** Longman, Jere. *Among the Heroes: United Flight 93 and the Passengers and Crew Who Fought Back.* HarperCollins, 2002: 108. **30.** Sperry, Paul. "Hijacker Shot Passenger on Flight 11: FAA Memo." WorldNetDaily, 27 Feb 2002. **31.** Sperry, Paul. "American Denies Giving Gun Info to FAA." WorldNetDaily, 27 Feb 2002. **32.** Sperry, Paul. "Did FAA Get Flight 11 Gun Story From FBI?" WorldNetDaily, 27 Feb 2002. **33.** All times are taken from "The Complete 9/11 Timeline" by Paul Thompson, which is a distillation of governmental and mainstream news reports. The timeline is available various places online, including <www.unansweredquestions.org/timeline/> and <www.cooperativeresearch.org/completetimeline/>. Reportedly, it will be released in book form at some point. **34.** <www.emperors-clothes.com>. **35.** See note #33. **36.** "President Meets with Displaced Workers in Town Hall Meeting: Remarks by the President in Town Hall Meeting" (transcript). White House Website, 4 Dec 2001. **37.** "President Holds Town Hall Forum on Economy in California: Remarks by the President in Town Hall Meeting with Citizens of Ontario" (transcript). White House Website, 5 Jan 2002. **38.** See endnote #33. **39.** See endnote #34. **40.** Chen, Edwin. "Bush Fled 'Harm's Way' With 9/11 Flights." *Los Angeles Times*, 22 May 2002. **41.** Donnelly, Sally.

"An Inside Job?" *Time*, 22 Sept 2001. **42.** Kelso, Paul, *et al.* "FBI Believes Plotters Planned to Seize Six Airliners for Attack." *Guardian* (London), 19 Sept 2001. **43.** Hedges, Stephen J. and Naftali Bendavid. "FBI Probes 5th Flight for Hijackers." *Chicago Tribune*, 18 Sept 2001. **44.** *Op cit.*, Donnelly. **45.** Gumbel, Andrew. "Hijack Squads 'Planned to Seize Eight Aircraft.'" *Independent* (London), 25 Sept 2001. **46.** Robinson, Walter V., and Stephen Kurkjian. "Officials Deny 3d Boston Plane Targeted." *Boston Globe*, 23 Sept 2001. **47.** Borger, Julian, and John Hooper. "Evidence of Six Hijacking Teams." *Guardian* (London), 13 Oct 2001. **48.** Unsigned. "Knives Hidden on Air Canada Plane." BBC News, 14 Oct 2001. **49.** *Op cit.*, Gumbel. **50.** Calderone, Joe. "Hijackings May Have Been an Inside Job." *Daily News* (New York), 25 Sept 2001. **51.** *Op cit.*, Donnelly. **52.** Koring, Paul. "5th hijack team may have been thwarted." *Globe and Mail* (Toronto), 15 Sept 2001: A3. **53.** Fletcher, Martin. "Hijack Suspects on Fifth Jet." *Times* (London), 22 Oct 2001. **54.** *Op cit.*, Robinson. **55.** Pate, James L. "Passengers Say Suspicious Flier Had Partners." *Washington Times*, 28 Sept 2001. **56.** *Op cit.*, Eggen, "Armed Groups" **57.** Von Drehle, David. "Bush Pledges Victory; Reagan National Closed Indefinitely." *Washington Post*, 14 Sept 2001: A01. **58.** Unsigned. "Terrorist Hunt." ABCNews.com, 12 Sept 2001. **59.** Eggen, Dan, George Lardner Jr., and Susan Schmidt. "Some Hijackers' Identities Uncertain." *Washington Post*, 20 Sept 2001: A01; Harrison, David. "Revealed: The Men With Stolen Identities." *Daily Telegraph* (London), 23 Sept 2001; Hopkins, Nick. "False Identities Mislead FBI." *Guardian* (London), 21 Sept 2001; Unsigned. "Hijack 'Suspects' Alive and Well." BBC News, 23 Sept 2001. **60.** *Op cit.*, Harrison. **61.** *Ibid.* **62.** Unsigned. "Calm Before the Crash." ABC News, 18 July 2002. **63.** Harkavy, Jerry. "FBI Affidavit: Flight Attendant Made Call To Report Hijacking." Associated Press, 5 Oct 2001. **64.** Unsigned. "The Last Moments of Flight 11." BBC News, 21 Sept 2001. **65.** Lichtblau, Eric. "Aboard Flight 11, a Chilling Voice." *Los Angeles Times*, 20 Sept 2001. **66.** Harkavy, Jerry. "FBI Affidavit: Flight Attendant Made Call To Report Hijacking." Associated Press, 5 Oct 2001. **67.** Unsigned. "One-way Tickets to Hell." *Sydney Morning Herald*, 15 Sept 2001. **68.** Cullen, Kevin, and Ralph Ranalli. "Flight School Says FBI Trailed Suspect Prior To Hijackings." *Boston Globe*, 18 Sept 2001. **69.** *Op cit.*, endnotes #66-68. **70.** Fisk, Robert. "What Muslim Would Write: 'The Time of Fun and Waste Is Gone'?" *Independent* (London), 29 Sept 2001. **71.** "Remarks Prepared for Delivery by Robert S. Mueller III, Director, Federal Bureau of Investigation." FBI Website, 19 April 2002; Lichtblau, Eric, and John Meyer. "U.S. Finds No Paper Trail in Terror Plot." Los Angeles Times Service. *Miami Herald*, 30 April 2002 **72.** Johnston, David, and James Risen. "Officials Say 2 More Jets May Have Been in the Plot." *New York Times*, 19 Sept 2001. **73.** Van Natta, Don, Jr., and Kate Zernike. "Hijackers' Meticulous Strategy of Brains, Muscle and Practice." *New York Times*, 4 Nov 2001. **74.** Wapshott, Nicholas. "Credit Card Trail Reveals Hijackers' Devices." *Times* (London), 24 May 2002. **75.** Fallis, David S., and Ariana Eunjung Cha. "Agents Follow Suspects' Lengthy E-Trail." *Washington Post*, 4 Oct 2001. Emphasis mine. **76.** "Transcript of United Airlines Flight

Focused On Attacks in U.S." *Washington Post*, 18 May 2002: A01. **105.** Eggen, Dan, and Bill Miller. "FBI Memo's Details Raise New Questions." *Washington Post*, 19 May 2002: A01. **106.** Hirsh, Michael, and Michael Isikoff. "What Went Wrong." *Newsweek*, 27 May 2002. **107.** *Ibid.* **108.** Shenon, Philip. "Early Warnings on Moussaoui Are Detailed." *New York Times*, 17 Oct 2002. Emphasis mine. **109.** "Secretary Rumsfeld Interview with Parade Magazine." Defense Department Website, 12 Oct 2001. **110.** Lewis, Neil A. "F.B.I. Chief Admits 9/11 Might Have Been Detectable." *New York Times*, 30 May 2002. **111.** Parry, Wayne. "Official: Many Signs Pointed to 9/11." Associated Press, 1 June 2002. **112.** Miller, Greg. "Congress Fattens Its Dossier on Sept. 11 Intelligence Errors." *Los Angeles Times*, 6 June 2002. **113.** Priest, Dana, and Juliet Eilperin. "'We Should Have' Known, Goss Says of 9/11." *Washington Post*, 12 June 2002: A12. **114.** Coile, Zachary. "Another Dot That Didn't Get Connected." *San Francisco Chronicle*, 3 June 2002. **115.** Sisk, Richard. "FBI, CIA Brass in a Sling." *Daily News* (New York), 6 June 2002. **116.** Unsigned. "Cheney Blasts September 11 Critics." CNN, 23 May 2002. **117.** "Poll: What Did the President Know?" CBS News, 21 May 2002. **118.** Stewart, Jim. "Ashcroft Flying High." CBS News, 25 July 2001. **119.** Doran, James. "Rushdie's Air Ban." *Times* (London), 27 Sept 2001. **120.** Executive Order 01-261, 7 Sept 2001. Taken from the [Florida] Governor's Office Homepage. **121.** Thomas, Evan, and Mark Hoseball. "Bush: 'We're at War'." *Newsweek*, 24 Sept 2001. **122.** Matier, Philip, and Andrew Ross. "Willie Brown Got Low-key Early Warning About Air Travel." *San Francisco Chronicle*, 12 Sept 2001. **123.** Welna, David. Report on Morning Edition. National Public Radio, 11 Sept 2001. (You can hear this clip on my Website <www.thememoryhole.org/tenet-911.htm>.) **124.** Ross, Brian, and Vic Walter. "Called Off the Trail?" ABC News, 19 Dec 2002. **125.** Rowley, Coleen. "Coleen Rowley's Memo to FBI Director Robert Mueller." *Time*, 3 June 2002. **126.** Gordon, Greg. "FBI Lawyer Who Rejected Moussaoui Search Is Given Award." *Star Tribune* (Minneapolis), 18 Dec 2002. **127.** Fournier, Ron. "Bush Opposes Independent Commission to Investigate Pre-Sept. 11 Terror Warnings." Associated Press, 23 May 2002; Holland, Steve. "Bush Opposes Independent September 11 Probe." Reuters, 23 May 2002; Mitchell, Alison. "Cheney Rejects Broader Access to Terror Brief." *New York Times*, 20 May 2002. **128.** Unsigned. "9/11 Panel Faces Time, Money Pressure." Associated Press, 21 Jan 2003. **129.** Unsigned. "Attacks Meeting to Be Closed to Public." Associated Press, 23 Jan 2003. **130.** Steinhauer, Jennifer. "Records of 9/11 Response Not for Public, City Says." *New York Times*, 23 July 2002. **131.** Haberman, Maggie. "FDNY Has to Open WTC Records." *Daily News* (New York), 6 Feb 2003. **132.** Lehmann, John. "Feds Oppose Suits vs. Airlines." *New York Post*, 25 June 2002. **133.** Ibarguen, Diego. "Gov't Role Granted in Sept. 11 Suits." Associated Press, 12 July 2002. **134.** Tanner, Adam. "FBI Head Not to Testify in German Sept 11 Trial." Reuters, 7 Jan 2003. **135.** Unsigned. "Use of Military Jets Jumps Since 9/11." Associated Press, 13 Aug 2002. **136.** Sobieraj, Sandra. "White House Mail Machine Has Anthrax." Associated Press, 23 Oct 2001. **137.** For more on

DESPITE THE LENGTH OF THIS ARTICLE, THERE ARE STILL PLENTY MORE CONTRADICTIONS, IMPOSSIBILITIES, UNBELIEVABLE COINCIDENCES, WITHHELD INFORMATION, INEXPLICABLE BEHAVIOR, IGNORED ANOMALIES, AND—ABOVE ALL—UNANSWERED QUESTIONS REGARDING THAT EPOCHAL DAY.

175." *New York Times*, 16 Oct 2001. **77.** Manning, Bill. "$elling Out the Investigation." *Fire Engineering*, Jan 2002. **78.** Unsigned. "Bush Asks Daschle to Limit Sept. 11 Probes." CNN, 29 Jan 2002. **79.** Hill, Eleanor. "Joint Inquiry Staff Statement, Part One." Presentation to congressional joint inquiry, 18 Sept 2002: 2. **80.** *Ibid.* Emphasis mine. **81.** *Ibid.*: 26. **82.** *Ibid.*: 15. **83.** *Ibid.* **84.** *Ibid.* **85.** *Ibid.*: 17. **86.** *Ibid.*: 16. **87.** *Ibid.*: 16. **88.** *Ibid.* Emphasis mine. **89.** *Ibid.*: 23. **90.** *Ibid.*: 29. **91.** *Ibid.* **92.** *Ibid.*: 30. Emphasis mine. **93.** Woodward, Bob, and Dan Eggen. "Aug. Memo Focused On Attacks in U.S." *Washington Post*, 18 May 2002: A01 **94.** Eggen, Dan, and Bill Miller. "Bush Was Told of Hijacking Dangers." *Washington Post*, 16 May 2002: A01. **95.** "Findings of the Final Report of the Senate Select Committee on Intelligence and the House Permanent Select Committee on Intelligence Joint Inquiry into the Terrorist Attacks of September 11, 2001." Website of the US Senate Committee on Intelligence, 11 Dec 2002. **96.** Kick, Russ. "September 11, 2001: No Surprise." *Everything You Know Is Wrong: The Disinformation Guide to Secrets and Lies*. Russ Kick, ed. New York: The Disinformation Company, 2002. **97.** Cooley, John K. "The U.S. Ignored Foreign Warnings, Too." *International Herald Tribune*, 21 May 2002. **98.** *Ibid.* **99.** Tyler, Patrick E., and Neil MacFarquhar. "Egypt Warned U.S. of a Qaeda Plot, Mubarak Asserts." *New York Times*, 4 June 2002. **100.** Clark, Kate. "Revealed: The Taliban Minister, the US Envoy and the Warning of September 11 That Was Ignored." *Independent* (London), 7 Sept 2002. **101.** Unsigned. "Condoleezza Rice Warned Sept. 6 About Imminent Terror Attack." NewsMax, 29 May 2002. **102.** Milligan, Susan, and Robert Schlesinger. "Panel Sets Wide Scope for Inquiry into 9/11." *Boston Globe*, 5 June 2002. **103.** Diamond, John. "U.S. Had Agents Inside al-Qaeda CIA Turns Over Clues; Hearings Open Today." *USA Today*, 4 June 2002. **104.** Woodward, Bob, and Dan Eggen. "Aug. Memo

this see Justin Raimondo's columns at Antiwar.com <www.antiwar.com/justin/jarchive.html>. Raimondo is due to have a book on the subject published by Verso Books in 2003. Working title: *The Terror Enigma: Israel and the 9/11 Connection*. **138.** Stein, Nicholas. "Five Degrees of Osama." *Fortune*, 22 Jan 2003. **139.** Unsigned. "New York City." People.com, 12 Sept 2001. **140.** Gkanz, James. "Diesel Suspected in 7 WTC Collapse." New York Times News Service. In *Chicago Tribune*, 29 Nov 2001. **141.** <www.unansweredquestions.net>. **142.** Kelley, Matt. "Three Committees to Probe Space Shuttle." Associated Press, 1 Feb 2003. **143.** "Senate and House Intelligence Committees Announce Joint Inquiry into the September 11 Terrorist Attacks." Website of US Senate Committee on Intelligence, 14 Feb 2002. **144.** Unsigned. "First Meeting of US Commission on Terrorist Attacks Will Be Closed to Public." Associated Press, 23 Jan 2003.

WAR AGAINST TERRORISM OR EXPANSION OF THE AMERICAN EMPIRE?

WILLIAM BLUM

This talk was delivered on October 16, 2002, at the University of Colorado in Boulder.

Good evening, it's very nice to be here, especially since the bombs have not yet begun to fall. I mean in Iraq, not Boulder; Boulder comes after Iraq and Iran if you folks don't shape up and stop inviting people like me to speak.

The first time I spoke in public after September 11 of last year, I spoke at a teach-in at the University of North Carolina. As a result of that, I and some of the other speakers were put on a list put out by an organization founded by Lynne Cheney, the wife of you-know-who. The organization's agenda can be neatly surmised by a report it issued, entitled "Defending Our Civilization: How Our Universities are Failing America and What Can Be Done About It." In the report and on their Website, they listed a large number of comments made by mainly faculty and students from many schools which indicated that these people were not warmly embracing America's newest bombing frenzy and were guilty of suggesting that some foreigners might actually have good reason for hating the United States, or what I call "hating US foreign policy."

Because of that listing, as well as things I wrote subsequently, I've gotten a lot of hate mail in the past year, hate email to be exact. I'm waiting to receive my first email with anthrax in it. Well, there are viruses in email—why not bacteria?

I DON'T THINK THAT PATRIOTISM IS ONE OF THE MORE NOBLE SIDES OF MANKIND.

The hate mail almost never challenges any fact or idea I express. They attack me mainly on the grounds of being unpatriotic. They're speaking of some kind of blind patriotism, but even if they had a more balanced view of it, they would still be right about me. I'm not patriotic. I don't want to be patriotic. I'd go so far as to say that I'm patriotically challenged.

Many people on the left, now as in the 1960s, do not want to concede the issue of patriotism to the conservatives. The left insists that they are the real patriots because of demanding that the United States lives up to its professed principles. That's all well and good, but I'm not one of those leftists. I don't think that patriotism is one of the more noble sides of mankind. George Bernard Shaw wrote that patriotism is the conviction that your country is superior to all others because you were born in it. And remember that the German peo-ple who supported the Nazi government can be seen as being patriotic, and the German government called them just that.

The past year has not been easy for people like me, surrounded as we've been by an orgy of patriotism. How does one escape "United We Stand" and "God Bless America"? And the flag—it's just all over. I buy a banana, and there it is, an American flag stuck on it.

And making heroes out of everyone—the mayor of New York, Rudy Giuliani, became a hero. On September 10 he was an arrogant, uncompassionate reactionary—suddenly he was a hero, even a statesman, speaking before the UN. George Bush also became a hero. People who called him a moron on September 10 welcomed him as hero and dictator after the eleventh.

In the play *Galileo*, by Bertolt Brecht, one character says to another: "Unhappy the land that has no heroes."

And the other character replies: "No. Unhappy the land that *needs* heroes."

Although I'm not loyal to any country or government, like most of you I am loyal to certain principles, like political and social justice, economic democracy, human rights.

The moral of my message to you is this: If your heart and mind tell you clearly that the bombing of impoverished, hungry, innocent peasants is a terrible thing to do and will not make the American people any more secure, you should protest it in any way you can, and don't be worried about being called unpatriotic.

There was, sadly, very little protest against the bombing of Afghanistan. I think it was a measure of how the events intimidated people. The events and the expanding police powers, led by Ayatollah John Ashcroft. I think it was also due to the fact that people felt that whatever horrors the bombing caused, it did get rid of some really nasty anti-American terrorists.

But of the thousands in Afghanistan who died from American bombs, how many do you think had any part in the events of 9-11? I'll make a rough guess and say "none." And how many do you think ever took part in any other terrorist act against the United States? We'll never know for sure, but my guess would be a number in the very low one digits, if that. Terrorist acts don't happen very often after all, and usually are carried out by a handful of men. So of all those killed by the American actions, were any of them amongst any of those few handfuls of terrorists, many of whom were already in prison?

And keep in mind that the great majority of those who were at a training camp of al Qaeda in Afghanistan were there to help the Taliban in their civil war—nothing to do with terrorism or the United States. It was a religious mission for them, none of our business. But we killed them or have held them under terrible conditions at the Guantanamo base in Cuba for a very long time now, with no end in sight, with many attempts at suicide there amongst the prisoners.

■■■■■■■■■■

It is remarkable indeed that what we call our government is still going around dropping huge amounts of exceedingly powerful explosives upon the heads of defenseless people. It wasn't supposed to be this way. Beginning in the late 1980s, Mikhail Gorbachev put an end to the Soviet police state; then the Berlin Wall came down and people all over Eastern Europe were joyfully celebrating a *new day*; and South Africa freed Nelson Mandela and apartheid began to crumble; and Haiti held its first free election ever and chose a genuine progressive as president. It seemed like anything was possible; optimism was as widespread as pessimism is today.

And the United States joined this celebration by invading and bombing Panama, only weeks after the Berlin Wall fell.

At the same time, the US was shamelessly intervening in the election in Nicaragua to defeat the Sandinistas.

> THE ENEMY WAS, AND REMAINS, ANY GOVERNMENT OR MOVEMENT, OR EVEN INDIVIDUAL, THAT STANDS IN THE WAY OF THE EXPANSION OF THE AMERICAN EMPIRE; BY WHATEVER NAME WE GIVE TO THE ENEMY—COMMUNIST, ROGUE STATE, DRUG TRAFFICKER, TERRORIST....

Then, when Albania and Bulgaria, "newly freed from the grip of communism," as our media would put it, dared to elect governments not acceptable to Washington, Washington just stepped in and overthrew those governments.

Soon came the bombing of the people of Iraq for 40 horrible days without mercy, for no good or honest reason, and that was that for our hopes of a different and better world. But our leaders were not through. They were soon off attacking Somalia, more bombing and killing.

Meanwhile they continued bombing Iraq for years.

They intervened to put down dissident movements in Peru, Mexico, Ecuador, and Colombia, just as if it was the Cold War in the 1950s in Latin America, and the 1960s, the 1970s, the 1980s, and still doing it in the 1990s.

Then they bombed the people of Yugoslavia for 78 days and nights.

And once again, last year, grossly and openly intervened in an election in Nicaragua to prevent the left from winning.

Meanwhile, of course, they were bombing Afghanistan and in all likelihood have now killed more innocent civilians in that sad country than were killed here on September 11, with more to come, as people will continue to die from bombing wounds, cluster-bomb landmines, and depleted-uranium toxicity.

And all these years, still keeping their chokehold on Cuba.

And that's just a partial list.

There was none of the peace dividend we had been promised, not for Americans nor for the rest of the world.

What the heck is going on here? We had been taught since childhood that the Cold War, including the Korean War, the Vietnam War, the huge military budgets, all the foreign invasions and overthrows of governments—the ones we knew about—we were taught that this was all to fight the same menace: The International Communist Conspiracy, headquarters in Moscow.

So what happened? The Soviet Union was dissolved. The Warsaw Pact was dissolved. The East European satellites became independent. The former communists even became capitalists. And nothing changed in American foreign policy.

Even NATO remained, NATO which had been created—so we were told—to protect Western Europe against a Soviet invasion, even NATO remains, bigger than ever, getting bigger and more powerful all the time, a NATO with a global mission. The NATO charter was even invoked to give a justification for its members to join the US in the Afghanistan invasion.

The whole thing had been a con game. The Soviet Union and something called communism per se had not been the object of our global attacks. There had never been an International Communist Conspiracy. The enemy was, and remains, any government or movement, or even individual, that stands in the way of the expansion of the American Empire; by whatever name we give to the enemy—communist, rogue state, drug trafficker, terrorist....

You think the American Empire is against terrorists? What do you call a man who blows up an airplane, killing 73 people? Who attempts assassinations against several diplomats? Who fires cannons at ships docked in American ports? Who places bombs in numerous commercial and diplomatic buildings in the US and abroad? Dozens of such acts. His name is Orlando Bosch; he's Cuban and he lives in Miami, unmolested by the authorities. The city of Miami once declared a day in his honor—Orlando Bosch Day. He was freed from prison in Venezuela, where he had been held for the airplane bombing, partly because of pressure from the American ambassador, Otto Reich, who earlier this year was appointed to the State Department by George W.

After Bosch returned to the US in 1988, the Justice Department condemned him as a totally violent terrorist and was all set to deport him, but that was blocked by President Bush, the first, with the help of son Jeb Bush in Florida. So is George W. and his family against terrorism? Well, yes, they're against those terrorists who are not allies of the Empire.

The plane that Bosch bombed, by the way, was a Cuban plane. He's wanted in Cuba for that and a host of other serious crimes, and the Cubans have asked Washington to extradite him to Cuba. To Cuba, he's like Osama Bin Laden is to the United States. But the US has refused. Can you imagine the reaction in Washington if bin Laden showed up in Havana and the Cubans refused to extradite him to the US? Can you imagine the reaction in the United States if Havana proclaimed Osama Bin Laden Day?

Washington's support of genuine terrorist organizations has been very extensive. To give just a couple of examples of the past few years: The ethnic Albanians in Kosovo have carried out numerous terrorist attacks for years in various parts of the Balkans, but they've been our allies because they've attacked people out of favor with Washington.

The paramilitaries in Colombia, as vicious as they come, could not begin to carry out their dirty work without the support of the Colombian military, who are the recipients of virtually unlimited American support. This, all by itself, disqualifies Washington from leading a war against terrorism.

Bush also speaks out often and angrily against harboring terrorists. Does he really mean *that*? Well, what country harbors more terrorists than the United States? Orlando Bosch is only one of the numerous anti-Castro Cubans in Miami who have carried out hundreds, if not thousands, of terrorist acts in the US, in Cuba, and elsewhere; all kinds of arson attacks, assassinations, and bombings. They have been harbored here in safety for decades. As have numerous other friendly terrorists, torturers, and human-rights violators from Guatemala, El Salvador, Haiti, Indonesia, and elsewhere, all allies of the Empire.

The CIA is looking for terrorists in caves in the mountains of Afghanistan at the same time as the Agency sits in bars in Miami having beers with terrorists.

What are we to make of all this? How are we to understand our government's foreign policy? Well, if I were to write a book called *The American Empire for Dummies*, page one would say: Don't ever look for the moral factor. US foreign policy has no moral factor built into its DNA. Clear your mind of that baggage which only gets in the way of seeing beyond the clichés and the platitudes.

I know it's not easy for most Americans to take what I say at face value. It's not easy to swallow my message. They see our leaders on TV and their photos in the press, they see them smiling or laughing, telling jokes; see them with their families, hear them speak of God and love, of peace and law, of democracy and freedom, of human rights and justice and even baseball. How can such people be moral monsters? How can they be called immoral?

They have names like George and Dick and Donald, not a single Mohammed or Abdullah in the bunch. And they even speak English. Well, George almost does. People named Mohammed or Abdullah cut off arms or legs as punishment for theft. We know that that's horrible. We're too civilized for that. But people named George and Dick and Donald drop cluster bombs on cities and villages, and the many

unexploded ones become land mines, and before very long a child picks one up or steps on one of them and loses an arm or leg, or both arms or both legs, and sometimes their eyesight. And the cluster bombs which actually explode do their own kind of horror.

But our leaders are perhaps not so much immoral as they are amoral. It's not that they take pleasure in causing so much death and suffering. It's that they just don't care—if that's a distinction worth making. As long as the death and suffering advance the agenda of the Empire, as long as the right people and the right corporations gain wealth and power and privilege and prestige, as long as the death and suffering aren't happening to them or people close to them, then they just don't care about it happening to other people, including the American soldiers whom they throw into wars and who come home—the ones who make it back—with Agent Orange or Gulf War Syndrome eating away at their bodies. Our leaders would not be in the positions they hold if they were bothered by such things.

It must be great fun to be one of the leaders of an empire, glorious in fact, intoxicating, the feeling that you can do whatever you want to whomever you want for as long as you want for any reason you care to give—because you have the power—for theirs is the power and the glory.

WASHINGTON'S SUPPORT OF GENUINE TERRORIST ORGANIZATIONS HAS BEEN VERY EXTENSIVE.

When I was writing my book *Rogue State* a few years ago, I used the term "American Empire," which I don't think I had seen in print before. I used the term cautiously because I wasn't sure the American public was quite ready for it. But I needn't have been so cautious. It's now being used proudly by supporters of the Empire. There's Dinesh D'Souza, the conservative intellectual at the Hoover Institution. Earlier this year he wrote an article entitled "In Praise of American Empire," in which he argued that Americans must finally recognize that the US "has become an empire, the most magnanimous imperial power ever."

Robert Kagan of the Carnegie Endowment writes: "And the truth is that the benevolent hegemony exercised by the US is good for a vast portion of the world's population. It is certainly a better international arrangement than all realistic alternatives."

And syndicated columnist Charles Krauthammer speaks of America's "uniquely benign imperium."

So that's how people who are wedded to American foreign policy are able to live with it: They conclude, and proclaim, and may even believe, that our foreign policy is a benevolent force, an enlightened empire, bringing order, prosperity, and civilized behavior to all parts of the globe. And if we're *forced* to go to war, we conduct a *humanitarian* war.

Well, inasmuch as I've devoted much of my adult life to documenting in minute detail the exact opposite, to showing the remarkable cruelty and horrific effects of US interventions on people in every corner of the world, you can understand, I think, that my reaction to such claims is: Huh? These conservative intellectuals—is that an oxymoron?—they are as amoral as the folks in the White House and the Pentagon. After all, the particles of depleted uranium are not lodging inside *their* lungs to keep radiating for the rest of their lives; the International Monetary Fund is not bankrupting *their* economy and slashing their basic services; it's not *their* families wandering in the desert as refugees.

The leaders of the Empire, the imperial mafia—Bush and Rumsfeld and Cheney and Powell and Rice and Wolfowitz and Perle—and their scribes as well, are as fanatic and as fundamentalist as Osama Bin Laden. And the regime change they accomplished in Afghanistan has really gone to their heads. Today Kabul, tomorrow the world.

So get used to it, world. The American Empire. Soon to be a major motion picture, coming to a theater near you.

■ ■ ■ ■ ■ ■ ■ ■ ■ ■

A while ago, I heard a union person on the radio proposing what he called "a radical solution to poverty: Pay people enough to live on."

Well, I'd like to propose a radical solution to anti-American terrorism: Stop giving terrorists the motivation to attack America.

Now, our leaders and often our media would have us believe that we're targeted because of our freedom, our democracy, our wealth, our modernity, our secular government, our simple goodness, and other stories suitable for schoolbooks. George W. is still repeating these cliches a year after 9/11. Well, he may believe it, but other officials have known better for some time. A Department of Defense study in 1997 concluded: "Historical data show a strong correlation between US involvement in international situations and an increase in terrorist attacks against the United States."

Jimmy Carter, some years after he left the White House, was unambiguous in his agreement with such a conclusion. He said:

We sent Marines into Lebanon and you only have to go to Lebanon, to Syria or to Jordan to witness first-hand the intense hatred among many people for the United States because we bombed and shelled and unmercifully killed totally innocent villagers—women and children and farmers and housewives—in those villages around Beirut.... As a result of that...we became kind of a Satan in the minds of those who are deeply resentful. That is what precipitated the taking of our hostages and that is what has precipitated some of the terrorist attacks.

The terrorists responsible for the bombing of the World Trade Center in 1993 sent a letter to the *New York Times* which stated, in part: "We declare our responsibility for the explosion on the mentioned building. This action was done in response for the American political, economical, and military support to Israel the state of terrorism and to the rest of the dictator countries in the region."

And finally, several members of al Qaeda have repeatedly made it quite plain in the past year that it's things like US support of Israeli massacres and the bombing of Iraq that makes them hate the United States.

I present more evidence of the same sort in one of my books, along with a long list of US actions in the Middle East that has created hatred of American foreign policy.

I don't think, by the way, that poverty plays much of a role in creating terrorists. We shouldn't confuse terrorism with revolution.

And the attacks are not going to end until we stop bombing innocent people and devastating villages and grand old cities and poisoning the air and the gene pool with depleted uranium. The attacks are not going to end until we stop supporting gross violators of human rights who oppress their people, until we stop doing a whole host of terrible things. We'll keep on adding to the security operations that are turning our society into a police state, and it won't make us much safer.

It's not just people in the Middle East who have good reason for hating what our government does; we've created huge numbers of potential terrorists all over Latin America during a half-century of American actions far worse than what we've done in the Middle East. I think that if Latin Americans shared the belief of many Muslims that they will go directly to heaven for giving up their life and acting as a martyr against the great enemy, by now we would have had decades of repeated terrorist horror coming from south of the border. As it is, there have been many non-suicidal terrorist attacks against Americans and their buildings in Latin America over the years.

There's also the people of Asia and Africa. The same story.

The State Department recently held a conference on how to improve America's image abroad in order to reduce the level of hatred. Image is what they're working on, not change of policies.

But the policies scorecard reads as follows: From 1945 to the end of the century, the United States attempted to overthrow more than 40 foreign governments and to crush more than 30 populist movements fighting against insufferable regimes. In the process, the US bombed about 25 countries, caused the end of life for several million people, and condemned many millions more to a life of agony and despair.

If I were the president, I could stop terrorist attacks against the United States in a few days. Permanently. I would first apologize—very publicly and very sincerely—to all the widows and orphans, the tortured and impoverished, and all the many millions of other victims of American imperialism. Then I would announce that America's global interventions have come to an end and inform Israel that it is no longer the fifty-first state of the union but—oddly enough—a foreign country. I would then reduce the military budget by at least 90 percent and use the savings to pay reparations to our victims and repair the damage from our bombings. There would be enough money. Do you know what one year's military budget is equal to? One year. It's equal to more than $20,000 per hour for every hour since Jesus Christ was born.

FROM 1945 TO THE END OF THE CENTURY, THE UNITED STATES ATTEMPTED TO OVERTHROW MORE THAN 40 FOREIGN GOVERNMENTS AND TO CRUSH MORE THAN 30 POPULIST MOVEMENTS FIGHTING AGAINST INSUFFERABLE REGIMES.

That's what I'd do on my first three days in the White House. On the fourth day, I'd be assassinated.

■ ■ ■ ■ ■ ■ ■ ■ ■

On page two of *The American Empire for Dummies*, I'd put this in a box outlined in bright red:

Following its bombing of Iraq, the United States wound up with military bases in Saudi Arabia, Kuwait, Bahrain, Qatar, Oman, and the United Arab Emirates.

Following its bombing of Yugoslavia, the United States wound up with military bases in Kosovo, Albania, Macedonia, Hungary, Bosnia, and Croatia.

Following its bombing of Afghanistan, the United States is now winding up with military bases in Afghanistan, Pakistan, Kazakhstan, Uzbekistan, Tajikistan, Kyrgyzstan, Georgia, and perhaps elsewhere in the region.

That's not very subtle, is it? Not really covert. The men who run the Empire are not easily embarrassed. And that's the way the empire grows, a base on every corner, ready to be mobilized to put down any threat to imperial rule, real or imagined. Fifty-seven years after World War II ended, the US still has major bases in Germany and Japan; and 49 years after the Korean War ended, the US military is still in South Korea.

A Pentagon report of a few years ago said:

Our first objective is to prevent the re-emergence of a new rival, either on the territory of the former Soviet Union or elsewhere.... [W]e must maintain the mechanisms for deterring potential competitors from even aspiring to a larger regional or global role.

The bombing, invasion, and occupation of Afghanistan have served the purpose of setting up a new government that will be sufficiently amenable to Washington's international objectives, including the installation of military bases and communications listening stations and, perhaps most important of all, the running of secure oil and gas pipelines through Afghanistan from the Caspian Sea region, which I'm sure many of you have heard about.

For years, the American oil barons have had their eyes on the vast oil and gas reserves of the Caspian Sea area, ideally with an Afghanistan-Pakistan route to the Indian Ocean, thus keeping Russia and Iran out of the picture. The oilmen have been quite open about this, giving very frank testimony before Congress, for example.

Now they have their eyes on the even greater oil reserves of Iraq. If the US overthrows Saddam Hussein and installs a puppet government, as they did in Afghanistan, the American oil companies will move into Iraq and have a feast, and the American Empire will add another country and a few more bases.

Or as General William Looney, the head of the US-UK operation that flies over Iraq and bombs them every few days, said several years ago:

If they turn on their radars we're going to blow up their goddamn missiles. They know we own their country. We own their airspace.... We dictate the way they live and talk. And that's what's great about America right now. It's a good thing, especially when there's a lot of oil out there we need.

We've gone through a few months now of a song and dance show that passes for debate, a debate about whether to attack a sovereign nation that has not attacked us, that has not threatened to attack us, that knows it would mean instant mass suicide for them if they attacked us. This debate is absurd not simply because Iraq is not a threat—by now, even the Martians must know that—but because our imperial mafia *knows* that Iraq is not a threat, at all.

They've been telling us one story after another about why Iraq is a threat, an imminent threat, a nuclear threat, a threat increasing in danger with each passing day, that Iraq is a terrorist state, that Iraq is tied to al Qaeda, only to have each story amount to nothing. They told us for a long time that Iraq must agree to having the weapons inspectors back in, and when Iraq agreed to this, they said, "No, no, that isn't good enough."

How soon before they blame the horror in Bali on Iraq?

Does any of this make sense? This sudden urgency of fighting a war in the absence of a fight? It does, I suggest, only if you understand that this is not about Saddam Hussein and his evilness, or his weapons, or terrorism. What it's about is that the Empire is still hungry and wants to eat Iraq and its oil and needs to present excuses to satisfy gullible people. And then they want to eat Iran.

The Empire, in case you missed it, is not content with merely the Earth; the Empire has been officially extended to outer space. The Pentagon proudly admits this, and they have a nice name for it. They call it "full-spectrum dominance," and for years now they've been planning to fight wars in space, from space, and into space. And that's a quote.

And if you're wondering "why now?" about Iraq, I think—as many have said—that the coming election plays a role. It's going to decide which party will control Congress, and there's nothing like a lot of talk about war and defending America to sway voters and make them forget about the economy and health care at the same time.

In addition to all the absurdities and lies they've been throwing at us, what I've found most remarkable and disturbing about this period has been the great absence in the mass media of the simple reminder that a US attack upon Iraq means bombs falling on people, putting an end to homes, schools, hospitals, jobs, futures. The discussion has focused almost entirely on whether or not to go after the evil Saddam and his supposed evil weapons. What it all means in terms of human suffering is scarcely considered worthy of attention. Is that not odd?

Also absent from the discussion is that over the course of several years in the 1990s, the UN inspectors found and destroyed huge amounts of chemical, biological, and nuclear weapons in Iraq. I'm sure that most Americans are convinced that Saddam got away with hiding virtually all his weapons and that he'll get away with it again if there's a resumption of the inspections. But that's not what happened. Scott Ritter, chief UN weapons inspector in Iraq, recently stated:

Since 1998 Iraq has been fundamentally disarmed; 90-95 percent of Iraq's weapons of mass destruction have been verifiably eliminated. This includes all of the factories used to produce chemical, biological, and nuclear weapons, and long-range ballistic missiles; the associated equipment of these factories; and the vast majority of the products coming out of these factories.

"THEY KNOW WE OWN THEIR COUNTRY. WE OWN THEIR AIRSPACE."—GENERAL WILLIAM LOONEY

And the director general of the International Atomic Energy Agency, Mohamed El Baradei, has written that his agency

dismantled extensive nuclear weapons-related facilities. We neutralized Iraq's nuclear program. We confiscated its weapon-usable material. We destroyed, removed or rendered harmless all its facilities and equipment relevant to nuclear weapons production.

Each of the big American bombing campaigns carries its own myths with it, but none so big as the one before last. I must remind you of that.

We were told that the US/NATO bombing of Yugoslavia in 1999 was to save the people of Kosovo from ethnic cleansing by the Serbs. And since the ethnic cleansing finally came to an end, the bombing seems to have worked. Right? First there was the ethnic cleansing, then came the bombing, then came the end of the ethnic cleansing. What could be simpler? I'm sure that about 90 percent of those Americans who think about such things firmly believe that, including many of you, I imagine.

But it was all a lie. The bombing didn't end the ethnic cleansing. The bombing *caused* the ethnic cleansing. The systematic forced deportations of large numbers of Kosovars—what we call ethnic cleansing—did not begin until about two days after the bombing began, and was clearly a reaction to it by the Serb forces, born of great anger and feelings of powerlessness due to the heavy bombardment. This is easily verified by looking at a daily newspaper for the few days before the bombing began, the night of March 23/24, and the few days after. Or simply look at the *New York Times* of March 26, page one, which reads:

[W]ith the NATO bombing already begun, a deepening sense of fear took hold in Pristina [the main city of Kosovo] that the Serbs would *now* vent their rage against ethnic Albanian civilians in retaliation. [Emphasis added.]

The next day, March 27, we find the first reference to a "forced march" or anything of that sort.

How is it possible that such a powerful lie could be told to the American people and that the people would swallow it without gagging? One reason is that the media don't explicitly point out the lies; at best, you have to read between the lines.

There's the story from the Cold War about a group of Russian writers touring the United States. They were astonished to find, after reading the newspapers and watching television, that almost all the opinions on all the vital issues were the same. "In our country," said one of them, "to get that result we have a dictatorship. We imprison people. We torture them. Here you have none of that. How do you do it? What's the secret?"

Can any of you name a single American daily newspaper that unequivocally opposed the US-NATO bombing of Yugoslavia three years ago?

Can any of you name a single American daily newspaper that unequivocally opposed the US bombing of Iraq eleven years ago?

Can any of you name a single American daily newspaper that unequivocally opposed the US bombing of Afghanistan?

Isn't that remarkable? In a supposedly free society, with a supposedly free press, with about 1,500 daily newspapers, the odds should be way against that being the case. But that's the way it is.

I suppose that now some of you would like me to tell you how to put an end to all these terrible and absurd things I've talked about. Well, good luck to all of us.

I could say that, personally, I proceed from the assumption that if enough people understand what their government is doing and the harm that it causes, at some point the number of such people will reach critical mass and some changes can be effectuated. But that may well be a long way off. I hope I live to see it.

I'm sure that if all Americans could see their government's bomb victims up close, see the body fragments, smell the burning flesh, see the devastated homes and lives and communities, there would be a demand to end such horror so powerful that even the imperial mafia madmen couldn't ignore it. But how to get Americans to see the victims? I and many of you don't need to see those terrible sights to be opposed to the madmen's policies, but most Americans do. If we could figure out why we have this deep empathy for the victims, this imagination, it might be a very good organizing tool.

Gandhi once said, "Almost anything you do will be insignificant, but you must do it." And the reason I must do it is captured by yet another adage, cited by various religious leaders: "We do these things not to change the world, but so that the world will not change us."

Sam Smith, a journalist in Washington, whom some of you are familiar with, in his new book makes the point that: "Those who think history has left us helpless should recall the abolitionist of 1830, the feminist of 1870, the labor organizer of 1890, and the gay or lesbian writer of 1910. They, like us, did not get to choose their time in history but they, like us, did get to choose what they did with it."

CAN ANY OF YOU NAME A SINGLE AMERICAN DAILY NEWSPAPER THAT UNEQUIVOCALLY OPPOSED THE US BOMBING OF AFGHANISTAN?

He then asks: Knowing what we know now about how certain things turned out, but also knowing how long it took, would we have been abolitionists in 1830, or feminists in 1870, and so on?

We don't know what surprises history has in store for us when we give history a little shove, just as history can give each of us a little shove personally. In the 1960s, I was working at the State Department, my heart set on becoming a Foreign Service Officer. Little did I know that I would soon become a ranting and raving commie-pinko-subversive-enemy of all that is decent and holy because a thing called Vietnam came along. So there is that kind of hope, as well.

■ ■ ■ ■ ■ ■ ■ ■ ■ ■

Let me close with two of the laws of politics which came out of the Watergate scandal of the 1970s, which I like to cite:

The First Watergate Law of American Politics states: "No matter how paranoid you are, what the government is actually doing is worse than you imagine."

The Second Watergate Law states: "Don't believe anything until it's been officially denied."

Both laws are still on the books.

For the source for anything referred to in the talk, please write to the author at <bblum6@aol.com>.

THE OTHERS
MOURNING THE DEAD, WHEREVER THEY MAY BE
HOWARD ZINN

After the attacks of September 11, 2001, the *New York Times* did what should always be done when a tragedy is summed up in a statistic: It gave us miniature portraits of the human beings who died on that day—their names, photos, glimmers of their personalities, their idiosyncrasies, how friends and loved ones remembered them.

As the director of the New York Historical Society said about what the *Times* did: "The peculiar genius of it was to put a human face on numbers that are unimaginable to most of us.... It's so obvious that every one of them was a person who deserved to live a full and successful and happy life. You see what was lost."

I was deeply moved, reading those intimate sketches—"A Poet of Bensonhurst," "A Friend, a Sister," "Someone to Lean On," "Laughter, Win or Lose." I thought: Those who celebrated the grisly deaths of the people in the Twin Towers and the Pentagon as a blow to symbols of American dominance in the world—what if, instead of symbols, they could see, up close, the faces of those who lost their lives? I wonder if they would have second thoughts, second feelings.

> I FEEL THAT MOST AMERICANS, YES, MOST AMERICANS WOULD BEGIN TO UNDERSTAND THAT THE WAR WE ARE WAGING IS A WAR ON ORDINARY MEN, WOMEN, AND CHILDREN.

Then it occurred to me: What if all those Americans who declare their support for Bush's "War on Terrorism" could see, instead of those elusive symbols—Osama bin Laden, al Qaeda—the real human beings who are dying under our bombs? I do believe they would have second thoughts.

I feel that most Americans (not those fanatics in Washington and around the country who are willing—like their counterparts in other parts of the world—to kill for some cause), yes, most Americans would begin to understand that the war we are waging is a war on ordinary men, women, and children. And that these human beings die because they happen to live in Afghanistan in villages in the vicinity of "military targets" (always vaguely, though confidently, defined) and that the bombing that destroyed their lives is in no way a war on terrorism because it has no chance of ending terrorism and is itself a form of terrorism.

But how can this be done—this turning of numbers into human beings? Unlike the vignettes in the *New York Times*, there are no available details about the dead men, women, and children in Afghanistan.

We would need to study the scattered news reports, usually in the inside sections of the *New York Times* and the *Washington Post*, but also in the foreign press—Reuters; Agence France-Presse; the *Times*, the *Guardian*, and the *Independent* of London (concentrating on the Western press to avoid charges that Middle-Eastern sources are tainted), as well as reports from Human Rights Watch.

These reports are mostly out of sight of the general public (indeed, they are virtually never reported on national television, where most Americans get their news), and so dispersed as to reinforce the idea that the bombing of civilians is an infrequent event, an accident, a mistake, unfortunate but necessary. ("Collateral damage," Timothy McVeigh said, using a Pentagon expression, when asked about the children who died when he bombed the federal building in Oklahoma City.)

Listen to the language of the Pentagon:

> We cannot confirm the report.... Civilian casualties are inevitable.... We don't know if they were our weapons.... It was an accident.... Incorrect coordinates had been entered.... They are deliberately putting civilians in our bombing targets.... The village was a legitimate military target.... It just didn't happen.... We regret any loss of civilian life.

After reports of the bombing of one village, Pentagon spokeswoman Victoria Clarke said, "We take extraordinary care.... There is unintended damage. There is collateral damage. Thus far, it has been extremely limited."

The Agence France-Presse reporter quoting her wrote: "Refugees arriving in Pakistan suggested otherwise. Several recounted how twenty people, including nine children, had been killed as they tried to flee an attack on the southern Afghan town of Tirin Kot."

Listening to the repeated excuses given by President Bush, Secretary of Defense Donald Rumsfeld, and the others, one recalls General Colin Powell's reply at the end of the Gulf War, when questioned about Iraqi casualties: "That is really not a matter I am terribly interested in."

If, indeed, a strict definition of the word *deliberate* does not apply to the bombs dropped on the people of Afghanistan, then we can offer, thinking back to Colin Powell's statement, an alternate characterization: "A reckless disregard for human life."

The denials of the Pentagon are uttered confidently half a world away in Washington. But there are on-the-spot press reports from the villages, from hospitals where the wounded lie, or from the Pakistan border where refugees have fled the bombs.

If we put these reports together, we get brief glimpses of the human tragedies in Afghanistan—sometimes the names of the dead and the villages that were bombed, sometimes the words of a father who lost his children, a brother who lost his sister, the ages of the children. We would then have to multiply these reports and, realizing there must be many unreported incidents, know the numbers go into the thousands.

> **MY INTENTION IS NOT AT ALL TO DIMINISH OUR COMPASSION FOR THE VICTIMS OF THE TERRORISM OF SEPTEMBER 11, BUT TO ENLARGE THAT COMPASSION TO INCLUDE THE VICTIMS OF ALL TERRORISM, ANY PLACE, ANY TIME, WHETHER PERPETRATED BY MIDEAST FANATICS OR AMERICAN POLITICIANS.**

A professor of economics at the University of New Hampshire, Marc Herold, has done a far more thorough survey of the press than I have: He lists location, type of weapon used, sources of information, and finds the civilian death toll in Afghanistan exceeding 3,500 as of August 2002, a sad and startling numerical juxtaposition with the victims of the Twin Towers.

The *New York Times* was able to interview friends and families of the New York dead, but for the Afghans, we will have to imagine the hopes and dreams of those who died, especially the children, for whom 40 or 50 years of mornings, love, friendship, music, sunsets, and the sheer exhilaration of being alive were extinguished by monstrous machines sent over their land by men far away.

My intention is not at all to diminish our compassion for the victims of the terrorism of September 11, but to enlarge that compassion to include the victims of all terrorism, any place, any time, whether perpetrated by Mideast fanatics or American politicians.

Surely we cannot, especially if we want to make the world different in this new century, this new millennium, huddle inside a circle of flags, singing national anthems, content with the artificially created "unity" of 4 percent of the world's population. Surely we must apply the Golden Rule ("Do unto others....") to all people everywhere. We forgot that at Hiroshima. We should not forget it again.

In that spirit, I present the following news items, hoping that there is the patience to go through them all, like the patience required to read the portraits of the September 11 dead, like the patience required to read the 58,000 names on the Vietnam Memorial.

■ ■ ■ ■ ■ ■ ■ ■ ■ ■

All articles are from October through December of 2001.

From a hospital in Jalalabad, Afghanistan, reported in the *Boston Globe* by John Donnelly on December 5:

In one bed lay Noor Mohammad, 10, who was a bundle of bandages. He lost his eyes and hands to the bomb that hit his house after Sunday dinner. Hospital director Guloja Shimwari shook his head at the boy's wounds. "The United States must be thinking he is Osama," Shimwari said. "If he is not Osama, then why would they do this?"

The report continued:

The hospital's morgue received 17 bodies last weekend, and officials here estimate at least 89 civilians were killed in several villages. In the hospital yesterday, a bomb's damage could be chronicled in the life of one family. A bomb had killed the father, Faisal Karim. In one bed was his wife, Mustafa Jama, who had severe head injuries.... Around her, six of her children were in bandages.... One of them Zahidullah, 8, lay in a coma.

The first report of civilian casualties, in an inside section of the *New York Times* (which has been the preferred placement for all stories of civilian deaths), came on October 10 from Barry Bearak, reporting from Peshawar, Pakistan:

Four security guards working the night shift were killed near Kabul when the local headquarters of a United Nations-supported organization in Afghanistan was struck during an air attack by the United States. "The totally innocent have been killed for no reason," the local supervisor, a man who uses the single name Usman, said. "We know we have four dead, but the bodies are so torn apart we don't know who is who."

In the *New York Times*, Barry Bearak, reporting December 15 from the village of Madoo, Afghanistan, tells of the destruction of fifteen houses and their occupants by American bombs.

"In the night, as we slept, they dropped the bombs on us," said Paira Gul, a young man whose eyes were aflame with bitterness. His sisters and their families had perished, he said.... The houses were small, the bombing precise. No structure escaped the thundering havoc. Fifteen houses, 15 ruins. "Most of the dead are children," Tor Tul said.

Another *Times* reporter, C.J. Chivers, writing from the village of Charykari, Afghanistan, on December 12, reported

a terrifying and rolling barrage that the villagers believe was the payload of an American B-52.... The villagers say 30 people died.... One man, Muhibullah, 40, led the way through his yard and showed three unexploded cluster bombs he is afraid to touch. A fourth was not a dud. It landed near his porch. "My son was sitting there.... [T]he metal went inside him." The boy

Zumarai, 5, is in a hospital in Kunduz, with wounds to leg and abdomen. His sister, Sharpari, 10, was killed. "The United States killed my daughter and injured my son," Mr. Muhibullah said. "Six of my cows were destroyed and all of my wheat and rice was burned. I am very angry. I miss my daughter."

An Agence France-Presse dispatch of October 24:

United Nations spokeswoman Stephanie Bunker said...at least 70 percent of people living in the major towns of Herat, Kandahar in the South and Jlalabad in the east had fled the bombing. Independent estimates put the number of people on the move from the three cities at around one million.

From the *Washington Post*, October 23, from Peshawar, Pakistan, by Pamela Constable:

"The world must know what is happening in Afghanistan," said Mohammed Sardar. "The terrorists and the leaders are still free, but the people are dying and there is no one to listen to us." Sardar, a taxi driver and father of 12, said his family had spent night after night listening to the bombing in their community south of Kabul. One night during the first week, he said, a bomb aimed at a nearby radio station struck a house, killing all five members of the family living there. "There was no sign of a home left," he said. "We just collected the pieces of bodies and buried them."

"Kandahar was completely destroyed. Everything has turned into piles of stones...." said refugee Abdul Nabi after his arrival at a makeshift refugee camp here. He said he had seen two groups of 13 and 15 corpses, which he believed were the remains of civilians, near bombed out trucks on the road between Herat and Kandahar.

> "INDEPENDENT ESTIMATES PUT THE NUMBER OF PEOPLE ON THE MOVE FROM THE THREE CITIES AT AROUND ONE MILLION." — AGENCE FRANCE-PRESSE

Again from the *Washington Post*, on October 24:

Qatar's al-Jazeera television—an independent global satellite network that broadcasts in Arabic—reported that US strikes had killed 93 people in the village of Chukar.... In Quetta, Pakistan, injured refugees crossing the border from Afghanistan reported that airstrikes on the town of Tarin Kot had killed at least 29 people when eight or nine homes were bombed.... Clarke [i.e., Pentagon spokesperson Victoria Clarke] said she had no information on the extent of casualties resulting from the bombing of the senior citizens home in Herat and the residential area northwest of Kabul.

Reporter Catherine Philip of the London *Times*, reporting October 25 from the border city of Quetta in Pakistan:

It was not long after 7 PM on Sunday when the bombs began to fall over the outskirts of Torai village.... Rushing outside, Mauroof saw a massive fireball rising from the ground and realized, in horror, that the bombs had fallen over the little cluster of houses a mile away where his sister and his other relatives were living.... Morning brought an end to the bombing and...a neighbor arrived to tell him that some 20 villagers had been killed in the blasts, among them ten of his relatives. "I saw the body of one of my brothers-in-law being pulled from the debris," Mauroof said. "The lower part of his body had been blown away. Some of the other bodies were unrecognizable. There were heads missing and arms blown off...." The roll call of the dead read like an invitation list to a family wedding: his mother-in-law, two sisters-in-law, three brothers-in-law, and four of his sister's five young children, two girls and two boys, all under the age of eight.

A *New York Times* report of October 26 from Washington, by Elizabeth Becker and Eric Schmitt:

American warplanes bombed and largely destroyed the same Red Cross complex in Kabul that they struck ten days ago, an error the Pentagon admitted tonight, saying it occurred because military planners had picked the wrong target.... The attack on the Red Cross buildings by two Navy fighter-bombers and two B-52s, came in two waves today...using satellite-guided bombs that wrecked and set ablaze warehouses storing tons of food and blankets for civilians. The Red Cross seemed stunned by the Pentagon's admission today: "Now we've got 55,000 people without that food or blankets, with nothing at all."

Human Rights Watch report, October 26, from Afghanistan:

At least twenty-three civilians, the majority of them young children, were killed when US bombs hit a remote village located near a Taliban military base.... Maroof, aged thirty-eight, lived at his farm located about one kilometer from the village and told Human Rights Watch that he had witnessed the attacks.... When he rushed to the village the next day, he found the family compound of his relatives in ruins, and villagers digging through the rubble. Twelve bodies of his relatives were recovered from the debris of the family compound. The dead included the two sons and two daughters of his twenty-five-year-old sister Rhidi Gul; Aminullah, aged eight; Raminullah, aged three; Noorjan, aged five; and Gulpia, aged four....

Twenty-five-year-old Samiullah was outside the village when the bombing raids began, and rushed home to rescue his family. When he arrived at his family compound, he found the bodies of his twenty-year-old wife

THE OTHERS
HOWARD ZINN

and three of his children: Mohibullah, aged six; Harifullah, aged three; and Bibi Aysha, aged one.... Also killed were his two brothers, Nasiullah, aged eight, and Ghaziullah, aged six, as well as two of his sisters, aged fourteen and eleven.

Reuters, October 28—Sayet Salahuddin reporting from Kabul:

A US bomb flattened a flimsy mud-brick home in Kabul Sunday, blowing apart seven children as they ate breakfast with their father. The last shattered a neighbor's house, killing another two children in one of the most gruesome scenes of Washington's three-week-old bombing of the Afghan capital.... Sobs racked the body of a middle-aged man as he cradled the head of his baby, its dust-covered body dressed only in a blue diaper, lying beside the bodies of three other children, their colorful clothes layered with debris from their shattered homes.

Washington Post Foreign Service, November 2, from Quetta, Pakistan, by Rajiv Chandrasekaran:

The thunder of the first explosions jolted Nasir Ahmed awake. The next few blasts led him to open his Koran and begin praying. Then, he said, the bombs fell on his house. As the mud-brick housing compound he shared with his extended family began collapsing, he grabbed his 14-year-old niece and scurried into a communal courtyard. From there, he said, they watched as civilians who survived the bombing run, including his niece and a woman holding her 5-year-old son, were gunned down by a slow-moving, propeller-driven aircraft circling overheard. When the gunship departed an hour later, at least 25 people in the village—all civilians—were dead, according to accounts of the incident provided today by Ahmed, two other witnesses and several relatives of people in the village.... Ahmed, another survivor and the relative of a wounded survivor were all interviewed separately, Oct. 22, in the village of Chowker-Karez, about 50 miles north of Kandahar.

"There were no Taliban in the village," said Ahmed.... "They just killed innocent people.... The plane saw us, and they opened fire. We don't understand why they did that."

The Pentagon confirmed that the village was hit by an AC-130 Spectre gunship on October 22, but officials said they believe the aircraft struck a legitimate military target. Asked about civilian casualties, the official said, "We don't know. We're not on the ground."

Shaida, 14, [said]..."Americans are not good.... They killed my mother. They killed my father. I don't understand why."

A *Newsday* report by James Rupert, published in the *San Francisco Chronicle*, November 24, from Kabul:

In the sprawling, mud-brick slum of Qala-ye-Khatir, most men were kneeling in the mosques at morning prayer on Nov. 6 when a quarter-ton of steel and high explosives hurtled from the sky into the home of Gul Ahmed, a carpet weaver. The American bomb detonated, killing Ahmed, his five daughters, one of his wives, and a son. Next door, it demolished the home of Sahib Dad and killed two of his children.

Ross Chamberlain, coordinator for the UN mine-clearing operations in much of Afghanistan [said]..."There's no such thing as precision bombing.... We are finding more cases of errant targeting than accurate targeting, more misses than hits."

New York Times, November 23, from Ghaleh Shafer, Afghanistan:

Most children in Afghanistan, lacking toys, play with what they find. In this tiny, dusty village they have been finding pieces of a cluster bomb. Three children were injured this week, and one teenager was killed, when they picked up undetonated remnants of a bomb dropped by American planes about a month ago. The bomb's initial impact killed 12 people, most from the same extended family. The village mourned, thinking it had seen the worst.... 10-year old Mohebolah Seraj went out to collect wood for his family, and thought he had happened upon a food packet. He picked it up and lost three fingers in an explosion. Doctors say he will probably lose his whole hand.... [H]is mother, Sardar Seraj...said that she cried and told the doctors not to cut off her son's whole hand....

> "SOBS RACKED THE BODY OF A MIDDLE-AGED MAN AS HE CRADLED THE HEAD OF HIS BABY, ITS DUST-COVERED BODY DRESSED ONLY IN A BLUE DIAPER, LYING BESIDE THE BODIES OF THREE OTHER CHILDREN, THEIR COLORFUL CLOTHES LAYERED WITH DEBRIS FROM THEIR SHATTERED HOMES." — REUTERS

The hospital where her son is being cared for is a grim place, lacking power and basic sanitation. In one room lay Muhammad Ayoub, a 20-year old who was in the house when the cluster bomb initially landed. He lost a leg and his eyesight, and his face was severely disfigured. He moaned in agony.... Hospital officials said that a 16-year-old had been decapitated.

A Reuters dispatch, published November 8 in the *Independent* of London:

The United Nations is warning of a "disaster of tremendous proportions" after US planes bombed a hydro-electric power station close to a vast dam in southern Afghanistan. UN officials say that the loss of electricity will increase the suffering of civilians in southern Afghanistan, which has already suffered massive damage from American air raids.

A *New York Times* report, December 2 from Alalabad, Afghanistan, by Tim Weiner:

According to Afghan commanders here in the far eastern part of the country, civilians are being killed in the American hunt for Osama bin Laden. The commanders, who are pro-American...say that four nearby villages were struck this weekend, leaving 80 or more people dead and others wounded.... The villages are near Tora Bora, the mountain camp where Mr. bin Laden is presumed to be hiding. A Pentagon spokesman said Saturday that the bombing of civilians near Tora Bora "never happened."

Eight men guarding the building [a district office building]...were killed, Hajji Zaman said. He gave the names of the dead as Zia ul-Hassan, 16; Wilayat Khan, 17; Abdul Wadi, 20; Jany, 22; Abdul Wahid, 30; Hajji Wazir, 35; Haji Nasser, also 35; and Awlia Gul, 37.... Ali Shah, 26, of Landa Khel, said, "There is no one in this village who is part of Al Qaeda."

"A SECOND 6-YEAR-OLD GIRL IN THE ROOM WAS PARALYZED FROM THE WAIST DOWN. X-RAYS SHOWED HOW A TINY SHARD OF METAL HAD NEATLY SEVERED HER SPINAL CORD." — *NEW YORK TIMES*

Muhammed Tamir is from the village of Gudara.... [I]t lies about three miles from a now famous mountain redoubt called Tora Bora, where the United States thinks Osama bin Laden may be hiding. "The Americans bombed on the third day of Ramadan," he said. "Then they bombed on the fifth day of Ramadan. Then they bombed on the eighth day of Ramadan." And then they bombed on the 13th day, the first of December. Witnesses said that at least 50 and as many as 300 villagers had been killed.

"We are poor people," Mr. Tahir said. "Our trees are our only shelter from the cold and wind. The trees have been bombed. Our waterfall, our only source of water— they bombed it. Where is the humanity?"

The *Boston Globe*, December 2, from Mengchuqur, Afghanistan, by David Filipov:

For two weeks, the US planes dropped cluster bombs in an effort to kill Taliban troops on the ground. The story is the same in all the villages that once formed the front line: Koruk, Qal Bad, Dashti-Archi, Taza Laqai, Garau. Everywhere, people have returned to find their houses destroyed. Everywhere, little bomblets lie unexploded. Everywhere, people continued to die.

From the *Independent* of London, December 3, reporting from Jalalabad, Richard Lloyd Parry:

A senior mujahedin commander said US strikes killed more than 100 civilians around Agam, 25 miles south of Jalalabad, on top of a least 70 killed in air raids on Saturday night.... [C]ommanders were already reeling from the attacks on Friday night and early Saturday when three villages were bombed, killing at least 70, and perhaps as many as 300, civilians in territory controlled by allies of the anti-terrorism coalition.

From the same paper, the next day:

The village where nothing happened.... The cemetery on the hill contains 40 freshly dug graves, unmarked and identical. And the village of Kama Ado has ceased to exist.... And all this is very strange because, on Saturday morning—when American B-52s unloaded dozens of bombs that killed 115 men, women and children—nothing happened.... We know this because the US Department of Defense told us so.... "It just didn't happen."

The *New York Times*, December 11, David Rohde, writing from Ghazni, Afghanistan:

Each ward of the Ghazni Hospital features a new calamity. In the first, two 14-year-old boys had lost parts of their hands when they picked up land mines. "I was playing with a toy and it exploded," said one of them, Muhammad Allah.... [A] woman named Rose lay on a bed in the corner of the room, grunting with each breath. Her waiflike children slept nearby, whimpering periodically. Early on Sunday morning, shrapnel from an American bomb tore through the woman's abdomen, broke her 4-year-old son's leg and ripped into her 6-year-old daughter's head, doctors here said. A second 6-year-old girl in the room was paralyzed from the waist down. X-rays showed how a tiny shard of metal had neatly severed her spinal cord.

From the *New York Times*, December 22:

[A]n attack by American warplanes on a convoy of trucks threatened to cast a shadow over the inaugural ceremonies [of the Interim Authority of Afghanistan]. The attack, southwest of Tora Bora, killed 65 people. American officials said the convoy was believed to be carrying Taliban or Al Qaeda leaders. But the Pakistan-based Afghan Islamic Press said it was carrying Afghan elders, tribal chiefs and other supporters of the new government on their way to the inauguration.

Reported in the *Chicago Tribune*, December 28 by Paul Salopek, from Madoo, Afghanistan:

Dusty mounds of rubble sit where buildings once stood. Sad artifacts of daily life are scattered across a wasteland of crater-gouged earth—buckets, shoes, shredded clothing. And there is the bruised smell of death: a nauseating reminder that 55 farmers and their livestock lie buried in the ruins of a US air strike.

"American soldiers came after the bombing and asked if any Al Qaeda had lived here," said villager Paira Gul. "Is that an Al Qaeda?" Gul asked, pointing to a child's severed foot he had excavated earlier from a smashed house. "Tell me," he said, his voice choking with fury, "is that what an Al Qaeda looks like?"

In four waves beginning in the predawn hours of December 1, US jets launched volleys of missiles and dropped guided bombs that obliterated the entire hamlet of 15 houses. Twenty-five days later, three ragged men—the only male survivors of the attack—were still picking through the debris, searching for the body parts of their families. "I swear to almighty Allah that we are not Al Qaeda or Taliban, we are farmers," said Abdul Hadi, whose wrinkled face and unkempt beard were covered with dust from digging. "We do not know why this happened to us. Only Allah knows."

Reuters, December 31, from Qalaye Niazi, Afghanistan:

US warplanes killed over 100 people in a raid on a village in eastern Afghanistan, residents said Monday.... At least one fighter jet, a B-52 bomber and two helicopters Sunday morning swooped down on the village of Qalaye Niazi.... Janat Gul said 24 members of his family were killed in the pre-dawn US bombing raid on Qalaye Niazi, and described himself as the sole survivor.... In the US Major Pete Mitchell—a spokesman for US Central Command—said: "We are aware of the incident and we are currently investigating."

The following day, which was New Year's Day, 2002, I looked in the *New York Times* and *Boston Globe*, who surely have better access to Reuters dispatches than I do, to find the above story. There was nothing. The next day, nothing in the *Globe*, but as part of a story in which an Afghan leader said he wanted the bombing to continue but expressed concern over civilian casualties, the *Times* talked of "reports that up to 100 villagers in Paktia Province had been killed in airstrikes overnight Saturday." It also quoted an American military commander, "This was a valid military target."

■ ■ ■ ■ ■ ■ ■ ■ ■ ■

The much-heralded "free press" of this country, by its failure to fully report on the terror visited daily on the people of Afghanistan, has become a handmaiden to the US government, and bears some responsibility for the continuation of this spurious "war on terrorism," for the deaths and mutilations reported in these articles.

The American people have been kept uninformed by government lies and media complicity and have little access to alternative information, so it is not surprising that a majority has supported what they have been led to think is a "war on terrorism."

I do believe that if they could see the consequences of the bombing campaign as vividly as we were all confronted with the horrifying photos of the Twin Towers collapsing and burning, and the victims' bodies being carried from the rubble, there would be a revulsion against such violence. If they saw on television, night after night, the blinded and maimed children, the weeping parents of Afghanistan, as we all saw day after day the awful photos of September 11, they might ask: Is this the way to combat terrorism?

Recall that Americans at first supported the war in Vietnam. But once the statistics of the dead became visible human beings—once they saw not only the body bags of young GI's piling up by the tens of thousands, but also the images of the napalmed children, the burning huts, the massacred families at My Lai—shock and indignation fueled a national movement to end the war.

I'm hoping that we can keep a double image in our minds—the American victims of September 11 and the Afghan victims of the misnamed "war on terrorism." That would be a first step towards a universal morality, beyond national borders, to think of all men and women, all children, everywhere, as our own.

| "'TELL ME,' HE SAID, HIS VOICE CHOKING WITH FURY, 'IS THAT WHAT AN AL QAEDA LOOKS LIKE?'" — *CHICAGO TRIBUNE*

ABUSE YOUR ILLUSIONS

US HOMELAND SECURITY: A BRIDGE FROM DEMOCRACY TO DICTATORSHIP

RITT GOLDSTEIN

America has changed. A leadership whose vision brought increasingly broad powers to the country's police, and one of every 32 adults to the penal system, is dominating today's political spectrum. Previously, in the turbulent era that was Vietnam, authoritarian leanings meant that security forces were repeatedly used in combating opposition to government policy. Then, as now, there were attempts to equate dissent with a lack of patriotism amounting to treachery. Dissenters were effectively marked as "the enemy," then treated as such.

As many recall, the ramifications were readily defined as the Ohio National Guard killed four protesting students at Kent State, with other killings occurring at places such as Jackson State. It was an era when violence toward dissenters was common, the security services feeling it "their duty" in helping the war effort.

Providing a sense of *déjà vu* for many, it was August 22, 2002, when police in Portland felt it "their duty" to assault nonviolent demonstrators. Both babies and very young children were among those pepper-sprayed. And in a statement cutting to the issue's very heart, the demonstrators vainly chanted, "We are not the enemy." But this unfolding nightmare has been years in the making.

As early as September 1, 1997, a *Time* article by a Hoover Institution research fellow, Joseph D. McNamara, warned that America must pursue security methods based upon law and communities' own democratic standards, not a reflection of "Berlin under the Nazis." But such warnings are dismissed as theatrical rhetoric, and so the most drastic changes have come, accelerated by the events of September 11.

> **FEMA'S NOT SO BENEVOLENT FACE PREVIOUSLY SHOWED ITSELF DURING THE REAGAN ERA, THE LAST TIME IT WAS PLACED IN A NATIONAL SECURITY ROLE.**

Now, as you read this, know that a secret American government genuinely exists in the country's shadows, one that can suspend your constitutional rights and subject America to martial law. Worst of all, this is not a product of conspiracy theory but presidential executive orders, orders to be implemented in the event of what the American public would accept as a "national crisis," a crisis which the prevailing political climate could quite easily provide.

Today, as terrorism's specter and warnings heighten apprehension, CBS News already having dubbed Attorney General John Ashcroft the "Minister of Fear," America's freedoms and democracy are indeed threatened by unseen forces.

While the Bush Administration has been repeatedly charged with wrongfully increasing the power of the Presidency, an all too possible avenue presently exists whereby George W. Bush could effectively declare a virtual American dictatorship. It would, of course, be a dictatorship declared in the name of freedom and democracy, and it would be achieved through FEMA.

FEMA is the Federal Emergency Management Agency, and for most of America the agency represents nothing more than a benevolent responder to domestic disaster. But far removed from far-right conspiracy theory, though unknown to most, FEMA does have a history of pursuing domestic intelligence and practicing for martial law and citizen internment. These activities were undertaken during the Reagan era, FEMA then facing censure for them. But today's circumstances are increasingly forming numerous parallels to the more darkly obscure pursuits of that era.

Of particular note, and equally obscure, is the fact that FEMA is today the federal agency "in charge of terrorism response." Under the White House's new "National Strategy for Homeland Security," FEMA is also acknowledged as the framework for the Department of Homeland Security (DoHS). The DoHS legislation confirms this. As Homeland Security Office spokesman Gordon Johndroe told the *New York Times*, "Our mission is not only to prevent against attacks, but to respond to them, and FEMA is the response mechanism in the government."

Unfortunately, FEMA critics of both the left and right have long warned of the agency's potential for assaulting the very foundations of America's freedoms.

FEMA's not so benevolent face previously showed itself during the Reagan era, the last time it was placed in a national security role. Then, according to Political Research Associates (PRA), the agency attempted to build a "military/police version of civil security." (As a footnote, the highly respected PRA is a small, progressive think tank specializing in threats from the right.)

What "threat" means here is internment camps, martial law, and the suspension of civil rights and the Constitution. PRA also cited a warning that "only the lack of a crisis big enough, a president willing enough, and a public aroused enough to permit it to be invoked, separates us from a possible dictatorship, brought about under current law, waiting to be implemented in the event of circumstances which can be construed as a 'national emergency.'" American democracy has become an endangered species.

Once a "national emergency" is declared, FEMA steps in…and while the route to martial law and effective dictatorship is clear, the path back is anything but so. Provisions for a return to so-called normalcy remain murky at best.

Illuminating FEMA's proposed DoHS role, a role vastly expanding its powers, congressional records illustrate that the DoHS is strongly modeled upon House bill HR 1158, a bill crafting the DoHS simply "by renaming the Federal Emergency Management Agency (FEMA) and merging the Coast Guard, the Customs Service, and the Border Patrol into the 'new agency.'" This quote is according to congressional records. In essence, the DoHS is essentially a vastly expanded and empowered FEMA.

> ## ACCORDING TO CNN, JOHN GOODMAN OF THE UNITED STEELWORKERS SAID OF THE SECURITY FORCES' ACTIONS, "I'VE WITNESSED THINGS IN THE LAST FOUR DAYS THAT I DIDN'T BELIEVE COULD HAPPEN IN AMERICA."

Providing a measure of comparison, FEMA today has 2,600 personnel; the DoHS is slated to have 170,000. Illustrating this other dimension of FEMA's potential new powers, UPI reported that the DoHS will have "more armed law enforcement officers than the Department of Justice, FBI, CIA or any US police agency."

And so, what had been found in the Reagan era to be one of the greatest potential threats to American democracy, has just become democracy's staunchest protector.

The fox has indeed come to guard the henhouse…and the watchdogs haven't barked.

The Homeland Security legislation will effectively transform a small but dangerous FEMA into a gigantic Homeland Security Agency. However, some more severe Administration critics have recently noted that there is an historical precedent for such homeland security measures. It is disturbing to note that the precedent they cite was commonly called "the SS, or Schutzstaffel (defense echelons)," and was created in Nazi Germany.

According to the *Washington Post*, Congress acknowledges that the DoHS will effectively change the face of FEMA from that of rescue worker to that of counterterrorism agent.

And in a period when the Nobel Peace Prize-winning American Friends Service Committee (a Quaker organization) is classified a "criminal extremist group," and President Bush has declared that those who are not with us are with the terrorists, questions need be raised regarding whom FEMA might respond against and how. Providing an insightful revelation, FEMA has already gone into limited operation to combat dissenters, doing so during the WTO meeting in Seattle in November/December 1999.

At that time, CNN reported that both regular and special forces troops were present to support FEMA's "security" role and "assist in coordinating a federal response" should a "terrorist" incident occur. A Seattle curfew was declared, the first since the one affecting Japanese-Americans during WWII. According to CNN, John Goodman of the United Steelworkers said of the security forces' actions, "I've witnessed things in the last four days that I didn't believe could happen in America."

But things are happening in America, and as the Department of Homeland Security's name implies, it is an organization whose purpose is both to safeguard the homeland and maintain order in it. Given what FEMA has planned and practiced for, the methods for the DoHS's pursuit of its latter mission are those generating substantive concerns. Even FEMA's Clinton-era director, James Lee Witt, had argued to keep FEMA out of the DoHS.

In this era of "the new McCarthyism," concerns exist that all citizens not of "pure" thought or blood can be suspect. Arab-Americans effectively heard this in Detroit when a member of the Civil Rights Commission raised the specter of internment camps, and as battered demonstrators in Portland discovered, the War on Terror also appears to be a War on Dissent.

At the time of FEMA's earlier abuses, then-FBI Director William Webster objected to FEMA's pursuing domestic intelligence "under the rubric of counterterrorism." Appreciating Webster's complaint, alarmed as to both the aim and scope of FEMA's efforts, then-Attorney General William French Smith charged that there were "serious policy and legal objections to an 'emergency czar' role for FEMA."

But cutting to the very root of today's concerns, Smith also conveyed alarm regarding what he perceived as a drift into an effective exaggeration of events. This created circumstances allowing what he termed "the expansion of the definition of severe emergencies to encompass 'routine' domestic law enforcement emergencies," potentially threatening the engagement of FEMA's draconian capabilities.

As for today's implications, Vietnam War-style peace demonstrations could conceivably be used as a well fabricated pretext for declaring a "national crisis." Recent developments have demonstrated that it is all too conceivable that dissenters could be marked as what John Ashcroft termed "enemy combatants."

Today, under the USA PATRIOT Act, the definition of terrorism has been substantively broadened to effectively include groups of activists. According to the Center for Constitutional Rights, this means that "environmental activists, anti-globalization activists, and anti-abortion activists who use direct action to further their political agendas are particularly vulnerable to prosecution as 'domestic terrorists,'" adding that there are concerns regarding political activism, as well. In a disturbing illustration, the US government's "'no fly' list, intended to keep terrorists from boarding planes, is snaring peace activists" at America's airports. This disquieting revelation appeared in the *San Francisco Chronicle* (September 27, 2002).

However, cutting to what many perceive as the way that the most authoritarian of measures could be accepted, US Civil Rights Commission member Peter Kirsanow said that should an attack occur, "the public would be less concerned about any perceived erosion of civil liberties than they are about protecting their own lives."

Meanwhile, since 9/11, considerable criticism of the Bush Administration's response has provided an alarming echo of former Attorney General Smith's warnings. But the Administration's secret shadow government, activated in the wake of 9/11, today highlights the most visible part of American democracy's unrealized threat, as well as providing the structure for G.W. Bush and FEMA to run America should a crisis be declared.

The *Washington Post* revealed the shadow government's existence on March 1, 2002, noting it was a part of Reagan-era national security initiatives. The Bush Administration explained the shadow government as a precaution to ensure the continuation of government in case of a terrorist attack. But the next day, the *Post* ran a subsequent headline, that the US Congress had been unaware that the shadow government existed. However, providing a curious question, present law provides for the Speaker of the House, followed by the President pro tempore of the Senate, to assume the presidency should the President and Vice President become unable to perform their duties. Questions indeed remain as to why Congress didn't know.

However, should the Constitution be suspended, control of the country passes to the President and FEMA alone, so it would be the executive branch of government which would oversee America, effectively eliminating the voices of Congress and the judiciary. And in this context, it should also be noted that the shadow government is physically located within a FEMA facility.

And so as Bush's "imperial presidency" continues what the *Detroit News* termed a "thinly veiled power grab," America has already witnessed an assault upon civil liberties, with discussion of martial law and internment camps also having begun. FEMA critics from both the left and right have charged that at the end of this path could be an exercise, either explicit or effective, of the "national crisis" executive orders, orders turning control of America over to Bush and FEMA, which is headed by former Bush/Cheney 2000 campaign manager Joe Allbaugh.

Nadine Strossen, president of the American Civil Liberties Union, had earlier distilled the dynamics of the present danger, charging that "the Administration has adopted a 'trust us, we're the government' attitude toward its critics and the American people. But for our democracy to thrive, Congress and the American public must cast a skeptical eye over any attempt by the executive branch to amass new unchecked powers."

When the origins of FEMA's dark side were secretly spawned during the Reagan era, it's known that FEMA planned and practiced for the imposition of martial law and the internment of so-called aliens and radicals. An exercise termed Rex-84 became public knowledge.

Mounted in cooperation with the Department of Defense (DoD), material presented by Political Research Associates highlights that Rex-84 was an exercise with the purpose of testing military capabilities in anticipation of "civil disturbances, major demonstrations." Civil defense became civil control. As part of Rex-84, individuals detained were to be held in rural internment camps.

Sharpening present concerns, on August 14, 2002, the *Los Angeles Times* ran an article entitled "Camps for Citizens: Ashcroft's Hellish Vision." As CNN/FindLaw summarized the issue, "We now are faced with a scary prospect—indefinite detention of multiple citizens because the government decides they are dangerous. The mere suggestion of camps or group detention facilities implies that the Executive is, in fact, considering using its newfound citizen-combatant detention program on a broader scale.... [I]f this sounds frightening, that's because it is."

SHOULD THE CONSTITUTION BE SUSPENDED, CONTROL OF THE COUNTRY PASSES TO THE PRESIDENT AND FEMA ALONE.

Illustrating FEMA's prior perspective on homeland security, a July 5, 1987, *Miami Herald* article reported that 1982-85 FEMA Director Louis Guiffrida's deputy, John Brinkerhoff, handled the martial law portion of FEMA's crisis planning. Based on a Brinkerhoff memo that the *Miami Herald* obtained, the crisis plan envisioned was said to be similar to one which Giuffrida had earlier developed to combat "a national uprising by black militants." Giuffrida's plan had provided for the detention "of at least 21 million 'American Negroes'" in "assembly centers or relocation camps."

The Reagan initiatives were drafted during the period when the US was considering the invasion of Nicaragua, a parallel to today's Iraq controversy. Details of FEMA's national security role subsequently emerged during the Iran-Contra scandal, which involved clandestine sales of arms to Iran, using the proceeds to fund US-backed Central American insurgents, the Contras. The Contra period has since been termed that of the "Dirty Wars," accused of creating Central American killing fields. The scandal marked a period when senior members of the Reagan Administration engaged in both questionable and criminal acts in the name of national security.

Iran-Contra lead to convictions for key Reagan figures such as John Poindexter and Elliott Abrams, both of whom serve in the present Bush Administration, as do a number of others from that period. Critics charge that this has provided an all too effective link to the policies pursued in that era.

In order to facilitate prospective Reagan-era internments, FEMA had begun assembling files on those whom they might target. Ominously, FEMA's Operation TIPS provided another echo of that time, having been designed as a vehicle where citizen-informants' reports would be "maintained and analyzed in a single (TIPS) database." Providing a curious footnote, the TIPS connection to FEMA was initially obscured, the TIPS Website originally calling the program "a project of the US Department of Justice." Thanks to the efforts of one Senator, the legislation creating the Department of Homeland Security specifically outlawed Operation TIPS, although it said absolutely nothing about other programs that might use the same tactics.

As regards FEMA's earlier dossier effort, according to investigative authors Ward Churchill and Jim Vander Wall, before the Reagan-era effort became extensive, FBI intervention halted it. The dossier episode detonated when the FBI challenged FEMA's right to pursue domestic intelligence, resulting in FEMA's turning over "12,000 political dossiers" to the Bureau.

It was a Reagan-era series of executive orders which reportedly granted FEMA powers to impose martial law, suspend the Constitution, and intern individuals during a so-called national crisis. Crisis was defined to include "violent and widespread internal dissent or national opposition against a US military invasion abroad."

With opposition to a war on Iraq growing, FEMA's definition of "crisis" again highlights an evolution of civil defense into civil control. And even if a formal crisis is not declared, speculation exists that a de facto drift into an effective deployment of FEMA's crisis powers could occur.

Present speculation also exists that a US Civil Rights Commission member, Bush appointee Peter Kirsanow, broached the idea of Arab-American internment as a so-called trial balloon, the Administration attempting to gauge public reaction. And almost simultaneously, on July 21, 2002, the New York Times headlined, "Wider Military Role in US is Urged," a necessary prelude for an evolution towards martial law. The Times article reported "a shift in thinking by many top Pentagon officials, who have traditionally been wary of involving the military in domestic law enforcement."

Giuffrida subsequently developed plans which, according to Reynolds and others, were designed to "legitimize the arrest and detention of anti-Vietnam war activists and other political dissidents," again highlighting a vision which transforms civil defense into civil control.

When Reagan became President, Giuffrida was appointed to head FEMA, promptly opening a "Civil Defense Training Center" based on CSTI. FEMA also worked with the Pentagon; their joint position paper, "The Civil/Military Alliance in Emergency Management," was a precursor to America's present debate regarding a law enforcement role for the military.

At present, the final contents and disposition of the Reagan security initiatives, part of a national crisis plan, remains beyond public knowledge. But in February 2002, the former FEMA executive who drafted the martial law/internment portions of the national plan, John Brinkerhoff, revealed that it was "approved by Reagan, and actions were taken to implement it." And so as critics of the current Bush Administration have increasingly charged, the greatest threat to America's freedom and democracy appears to be emanating from a leadership cloaking the most authoritarian of measures as our liberty's defense.

THE ROOTS OF TODAY'S EXTRAORDINARY CONCERNS WERE INITIATED BY REAGAN DURING THE PERIOD THAT HE WAS CALIFORNIA'S GOVERNOR.

Earlier, Secretary of Defense Donald Rumsfeld had said that the newly established Northern Command—in charge of "supporting homeland defense"—"will provide for a more coordinated military support to civil authorities such as FBI, FEMA and state and local governments."

According to the White House's Website, today's FEMA "will continue to change the emergency management culture from one that reacts to terrorism...to one that proactively helps communities and citizens avoid becoming victims." However, FEMA's prior rationale for domestic spying and the prospective internment of individuals was their alleged threat to their own communities. And it's no small paradox that FEMA's prior debacle, and conflict with the FBI, were a direct outgrowth of FEMA's attempt to legitimize the pursuit of disturbingly authoritarian measures under the very cloak of counterterrorism.

The roots of today's extraordinary concerns were initiated by Reagan during the period that he was California's Governor. According to Diana Reynolds—whose 1990 article "The Rise of the National Security State" laid bare the foundations of present concerns—in 1971 Reagan reportedly inaugurated the idea of utilizing the military and law enforcement to combat dissent, creating the California Specialized Training Institute (CSTI), a "counterterrorism training center." Present-day implications are amply provided by a revealing passage in the October 2001 Journal of Homeland Security. There, current Homeland Security notable John Brinkerhoff, Giuffrida's former deputy at FEMA, described CSTI as an institute which "trained state employees in emergency management."

Reagan also appointed Louis Giuffrida as his "Emergency Czar."

BILL OF RIGHTS, R.I.P.
A GUIDE TO PROVISIONS OF THE USA PATRIOT ACT AND FEDERAL EXECUTIVE ORDERS THAT THREATEN CIVIL LIBERTIES
NANCY TALANIAN

On October 26, 2001, President Bush signed into law the USA PATRIOT Act (an acronym for "Uniting and Strengthening America by Providing Appropriate Tools Required to Intercept and Obstruct Terrorism"). Passed hurriedly (many Congressmen stated later they had not even had time to read the law), it creates a new crime, "domestic terrorism," so broadly defined that it could conceivably apply to otherwise legal acts of civil disobedience and dissent.

The USA PATRIOT Act gives the FBI and the CIA greater rights to wiretap phones, monitor email, break into homes and offices without prior notification, and survey medical, financial, and student records.

The Justice Department has also dismantled regulations against COINTELPRO operations that were enacted following abuses of the civil rights and peace movements of the 1950s, 1960s, and 1970s.

The dangers of the USA PATRIOT Act are augmented by a Bureau of Prisons order allowing federal agents to abridge the attorney-client privilege by eavesdropping on conversations between lawyers and their clients held in federal custody.

The Administration has ordered secret military tribunals for suspected terrorists. In addition to being unfair and unnecessary, the US threat of using military tribunals increases the likelihood that US citizens will be treated accordingly overseas, and decreases the likelihood that other governments will be willing to extradite suspected terrorists or other parties wanted by the US.

Under this Act and other legislation, noncitizens are being deported or detained indefinitely without judicial appeal.

The Websites of the following organizations contain excellent analyses of the provisions of the USA PATRIOT Act and various federal executive orders passed since September 11, 2001, that threaten civil liberties:

- American Civil Liberties Union <www.aclu.org>
- Electronic Frontier Foundation <www.eff.org>
- National Lawyers Guild <www.nlg.org>
- People for the American Way <www.pfaw.org>

Congress showed its concern about certain sections of the Act relating to enhanced surveillance by including in Section 224 a "sunset" provision. We are also concerned about the powers for enhanced surveillance, and so we call upon Congress to accelerate the sunset provision so that the sections expire immediately rather than on December 31, 2005.

We are concerned not only that the government is using its new powers but is refusing to provide unclassified information under the Freedom of Information Act on how it is using them, such as who is being detained. The refusal prevents anyone, including citizens, the media, federal judges, and members of Congress, from knowing whether the powers have been or are being abused. We believe the enhanced secrecy imposed by the Administration makes it all the more imperative that Congress repeal unwarranted and unnecessary powers that provide little or no security but that clearly threaten our civil liberties.

What follows is a brief summary of some of the provisions of the USA PATRIOT Act (USAPA) and federal executive orders that threaten our rights as guaranteed by the Bill of Rights. We recommend that these sections be repealed.

_AMENDMENT I

"Congress shall make no law respecting an establishment of religion, or prohibiting the free exercise thereof; or abridging the freedom of speech, or of the press; or the right of the people peaceably to assemble, and to petition the Government for a redress of grievances."

Title or Provision:
USAPA §802: Definition of domestic terrorism.

What It Says/What It Changes:
Creates a new crime, "domestic terrorism," which it defines as "acts dangerous to human life that are a violation of the criminal laws of the United States or of any State" and that "appear to be intended...to influence the policy of a government by intimidation or coercion."

How It Can Be Misused:
Broad definition may be used against activists exercising their rights to assemble and to dissent.

Title or Provision:
USAPA §215: Access to records and other items under the Foreign Intelligence Surveillance Act.

What It Says/What It Changes:
Permits the FBI to seek records from bookstores and libraries of books that a person suspected of terrorism has purchased or read,

or of his or her activities on a library's computer. Also places a gag order to prevent anyone from disclosing that they have been ordered to produce such documents.

How It Can Be Misused:
Puts people at risk for exercising their free speech rights to read, recommend, or discuss a book or to write an email. Also denies booksellers and library personnel the free speech right to inform anyone, including an attorney, that the FBI has asked for someone's reading list.

Title or Provision:
Attorney General Ashcroft's edict for increased surveillance of religious and political organizations.

What It Says/What It Changes:
Rescinds anti-COINTELPRO regulations and authorizes the FBI to monitor and surveil religious groups and political groups without evidence of wrongdoing.

How It Can Be Misused:
Opens the door to COINTELPRO operations, which were used in the past to harass and to intimidate people who disagreed with the government on issues such as civil rights and the Vietnam War.

Title or Provision:
Attorney General Ashcroft's edict subverting Freedom of Information Act requests.

What It Says/What It Changes:
Replaced Attorney General Janet Reno's previous guidelines to agencies for fulfilling FOIA requests, which were to make allowable discretionary disclosures except where there was "demonstrable harm." Ashcroft tells agencies that "decide to withhold records, in whole or in part," that they "can be assured that the Department of Justice will defend your decisions unless they lack a sound legal basis or present an unwarranted risk of adverse impact on the ability of other agencies to protect other important records."

How It Can Be Misused:
Enables federal agencies to ignore many FOIA requests for unclassified information. For example, the Administration has used this edict to keep secret the names of detainees held for long periods, and to close their hearings.

Title or Provision:
Attorney General Ashcroft's approval of a Bureau of Prisons emergency surveillance order.

What It Says/What It Changes:
Removes requirement to obtain judicial permission before listening in on conversations between prisoners (both prior to trial and convicted) and their attorneys.

How It Can Be Misused:
Abridges freedom of speech.

_AMENDMENT IV

"The right of the people to be secure in their persons, houses, papers, and effects, against unreasonable searches and seizures, shall not be violated, and no Warrants shall issue, but upon probable cause, supported by Oath or affirmation, and particularly describing the place to be searched, and the persons or things to be seized."

This amendment forms a substantial basis of the constitutional right to privacy.

Title or Provision:
USAPA §203: Authority to share criminal investigative information.

What It Says/What It Changes:
Permits law enforcement to give CIA sensitive information gathered in criminal investigations, including wiretaps and Internet trapping.

How It Can Be Misused:
No court order is required. CIA may share the information with other agencies and with foreign governments.

Title or Provision:
USAPA §218: Foreign intelligence information.

What It Says/What It Changes:
Amends Foreign Intelligence Surveillance Act (FISA) by eliminating the need for the FBI to show "probable cause" before conducting secret searches or surveillance to obtain evidence of a crime.

How It Can Be Misused:
Eliminates judicial supervision by giving the FBI the ability to gather "foreign intelligence information" without a warrant, unless the evidence sought is to be used in a criminal proceeding. Former standard of "foreign intelligence information" is weakened.[1] Agent may now say that foreign intelligence is relevant or plays a part in the investigation. "Probable cause" of a crime is no longer needed.

Title or Provision:
USAPA §206: Roving surveillance authority (a/k/a "roving wiretaps") under the Foreign Intelligence Surveillance Act of 1978.

What It Says/What It Changes:
Extends roving wiretap authority to "intelligence" wiretaps authorized by the Foreign Intelligence Surveillance Court.

How It Can Be Misused:
These wiretaps may be authorized secretly. Expands the power broadly by tapping any device used by a terrorist suspect, regardless of who is using the device at the time.

Title or Provision:
USAPA §213: Authority for delaying notice of the execution of a warrant (a/k/a "sneak and peek").

What It Says/What It Changes:
Permits the government to search your home with no one present and to delay notification indefinitely. Court may authorize delayed notification "if the court finds reasonable cause to believe that providing immediate notification...may have an adverse result."

How It Can Be Misused:
Unlike the former "knock and announce" policy, a person whose home is to be searched cannot view the warrant to make sure the address is correct or to make sure that the agent adheres to the warrant's description of what is to be searched.

Title or Provision:
USAPA §215: Access to records and other items under the Foreign Intelligence Surveillance Act.

What It Says/What It Changes:
Relaxes requirements and extends capabilities of FISA by enabling anyone within the FBI down to rank of Assistant Special Agent in Charge to request a court order for tangible items sought for an investigation "to protect against international terrorism or clandestine intelligence activities." The judge must give permission if an agent has so certified.

For example, it permits the FBI to seek records from bookstores and libraries of books that a person has purchased or read, or of his or her activities on a library's computer. It also places a gag order to prevent anyone from disclosing that they have been ordered to produce such documents.

Eliminates the former test, that "there are specific and articulable facts giving reason to believe that the person to whom the records pertain is a foreign power or an agent of a foreign power."

How It Can Be Misused:
No legitimate checks and balances; rather, the judge becomes a "rubber stamp." No privacy protection for US citizens or legal residents acting legally. Transfers power from the judiciary to the executive branch.

Title or Provision:
USAPA §411: Definitions relating to terrorism.

What It Says/What It Changes:
Allows Secretary of State to designate as a "terrorist organization" any foreign or domestic group that has engaged in a violent activity.

How It Can Be Misused:
Lowers standard for terrorist designation; possibility of groups that dissent peacefully being so designated as the result of an action by an agent provocateur.

Title or Provision:
USAPA §412: Mandatory detention of suspected terrorists; *habeas corpus*; judicial review.

What It Says/What It Changes:
Gives Attorney General broad powers to certify immigrants as risks.

How It Can Be Misused:
Reduces previous standard from "probable cause."

Title or Provision:
Attorney General Ashcroft's edict for increased surveillance of religious and political organizations.

What It Says/What It Changes:
Rescinds anti-COINTELPRO regulations and authorizes the FBI to monitor and surveil religious groups and political groups without evidence of wrongdoing.

How It Can Be Misused:
Reduces standard for surveillance from "probable cause."

Title or Provision:
Attorney General Ashcroft's approval of a Bureau of Prisons emergency surveillance order.

What It Says/What It Changes:
Removes requirement to obtain judicial permission before listening in on conversations between prisoners (both prior to trial and convicted) and their attorneys.

How It Can Be Misused:
Constitutes "unreasonable searches" without the necessity to meet the standard of "probable cause."

Title or Provision:
Attorney General Ashcroft's TIPS program.[2]

What It Says/What It Changes:
Sets up a system for up to 2 million Americans (more than were involved in the heyday of East Germany's Stasi) to secretly provide information to the government about any persons whom they consider suspicious, and for the government to set up a file on these persons.

How It Can Be Misused:
May potentially damage someone's record due to innocent activities that are misunderstood or are invented or enhanced by the caller because of a personal vendetta. How the "tips" would be used has been neither reported nor approved, nor have there been assurances that anyone who is reported as "suspicious" will be confronted with the evidence against him/her and given an opportunity to correct it.

_AMENDMENT V

"No person shall be held to answer for a...crime, unless on a presentment or indictment of a Grand Jury..., nor shall be compelled in any criminal case to be a witness against himself, nor be deprived of life, liberty, or property, without due process of law."

Title or Provision:
President Bush's military order.

What It Says/What It Changes:
Establishes trials by military tribunal, at President's discretion, for noncitizens.

How It Can Be Misused:
Denies "due process of law," which applies not only to citizens but to all "persons" in the United States. Allows secret evidence and hearsay to be used against the accused.

Title or Provision:
President Bush's order designating "enemy combatants."

What It Says/What It Changes:
Allows committee of Attorney General, Defense Secretary, and CIA Director to label *citizens* and noncitizens as "enemy combatants," placing them in military custody, holding them in detention indefinitely, interrogating them, and denying them communication with outsiders or judicial review.

How It Can Be Misused:
No opportunity to prove innocence. Denial of "liberty...without due process of law."

Title or Provision:
USAPA §412: Mandatory detention of suspected terrorists; *habeas corpus*; judicial review.

What It Says/What It Changes:
Gives Attorney General broad powers to certify immigrants as risks.

How It Can Be Misused:
Deprives immigrants of "liberty...without due process of law."

Title or Provision:
Attorney General Ashcroft's approval of a Bureau of Prisons emergency surveillance order.

What It Says/What It Changes:
Removes requirement to obtain judicial permission before listening in on conversations between prisoners (both prior to trial and convicted) and their attorneys.

How It Can Be Misused:
A prisoner may be made to be a witness against himself or herself.

Title or Provision:
Attorney General Ashcroft's edict for increased surveillance of religious and political organizations.

What It Says/What It Changes:
Rescinds anti-COINTELPRO regulations and authorizes the FBI to monitor and surveil religious groups and political groups without evidence of wrongdoing.

How It Can Be Misused:
An unsuspecting participant in a religious or political meeting may be "compelled to be a witness against himself."

_AMENDMENT VI

"In all criminal prosecutions, the accused shall enjoy the right to a speedy and public trial, by an impartial jury of the State and district wherein the crime shall have been committed...and to be informed of the nature and cause of the accusation; to be confronted with the witnesses against him; to have compulsory process for obtaining witnesses in his favor, and to have the Assistance of Counsel for his defence."

Title or Provision:
USAPA §412: Mandatory detention of suspected terrorists; *habeas corpus*; judicial review.

What It Says/What It Changes:
Gives Attorney General broad powers to certify immigrants as risks.

How It Can Be Misused:
Infringes upon the rights "to a speedy and public trial, by an impartial jury of the State and district..., to be informed of the nature and cause of the accusation, to be confronted with the witnesses against him," and "to have the Assistance of Counsel for his defence."

Title or Provision:
President Bush's order designating "enemy combatants."

What It Says/What It Changes:
Allows committee of Attorney General, Defense Secretary, and CIA Director to label *citizens* and noncitizens as "enemy combatants," placing them in military custody, holding them in detention indefinitely, interrogating them, and denying them communication with outsiders or judicial review.

How It Can Be Misused:
Infringes upon the rights "to a speedy and public trial, by an impartial jury of the State and district..., to be informed of the nature and cause of the accusation, to be confronted with the witnesses against him," and "to have the Assistance of Counsel for his defence."

Title or Provision:
Attorney General Ashcroft's approval of a Bureau of Prisons emergency surveillance order.

What It Says/What It Changes:
Removes requirement to obtain judicial permission before listening in on conversations between prisoners (both prior to trial and convicted) and their attorneys.

How It Can Be Misused:

A prisoner who knows that law enforcement may listen in on conversations with an attorney may forgo the right to ask for counsel to aid in his or her defense.

_AMENDMENT VIII

"Excessive bail shall not be required, nor excessive fines imposed, nor cruel and unusual punishments inflicted."

Title or Provision:

USAPA §412: Mandatory detention of suspected terrorists; *habeas corpus*; judicial review.

What It Says/What It Changes:

Gives Attorney General broad powers to certify immigrants as risks.

How It Can Be Misused:

May result in "cruel and unusual punishments" (deportation).

Endnotes

1. The Foreign Intelligence Surveillance Administration (FISA) issued a surprising opinion in May 2002, which rejected the Justice Department's request for information-sharing between counterintelligence and prosecutors because it would not effectively protect privacy rights. **2.** In late November 2002, Operation TIPS was formally outlawed by the Homeland Security Act. However, the law says absolutely nothing about similar citizen-informant programs that may be set up under a different name.

Editor's Note: Nancy Talanian is the founder of the Bill of Rights Defense Committee <www.bordc.org>, which urges cities, towns, and counties to pass resolutions rejecting the PATRIOT Act and protecting the constitutional rights of citizens. As of the beginning of 2003, 23 communities—including Berkeley, Flagstaff, Oakland, Denver, Boulder, Amherst, Cambridge, and Detroit—had passed such a resolution, and efforts were underway in at least 70 other communities.

CREATING PANAMA FOR FUNDS AND PROFIT
THE COUNTRY'S INDEPENDENCE WAS ENGINEERED BY TYCOONS AND POLITICIANS IN THE US
OVIDIO DIAZ-ESPINO

On November 4, 1903, at 1:30 in the afternoon, 500 Colombian soldiers menacingly circled the Atlantic terminal of the American-owned Panama Railroad Company. They raised their loaded rifles and aimed at the American employees defending the front entrance of the wooden building. Inside, silver-haired Civil War veteran Colonel James Shaler, the railroad's superintendent, raised the American flag over the flagpole. This was the pre-arranged signal to Commander Hubbard of the U.S.S. *Nashville* to land his troops. Within minutes, 42 well-armed American Marines landed to face the Colombians and secure the independence of Panama.

Teddy Roosevelt's decision to send troops to the Isthmus of Panama in 1903 and seize the province of Colombia was the critical event that permitted the construction of the Panama Canal in 1914, which Roosevelt called the single "greatest accomplishment" of his eight years in office. However, Roosevelt later denied any involvement with the independence of Panama. In his State of the Union address in 1904, he claimed that Panamanians rebelled because they were tired of the injustices committed by the Bogota government and thus "rose literally as one man." ("Yes, and the one man was Roosevelt," added Senator Edward Carmack.) Only after the revolution in Panama City had been consummated, Roosevelt assured, did United States troops intervene, and then only to preserve the functioning of the railroad pursuant to treaty rights. "I think proper to say, therefore, that no one connected with this government had any part in preparing, inciting, or encouraging the revolution on the Isthmus of Panama."

> TEDDY ROOSEVELT'S DECISION TO SEND TROOPS TO THE ISTHMUS OF PANAMA IN 1903 AND SEIZE THE PROVINCE OF COLOMBIA WAS THE CRITICAL EVENT THAT PERMITTED THE CONSTRUCTION OF THE PANAMA CANAL IN 1914

Even though his claims run against the weight of historical evidence, for the last century, his version became the official story espoused in schoolbooks in the United States and Panama, and written about by historians of the Panama Canal and of Roosevelt even today. As recently as November 2002, during the 99th anniversary of the independence of Panama from Colombia—as the entire government of the republic, including President Mireya Moscoso, her cabinet, and all members of the National Assembly, gathered to lay wreaths at the tomb of the country's first President and officially kick off the celebrations leading to the 100-year anniversary of independence on November 3, 2003—the official historian dedicated his entire reflections and speech to attack "those who claim that Panama was created by Washington and Wall Street," and argued that such claims constitute "gutsy irresponsible accusations which are not based on sustainable documentation." *La Prensa*, Panama's leading newspaper, carried the comments on the first page of the November 3rd edition with big headlines stating: "WASHINGTON DID NOT CREATE PANAMA... INDEPENDENCE AROSE FROM THE GENUINE WANTS OF PANAMANIANS."

But like it or not, the evidence reveals that behind the Panamanian nation's independence and Teddy Roosevelt's gunboat diplomacy was a dark alliance between the bankrupt French Panama Canal Company and a secretive syndicate of Wall Street financiers aiming to remap the world to line their pockets. As the *New York Times* said in 1906: "[T]he history of the Panama Canal is one long track and trail of scandal. There has been scandal in the remote past, in the recent past, there is some now and we fear there will be more in the future."

■■■■■■■■■■

For 400 years, cutting a strait through the mountains and jungles of Panama to join the Pacific Ocean with the Atlantic Ocean had been the fractured dream of European nations who sought access to the Pacific. In 1879, Ferdinand de Lesseps, the visionary French promoter who built the Suez Canal, went against all advice and turned his attention to the centuries-old dream of building the Panama Canal.

He chartered the Compagnie Universalle Pour le Canal Interoceanic, its stated purpose to build *la grande enterprise*. It was the greatest human undertaking ever attempted. The cost was calculated at $240 million dollars, twice that of the Suez Canal. The time for construction was estimated at twelve years, also twice as long as that of Suez. The excavation was expected to be finished by 1899, but by that time only a fifth had been completed.

De Lesseps had made crucial engineering mistakes, such as demanding a sea-level canal and underestimating the difference between the dry deserts of Suez and the humid, muddy land in Panama. Also, tuberculosis, yellow fever, and malaria had killed or seriously debilitated two of every three workers. In December 1889, unable to raise more money to continue the work, the French hero had no choice but to declare that *la grande enterprise* was dead.

The Compagnie Universalle's bankruptcy was a failure of unimaginable proportion. Thousands of peasants throughout Europe who had invested their life savings in the company saw their money evaporate. Outraged, the public demanded the guillotine for those responsible. Several of the organizers, including the family of de Lesseps and Gustave Eiffel, the builder of the Eiffel tower and the Statue of Liberty, were imprisoned for fraud and misfeasance of the investors' funds.

A new company acquired the assets of the old company and launched a campaign to raise enough capital to begin again, but it was mere fantasy. In Panama, all that remained of the original company were a few rusting dredges, and most of the excavation had disappeared under tropical mudslides. The only valuable asset was the concession to build the canal granted by Colombia, of which Panama was a province, but this was set to expire in a few years. France's only real hope of recouping some of its investment was to sell the rights to build the Panama Canal to the United States.

France knew that the United States had wanted to build an isthmian route since the 1840s to facilitate the massive migration spurred by the California Gold Rush. However, given the bankruptcy of the French, public sentiment in the United States supported the long cherished plan to build a canal through Nicaragua, using its two lakes, Lake Managua and Lake Nicaragua.

For France, an American-built Nicaragua Canal meant the loss of its $250 million investment. The French thus sought to sway American opinion by any means. They knew something about a Wall Street lawyer who was an expert in bankrupt companies, William Nelson Cromwell.

On January 26, 1896, Maurice Hutin, president of the Compagnie Nouvelle, paid a visit to the mahogany-paneled offices of Sullivan & Cromwell at 41 Wall Street. He came to sign up Cromwell's services in convincing the United States government to acquire the rights to build the Panama Canal from the bankrupt French company. Cromwell gave his guest an enthusiastic reception. From that moment, the destiny of *la grande enterprise* and the dream of centuries rested on the shoulders of the man who, according to Joseph Pulitzer's *World*, with his "masterful mind, whetted on the grindstone of corporation cunning, conceived and carried out the rape of the Isthmus."

■ ■ ■ ■ ■ ■ ■ ■ ■ ■

A little man, Cromwell was "strikingly pretty, with aquiline features and a mane of white wavy hair which added to his air of authority and made him conspicuous in any company." Nicknamed "the Fox" by his opponents, he was controlling, shameless, and utterly persuasive. "No life insurance agent could beat him," a reporter wrote, "he talks fast and when he wishes to, never to the point." With his "wizardry with figures and an intellect like a flash of lighting that swings with the agility of an acrobat," he planned all his movements in advance.

His clients included J.P. Morgan, whom he helped to create the United Steel Corporation, the biggest company in the world, and Edward Harriman, whom he assisted in designing the complex finances and mergers that led to the first transcontinental railroad company.

He offered more than a law firm did: He had press agents, accountants, and politicians that helped him lobby his cases in Washington.

He had intimate relations, "susceptible of being used to advantage," with men possessing influence and power in all circles, including political, financial, and in the press. His specialty was bankrupt companies. He was the obvious choice for the Compagnie Nouvelle du Canal Interoceanic to turn to when they needed a miracle.

TUBERCULOSIS, YELLOW FEVER, AND MALARIA HAD KILLED OR SERIOUSLY DEBILITATED TWO OF EVERY THREE WORKERS.

On December 2, 1898, Cromwell went to Washington, DC, to convince President McKinley and Congress to build the Panama Canal, but found himself against an entrenched Nicaragua lobby. Since the failure of the Panama route, important politicians and businessmen with great influence in Washington had gotten Congress to pass an act to build the Nicaragua Canal. Louisiana Senator John Tyler Morgan, Chairman of the Interoceanic Affairs Committee, had introduced a bill dedicating United States funds to the construction of the Nicaragua Canal, and everything indicated that it would pass. William Randolph Hearst's *New York Herald* expressed the popular opinion when it said:

The Nicaragua Canal project is a purely national affair, conceived by Americans, sustained by Americans, and if later on constructed, operated by Americans according to American ideas, and for American needs. In one word, it is a national enterprise.

Cromwell spearheaded his campaign with an official audience with President McKinley. The President was not convinced in the least, and on December 5 sent his message to Congress in which he supported the Nicaragua bill and recommended providing government funds to build the Nicaragua Canal.

Cromwell decided to encounter Senator Morgan face-to-face. Few dared oppose the Southern Democrat, as he had a tendency to get angry and to attack viciously. Short-statured, with thin white hair, a piercing, unblinking gaze, and a stern expression, he had been in the Senate for eighteen years, and at age 77, was one of its oldest, most influential, and hardest-working members. Independent in his thinking, rigorous, he was uncompromising in any matters regarding the Nicaragua Canal.

Morgan was motivated by an idea of what a Nicaragua Canal would mean to the battered post-Civil War Southern states. He foresaw the world markets opening to Southern lumber, ore, iron, and manufactured goods, and his own popularity rising at home. Morgan also believed the Nicaragua route to be superior: Nicaragua was much closer to the United States; it offered the lowest pass anywhere on the cordillera of Central America; and it provided as much as 100 miles of navigable lakes and rivers. In addition, Morgan saw Nicaragua as a much more stable country than Colombia, which had been ravaged by a 50-year civil war. In short, building the Nicaragua Canal had become the centerpiece of Senator Morgan's politics. Cromwell sought to hinder his life-long quest.

In the Senator's office on Capital Hill, Cromwell demanded a chance to espouse the advantages of Panama during the upcoming Senate

CREATING PANAMA FOR FUNDS & PROFIT
OVIDIO DIAZ-ESPINO

debates, but Morgan threw him out of his office. The next day, the Senator discharged his fury before his Committee with a violent attack on the "Panama lobby of Cromwell."

Morgan's attack only served to anger Cromwell and create a personal challenge for the Fox. He had been one of the biggest donors to the Republican Party during the 1896 presidential campaign, and many prominent Congressmen and Senators owed him favors. He visited and castigated them for allowing Senator Morgan and the Democrats to be immortalized with a canal bill, especially during an election year. When he realized that arguments were not enough, Cromwell promised the politicians enormous contributions for their upcoming campaigns.

> **HE PROPOSED CREATING AN AMERICAN COMPANY OWNED BY IMPORTANT AMERICAN CAPITALISTS (INCLUDING HIM-SELF) TO BUY THE ASSETS OF THE COMPAGNIE NOUVELLE AND THEN SELL THEM TO THE UNITED STATES GOVERNMENT.**

Cromwell then turned his attention to securing the support of the most powerful man in Washington, the Chairman of the Republican Party, Senator Mark Hanna. At age 64, the portly and electrifying Ohio Senator looked weak as he carried a cane for his limp, but "his wide eyes and slightly protuberant ears made him a perpetually attentive adolescent." The Republican Party was known for its open alignment with big business, and Hanna was its leader in Congress. For his open support of the railroads and monopolies, the press nicknamed him Mark "Dollar" Hanna. To assure his support, Cromwell presented a $60,000 donation to the Republican Party, compliments of his client, the Compagnie Nouvelle, an outrageously large donation which surpassed even the Rockefeller Standard Oil Company $50,000 gift to the Republican Party that year. "Dollar" Hanna did not think twice about taking the money, even though it came from a foreign company.

As a result of his peddling influence over the Republicans, Cromwell got them to block the Nicaragua Canal bill and got Congress to approve the creation of an Isthmian Canal Commission to investigate all canal routes, including Panama.

Cromwell had simply bought time. Now he needed to convince the commission, the American public, and members of Congress to support Panama.

■ ■ ■ ■ ■ ■ ■ ■ ■ ■

Cromwell's first tactical move was to convince the members of the Isthmian Canal Commission to travel to Paris instead of Central America. He wanted to keep them from seeing the rusting machinery that the French had left in the treacherous mountains of Panama, and he also knew that in Paris, Panama, not Nicaragua, would be the only subject of conversation.

In Paris, the little American lawyer wined and dined the distinguished Americans and, in his newfound role as engineer, convinced them to offer $40 million for the French company rights, even though the concession granted by Colombia was due to expire in just over two years.

After the American delegates left, Cromwell stayed in Paris to pursue a personal agenda. He pressed the French Company to accept a more aggressive plan, which he called the "Americanization of the Panama Canal." He proposed creating an American company owned by important American capitalists (including himself) to buy the assets of the Compagnie Nouvelle and then sell them to the United States government. He got the support of the "penalized stockholders" of the Compagnie Nouvelle, including former head engineer Philip Bunau-Varilla, Charles de Lesseps, and Gustave Eiffel.

Cromwell returned to New York and immediately began to interest important capitalists in joining his scheme. The first person he visited was the enigmatic J.P. Morgan. A few weeks later, Cromwell and Morgan's personal attorney incorporated the Panama Canal Company of America. The subscribers included some of the most influential financial tycoons in America, including J.P. Morgan; J.E. Simmons; Kuhn, Loeb & Co.; Levi Morton; Charles Flint; and John Seligman, as well as some Washington insiders, such as Douglas Robinson, Roosevelt's brother-in-law, and Henry Taft, brother of Secretary of War (and later President) William Taft.

The American press covered the peculiar event. On December 28, 1899, the *New York Times* published the headline: "French Stockholders Shares Taken by American Financiers. J.P. Morgan Interested in the Project to Americanize the Great Waterway," while the *World* declared that "capitalists having secured control of the French company… Americans to build the Panama Canal." However, in France, the liquidator of the Compagnie Nouvelle found out about the Fox's machinations in the United States and got a French tribunal to rule that the company could not sell its assets to the Americans without the consent of its more than 100,000 shareholders. The board of directors was forced to resign three days later.

With the decision of the French court that the company could not sell its assets, Cromwell's plan seemed dead, but only temporarily. Some months later, in May 1901, a rumor spread in Paris that between May 25, 1900, and June 6, 1901, a confidential "Memorandum of Agreement" was signed by sixteen American capitalists and politicians to speculate on the stock of the Compagnie Nouvelle.

According to the secret sources, the Americans planned to buy the shares quietly in the Paris bourse and from small shareholders scattered throughout the country. Since the collapse of the de Lesseps company, everyone believed the project was dead and that the French stock was worthless. Actually, bonds of the company were sold in France for about 3 percent of their face value. The syndicate sent word to the "penalized" banks of the Compagnie Nouvelle, including Credit Lyonnais, which was headed by Maurice Bo, a member of the syndicate, to quietly buy up the bonds of the Compagnie Universalle. The small holders of the canal paper hastened to take advantage of the gift laid at their doors, for the shares for many years had been considered practically worthless by thousands of peasants. All the bonds were purchased for about $3.5 million. The syndicate then embarked on a mission to convince the United States to buy their company for $40 million, and thus reap a huge gain (equal to about $1 billion today). The scheme was a gamble, but the rewards enormous.

However, when the President of the Compagnie Nouevelle, Maurice Hutin, heard the rumors, he was outraged. On July 1, 1901, Hutin sent a letter to Cromwell dismissing him as general counsel and representative in the United States. The consequences of his dismissal were immediate. On November 1, the Isthmian Canal Commission issued a unanimous preliminary report in favor of the Nicaragua route.

With Cromwell sidelined and the Commission supporting Nicaragua, all the obstacles for a swift approval of its route were removed. On January, the House of Representatives quickly debated and passed a bill approving the construction of the Nicaragua Canal, and later that month, Secretary of State John Hay and the government of Nicaragua signed a formal treaty for the construction of the canal. Only the Senate approval was needed for the treaty, and it seemed as if there would be no opposition. The death bells for Panama had begun to toll.

That fall, however, something unexpected occurred. Theodore Roosevelt was rushed into power when an anarchist in Buffalo assassinated President McKinley. A window for Panama suddenly opened.

■ ■ ■ ■ ■ ■ ■ ■ ■ ■

Upon hearing the news that Roosevelt had been sworn in, Senator Hanna is said to have remarked, "Now look! That damned cowboy is President of the United States." At age 42, T.R. was the youngest man ever to become President. A proponent of the "strenuous life," while in the White House he boxed, wrestled, practiced jiu-jitsu, hunted wild animals, rode horses, played tennis, hiked, and in winter, skinny-dipped in the icy waters of the Potomac. His most sedentary activities included reading up to two books per day.

Roosevelt spoke vigorously, striking the air with his fist for emphasis, while moving his head from side to side with almost every phrase. He was impetuous by nature, and pursued his goals with unfettered intensity. A Colombian Ambassador warned his government to be careful with "the President's vehement character," as well as "the persistence and decision with which he pursues the things to which he commits."

Politically, Roosevelt attacked corruption and fought against monopolies such as Rockefeller's Standard Oil Company and J.P. Morgan. In Panama, however, he was willing to collude with them to promote an even mightier goal: to make the United States the most powerful nation in the world. He sought to end the American isolationism that persisted throughout the nineteenth century, and he found In Panama an arena in which to promote his vision of America.

Roosevelt's ascendancy at first seemed to be a blow for the Panama lobby. During his tenure as Vice President, Cromwell had not even bothered to lobby him. More than any President, he was the embodiment of the public sentiment, which favored Nicaragua. However, at the same time his ascendancy opened an opportunity to undo a decade of debates, since T.R., unlike McKinley, was not the kind of man who was going to let a commission or even

Congress make one the most important decisions of his presidency. As one commentator put it, he "set out to be the bride at every wedding, the corpse at every funeral."

Under the encouragement of Cromwell, Hanna and an eminent engineer and member of the Isthmian Canal Commission visited Roosevelt and stressed to him the superiority of Panama from a military point of view. If the United States built in Nicaragua, nothing prevented the British or another European power from finishing the work of the French in Panama. A Panama Canal, in turn, would be superior to a route through Nicaragua because a ship could more quickly make the crossing from one ocean to the other.

Roosevelt, who had fought in the Spanish War in Cuba, had witnessed the agonizing voyage of the *Oregon* as it inched its way from San Francisco to Havana through the Cape of Horn, only to arrive after the war had ended. He therefore knew the importance of speed if ever the United States had to face a powerful European navy. Thus, despite the evidence showing that Nicaragua was superior to Panama and that a canal through Panama might be impossible to build, in December, Roosevelt called the members of the Isthmian Canal Commission to his office and asked each of them individually to reconsider their recommendation. Under intense pressure, the Commission had no choice but to reverse its prior vote. Roosevelt then told his friend Senator Spooner to propose a bill for the construction of "his ditch" through the mountainous Isthmus of Panama.

A stupefied and outraged press called upon the Senate to disregard the recommendation of the President and of the Isthmian Canal Commission, and to approve the Nicaragua route. The *New York Herald* published an editorial saying that the recommendation "could not counterbalance the weight of the national sentiment in favor of Nicaragua." Senator John Tyler Morgan pledged a vitriolic attack against the defenders of Panama.

To prepare for the debate, the "penalized stockholders" of the Compagnie Nouvelle sent the enigmatic Philip Bunau-Varilla to the United States. Since 1879, Bunau-Varilla had dedicated his life to the construction of the Panama Canal. Plump, stiff, exceedingly vain, his chest always erect, he wore a perfectly manicured moustache waxed to fine spikes.

A former head engineer of de Lesseps' company, he had worked behind the scenes since the French company went bankrupt to raise the money to begin construction again. He prepared maps, plans, and budgets, and went on a campaign to "Preach the Truth in the Highways" about the "Idea of the Canal." In his memoirs, he insisted that he did it independently as a crusade of faith for the "Glory of France." However, Bunau-Varilla owned 11,000 shares of the Compagnie Nouvelle. If the United States bought the concessions, he would become a very rich man.

When Bunau-Varilla arrived in New York, he knew what his mission would be. "I was embarking on an apparently impossible trip. It was nothing more nor less than to change the settled opinion of eighty million men." He secured appointments with Hanna and other influ-

IN PANAMA, HOWEVER, HE WAS WILLING TO COLLUDE WITH THEM TO PROMOTE AN EVEN MIGHTIER GOAL: TO MAKE THE UNITED STATES THE MOST POWERFUL NATION IN THE WORLD.

ential businessmen and politicians by hiding in corners and corridors where he knew his prey would appear, usually arranged by someone on his pay. When the Americans saw the stiff Frenchman with his ornamentally waxed mustache, they snickered. But despite his comical appearance, Bunau-Varilla was astute, audacious, cynical, and incredibly convincing, especially in matters regarding the Panama Canal.

To prepare for the debates, Bunau-Varilla and Cromwell literally wrote the minority report that Senator Mark "Dollar" Hanna presented. The debates started with Senator Morgan attacking the political instability in Colombia and Panama, their "mixed and turbulent people." It would be merely a matter of time, he announced prophetically, before the United States would have to take Panama by force. "It would poison the minds of people against us in every Spanish-American republic in the Western Hemisphere, and set their teeth on edge against us." The Senator then extolled the virtues of Nicaragua, "where all the people are anxiously awaiting the coming of the United States to their assistance, with eager hopes and warm welcome, to their fertile, healthy, and beautiful land." He finished with an appeal to his Old South: "I hope to see the water of the Gulf of Mexico and of the Caribbean Sea…as busy with commerce as the Bay of San Francisco."

The following day, a weary and ailing Senator Hanna "limped down the aisles of the Senate" and decided, though unprepared, to address his colleagues. Hanna delivered the best speech of his eminent career. Unlike Morgan, he spoke softly, without emotion, recounting the virtues of Panama in a businesslike and factual manner, occasionally taking material from an aide and using the large visuals provided by Bunau-Varilla and Cromwell.

He began with an exposition of the volcanic dangers of Nicaragua. Bunau-Varilla had produced a large map of volcanoes in Central America, with still-active volcanoes marked red, and the extinct volcanoes marked black. Nicaragua had eight active sites, Panama zero. He presented a pamphlet that Bunau-Varilla had prepared about the advantages of Panama. He summarized its content in an almost mechanical fashion: One, a Panama Canal would be shorter; two, it would have less curvature; three, the time of transit would be less than half that of Nicaragua; four, it has fewer locks, etc. When Senator Mitchell of Oregon, a Nicaragua supporter, tried to interrupt Hanna to question the sources of his report, Hanna replied, "I do not want to be interrupted, for I am very tired."

Hanna didn't want to admit that Cromwell and Bunau-Varilla provided him with all the data, charts, and maps that he relied on during his speeches. The two lobbyists sat together in the gallery, occasionally advising the Senator through pageboys. The opposition became quite annoyed, and at one point, Senator Morgan openly accused Cromwell of writing Hanna's minority report; the accusation went unchallenged. At a later date, he said, "I warn that distinguished citizen wherever he may be to beware of Mr. Cromwell." In yet another speech, he referred to Cromwell, dramatically looking up at him, "I suppose he is in the gallery listening to me as he always is."

One of the most serious accusations the Panama lobby made was that of volcanic eruption in Nicaragua. The Nicaraguan government and the US Embassy in Managua maintained that the eruption never took place and that no active volcanoes existed in Nicaragua. Bunau-Varilla searched in Washington for an official document from the Nicaraguan government acknowledging the abundance of active volcanoes, and found a postage stamp showing a beautiful volcano belching forth in magnificent eruption. He pasted his precious stamps on sheets of paper. On the top of each was written, "Postage Stamps of the Republic of Nicaragua, An official witness of the volcanic activity of Nicaragua," with a note:

Look at the coat of arms of the Republic of Nicaragua; look at the Nicaraguan postage stamps. Youthful nations like to put on their coats of arms what best symbolizes their moral domain or characterizes their native soil. What have the Nicaraguans chosen to characterize their country on their coat of arms, on their postage stamps? Volcanoes!

The stamps arrived on the Senators' desks on June 16, just three days before the vote. They had the desired effect: Senator Gallinger asked the Senate if it were reasonable to undertake this colossal work in a country which had taken as the emblem on its postage stamps a volcano in eruption. Many Senators who had been ambivalent were won over to the side of Panama.

During its last days, the debate became especially heated. On June 19, it ended. The gallery filled up; the press awaited the most important decision by Congress in years. Everyone knew it would be extremely close, and Morgan claimed that he had the votes to win. The decision came in the afternoon: 42 to 34 in favor of Panama.

The Spooner Bill gave preference to Panama, provided that a satisfactory treaty could be negotiated with Colombia. Otherwise, the President would have to construct the Nicaragua Canal. During the Congressional debates, Colombia had already issued troubling statements about its willingness to grant its consent. Senator Hanna encouraged President Roosevelt to rely heavily on Cromwell during the sensitive negotiations. This is exactly what T.R. did.

■ ■ ■ ■ ■ ■ ■ ■ ■ ■

When Congress adopted the Panama Canal route in June 1902, Secretary of State John Hay called upon Cromwell to write and negotiate the treaty with Colombia, even though he also represented the interests of the French shareholders.

Hay was already badly predisposed to negotiations with Colombia. Smart and stocky, with a stiff posture and a gigantic moustache that curled back toward his ears, he had the air of a high school principal. His experience in international relations was unrivaled. He had served as British Ambassador before he reluctantly accepted the post of Secretary of State for McKinley and later for Roosevelt. He had approved the annexation of the Philippines, had dispatched a dangerous relief expedition to rescue Americans in China during the Boxer Rebellion, and had described the Spanish-American conflict as a "splendid little war." In Panama, however, he found a challenge that matched his abilities.

Hay shared Roosevelt's view that South American diplomats were "dago ambassadors from powerless, insignificant countries." He complained that negotiating with Colombians was "like holding a squirrel in your lap" because Colombia changed its diplomats in Washington so frequently.

Colombia had not had a legation in Washington for years because of the civil war that was ravaging the country. The war pitted rebel Liberal Party troops against the ruling Conservative Party led by President José Manuel Marroquín. A bearded 80-year-old professor and feeble scholar who overthrew his own President in a *coup d'etat* in 1900, he never fully consolidated his power. As a result, government departments acted independently of one another. Rebel troops were at the gates of Bogota, and confusion reigned throughout the country, but even so, Marroquín insisted on giving directions to his diplomats in Washington.

HAY SHARED ROOSEVELT'S VIEW THAT SOUTH AMERICAN DIPLOMATS WERE "DAGO AMBASSADORS FROM POWERLESS, INSIGNIFICANT COUNTRIES."

During the Senate debates, Marroquín instructed Colombian Ambassador José Vicente Concha to demand a $20 million down payment, a $600,000 annuity, and a 100-year lease. Secretary Hay counter-offered with a $7 million down payment, a $10,000 annuity, and a perpetual lease. For months, Cromwell went back and forth between Concha and Hay, and managed to extract a compromise deal.

However, when Congress adopted the Spooner Act in June 1902, the United States required not a lease, but an absolute and perpetual cession of the land. Cromwell prepared an amendment to the treaty he himself had drafted and submitted it to Concha on July 1902.

Concha immediately objected. He sent a telegram to President Marroquín urging his government to reject the proposed amendment, which he considered to be an affront to Colombian sovereignty. He expected President Marroquín to heed his advice, but the President cabled back telling him to accept the proposal. "In order to render the amendments to memorandum presentable to our Congress, demand ten million cash and annuity of six hundred thousand after 14 years," the cable said.

Concha was stunned by Marroquín's response; he could not comprehend how Colombia could so easily cede its sovereignty. He did not know that Marroquín had reached an agreement whereby American troops would invade Panama to quash the Liberal Party troops that had almost taken over the entire province, and in exchange he would sign the proposed treaty.

On September 16, the U.S.S. *Cincinnati* landed in Colon with more

than 200 American Marines. They seized the railroad trains, and for the next three months they held Panama City and Colon under siege, disarming the rebel forces. The US troops' siege gave Marroquín sufficient time to bring reinforcements from Colombia, and the Panamanian Liberal revolt was summarily quashed. Unaware of Marroquín's plot, Concha was so outraged by the United States' invasion and by Marroquín's consent that he lost the capacity to deal with Americans at all, and he resigned. Before he did so, he sent home a bitter note, railing against the United States:

This uncle of ours can settle it all with a single crunch of his jaws. The desire to make themselves appear as the nation most respectful of the rights of others forces these gentlemen to toy a little with their prey before devouring it.... My presence here is not only useless—it is improper."

When Concha left the United States, he turned the legation over to 50-year-old Dr. Tomás Herrán, a refined, intelligent, and somber-looking man. Mindful of Roosevelt's character, Herrán advised Marroquín to try to get the best pecuniary advantages possible, but to sign the treaty if the United States gave an ultimatum. Cromwell delivered such ultimatum in early January.

The Hay-Herrán treaty was signed at Secretary Hay's Lafayette Square house on the evening of January 23, 1903. Cromwell was the sole witness, and Hay gifted to him the pen used in recognition of his fine work.

Roosevelt submitted the treaty for ratification to the US Senate the day after, but Senator Morgan filibustered for the remainder of the winter term, ensuring the closing of the session without a vote. T.R. called a special session of Congress, and ten days later the little Colonel fell on the floor physically exhausted. On the same afternoon of March 10, the treaty was ratified.

The treaty also had to be ratified by the Colombian Congress, a mere formality that became an unbearable task due to Colombia's hunger for more money.

■ ■ ■ ■ ■ ■ ■ ■ ■ ■

Colombia had not had a Congress since 1898, when Marroquín overthrew his government, but he decided to submit the canal ratification to a Congress. This angered the Americans, who could not understand why Marroquín would do so given that he had *de facto* powers to ratify the treaty himself by executive decree. The reason is that Marroquín was hatching a secret plan.

Colombians reasoned that since the French concessions lasted only until October 1904, Colombia had as much right to the machinery, land, and railroad as the French, who were getting four times as much. But since the United States was unwilling to pay a cent more, Marroquín planned to demand at least $15 million of the $40 million that the Compagnie Nouvelle was receiving, and this way the two would share the money half and half. If the Compagnie Nouvelle refused to share its payment with Colombia, he would then personally select delegates who would oppose the treaty. Once it was rejected, he would have an excuse to negotiate better terms with the United States.

Marroquín's decision was well thought-out and reasonable. If Colombia managed to delay the negotiations for just over a year, at that time Colombia would take control of the French investment, and sell the concessions to the United States for $25 million. Marroquín's errors were to think he could outsmart Cromwell and to underestimate the influence that the Wall Street lawyer exerted over Secretary Hay and Teddy Roosevelt.

In mid-April, Cromwell received an alarming dispatch from the Bogota government demanding from the Panama Canal Company part of the $40,000,000 that it would receive from the United States. A furious Cromwell immediately scheduled conferences with Hanna, Hay, and Roosevelt, and began a campaign to discredit Colombia's request. He asserted that the Colombian action was an attempt to blackmail and extract more money from the US government, most likely to pad the private vaults of Marroquín and his cronies. Hanna saw this as a dispute between Colombia and the French company that did not concern the United States. Nevertheless, on April 28, Cromwell got Secretary Hay to wire a message to Bogota that he himself had drafted, stating unequivocally that the United States opposed Colombia's attempt to seek money from the Compagnie Nouvelle. "The United States considers this suggestion wholly inadmissible," a cable sent by Hay to Colombia asserted. Colombia reacted by dropping the request, but with a warning that the treaty would most likely be rejected.

A few days before the final vote of the Colombian Congress, the *New York Herald* outlined the choices available to President Roosevelt: to fight Colombia; to move in accordance with the Spooner Act and construct the canal in Nicaragua; to continue to negotiate with Colombia until something happened. The *Herald* then predicted that "persons interested in getting the $40,000,000 for the Panama Canal are of course eager that this government shall go ahead and seize the property, even though it leads to war."

BETWEEN 1857 AND 1902, THERE WERE SEVEN US INVASIONS OF PANAMA TO QUASH LOCAL REBELLIONS THAT COULD HAVE LIBERATED PANAMA.

On August 12, the Colombian Congress defeated the treaty by unanimous vote. On August 13, Senator Shelby Cullom returned from the President's Sagamore Hill summer home and told the press, "We might make another treaty not with Colombia, but with Panama."

■ ■ ■ ■ ■ ■ ■ ■ ■ ■

Aging and of slight build, with receding white hair, a walrus moustache, a worried look, and stiff posture, Dr. Manuel Amador Guerrero appeared at first glance to be an unlikely candidate to lead a revolution. In 1903, at age 70, he would have been happy to spend his days resting in a hammock at his comfortable sea-front home in Panama City with his young and beautiful wife, if José Agustín Arango had not recruited him to join a secessionist movement.

Tall and robust, with a gigantic white beard, a stern face, and an air of confidence and dignity, Arango was the lawyer for the Panama Railroad. His offices were directly across from Amador's. The two of them had been chosen to lead the revolution by the representative of the Panama Railroad & Steamship Co. in the United States, their boss, William Nelson Cromwell.

When Amador and Arango set out to foment a revolution in the summer of 1903, Panamanians didn't trust Washington's intentions. For more than 70 years, Panamanians had tried unsuccessfully to secede from Colombia. The attempted independence movements were usually not quashed by Colombian forces; rather, the Bogota government would ask the United States to send troops to the Isthmus to put down the rebellion and reclaim its sovereignty under the terms of the Bidlack-Herrán treaty signed in 1846.

Pursuant to the terms of the treaty, Colombia gave Americans the "right of transit across the Isthmus of Panama," which permitted the construction of the first transcontinental railroad. In exchange the United States not only guaranteed "that the free transit from one to the other sea may not be interrupted," but it pledged to protect and guarantee "the rights of sovereignty and property which New Granada [Colombia] has and possesses over said territory…"

The "neutrality clause," as it became known, meant that the United States was under obligation not only to protect Panama against invasions by foreign powers, but also to quash local rebellions and uprisings that were trying to liberate Panama from the rest of Colombia. In fact, the United States' invasions became Colombia's main weapon to prevent Panama from reaching independence. Between 1857 and 1902, there were seven US invasions of Panama to quash local rebellions that could have liberated Panama. Only a few months earlier, in September 1902, US Marines dismantled the Liberal rebel forces that could have liberated Panama.

Given this past, promises uttered by Washington to free the Isthmus were interpreted in Panama as warnings intended to bully Bogota into ratifying the canal treaty. Most likely, no one would have made a move if the two railroad company employees didn't believe that they could overcome 50 years of history by placing their trust in the Wall Street lawyer.

In early July, José Agustín Arango asked Panama Railroad Captain James Beers to travel to New York to see if he could procure Cromwell's support for a revolution. Beers came back with an upbeat response. As a result, on August 1903, Amador traveled to the United States to meet with Cromwell personally. He thought that Cromwell would take him to see Hay and Roosevelt to get their express support for the secessionist movement. But to his dismay, Cromwell would not see him. Even though Amador visited him many times, Cromwell refused to get involved in the details of the revolutionary plans in order to protect the concessions of the Panama Railroad Company, which would be lost if the railroad employees were caught planning a revolution.

Cromwell thus disappeared from sight. But before he left the scene, he mapped out the strategy for the liberation of Panama and left its execution in the hands of his French counterpart, Philip Bunau-Varilla.

During the next two months, Bunau-Varilla and Amador secretly met many times in Room 1162 of the Waldorf Astoria, the "birthplace of Panama." The Frenchman brokered a deal between the desire of Amador for a full US military operation and the desire of Hay and T.R. for the US to appear as a nation that respected the rights of Colombia and was acting pursuant to the 1846 treaty. Thus, instead of the invasion and annexation that Amador hoped for, Bunau-Varilla presented a most unusual, very capitalist independence movement for Panama.

Panamanians would declare Panama City and Colon independent, propelling the Colombians to send troops to regain the territory. The United States would prevent the landing of Colombian troops under the excuse that they were protecting the railroad to "maintain free transit across the Isthmus" and to enforce the "no fighting within gunshot distance of the railway" policy as provided under the 1846 treaty. The rest of the country would be liberated later.

Instead of guns, Panamanians would be given enough money to bribe the Colombian troops stationed in Panama to leave. They figured that $100,000 would be sufficient. J.P. Morgan & Co. would loan this amount. Upon ratification of the treaty, Panama would receive the $10,000,000 payment that was due to Colombia and would pay off its loans to Wall Street.

> **TO KEEP THE COLOMBIAN TROOPS FROM FIGHTING, THE PANAMANIAN PATRIOTS RELIED ON THEIR SUPPLY OF WALL STREET DOLLARS TO BRIBE THE OFFICERS TO GO HOME.**

But there was a catch: Bunau-Varilla demanded that he be given the authority to negotiate and sign the Panama Canal treaty between Panama and the United States. He claimed that he needed to ensure that the treaty was signed without delays soon after independence was declared. Amador objected to his request under the grounds that it would offend Panamanian nationalism if a foreigner were given the right to sign the treaty. Bunau-Varilla then threatened to withdraw United States government support, and Amador reluctantly consented. With these plans arranged, Amador returned to Panama and immediately began to plan the independence of Panama.

■ ■ ■ ■ ■ ■ ■ ■ ■ ■

My book, *How Wall Street Created a Nation*, pieces together hour by hour the dramatic and almost comical events that led to the independence of Panama, including the attempts to enlist Colombian generals with money, the mistakes they made, the lies they invented, and the schemes that went right and the ones that went wrong.

This most unusual revolution was entirely bloodless—only a donkey and a man from China accidentally died during the independence movement. The official story is that the United States warships prevented Colombian troops from disembarking on the Isthmus to retake Panama by force, and thus a war was avoided. However, Colombia had hundreds of troops stationed in Panama City and Colon, and an additional 500 *Tiradores*, or expert riflemen, disembarked on November 3 in Colon to face an American force of only 40 Marines.

To keep the Colombian troops from fighting, the Panamanian patriots relied on their supply of Wall Street dollars to bribe the officers

to go home. Generals and captains guarding Panama City were paid $35,000 each to stay put, while on the Atlantic, Colonel Shaler bought the good grace of the violent captain in charge of the Colombian troops with $8,000, and shipped his troops in a British Royal Mail steamer back to Cartagena.

Soldiers also got their share. On November 4, the birthday of bribery, Amador went to the Chiriquí barracks to meet the Colombian battalion. General Huertas had his men gathered and was trying to hearten them to stand firmly by the revolution, but they were frightened. Amador spoke to them:

> Boys, at last we have carried through our splendid work. The world is astounded at our heroism. Yesterday we were but slaves of Colombia; to-day we are free. Have no fears. Here we have the proof [holding up a sheet of paper with the American coat of arms] that our agent in the United States, Señor Bunau-Varilla, gave us. Panama is free!... Free sons of Panama, I salute you. Long live the Republic of Panama! Long live President Roosevelt! Long live the American Government!

Amador then sent a paymaster to the Government Palace to bring boxes full of coins. Each soldier received 50 dollars in gold. Such was the bounty that was handed out by the patriots to Colombians (not to mention to themselves) that $100,000 did not suffice, leaving the country indebted to J.P. Morgan & Co from day one of its existence.

With the independence of Panama secured, the only condition that had to be met before the speculators got their hands on the $40 million payment was the signature of a treaty between the new Republic of Panama and the United States. To avoid troubles this time, the speculators ensured that Bunau-Varilla treaty got the right to negotiate the treaty on behalf of Panama.

■ ■ ■ ■ ■ ■ ■ ■ ■ ■

The silence of Washington, which for three days didn't recognize the new republic, unnerved the Panamanian patriots, who were afraid that the US would take away its support as it had done throughout the nineteenth century. This would leave the Panamanians to be massacred by the much more powerful and numerous Colombians, who were seething with war spirit and sending dozens of ships to take over the rebellious Isthmus.

Bunau-Varilla led the Panamanians to believe that he was the key to recognition, and he conditioned his help on getting the appointment as minister of Panama with the right to negotiate and execute the treaty on behalf of the new republic.

The Panamanians did not want to grant Bunau-Varilla the appointment he sought but instead wanted Amador, who had departed for Washington, to negotiate and sign the treaty. However, in several angry cables to Panama, Bunau-Varilla threatened that if they did give him his appointment, he would ensure that Roosevelt took away the warships.

In reality, Bunau-Varilla had nothing to do with the decision of Roosevelt and Hay, who had already decided to recognize the new republic once the Colombian troops had left Colon. While the troops occupied Colon or Panama City, they could not claim that the provisional government was the *de facto* government of the Isthmus. Indeed, a few hours after the Colombian troops left, at 12:51 PM on November 6, Secretary Hay recognized the new republic of Panama.

In Panama, the news caused celebration. To the revolutionaries, Bunau-Varilla was responsible because the cable from Hay had been received only hours after they had sent the telegram asking Bunau-Varilla to intervene on their behalf. Unaware that he had nothing to do with the recognition, at 6:45 in the evening, the Panamanians sent to him the following cablegram:

The Junta of Provisional Government of Republic of Panama appoints you Envoy Extraordinary and Minister Plenipotentiary near the Government of the United States of America with full powers for political and financial negotiations.

That same day, Bunau-Varilla learned that Amador had sailed for New York. He calculated that it would take about six or seven days for the ship to dock there and another day for the delegates to make it to Washington, DC. He set out to accomplish his "high mission," that is, to sign the treaty before the Panamanians arrived. "To prevent any injurious action on their [the Panamanians'] part," he told Hay, "it was necessary that on their respective arrivals, they would be met not with arrangements for the signing of a treaty, which they might defeat, but with definitive and accomplished facts…. Success was more than ever the price of rapidity of movement."

Since the Panamanians were expected to arrive soon, Bunau-Varilla did not have much time. On the evening of Sunday, November 16, Bunau-Varilla received a draft of the treaty from Hay. It was essentially the Hay-Herrán Treaty with a few minor modifications. Bunau-Varilla stayed up all night reading the draft, sleeping only between midnight and 2:00 AM. By dawn, he had decided that it would not do. "I was thus led to the conclusion that the indispensable condition of success was to draft a new treaty, so well adapted to American exigencies, that it could challenge any criticism in the Senate."

From the Hay-Herrán treaty, he decided to leave intact only the principles of neutrality of the interoceanic passage; the equality in the treatment of all flags, whether American or non-American; and the attribution of the indemnity of $10 million to Panama. Every other concession that Concha had demanded would be deleted. Instead of listing the attributes of sovereignty which the United States would receive inside the Zone, he decided to grant a "concession of sovereignty *en bloc*." That is, Panama would have no rights in the Canal Zone, as if it were not Panama's territory. The concession, instead of being granted for 100 years and renewable, would be in perpetuity.

The changes amounted to Panama giving away the land to the United States. As an historian later said, "How could the Canal Zone be said to belong to Panama, if neither the government nor the people of Panama had any rights there, or any prospect of ever receiving their rights again till the end of time?"

Bunau-Varilla's decision was an act of treachery. As a representative of Panama, his job was to negotiate the best deal for the country, but he actually made it worse. At the very least, he could have simply signed and sent back the treaty as Hay had drafted it. His fear that Congress might reject it was unfounded, since a treaty with similar terms had already been approved by the US Senate only six months earlier.

Despite some hesitations from Secretary Hay to sign such an unjust treaty, on November 18, he and Bunau-Varilla met at Lafayette Square and dipped their pens in an inkwell that belonged to Abraham Lincoln to sign the Panama Canal treaty. This occurred merely eighteen days after the revolution, and a few hours before the Panamanian delegation arrived in Washington, DC.

Bunau-Varilla went to the railroad station to meet the Panamanian delegation. When he saw them disembarking, he called out, "The Republic of Panama is henceforth under protection of the United States. I have just signed the Canal Treaty!" Amador nearly fainted. Federico Boyd was livid, and Panamanians later claimed that he spat in Bunau-Varilla's face.

Despite the attempt by Panamanians to open the negotiations again, Washington would not budge. The Hay-Bunau-Varilla treaty was ratified by the Panamanian Junta only three days after it was signed, and by the US Senate a few months later with hardly any debate.

PANAMA WOULD HAVE NO RIGHTS IN THE CANAL ZONE, AS IF IT WERE NOT PANAMA'S TERRITORY. THE CONCESSION, INSTEAD OF BEING GRANTED FOR 100 YEARS AND RENEWABLE, WOULD BE IN PERPETUITY.

Since its signature, the Panama Canal Treaty incited a whirlwind of controversy and remained the thorniest issue in the relations between the United States and Panama throughout the twentieth century. In fact, the treaty was so one-sided that Secretary Hay, who willingly participated in the injustice, later confessed to Senator Spooner that the new treaty was "very satisfactory, vastly advantageous to the United States, and we must confess, with what face we can muster, not advantageous to Panama…. You and I know too well how many points there are in this treaty to which a Panamanian patriot could object." During the Senate ratification debates, a Nicaragua supporter had to admit that "we have never had a concession so extraordinary in its character as this. In fact, it sounds very much as if we wrote it ourselves."

With the treaty signed, all the conditions for the $40 million payment were fulfilled. Not surprisingly, the Panamanians weren't the only ones clamoring to dip their hands into the vaults of the American Treasury. William Nelson Cromwell and J.P. Morgan also sought to control the booty.

■ ■ ■ ■ ■ ■ ■ ■ ■ ■

After the revolution was complete and the treaty hastily signed by Bunau-Varilla and Secretary Hay, Cromwell visited T.R. and asked him to appoint J.P. Morgan for transactions between the United States,

Panama, and the Compagnie Nouvelle. Despite the objections of the Secretary of the Treasury, who thought Treasury should make the payments, T.R. consented. Cromwell and J.P. Morgan now had control over the disbursement of the single largest payment in history.

The $50 million payment for an area 30 miles long and ten miles wide exceeded the amount paid by the United States for the combined territories of Louisiana ($15 million), Alaska ($7.2 million), and the Philippines ($20 million). Neither the press nor Congress could fathom how the US could pay so much for what they considered nearly worthless assets. They knew that Wall Street was reaping a huge profit, but they were powerless to stop it.

Word immediately broke in France and in the United States that Panama had been a syndicate's gamble. On February 4, 1904, the New York Times reported that the president of a large French national bank had said that roughly half of the money would stay in the United States.

Despite the rumors, Roosevelt put an end to the speculation when he exclaimed, "Let the dirt fly!" to start the Herculean task of building the Panama Canal. The engineering, medical, and administrative challenges were so great that few cared to know how the rights to build the canal had been obtained. With everyone involved keeping silent, the public thus came to believe Roosevelt's statements that the actions of his government had been "as free from scandal as the public acts of George Washington or Abraham Lincoln" and "as clean as a hound dog's teeth." In various pronouncements, T.R. alleged that in the history of the United States, there was no "more honorable chapter than that which tells of the way in which our right to dig the Panama Canal was secured.... Every action taken was not merely proper, but was carried in accordance with the highest, finest and nicest standards of public and government ethics."

■ ■ ■ ■ ■ ■ ■ ■ ■ ■

The controversy resurfaced several times during the first decade, leading to three congressional investigations and a Supreme Court case. However, in 1911 the mighty T.R. crashed the deliberations with a speech at the Greek Theater in the University of California at Berkeley. Roosevelt had decided to seek the presidency again; for years, he had been denying his complicity in the Panamanian Revolution, but with the Canal, the greatest man-made work of all time, nearly completed, he realized the value of accepting credit for what he had done:

The Panama Canal I naturally take special interest in because I started it. [Laughter and applause.]

There are plenty of other things I started merely because the time had come to whoever was in power would have started them.

But the Panama Canal would not have been started if I

had not taken hold of it, because if I had followed the traditional or conservative method I should have submitted an admirable state paper occupying a couple of hundred pages detailing all of the facts to Congress and asking Congress consideration of it.

In that case there would have been a number of excellent speeches made on the subject in Congress; the debate would be proceeding at this moment with great spirit and the beginning of work of the canal would be fifty years in the future. [Laughter and applause.]

Fortunately the crisis came at a period when I could act unhampered. Accordingly I took the Isthmus, started the canal and then left Congress not to debate the canal, but to debate me." [Laughter and applause. Emphasis added.]

"I took the Isthmus" was a proud and boastful statement characteristic of Roosevelt, "the kind of exaggeration that he liked to make." It was also a misleading statement, for it dismissed the importance of Cromwell, Hanna, Amador, Bunau-Varilla, and others. Nevertheless, his statement traveled the world with remarkable speed. Riots broke out in many Latin American cities, and Colombia immediately demanded that the United States apologize and pay sizable reparation for the country's loss. More important, to critics and supporters alike, Roosevelt's statement, "I took the Isthmus," would be remembered as the best explanation of what happened in Panama in 1903. It became a symbol of Teddy Roosevelt's "gunboat diplomacy." Now that the President had stated his version of events, no other explanation would do.

From that moment on, allegations about a syndicate that had speculated on French shares and fomented a revolution in Panama would be dismissed. Later, even Roosevelt would deny any involvement with Wall Street. In his autobiography, he devoted an entire chapter to the Panama Canal; he discussed Bunau-Varilla's role but made no mention of Cromwell. Not only had Roosevelt "taken the Isthmus," he also eliminated the possibility of further investigation and scrutiny about Wall Street's role in the creation of the Panama Canal.

With the advent of World War I, the conspiracy and the "long track and trail of scandal" that had seemed so obvious to people living during the first years of the century were forgotten, except in Latin America, where the "taking" of Panama was the first of many selfish acts perpetrated by the United States and its powerful businesses on Latin Americans in the twentieth century.

In summary, in America at the turn of the century, Wall Street tycoons saw the synergies between three powerful forces: Teddy Roosevelt's hunger for territory in which to build an Isthmian canal, Panama's century-long quest for freedom, and Wall Street's greed. William Nelson Cromwell created a syndicate and a brilliant scheme that perfectly synthesized these forces, then executed it flawlessly.

RIOTS BROKE OUT IN MANY LATIN AMERICAN CITIES, AND COLOMBIA IMMEDIATELY DEMANDED THAT THE UNITED STATES APOLOGIZE AND PAY SIZABLE REPARATION FOR THE COUNTRY'S LOSS.

In the process, Wall Street created a nation, realized for mankind the centuries-old dream of building the Panama Canal, and then made sure that "grass grew over the episode." American capitalism functioned exactly as it was supposed to do: The plan was lavishly profitable and immensely beneficial.

"A TRUTH SO TERRIBLE"
ATROCITIES AGAINST GERMAN POWs AND CIVILIANS DURING AND AFTER WWII

JAMES BACQUE

The news that the United States Army maintained death camps for German prisoners after World War II was suddenly revealed to the US media in 1989. Reviewing the book *Other Losses*—in which I revealed the deaths of some 900,000 to 1,000,000 prisoners in French and American captivity—*Time* magazine said it was "stunning." It quoted the famous American historian Stephen E. Ambrose, who said that the book revealed "a major historical discovery.... [W]e as Americans can't duck the fact that terrible things happened." He repeated these thoughts on the *CBS Evening News*. I was interviewed on *Good Morning America* and many other programs in North America and Europe.

Probably none of this would have happened had Steve Ambrose not helped me in the final stages of manuscript preparation. On the advice of the British historian M.R.D. Foot, Ambrose read the final draft and wrote to me on June 6, 1988, as follows:

I have now read *Other Losses* and wish I had not. I have had nightmares every night since I started reading.... [Y]ou have a sensational if appalling story and it can no longer be suppressed, and I suppose (in truth, I know) it must be published.... I'm not as convinced as you are that Ike played so absolutely central a role.... [T]here were clearly things going on that were not central to him and to which he paid less attention than he should have. Maybe that is all rationalization on my part.... But again, you have the goods on these guys, you have the quotes from those who were present and saw with their own eyes.... You really have made a major historical discovery, the full impact of which neither you nor I nor anyone can fully imagine. Many will curse you; many will denounce you, many will argue with you; most will try to ignore you....

Sincerely
Stephen E. Ambrose

PS I have written at length about your script to Alice Mayhew, my editor at Simon and Schuster.[1]

A few weeks later, I went to Steve's cottage in Wisconsin to go over details with him. We spent several days there while he outlined his objections and suggestions for improvement. I carried out the major ones and many minor ones. Later, by correspondence he advised and helped again.

The book was published in Canada and Germany in the autumn of 1989. The reaction was powerful. The US State Department immediately issued a bewildered denunciation. A US network TV crew set up at my publisher's office in Toronto to interview him. Foreign rights were sold at the Frankfurt Book Fair, the largest gathering of the publishing industry. The German paper *Die Zeit* ran an approving, full-page review.

As a result of the international publication, my publishers and I received thousands of letters from ex-prisoners scattered round the world. Most of them thanked me fervently for telling a story which they had thought would remain their bitter secret forever. So many letters were received by *Die Welt* that the editors had to print a notice asking readers to stop submitting them.

■ ■ ■ ■ ■ ■ ■ ■ ■ ■

The atrocity began in the spring of 1945 when the US State Department unilaterally and secretly abrogated the Geneva Convention covering prisoners of war, at the request of General Eisenhower.[2] The cover-up began simultaneously at a press conference in Paris where Eisenhower was asked about prisoners of war and the Convention. He replied, "If the Germans were reasoning like normal human beings they would realize the whole history of the United States and Great Britain is to be generous toward a defeated enemy. We observe all the laws of the Geneva Convention."[3] The deception remained official US government policy for years. In 1947, the International Committee of the Red Cross was officially misinformed by Acting Secretary of State Dean Acheson, that even if prisoners were officially downgraded in status from the "prisoner of war" category to "disarmed enemy forces," there was no difference in the actual treatment.[4]

By June 15, 1945, some 5,224,310 prisoners had been taken by Eisenhower in his command in northwest Europe. Many hundreds of thousands more were captured by the US Army command under General Mark W. Clark in Italy. The British and Canadian armies captured some 2,000,000 more, and the Russians took in 2,389,560. The Russians also imprisoned 271,672 civilians as sub-

> "[Y]OU HAVE A SENSATIONAL IF APPALLING STORY AND IT CAN NO LONGER BE SUPPRESSED, AND I SUPPOSE (IN TRUTH, I KNOW) IT MUST BE PUBLISHED." —STEPHEN AMBROSE

stitutes for captive soldiers who had died or escaped during transfer from the Army camps at the front to the KGB camps in the rear.[5]

In the Eisenhower camps, starting in April 1945, most of the prisoners were given no shelter at all, very little food, and—for long periods—no water. They were simply herded through the barbed-wire gates, deprived of their pay-books and ID discs, and left to starve in a field under the open sky. General Richard Steinbach, put in charge of a group of camps near Heilbronn in southwest Germany late in 1945, said, "The conditions were terrible. I was amazed and disgusted at the same time.... I immediately sent to the railhead for supplementary rations...."[6]

Professor Martin Brech, formerly a guard at Camp Andernach in Germany, said that the 50,000 men there were starving. He fed some with loaves of bread through the wire and was told by his superior officer, "Don't feed them. It is our policy that these men not be fed." Later, at night, Brech sneaked some more food into the camp, and the officer told him, "If you do that again, you'll be shot."[7]

Lieutenant Colonel Henry W. Allard, in command of camps in France in 1944, even before the Geneva Convention was secretly denounced, said, "The standards of PW camps in the Com Z [communications zone] in Europe compare as only slightly better, or even, with the living conditions of the Japanese PW camps our men tell us about, and unfavourably with those of the Germans."

One of the prisoners, Charles von Luttichau, who was half-American, has written:

To sleep, all we could do was to dig out a hole in the ground with our hands, then cling together in the hole. We were crowded very close together. Because of illness, the men had to defecate on the ground. Soon, many of us were too weak to take off our trousers first. There was no water at all at first, except the rain, then after a couple of weeks we could get a little water from a standpipe.... More than half the days we had rain.... [M]ore than half the days we had no food at all. On the rest we got a little K ration. I could see from the package they were giving us one tenth of the rations they issued to their own men. So in the end we got perhaps five per cent of a normal US Army ration. I complained to the American camp commander that he was breaking the Geneva Convention, but he just said, 'Forget the Convention. You haven't any rights.' Within a few days, some of the men who had gone healthy into the camp were dead. I saw our men dragging many dead bodies to the gate of the camp where they were thrown loose on top of each other onto trucks which took them away.[8]

General Steinbach blamed Secretary of the Treasury Henry C. Morgenthau for the treatment inflicted on the prisoners. He has written in his memoirs, "This was caused by the Morgenthau Plan. His objective was vengeance rather than promoting US national objectives."

The conception of the Morgenthau Plan for the postwar treatment of

EISENHOWER SAID HE THOUGHT THE GERMANS HAD "PUNISHMENT COMING TO THEM."

Germany by the United States has been described by an eyewitness, who wrote down his notes immediately after a meeting between Secretary Morgenthau and General Eisenhower in England in August 1944:

Actually, it was General Dwight D. Eisenhower who launched the project.... The subject first came up at lunch in General Eisenhower's mess tent. Secretary Morgenthau, Assistant to the Secretary Harry D. White and I were there. White spoke of Germany, which was now certain to be defeated.... White said, "I think that we should give the entire German economy an opportunity to settle down before we do anything about it."

Here Eisenhower became grim, and made the statement that actually sparked the German hardship plan. "I am not interested in the German economy and personally would not like to bolster it if that will make it any easier for the Germans." He said he thought the Germans had "punishment coming to them.... [T]he whole German population is a synthetic paranoid.... I would like to see things made good and hard for them for a while.... I will tell the president myself if necessary."[9]

Colonel Philip S. Lauben, who was in charge of the German Affairs Branch of SHAEF (Supreme Headquarters Allied Expeditionary Force), and who also negotiated prisoner transfers among the French, British, and Americans, saw the camps in eastern France. He told me, "The Vosges was just one big death camp." Captain Fred Siegfriedt, a guard officer in an American Vosges camp, has written: "It just broke your heart to see it." Captain Ben H. Jackson said, after seeing one camp, "I could smell it a mile away. It was barbaric."[10]

Konrad Adenauer, a former mayor of Cologne who was later picked by the Allies as Chancellor of a reconstructed Germany, was being interviewed by US Army personnel on June 22, 1945:

I know that in the winter of 1941-42 the Russian prisoners were very badly treated by the Germans and we ought to be ashamed of the fact, but I feel that you ought not to do the same thing.... German prisoners too in American camps ate grass and picked leaves from the trees because they were hungry exactly as the Russians unfortunately did.... Please allow me to say frankly, in very important matters...the Allies have used the same methods as the Germans unfortunately used. It is true that in the use of these methods they do not go to the same extremes, but the methods are the same.[11]

(In referring to the methods that the Allies used, which did not go as far as the Germans, we have to remember that in June 1945, the Allies had scarcely begun their program of pillage and massacre. In a speech in Switzerland in 1949, Adenauer referred to the deaths of six million Germans that had been caused by the Allies.)

Approximately 700,000 to 750,000 people died in US captivity, and many hundreds of thousands more were turned over to the French in dying condition, to be used as slave labor. Of the French prisoners, some 250,000 died.

The American camps in Italy, where Clark commanded during the war, displayed few of the stigmata of the Eisenhower camps. In fact, when Clark became Political Commissioner in Austria, he went out of his way to improve the treatment of prisoners who had been

"AS ONE SPEAKS TODAY OF DACHAU, IN TEN YEARS PEOPLE THROUGHOUT THE WORLD WILL SPEAK ABOUT CAMPS LIKE SAINT PAUL D'EYJEAUX." —LE MONDE

abused under Eisenhower's regime. He wrote a memo "for files" (i.e., not for immediate circulation) in which he said, "When I first came to Austria from Italy, General Keyes told me of the deplorable conditions which existed in the Ebensee Camp, mostly due to overcrowding and to lack of proper nourishment." He took steps to alleviate the "critical situation which exists there." These included sending in a medical team, increasing the food ration, and directing that the "overcrowding be released."[12]

News of the camps was easy enough for Eisenhower to control, because he maintained tight censorship in the occupied country. Control was so strict that even the court newspaper, the *New York Times*, complained a little. But when the French began demanding some German prisoners to use as slaves—again in contravention of the Geneva Convention—the tight censorship began to burst. In September and October 1945, a young French reporter named Jacques Fauvet printed two stories in *Le Monde*, one of which stated: "As one speaks today of Dachau, in ten years people throughout the world will speak about camps like Saint Paul D'Eyjeaux," where 17,000 people taken over from the Americans in late July were dying so fast that within a few weeks two cemeteries of 200 graves each had been filled. By the end of September, the death rate was over 21 percent per year, about eighteen times the ambient European death rate.

Fauvet continued:

People will object that the Germans weren't very particular on the manner of feeding our men, but even if they did violate the Geneva Convention, that hardly seems to justify our following their example.... People have often said that the best service we could do the Germans would be to imitate them, so they would one day find us before the judgement of history, but...we didn't suffer and fight to perpetuate the crimes of other times and places.[13]

Some people have suggested that it was inevitable that the German prisoners would die because of "the chaos" in the country and because there was a "world food shortage" caused by the war, which had been started by the Germans. In fact, the US Army denied the Germans food that was parked right beside the camps. Captain Lee Berwick of the 424th Infantry, who commanded the guard towers at Camp Bretzenheim, has said that he cannot under-

stand the accusation in *Other Losses* that prisoners in his camp starved to death. He told me, "Food was piled up all round the camp fence." Prisoners there saw crates piled up "as high as bungalows." Yet the official US Army ration book for the camp, stolen after the war by a German trusty who presented me with a photocopy, shows that the ration per person was 600-850 calories per day. Sometimes the prisoners got nothing.

This was in line with General Eisenhower's policy to starve the men, adumbrated in a letter his military government sent on May 9, the day after VE Day in the west, by urgent special courier to all the leaders of the German towns and *laender*. This reads in part:

[U]nder no circumstances may food supplies be assembled among the local inhabitants in order to deliver them to the prisoners of war. Those who violate this command and nevertheless try to circumvent this blockade to allow something to come to the prisoners place themselves in danger of being shot."[14]

Some women taking food to the starving were indeed shot by the Americans and by the French. That these conditions were deliberately imposed is certain from the fact that no such mass die-off occurred in the British and Canadian camps. The British and Canadians were able to treat their prisoners well enough that every one of the scores who have reported to me have said that there were no widespread atrocities and certainly no mass deaths.

After the victory, the British and Canadians at first kept their prisoners in their original units, allowing them to billet themselves wherever they could. There were at first no British-Canadian camps at all in Germany. The prisoners stayed where they were told because they were fed daily in a big central facility, such as an hotel or railway station. Many were released early to help in Operation Barleycorn, to bring in the skimpy harvest. Although several of the later British-Canadian camps have been sharply criticized for filthy conditions, I have never found any documentary or anecdotal evidence pointing to an unusually high death rate. Certainly Germans who had survived both British and American camps said that the worse by far were the American camps.

Nor is it true that food had to be conserved in Germany because of a shortage throughout the world. In fact, production at the end of the war all over the world was down between 5 percent and 9 percent from prewar levels, a minor reduction considering the enormous amount of luxury food still being produced, as for instance whiskey, meat, and beer made from grain. US Secretary of War Robert Patterson said repeatedly there was no food shortage; the big problem was allocating it on a priority basis.

■ ■ ■ ■ ■ ■ ■ ■ ■ ■

In any case, the Germans were actually prevented from growing food. This was accomplished by a series of measures whose purpose and result was starvation. About 25 percent of the best farmland was confiscated by the Poles and Russians. All the Germans remaining there in 1945 were expelled, starving and penniless, and forced into rump-

Germany, where they had to remain because emigration was forbidden. Germany was transformed into one great prison, filled with starving, penniless people seeking shelter and work.

Simultaneously, the nation's surviving young men were reduced by the Allied death camps, or so weakened that they died soon after release. The Allies also reduced German fertilizer production by about 80 percent. They confiscated so many factories, machine tools, raw materials, and finished goods of all kinds, including patents, that German industrial production—which had increased throughout the war despite bombing—was reduced in the first six months of the occupation to about 25 percent of prewar levels.

The Allies agreed at their final wartime conference at Potsdam in July-August 1945 that they would take about $20 billion in reparations, but the actual amount was many times bigger. Nearly all the exports from Germany for years after the war were deemed to be reparations, depriving the Germans of foreign exchange to import food. The American economic historian John Gimbel defined the reparations policy quite simply as "plunder."[15]

Court historians have covered over the savage assault on the civilians with soothing words about the Marshall Plan, but Gimbel has revealed much of what happened:

Historians of the Marshall Plan have fallen into a familiar trap. They have [described] what must have been the reasons for the origin of the Marshall Plan...by extrapolation rather than by interpretation of documents, sources and contemporary evidence. Government officials are not averse to misleading the public.... [T]hey told the American people or whomever what they wanted to tell them...without regard for what was true and accurate.

Even George C. Marshall, much revered in the US—as is Eisenhower—deceived the world. Responding to criticism levelled at him by the Soviets during a meeting of Foreign Ministers in Moscow in 1947, he denounced the Soviet Minister, Vyachaslav Molotov, for saying that the Americans were taking valuable reparations without reporting them in the official reparations account. Gimbel comments, "Marshall responded angrily—a manner quite uncharacteristic of him, as an esteemed observer commented.... [T]his was distorted, misleading and propagandistic."

All of these measures resulted in desperate conditions. A US Navy doctor on the scene, Albert R. Behnke, wrote: "From 1945 to the middle of 1948 one saw the probable collapse and destruction of a whole nation. Germany was subjected to physical and psychic trauma unparalleled in history." Somewhere between nine and thirteen million people died prematurely in the slaughter between 1945 and 1950.[16]

■ ■ ■ ■ ■ ■ ■ ■ ■ ■

How is it that such widespread suffering was inflicted, that millions

of people were starved to death, that the worst ethnic cleansing in human history was carried out, the UN Declaration of Human Rights betrayed, the Geneva Convention denied, without all of this being noticed, reported, and denounced in the Western press?

The answer is complicated, but it begins with the deliberate cover-up instituted by Eisenhower and the officers around him. The Army, accustomed to using deception and camouflage during wartime, naturally carried on the policy afterwards, especially vis-à-vis the enemy. One officer who witnessed such covering up was Lieutenant Ernest F. Fisher, of the 101st Airborne, who later was promoted to colonel and became an official US Army historian. In spring 1945, he was ordered to take part in an investigation of allegations of crimes by US soldiers against Germans. At the end, he said, "It was a whitewash."

The press was hampered in its work by its status in Germany as part of the occupying forces under the direct command of the Army. Nothing displeasing to the military was likely to be published because the usefulness of the reporter would be ended when he was expelled to the States, as one was in May 1945. Another reason for the failure to expose the atrocities was the role that most of the commercial press plays in Western society, part cheerleader for the government team, part self-absorbed observer of its own antics. But deliberate, prolonged, and skilled cover-up was the main reason.

As it began in 1945, so it continues to this day. Apologists for the American Army and for Eisenhower have said in effect that although no such events occurred, they were caused by the Germans themselves. This absurd thesis states that they started the war, causing so much devastation that widespread suffering was inevitable. And that this deserved suffering was not serious. Conveniently overlooked are the facts that Britain and France declared war on Germany in 1939, not the other way around; that nearly all the devastation in Germany itself was caused by the Allied air-raid assaults on civilian targets; and that Allied postwar policy sought to reduce German industrial and agricultural production to below starvation levels.

Stephen E. Ambrose played an almost incredible role in these events. At first, in the spring of 1988, he was honest, shocked, and helpful. He told me, "You have the broad outline of a truth so terrible that I really can't bear it." In the spring of 1989, just a few months before publication of *Other Losses*, he met Col. Dr. Ernest F. Fisher at a conference in Washington to hand him a copy of the galleys (Fisher had helped me with the research and with a foreword). Ambrose told Fisher, "This book destroys my life's work." A few months later, at a conference in Vancouver just after the book was published, a student asked him why, as Eisenhower's biographer, he had not discovered the story himself. Ambrose replied that he had not thought of looking at the prisoner of war records. Perhaps he began feeling the embarrassment of missing a story which had been uncovered by an amateur. Nevertheless, he continued his public support, for a little while, probably driven by his agonized conscience.

Then he went to the Army War College at Carlisle Barracks in Pennsylvania. There, in the autumn of 1989, he backtracked. He

| SOMEWHERE BETWEEN NINE AND THIRTEEN MILLION PEOPLE DIED PREMATURELY IN
| THE SLAUGHTER BETWEEN 1945 AND 1950.

began to organize an academic conference on the subject of Eisenhower and the German prisoners. The papers presented there by his friends—the Ike-minded—eventuated in a dim-witted book loaded with pseudo-academic trappings like a donkey under a howdah. This was *Eisenhower and the German POWs*, edited by Ambrose and Gunter Bischof. Soon after the conference, Ambrose wrote to the *New York Times,* suggesting that he review my book for them, although it had not been published in the US. They accepted despite their policy of not allowing people closely connected to the preparation of a manuscript to review the resulting book. In the review he cited the results of the conference in support of his criticism, but once again his natural honesty shone through the camouflage. He wrote, "our conclusion was that when scholars do the necessary research, they will find Mr Bacque's work to be worse than worthless. It is seriously—nay spectacularly—flawed in its most fundamental aspects." Don't you love the way that Ambrose predicts what the research will find, and then, shifting to the present tense, presents the conclusions *without* the research?

The Ike-minded at the conference did almost no original research on prisoners of war but instead relied on a series of books subsidized by the German government, about the missing prisoners of war. These books were edited by a former Nazi Party member and mercenary historian for the Third Reich, Dr. Erich Maschke. This odd interest of the German government—in subsidizing and controlling a series of history books by academics—arose because the government wished to respond to public demand for information about 1.5 million prisoners of war still missing from their homes in the 1960s. The purpose of the series was described by the German Foreign Minister, Willy Brandt, who controlled Maschke:

[I]t was decided with the approval of the Foreign Office to print them [the books] with the FO's stamp of approval…to exclude misunderstanding, with a modest publication…and to avoid provoking a public discussion at home and abroad…[which would] open old wounds and would not serve the reconciliation efforts of the Federal Republic's foreign policy."[17]

In plain language this meant that Brandt wanted to be seen as doing something to quell the anger and sorrow of the German families grieving for the fate of their million and a half husbands, friends, sons, fathers, and brothers still missing after 24 years of Allied captivity. To shift the blame for American and French atrocities onto the Soviets was the purpose of the Maschke series.

The writer of the one slim volume concerning Germans in American hands, Kurt W. Bohme, nowhere cites the most authoritative source for statistics on prisoners of war held by Americans: the Modern Military Records section of the US National Archives. These contain many thousands of pages of documents which describe much of the fate (though not in plain language) of the German prisoners. It is very doubtful that Bohme even visited the archives at all, because he quotes no documents that he could not have gotten from official US Army publications. If the papers were open to him, how could he have missed the story that Col. Fisher and I discovered there? If they were closed to him, one must ask why. His work was closely controlled by a NATO ally, West Germany, and if it were true that the US Army had nothing to hide, as Ambrose contended, why did the Army not offer the papers to this person commissioned to quell a controversy "without opening a public discussion"?

Bohme, faithful to his government's purpose, tells the world that civilians frequently brought food to several of the US camps, without mentioning the eyewitnesses who saw people being shot for doing just that, in line with Eisenhower's edict against civilians bringing food. Not only were hundreds of thousands of such eyewitnesses available to Bohme, the archives of all German towns, villages, and *laender* contain hundreds of copies of Eisenhower's letter forbidding civilians to bring food to the camps. It was in the village of Langenlonsheim that the copy I have was found, 40 years after it had been sent.

THE NICKNAME FOR THE CAMPS AMONG THE PRISONERS WAS "THE SLOW DEATH CAMPS."

Furthermore, Bohme reproduces a pretty photograph of tents for prisoners of war purportedly at Heilbronn. But no barbed wire or guard towers are visible in the photograph, whose horizon is far away. It is hard to believe that the tents were for prisoners of war. General Richard Steinbach, the commander, had said of this camp that before he took over in October, the prisoners "were moved into a field and told to make camp. The weather was rainy and cold. They dug caves and holes in the ground to try to keep warm." On taking over, he had to order in "tentage" so that the POWs would be "properly housed." So, even if Bohme's tents were for prisoners, they did not arrive until the men had been dying of exposure and starvation for six months, since April. As for Bohme's nice picture of the women arriving with food, Steinbach says the prisoners got only 1,000 calories per day. The prisoners at Bretzenheim were lucky to get their allotted 650-800. The nickname for the camps among the prisoners was "the slow death camps."

Many are the Maschke volumes on the atrocities committed by the Soviets, though Maschke consulted no original documentary sources at all, since they were locked away in the KGB archives in Moscow. The Maschke volumes are no better than deceit in defense of the Americans and French, and in criticism of the Soviets for atrocities even greater than those they had actually committed.

During the height of the controversy between Ambrose and myself over the statistics, the KGB archives were opened. I went to Moscow in 1992 and 1993 to work in that gloomy building. I never saw or heard that anyone from Ambrose's team or from the United States Army Center for Military History had been there, or was expected. The reason became clear as soon as I saw the Bulanov report on the fate of Second World War prisoners in Soviet hands. This report, supplemented by a subsidiary report on seized civilians, showed that the Soviets had taken in far fewer German prisoners than the Maschke series had reported. And that a total of just over 500,000 had died. Subtracted from the 1.5 million missing—a figure which no one had ever disputed—this left about one million to be accounted for. This was the accounting which had already appeared in *Other Losses.*[18]

Ambrose and the Ike-minded virtually admitted that they were suppressing the story. Ambrose had begun his 1988 letter to me with the admission that the story "can no longer be suppressed." He and his cohorts often admitted they had no facts to rebut the book, then rebutted away, regardless. They said that they preferred their own estimates to the documents in the archives. Eisenhower and the State Department had begun this process in 1945, but it was reinforced by Drew Middleton, writing in the *New York Times* in 1945. Middleton, one of the *Times'* star correspondents during the war, had written several stories defending Eisenhower against the charges brought by Fauvet in *Le Monde*. In one of the stories, he said that he had visited the camps and found none of the evil conditions that made Fauvet compare St. Paul D'Eyjeaux to the infamous Nazi camp at Dachau. In 1988, when the final draft of my manuscript was ready, I phoned Middleton, described briefly what I had discovered, and asked him for an interview.

Sucking on a pipe in his narrow cranny of an office in the *Times* building, he calmly told me, "I am not surprised that you were able to dig up some bad things from that time." He then admitted that he had not visited the camps themselves, but had only driven by. I offered to show him the full manuscript so he could check it out, because it proved that either he had made a vast error or had lied to cover up a tremendous American war crime committed by the general who became President. Middleton scoffed at the offer. "Don't worry about me," he said.

I was shocked. As Ambrose had said, I had the goods on these guys, but Middleton did not care. This really impressed me—and I am still impressed—that those who do such dreadful things or who cover them up are so powerful that even the threat of exposure does not perturb them.

This confidence is not confined to the Americans. Sir Michael Howard, writing in the *Times Literary Supplement*, admitted that he is an "innumerate historian" not qualified to judge the statistical analysis in *Other Losses*. He develops a "criterion" to help him along. This is "the criterion of inherent probability," which relieves him not only of the need to do research but of the need to understand research set plain before him. Howard writes, "Which is in fact the more probable explanation; that a million German prisoners quietly died in American hands in 1945 without anyone noticing, or that the American authorities...made mistakes in their initial figures...?" Which of course not only gets him out of having to understand research, but also cynically ignores that a million and a half Germans had never come home from Allied captivity. For Howard, the fate of these people is as nothing compared with the need to defend the flightless swans of academe from the terrorist raid that *Other Losses* represents to them.

One would think that sloth could go no further, but Professor Stefan Karner of Graz, Austria, succeeds. He actually went to Moscow and saw the Bulanov report. Having seen it, he decided it was not there. Or at least, that it did not mean what it said. What he did find in Moscow were estimates. His own. He does not present a single valid reason for doubting the Soviet figures, which of course had been kept secret by the Soviets because they are irrefutable evidence of an enormous atrocity against people of many nations. The Soviet figures for captures and deaths of Japanese prisoners, Polish

officers and civilians, and German civilians had already been independently corroborated by the Japanese, Poles, and Germans themselves. There is not the faintest doubt about the accuracy of the KGB figures. And there is no archival or documentary or anecdotal support for the Maschke, Ambrose, or Karner figures on prisoner deaths. They are all fiction.

Perhaps the best insight into the minds of historians was displayed by the mayor of Rheinberg during an interview with me in autumn 1988. I already knew that many thousands of prisoners had died in the camp in 1945, but I was curious to find out what the town archives had to say about the deaths, since all deaths in Germany must be reported to the local authorities. I asked the mayor how many prisoners had died there, and he gave me an absurdly low figure, somewhere around 500. I said, "Do you believe that?" He looked uncomfortable and said, "No."

"Then why do you give out the figure?"

"We have to say something."

Ambrose and the Ike-minded have for many years been helped by various agencies of Western governments to suppress the story that he said "can no longer be suppressed." After Ambrose had begun to change his policy towards these revelations, the US State Department issued denunciations of me and my work, and the Center for Military History in Washington, led by Albert E. Cowdrey, orchestrated deceptive rebuttals that appeared on the BBC, in the *New York Times* and Ambrose's book about German PoWs. The Royal Canadian Mounted Police interfered with one of my witnesses and with a reporter for a newspaper in western Canada.

I suspected that I was being watched, but I had no solid proof until I met a former Deputy Commissioner of the Royal Canadian Mounted Police, who told me that my transatlantic phone calls to my publisher in Toronto were intercepted by American computers, and the contents misrepresented to reviewers and TV producers. My baggage was confiscated by British Airways at Heathrow and my computer held by them for many hours. The ex-Mountie told me that my hotel room in Paris was burgled by French government security agents, and I was followed by them in France. Mail sent to me from London and from Cologne was opened, and some of it was stolen.

MY BAGGAGE WAS CONFISCATED BY BRITISH AIRWAYS AT HEATHROW AND MY COMPUTER HELD BY THEM FOR MANY HOURS.

A former KGB colonel hired a lawyer in Toronto to harass me and the editors at my book publisher and at the magazine which had first published my work. Subsequently, both magazine and book publisher turned down my next work in the same vein, then denied that they had been intimidated.

When I asked the former Mountie why the various agencies were so interested in my historical research, he said, "They want to know who you're working for. Especially since you went to Moscow."

I replied, "I work for my readers." He laughed.

Because Stephen E. Ambrose and his cohorts have done such a good job in suppressing the news, the American public has been kept in ignorance of the crimes committed in their name by Eisenhower, crimes which are now probably being repeated. An eerie reminder of those postwar days has recently come to light with the capture of the Taliban prisoners who were flown to Guantanamo, Cuba. Now, as in 1945, the US government unilaterally has suspended the Geneva Convention. Now, as in 1945, there are serious allegations of mistreatment of prisoners of war. Now, as in 1945, the Canadian Army, having captured prisoners, refused to turn them over to the Americans because they took their obligations to the Geneva Convention seriously. However, the spineless Canadians of 2002 soon caved in to the Americans and handed over their Taliban prisoners.

BECAUSE THE ALLIES MASSACRED GERMANS BY STARVATION, IT WAS NECESSARY NOT ONLY TO DENY THE RESULTING DEATHS BUT ALSO TO EUPHEMIZE, DEPRECATE, IGNORE, EVADE, AND RE-CATEGORIZE THE STARVATION ITSELF.

Ambrose and company have kept the American public from having an informed debate about the wisdom of allowing the Army to tell the State Department to abandon the Geneva Convention whenever it suits the Army. Which is usually when the prisoners need it most. They have also helped to damage historical memory of great acts of generosity carried out by Canadians and Americans together in 1945-49. Because the Allies massacred Germans by starvation, it was necessary not only to deny the resulting deaths but also to euphemize, deprecate, ignore, evade, and re-categorize the starvation itself. This necessarily meant hiding the vast extent of the aid that people in Canada and the US sent to Germany after 1946 to alleviate the suffering. The full story of this weird contradiction was not presented to the public until 1998, when my book *Crimes and Mercies* was published in Canada, the UK, and Germany. In brief, Canada and the US, partly through government agencies and partly by NGOs, sent so much food abroad to relieve world suffering that one of the chief administrators of aid, Herbert Hoover, said that 800,000,000 lives had been saved between 1945 and 1948. This astounding figure comes from a well-informed and credible source, and is confirmed by several others.

Food and other aid in significant quantities did not begin to reach Germans until late 1946. Until then, most aid sent to Europe was distributed by UNRRA to non-Germans. The first Germans to be helped were schoolchildren, who nicknamed the aid "Hooverspeise," after the former President. One child drew a touching map of wheat being loaded onto trains in Canada, then shipped from Montreal to his schoolroom. The change in American policy came largely as a result of speeches in the Senate—widely ignored in the US press—by a few Senators who had been appalled by what they had seen during recent junkets to Germany. Gradually the Morgenthau Plan was abandoned, and the merciful Marshall Plan came into operation in 1948. In my opinion, there has never been a clearer demonstration of the power of public opinion than this change. Even though the events themselves were usually hushed up by the press, returning soldiers and the Senate speeches spread the word, and the generosity native to Americans compelled the government and the NGOs to act.

Crimes and Mercies, a bestseller in Canada, recently reprinted in Germany, has been denied to the American public by Ambrose & Co. Fifteen publishers have turned down the manuscript, including Little, Brown, the parent company of the UK publisher. Koreans can get this hair-raising and inspiring book about American generosity and terrorism, but not Americans. Such is the power of deceit in the hands of Ambrose, the *New York Times*, and their friends.

Well, poor old Steve has died, his reputation buried in contempt. It sounds strange, but I continued to like him through all the lies he told. He had a rough, direct charm that seldom failed; his original, unplagiarized writing was interesting; and he knew the truth when he saw it. If only he had kept on telling it.

I once told him, "Steve, if you want to teach history, you must first let history teach you." I think he thought that I was just a meddling fool.

Endnotes

All references to *Other Losses* mean the edition of 1999.

1. Letter in the author's possession. **2.** *Other Losses*: 27. **3.** Quoted in Butcher, Harry C. *My Three Years With Eisenhower*. New York: Simon & Schuster, 1946: 789. **4.** Acheson to E. Gloor, ICRC, Geneva, 17 March 1947. In 740.00114 EW/2-1447, State Department Archives, Washington, DC. **5.** *Op cit.*, *Other Losses*, Introduction and Appendix One. **6.** Unpublished memoirs of General Steinbach in author's possession. **7.** For sources for Brech and Allard, see *Other Losses*. **8.** Interviews with the author, Washington, DC, 1987-8. **9.** *Op cit.*, *Other Losses*: 197-8. **10.** For sources for Lauben, Siegfriedt, and Jackson, see *Other Losses*. **11.** I was sent the photocopy by Prof. Peter Hoffmann of McGill University who found the original in the US National Archive, RG 226 OSS R&A, XL 12708. See *Other Losses* Epilogue. **12.** Memo dictated by General Clark "for files," 30 Aug 1945, Citadel Archives, Charleston, North Carolina. **13.** *Le Monde*, 30 Sept-1 Oct 1945. Bibliotheque Nationale, Paris. **14.** *Op cit.*, *Other Losses*, Introduction: xxxii - xxxiii. **15.** For a full discussion of food and reparations, see *Crimes And Mercies*, and/or Gimbel, John. *Science, Technology and Reparations: Exploitation and Plunder in Post-war Germany*. Stanford, CA: Stanford University Press, 1990. **16.** *Op cit.*, *Crimes And Mercies*. The evidence is chiefly from German census information and from memoranda by Robert Murphy, whose papers are in the Hoover archives in Stanford. **17.** Brandt to Bundestag, 25 April 1969. **18.** The Soviet statistics are fully discussed in *Other Losses* and *Crimes and Mercies*. They also appear in Krivosheyev, G.G. (ed.). *Soviet Casualties and Combat Losses in the 20th Century*, Greenhill and Stackpole Books, 1997.

"A TRUTH SO TERRIBLE"
JAMES BACQUE

INSIDE SCIENCE'S CLOSET
RICHARD ZACKS

Editor's Note: This article is excerpted from the chapter "Science" in *An Underground Education* by Richard Zacks (Doubleday, 1997).

_TAKING A BITE OUT OF NEWTON'S APPLE

Isaac Newton sat in the summer heat in 1666; the 24-year-old pondered; he scratched his nose. An apple konked him on the noggin and he discovered gravity.

That story makes it into almost every textbook.

Voltaire, one of the world's wittier and more mischievous men, spread the tale in his brief bio of Newton. The philosopher said he heard it from Newton's niece, Catherine Barton Conduitt, who lived with Newton for 20 years.

However, Sir Isaac never once recorded the story in his voluminous published works or letters. And Newton never mentioned the falling *pomme* to two learned men who interviewed him extensively on the development of his gravity theory.

One German astronomer, Karl Friedrich Gauss, gave perhaps the best explanation of where the apple story came from. Wrote Gauss: "The history of the apple is too absurd. Whether the apple fell or not, how can anyone believe that such a discovery could in that way be accelerated or retarded? Undoubtedly, the occurrence was something of this sort. There comes to Newton a stupid importunate man who asks him how he hit upon his great discovery. When Newton had convinced himself what a noodle he had to do with and wanted to get rid of the man, he told him that an apple fell on his nose; this made the matter quite clear to the man, and he went away satisfied."

Splinters from that apple tree have been sold as "holy relics" in England.

_THE *REST* OF NEWTON'S LIFE

The plague struck in 1664, soon closing Cambridge University for eighteen months. Twenty-two-year-old Isaac Newton—instead of trying to tan that pale body or play tennis—used the forced recess to make some of the most startling scientific discoveries in the history of the human race: the law of gravity, laws of motion, the binomial theorem and method of fluxions (roots of calculus), and spectrum theory in optics (that would lead to the reflecting telescope).

But what did Newton (1642-1727) do with the rest of his long life? He lived to be 85. Certainly, he pursued further work on some of the above, but his two major preoccupations for half a century were alchemy and theology. (Minor interests were checking prophecies and determining the chronology of the long-lost kingdoms.)

Isaac Newton wrote more than one million words on religion— almost all unpublished and never intended for publication, according to *The Religion of Isaac Newton* by Frank Manuel.

"For two hundred years thereafter most of the manuscripts were suppressed, bowdlerized, neglected or sequestered, lest what were believed to be shady lucubrations tarnish the image of the perfect scientific genius," observes Manuel. ("Lucubrations" are overwrought studies.)

Newton wrote such page-turners as *Paradoxical Questions Concerning the Morals and Actions of Athanasius and his Followers*, *A Treatise on Revelation*, commentaries on Latin translations of the Talmud, investigations into the apocalypse, and much more.

> SIR ISAAC—WHO WAS RAISED AN ANGLICAN—PUT HIS AWESOME MATHEMATICAL POWERS TO WORK TO COMPUTE WHEN THE CHURCH OF ROME WOULD BECOME THE ELEVENTH HORN OF THE FOURTH BEAST IN PROPHET DANIEL'S VISION.

In a word, Newton's obsessive religious investigations and fractious Bible study have proved disturbing to biographers and fellow scientists wanting to celebrate the man's remarkable scientific achievements.

As Robert Frost remarked, well-rounded figures roll, and Newton was anything but, being rather a mass of spiky extremes.

Here's a taste of Newton's more accessible religious thoughts from a fragment, *Of the Faith which was Once Delivered to the Saints*: "If God be called...the omnipotent, they take it in a metaphysical sense for God's power of creating all things out of nothing whereas it is meant principally of his universal irresistible monarchical power to teach us obedience."

There is absolutely no way to summarize Newton's million words on religion, to boil them down to some pithy phrase on the relation of science and religion, of reason and faith. Most of his biographers have ignored the challenge, and a glance at some of the text makes it a pardonable offense.

For instance, published after his death was *Observations upon the Prophecies of Daniel and the Apocalypse of St. John*. In it, Sir Isaac—who was raised an Anglican—put his awesome mathematical powers to work to compute when the Church of Rome would become the eleventh horn of the fourth beast in prophet Daniel's vision. Newton's tally came to 1,260 solar years, and he therefore predicted the Catholic Church's downfall between the years 2035 and 2054. Being a seasoned scientist, he left a margin of error.

Alchemy. Although alchemy is now considered greed-driven quackery, in the mid-seventeenth century, it was still a fairly respected branch of study. Among Newton's unpublished writings, scholars have found more than 650,000 words on alchemy. "Its evident appeal to generation after generation of adepts is inaccessible to the modern critical intellect," observes Betty Jo Teeter Dobbs in *The Foundations of Newton's Alchemy*. Here, here.

Newton's notes are packed with the confusing symbols alchemists employed in their research. Here are some experiment notes: "Its fumes strangely open & volatize minerall bodys as of Antimony in making it Butter, and [45-degree forward upward angle arrow] grosly beaten Venetian Sublimate opens [45-degree backward downward arrow] Copper cemented with it so as to..."

Some scholars have speculated that Newton's alchemy experiments might have caused him to suffer from long-term lead and mercury poisoning. Newton's life is packed with surprises for the modern reader—perhaps the most surprising of all is that he died a virgin, and proud of it.

_KEPLER PREDICTS COLD WEATHER AND LOTS OF TURKS

Johann Kepler (1571-1630), one of the greatest astronomers ever to live, made more money doing horoscopes than he did from his research. Although he had misgivings about *charlatans* performing astrology, he ultimately justified his own work: "It still remains that people are distinguished from one another more by heavenly bodies than by institutions and habit." And he stated that the alignments of the planets at birth stamped a person's character for life, and he "boasted" that he could discern future behavior and opportunities from checking planetary positions.

JOHANN KEPLER (1571-1630), ONE OF THE GREATEST ASTRONOMERS EVER TO LIVE, MADE MORE MONEY DOING HOROSCOPES THAN HE DID FROM HIS RESEARCH.

One of Kepler's first career breaks came when his "astrological calendar" for 1595 predicted extreme cold and a Turkish invasion. He was right on both scores. (Some peasants, it was recorded, blew their frozen noses right off their faces; and no one could deny the onslaught of the Turks.)

The Holy Roman Emperor Rudolph II—who appointed Kepler "Imperial Mathematician"—gave Kepler plenty of astrology homework: Rudolph wanted to know about the planetary alignment at the birth of Augustus Caesar and Muhammad; he wanted a critique on astrological predictions about a battle raging between Venice and Pope Paul V; he wanted to know the meaning of the New Star of 1604 that sparked "Day of Judgment" predictions.

One of Kepler's horoscopes begins: "I might truthfully describe this man as one who is alert, quick, industrious, of restless disposition, with a passionate..."

Astrology was taken very seriously at the time. (Nancy Reagan would have been deeply respected for turning to Joan Quigley.) Many university-trained doctors turned to astrology to know when and how much to bleed a patient, or when to schedule an operation. A patient's astrological sign (denoting fieriness or earthiness) might also dictate the proper treatment.

Kepler, for his part, tried to downplay the telling the future side of his job. Nonetheless, having grown accustomed to daily meals, Kepler filled volumes with his "calendars," horoscopes, special astro-studies, and yes, even predictions. He also found time to discover his three planetary laws that paved the way for Newton and gravity. For those of you who snoozed that afternoon, those laws are: the elliptical path of the planets, increased orbital speed closer to the Sun, and the relation between orbital duration and distance from the Sun.

_FRANCE CUTS OFF ITS MOST BRILLIANT HEAD, 1794

Antoine Lavoisier (1743-1794), often called the "father of modern chemistry," used precise laboratory methods to identify and name hydrogen and oxygen. His research helped debunk the reigning phlogiston nonsense and his *Elementary Treatise on Chemistry* (1789) paved the way for chemical research. In May 1794, Lavoisier inserted his head through the window of Dame Guillotine, the heavy blade descended, the crowd roared.... But why did the Republic execute its leading scientist?

Lavoisier, an aristocrat, had invested his inheritance in buying a share in tax farming, a business that had nothing to do with raising crops. These rich entrepreneurs harvested taxes, collecting royal duties from the people on numerous goods, including tobacco and salt, in exchange for a percentage. (Imagine a privatized IRS run by a clique of wealthy Americans.) They literally carved the country up into districts and had a standing army of 20,000 often brutal men, who, upon the merest suspicion, had the legal right to pole-ax doors and search homes.

Lavoisier, truth be told, *did* apply his considerable genius to various tax-farm problems, and even helped design and build an enormous wall around parts of Paris to thwart smugglers. On the flip side, Lavoisier used his profits from tax collecting to finance his chemistry experiments.

Of all the villains hated by the French working class, these tax farmers, especially the so-called Farmers-General, probably topped the list, since they set prices for all kinds of daily food items. It was at one of the more crowded public executions that Antoine Lavoisier—along with fellow tax farmers—was guillotined. Their remains, including Lavoisier's body and head, were tossed in unmarked mass graves in the cemetery of Parc Monceaux.

_NOBEL PRIZE ADULTERY: MADAME CURIE

When Madame Curie (1867-1934) was accused of adultery in 1911, her good friend Albert Einstein rose to her defense: "She is not attractive enough to become dangerous for anyone," he declared. Thank you, Albert.

The Nobel Prize committee reacted a bit differently. One committee member begged her *not* to come to Stockholm to accept her upcoming unprecedented *second* Nobel Prize, advising her to stay in Paris and clear her name. Madame Curie refused. "The prize has been awarded for the discovery of radium and polonium," she wrote back. "I believe there is no connection between my scientific work and the facts of my private life." How charmingly naïve.

This scandal has been largely forgotten in the glare of Madame Curie's halo, her enshrinement on everyone's short list as one of the world's most brilliant, most accomplished women.

She belongs on that list, and part of the reason is how she reacted to that scandal. She could have let the Nobel committee bully her into not accepting her award; she could have given up research. She could have moved back in with her family in Poland. While she sat in her apartment that November 1911, pondering these decisions, she could hear French crowds outside chanting: "*A bas l'étrangère, la voleuse de maris!*" ("Down with the foreigner, the thief of husbands!")

Manya Sklodowska, native of Poland, married her teacher, Pierre Curie, and the two of them, in perhaps the most successful marital collaboration in history, did pioneer research in discovering radioactive elements, key breakthroughs in the route to atomic energy. While Pierre focused more on the theoretical, Marie spent years shoveling and stirring *tons* of pitchblende in a warehouse-like lab to isolate a precious decagram of radium. *Her* chemical experiments would prove *their* theoretical physics.

> THE STORY BROKE IN PURPLE PROSE ON NOVEMBER 4 IN *LE JOURNAL*: "THE FIRE OF RADIUM LIT A FLAME IN THE HEART OF A SCIENTIST AND THE SCIENTIST'S WIFE AND CHILDREN ARE NOW IN TEARS."

The genuinely enamored couple had no idea of the dangers of radioactivity. In fact, they sent samples by mail to a handful of choice friends around the world. A scientist in Iceland commented on how nicely it glowed. Pierre even tried wrapping a barium-laced bandage around his arm for ten hours and then carefully observing the 52-day healing period that followed.

The Curies were rewarded with a joint Nobel Prize for Physics in 1903, the first time a woman had ever received the then-fledgling prize. The popular press fussed over her, and the Women's Movement not surprisingly embraced her as a hero.

The Curies' collaboration and their happy marriage was suddenly cut short when absentminded Pierre stepped off the curb and was run over by a horse-drawn wagon in 1906, his skull crushed by a wheel of the six-ton vehicle hauling military uniforms. Devastated, Marie immersed herself in work, and that work would lead to her being selected in 1911 to become the first *person*—male or female—ever to win a second Nobel Prize.

In France, at the time, successful men could take mistresses so long as they appeared in polite society with their wives. That was acceptable, but Marie Curie, a successful 43-year-old widow, taking up with 38-year-old Paul Langevin, a dapper, married father of four, apparently was not.

The story broke in purple prose on November 4 in *Le Journal*: "The fire of radium lit a flame in the heart of a scientist and the scientist's wife and children are now in tears."

Langevin's wife, who had been suspicious for a while, had somehow gotten a hold of the couple's love letters. Perhaps her fury was a bit aroused when she read that Madame Curie had written Paul to make sure to avoid getting his wife pregnant, since another baby would dishonor Marie in the eyes of their friends who knew about their affair. Her love letters, which sparkle with desire, reveal that she had hopes they could one day live together openly.

Langevin's wife, Jeanne, sued for divorce and leaked documents to the media, but before the trial, scheduled for early December, both sides agreed to a settlement.

The French press for the most part hammered Madame Curie, whipping up some xenophobia about Polish émigrés breaking up French homes; the French Academy of Sciences, legendary for pig-headed snobbery, acted true to form and voted not to elect her. But she defied the Nobel Prize committee, which had already selected her, and despite being ill, traveled to Stockholm to accept her award.

However, she devoted the last two decades of her life exclusively to research, and colleagues say that Madame Curie, by nature intense and taciturn, often became downright dour and dictatorial. She only acted more warmly with her family and a very tight circle of friends

Paul Langevin eventually reconciled with his wife, who later gave her blessing to Paul's keeping a mistress, this time an acceptable one, a secretary.

_THE NOBEL DYNAMITE BLASTING CAP AWARD FOR PEACE

What about the Exxon award for environmental safety? Or the Adolph Hitler award for ethnic tolerance? Or the John F. Kennedy award for marital fidelity? They have a certain irony, if not outright hypocrisy.

It is the same with the Nobel Peace Prize, only most of us have forgotten who Alfred Nobel was.

On April 13, 1888, the Swedish engineer woke up in Paris and read his obituary. The French newspaper had accidentally run an obit for him when actually it was his brother *Ludwig* who had died. Alfred was shocked to see himself portrayed as the Merchant of Death, the man responsible for escalating the arms race.

Nobel had invented dynamite, blasting caps, smokeless gunpowder, and blasting gelatin; he had made high-powered explosives much easier and safer to use, and he was quite proud of how this power had been unleashed to mine precious minerals and to build roads, railways, and canals. "Despite nine centuries of gunpowder," states Donovan Webster in *Aftermath: The Landscape of War*, "weaponry had not really changed until Nobel's discoveries boosted the bloody art of war from bullets and bayonets to long-range high explosives in less than twenty-four years, forever altering the way armies killed one another."

Nobel (1833-1896) was horrified to see himself portrayed as some kind of bellicose monster. He came up with a shrewd spin control plan for the family name. With his vast wealth and 350 patents, he decided he would create prizes to be awarded in physics, chemistry, medicine, literature, and peace. In a world now overrun with awards (mostly commercial self-promotion disguised as meritocracy), the Nobel Prizes have evolved into perhaps the planet's most prestigious prizes. Past winners in various categories have included Einstein, Sartre, Schweitzer, Faulkner, Martin Luther King, and darkly humorous picks like Henry Kissinger.

> OF THE BILLIONS OF PEOPLE WHO HAVE HEARD OF THE NOBEL PRIZES, VERY FEW NOWADAYS EVER THINK OF LONG-RANGE ARTILLERY SHELLS OR OF THE ESTIMATED 100 MILLION DEATHS BY WAR IN THE CENTURY SINCE ALFRED NOBEL FIRST HELPED REVOLUTIONIZE THE ART OF KILLING.

Of the billions of people who have heard of the Nobel Prizes, very few nowadays ever think of long-range artillery shells or of the estimated 100 million deaths by war in the century since Alfred Nobel first helped revolutionize the art of killing.

_REJECTEES WIN NOBEL PRIZE

The world-respected scientific journal *Nature*, taking advice from its panel of experts, chose to refuse to publish Enrico Fermi's research on beta-decay, H.C. Urey's work on heavy hydrogen, and Hans Krebs' work on the citric acid cycle. All three went on to win Nobel Prizes.

The same happened to Rosalyn Yallow at *Science*, where her future Nobel Prize work on radioimmunoassay was tossed in the circular file. Her process is now used in almost every hospital lab.

Sources

Newton: Madigan, Carol, and Ann Elwood. *Brainstorms and Thunderbolts: How Creative Genius Works*. New York, 1983; Dobbs, Betty Jo Teeter. *The Foundations of Newton's Alchemy*. Cambridge, 1975; Manuel, Frank. *The Religion of Isaac Newton*. Oxford, 1974; Skrabanek, Petr, and James McCormick. *Follies and Fallacies in Medicine*. Buffalo, 1990.

Kepler: Caspar, Max. *Kepler*. Tr. C. Doris Hellman. New York, 1993; *op cit.*, Skrabanek.

Lavoisier: Donovan, Arthur. *Antoine Lavoisier: Science, Administration and Revolution*. Oxford, 1993; Schama, Simon. *Citizens: A Chronicle of the French Revolution*. New York, 1989.

Curie: Langevin, Andre. *Paul Langevin, mon père: l'homme et l'oeuvre*. Paris, 1971; Marbo, Camille. *Souvenirs et recontres à travers deux siècles*. Paris, 1967; Quinn, Susan. *Marie Curie: A Life*. New York, 1995.

Nobel: Webster, Donovan. *Aftermath: The Landscape of War*. New York, 1996.
Rejectees: Op cit., Skrabanek.

OUR BACK PAGES
THE NOSTALGIA INDUSTRY AND "GOOD OLD DAYS" MYTHOLOGY
MICKEY Z.

Mythology, for most Americans, evokes images of Zeus, Hercules, and Thor; it's something the primitive ancients engaged in before modernity reared its enlightened head. But the US is a nation built upon a foundation of myth, and many forms of mythology have taken hold: free markets, Western supremacy, the cult of science and technology, and fundamentalist demagoguery, to name a few. Such deeply held tenets could only become acceptable in a society consciously and purposefully conditioned to worship wealth, consumerism, and the unquestioned preservation of power at any cost.

That same society might be quite receptive to the alluring appeal of the "good old days." You're familiar with this concept, I'm sure. The days when you could leave your doors open, sex was for the bedroom, men wore ties and hats, and women knew their place. "Girls were girls, and men were men," as the *All in the Family* theme song goes. Here's how conservative columnist, Linda Bowles, recently described the concept in all seriousness: "There was a time, let's call them the good old days, when parents could send their little children off to school with full confidence they would be in good hands."[1]

And some good old days, it seems, were better than others.

Tom Brokaw, in his best-selling book, *The Greatest Generation*, informs those who came of age during the era of Reagan and Rambo that those who came of age during the Depression and WWII were "the greatest generation any society has ever produced." This was a generation that would take its rightful place alongside those "who had converted the North American wilderness into the United States," Brokaw declares without a hint of irony.[2]

> IF THE GOOD OLD DAYS INVENTION IS ACCURATE, THEN THE WARS FOUGHT, THE BUSINESSES STARTED AND SUBSIDIZED, THE LEGISLATION PASSED, THE CULTURE CREATED, AND THE LEADERS ELECTED IN THE GOOD OLD DAYS GET A FREE RIDE ON ITS COATTAILS.

The danger inherent in the good old days myth is twofold. Like all myths, its mere existence makes other illusions easier to swallow. If the good old days invention is accurate, then the wars fought, the businesses started and subsidized, the legislation passed, the culture created, and the leaders elected in the good old days get a free ride on its coattails. We become a nation of people gazing backward for innocence lost rather than looking ahead for how to apply lessons learned. This is the second danger of the good old days fiction: disempowerment.

By accepting that "the greatest generation any society has ever produced" roamed the earth some 50 to 70 years ago, we surrender new ideas and embrace whitewashed nostalgia. The answers, we acknowledge, are found in the past; all we have to do is slam on the brakes and throw our SUVs in reverse.

A valuable step in fostering a more forward-thinking approach would be to expose the good old days for what they were—a mixed bag of good and not so good—like all such "days." If we don't buy into the mythology, it's harder to convince us that most or all the solutions lie in the past.

Howard Zinn reminds us that "history involves the selection and arrangement of facts." Challenging that selection and arrangement is more than can be done in any one article. The following look at the good old days from the late 1800s to the 1950s is merely a nudge in a new direction.

■ ■ ■ ■ ■ ■ ■ ■ ■ ■

"Life in the 1800s has taken on an almost Utopian quality in the minds of many Americans," writes historian Dennis N. Randall. "The images associated with this era of our history are, on the surface, pleasant to recall: one room school houses with a heavy dose of the 3 Rs [i.e., reading, 'riting, and 'rithmetic]; rugged self-reliance; living close to the earth, no income tax, steam-powered railroads and individual freedom."[3]

The 1800s were hardly the good old days of "individual freedom" for the African slaves. Even the Great Emancipator himself, Abe Lincoln, admitted in 1862: "If I could save the Union without freeing any slaves, I would do it—if I could save it by freeing all the slaves, I would do it—and if I could do it by freeing some and leaving others alone, I would also do that."[4] The post-Civil War period was hardly cause for celebration. Between 1882 and 1903, 2,060 blacks were lynched across the United States.[5] Unknown to most people, hundreds of whites were also lynched, usually—but not always—by other whites, according to the venerable Tuskegee Institute.

As for steam-powered railroads as icons of nineteenth-century utopia, one might want to ask America's indigenous population, many members of which were relocated or exterminated to make room for intercontinental railways. According to the US Bureau of

Indian Affairs, the estimated pre-1492 population of what is now called the United States ranges from 5 million to 15 million. By the good old days of the late 1800s, that number was down to 25,000. (Today, there are roughly 2 million people claiming Indian ancestry living in the US.)[6] Those who built the railroads probably didn't envision themselves as living in a special time. From 1898 to 1900, US railroads lost as many workers to accidents as the entire British Army did in its three-year Boer War.[7]

Workplace accidents were not the only concerns of nineteenth-century US workers.

An average worker could expect to earn between 50 and 75 cents a day. A woman lucky enough to find a paying job earned far less than a man. Her standard wage was anywhere from half to two-thirds less than her male counterpart. "Unions were almost unheard of," writes Randall.

"POLICE CLUBS ROSE AND FELL. WOMEN AND CHILDREN RAN SCREAMING IN ALL DIRECTIONS."

Male or female, those workers lived through many nineteenth-century depressions. In the 1870s, for example, things got so bad that 90,000 workers had to sleep in police stations throughout New York City. In January of 1874, a parade of demonstrating workers was diverted from City Hall and ended up at Tompkins Square, where police told them they couldn't hold a meeting. Here's how one newspaper reported what ensued:

Police clubs rose and fell. Women and children ran screaming in all directions. Many of them were trampled underfoot in the stampede for the gates. In the street bystanders were ridden down and mercilessly clubbed by mounted officers.[8]

More than 43,000 families in New York City were evicted in 1884 because they couldn't pay rent.[9] In 1887, nearly three million workers lost their jobs. "Many families lost their homes or were thrown out of their city tenements," Randall reports. "Thousands of homeless families lived on the streets of major cities."[10]

Another economic crisis hit in 1893 and lasted for five years. Four million workers lost their jobs, and almost one in five workers was unemployed.[11] When the economy began an upswing, a new breed of worker had entered the job market: children. Nearly a million children under fifteen worked in factories across America at the turn of the century. They were paid between $1.50 and $2.50 a week for up to 84 hours of work.[12] This actually represented an improvement for many children on the streets of Manhattan, such as the newsboys.

The newsboy screaming out headlines on a crowded street corner is a quintessential good old days image, but this character has undergone a bit of nostalgic cleansing. The newsboys were subject to some unwritten rules. Youngsters sold papers until the age of ten, when they moved up to boot blacking. The morning editions were reserved for kiosk vendors, leaving the evening papers and extras for the youthful hawkers. Surviving as a newsboy involved fierce battles for turf and the papers themselves. Even so, those lads who rose to the "top" of their profession were still only earning an average of 30 cents a day in the 1870s and the vast majority were homeless.[13] By 1880, an estimated 100,000 homeless children wandered the streets and back alleys of New York City.[14]

For female children (with or without homes), the "age of consent" in many states in the late 1800s was as low as nine or ten. "Which makes a mockery of the term," remarks author and social critic Stephanie Coontz.[15]

Further shattering the family values façade of the good old days, during the 1880s, the US had more divorces per year (25,000) than any other industrialized nation.[16]

On the political front, by the late eighteenth century, according to historian Howard Zinn, the US government was "behaving as Karl Marx described a capitalist state: pretending neutrality to maintain order, but serving the interests of the rich." When Grover Cleveland (Democrat) was elected President in 1884, robber baron Jay Gould wired him: "I feel…that the vast business interests of the country will be entirely safe in your hands."[17]

What was the source of Gould's confidence? To begin with, one of President Cleveland's chief advisers was William Whitney, a millionaire corporate lawyer who married into the Standard Oil fortune. Republican Benjamin Harrison, a man whose main qualification was working for the railroads as a lawyer, succeeded Cleveland in the White House. In 1877, Harrison prosecuted railroad strikers in federal courts. Still, he was bumped out of the White House in 1892 when Grover Cleveland (still a Democrat) reclaimed his throne. In light of this development, robber baron Andrew Carnegie received a letter from the manager of steel plants, Henry Clay Frick. "I am sorry for President Harrison," Frick wrote, "but I cannot see that our interests are going to be affected one way or the other by the change in administration."[18]

Right on cue, President Cleveland used US troops to break up "Coxey's Army," a demonstration of unemployed men who had come to Washington.

It's no wonder that of the 20 million immigrants who came to America between 1820 and 1900, five million skipped out on the good old days to return to their place of origin.[19]

■ ■ ■ ■ ■ ■ ■ ■ ■ ■

As the new century dawned, life expectancy was a mere 47.3 years,[20] and industrial pollution had grown so pervasive that the term "smog" was coined in 1905.[21] Even looking back through the prism of modern capitalism, inequality was remarkably unchecked in the first decade of the 1900s. Ninety-five percent of executives came from the upper or upper-middle classes, and less than 3 percent of them started as poor immigrants or farm children.[22] "By 1904," Howard Zinn writes, "318 trusts with capital of more than seven billion dollars, controlled 40 percent of the US manufacturing."[23]

Between 1900 and 1909, the burgeoning American empire used armed forces to intervene abroad in China, Colombia, Honduras, Dominican Republic, Syria, Abyssinia, Panama, Korea, Cuba, and Nicaragua.[24]

Inequity advanced in the following decade, with the top 1 percent of Americans receiving more than one-third of personal income, while the bottom fifth got less than one-eighth.[25] "Our democracy is but a name," declared Helen Keller in 1911. "We vote? What does that mean? It means that we chose between two bodies of real, though not avowed, autocrats. We choose between Tweedledum and Tweedledee."[26] Keller's words only referred to men, of course, as women were still barred from voting in the US at the time.

■ ■ ■ ■ ■ ■ ■ ■ ■ ■

The years 1910 to 1919 also saw the deportation of Emma Goldman and Alexander Berkman, the Black Sox scandal, US citizenship imposed on Puerto Rico without the approval or consent of the indigenous population, and of course, World War I.

As I write this, the US government and the corporations that own it are poised for another exercise in international criminality. This time it's an escalation of the assault on Iraq. Were things different for US foreign policy during the good old days of the early 1900s? The First World War provides an instructive answer.

In what has been called "perhaps the most effective job of large-scale war propaganda which the world has ever witnessed," the Committee on Public Information, run by veteran newspaperman George Creel, used all available forms of media to promote the noble purpose behind World War I (i.e. to make the world safe for democracy). The Creel Committee (as it came to be known) was the first US government body set up strictly for the purpose of issuing outright propaganda. It published 75 million books and pamphlets, had 250 paid employees, and mobilized 75,000 volunteer speakers known as "four minute men," who delivered their pro-war messages in churches, theaters, and other places of civic gatherings. The idea, of course, was to give war a positive spin.

Although Woodrow Wilson won reelection in 1916 on a promise of peace, it wasn't long before he severed diplomatic relations with Germany and proposed arming US merchant ships—even without congressional authority. Upon declaring war on Germany in December 1917, the President proclaimed, "Conformity will be the only virtue and any man who refuses to conform will have to pay the penalty."

The masses got the message:

• Fourteen states passed laws forbidding the teaching of the German language.

• Iowa and South Dakota outlawed the use of German in public or on the telephone.

• From coast to coast, German-language books were ceremoniously burned.

• The Philadelphia Symphony and the New York Metropolitan Opera Company excluded Beethoven, Wagner, and other German composers from their programs.

• German shepherds were renamed Alsatians.

• Sauerkraut became known as "liberty cabbage."

• Even Irish-American newspapers were banned from the mails because Ireland opposed England—one of America's allies—as a matter of principle.

In a forerunner of today's Patriot Act, the good old days offered the Espionage Act, passed in June 1917. The act read in part: "Whoever, when the United States is at war, shall willfully cause or attempt to cause insubordination, disloyalty, mutiny, or refusal of duty in the military or naval forces of the United States, shall be punished by a fine of not more than $10,000 or imprisonment of not more than 20 years, or both."[27]

Perhaps the best-known target of the act was noted Socialist Eugene V. Debs who, after visiting three fellow Socialists in a prison in June 1918, spoke across the street from the jail for two hours. He condemned war and capitalism. For this, he was arrested, found guilty of subversion, and spent over two years in prison. Before sentencing, Debs famously told the judge: "Your honor, years ago, I recognized my kinship with all living beings, and I made up my mind that I was not one bit better than the meanest on earth. I said then, and I say now, that while there is a lower class, I am in it; while there is a criminal element, I am of it; while there is a soul in prison, I am not free."[28]

Roughly 900 others also did time, thanks to the Espionage Act—which is still on the books today.

Besides WWI battles, between 1910 and 1919, the US sent troops into Nicaragua, Honduras, China, Panama, Cuba, Turkey, Mexico, Haiti, and Soviet Russia.[29]

■ ■ ■ ■ ■ ■ ■ ■ ■ ■

In the Roaring Twenties, only 56 percent of students graduated high school,[30] the divorce rate was nearly as high as in the 1960s,[31] and 60 percent of American families earned less than the amount considered necessary to meet basic human needs: $2,000 a year.[32] After touring the poorer districts of New York in 1928, a shocked Mayor Fiorello La Guardia was heard to say: "I confess I was not prepared for what I actually saw. It seemed almost incredible that such conditions of poverty could really exist."[33]

That same year, Emma Goldman remarked: "If voting changed anything, they'd make it illegal."[34] If voting could have changed anything, during the years from 1920 and 1929, the US might not have gotten away with sending troops into China, Guatemala, Siberia, Panama, Costa Rica, Turkey, Honduras, and Nicaragua.[35]

The 1920s also gave us Prohibition, the anti-Catholic bias that brought down Al Smith's 1928 presidential bid, the Sacco and Vanzetti case, the Teapot Dome scandal, and then of course, the stock market crash of 1929.

Many look back to the Great Depression as a time when Americans courageously rallied together to survive economic catastrophe, a time of unity. When researching my book, *Saving Private Power*, I came across plenty to counter this conviction—far too much to document here. For the sake of illustration, let's focus on the plight of one group of struggling Americans: the Bonus Army.

In the spring and summer of 1932, unemployed World War I veterans, government bonus certificates in hand, got the idea to demand payment on the future worth of those certificates (they were issued in 1924, to be paid off in 1945). Anywhere from 17,000 to 25,000 former doughboys and their families formed a Bonus Expeditionary Force, otherwise known as the "Bonus Army." They marched on Washington and picketed Congress and the President.

Arriving from all over the country, with wives and children or alone, they huddled together, mostly across the Potomac River from the Capitol, in what were called "Hoovervilles," in honor of the President, who adamantly refused to hear their pleas. Shacks, tents, and lean-tos sprung up everywhere, and the government and newspapers decided to play the communist trump card for the umpteenth time. Despite the fact that the Bonus Army was 95 percent comprised of veterans, the entire group was labeled "Red agitators"—tantamount to declaring open season on them. Right on cue, Hoover called out the troops, which included three soon-to-be heroes.

The commander of the operation was Douglas MacArthur; his young aide was Dwight D. Eisenhower. George S. Patton led the Third Cavalry—which spearheaded the assault.

The US Army assault on July 28, 1932, included four troops of cavalry, four companies of infantry, a machine-gun squadron, and six tanks. After marching up Pennsylvania Avenue, soldiers lobbed tear gas and brandished bayonets as they set fire to some of the tents. In a flash, the whole Bonus Army encampment was ablaze. Three lives were lost: two veterans and an 11-week-old baby. In addition, an 8-year-old boy was partially blinded by gas, two policemen had their skulls fractured, and a thousand veterans suffered gas-related injuries. After this impressive military success, the members of the Bonus Army were forced to leave Washington, and many of them joined the other two million or so Americans who lived their lives on the road during the Great Depression.[36]

Less than ten years later, MacArthur, Patton, and Eisenhower would be earning a place in history books by sending many of those same disenfranchised poor to grisly deaths on the battlefields of Europe and the Pacific. The greatest generation was about to march off to war.

■ ■ ■ ■ ■ ■ ■ ■ ■ ■

How does the WWII era hold up? Let's take a brief look.

Unity and solidarity? There were some 14,000 strikes involving nearly seven million workers during the war years. "In 1944 alone," writes Howard Zinn, "a million workers were on strike, in the mines, in the steel mills, in the auto and transportation equipment industries."

Family values? The divorce rate in 1940 was 16 percent; by 1944, it had jumped to 27 percent. There were 600,000 divorces in 1946. Between 1939 and 1945, illegitimate births in the US rose by 42 percent. The venereal disease rate for girls fifteen to eighteen in New York City increased 204 percent between 1941 and 1944.[37]

Education? In 1940, 60 percent of all American students dropped out of school. Today, less than 25 percent do. That same year, the United States Navy gave a group of recent high school graduates a test that, in part, called upon them to add, subtract, multiply, divide, and use fractions. Sixty percent of those tested failed.[38]

Race? In 1948, now-Senator Strom Thurmond ran for President on the slogan "Segregation Forever."[39]

Tolerance? Homosexual veterans were frequently denied benefits under the G.I. Bill.[40]

Morality? In late 1993, then-Energy Secretary Hazel O'Leary released documents about secret nuclear experiments on American citizens. Immediately after Hiroshima and Nagasaki, nuclear researchers set about, at any cost, to discern the effects of plutonium on the human body. Peter Montague, director of the Environmental Research Foundation, explained:

FROM COAST TO COAST, GERMAN-LANGUAGE BOOKS WERE CEREMONIOUSLY BURNED.

There were two kinds of experiments. In one kind, specific small groups (African-American prisoners, mentally retarded children, and others) were induced, by money or by verbal subterfuge, to submit to irradiation of one kind or another. In all, some 800 individuals participated in these "guinea pig" trials. In the second kind, large civilian populations were exposed to intentional releases of radioactive isotopes into the atmosphere.

These vile experiments cannot genuinely be dismissed as a momentary lapse amidst a well-intentioned, post-"Good War" paranoia. The declassified documents on US radiation experiments stretch three miles long.[41]

Democracy? After the US dropped atomic bombs on civilians to close out one war, the good guys in the good old days were laying the groundwork for a future war: The Japanese had displaced the French in ruling Southeast Asia, and when WWII ended, the Viet Minh could have filled that void. The Viet Minh was a broad coalition of communists led by Ho Chi Minh. In 1945 and 1946, William Blum reminds us that Ho wrote "at least eight letters to President Truman and the State Department asking for America's help in winning Vietnamese independence from the French." Ho Chi Minh had also appealed to the US for help after WWI with the same result: rejection. This came despite the facts that the Viet Minh had worked with the forerunner of the American CIA and Ho Chi Minh himself admired US democracy. "Ho trusted the US more than he did the Soviet Union and reportedly had a picture of George Washington and a copy of the American Declaration of Independence on his desk," Blum explains.[42] Within ten years, the fallout from this rejection would set America on its path towards invasion.

Greatest Generation? A March 1938 survey showed that 41 percent of Americans believed that "Jews have too much power in the United States," and a US Army poll taken as the war was ending, in September 1945, found that an astonishing 22 percent of GIs thought the Nazi treatment of the Jews was justified. Another 10 percent labeled themselves "unsure."[43] A December 1945 *Fortune* poll revealed that nearly 23 percent of Americans questioned wished the US could have dropped "many more [atomic bombs] before the Japanese had a chance to surrender."[44]

Toss in the firebombings of Dresden and Tokyo, the recruitment of Nazi war criminals to start the Central Intelligence Agency, and the internment of Americans of Japanese, German, and Italian descent, and one might wonder what the "worst generation" would have looked like.

■ ■ ■ ■ ■ ■ ■ ■ ■

When discussing Pat Robertson and his "fellow Puritans," the American Civil Liberties Union (ACLU) explained that they "like to paint a picture of America in the 1950s as a better, more virtuous place, a prosperous nation of properly respectful citizens curled up beneath a warm quilt of moral security. A Norman Rockwell vision of life that was suddenly destroyed when the godless catastrophe that was the 1960s turned us away from virtue."[45]

"Contrary to popular belief," responds Stephanie Coontz, "*Leave it to Beaver* was not a documentary."[46]

To believe the 1950s were the true good old days depicted in film and on TV would be to ignore the facts that 25 percent of Americans (some 40 to 50 million people) were poor in the mid-1950s[47] and that life expectancy in 1950 was only 68.2 (compared to 76.7 in 1999).[48] By the end of the decade, only half the US population had savings, and one-quarter had no liquid assets at all.[49]

Robertson and his ilk surely aren't aware that 97 out of every 1,000 girls between the ages of fifteen and nineteen gave birth during that decade (compared to 52:1000 in 1983). They must now know about the 80 percent increase in out-of-wedlock babies placed for adoption from 1944-55.[50]

Were the 1950s a "better, more virtuous place" for women and minorities? In 1956 alone:

• Autherine Juanita Lucy, 26, became the first African American ever admitted to a white public school or university. In less than a week, she was suspended because her presence incited violence from a white mob.

• *Life* magazine published interviews with five male psychiatrists who believed female ambition was the root of mental illness in wives, emotional upsets in husbands, and homosexuality in boys.

• The first lobotomy in the US was performed at George Washington University Hospital on a 63-year old woman. Some surgeons looked upon the controversial operation as a cure for the "mad housewife" syndrome.[51]

During the 1950s, there were US-sponsored coups in Iran and Guatemala, yet another military intervention in Haiti, and the escalation of that great catalyst for 1960s change: the Vietnam War.

As explained earlier, the US invasion of South Vietnam didn't materialize out of thin air in the mid-1960s. US involvement was direct and intense during the golden age of the 1950s. By 1954, US aid to French efforts in Indochina reached $1.4 billion or 78 percent of the French budget for the war.[52] While Americans sat in front of their brand new televisions and dreamed dreams of suburbs, two-car garages, and a better life through technology, the US war machine was leading the nation down the path to a decade of deep division, war crimes, and (some) change.

■ ■ ■ ■ ■ ■ ■ ■ ■

"The simple truth is that the 'good old days' were never that good for the vast majority of the people who lived them," concludes Dennis N. Randall. "We cannot expect to return to a past that never really existed. History is written by the victors. It is usually written for, by, and about the wealthy and influential people of the times."

BETWEEN 1939 AND 1945, ILLEGITIMATE BIRTHS IN THE US ROSE BY 42 PERCENT.

"It would be as foolish to think things are always getting better as it is to assume they're steadily worsening," adds historian Richard Shenkman

There's a Hebrew proverb urging all those faced with two options to choose the third. If the good old days weren't as good as we've been told and most of us can agree that things really suck now, perhaps the choice is no longer between yesterday and today.

Perhaps the third option is to make sure tomorrow is better.

Endnotes

1. Bowles, Linda. "The Good Old Days." Syndicated column, 17 July 2001. **2.** Brokaw, Tom. *The Greatest Generation*. New York: Random House, 1998: xxx. **3.** Randall, Dennis N. "How Good Were They…Really? The Good Old Days: Myth vs. Reality." Website of the Jones River Village Historial Society <kingstonuu.org/jrvhs/>. **4.** Davis, Kenneth C. *Don't Know Much About The Civil War: Everything You Need to Know about America's Greatest Conflict but Never Learned*. New York: Avon Books, 1996: 206. **5.** *Op cit.*, Randall. **6.** Rendall, Steve, Jim Naureckas, and Jeff Cohen. *The Way Things Aren't: Rush Limbaugh's Reign of Error*. The New Press, 1995: 48. **7.** *Op cit.*, Randall. **8.** See my book, *Forgotten New York: Small Slices of a Big Apple*. Seaburn Books, 2002. **9.** Shenkman, Richard. *Legends, Lies, and Cherished Myths of American History*. HarperPerennial, 1989: 160. **10.** *Op cit.*, Randall. **11.** *Ibid.* **12.** *Ibid.* **13.** *Op cit.*, *Forgotten New York*. **14.** *Op cit.*, Randall. **15.** Coontz, Stephanie. *The Way We Never Were: American Families and the Nostalgia Trap*. New York: Basic Books, 1992: 184. **16.** *Op cit.*, Shenkman: 74. **17.** Zinn, Howard. *The People's History of the United States: 1492-Present*. New York: HarperPerennial, 1995: 252. **18.** *Op cit.*, Zinn: 254. **19.** *Op cit.*, Shenkman: 107. **20.** *The World Almanac and Book of Facts*. World Almanac Books, 2002: 877. **21.** Mescher, Virginia. Review of *The Good Old Days: They Were Terrible* by Otto L. Betterman. Website of the 42nd Virginia Infantry Regiment, 1997. **22.** Loewen, James W. *Lies My Teacher Told Me: Everything Your American History Textbook Got Wrong*. The New Press, 1995: 203. **23.** *Ibid.*: 342-3. **24.** Blum, William. *Killing Hope: US Military and CIA Interventions Since World War II*. Monroe, Maine: Common Courage Press, 1995: 449. **25.** *Op cit.*, Loewen: 204. **26.** *Op cit.*, Zinn: 337. **27.** For more on propaganda during World War I and ensuing wars, see my book: *Saving Private Power: The Hidden History of "The Good War"*. New York: Soft Skull Press, 2000. **28.** *Op cit.*, Zinn: 359. **29.** *Op cit.*, Blum: 449-51. **30.** *Op cit.*,

A US ARMY POLL TAKEN AS THE WAR WAS ENDING, IN SEPTEMBER 1945, FOUND THAT AN ASTONISHING 22 PERCENT OF GIs THOUGHT THE NAZI TREATMENT OF THE JEWS WAS JUSTIFIED.

Shenkman: 152. **31.** *Ibid*.: 74. **32.** *Ibid*.: 160. **33.** *Op cit*., Zinn: 376. **34.** Northern Sun Merchandising catalog, Fall/Winter 2002/3: 5. **35.** *Op cit*., Blum: 451. **36.** For more documentation, see *Saving Private Power*. **37.** Adams, Michael C.C. *The Best War Ever: America and World War II*. Baltimore: The Johns Hopkins University Press, 1994: 35. **38.** Schlechty, Phillip C. "Were They Really the Good Old Days?" Website of District School Board of Collier County. Schlechty is the founder and CEO of the Center for Leadership in School Reform. **39.** *Op cit*., Rendall, *et al*.: 48. **40.** For more documentation, see *Saving Private Power*. **41.** *Op cit*., Adams: 89. **42.** *Op cit*., Blum: 123. **43.** Herzstein, Robert Edwin. *Roosevelt and Hitler: Prelude to War*. Paragon House, 1989: 156. **44.** Dower, John W. *War Without Mercy: Race and Power in the Pacific War*. Pantheon Books, 1986: 54. **45.** American Civil Liberties Union. "Background Information: 'The Good Old Days.'" ACLU, 1998. **46.** *Op cit*., Coontz: 29. **47.** *Ibid*.: 29. **48.** *Op cit*., *Almanac*: 877. **49.** *Op cit*., Coontz: 30. **50.** *Ibid*.: 39. **51.** Carabillo, Toni, *et al*. *The Feminist Chronicles, 1953-1993*. Los Angeles: Women's Graphics, 1993. **52.** *Op cit*., Blum: 123.

THE SECRET BEHIND THE CREATION OF THE UNITED NATIONS
US INTERCEPTED ALLIES' ENCRYPTED COMMUNICATIONS
STEPHEN SCHLESINGER

THE UNITED STATES INTERCEPTED THE CONFIDENTIAL DIPLOMATIC CABLE TRAFFIC OF ITS ALLIES IN THE SIX MONTHS BEFORE AND THE TWO MONTHS DURING THE 1945 CONFERENCE THAT DRAFTED THE CHARTER OF THE UNITED NATIONS. IT USED THIS PURLOINED INFORMATION TO INFLUENCE THE OUTCOME OF THAT MEETING AND, THUS, THE STRUCTURE OF THE UN.

The interception of foreign diplomatic traffic by the United States played a major role in enabling America to fashion the United Nations into the organization it wished at the San Francisco conference in 1945. The United States, the primary strategist behind the creation of the UN, had a war-created cryptanalytic program that included the interception and solution of the embassy cables not only of its enemies, but also of its allies and of neutrals. As World War II wound down, America employed it to uncover the interests of the San Francisco participants in order to mold the organization's charter to its liking.

Secret US files released in 1993 under the Freedom of Information Act reveal how Pentagon operatives eavesdropped on friendly nations in the weeks leading up to the San Francisco meeting to find out how they were preparing for it and during the two months of the conference to find out how they were reacting to it. These documents suggest that, in producing a United Nations that the United States envisaged, it was indulging not only in altruism but also in national self-interest. Such revelations indicate that, in retrospect, some revisions in conventional historical judgments on the origins of the United Nations may now be in order.

The 635 pages of diplomatic messages came from the Army's Signal Security Agency, which broke codes and solved intercepts, and its Special Branch, which evaluated, edited, and distributed them as "Magic" Diplomatic Summaries. These summaries reported information obtained from intercepted and solved foreign diplomatic cryptograms. Reproduced in purple ink by the Ditto process and issued daily, they averaged fifteen pages each. All were divided into three categories—military, political, and economic—and, where needed, into two others: psychological and subversive and miscellaneous. Sometimes annexes amplified some items or gave the full text of important documents; occasionally maps were included. Within each category, headings described the subject of the intercept or intercepts. The scope was extremely great, ranging from German military plans as reported by the Japanese ambassador to Afghan attitudes to Japanese intelligence activities. The documents do not include any British or Soviet messages.[1]

The "Magic Summaries" reveal that:

• Washington knew in advance the negotiating positions of almost all of the 50 countries that assembled in San Francisco.

• On key issues—whom to admit to the UN, decolonization, the Security Council veto, the role of smaller countries, even Soviet views—the US had crucial intelligence beforehand.

• Most nations, including the US, sought to push their own interests over those of the world community.

• The US apparently used its surveillance reports to set the agenda of the UN, to control the debate, to pressure nations to agree to its positions, and to write the UN Charter mostly according to its own blueprint.

Whether the US was morally right to make use of Ultra—as the solutions were covernamed—is not an easy question to answer; America found itself in desperate times in the 1940s. Undoubtedly every country that had the ability to intercept cable traffic was ready to take advantage of this capacity to ferret out as much as possible about the strategies of other governments. And surely the creation of as important a body as the UN, given past historic failures, also merited special attention. Still, Ultra was not the proper way to treat allies and was of dubious legality.[2]

But President Franklin D. Roosevelt knew he was going to have a difficult time pushing through the US Senate a complicated UN structure, even if designed in large part to forestall another League of Nations-style disaster. Isolationist sentiment was still strong in the land. To make the United Nations palatable to Congress, Roosevelt—beginning at a conference of the leading Allied nations he convened on August 21, 1944, at Dumbarton Oaks, a study center in Washington—campaigned for a Security Council tightly controlled by the major powers.[3] The United States, Great Britain, the

Soviet Union, and China agreed at Dumbarton Oaks to the draft outlines of the United Nations, which provided for a General Assembly with rather modest authority, a Secretariat subject to major power control, a Military Staff Committee composed of the Big Five (the four nations that met at Dumbarton plus France, which was also invited to be the fifth permanent Council member), and, of course, the all-powerful Security Council, an 11-member body of which the Big Five were to be permanent members with veto powers.

The adoption of the latter veto provision, which at first was left in limbo at Dumbarton Oaks, reflected FDR's belief that the Security Council would actually run the United Nations and that, since these five nations were the only ones that possessed the forces to police the world, this prerogative was required. Extending the veto to all nations (as had been done for the Executive Council of the League of Nations) would invite gridlock and inaction. Four months later, at Yalta, Churchill and Stalin, at FDR's insistence, completed voting procedures reflecting this veto system for the United Nations.

With these building blocks in place, FDR believed in the spring of 1945 that his special conception of the United Nations would have the best chance of acceptance by the other nations of the world. Not only was it in America's national interest, but it basically met the needs of all the earth's capitals. Still, he anticipated that smaller countries would fear the expansive authority of the organizing nations and would probably dispute the draft UN Charter. He knew he would probably have to twist arms to get his way.

The intercepted diplomatic notes nonetheless show that in the months leading up to the San Francisco conference, which began April 25, 1945, as well as during the two-month meeting itself, the US used information from its codebreaking to help get its way on the UN issues about which it vitally cared.

_ARGENTINA

One of the most vexing questions facing the conference from the onset was whether Argentina should be admitted. Soviet Premier Joseph Stalin opposed the admission of Argentina on the grounds that it was a crypto-Nazi country that had helped Hitler during the war. The "United Nations" was, in Stalin's reasoning, originally a wartime alliance of nations opposed to the Axis, not yet a global security organization, and thus like-minded countries should be its members. Most Latin American nations, however, for reasons of hemispheric solidarity, threatened to boycott the UN if Argentina's application were turned down. Although the US had objected to Argentina's neutrality during nearly all of the war, Washington knew that it had to resolve the question of Argentina's admission or face the possibility that either Moscow or Latin America would refuse to join the UN, crippling the fledgling organization from the outset.

The general outlines of the Argentine dispute were known to the US through the diplomatic contacts of Roosevelt's coordinator of inter-American affairs, Nelson Rockefeller. But Ultra told the United States precisely what tactics the Latin nations were beginning to pursue on Argentina's behalf and what actions Moscow was, in turn,

taking to prevent its admission.

Hemispheric countries, according to Ultra, already were aware that Roosevelt was sidestepping an urgent Argentine proposal in late 1944 to convene a meeting of the Pan American Union on postwar hemisphere problems. Argentina, which had severed its relations with Germany and Japan in January, was going to present its arguments for a continued neutrality at this meeting. Instead, Washington, to isolate Argentina within the Americas in order to force it to abandon its position, suggested that the Latin republics that had collaborated with Washington in the war effort meet in a conference outside the Pan American Union in Mexico and there consider the Argentine request.[4] The United States may have supposed that, once it induced Buenos Aires to abandon its neutrality and declare war on Germany, it could recast that nation into a more acceptable applicant for UN membership.

THE US APPARENTLY USED ITS SURVEILLANCE REPORTS TO SET THE AGENDA OF THE UN, TO CONTROL THE DEBATE, TO PRESSURE NATIONS TO AGREE TO ITS POSITIONS, AND TO WRITE THE UN CHARTER MOSTLY ACCORDING TO ITS OWN BLUEPRINT.

The Ultra intercepts enabled the United States to track the reaction to FDR's proposal around the hemisphere. For example, it read an Ecuadorian message of December 30, 1944, to its chargé in Washington, Duran Ballen, instructing him to tell representatives of Chile and Colombia that Ecuador would back Buenos Aires' request. In his answer, Ballen stated that since sixteen Latin countries had already accepted invitations to the conference, he advised de-emphasizing strong support for Argentina at the Pan American Governing Board. "I therefore suggest that I limit myself to stating Ecuador's point of view without seeking to contradict the plans prepared by nearly all the other countries," he wrote in a message that US officials undoubtedly read with satisfaction. Ballen then did what he had proposed.[5]

US codebreakers also solved a dispatch of January 6, 1945, from the Argentine chargé in Washington to his government. This reported that the Chilean ambassador was assuring him that the conference in Mexico—now scheduled for February—"should not be considered as an unfriendly act toward Argentina but rather as a means for reaching a solution." The Chilean soothed the Argentinean. Perhaps the meeting would "convert" itself into the Pan American Union conference on postwar problems that Argentina wanted. In a message to its Washington embassy, Chile's foreign ministry said that it had turned down a US request that it demand the Pan American Governing Board rebuff Buenos Aires' entreaty. And a day earlier, the Chilean ambassador in Brazil informed Santiago that Brazil's acting Foreign Minister, while not approving of the Mexican parley, nevertheless planned to attend it.

In mid-February, shortly before the assemblage in Mexico City, another flurry of messages scanned by Ultra reported on new developments in Latin attitudes on the Argentina problem. Paraguay now proposed to Colombia, Ecuador, and Venezuela that pressure be put on Argentina directly to join the Allied war effort. Colombia, though, objected to that course as likely to be "badly received" and offered a gentler plan.

All of these tidbits may have helped Washington intensify pressure on the other Latin countries—both within and without the Mexico meeting—to compel Argentina to reassess its ideological course.[6] For example, the Chilean envoy in Washington telegraphed Santiago in mid-January about a luncheon with Nelson Rockefeller at the Cuban embassy. He and seven other ambassadors agreed there that Buenos Aires had to be told to "adopt concrete and effective measures to eradicate the conviction of all the American peoples that she has been antagonistic toward the democracies of the continent..." The relentless US blitz against Buenos Aires was gradually generating a hemispheric condemnation that was starting to be felt by Argentine officials—at least those in Washington. Around the time of the Rockefeller lunch, the Argentine chargé in Washington informed his government that, while the Mexico conference would

> ## "MR. EDEN EXPLAINED TO ME THAT THE IDEA [OF THE TRUSTEESHIP] WAS AN AMERICAN ONE AND WOULD PERMIT THE UNITED STATES TO LAY HANDS CHASTELY ON THE JAPANESE ISLANDS IN THE PACIFIC."

"cover a discussion of the diplomatic misunderstanding" (copying the same word as one of his Latin colleagues), his country might have to think about a compromise.[7]

By March 21, 1945, the Argentine military attaché in the US cabled President Farrell of Argentina that it was "decidedly advisable" for Buenos Aires to back an idea recently floated by its foreign minister: The country should hold a plebiscite for or against a declaration of war against Germany and Japan.

Ultra enhanced Washington's ability to anticipate objections from Argentina, evaluate shifts in the mood of Argentina, and calibrate the growing demands upon Argentina by its neighbors. On March 27, 1945, Argentina entered the war against the Axis powers.[8]

Ecuador now tried to convince the other recalcitrant party to this drama, the USSR, to reconsider its opposition to Argentina's admission to the UN. Ecuador enlisted Peru, Mexico, Cuba, Panama, Venezuela, and Brazil in this campaign. On April 7, Colombia's Foreign Minister instructed his envoy in Moscow to tell the Soviet regime that if it were now to oppose Buenos Aires, "we fear it would be a bad beginning for her relations with the American countries, which, for the most part, have established relations with Russia without much conviction and against considerable internal opposition."[9] With this information, the US was in a position in its negotiations with Moscow at San Francisco to persuade Stalin's envoys to admit Argentina, thereby placating the Latins.[10]

_COLONIES

A second great dispute arose over the US desire to establish a Trusteeship Council at the UN. Both the British and French feared that such a body might force them to give up their colonies after the war. Through Ultra, the US became keenly aware of French appre-

hensions as early as mid-January 1945. France's provisional Foreign Minister, Georges Bidault, telegraphed his ambassador in Washington about reports that the Americans at a preliminary UN conference were pressing for an international UN committee for colonies modeled on the controversial Mandates Commission of the League of Nations. A French emissary reassured Bidault on the matter: "The American tendency of hastening the normal evolution of colonies toward autonomy, dominion status, or independence was met by objections—and even the protests—of qualified delegates...including ours."[11] But the issue was not dead.

After the Yalta meeting in early February (from which the French had been excluded), the French representative in Moscow sought out Soviet Foreign Minister Vyacheslav Molotov to obtain additional assurances that the UN would not act against Paris' colonial possessions. Molotov responded that Paris should take the matter up with the White House, which, he said, was now assuming primary responsibility over the colonial matter. In any event, he informed the French, a system of "trusteeship" had been "defined only in principle" at Yalta.[12] Solutions of French intercepts revealed these discussions to the Americans.

The French later shared their concerns with the British. After meeting with British Foreign Secretary Anthony Eden in London, Bidault, according to Ultra, expressed his satisfaction with the results: "Mr. Eden explained to me that the idea [of the trusteeship] was an American one and would permit the United States to lay hands chastely on the Japanese islands in the Pacific. The system is not to be applied to any region in Europe nor to any colonies belonging to the Allied countries. The English are determined that no misunderstanding arise in this regard." In their talks, Eden and Prime Minister Winston Churchill approved a continuation of France's "privileged position" in Syria and Lebanon.[13]

But the French, not convinced of the British assurances, undertook a broader offensive to protect their colonies. For example, they convened talks in Paris between General Charles de Gaulle and the Foreign Minister of the Netherlands, which also had overseas territories. Both men agreed, according to Bidault, on "the impossibility of surrendering to an international authority any of their colonies." By early April, Bidault wired all his envoys that France would flatly reject any plan of international control "over all or part of her colonial empire or of the countries placed under her protection." She would, moreover, uphold trusteeships for former Japanese or Italian territories. Bidault told the Greek ambassador that the US was promoting trusteeships simply because it "wants to exercise influence on other people's colonies for selfish political and economic reasons."[14]

The codebreaking helped shape US policy. Just as the San Francisco conference was commencing, the US began to reassess its thinking about France. It wanted France to join the Security Council and drop its championship of smaller nations opposed to the Big Five rule. It started easing its pressure somewhat on the trusteeship issue. America's conciliatory stance and respect toward France's *amour-propre* had an immediate calming influence, the Ultra documents show.

Paris began displaying more pragmatism on the colonial issue. A French official in the US with experience in territorial problems advised his home office midway through the conference that France should not "turn down a text in which independence is set as the eventual goal for trusteeship, for we would be approximately the only ones to do so." By the end of the San Francisco conference, Bidault himself was imploring his delegates to get UN approval for an impartial commission to investigate France's treaty status in Syria and Lebanon. At the conference's conclusion, France's verdict on trusteeship was now cautiously favorable and no longer harshly antagonistic. Its delegate wrote Paris: "The settlement of the trusteeship problem fulfills in broad outlines the instructions of the French government."[15] American diplomacy, guided in part by intelligence from Ultra, had maneuvered France into a satisfactory stand-down.

_VETO POWER

The third serious matter that roiled UN members from the outset was the exclusive veto power over UN actions that the Big Five as permanent members of the Security Council would hold. Before the conference, Washington had had hints of the profound misgivings of certain mid-sized countries about this allocation of power. France had provisionally turned down becoming the fifth permanent member of the Security Council (after the US, the Soviet Union, China, and the United Kingdom) with the accompanying right to the veto because of its ire over its exclusion from Yalta. It criticized the veto and held to a romantic notion of becoming the leader of the UN's smaller nations.

In the months preceding the San Francisco conclave, FDR also privately clashed with Stalin over the breadth of the veto. Stalin wanted the power to bar even discussion of issues in the Security Council, not merely to prevent action by the Security Council, as FDR wished. Whatever the source, FDR's effort to get the veto in any form was in much more serious trouble from UN members than many historians have previously thought.

First, US intelligence obtained a message in mid-March 1945 from the Chilean Foreign Minister offering his "personal opinion" to his envoys that "the procedure devised at the Crimea Conference [Yalta] for voting in the Security Council is not in accord with the sovereign equality of all peace-loving states and, in operation, would put the permanent members of the Council above the law which will govern all nations." The Minister requested his diplomats abroad find out how other countries regarded the special status of the great powers at the UN. He received at least five replies—from Costa Rica, Cuba, Italy, Switzerland, and the Vatican—agreeing with Chile's reservations. This group was probably representative of the 50 states that were to convene at San Francisco, and their reservations suggested that an alarmingly large opposition to the US position was in the making.[16]

In a dispatch in late March, Turkish officials also expressed doubts about the voting procedures. They told French diplomats in Ankara that the setup "seemed destined to make lawful the projects of the large powers against the small—with the system of voting in the Security Council ensuring them impunity." The Turks warned that "the small states are inevitably going to be reduced to the status of satellites of the great." They also feared that bilateral alliances—for example, their 1939 mutual assistance pact with Great Britain—

could be overridden during a crisis by the veto, say, with the USSR. But they also conceded the "futility" of modifying the UN Charter. Instead they hoped to increase "the number of non-permanent members on the Security Council from six to nine in order to give the Great Powers a less preponderant majority."[17]

Likewise, France's initial worries with respect to Security Council procedures grew as the conference neared. In early March, Bidault instructed his ambassador in Moscow to advise the Soviets of his concern that, under the veto arrangement, regional and bilateral treaties could be "subordinated to the previous agreement of the Security Council." This is dangerous, he added, because the "automatic nature of regional pacts is...the essential element of collective security..." The French enlisted the Belgians and sounded out the British on an amendment to "clarify" the section on regional agreements in the UN Charter.[18]

With such intelligence data, the United States was able to develop its arguments on behalf of the veto well in advance and thus disable the opposition. Washington contended that, as a matter of Realpolitik, there simply was not going to be a viable UN organization unless the four or five most powerful nations received the veto. Without it, none of these countries, the US insisted, would entrust any of its sovereignty to an international group, especially not to an intrusive and powerless League of Nations-like body. The US Congress, for instance, would not ratify the pact and probably would allow America to return to isolationism. Nor would the Soviets join without the veto. And, as a matter of practicality, US delegates added, the other countries in the United Nations would never have enough weapons or influence to impose UN edicts on the great powers except with the concurrence of the Big Five themselves. Finally, even with an organization that might distribute authority in a way that would seem unsatisfactory to lesser powers, the superpowers would still always remain in the dock of world opinion. This would stabilize the peace system better than none at all.

> **FDR'S EFFORT TO GET THE VETO IN ANY FORM WAS IN MUCH MORE SERIOUS TROUBLE FROM UN MEMBERS THAN MANY HISTORIANS HAVE PREVIOUSLY THOUGHT.**

Alerted to France's hesitancy by its reading of the French diplomatic transmissions, Washington decided to focus its campaign for the veto on Paris, which had now made itself the leader of the recalcitrant member-states. As the San Francisco conference commenced, America intensified its overtures to France to reconsider its decision to forgo its role as the fifth permanent member of the Security Council. This approach, coming at a time when France was finding it increasingly difficult to act as the champion of the smaller nations, and flattering France's pretensions to being a great power and salving its hurt over Yalta, reignited the Quai d'Orsay's interest.[20] The French soon decided to accept their earlier assigned spot on the Security Council. With France's decision, the campaign to thwart the veto collapsed.

French diplomats saw fresh virtues in the arrangement, Ultra showed. While ostensibly staying above the battle, they were signaling a change of heart. The French UN delegate cabled Paris:

THE TURKS WARNED THAT "THE SMALL STATES ARE INEVITABLY GOING TO BE REDUCED TO THE STATUS OF SATELLITES OF THE GREAT."

"However far apart we [the Four Powers and the small and medium powers] still are, a conciliatory solution is not impossible, for everyone is beginning to realize that the veto is a necessity and that its limits could not be further defined without risks for which no one wishes seriously to assume responsibility." Later, in summing up his country's achievements at San Francisco, the French delegate reflected: "[A]lthough it [the veto] may in some cases seem an annoyance—and a very grave annoyance—it may also in others be a means of preventing the Council from meddling unduly in affairs which are our own or which we intend to settle through other channels."[21]

Finally, discussions at San Francisco had rendered moot the concern of France and Turkey that bilateral and regional pacts would be undermined by the veto. Several Ultra dispatches showed that France no longer worried about this. The American victory was complete.

_US-SOVIET RELATIONS

The fourth event of importance illuminated by the Ultra files were the chronically touchy US-Soviet relations. Intercepted cables—none of them Soviet—contained conflicting assessments of Soviet intentions. On the one hand, they showed the Soviets holding firm to their agreement with FDR forged at Yalta, which had included a commitment to free elections in Poland. On the other hand, Moscow's surreptitious resistance to democratic government in Poland, and its heavy-handed pressures on such border countries as Iran and Turkey, revealed a Soviet Union that was growing increasingly obstinate about its territorial security. Ironically, even after the intercepts disclosed potentially alarming Russian moves, the United States remained puzzled about Moscow's intentions and unsure of how to act toward Stalin. American reactions swung between confrontation and conciliation.

Washington learned from intercepted messages, for example, that Moscow, at least in private conversations with some European powers, was treating the Yalta agreements as sacrosanct. Just days after Yalta, Molotov told the French ambassador to the Soviet Union—according to that envoy's dispatch to Paris on February 19—that Stalin had expressed great confidence at the outcome of the meeting with Roosevelt and Churchill. And Molotov, according to the official, said that Stalin guaranteed that France would receive "an equal place" with Great Britain, Russia, and the US at the UN.[22]

But Stalin was not willing to jeopardize his agreements with Washington and London to please Paris over the latter's aggressive insistence that the three powers reword the joint summons to San Francisco—an invitation in which France had been asked to join by Moscow—to promise preservation of regional and bilateral pacts. The French ambassador messaged home his guess as to why the Soviets refused to rephrase the invitation: "I have reason to believe that at the present stage one of the prime concerns of Soviet policy is carefully to avoid anything that could weaken the assertion of perfect unity of viewpoint and action proclaimed by the Three Powers

meeting at Yalta." Why? Because, he concluded, Moscow was "the principal beneficiary of the accord."[23]

On the other hand, America was picking up ominous reports from foreign emissaries in Moscow and elsewhere concerning Poland and other Soviet border nations. The crux of the issue with respect to Poland was Stalin's demand that his puppet regime in Lublin be admitted to the UN and the US response that Stalin first democratize Lublin by including members of the prewar Polish government-in-exile in London. At Yalta, Stalin had agreed to a three-way British-American-Soviet commission to try to work out a coalition government in Poland. But Washington soon knew from the Ultra records and from its own ambassador in Moscow, Averell Harriman, that Stalin was reneging on that deal. France's delegate to Stalin's puppet regime in Lublin wired Paris that Lublin's policies were gradually turning it into a "quasi-protectorate" of the Soviet Union. Meantime, in early March, France's Moscow envoy reported that the commission was "running into great difficulties" because, according to information from Harriman, the Soviets didn't like "the choice of Polish leaders to be consulted." By mid-March, the French diplomat had had conversations with Poland's pro-Russian emissary to Moscow and informed Paris that the Soviets would probably impose their own regime on Poland.[24]

The impasse over Poland persisted for weeks, gravely imperiling the United Nations' ratification. Stalin was, according to some observers, on the edge of aborting the whole idea of a global organization—a "Western" idea about which he was never enthusiastic—over the matter. Eventually President Harry Truman, in the midst of the San Francisco conference, sent the late FDR's closest confidante—the seriously ill Harry Hopkins, who knew Stalin from past encounters—as his emissary to the Soviet leader to work out a settlement on Lublin. Hopkins, though terminally ill, arrived in Moscow in late May and conferred with the Soviet chieftain for ten days.

Hopkins eventually obtained Stalin's agreement to a high-level meeting in Moscow on the beleaguered nation's future to be supervised by the three-way commission. The French liaison in London to the Polish government-in-exile learned of the Hopkins deal from his contacts and, in a message read in Washington, informed Paris in early June that the meeting would include all Polish leadership inside and outside the country. But he noted that the Polish exiles were disappointed that so few representatives of the democratic parties had been invited.

Harriman later told the French in mid-June that "it is not impossible that a successful conclusion will be reached" at the upcoming Moscow conclave on Poland. By the end of June, the session did produce a Provisional Government of National Unity that nominally included members of all political parties; as a result of this settlement, by early July, the US and Great Britain formally recognized the regime and thereafter it gained UN membership. Ultra had warned Washington how stubborn and unyielding Stalin was likely to be on Poland and thereby had encouraged a US back-down on the issue.

During this time, Washington had taken its own action to ward off what it saw as a potential Soviet intrusion in its own sphere of influence in Latin America. It began to caution Latin states throughout the hemisphere against Communist subversion. Ultra revealed that a Venezuelan diplomat telegraphed his home office on May 7 after a session with Rockefeller, the coordinator of inter-American affairs, that "Rockefeller communicated to us the anxiety of the United States government about the Russian attitude." American officials, the envoy wrote, were "beginning to speak of Communism as they once spoke of Nazism, and are invoking continental solidarity and hemispheric defense against it."

Still, as the Ultra documents illuminate, even as it maneuvered its way between various Soviet moves and countermoves, the United States continued to concentrate on the main target at hand—overcoming the Soviet Union's reservations about the United Nations, especially on such matters as Argentina's admission, the breadth of the veto, and Poland. Thus it showed a distinct unwillingness to allow any of these outside events to derail the conference. While FDR at Yalta, and Truman in his first days in office, bargained hard on most issues with Stalin and Molotov, both always judged that the US national interest in establishing the UN made it necessary to accommodate Stalin where otherwise they might have challenged him.

HELPED BY ULTRA, WASHINGTON BY AND LARGE ACHIEVED WHAT IT WANTED: A SECURITY COUNCIL CONTROLLED BY THE FIVE ALLIES, A WEAKER GENERAL ASSEMBLY, AND A MALLEABLE SECRETARIAT AND MILITARY COMMISSION.

At Yalta, FDR accepted the dictator's desire for three votes at the UN (one for the Soviet Union, and one for each of its "territories," the Ukraine and Byelorussia). Truman eventually backed a vague settlement of the Polish situation and gave in on a host of other protocol matters at San Francisco. In turn, though, the US gained Stalin's assent to what is now generally regarded as an essential international body. That that assent was a necessity was well understood even then. As the Undersecretary of State, Sumner Welles, wrote a few years later, without the UN "war between the Soviet Union and Western powers would already have been inevitable, and the fate of our civilization would today be trembling in the balance."[25]

■■■■■■■■■■

The San Francisco conference ended in late June 1945. Helped by Ultra, Washington by and large achieved what it wanted: a Security Council controlled by the five Allies, a weaker General Assembly, and a malleable Secretariat and military commission (though the latter soon vanished in the Cold War mists). The Ultra intercepts gave the United States advance warnings about problems with members' admissions to the UN, with decolonization, with the veto, and with US-Soviet relations—all essential to America's various bargaining positions. The Ultra intelligence thus gave Washington an edge in its public and in its behind-the-scenes efforts at the conference.

In the spring of 1945, the US already had a very big edge—Franklin Roosevelt had formally crafted the idea for the United Nations; he had organized the founding meeting in an American city (incidentally making interception easier for the Americans); nearly every country in the world wanted to join it; and the United States was now the most powerful nation on earth, possessing the richest economy and the strongest military. Nonetheless, Washington had to be absolutely certain of gaining its objectives at San Francisco, or the United

Nations it desired might have fallen apart. America consequently used every weapon in its arsenal, including one of its most secret—Ultra. And it achieved what it sought.

Endnotes

1. The National Archives and Records Administration, Record Group 457 (Records of the National Security Agency / Central Security Service),"'Magic' Diplomatic Summaries," 1942-1945. The NSA declassified portions of the summaries for me October 28, 1993, on the basis of my request of August 13, 1993, under the Freedom of Information Act. All are from 1945. The intercept numbers on the declassified portions were found in the full summaries by David Kahn, and sources in each summary are cited below by date (excluding "1945") and page. For the organization and operation of Special Branch, which produced and distributed the summaries, see Kahn, David. "Roosevelt, Magic, and Ultra" *Cryptologia* 16 (Oct 1992), 289-319. **2.** Under the Federal Communications Act of 1934, "no person receiving...any interstate or foreign communication by wire or radio shall divulge or publish the existence, contents, substance...thereof...to any person other than the addressee..." (18 United States Code 605). **3.** See Hilderbrand, Robert. *Dumbarton Oaks: The Origins of the United Nations and the Search for Postwar Security*. Chapel Hill: University of North Carolina Press, 1990. **4.** January 6: 7-9. See also "The Inter-American Conference on Problems of War and Peace. Held at Mexico City, February 21-March 8, 1945 (The Chapultec Conference)," in United States, Department of State, *Foreign Relations of the United States: Diplomatic Papers, 1945, 9: The American States* (Washington, DC: Government Printing Office, 1969): 1-153; also 223-30. **5.** *Ibid.* **6.** January 8: 4-6; January 11: 9. **7.** January 19: 9-12; January 22: 13. **8.** March 26: 5-6. **9.** April 16: 10-1. **10.** George McJimsey says in *Harry Hopkins: Ally of the Poor and Defender of Democracy* (Cambridge, MA: Harvard University Press, 1987), page 382, that Stalin gave in on Argentina's seating after "both Hopkins and Stalin were willing to concede issues that lay in the other's area of special interest." **11.** February 6: 5-7. **12.** February 24: 8-10. **13.** March 6: 8-11. **14.** March 29: 9-10; April 12, 6-8; April 14: 8-10. **15.** June 5: 14-5; June 25: 7-9; June 30: 4-6. **16.** April 11: 12-3. **17.** April 13: 7-9. **18.** March 7: 6-8; March 9: 6-7. **19.** Eichelberger, Clark. *Organizing for Peace: A Personal History of the United Nations*. New York: Harper & Row, 1977: 165; Luard, Evan. *Conflict and Peace in the Modern International System*. New York: Macmillan, 1988: 212-5; Truman, Harry. *Memoirs: Years of Decision*. New York: Doubleday, 1955: 284-5; Welles, Sumner. *Seven Decisions That Shaped History*. New York: Harper, 1950: 185. **20.** *Op cit.*, Hilderbrand: 40, 120-1; *New York Times*. "France Lining Up With Big Powers" (25 April 1945), "France's Position Put by De Gaulle" (26 April 1945), "France Position Still in Doubt" (28 April 1945), "Hints France Asks Major-Power Role" (3 May 1945). **21.** June 30: 4-6. **22.** February 26: 8-10. **23.** March 16: 6-7. **24.** March 10: 8-9; March 22: 7-9. **25.** *Op cit.*, Welles: xviii.

ONE GIANT LEAP—BACKWARD
AMERICA'S FORGOTTEN FEMALE ASTRONAUTS
STEPHANIE NOLEN

Jerrie Cobb was in the heart of the Amazon jungle. It was a summer night, and the air was dense and hot. She lay in a rough woven hammock strung between a wingtip and a door of her grounded twin-engine Islander plane. She looked up and tried again to count the stars. Then there was a crackle from the radio.

She scrambled into the cockpit and fiddled with the dials, trying to bring in the voice. It was a priest at a missionary station a couple of hundred miles away, calling with news: A few hours earlier, two American men, Neil Armstrong and Buzz Aldrin, had walked on the Moon. It was July 20, 1969.

Cobb leaned out of the cockpit and pulled herself up on to the wing. She did a little dance from the tip of one wing to the end of the other. "Vaya con Dios," she whispered up at the night sky.

And then she looked down at the ground around her, and spoke again.

"It should have been me."

■ ■ ■ ■ ■ ■ ■ ■ ■ ■

When astrophysicist Sally Ride became the first American woman in space in 1983, there was a media frenzy. Canadian physician Roberta Bondar won her share of headlines when she was launched in 1992. And reporters couldn't get enough of a gentle US Air Force Lieutenant Colonel named Eileen Collins, who became the first woman to actually fly the space shuttle and then the first woman to command an American space mission.

But shuttle launches barely make the news today, and with women making up a quarter of the National Air and Space Administration's astronaut corps, there is routinely one female on each flight.

The issue of female astronauts barely made the news in 1960, too. And you won't find the story in American history textbooks. But just at the dawn of the women's movement, a group of superbly qualified female pilots was poised to lead the country into space. As it turned out, their country wasn't ready for them.

Americans heard the crack of the starter's gun in the race for space on October 4, 1957, when the Soviet Union launched Sputnik, the first satellite. The American military scrambled to match the achievement but produced a string of failures. In 1958, President Dwight Eisenhower, taking a pounding over the "space gap," created the National Aeronautics and Space Administration (NASA) and charged it with getting a human being into space before the Soviets did.

The President ruled that Air Force test pilots, elite flyers with security clearance who were already on his payroll, would be best suited for the new job, and a group of 30 men (military flying would not be open to women for another 30 years) was dispatched for medical screening—by Dr. Randy Lovelace, a pilot and a pioneer in aerospace medicine who now headed NASA's Life Sciences Committee, at his clinic in Albuquerque, New Mexico.

In 1959, no one had ever traveled beyond the pull of gravity, and no one knew what being in space would do to the human body: Would the heart cease to beat? Would eyeballs drift out of sockets? Would food stick in the throat? The Lovelace doctors did every test they could think of. They tried to shake the pilots' bones with blasts of sound, induced vertigo, analyzed every bodily fluid they could wring out of the men, subjected them to extremes of temperature, and pushed them to the point of exhaustion.

With rockets blowing up or fizzling on the launch pad, NASA needed some good news, and on April 9, 1959, it introduced the word *astronaut*—and seven men to whom it gave the title—to the public: There were three Air Force pilots (Deke Slayton, Gordon Cooper, Gus Grissom), three Navy pilots (Walter Schirra, Alan Shepard, Scott Carpenter) and one Marine, John Glenn. Asked by a reporter which one would be the first in space, each of the seven immediately raised a hand. Glenn raised both hands.

> ## AT THE DAWN OF THE WOMEN'S MOVEMENT, A GROUP OF SUPERBLY QUALIFIED FEMALE PILOTS WAS POISED TO LEAD THE COUNTRY INTO SPACE.

The men were all white Protestants from small towns, married with children. Four were named for their fathers; three were military-college graduates. This, America was told, was what an astronaut looked like. The country swooned at this image of laconic bravery and pinned its hopes for the space race on seven pairs of broad shoulders. Dr. Lovelace sat up on the dais with them and described their testing ordeals.

Five months later, at an aviation conference, he met Jerrie Cobb.

In September 1959, Geraldyn Cobb was 28 and an internationally renowned pilot. She had been flying since she was twelve, taught by her father, who tied wood blocks on the pedals of his Waco biplane so her feet could reach them. Now she flew for the Aero Design and Engineering Company in Oklahoma City, one of only two or three women in the United States with a senior aeronautics post.

She had set world records for altitude, distance, and speed in the Aero Commander, and just that summer she had been awarded the Gold Wings of the Fédération Aéronautique Internationale in Paris, one of aviation's highest honors.

Freckled, shy, her hair in a long, blond ponytail, she didn't look a pilot—but when Dr. Lovelace heard about her three world records and her 7,000 hours in the cockpit, he had an idea.

NASA's engineers were struggling with the design of their first space capsule. They could not get it small or light enough to launch. But if the pilot were 40 precious pounds lighter, and required less food, fewer heavy oxygen canisters—that might be enough. A Redstone rocket, the country's largest, just might be able to launch that capsule, with a lighter, female passenger.

The doctor pulled Cobb aside. "Medical and psychological investigations," he explained, "have long shown that women are better than men at withstanding pain, heat, cold, loneliness, and monotony," and all of those were sure to be factors in spaceflight. But there was no research on how women held up in space-stress tests.

Cobb was startled to hear it. The space race was consuming America, and the nation knew all about the elaborate tests of the Mercury 7—but nobody had looked at women?

He told her the last testing of female pilots was done on the Women Airforce Service Pilots (WASPs) in World War II, a corps of 1,200 female ferry pilots. Research showed that they had been better able to tolerate isolation and extremes of temperature than male pilots. But there had been no further study in fifteen years; Dr. Lovelace thought it was high time to return to the question.

With an Air Force general he knew, he was designing a "girl astronaut" program for the Air Research and Development Command, the experimental wing of the Air Force trying to get America into space. And he had a question for Cobb: "Would you be willing to be a test subject for the first research on women as astronauts?"

He made the offer to a woman who had been flying since she was twelve at the cost of all else, ever faster and higher, pushing planes so far up into the darkening blue that her hands froze to the controls.

Would she volunteer for astronaut testing? Oh, yes.

■ ■ ■ ■ ■ ■ ■ ■ ■ ■

Cobb arrived in Albuquerque on a chilly Valentine's Day in 1960, but there was nothing romantic about the instructions that awaited her:

Have nothing to eat or drink, not even gum. Do an enema at night, another in the morning, and report to the lab at 8 AM.

She was "Unit 1, Female." There were dozens of blood tests, and more than 100 X-rays, pictures of every bone she had. She blew into tubes while doctors listened for the smooth flow of blood between the chambers of her heart (tiny defects could explode in a rapidly-decompressing space capsule). They strapped her to a table and hung her tilted at 65 degrees while every five minutes an EKG recorded the function of her cardiovascular system.

And when she sat back in an innocuous-looking chair in the otolaryngologist's office, he used a huge syringe to inject supercooled, 10-degree-Fahrenheit water deep into her ear. The water froze her inner-ear bone, inducing vertigo. "I felt the water hit my inner ear, and almost immediately the ceiling began to whirl and became a multiple of spinning blobs. My right hand fell off the chair, and I couldn't lift it back. I knew what was going on, but I couldn't focus my eyes or control my equilibrium." A nurse stood over her with a stopwatch, clocking how long it took her to regain her balance.

Next they put her on an exercise bicycle, covered her in electrodes, and had her pedal in time to a metronome—and every minute, they added drag to the rear wheel, so it felt like going up an ever-steeper incline. She puffed into a gauge while a ring of doctors stood around, watching. The metronome kept ticking, and she kept pedaling. And pedaling. Finally, as her pulse rate hit 180 (the point just before unconsciousness), they told her she could stop.

The test determined how far a person could continue once the point of exhaustion was reached—Cobb found "that extra push" deep within herself, knowing that the Mercury men had beaten this bike.

She had passed the first round. But it wasn't over yet. Next, Dr. Lovelace arranged for her to "fly" the Multi-Axis Spin Test Inertia Facility (MASTIF) housed at NASA's Lewis Research Center in Cleveland. It was a huge, three-way gyroscope, the size of a house, with three separate steel frames nested one inside another so that each could spin independently. It was designed to test a pilot's ability to control roll, pitch, and yaw, the three axes on which a plane or spacecraft turns. A pilot sometimes fights against one, or maybe two. Spinning in space, a capsule could oscillate on all three, and the pilot would have to fire rocket thrusters to still the spinning.

Cobb reported to the lab that housed the monster, christened the "Vomit Comet" by the Mercury 7—Alan Shepard, they say, hit the chicken switch on his first flight. Outfitted in an orange flight suit and a helmet, she climbed up into a rig about the same size as the Mercury capsule and slid onto the contoured couch, facing an instrument panel. Technicians strapped her to the seat with a chest harness, then tied down her legs, waist, and helmet. Then the machine began to move, faster and faster, until it was spinning on all three axes at once at 30 revolutions a minute.

ONE GIANT LEAP—BACKWARD
STEPHANIE NOLEN

"First the thing started to pitch, and if I hadn't been fastened in, I would have been tossed right off the couch," Cobb recalled. "Then as the pitch reached peak speed, I felt the roll start. I was twisting, twisting like a toy, and going head-over-heels at the same time." When the yaw set in, her vision blurred and her stomach churned, as if she were on a dozen amusement-park rides at once—and Cobb avoided those rides.

She forced her eyes to focus. Using her hand control, she had to guide the capsule out of each spin—but if she pushed too far, too fast, or not enough, the spinning got wilder. One by one, she stopped the gyrations, until suddenly, the machine was tamed.

> **COBB'S LONG, BLONDE HAIR MADE THE FIRST PARAGRAPH OF EVERY STORY. *TIME* HELPFULLY PUT THE 36-27-34 MEASUREMENTS OF THE "ASTRONAUTRIX" IN THE SECOND.**

She rode it a few more times, and in the end, the MASTIF handlers said her response was exceptionally quick. "And don't worry," they added, "the space capsule won't be nearly as bad."

Cobb took more tests that summer: Escaping from a spinning, crashed "spaceship" in a deep water tank, taking a jet through a punishing round of high G-force rolls, and a whole week of psychological grilling. Jay Shurley, a military psychiatrist, put her through his pioneering isolation-tank test, immersing her in a soundproof, lightproof, eight-foot tank of water heated to her exact body temperature. At the time, the tank was the closest thing scientists had to mimic the isolation of space.

Cobb climbed in—and at the end of nine hours quietly asked over the microphone if she had done enough. None of the previous female subjects had lasted more than six hours, and no man more than six-and-a-half. "Probably not one in 1,000 persons would be capable of making such a lengthy isolation run," Dr. Shurley wrote.

■ ■ ■ ■ ■ ■ ■ ■ ■ ■

Dr. Lovelace made Cobb's extraordinary results public at the Space and Naval Medicine Congress, an international convention of aerospace scientists held in Stockholm in August. "We are already in a position to say that certain qualities of the female space pilot are preferable to those of her male colleague," he told the audience, adding that the tests to date were purely research—but would continue.

It is unlikely Dr. Lovelace made Cobb's results public without first talking to his colleagues at NASA. With Cobb, he was already using words such as "woman-in-space program," but in Stockholm he was cautious. Perhaps he was playing politics by going public.

"Nobody else was doing it, except maybe the Russians," his clinic colleague Donald Kilgore says now. "He wanted to be on the record about there being something special about female candidates."

His announcement delighted American reporters. "Moon Maid's Ready!" said one headline. "Astronette!" said another. Cobb's long, blonde hair made the first paragraph of every story. *Time* helpfully put the 36-27-34 measurements of the "astronautrix" in the second.

Dr. Lovelace, meanwhile, was determined to find out if his one stellar subject was an aberration or whether there might be more potential "girl astronauts." He asked if Cobb knew any other women with her kinds of hours as a commercial pilot. She listed the handful she knew from the aviation industry and the women's transcontinental air races. In late 1960, he sent out a first stack of letters, asking the women if they were interested in being tested as "potential women astronaut candidates" and warning them to keep their participation secret.

In ones and twos, over the next few months, 20 women made their way to the Lovelace Clinic. There was a petite, flirtatious Texan named Jerri Truhill, who made her living test-flying secret military equipment. An Ohio schoolteacher named Jean Hixson, who served as a test pilot for the WASPs in World War II, the only time women were allowed to fly for the US military. Jan and Marion Dietrich, a pair of vivacious twins from California who had been flying since they were little girls. A crusty, stubborn crop-duster turned Fire Service pilot named Irene Leverton from Chicago. Janey Hart, the daughter of a millionaire auto industrialist, wife of a Senator, mother of eight, and at 40 a public feminist and helicopter pilot. And a 20-year-old New Mexico native named Wally Funk, who was working as a flight instructor on an Air Force base.

At the end of the summer of 1961, Dr. Lovelace had thirteen women whose scores mirrored Cobb's, and he began to make plans to bring them to the naval base at Pensacola, where he would test them in jet-flying and winnow the group down further.

By now, the doctor had a partner. He had asked his friend Jackie Cochran for help in finding candidates, and, as she had a way of doing, she had decided that she had better run things. She was, in 1960, one of the most powerful women in the country. She always claimed to have been an orphan who grew up dirt-poor and near-illiterate in a Florida mill town, but she learned to be a hairdresser, and by the time she was in her early twenties, she had moved to New York and founded an eponymous cosmetics company that rivaled Estée Lauder's.

She also fell in love with flying, and in 1938 was the first woman to win the Bendix Air Race, the country's most storied competition. She married a billionaire stock tycoon named Floyd Odlum, became a close friend of Amelia Earhart's, the confidante of generals and Presidents. In the 1940s, she founded and led the WASP. Then she took up jet flying, and in 1953 became the first woman to break the sound barrier.

When she heard that Dr. Lovelace thought women belonged in space, she immediately decided she would be first. But her old friend broke the news that, in her early fifties, she was too old. If she couldn't go, then she was going to decide who did—and she didn't much like Cobb, one of her few rivals for newspaper headlines and air records.

Nonetheless, Cobb had become the face of the women-in-space program. NASA's director, James Webb, named her his consultant on the issue. Some of the impetus was removed when NASA managed to launch a man, Alan Shephard, in a fifteen-minute suborbital shot in May. But the Soviets had launched two cosmonauts, and both had orbited the earth. In private and on the lecture circuit, Cobb said the US had one space "first" well within its grasp—launching a woman.

Meanwhile, the other women (whom Cobb had taken to addressing in correspondence as the Fellow Lady Astronaut Trainees, or FLATs) were all due in Pensacola on September 17, 1961. They had arranged for people to look after their children, and four of them had to quit their precious flying jobs because their bosses didn't like the idea of women messing with the space program. But they weren't going to miss this opportunity.

On September 16, Jerri Truhill was at home in Dallas, saying good-bye to her kids; her husband Lou had filed for divorce, fed up with his independent wife, but that wasn't enough to stop her. She was just trying to figure out what to pack when the doorbell rang. It was a Western Union delivery boy. Dr. Lovelace's telegram said:

REGRET TO ADVISE ARRANGEMENTS AT PENSACOLA CANCELLED, LETTER WILL ADVISE OF ADDITIONAL DEVELOPMENTS WHEN MATTER CLEARED FURTHER.

But there never was another letter. Cobb flew to Washington and banged on doors; NASA and the Navy shrugged her off. Dr. Lovelace was strangely silent. She got no explanation for the abrupt cancellation. Cobb enlisted the help of Janey Hart, the Senator's wife. The word "discrimination" was just beginning to be used on matters of gender and jobs, and after months of lobbying, the women managed to get a couple of politicians interested.

■ ■ ■ ■ ■ ■ ■ ■ ■ ■

Cobb and Hart met outside a hearing room on Capitol Hill on July 17, 1962. They took their seats at the witness table, facing the row of representatives on the House Space Committee. Ten of the twelve were men, and all but one of those a war veteran. The chairman called on Cobb almost immediately. Feeling her stomach knot, she reminded herself how angry she was and that this might be her only chance.

She told them how she was chosen, and about the tests, and for the first time she made public the names of the other ten women. "We seek, only, a place in our nation's space future without discrimination. We ask as citizens of this nation to be allowed to participate with seriousness and sincerity in the making of history now, as women have in the past."

She outlined the medical and scientific reasons why it made sense to use women, then appealed to national pride:

We have seen the reflected pride of the entire free world in the accomplishments of US Astronauts Shepard, Grissom, Glenn, and Carpenter. All Americans, and certainly all pilots salute them. Now we who aspire to be women astronauts ask for the opportunity to bring glory to our nation by an American woman becoming first in all the world to make a spaceflight.

The next speaker was introduced as, "Mrs. Philip Hart, an excellent wife and mother, as well as a pilot." Poised and calm, she spoke

lightly but with great seriousness. "It is inconceivable to me that the world of outer space should be restricted to men only, like some sort of stag club." But Hart knew that she could not win this case arguing discrimination; she knew how to play politics.

"Above all," she said, "I don't want to downgrade the feminine role of wife, mother, and homemaker. It is a tremendously fulfilling role. But I don't think, either, that it is unwomanly to be intelligent, to be courageous, to be energetic, to be anxious to contribute to human knowledge."

One of the committee members noted that the Mercury astronauts were all jet test pilots, while few of the FLATs had jet time. Cobb patiently explained that women pilots were barred in the Air Force, which did almost all the jet-flying at the time. She didn't think it was a problem, but if NASA did, they should simply let them do the jet runs they had been set for, and see how they performed.

Cobb spoke eloquently of the women's thousands of hours of "equivalent experience"—"flawless judgment, fast reaction, and the ability to transmit that to the proper control of the craft"—earned "the hard way," in as many as 10,000 hours and a million miles in flight.

The committee asked why their program was terminated so abruptly, but the women could only shrug and say they had no idea. So the floor was turned over to the day's star witness: Jackie Cochran. There was no love lost between Cochran and Cobb, but Cochran was the only woman in the country with real jet experience, and she had the political connections that could help them. Cochran was the one who could make this happen.

> "IT IS INCONCEIVABLE TO ME THAT THE WORLD OF OUTER SPACE SHOULD BE RESTRICTED TO MEN ONLY, LIKE SOME SORT OF STAG CLUB."

Instead, she arranged her papers, listed off her hundreds of qualifications, and bluntly made her point: "I do not believe there has been any intentional or actual discrimination against women in the astronaut program to date." Since there was no pressing need for more astronauts, "and there is no shortage of well-trained and long-experienced male pilots," there was no need for women.

Cochran had testified before Congress before: In 1943 she defended her WASPs, when critics alleged, among other things, that it was a waste to train them to fly since they just went off and got married anyhow. But now she invoked the exact argument she had once fought: "You are going to have to, of necessity, waste a great deal of money when you take a large group of women in, because you lose them through marriage."

A few committee members bridled, noting that this argument would bar women from all the professions—and that all the male astronauts were married with children. "They didn't have [the babies]," Cochran snapped back.

As the committee prepared to break up for the day, she leaned forward with one last comment. "Even if we are second in getting a woman into the new environment," said the greatest female pilot in the country to the members of Congress, "it's better than to take a chance on having women fall flat on their faces."

The next day it got worse. Now it was NASA's turn at the witness table, and the space agency had sent its stars, Scott Carpenter and John Glenn—the nation's hero, who had made his orbital flight five months before and finally given the United States an unblemished achievement in space. The galleries were packed with Representatives and Senators who came to hear the astronauts.

First, NASA's director of Spacecraft and Flight Missions outlined the criteria the agency was using to select astronauts. Then, Colonel Glenn smoothly assured the committee that NASA had plenty of astronauts; they weren't looking for more. "[But] if we can find any women that demonstrate that they have better qualification for going into a program than we have going into that program, we would welcome them with open arms," Glenn added.

The committee members dissolved in laughter, and he played it up. "For the purpose of my going home this afternoon, I think that should be stricken from the record."

"THE FACT THAT WOMEN ARE NOT IN THIS FIELD IS A FACT OF OUR SOCIAL ORDER." — ASTRONAUT JOHN GLENN, 1962

The astronauts and the politicians went back and forth over the issue of whether the women should be given a chance to prove themselves in jets or simulators, before Glenn leaned forward and neatly put into words what most of those in the room had been thinking—and closed the debate on female astronauts in the United States for 20 years.

"I think this gets back to the way our social order is organized, real-

ly. It is just a fact. The men go off and fight the wars and fly the airplanes and come back and help design and build and test them. The fact that women are not in this field is a fact of our social order."

■ ■ ■ ■ ■ ■ ■ ■ ■ ■

None of the FLATs ever got to space. Though they couldn't know it, some of the most powerful people in the country were secretly working against them. Lyndon Johnson personally killed off any last hope of their joining the space program, only months before he pushed into law the Civil Rights Act, making it illegal to discriminate on the basis of gender. Nobody in the United States saw any glory in having the most prestigious of American jobs being carried out by a girl with a ponytail.

And so the Soviets won this space race, too, launching cosmonaut Valentina Tereshkova in June 1963.

Most of the FLATs went back to their lives—they found new jobs and kept flying. Most still fly today. But four did not give up the dream. Wally Funk, for instance, has contracted with a private space-tourism company that promises to launch her within a couple of years.

Cobb ran away to the Amazon jungle to serve as a missionary pilot shortly after the Congressional hearings and has lived there ever since. But she is now, at 71, the subject of an international lobby directed at NASA, whose supporters include Hillary Clinton and the National Organization for Women.

"I would give my life to fly in space," Cobb says. "I would have then. I would now."

Reprinted with permission from the Globe and Mail *(Toronto). Based on the research for Stephanie Nolen's book* Promised the Moon: The Untold Story of the First Women in the Space Race *(Penguin Books Canada, 2002).*

THE LILLY SUICIDES
RICHARD DeGRANDPRE

William Forsyth met and married his wife June in 1955. After two years of military service in West Germany, Bill left with June for Los Angeles, where Bill had grown up. Soon after arriving, Bill bought several Volkswagens and started a rental car business near the LA airport. Times were tough at first, but the business eventually caught on. Soon Bill and June had two kids, Susan and Bill Jr., and the business and other property investments continued to grow. Then in 1986 they cashed in. Four years later, after living almost his entire life in California, Bill and June retired to Maui, where Bill Jr. lived. Bill Forsyth was 61 at the time. June was 54.

As is often the case with seniors who suddenly leave their home behind for the romance of a new life, the transition was difficult for Bill Forsyth. The Hawaii move did not sit well with him, although his wife was content, even thriving. Personal difficulties led to marital difficulties. But marriage counseling seemed to help, and there was a general sense in the family that Bill was working through his difficulties. Three years after the move to Maui, with Bill still feeling unsettled, a local psychiatrist prescribed Prozac. Despite giving the diagnosis of depression, the psychiatrist, who had been seeing Bill since the previous year, did not believe him to be seriously depressed or suicidal. Indeed, Bill Forsyth had never spoken of or attempted suicide, nor had he any history of violence, domestic or otherwise.

After his first day on Prozac, Bill was feeling as you might expect if you've read Peter Kramer's *Listening to Prozac*. He was "better than well." The next day, however, he felt horrible, and for the first time put himself under hospital care. After ten days Bill felt well enough to leave the hospital. He was still taking Prozac. Everyone seemed to agree that he was doing better, and the family scheduled a boat trip for the next day. When his parents failed to show that afternoon, Bill Jr. went to their home, where he found his parents lying in a pool of blood. After taking Prozac for eleven days, Bill Forsyth had taken a serrated knife from the kitchen and stabbed his wife fifteen times. Then he took the knife, fixed it to a chair, and impaled himself on it.

Depressed people sometimes do desperate things. Yet these were senseless acts that, at least for those who knew Bill Forsyth, were simply unimaginable. For his two grown children the only possible explanation was the drug. And so Bill Jr. and Susan decided to sue. Their lawyers would later argue that Prozac can produce a kind of psychological hijacking—a bizarre and nightmarish syndrome, unique to the Prozac family of drugs, marked by suicidal thoughts, extreme agitation, emotional blunting, and a craving for death. They would also argue that the company knew of these risks and, instead of warning doctors to look out for them, worked vigilantly to sweep them under the rug.

The Forsyth case was not the first wrongful death suit to be brought against Eli Lilly, nor was it the first to make it to trial. The first, known as the Fentress case, concerned the events of an early September morning in 1989, when Joseph Wesbecker walked into the Louisville printing plant where he had been working, armed with an AK-47 and some handguns, and began shooting.[1] "I'm sorry, Dickie," he told a fellow worker before shooting him five times. When it was over, Wesbecker had shot 20 people, killing eight, and then shot and killed himself. One month prior to the shooting, Wesbecker had been put on Prozac. Whether Prozac made him do it, we'll never know. One thing we do know, though, is it did not make him better than well.

The Fentress case, named after Joyce Fentress, now a widow, and one of the several plaintiffs who sued after the Wesbecker rampage, was the first of 160 cases pending against Prozac in the fall of 1994. By this time Prozac already represented about a third of all Lilly's income, some $2 billion. Suits were filed by families of people who had committed suicide while on Prozac, families of those who had been murdered by persons on the drug, and individuals who had

WHEN HIS PARENTS FAILED TO SHOW THAT AFTERNOON, BILL JR. WENT TO THEIR HOME, WHERE HE FOUND HIS PARENTS LYING DEAD IN A POOL OF BLOOD.

themselves been harmed while taking Prozac, including a woman who worked for Eli Lilly as a sales rep. Many of these cases were dismissed. Others were settled, some for large sums. But Lilly would not settle the Fentress case. Wesbecker was a nut, they believed, and his case would send the right message: Settle rather than take Lilly to court, because you'll lose.

And they had a point. At least a year before starting on Prozac, Wesbecker began buying guns and ammunition and making threats. He also had a history of psychological problems, which had led Wesbecker to be placed on several psychiatric drugs before being put on Prozac. Other aspects of the case, however, were curious, if not compelling. After a month on Prozac, Wesbecker returned to his psychiatrist, who found him a changed man. He was agitated, his mood was erratic, and his behavior was even stranger than usual. Coleman, the psychiatrist, tried to persuade Wesbecker to go off the drug, which he saw as responsible for his agitation, and return to the hospital for further evaluation. Wesbecker went to work instead.

After the Wesbecker rampage, Eli Lilly also went to work, building a case against Wesbecker, which included approximately 400 depositions taken from people who knew him. Lilly's attorneys were determined to show that Wesbecker's madness was the product of a poor childhood environment and abnormal psychological development. The very company that relies on marketing copy to sell the idea that depression is an internal problem of biochemistry was, in other words, turning away from its biochemical theories, blaming the outer environment instead. Helped somewhat by their expert witness, anti-psychiatry hell-raiser Peter Breggin, the plaintiffs' lawyers saw the contradiction: If Lilly's drug worked by chemically altering mood and behavior, why might it not also be possible that their drug caused the disastrous mood and behavior changes noted by Wesbecker's psychiatrist just prior to the rampage?

The plaintiffs' lawyers also wanted the jury to know that Lilly had a history of concealing bad news about its drugs, a history that suggested a pattern of placing company profits ahead of public health and safety. In 1985, Lilly and a chief medical officer had pleaded guilty to 25 criminal counts of failing to report adverse reactions for its anti-inflammatory drug Oraflex, including four deaths, to the FDA (eventually the FDA linked the drug to several dozen deaths in the US and several hundred abroad). But the judge in the Fentress/Wesbecker case, John Potter, said no. The material was unfairly prejudicial and would not be allowed in. But then Lilly's lawyers blundered by repeatedly introducing testimony that it had always taken the reporting of adverse drug affects seriously. This opened the door to rebuttal, plaintiffs' lawyers argued, and Judge Potter finally agreed.

But the jury never heard the plaintiffs' lawyers present the evidence. During a brief recess that followed Potter's reversal, Lilly's lawyers got together with plaintiffs' lawyers and made a secret deal. The plaintiffs would allow the case to go forward without presenting the damaging Oraflex evidence, and Lilly would in turn pay to the plaintiffs in the case what has since been described as a sum that "boggles the mind." And this is just what happened. The evidence was not presented, the jury returned a verdict in favor of Lilly, Judge Potter dismissed the case, and Lilly and its lawyers claimed total victory. "We are pleased—although not surprised—by the decision," Randall L. Tobias, Lilly's then-chairman and -CEO, told the *New York Times*. "We have proven in a court of law, just as we have to more than 70 scientific and regulatory bodies all over the world, that Prozac is safe and effective. Our hearts go out to the victims of the terrible tragedy.… But the members of the jury...came to the only logical conclusion—that Prozac had nothing to do with Joseph Wesbecker's actions."[2]

Still, Judge Potter suspected something was amiss. While the jury was deliberating in the case, a juror had come forward to say that she had overheard settlement negotiations going on in the hallway. Then some months later, during the course of a divorce hearing involving one the plaintiffs in the case, it was revealed that he was expecting a substantial pay-off from Eli Lilly. Judge Potter drew his own conclusion and, in April 1995, filed a motion to amend his post-trial order, declaring that the case had not been won by Lilly, but settled. Lawyers on both sides filed their objections with Kentucky's

appeals court. Two months later, the appeals court ruled against Potter, arguing that he no longer had jurisdiction. The case was then appealed to the Kentucky Supreme Court. At this point the stakes had apparently become too high, as lawyers from both sides finally capitulated. They acknowledged that they had conspired to settle without settling, and on May 23, 1996, the Kentucky Supreme Court decided unanimously in favor of Judge Potter. Lilly had settled the case, not won it.

> IN 1985, LILLY AND A CHIEF MEDICAL OFFICER HAD PLEADED GUILTY TO 25 CRIMINAL COUNTS OF FAILING TO REPORT ADVERSE REACTIONS FOR ITS ANTI-INFLAMMATORY DRUG ORAFLEX, INCLUDING FOUR DEATHS, TO THE FDA.

The Fentress/Wesbecker case revealed much about the back-alley tactics of Eli Lilly. "The history of Prozac litigation reads like a mystery thriller," writes Michael Grinfeld in *California Lawyer* magazine, "filled with allegations of backroom deals, hidden agendas, and unethical behavior." What the trial did not do, however, was answer the central questions of the case: would Wesbecker have committed his rampage had he never been put on Prozac, and might the rampage have been avoided altogether if the drug company had warned doctors like Wesbecker's to be on the lookout for signs of drug-induced agitation? The case against the Prozac family of antidepressants, known as the SSRIs, was not coming to an end. It was only just beginning.

_II

In March 1999, the Lilly case involving the Forsyth suicide-homicide finally made it to trial, in United States District Court in Honolulu. "I know that with all their power and money I don't have much of a chance," said the daughter, Susan Forsyth, "but I feel like I have to try."[3] There was some hope, however, as Prozac's maker was facing a different legal team than in the Fentress case, and a new expert witness: David Healy.

The recruitment of Healy into the case was important.[4] David Healy is an internationally renowned psychiatrist as well as an historian of psychiatric medicine. Author of several books, including *The Antidepressant Era* and *The Creation of Psychopharmacology* (both published by Harvard University Press), Healy has the British equivalent of both an M.D. and a Ph.D. Prior to his involvement in any litigation involving the pharmaceutical industry, Healy had already raised a number of questions about the selective serotonin reuptake inhibitors, or SSRIs. He had asked whether they were best classified as antidepressants rather than as anti-anxiety drugs, and he had asked in an article whether the SSRIs might produce agitation and other problems with an unusual frequency. Most important, Healy wasn't a radical, nor was he an outsider of the pharmaceutical or psychiatric establishment. Healy had a record of doing research and consulting for various drug companies, and he was not against prescribing Prozac or other psychiatric drugs.

Unlike the example of the tobacco industry, drug companies do not place an importance on executives and scientists remaining in the fold, and many CEOs come from outside the industry. This means that there is a high rate of turnover, and a continual loss of institutional knowledge in the industry. It also means that, with pretrial discovery laws forcing Lilly—and later Pfizer and SmithKline—to allow Healy into their archives, he would be as close to an industry insider as the public was going to get. And he had plenty to say.

Pointing to Lilly's own internal documents, Healy showed that the company was well aware that its drug would, in a minority of cases, produce a psychological state like the one that overwhelmed William Forsyth, a key ingredient of which is a bizarre form of inner torture known as akathisia. Moreover, Healy argued that the company knew of this potentially catastrophic reaction prior to seeking FDA approval, and he showed that they had gone to great lengths to conceal it.

In 1978, ten years before fluoxetine would be branded as Prozac and brought to market in the US, initial clinical trials began. Minutes from meetings of Lilly's Prozac project team in July and August of that year noted:

Some patients have converted from severe depression to agitation within a few days; in one case the agitation was marked and the patient had to be taken off [the] drug.... There have been a fairly large number of reports of adverse reactions.... Another depressed patient developed psychosis.... Akathisia and restlessness were reported in some patients.... In future studies the use of benzodiazepines to control the agitation will be permitted.

And it was this use of benzodiazepines—anti-anxiety drugs like Librium, Valium, and Xanax—that greased the rails for Prozac's eventual approval. The FDA relied only on a handful of studies submitted by Lilly, which the FDA has since described as "adequate and well-controlled trials which provided evidence of [Prozac's] efficacy."[5] Of these studies, most permitted the simultaneous use of benzodiazepines and similar drugs, and about a quarter of the patients took them. As clinicians have since discovered, benzodiazepines are effective in reducing the Prozac-induced agitation that can lead to violence.[6] If Prozac could cause self-mutilation, suicide, or even murder in some users, these studies would never have revealed it.

But of course others would. Lilly's own internal records show a letter sent to them from the British Committee on Safety of Medicines (the British FDA equivalent) in May 1984, expressing concerns over clinical trial data they had seen: "During the treatment with the preparation [Prozac] 16 suicide attempts were made, two of these with success. As patients with a risk of suicide were excluded from the studies, it is probable that this high proportion can be attributed to an action of the preparation [Prozac]." Similar concern was expressed by the Bundes Gesundheit Amt (the German FDA equivalent) in 1985. By this time Lilly was well aware that they had a problem, summed up nicely by FDA scientist Martin Brecher, who, after noticing Lilly's effort to obscure the problem, wrote to Lilly saying, "I am skeptical whether dichotomizing on the basis of the presence or absence of poisoning with an antidepressant will provide any insight.... Most of the fluoxetine [Prozac] suicides have not been by overdose, but rather by gunshot, jumping, hanging or drowning."

By 1986, clinical-trial studies comparing Prozac with other antidepressants showed a rate of 12.5 suicides per 1,000 users of Prozac compared to only 3.8 per 1,000 on older, non-SSRI antidepressants, and 2.5 per 1,000 on placebo.[7] An internal Lilly document dated March 29, 1985, also quantified the problem:

The incidence rate [of suicide] under fluoxetine [Prozac] therefore purely mathematically is 5.6 times higher than under the other active medication imipramine.... The benefits vs. risks considerations for fluoxetine currently does not fall clearly in favor of the benefits. Therefore, it is of the greatest importance that it be determined whether there is a particular subgroup of patients who respond better to fluoxetine than to imipramine [a non-SSRI antidepressant], so that the higher incidence of suicide attempts may be tolerable.

After Prozac's entry into the market in 1988, reports quickly surfaced, confirming that the beast Lilly saw in the laboratory had now, without warning, been unleashed upon the public. In 1990, three years before Bill Forsyth killed his wife and himself, a report appeared in the *American Journal of Psychiatry* on the "Emergence of Intense Suicidal Preoccupation During Fluoxetine [Prozac] Treatment." Two Harvard psychiatrists, Martin Teicher and Jonathan Cole, and a registered nurse, Carol Gold, described cases in which patients developed serious preoccupations with suicide soon after being given Prozac.[8] They concluded:

We were especially surprised to witness the emergence of intense, obsessive, and violent suicidal thoughts in these patients.... No patient was actively suicidal at the time fluoxetine treatment began. Rather, all were hopeful and optimistic.... Their suicidal thoughts appear to have been obsessive, as they were recurrent, persistent, and intrusive.... It was also remarkable how violent these thoughts were. Two patients fantasized, for the first time, about killing themselves with a gun (cases 4 and 5), and one patient (case 6) actually placed a loaded gun to her head. One patient (case 3) needed to be physically restrained to prevent self-mutilation. Patient 2, who had not had prior suicidal thoughts, fantasized about killing himself in a gas explosion or a car crash.

The report by the Harvard psychia-

"THE INCIDENCE RATE [OF SUICIDE] UNDER FLUOXETINE [PROZAC] THEREFORE PURELY MATHEMATICALLY IS 5.6 TIMES HIGHER THAN UNDER THE OTHER ACTIVE MEDICATION IMIPRAMINE.... THE BENEFITS VS. RISKS CONSIDERATIONS FOR FLUOXETINE CURRENTLY DOES NOT FALL CLEARLY IN FAVOR OF THE BENEFITS." — INTERNAL LILLY DOCUMENT

THE LILLY SUICIDES
RICHARD DeGRANDPRE

trists prompted responses from clinicians describing similar cases. That Teicher and colleagues were on to something came as no surprise, moreover, as these were not the findings of amateurs. Jonathan Cole, the second author of the study, had a career that dates back to the 1950s, and he has been described by Pfizer, the maker of the SSRI Zoloft, as a "pioneer" in the field of psychopharmacology. Referring to the Teicher/Harvard report during the Forsyth trial, David Healy told the court that Jonathan Cole "is a man who has seen suicidal ideation and yet he and colleagues were saying that what they witnessed in this instance was something different. These are not investigators who would have easily been deceived by the ordinary kind of suicidal ideation that occurs in depression."[9]

In July 1992, another article appeared, this time in the *Archives of General Psychiatry*. Like the Harvard report, the article had two senior researchers among its authors, William Wirshing and Theodore Van Putten, the latter a leading expert on akathisia. They stressed in the report that, prior to going on Prozac, none of their patients "had a history of significant suicidal behavior; all described their distress [while on Prozac] as an intense and novel somatic-emotional state; all reported an urge to pace that paralleled the intensity of the distress; all experienced suicidal thoughts at the peak of their restless agitation; and all experienced a remission of their agitation, restlessness, pacing urge, and suicidality after the fluoxetine [Prozac] was discontinued."

The finding that these problems emerge soon after a selective-serotonin drug is taken, then disappear soon after the drug is withdrawn, provides compelling evidence, David Healy came to believe, that the problem is often the drug and not the so-called disease. Anthony Rothschild and Carol Locke, also of Harvard Medical School and McLean Hospital, reported three such cases in the *Journal of Clinical Psychiatry* in December 1991. All three patients, the authors note, "were reexposed to fluoxetine [Prozac] after having previously made a serious suicide attempt during fluoxetine treatment."

The first case involved a 25-year-old woman with a three-year history of depression. Two weeks after starting Prozac, and three days after having her dose increased from 20mg to 40mg, she escaped from the hospital and jumped off the roof of a building. After jumping, she hit a landing, compound fracturing both her arms and legs. With the patient now in a wheelchair, the psychiatrists tried Prozac on her a second time. Eleven days later she noted that she was having the same adverse effects as when previously given Prozac, stating, "I tried to kill myself because of these anxiety symptoms. It was not so much the depression." All adverse reactions disappeared within three days after the drug was terminated a second time.

The second case involved a 47-year-old man with an eight-year history of depression. He began experiencing severe restlessness and anxiety within two weeks of starting Prozac, from which he said death would be a welcome relief. He then jumped from a cliff, but had his fall broken by a tree. Put in psychiatric care, he was put on Prozac a second time. And when his dose was increased from 20mg to 40mg, the adverse reaction returned, prompting the comment that "this is exactly what happened the last time I was on fluoxetine [Prozac], and I feel like jumping off a cliff again." All adverse reactions disappeared 24 hours after being put on an additional drug.

Finally, the third patient was a 34-year-old woman with a fourteen-year history of depression. About a week after the Prozac dosage was increased from 40mg to 60mg, she jumped off the roof of a tall building, landing on a balcony, and suffering a fractured femur. In psychiatric care, she was put on Prozac again and, after having her dose increased, this time from 20mg to 40mg, she stated that the restlessness produced by the drug was making her feel "crazy," and that she was feeling just like she did before her last suicide attempt.

WITH THE PATIENT NOW IN A WHEELCHAIR, THE PSYCHIATRISTS TRIED PROZAC ON HER A SECOND TIME.

Reflecting on these cases, Rothschild and Locke stressed, "Patients need to be reassured that the overwhelming symptoms being experienced are the side effects of medication and are treatable.... Our patients had concluded their illness had taken such a dramatic turn for the worse that life was no longer worth living." Thus it seems that not only are Prozac suicides and homicides a hidden reality, the agitation and violent thoughts that precede them are likely to be misinterpreted as a sign of the very problems that the drug is said to treat. This is a horrible irony that Lilly had learned to exploit with earlier drugs, repeating the claim over and over that it's not the drug but the disease. "Prozac tends to be used by people with psychiatric problems," commented one Lilly executive. "Some people with psychiatric problems happen to be violent."

Doing what Lilly and the other manufacturers of SSRIs have failed to do all along, warn physicians to watch for agitation and increased suicidality soon after starting patients on an SSRI (or upping their dose), is crucial, as physicians are not otherwise likely to monitor them during the first weeks of drug use—Joseph Wesbecker being a case in point. Of course, this is partly why Lilly has worked so stubbornly to avoid having to issue a warning, fearing that the extra burden would reduce physicians' willingness to prescribe the drug. After all, a major factor in Prozac's immediate success was that it is taken only one time daily—"the safe and effective new medication, easy for both prescriber and patient."

Rather than doing this, and rather than remaining quiet on the subject, Lilly has actually fought in the other direction, declaring that these side effects are in fact proof of the existence of the disease. What has been happening as a result is illustrated in a case described in the Teicher/Harvard report. A 19-year-old college student had developed "disturbing and self-destructive thoughts" two weeks after starting on Prozac. When the dose was increased from 20mg to 40mg, her problems became worse, and then worse again after the dose was increased to 60mg. Still convinced that "it's not the drug but the disease," the doctors increased the young woman's dose yet another time, to 80mg. At this point she begin violently banging her head and mutilating herself.

_III

Growing reports suggesting that Prozac might be unsafe at any dose had Lilly running scared. One executive stated in an internal memo in 1990 that, if Prozac is taken off the market, the company could "go down the tubes."[10] Responding to concerns expressed by the FDA, Lilly agreed to conduct a study examining the question of whether Prozac induced aggression and suicidal thoughts. The result, known as the Beasley study, appeared in the September 21, 1991, issue of the *British Medical Journal*.[11]

> **ALSO AMONG THE DOCUMENTS WAS EVIDENCE THAT THE COMPANY HAD DRAFTED WORDING FOR A PACKAGE INSERT FOR PROZAC STATING: "MANIA AND PSYCHOSIS MAY BE PRECIPITATED IN SUSCEPTIBLE PATIENTS BY ANTIDEPRESSANT THERAPY."**

The study, authored by Lilly employees, including psychiatrist Charles Beasley, looked and sounded like good science. On the surface it represented the data pooled to date comparing Prozac with either older, non-SSRI antidepressants or placebo. In fact, the data had been hand-picked to favor the company.[12] The analysis dealt with 3,065 patients, less than 12 percent of the total data in clinical-trial studies at that time. Among those who were left out was the very population most likely to become suicidal—the 5 percent or so of patients who dropped out of the clinical trials because they experienced unpleasant side effects after taking Prozac. The report also made no mention of the dozen or so suicides that had already occurred in Prozac's clinical trials, a number that, given the population being studied—primary-care out-patients rather than severe depressives—would be expected to be near zero.

The Beasley study was submitted first to the *New England Journal of Medicine* but was rejected. Publication in the *British Medical Journal* was not as high profile, but it would have to do. And it did. After seeing the report and after receiving continued assurances from Lilly that its drug does not lead to extreme acts of violence, the FDA's Psychopharmacological Drugs Advisory Committee gave the drug a new lease on life in September 1991. To a great sigh of relief at Lilly, the committee's report stated that there was "no credible evidence of a causal link between the use of antidepressant drugs, including Prozac, and suicidality or violent behavior." From this moment on, instead of having to defend the safety of its antidepressant, Lilly could simply stand behind the "independent" conclusions of the FDA: "Our experience with Prozac does not show a cause-and-effect relationship between it and suicidal thoughts or acts. Our safety track record has been well established," notes an Eli Lilly spokesperson. Prozac was saved.

It wasn't until the Fentress and Forsyth trials that Lilly's internal documents surfaced, revealing the depth of the deception. This included the statements from the Prozac working group in 1978, acknowledging problems with akathisia and drug-induced psychosis.[13] Also among the documents was evidence that the company had drafted wording for a package insert for Prozac stating: "Mania and psychosis may be precipitated in susceptible patients by antidepressant therapy." This warning never made it into the final package insert, of course, but similar wording ended up being required before Lilly could sell Prozac in Germany, as Fluctin.

And there was a memo dated October 2, 1990, which referenced an upcoming Prozac symposium in which the issue of suicidality was to be discussed. One Lilly employee queried another: "Then the question is what to do with the 'big' numbers on suicidality. If the report numbers are shown next to those for nausea, they seem small."

There was also a series of memos concerning two Taiwanese doctors who had completed a study entitled: "Suicidal Attempts and Fluoxetine (Prozac) Treatment." In a memo dated April 8, 1992, a Lilly employee reports: "Mission accomplished. Professor Lu will not present or publish his fluoxetine [Prozac] vs. maprotiline suicidality data."

A similar case was that of Robert Bourguignon, a Belgian doctor who, after soliciting his colleagues' experiences regarding suicidality and other side effects concerning Prozac, was sued by Lilly. A cease-and-desist order was issued, but Bourguignon eventually prevailed. The result of the survey, "Dangers of Fluoxetine," appeared in *The Lancet* in 1997. Bourguignon cites eleven reports of serious events in the paper, examples of which included severe nervousness, suicidal thoughts, and "paranoid psychosis."[14]

Lilly had also canceled a clinical trial being conducted at a hospital in Indianapolis, Lilly's hometown. While researchers doing trials for Lilly often obscured problems with akathisia by coding it as simple nervousness or anxiety, the chief researcher in the trial, Joyce Small, was actually coding akathisia as akathisia. No doubt Lilly was displeased to find out that she was also finding the problem in nearly one out of ten patients taking Prozac.[15]

Another finding, not involving case studies, also raises questions about violence with the SSRIs. Although rates of suicide were four times higher for men than women throughout the latter half of the twentieth century, women taking SSRIs suddenly and mysteriously show the same rate of suicide as men taking SSRIs. Whether Prozac and other SSRIs produce agitation and suicidal obsessions more often in women is not clear, since women are more than twice as likely to be taking SSRIs. What is clear is that, despite their high rate of antidepressant use, women taking them do not lower their risk, but rather acquire the same, higher risk of suicide as men.

In the face of all the case reports and all the epidemiological statistics, and in the face of more than 200 lawsuits claiming a link between Prozac and violence, Lilly continued throughout the 1990s to promote the view that their drug actually lowers suicide risk. "The over 10,000 patients who have been on clinical trials where people have looked at suicidality," commented a vice president of clinical investigations at Lilly on the ABC news show *20-20*, "have shown without a doubt that these drugs do not increase suicidal ideation or suicide potential. In fact, they do just the opposite: They reduce it."

Prior to the SSRIs, the rate of suicide in those using antidepressants on an outpatient basis (i.e., without hospitalization) was only about 30 suicides per 100,000 years of patient use, which is roughly the same rate of suicide as the general population.[16] However, the suicide rate for Prozac from a 1995 study published in the *British Medical Journal*, which looked at ten antidepressants used by a total of 170,000 people in the United Kingdom, was 189 suicides per 100,000 years. In contrast to the claims of Lilly executives, this suggests a six-fold increase in suicide for Prozac relative to older, non-SSRI antidepressants, a number that is similar to Lilly's own internal assessment from 1985, which acknowledges a risk that was "5.6 times higher than under the other active medication imipramine."

There is, however, a way to test the theory once and for all, which is to give the drugs to people who have no history of depression or violence. Evidence of just this kind came unexpectedly from David Healy himself.

Back in North Wales, Healy was conducting what is called a healthy volunteer study.[17] Twenty volunteers were recruited, half of whom were given the SSRI Zoloft for two weeks, and the other half of whom were given a non-serotonin antidepressant (Edronax) for two weeks. Afterwards, following a two-week "washout" period, each was given the other drug for an additional two weeks. Healy had designed the study to compare people's experience of being on one drug vs. another, but before he knew it, he had two healthy volunteers who became dangerously agitated and suicidal—and both were on the SSRI Zoloft.

Healy was surprised, but he would not stay surprised. Months later he would discover an unpublished study Pfizer conducted in the 1980s in which healthy female volunteers were given either Zoloft or placebo. The study was canceled four days later because all those receiving Zoloft were complaining of problems of agitation and apprehension. Healy's case was not this bad; in fact some of the healthy volunteers rated the Zoloft experience positively. One of those who didn't was a 30-year-old woman who, one week after starting Zoloft, began having nightmares about having her throat slit. Within two weeks she became suicidal. Obsessed with an idea that has struck others highjacked by SSRIs, that she should throw herself in front of a car, she felt "it was as if there was nothing out there apart from the car, which she was going to throw herself under. She didn't think of her partner or child."

Adverse reactions like this cannot easily be blamed on psychiatric instability, given the population, and a rate of ten percent makes it clear that such results are not so rare as to be negligible. Nevertheless, these are normal volunteers, and most readers will probably see the ambiguity that still remains in cases like William Forsyth's. Did the drug cause him to do it? Did it simply precipitate the inevitable? Or did it have no bearing at all on the events of March 3, 1993? No doubt this ambiguity played a part in why, despite David Healy's testimony and the surfacing of the Lilly papers in the Forsyth trial, the jury found once again in favor of Lilly.

_IV

The challenges plaintiffs' lawyers face in cases like William Forsyth's are considerable. There can be overwhelming evidence against a drug and its manufacturer, but such evidence may not be enough if it's still ambiguous when applied to the case at hand. This is especially true for the SSRIs, since suicides and homicides occur unexpectedly even when no drugs are involved. To use an analogy, a die that comes up six on every roll is clearly biased, but how does one know, on any particular role, whether a six might not have come up anyway?

Still, not all tragedies involving the SSRIs have been overwhelmed by ambiguity. The Australian David Hawkins was freed from prison in May 2001, after a Supreme Court judge said his actions, which included the killing of his wife, were wholly out of character. Two days after going on Zoloft, the 74-year-old Hawkins strangled his wife, then set out but failed to kill himself by carbon-monoxide poisoning. "But for the Zoloft," said the judge, "which he took on the morning of August 1, 1999, it is overwhelmingly probable that Mrs. Hawkins would not have been killed on that morning."

A month after Hawkins' release, in a case in federal court in Cheyenne, Wyoming, a jury found against SmithKline Beecham (now GlaxoSmithKline), the maker of the drug Paxil. This was the case of Donald Schell. After complaining of anxiety, stress, and possible depression, the 60-year-old Schell was diagnosed as having mild depression and, like most SSRI users, was prescribed the drug by his family doctor. He was given promotional samples of Paxil, and two days later—the same two days of SSRI use that preceded David Hawkins' murder of his wife—Schell committed the most violent act in recent Wyoming history. The jury in the case concluded that the SSRI can cause some individuals to commit suicide and homicide, and did just that in the case of Donald Schell, who, on February 13, 1998, shot to death his wife, his adult daughter, his infant granddaughter, and then himself.

> "BUT FOR THE ZOLOFT," SAID THE JUDGE, "WHICH HE TOOK ON THE MORNING OF AUGUST 1, 1999, IT IS OVERWHELMINGLY PROBABLE THAT MRS. HAWKINS WOULD NOT HAVE BEEN KILLED ON THAT MORNING."

The award of $6.4 million against SmithKline Beecham was the first case to be lost in court by any manufacturer of an SSRI. Known as the Tobin case—Tim Tobin was the husband of Donald Schell's deceased daughter—the trial took two weeks to complete, after which the jury returned with a unanimous verdict in only three and a half hours. The company had faced a more experienced legal team—the core of which was the same as in the Forsyth case, including expert witness David Healy—and a different and apparently more effective legal strategy: In the Forsyth case, plaintiff's lawyers focused on the man, William Forsyth, but in the Tobin case they focused on the company.

Also, as Healy revealed in the trial, there was much in SmithKline's records to warrant concern about the company's behavior and their drug. SmithKline had carefully researched Paxil and in the process had produced plenty of evidence that the drug posed the same kind of dangers as Prozac, yet did nothing about them. Among SmithKline's internal files were 34 healthy volunteer studies involving company employees. They showed that, even though these people had no noted problems of depression or anxiety, 25 percent experienced some degree of agitation after taking Paxil.[18] These studies were not conducted by psychiatrists, however, and those that had been were missing unaccountably from the company archive. Healy did find a note, though, which made reference to one. On it the investigating psychiatrist wrote that he'd never seen such a high incidence of problems in a healthy volunteer study.

Healy also discovered other problems—problems that spoke to the

> **THREE DAYS AFTER STARTING PROZAC, A 58-YEAR-OLD MAN BEGAN HAVING SUICIDAL THOUGHTS AND TRIED TO HANG HIMSELF WITH A ROPE, PROMPTING A DISCONTINUATION OF THE DRUG AND, FOUR DAYS LATER, A COMPLETE DISAPPEARANCE OF HIS SUICIDAL IDEATION.**

myriad of other adverse reactions one can experience when taking an SSRI. In addition to agitation, akathisia, suicidal thoughts, and violence, the SSRIs also produce physical dependence in many users. A class-action complaint against the maker of Paxil notes:

Currently, on one website alone there are 1,359 electronic signatures of persons complaining to the GlaxoSmithKline Corporation about withdrawal reactions they have suffered from Paxil. Given that the signatures provide the full name of each person, many of who provided their e-mail addresses and lengthy commentary, this is a reliable example of the numerosity of the persons suffering from Paxil withdrawal. Over the past two years, plaintiffs' attorneys have been individually contacted by approximately 500 Paxil withdrawal victims. The pain and suffering experienced by each of these individuals is the direct result of GlaxoSmithKline Corporation's failure to warn users of Paxil's addictive nature, the drug's inducement of physical or psychologic dependency, and its infliction of dependency/withdrawal syndrome when the patient's Paxil dosage is reduced or terminated.[19]

This complaint is consistent with what David Healy had found while researching the SmithKline archives. In one healthy volunteer study conducted within the company, researchers had found that, upon drug discontinuation, as many as 85 percent of the volunteers suffered agitation, bizarre dreams, insomnia, and other adverse effects. Healy noted that as much as half of the healthy volunteers taking part in the study showed symptoms that indicated they were becoming physically dependent on the drug. The example of Lisa, a woman participating in an online chat session on antidepressants, illustrates the nature of the problem: "I was addicted to Effexor. Was horrified of the thought of going without it—and for good reason!! I don't think the physical/mental dichotomy makes sense. If you can't get by without the stuff, you're addicted. Effexor IS addictive, I'm off the stuff, but I've never been so physically sick in my life as when I was in withdrawal..."[20]

There is also a substantial problem of sexual side effects with the SSRIs, with perhaps as many as 70 to 80 percent of users experiencing lowered sex drive and impotence. Beyond this, there are a variety of more minor side effects, including nausea, insomnia, nightmares, fatigue, drowsiness, weakness, loss of appetite, tremors, dry mouth, sweating, and even yawning. The one characteristic of the SSRIs that is preferred over the older, tricyclic antidepressants is that it's difficult to overdose on the SSRIs. Of course, this hardly matters when, as illustrated in the following cases, the drug itself precipitates suicide and other forms of violence.

— Fifteen days after starting Prozac, the 56-year old singer known as Del Shannon died after he shot himself in the head with a .22-caliber rifle.

— Ten days after starting Prozac, a 41-year-old woman began experiencing a longing for pain, which she satisfied by mutilating her legs, stomach, thighs, arms, and torso, along with six suicide attempts, all of which ended abruptly after she was taken off the drug.

— Three days after starting Prozac, a 58-year-old man began having suicidal thoughts and tried to hang himself with a rope, prompting a discontinuation of the drug and, four days later, a complete disappearance of his suicidal ideation.

— Within a week after having her dose of Prozac gradually increased from 20mg to 60mg, a 28-year-old woman began to suffer akathisia and started fantasizing about jumping out of the hospital window, which prompted the discontinuation of Prozac and, in about a week, the elimination of all adverse effects.

— Twenty-four hours after accidentally increasing his dose of Prozac from 60mg to 80mg, a 44-year-old man began making superficial cuts to his throat, wrist, and abdomen while driving. This behavior disappeared 24 hours after decreasing his dose.

— Two weeks after starting Prozac, a 32-year-old woman felt better, except that she began experiencing restlessness and out-of-control feelings, which led her to state that "I feel like I need to hold onto my chair or else I'll jump out the window." All of this disappeared several days after discontinuing Prozac.

— Eleven days after starting Prozac, a 63-year-old Englishman suffocated his wife and then jumped off a 200-foot cliff.

— Several weeks after starting Zoloft, a 35-year-old man stabbed his wife and two children while in their home, then killed himself with a .22-caliber rifle.

— Six days after starting Prozac, a 60-year-old woman stabbed and slashed herself more than 60 times as her husband ate breakfast in the kitchen; she died the next day.

— One week after his parents were told of a "terrific" new medicine called Zoloft, a 13-year-old boy went into his bedroom closet and, while his family slept, killed himself by hanging.

— Almost three months after her dose of Prozac was doubled, a woman living in Randolph, Vermont, used a .22-caliber pistol to shoot and kill her 8-year-old son, her 4-year-old daughter, and herself.

— Several days after Brynn Hartman was given Zoloft samples by her child's psychiatrist, she shot and killed her husband, comedic actor Phil Hartman, while he slept, and then, four hours later, shot and killed herself.

Two weeks after being prescribed Prozac, a 46-year-old man finished cleaning out the milking parlor on his farm, returned to the house, and shot himself in the forehead with a .22-caliber rifle.

— A few days after starting on Prozac, a 17-year-old boy complained that the drug was "messing with [his] mind" and, a few days later, hanged himself in his bedroom.

Tragic events like these litter the communities and countrysides of North America and Europe. Few of them ever make the headlines, however, buried instead behind the confusion and secrecy that so often marks sudden family tragedies. Before the Forsyth case made it to trial, in March 1999, 2,000 Prozac-associated suicides had been reported to the FDA, recorded on the their "adverse event system." At least a quarter of these include explicit references to agitation and akathisia. Based on years of drug monitoring, the FDA has concluded that only about 1 percent of serious and fatal adverse drug events are ever reported on the system. This means that, as David Healy has concluded, as many as 200,000 Prozac-related suicides had taken place by 1999, 50,000 of which are likely to have been precipitated by an extreme state of agitation. And this is only for Prozac. The total number of suicides for all SSRIs, including Paxil, would of course be larger.

Still, with the cult of the SSRI many millions strong, these cases are relatively rare. They are exceptional cases, people believe, and must therefore be weighed against the millions of others living happily in Prozac nation. There is, however, another, more chilling possibility. If most everything that Lilly says is false about Prozac turns out to be true, what if most everything that they say is true about Prozac turns out to be false? What if, counter to the media hype that ushered in the Prozac revolution, the SSRIs actually offer few real benefits over older, akathisia-free antidepressants, like Tofranil and Elavil? Might all this death and destruction be for naught? Viewed from the outside, this seems a certain impossibility. From the inside, however, it looks like an all too likely conclusion.

| **ALTHOUGH DIFFICULT TO IMAGINE TODAY, DEPRESSION WAS STILL UNDERSTOOD TO BE A RARE CONDITION IN THE 1950S, AND THERE WAS A COMMONSENSE DISTINCTION MADE BETWEEN DEPRESSION AND UNHAPPINESS.**

_V

The true story of the SSRIs begins in the 1950s, when the use of antidepressants was confined almost exclusively to cases of clinical depression. Although there was some suggestion at the time that the new antidepressant imipramine (Tofranil) might actually make some patients feel "better than well," it was also true that, as David Healy writes in The Antidepressant Era, "no one was interested in imipramine in 1958." Neither was anyone interested in feeling better than well, especially if it required pumping powerful chemicals into one's brain.

Although difficult to imagine today, depression was still understood to be a rare condition in the 1950s, and there was a commonsense distinction made between depression and unhappiness. "Depression as it is now understood both by clinicians and laypeo-

ple is an extremely recent phenomenon," continues Healy, "and one that is largely confined to the Western world." The rate of depression in the 1950s was estimated at about 50 people per million, an estimate that would grow to 100,000 per million by the end of the century. This is a 2,000-fold increase in what is ostensibly a hereditary disease. What happened during these years is not that a disease was discovered, nor its cure. What happened is that, because of ongoing changes in the drug marketplace, the pharmaceutical industry began to take an interest in depression.

Drug companies have always viewed the general public as a huge legal market for selling mind-altering drugs. And it has been one since the nineteenth century. Immediately prior to the SSRIs, the prescription drug market focused not on depression and antidepressants (the tricyclics) but on anxiety and anti-anxiety drugs (the benzodiazepines). When introduced in the 1960s, drug-makers declared the benzodiazepines, also called anxiolytics, to be powerful yet nonaddictive. The market for barbiturates (Nembutal, Seconal) was collapsing at the time, as they no longer lived up to the same claim, that they were powerful yet nonaddictive. This encouraged widespread promotion of the benzodiazepines, followed by widespread prescribing and use, with drugs like Valium becoming the most popular prescription drugs of all time. As long as millions of Americans were taking benzodiazepines, there would be no popular market for antidepressants.

Beginning in the 1980s, however, things began to change. Fewer and fewer doctors were willing to prescribe benzodiazepines to treat every psychological whim and woe, waking up to the fact that, as it was with the barbiturates, and now the SSRIs, those most interested in these drugs were also likely to develop a stubborn dependence on them. A 1983 study notes, "In the past 3 years there has been a dramatic change in medical attitudes to the prescribing of benzodiazepines. Before 1980 these drugs were regarded as not only safe and effective anti-anxiety drugs and hypnotics but also free of important unwanted effects. Since then there has been rising alarm about the risks of pharmacological dependence after regular consumption of these drugs."[21] The peak year for benzodiazepine use in the United States was 1973, when over 80 million prescriptions were filled. By 1986, this number had fallen to 61 million. As the number continued to decline, a hole in the domestic drug market began to open. And the SSRIs were just the drugs to fill it.

Synthesized in the early 1970s, Prozac was in fact the fourth SSRI to come to market (not the first, as Lilly had claimed).[22] The first was a drug called zimelidine (Zelmid), developed by the European drug company Astra. Lilly scientists David Wong, Bryan Molloy, and Ray Fuller began the search for a 5-hydroxytryptamine (serotonin) reuptake inhibitor on May 8, 1972.[23] Although the goal was to produce a drug that acted more selectively on serotonin in the brain (and could be patented accordingly), what was less clear was what the drug would be useful for. Shortly thereafter, Lilly's drug 110140—a.k.a. fluoxetine and Prozac—was born.

After the drug succeeded in not killing laboratory animals in initial exploratory studies (but turned cats from friendly to growling and hissing), Lilly began to look into what possible market might exist for its new compound. At a meeting in England around this time, psychopharmacologist Alec Coppen suggested that it might be useful as an antidepressant.[24] The response he received from Lilly was that, of all its possible uses, this was not one of them.[25] Lilly had its eye on Prozac, not as an antidepressant drug—nor a PMS, obsessive-compulsive disorder (OCD), nonsmoking, shyness, or anxiety drug—but as an antihypertensive drug (that is, to lower blood pressure).

By the 1980s, however, attitudes at Lilly had changed, although not because of any breakthrough in medicine or science. Astra's zimelidine had appeared on the market as a new (and patented) antidepressant, joined shortly thereafter by two other SSRIs (a patent is important because it ensures exclusivity for the compound, which then allows for higher pricing). With the benzodiazepine market collapsing, Lilly also began to see a larger market possibility in treating depression, which would be much the same population that had been taking the benzodiazepines. "The emergence of depression in this sense coincides with the development of the SSRIs," writes David Healy in The Creation of Psychopharmacology,

which in the mid-1980s appeared capable of being developed as either anxiolytics or antidepressants. After the benzodiazepine crisis, the industry had a new set of compounds to sell, but its new offerings did not meet the demand from the marketplace. And indeed since their initial launch as antidepressants, various SSRIs have been licensed for the treatment of panic disorder, social phobia, post-traumatic stress disorder, OCD, and other anxiety-based conditions. Indeed, for some of the SSRIs, contrary to popular perceptions, it has simply not been possible to show that they are effective in treating classic depressive disorders.

The turning of Prozac into an antidepressant is mirrored in the case of Paxil, which was also developed in the 1970s. Paxil didn't make it to market until 1993, however, delayed by the prevailing wisdom at SmithKline that although new patented antidepressants (the SSRIs) were coming on the market, they were not as effective as the existing tricyclics.[26] Trapped in a momentary spell of pharmacological honesty, SmithKline failed to grasp that when it comes to heavily promoted drugs like Prozac, being more effective needn't have anything to do with it. Of course, the spell has since worn off. Paxil would go on to become a popular drug in the antidepressant market in the 1990s, and would be an effective backdoor for reentering the anxiety market. "From the beach-head of depression," writes David Healy, "raids can subsequently be launched on the hinterlands of anxiety." Or, as GlaxoSmithKline put it in 2001, "Millions suffer from chronic anxiety. Millions could be helped by Paxil."

With benzodiazepine sales a shadow of what they once were, the number of prescriptions filled for antidepressants in the US in 1989 more than doubled. Less than two years after its release, sales for Prozac nearly tripled, from $125 million to $350 million, which was more than the total annual US sales for all other antidepressants combined. By 1990, when the cover of Newsweek announced "A Breakthrough Drug for Depression," Prozac had become the most frequently prescribed antidepressant of all time. And the antidepressant market continued to grow. Annual Prozac sales reached the $1 billion mark in 1993. By 1999, Prozac would become the number-three-selling drug in the entire market of prescription pharmaceuticals, with more than 76 million prescriptions filled. In fact, more than 3 billion doses of SSRIs were consumed in 1999. In 2000, annual antidepressant sales reached the $10-billion mark, with the US making up 70 percent of world sales for the drug.

Meanwhile, in Japan, the Prozac revolution never happened. Because the Japanese had experienced fewer problems with benzodiazepines, their sales remained strong, and this left little market in which to engineer a Prozac revolution.

_VI

It was not at Eli Lilly but at SmithKline that the concept of the selective serotonin reuptake inhibitor was minted, although all the makers of SSRIs quickly embraced it to promote their serotonin drugs. Like the "Pentium" concept used to sell Dell, Gateway, and other computers, the SSRI concept was a brilliant marketing device. Beyond its cleverness, however, the SSRI concept never had much to support it. Paxil, Zoloft, Prozac, Celexa, and Luvox are all considered SSRIs, but the term "selective" has since acquired a popular meaning that goes far beyond the one intended. The SSRIs are not selective in what they treat, or even claim to treat, since they are now hailed as cure-alls for everything from PMS to panic attacks to smoking to shyness.

> LILLY HAD ITS EYE ON PROZAC, NOT AS AN ANTIDEPRESSANT DRUG—NOR A PMS, OBSESSIVE-COMPULSIVE DISORDER, NONSMOKING, SHYNESS, OR ANXIETY DRUG—BUT AS AN ANTIHYPERTENSIVE DRUG (THAT IS, TO LOWER BLOOD PRESSURE).

Nor are they selective in their biochemical actions in the brain. While the older tricyclics act directly on two neurotransmitter chemicals in the brain—namely, serotonin and norepinephrine—the SSRIs affect only the former. Hence the name "selective serotonin reuptake inhibitors." But this is not all they do. The SSRIs may not directly impact on norepinephrine, but they do directly affect other biochemical systems, including those involving dopamine. And after acting directly on these systems, the SSRIs produce a cascade of secondary and tertiary biochemical and cellular effects, all of which remain poorly understood. While an initial dose of Prozac has been shown to increase serotonin activity in an area of the brain known as the substantia nigra, for example, long-term use has been shown to produce just the opposite effect.

What is clear about the SSRIs, or at least should be, is that people don't experience unhappiness or depression simply because they suffer a chemical imbalance of serotonin in the brain. While some SSRIs are more selective in their serotonin specificity than others (Celexa), and some are more potent in causing serotonin release than others (Luvox), these differences do not translate into one SSRI being more effective than another. Also, since drugs like Prozac raise serotonin levels almost immediately, it's hard to see how this can explain the therapeutic effects of SSRIs, which take days or weeks to be achieved.

Despite these basic pharmacological facts, Lilly and other SSRI-makers succeeded in the 1990s in convincing the public that a breakthrough had taken place in the brain and pharmacological sciences, with the SSRIs designed specifically to correct a biochemical imbalance now known to be a central cause in depression. "To help bring serotonin levels closer to normal," Lilly claimed in ads in popular magazines in the 1990s, "the medicine doctors now prescribe most often is Prozac." Suddenly anyone feeling down and depressed was presented with the possibility that perhaps they too suffered from low levels of serotonin. As Peter Kramer tells it in *Listening to Prozac*, the mainstay of antidepressants before the SSRIs—imipramine—"is 'dirty' in its main effects and its side effects because it affects both norepinephrine and serotonin. Once imipramine's mechanism of action was understood, pharmacologists set out to synthesize a 'clean' antidepressant."

The frequent claim that a revolution had taken place in psychiatric science also has little in the way of evidence to support it. Consider two articles from popular magazines. The first, a lead *Newsweek* article in 1994, "Beyond Prozac," claimed: "Research that once mapped the frontiers of disease—identifying the brain chemistry involved in depression, paranoia and schizophrenia—is today closing in on the chemistry of normal personality." Yet, three years later, in *Time* magazine, another article states that these aspects of the brain are not at all understood:

ANTIDEPRESSANTS LIKE EDRONAX SHOW THAT DIRECT ACTIONS ON SEROTONIN MAY NOT EVEN BE NECESSARY TO PRODUCE AN ANTIDEPRESSANT EFFECT.

For depression, bulimia, obesity and the rest of the serotonin-related disorders, however, no one knows for sure what part of the brain is involved or exactly why the drugs work.... The entire history of serotonin and of drugs that affect it has been largely a process of trial and error marked by chance discoveries, surprise connections and unanticipated therapeutic effects.... The tools used to manipulate serotonin in the brain are more like pharmacological machetes than they are like scalpels.

This 1997 *Time* article, "The Mood Molecule," nevertheless goes on to affirm the notion that SSRIs offer something positively unique:

In the 1960s, a second class of antidepressants emerged.... [They] had major side effects, though, including profound drowsiness and heart palpitations. The reason, scientists generally agreed, was that they affected brain chemistry too broadly. The research seemed to point to serotonin as the most important mood-enhancing chemical, though not the only one, and so neurochemists set about looking for a drug that would boost the influence of serotonin alone. In 1974, after a decade of work, Eli Lilly came up with Prozac, first of the so-called selective serotonin reuptake inhibitors, or SSRIs, and it was finally approved by the FDA in 1987.

The article contradicts itself, however, when it suggests that a new antidepressant has arrived on the market that acts not on serotonin but on the very neurochemical said to be irrelevant to depression, norepinephrine:

Psychiatrists in Europe are buzzing about a new drug, reboxetine, that has just been approved for use in Britain and seems to be even more effective than Prozac for severely depressed patients. Marketed under the brand name Edronax, it totally ignores serotonin and targets another brain chemical, norepinephrine, which is also known to have a powerful effect on mood.

At this point the *Newsweek* article brings us full circle, pointing out that another recent drug, Effexor, works even more effectively than the SSRIs, which it does by acting on both norepinephrine and serotonin: "Effexor...enhances both serotonin and norepinephrine, a second chemical messenger affecting mood. With its broader effect, Effexor should help some depressed patients who don't respond to Prozac."

While selectively targeting serotonin may be the key to producing akathisia, self-mutilation, suicide, and murder, it should be clear, even from these stories, that it's not the key to raising people's moods. Antidepressants like Edronax show that direct actions on serotonin may not even be necessary to produce an antidepressant effect. In fact, the trend at the end of the century was away from SSRIs and toward a new (or at least newly patented) set of compounds that act on both norepinephrine and serotonin.

After losing its patent on Prozac, Lilly announced late in 2001 that it was hoping to market a new and putatively more effective antidepressant than Prozac late in 2002. The drug, duloxetine, has been dubbed a "dual-action" agent because, as noted on Lilly's Website, it "enhances levels of two important brain chemicals," serotonin and norepinephrine. A presentation on the drug by Lilly scientists at the meeting of the New Clinical Drug Evaluation Unit at the National Institute of Mental Health concluded: "The increased extracellular levels of serotonin and norepinephrine produced by duloxetine administration suggests it would enhance serotonin and norepinephrine neurotransmission and is expected to be efficacious in the treatment of major depression." So much for Prozac being a breakthrough antidepressant tailored to fit with the latest scientific knowledge.

Fortunately for Lilly, the media have a poor memory. In December 2001, the *Boston Globe* began hyping Lilly's future drug, stating: "While Prozac and drugs like it increase the amount of the chemical serotonin in the brain, duloxetine and Effexor enrich the supply of two important mood-boosting chemicals: serotonin and norepinephrine. Because these drugs have two different mechanisms of action, rather than one, doctors believe they may be more effective than Prozac-like drugs at improving patients' moods and might help more seriously depressed people."

VII

The SSRIs look be on their way out, no doubt in part because of the risks of continuing to push "selective serotonin" drugs. The cult of the SSRI is, however, still going strong. The SSRIs are magic bullets, the public has come to believe, with any suggestion to the contrary met with a rash of cries and complaints.

Thus, in 1999, when science writer John Horgan wrote an op-ed piece called "Placebo Nation" in the *New York Times*, letters poured in complaining that new antidepressants like Prozac have helped millions of people, improving countless lives. That Horgan's message provoked a response was hardly surprising, implying as it did that individuals taking Prozac and other antidepressants might be benefiting not just from the package—that is, the pharmacological ingredients—but from the handling—that is, the experience of treatment. For those who have seen their mood brighten after taking Prozac, Paxil, Zoloft, or any other antidepressant for that matter, such a suggestion likely comes as a slap in the face. Prozac is not a placebo, it's a *selective serotonin reuptake inhibitor*, an SSRI!

Indeed, it is. But this was not Horgan's point. Like any other psychoactive drugs, including cocaine and Ritalin, Prozac's antidepressant effects are inseparably bound with the same psychosomatics that swamp all other moments of drug use. A placebo response might be taking place, Horgan was suggesting, with the act of taking the drug setting into motion a powerful psychological shift from hopelessness to hopefulness.[27] Prozac has real effects, and in some users these effects may very well produce "fantastic results," "a blessed relief," "a brighter, more cheerful mood," and other "awesome results."[28] But placebo effects are every bit as real as pharmacological ones, and their indistinguishability during drug use means that knowing what is and is not an effect of the latest mood molecules is not as easy to discern as one might like to think.

> TO THEIR SURPRISE, PARK AND COVI FOUND THAT EACH INDIVIDUAL TAKING THE SUGAR PILLS EXPERIENCED A REDUCTION IN PSYCHOLOGICAL DISTRESS.

A case in point was a compound that Merck pharmaceuticals synthesized, MK-869. In the realm of psychiatric medicine, concerns over placebo effects loom large, for in order to obtain FDA approval, drug companies must show that their drugs can outperform a placebo. As recounted in a *Science* magazine article entitled "Can the Placebo Be the Cure?," early clinical trials led Merck to think its new compound had great promise as an antidepressant, and with fewer side effects than other antidepressants, Prozac included.[29] On January 22, 1999, however, all bets were off, as Merck announced that they would not seek FDA approval for their new compound. The reason? While the latest data suggested that the drug was indeed effective in treating depression, it was no more effective than a placebo. "A novel compound—a Merck invention known as MK-869—then in several clinical trials, seemed set to become a new millennium drug for millions of people who take antidepressant medication every day. The news [that MK-869 would be shelved] was a downer for Merck and Wall Street: the price of the company's stock dropped 5% on the day Merck broke the news."

Drug companies are not the only ones to face the placebo challenge. The same problem applies to any drug user who, after popping a pill, wants to know what is and is not an effect of the drug. For those reporting positive drug experiences while on SSRIs, which may take days or weeks to occur, the question remains: Can one always be so sure that the effect is really because of the drug? Might it be at least partly a placebo effect? This may appear to be the same question as is asked of juries in cases like William Forsyth's, except for one important difference: Placebo effects rarely if ever include reactions like self-mutilation, suicide, and murder. A 1965 report in the *Archives of General Psychiatry* illustrates why we cannot simply assume that the psychological effects of a drug are just that and nothing more.

Lee Park and Lino Covi, two young psychiatrists at Johns Hopkins University, revealed some of these psychodynamics when they asked what would happen if their patients were given a placebo and told as much. To answer the question, they took fifteen newly admitted anxious and depressed patients and told them the following: "Many people with your kind of condition have been helped by what are sometimes called 'sugar pills,' and we feel that a so-called sugar pill may help you, too.... A sugar pill is a pill with no medicine in it at all.... Are you willing to try this pill?" Of the fourteen individuals who said yes to this question (all but one individual), all kept their second appointment, and all but one reported taking at least two-thirds of the prescribed pills.

To their surprise, Park and Covi found that each individual taking the sugar pills experienced a reduction in psychological distress. The average "distress score" was reduced by 43 percent, meaning that a majority of them felt "quite a bit" better after a week of taking sugar pills. When asked to explain why they might be feeling better, given they were taking only sugar pills, nine of the participants pointed to the pill, five of which actually suspected or insisted that they were given an active medicine rather than a placebo. Of the remaining five, two attributed their improvements to the doctor's care rather than the pills, and three pointed to self improvement.

Among the former, one was a 45-year-old man, described as being rigid, resistant to influence, and suffering from "agitated depression." The man had experienced severe insomnia, loss of appetite, feelings of despair, death wishes, and some somatic (i.e., bodily) symptoms. During the interview he testified to a reduction in all symptoms, except for his lack of appetite. At the start of the interview he immediately declared: "It wasn't a sugar pill; it was medicine!" He also noted that upon taking the pills he was able to think more clearly, which led to a positive change in his attitude about his problems and the future. In addition to positive psychological effects, the man also reported clear side effects of the pills, including dry mouth and butterflies in the stomach. When asked about his improvement, he implied that perhaps he was falsely told he was being given a placebo so that he would attribute the improvement to himself rather than the medication.

A second individual who had this experience was a 24-year-old woman with three children. She was clearly depressed and complained of insomnia, anorexia, irritability, and tension. After a week of taking sugar pills, she also testified that "they're not sugar pills...because they worked." This woman was in fact very skeptical of a placebo being effective for anyone, and stated that the pills she received were actually more effective than other medications she had previously taken. She noted that she was feeling better than she had in the past 20 years and was pleased with the idea of continuing with the same doctor and pills.

Clearly, the testimonials people offer in favor of a drug do not have to be accurate to be strong. Determining what is and is not an effect of a drug requires extracting the drug effect from a whole range of ongoing experiences, which will not necessarily be easy; it may even be theoretically impossible, as these pharmacological and nonpharmacological effects do not occur side by side in two separate realms of consciousness, but rather are experienced in combination, with the biopsychosocial whole adding up to more than the sum of the parts.

The matter is further complicated by the fact that, according to reviewers of the antidepressant literature, most users of SSRIs are in fact active placebo responders. As the *New York Times* summarized, "A [1998] review of placebo-controlled studies of modern antidepressant drugs found that placebos and genuine drugs worked about as well." This means that much of the credit given to the SSRIs should be attributed to the placebo effect instead. The report cited by the *Times* was one of three meta-analyses of the antidepressant literature that appeared in the 1990s, each of which independently concluded that placebo effects account for much of the effectiveness of the antidepressants.[30] Overall, about two-thirds of the effectiveness attributed to the SSRIs appears to be due to the placebo effect.

These numbers may seem confusing. People often associate a placebo effect with a placebo, and thus view drug effects and placebo effects as mutually exclusive. How can a drug effect really turn out to be partly or largely a placebo effect? In truth, placebo effects are just another way of saying that nonpharmacological factors can contribute significantly to so-called drug effects. If placebo effects are mobilized by beliefs and expectations, as they most certainly are, then what could be better than an active drug for launching the placebo effect? While some individuals will respond positively to SSRIs and not at all to placebos, a majority of individuals will experience the blessings of both pharmacological and nonpharmacological factors working in combination.

| **OVERALL, ABOUT TWO-THIRDS OF THE EFFECTIVENESS ATTRIBUTED TO THE SSRIs APPEARS TO BE DUE TO THE PLACEBO EFFECT.**

One arrives at the same conclusion when looking at the four studies Lilly submitted to the FDA for drug licensing.[31] Here it becomes clear that the dangerous adverse effects of Prozac might have been moot if the FDA had just upheld rigorous scientific standards. That is, had they relied only on data from patients receiving Prozac alone, Lilly's drug might have gone the way of Merck's MK-869. This conclusion stems from the fact that when the results of the 135 patients taking benzodiazepines are removed from the data set that Lilly submitted to the FDA, the statistical advantage of Prozac over placebo vanishes. That a benzodiazepine might make Prozac look like an effective antidepressant comes as no surprise, moreover, since anxiety

has long been known to play a role in depressive syndromes. As for the fourth study Lilly submitted, which prohibited the concurrent use of anti-anxiety drugs, it never showed an effect to begin with; that is, there was never any statistically significant difference between Prozac and placebo.

_VIII

To many, the placebo effects here will seem like a contradiction. How can the SSRIs be linked to suicides and homicides, yet for many users be effective only as a placebo? But this is also a confusion, as there is no contradiction in suggesting that a drug is powerful, yet not very powerful in doing what it's claimed to do. In fact the very creation of the FDA, as well as the passage of the Food, Drug, and Cosmetic Act of 1938, were motivated by this very scenario, that while a variety of commercial drug products had little hope of ever working except as a placebo, their active ingredients nevertheless posed a clear hazard to the public health.

And so goes the story of the SSRIs, sadly, many decades later. The spell of pharmacological magicalism was cast, Prozac was raised up as the latest panacea for medicating the malaise of everyday modern life, and millions of people were exposed to a group of drugs that were more toxic, more expensive, and less effective than drugs already existing. Given the powers of the prescription marketing machine, and given the subsequent trend back to drugs that act on neurochemicals other than serotonin, it should be clear that Prozac was not even necessary for the "Prozac revolution" to occur. Any number of non-SSRI antidepressants might have been fashioned for the revolution, just as they are being fashioned now for the next one. Shrink-wrapped with the same promise of becoming "better than well," these new wonder drugs could have given the people just what they wanted, and without all the wreckage.

Endnotes

1. See Cornwell, John. *The Power to Harm*. New York: Viking, 1996. **2.** Read Grinfeld, Michael Jonathan. "Protecting Prozac." *California Lawyer* (Dec 1998). **3.** Read Boseley, Sarah. "They Said It Was Safe." *Guardian* (London), 30 Oct 1999. **4.** Read "Healy General Causation Report" and "Zoloft Suicide: Causal Mechanisms: The Healy Report" at <www.justiceseekers.com>. **5.** Read Medawar, Charles. "The Antidepressant Web." *International Journal of Risk & Safety in Medicine* 10 (1997): 75-126; find at <www.socialaudit.org.uk>; see also, Breggin, Peter R. *Talking Back to Prozac*. New York: St. Martin's Press, 1994. **6.** Read, for example, Wirshing, William C., *et al.* "Fluoxetine, Akathisia, and Suicidality: Is There a Causal Connection?" *Archives of General Psychiatry* 49 (1992). **7.** Read "Zoloft Suicide: Causal Mechanisms: The Healy Report" at <www.justiceseekers.com>. **8.** Read Teicher, Martin H., *et al.* "Emergence of Intense Suicidal Preoccupation During Fluoxetine Treatment." *American Journal of Psychiatry* 147.2 (Feb 1990). A total of six cases were reported: Case 1 was a 62-year-old woman who began experiencing suicidal thoughts and other adverse side effects eleven days after starting Prozac but then experienced a complete reversal of these effects three days after stopping the drug. She described the experience as "uniquely bad," stating that "death would be a welcomed result." Case 2 was a 39-year-old man who developed a serious preoccupation with suicide and fantasies of self-destruction one month after starting Prozac. The sudden change in his manner led his elderly mother and former wife both to make "emergency calls" to his medical-care providers. Several weeks after the drug was discontinued, there were no signs of any Prozac-related problems. Case 3 was a 19-year-old female college student who developed "disturbing and self-destructive thoughts" two weeks after starting Prozac. When the dose was increased from 20mg to 40mg, the

SHE IMPROVED MARKEDLY AFTER PROZAC WAS DISCONTINUED.

problems became worse, and then worse again after the dose was increased to 60mg. Inexplicably, she then had her dose increased to 80mg, which led her to banging her head and mutilating herself. She did not show marked improvement until three months after the drug was discontinued. Case 4 was a 39-year-old woman who experienced a worsening of depression and the emergence of suicidal thoughts two weeks after starting Prozac. For the first time she began to have thoughts of buying a gun and killing herself. She improved markedly after Prozac was discontinued. Case 5 was a 39-year-old woman who, after going on Prozac, experienced the return of suicidal thoughts for the first time in years. However, "in contrast to her past experience with suicidal feelings, she now embraced these impulses and hid them from the clinicians." Suicidal thoughts diminished about eleven days after Prozac was discontinued. Case 6 was very similar to Case 4. **9.** From David Healy's testimony to the court in United States District Court, *Susan Forsyth vs. Eli Lilly and Company*, Civil No. 95-00185. **10.** Read Boseley, Sarah. "They Said it was Safe." *Guardian* (London), 30 Oct 1999. Excellent follow-up articles by Boseley can be found at www.guardian.co.uk. **11.** See Beasley, C.M., B E. Dornseif, and J. C. Bosomworth. "Fluoxetine and Suicide: A Meta-analysis of Controlled Trials of Treatment for Depression." *British Medical Journal* 303 (1991). **12.** Read Healy, David. "From the Psychopharmacology File." *The Psychopharmacologists*. London: Altman, 1996. (His collection of interviews.) The 1995 report by S. Jick, A. D. Dean, and H. Jick, "Antidepressants and Suicide," offers a more credible comparison of suicide rates for Prozac. Looking at ten antidepressants used by a total of 170,000 patients in primary-care settings in the United Kingdom, these researchers found that Prozac, the only SSRI included in the study, was associated with at least twice as high a rate of suicide as other antidepressants. The reported rate of suicide for Prozac in the Jicks study was about 189 suicides per 100,000 years of patient use of the drug (patient years are calculated because individuals taking older drugs will have often taken them for longer periods). Lilly claims that this rate is lower than the overall rates of suicide with depressed patients, which is about 600 suicides per 100,000 years. But this higher rate derives from data for severely depressed patients only, whereas the vast majority of people taking Prozac experience only mild to moderate depression. As Lilly's own packaging stated in 1996, Prozac's efficacy "was established in 5- and 6-week trials with depressed outpatients…. [T]he antidepressant action of Prozac in hospitalized depressed patients has not been adequately studied." **13.** See also, Meltzer, *et al*. "Extrapyramidal Side Effects and Increased Serum Prolactin Following Fluoxetine, a New Antidepressant."

Journal of Neural Transmission 45 (1979). **14.** Read Bourguignon, Robert. "Dangers of Fluoxetine" *The Lancet* (18 Jan 1997). **15.** From David Healy's testimony to the court in United States District Court, *Susan Forsyth vs. Eli Lilly and Company*, Civil No. 95-00185; another study puts rate as high as 25 percent. Read Lipinski, J. F., G. Mally, P. Zimmerman, and H. G. Pope. "Fluoxetine Induced Akathisia: Clinical and Theoretical Implications." *Journal of Clinical Psychiatry* 50 (1989). **16.** The statistic "years of patient use" is used because it controls for the fact that older antidepressants have been used for longer periods than others; see *op cit.*, Healy, "From the Psychopharmacology File." **17.** Read Healy, David. "Antidepressant Induced Suicidality." *Primary Care Psychiatry* 6 (2000). **18.** Read Boseley, Sarah. "Murder, Suicide." *Guardian* (London), 11 June 2001. **19.** Go to <www.quitpaxil.org>. **20.** Emphasis in original; quoted in *op cit.*, Medawar. **21.** Read Tyrer, P., and R. Owen. "Gradual Withdrawal of Diazepam After Long-Term Therapy." *The Lancet* (June 1983). **22.** See *op cit.*, Healy, *The Antidepressant Era.* **23.** See Wong, D.T., *et al*. "Prozac (Fluoxetine, Lilly 110140), the First Selective Serotonin Reuptake Inhibitor and an Antidepressant Drug: Twenty Years Since its First Publication." *Life Sciences* 57 (1995). **24.** See *op cit.*, Healy, *The Antidepressant Era.* **25.** *Ibid.* **26.** *Ibid.* **27.** As a review of antidepressant effectiveness in the *Journal of the American Medical Association* concluded in 1964, "[D]epression is, on the whole, one of the psychiatric conditions with the best prognosis for eventual recovery with or without treatment. Most depressions are self-limited and the spontaneous or placebo-induced improvement rate is often high. For example, in a series of nine controlled studies on hospitalized patients, 57% of the patients given placebo therapy showed improvement in two to six weeks." Cole, J. O. "Therapeutic Efficacy of Antidepressant Drugs, a Review." *JAMA* 190 (1964). **28.** Praise for SSRIs from an online chat session; quoted in *op cit.*, Medawar. **29.** 9 April 1999 issue. **30.** Read Kirsch, I., and G. Sapirstein. "Listening to Prozac and Hearing Placebo." *Prevention and Treatment*, an online journal of the American Psychological Association (June 1998) <www.apa.org>. Kirsch and Sapirstein reported that nearly all the variation in the efficacy of antidepressants across studies could be accounted for by variation in the magnitude of the placebo effect; they also found that active placebos—drugs that should have no pharmacological or clinical efficacy in the treatment of depression—were just as effective as were the antidepressants. See also, Fisher, S., and R.P. Greenberg. *The Limits of Biological Treatments for Psychological Distress.* Hillsdale, NJ: Erlbaum, 1998. For an excellent overview of these ideas, see Fisher, S., and R. Greenberg. "Prescriptions for Happiness." *Psychology Today* (Sept/Oct 1995). **31.** See *op cit.*, Breggin.

"The Lilly Suicides" is excerpted from the forthcoming book, The Cult of Pharmacology, *to be published by Duke University Press.*

THE FLUORIDATION FRAUD
ROBERT STERLING

In January 2000, California Assemblywoman Audie Bock introduced bill AB 1729 to the Golden State legislature. On the surface, Bock's bill was a modest proposal: It would require that public water systems which add fluoride ensure that no substances classified as either a pesticide or a hazardous waste be used, and that the substance added be approved as safe and effective for that use by the Food and Drug Administration. Again, on the surface, the bill was hardly objectionable. Nobody favors the dumping of pesticides or toxic waste into public drinking waters, and certainly the FDA could set reasonable standards to ensure the chemicals used be beneficial to the health of the public. Which, after all, is what water fluoridation is all about, right?

There was little opposition to the bill. Then again, perhaps it was minimal because the bill was unable to get much support in the first place. Bock, an independent elected from the Green Party, couldn't find allies in either of the two corporate-dominated parties.

Nonetheless, one group with impressive political pull did take some time to oppose the bill: The League of California Cities, an association of city officials founded in 1898. Their opposition to the bill was stated rather plainly: "Because no product or technology exists that would meet the specifications established in the bill, those cities that currently add fluoride would be required to stop and those that plan to add fluoride in the future would be unable to do so. It is clear that AB 1729 is a back door attempt to prohibit fluoridation of drinking water."

To the League's credit, their argument against the bill was completely accurate. There currently is nothing on the market that meets the requirements that Bock set forth. And while the motives of Bock can only be guessed at, it is implausible that she could have proposed the bill without understanding its widespread ramifications. (For the record, Bock had this to say when she proposed the bill: "We must ensure the dental health of California's children. However, we must also ensure that the chemicals we use do not themselves pose a severe health risk.") Left unsaid with their opposition were the implications of the facts they'd agreed to: The League stated that the bill "would require that public water systems that add fluoride meet several technical and operating criteria," without listing the specific requirements to avoid this rather touchy detail.

Jeff Green, director for the California Citizens for Safe Drinking Water, had this to say about the bill: "Opposition's only arguments contradict themselves; that testing is not necessary; that testing has already been done; that if you require testing, it will stop all fluorida-

tion, as none of the fluorides will pass all of the tests.... One Capitol hallway rumor says that the Bill is great but many want it to go away."

They got what they wanted. The bill was pulled prior to any staff analysis or hearing for it. There's nothing new here, as pro-fluoride forces have long dominated the debate over water fluoridation. They've even been aided by one of the greatest comedies in film history; anti-fluoridation activists are lumped in the minds of many with the paranoid ravings of Sterling Hayden's General Jack D. Ripper in *Dr. Strangelove*.

> AT THE TIME, THE LEADING PRODUCER OF FLUORIDE IN AMERICA WAS THE ALUMINUM COMPANY OF AMERICA (ALCOA). NOT THAT THEY WANTED TO BE—IT'S JUST THAT FLUORIDE IS A MAJOR WASTE BYPRODUCT OF ALUMINUM PRODUCTION.

Still, as humorous as the image of fluoride's development provided by the John Birchers of the world may be—a cabal of omnipotent communists hell-bent on world domination, using fluoride to sap freedom-loving people of their precious bodily fluids—the image provided by the pro-fluoride forces is just as absurd. For, if we are to believe the official line, 60 years ago (in a country that still has no universal health-care system) health officials became so obsessed with the issue of preventing cavities in children that they made it a mission to combat the cavity menace by any means necessary.

■ ■ ■ ■ ■ ■ ■ ■ ■ ■

The real history of water fluoridation begins in the 1930s. At the time, the leading producer of fluoride in America was the Aluminum Company of America (Alcoa). Not that they wanted to be—it's just that fluoride is a major waste byproduct of aluminum production. Alcoa was hardly alone, as fluoride has been a widespread form of waste since the Industrial Revolution. As early as 1850, industrial pollution tied to fluoride emissions was known to be poisonous to crops, livestock, and people, and (as fluoridation opponents like to point out) it was best known to the public as a rat poison. Health concerns increased, especially as the waste found its way into water supplies. In 1931, it was ironically a dentist, named H. Trendley Dean, who identified the dangers of fluoridated water, as he was dispatched to remote areas where drinking water contained high concentrations of natural fluoride. His conclusion: Teeth in these high-fluoride towns had mottled tooth enamel and became discolored and eroded. (This is the first sign of fluorosis, or fluoride poisoning.)

Left at that, such a report would seem to be a major indictment of fluoridated water. But turning lemons into lemonade, Dean also stated that it appeared there were fewer cavities in the teeth of people in these areas. Thus, he recommended further study into the possibility that a lesser, so-called "optimal" level of fluoride in the water would actually be beneficial to dental health.

Why would Dean try to put such a happy spin on his research? At the time, he was working for the US Public Health Service, which was under the jurisdiction of the Treasury Department. In 1931, the Treasury Secretary was Andrew Mellon, a founder and major stockholder of Alcoa.

The silver lining in dental fluorosis was supposedly confirmed in 1939, after biochemist Gerald J. Cox fluoridated lab rats and brashly concluded that fluoride reduced cavities. As he put it, "The case should be regarded as proved." Cox added that the "present trend toward complete removal of fluoride from water and food may need some reversal." He then came up with a proposition based on his apparently proven research that fluoride should be added to water as a public health measure. Rather coincidentally, at the time Cox worked for the Mellon Institute, the research lab for Alcoa. In other words, the first advocacy of water fluoridation came from a shill for the industry that conveniently mass-produced it as waste.

The Mellon family and Alcoa are pretty difficult to top as political influence peddlers, but in the case of water fluoridation, this was actually achieved. During World War II, another organization was tied to promoting fluoridation: the Pentagon. Besides the stepped-up production of Alcoa aluminum for fighters and bombers, the military had another little program that was heavily tied to fluoride, the Manhattan Project. This was kept secret for over 50 years, and was only uncovered by reporters Joel Griffiths and Chris Bryson in 1997 working with declassified papers. (They received a Project Censored Award for their work.) Griffiths and Bryson stated:

Fluoride was the key chemical in atomic bomb production, according to the documents. Massive quantities—millions of tons—were essential for the manufacture of bomb-grade uranium and plutonium for nuclear weapons throughout the Cold War. One of the most toxic chemicals known, fluoride emerged as the leading chemical health hazard of the US atomic bomb program, both for workers and for nearby communities, the documents reveal.

> **"ONE OF THE MOST TOXIC CHEMICALS KNOWN, FLUORIDE EMERGED AS THE LEADING CHEMICAL HEALTH HAZARD OF THE US ATOMIC BOMB PROGRAM, BOTH FOR WORKERS AND FOR NEARBY COMMUNITIES, THE DOCUMENTS REVEAL."**

Much of the concern surrounding fluoride was due to a major 1943 accident involving the Manhattan Project. A DuPont plant in Deepwater, New Jersey, dumped fluoride in the local air and water. Cows, horses, and poultry became sick and died; crops were destroyed; and farm and DuPont workers complained of illnesses. The locals were discovered to have abnormally high levels of fluoride in their blood. Due to this incident, the first lawsuit against the atomic bomb program was filed—not over radiation, but due to fluoride poisoning. The Pentagon blocked revealing how much fluoride had been released, citing national security, and due to continued stonewalling the lawsuit was eventually settled for a minimal sum.

Nonetheless, faced with the prospect of widespread fluoride lawsuits (that threatened to undermine the atomic weapons program) the Pentagon did the only logical thing: They covered it up. Much of the original supposed proof of the safety of fluoride in low doses came from scientists secretly ordered to provide "evidence useful in litigation" over fluoride exposure. Perhaps the most darkly comical (and important) example of this influence was the publication of a study on the effects of fluoride in the August 1948 *Journal of the American Dental Association*. In this key piece in the history of water fluoridation, Peter P. Dale and H. B. McCauley, both of whom worked on the Manhattan Project, claimed that workers in a fluoride-producing factory for atomic weapons had fewer cavities than would be expected. In fact, this was true. However, what the published report failed to mention was that most of the men had no teeth left, hence the lack of cavities. This minor detail was duly noted in the original classified report, also written by Dale and McCauley.

The influence of the Pentagon was felt quickly: The first public water fluoridation program in the US was begun in 1945 (before Hiroshima and Nagasaki) at Grand Rapids, Michigan. It was publicly labeled an experiment to test the safety and benefits of water fluoridation by comparing the town with nearby Muskegon. (In other words, the entire community became guinea pigs.) Oddly, although the experiment was supposed to be a fifteen-year study, it ended in 1947, when Muskegon itself became an early-fluoridated community, a rather unusual breach of protocol. A cynic may suggest that negative results were already clear, and the Muskegon fluoridation was to cover up the evidence.

Newburgh, New York, followed Grand Rapids in May 1945, and this program had major ties to the Manhattan Project. (Although it was implemented shortly after Grand Rapids, planning had begun in 1943, making it the model for all fluoridation programs, including Grand Rapids.) The chairman of the committee who pushed for the program was Dr. Harold C. Hodge. The Manhattan Project's chief of fluoride toxicity studies, he concealed his military connections, as did three others involved with the project.

In 1947, Oscar Ewing was appointed head of the Federal Security Agency, which was then in charge of the Public Health Service. Ewing was a lawyer for Alcoa, which paid him an annual salary of $750,000, and so was likely aware of the corporation's fluoride litigation. Ewing pushed for a national water fluoridation program, and his point man for the program was Edward L. Bernays. Bernays, the nephew of Sigmund Freud, is known as "the father of public relations" for his pioneering work on mass manipulation. He authored a book in 1928 titled *Propaganda*. In it, he wrote, "Those who manipulate this unseen mechanism of society, constitute an invisible government which is the true ruling power of our country..."

Under Bernays, the propaganda campaign to promote fluoridation went into hyperdrive. In a curious display of timing, the chief opponent of fluoridation in the public mind suddenly became the John Birch Society and other right-wing groups, who decried the process as a nefarious communist plot (and thus providing the archetype for General Ripper). The JBS, a group whose founding was tied to right-wing industrialists and military officials, strangely chose not to emphasize the connection of big business and the Pentagon to the push behind fluoridation in their commie conspiracy. (To give the Birchers their due, they have emphasized that point in recent years.)

Of course, there may be a non-conspiratorial explanation for the sudden right-wing opposition to fluoridation. Ewing, an avowed liberal, tied fluoridation to his desired nationalized health system. Whatever the reason behind the sudden right-wing opposition, the effect is still in place. Despite the creepy history behind the push for fluoridation, it is still considered, perversely, a "liberal" proposition. As Murray Rothbard, the libertarian economic philosopher once put it:

It has always been a bit of mystery to me why left-environmentalists, who shriek in horror at a bit of Alar on apples, who cry "cancer" even more absurdly than the boy cried "Wolf," who hate every chemical additive known to man, still cast their benign approval upon fluoride, a highly toxic and probably carcinogenic substance. And not only let fluoride emissions off the hook, but endorse uncritically the massive and continuing dumping of fluoride into the nation's water supply.

While this writer may not agree with all of Rothbard's statement, his main point is a good one.

■ ■ ■ ■ ■ ■ ■ ■ ■ ■

At this point, it seems almost unnecessary to mention that over 90 percent of water fluoridation is now done via hydrofluosilicic acid and sodium silicofluoride, overwhelmingly from waste products of the phosphate fertilizer industry. As noted by Janet Allen in *Whole Life Times*: "Only 23% fluoride in concentration, it's combined with other contaminants in an acid swill of industrial waste that contains varying amount of arsenic, cadmium, lead, mercury, and uranium, depending upon the phosphate mining operations of the day. Also included is a potpourri of other chemicals resulting from various manufacturing processes: diesel fuel, kerosene, chlorides, sulfides, polymers, defoamers, and possibly hexavalent chromium (chromium 6)." The last entry may raise some eyebrows from pop-culture buffs. Chromium 6 was the chemical poisoning the town of Hinkley, California, cited in the film *Erin Brockovich*. The mixture is indeed classified as a Class I toxic waste.

| "THE KIDNEYS OF THE CONTROL RATS DRINKING NON-FLUORIDATED WATER REMAINED NORMAL."

Still, just because the fertilizer industry, Alcoa, DuPont, the Mellon family, the Defense Department, and a self-admitted propaganda expert have colluded to promote the dumping of an industrial-nuclear-toxic waste into public waters doesn't prove that it's a bad idea. After all, there are numerous studies that prove its benefit to the public, right?

The main problem with such claims should be pretty self-evident by now: The primary sources of funding for the vast majority of the studies were the Pentagon and the Atomic Energy Commission (AEC), both of which had a policy to promote fluoridation and conceal any evidence adverse to the cause. This is even more problematic than it sounds. According to Noam Chomsky, 90 percent of all federal funds for research during the 1940s and 1950s came from these two institutions. Thus, not only was it difficult to get funding for studies which investigated fluoride dangers, you also risked being blacklisted by the two most overwhelmingly powerful funding sources going.

Case in point on how the suppression continues today: In 1995, Dr. Phyllis Mullenix, former head of toxicology at Forsyth Dental Center in Boston, published a study on rats that concluded fluoride was a powerful central nervous system toxin and might adversely affect human brain functioning even at low doses. Until that point, there had been no published studies in the US of fluoride's effects on the human brain. She applied for a grant to further her studies but was denied by the US National Institutes of Health. A NIH panel told her in no uncertain terms that "fluoride does not have central nervous system effects." Thus, that avenue of scientific inquiry has been shut down.

Among the classified papers uncovered by Griffiths and Bryson is this April 29, 1944, Manhattan Project memorandum:

Clinical evidence suggests that uranium hexafluoride may have a rather marked central nervous system effect.... It seems most likely that the F [code for fluoride] component rather than the T [code for uranium] is the causative factor.... Since work with these compounds is essential, it will be necessary to know in advance what mental effects may occur after exposure.

On the same day, this research was given the greenlight. In other words, over 50 years before Mullenix's denied request to study the subject, the Pentagon had done precisely that in secret.

What were the results of the research? They weren't found in the papers, which would indicate they are likely still classified. Needless to say, it seems unlikely that it would remain classified if the studies concluded that fluoride doesn't affect brain functions.

The research proposal attached to the 1944 memo was also missing, but the author is indicated in the files: Dr. Harold Hodge, the man behind the Newburgh fluoridation program. Curiously, Hodge also was brought in as a consultant for Dr. Mullenix's research, yet not once did he mention his work 50 years earlier on the same subject.

(Hodge's fluoride studies were conducted at the University of Rochester, where other hospital patients were secretly injected with toxic doses of radioactive plutonium, one of the more shocking human radiation experiments of the Cold War yet uncovered.)

Despite these admitted obstacles in research, here is just a sample of some of the problems linked with water fluoridation in studies:

Skeletal Fluorosis, Osteoporosis, and Arthritis. In 1944, the *Journal* of the *American Dental Association* ran another article warning that fluoridated water causes osteoporosis, goiter, and spinal disease. At the time, the article stated that "the potentialities for harm far outweigh those for good." Bone is collagen, and fluoride disrupts the formation of enzymes necessary for collagen production. Fluoride also causes low blood calcium, as well as the buildup of calcium stones and crystals in the joints and organs. A 1990 *Journal of the American Medical Association* study of 541,000 cases of osteoporosis found a definite connection between hip fractures in women over 65 and fluoride levels. A 1978 study by Yale University discovered that doses as low as 1 ppm of fluoride (the "optimal" level long pushed by promoters) decrease bone strength and elasticity, making fracture more likely.

Dr. Paul Connett (author of *50 Reasons to Oppose Fluoridation*) notes, "Hip fracture is a very serious issue for the elderly, as a quarter of those who have a hip fracture die within a year of the operation, while 50 percent never regain an independent existence." This is no minor bone to pick. On October 24, 2002, the Centers for Disease Control and Prevention announced that 69.9 million American adults (one in three) suffer from arthritis, a phenomenon that has spread over the past 50 years. Skeletal fluorosis in early stages causes chronic joint pain and can lead to hip fractures and bone cancer. Because the symptoms mimic arthritis, the first two clinical phases of skeletal fluorosis could be easily misdiagnosed. Arthritis, hip fractures, and bone cancer are now at epidemic levels in the United States.

Thyroid Disorders. As noted by Mary Shomon, author of *Living Well With Hypothyroidism* (HarperCollins, 2000): "Fluoride had been used for decades as an effective anti-thyroid medication to treat hyperthyroidism [too much thyroid hormone] and was frequently used at levels below the current 'optimal' intake of 1 mg/day. This is due to the ability of fluoride to mimic the action of thyrotropin (TSH). It makes sense, then that out of the over 150 symptoms and associations of hypothyroidism [too little thyroid hormone], almost all are also symptoms of fluoride poisoning." Thyroid problems are also running in epidemic levels in the US.

Kidney Damage. Polyuric nephropathy (a kidney disease characterized by excess urination) is a major manifestation of fluoride toxicity in its early stage. Three Cornell University scientists gave drinking water with varying amounts of fluoride (none, one, five, and ten ppm) to 86 albino rats for 520 days (an average rat's lifetime). In these experiments with small amounts corresponding to human intake, they found changes in the tubules similar to those from larger doses in short-term experiments. The kidneys of the control rats drinking non-fluoridated water remained normal.

Damage from Other Contaminants. It's worth repeating the list of contaminants found in the common "fluoride" acid swill: arsenic, cadmium, lead, mercury, and uranium. Even without chromium 6, that's an objectionable list of chemicals to systematically dump into water. Fluoride has the ability to act synergistically with other toxic minerals in drinking water.

Effects on the Brain. Aside from the work of Drs. Mullenix and Hodge (one unfinished and unfunded, the other classified), there's other evidence of damage to the brain caused by fluoride. In 1992, a team of New York scientists said rat studies link behavior changes and brain-cell damage to aluminum and fluoride in water. As the *Wall Street Journal* reported, "Rats fed the highest doses developed irregular mincing steps characteristic of senile animals, in contrast with the long and regular strides of animals in their prime. In addition, the rats lost their normal ability to distinguish the scent of banana, which is their favorite, from lemon."

Of course, the evidence of effects on the brain was there even before the end of WWII: The first mass water fluoridation operation was in Nazi concentration camps, to put prisoners into calm submission. Today, it is a basic ingredient in Prozac (*fluoxetene*

> "[F]LUORIDE IS A CARCINOGEN BY ANY STANDARD WE USE. I BELIEVE EPA SHOULD ACT IMMEDIATELY TO PROTECT THE PUBLIC, NOT JUST ON THE CANCER DATA, BUT ON THE EVIDENCE OF BONE FRACTURES, ARTHRITIS, MUTAGENICITY AND OTHER EFFECTS."

hydrochloride), the "date-rape drug" Rohypnol (*flunitrazepam*), and sarin nerve gas (isopropyl-methyl-phosphoryl *fluoride*).

The Big C. In 1987, the National Cancer Institute provided epidemiological evidence of a relation between cancer incidence and water fluoridation. A 1990 National Toxicology Program study discovered that male rats developed osteosarcoma (a rare bone cancer) from fluoride treatment. The Okinawa Islands (in the south of Japan and under US control from 1945 to 1972) were fluoridated. The relationship between fluoride concentration in drinking water and uterine cancer mortality rate was studied in 20 municipalities there. A significant positive correlation was found, even after adjusting for the potential confounding variables.

The time trends in the uterine cancer mortality rate appear related to changes in fluoridation practices. As early as 1976, Dr. Dean Burk, chief chemist of the National Cancer Institute, stated before Congress: "In point of fact, fluoride causes more human cancer death, and causes it faster than any other chemical." In 1977, he and Dr. John Yiamouyiannis—the biochemical editor for Chemical Abstracts Service, and the Science Director of the National Health Federation—completed a gigantic research project that compared cancer death rates in ten fluoridated and ten non-fluoridated US cities between 1940 and 1970. For the first ten years, when none of the 20 cities was fluoridated, the average cancer deaths were virtually identical. But after 1950, there was a major increase in cancer deaths in every single one of the fluoridated cities, while the non-fluoridated cities remained clustered together at a much lower level of death.

William Marcus, senior science adviser and toxicologist for the Environmental Protection Agency, summed it up best in 1990 (he was soon after fired from his job, and had to fight in court to regain his position): "[F]luoride is a carcinogen by any standard we use. I believe EPA should act immediately to protect the public, not just on the cancer data, but on the evidence of bone fractures, arthritis, mutagenicity and other effects."

THE FLUORIDATION FRAUD
ROBERT STERLING

. . . .

But hey, it's good for the teeth, right?

Well, maybe. Keep in mind, the first signs of fluoride toxicity appear in the teeth, so the original dental investigations were about its danger to teeth, not its benefits. As noted by Nicholas W. Hether (manager of product purity and regulatory sciences at the Gerber Products Company) in the Winter 1998 issue of *Pediatric Basics*: "In 1993 the Board on Environmental Studies and Toxicology of the National Research Council (NRC) reported that, in the absence of fluoride intake from other sources, fluoridation of municipal drinking water supplies at the recommended concentrations may result in mild to very mild dental fluorosis in about 10% of the population."

That said, here's a list of some of the curious suppressed evidence that has been compiled by health expert and fluoridation opponent Gary Null:

• "In British Columbia, only 11% of the population drinks fluoridated water, as opposed to 40-70% in other Canadian regions. Yet British Columbia has the lowest rate of tooth decay in Canada. In addition, the lowest rates of dental caries within the province are found in areas that do not have their water supplies fluoridated." (Source: A.S. Gray, *Canadian Dental Association Journal*, October 1987, pp. 76-83).

• "In 1986-87, the largest study on fluoridation and tooth decay ever was performed. The subjects were 39,000 school children between 5 and 17 living in 84 areas around the country. A third of the places were fluoridated, a third were partially fluoridated, and a third were not. Results indicate no statistically significant differences in dental decay between fluoridated and unfluoridated cities." (Source: John Yiamouyiannis, *Fluoride*, Vol. 23, 1990, pp. 55-67.)

• "A World Health Organization survey reports a decline of dental decay in western Europe, which is 98% unfluoridated. They state that western Europe's declining dental decay rates are equal to and sometimes better than those in the U.S." (Source: Center for Health Action, March 30, 1990.)

• "A 1992 University of Arizona study yielded surprising results when they found that 'the more fluoride a child drinks, the more cavities appear in the teeth.'" (Source: *Clinical Pediatrics*, November 1991.)

• "A follow-up of a study of the town of Kuopio, Finland six years after fluoridation was discontinued found no increase in dental caries [cavities]. The authors conclude that fluoridation was unnecessary to begin with." (Source: L. Seppa, S. Karkkainen, and H. Hausen. "Caries Trends 1992-1998 in Two Low-Fluoride Finnish Towns Formerly With and Without Fluoridation." *Caries Res* 34.6, Nov-Dec 2000, pp. 462-8).

• "A 1999 New York State Department of Health study of 3,500 7-14-year-olds shows that children in fluoridated Newburgh, New York, have no less tooth decay but significantly more dental fluorosis than children from Kingston, New York, which has never been fluoridated. Since 1945, children of the two towns have been examined periodically in order to demonstrate that fluoridation reduces tooth decay. 'This new research shows the experiment has failed,' the report concludes." (Source: J.V. Kumar and P.A. Swango. *Community Dent Oral Epidemiol* 27.3, June 1999, pp. 171-80.)

If that isn't enough, a 2001 *Journal of the American Dental Association* article admits the fluoride that is swallowed and incorporated into teeth is "insufficient to have a measurable effect" on reducing cavities. This is a mind-blowing revelation, coming as it does from the very seat of the dental establishment. (See "The Science and Practice of Caries Prevention" by J.D.B. Featherstone in the *Journal of the American Dental Association* 131, 2001, pp. 887-899.)

Dr. Hardy Limeback is the head of preventive dentistry at the University of Toronto and has long advocated water fluoridation. In 1999, he performed a literature review which resulted in his conclusion that any cavity-protection from fluoride comes from applying it to the teeth, not swallowing it. (In fact, any positive effect from the swallowing of fluoride would likely be caused by the damage it does to enzyme systems, something fluoridation supporters prefer to not advertise.) In an interview with Gary Null, Dr. Limeback stated:

Dental decay rates in North America are so low that water fluoridation provides little to no benefit whatsoever these days. In fact, studies show that when you turn the water fluoridation taps off and look for dental decay rates, they don't move whatsoever. There is no increase in dental decay when you stop fluoridating.

Of course, if topical treatment of fluoride really is what causes its benefits (and even that is highly debatable), there seems to be a simpler, safer, and arguably more effective solution to ensuring dental health in children: promotion of brushing with fluoridated toothpaste, along with dental education and free daily fluoride rinses in public schools. And while they are teaching them the importance of brushing and the benefits of topical fluoridation, they can also inform the little tykes that fluoridated toothpaste, despite its sweet taste, is not meant to be swallowed, emphasizing a little note found on the back of all fluoride toothpaste tubes: "If you accidentally swallow more than used for brushing, get medical help or contact a Poison Control Center right away." (The label on fluoridated toothpaste also warns to keep "out of the reach of children under 6.")

A 2001 *JOURNAL OF THE AMERICAN DENTAL ASSOCIATION* ARTICLE ADMITS THE FLUORIDE THAT IS SWALLOWED AND INCORPORATED INTO TEETH IS "INSUFFICIENT TO HAVE A MEASURABLE EFFECT" ON REDUCING CAVITIES.

Such a project could be done in a cost-effective manner, and it would give those opposed a chance to opt out. Which, of course, is the bigger principle here. After all, in the end, no matter what any study concludes, a study is just that. It is just information; meanwhile, every person has to live with the consequences of what they put in their own body. And not every person is affected in the same way by the same stimulus. Especially with as powerful of a chemical as fluoride, to indiscriminately dose a population without regard for the variance in response is pure medical recklessness. Water fluoridation deprives people of the basic right to choose what goes in them. To those who are for abortion rights and drug legalization for moral reasons, the argument against water fluoridation is one and the same.

This is no trivial issue. Fluoride, after all, is really a medication when ingested, and the medication of a group of people without their consent is a violation of the Nuremberg code of human rights. Thus, fluoridation can rightly be considered a crime against humanity.

Some may object to this, claiming it is mere hyperbole, and point out that other dangerous chemicals, most notably chlorine, are added to the water supply. This is true, but there's one important difference: When chlorine and other chemicals are added, it is to treat the water and kill dangerous pathogens such as cholera, typhoid, and dysentery. Yes, there are dangers with other chemicals, and the dangers should rightly be debated, but at least it's an honest argument. In the case of water fluoridation, however, one has the unique phenomenon of a mixture added to water not to maintain the integrity of the water supply but to somehow "enhance" it.

At least that's the official line on fluoridation, but the numbers speak much louder. As Janet Allen noted in the *Whole Life Times*, the neutralization of Class I toxic waste costs at least $1.40 per gallon. This leads to the strong motivation for secret and illegal dumpings, but to dump toxic waste into the water can lead to fines and criminal punishments. Yet, magically, under the policy of "fluoridation," suddenly this expensive waste is no longer a cost but, instead, a potential profit center. And rather than being punished for secretly dumping quantities of waste in the water, corporations are rewarded for dumping even larger amounts in the water as matter of policy.

For all the billions saved and earned by the military-industrial complex because of water fluoridation, however, the most important number comes from Drs. Burk and Yiamouyiannis:

30,000 to 50,000 deaths each year from various causes may now be attributable to fluoridation. This total includes 10,000 to 20,000 deaths attributable to fluoride-induced cancer every year.

Does this sound like an exaggeration? Consider that fluoride is more toxic than lead, and not quite as toxic as arsenic. In April 2001, there was deserved outrage in the US over the Bush Administration's decision to weaken regulations limiting arsenic in water. Rather than changing the limit to 10 parts per billion, the decision was made to leave it at 50 ppb. Lead is at 15 ppb. Meanwhile, fluoridated water has, on average, over 1 part per million, not billion, or one thousand ppb, which is twenty times the higher arsenic level chosen.

All of which makes the promotion of fluoridation perhaps the most amazing scam of the twentieth century. There perhaps has been no better example of how an inherently dangerous product linked to poison, pollution, and weapons of mass destruction has been transformed in the public's eye into a paragon of health. It is the ultimate con job in terms of mass manipulation, the perfect emblem of the "toxic sludge is good for you" mentality promoted by the poison-PR industry. Uncle Sigmund would be proud.

"IF YOU ACCIDENTALLY SWALLOW MORE THAN USED FOR BRUSHING, GET MEDICAL HELP OR CONTACT A POISON CONTROL CENTER RIGHT AWAY." — WARNING OF ALL TUBES OF FLUORIDE TOOTHPASTE

Websites for Further Research

The Advisory Committee on Human Radiation Experiments Report, 1995 <tis.eh.doe.gov/ohre/roadmap/achre/>

Earth Island Journal Special Section Fluorides and the Environment <www.earthisland.org/oijournal/fluoride/fluoride_index.html>

Fluoride Action Network <www.fluoridealert.org>

Gary Null's Natural Living <www.garynull.com>

NoFluoride.com

Sources

Allen, Janet. "Water That's Hard to Swallow: Fluoride in L.A.'s Taps." *Whole Life Times* 2002. <http//www.wholelifetimes.com/la_fluoride.html>

Bernays, Edward L. *Propaganda*. New York: Liveright, 1928.

Bock, Audie. AB 1729: The California Fluoride Product Quality Control Act. Read it at <www.nofluoride.com/AB1729.htm>.

Borkin, Joseph. *The Crime and Punishment of I.G. Farben*. New York: Pocket Books, 1979.

Bragg, Paul C., and Patricia. *Water: The Shocking Truth* (revised edition). California: Health Science, 1999

Caldwell, Gladys, and Philip E. Zanfagna, MD. *Fluoridation and Truth Decay*. California: Top-Ecol Press, 1974.

Chase, Marilyn. "Rat Studies Link Brain Cell Damage With Aluminum and Fluoride in Water." *Wall Street Journal*, 28 Oct 1992.

Chomsky, Noam, et al. *The Cold War and the University: Toward an Intellectual History of the Postwar Years*. New York: New Press, 1998.

Clark, Dr Hulda Regehr. *The Cure for All Diseases*. California: New Century Press, 1995.

Connett, Paul, Ph.D. "50 Reasons to Oppose Fluoridation." Fluoride Action Network, 6 Mar 2001.

Paul, Ellen, and Michael Connett. "Fluoridation: Time for a Second Look?" *Rachel Enviroment and Health News* 724 (10 May 2001).

Dale, Peter P., and H.B. McCauley. "Dental Conditions in Workers Chronically Exposed to Dilute and Anhydrous Hydrofluoric Acid." *Journal of the American Dental Association* 37.2 (Aug 1948). .

Dean, H. Trendley, MD. "Further Studies on Minimal Threshold of Chronic Endemic Dental Fluorosis." *Public Health Reports*, vol. 62 (1937).

Green, Jeff. "Update On AB1729." California California Citizens for Safe Drinking Water

THE FLUORIDATION FRAUD
ROBERT STERLING

CONSIDER THAT FLUORIDE IS MORE TOXIC THAN LEAD, AND NOT QUITE AS TOXIC AS ARSENIC.

Website, 23 Apr 2000.

Griffiths, Joel. "Fluoride: Commie Plot or Capitalist Ploy." *Covert Action Quarterly* 42 (Fall 1992).

Griffiths, Joel. "Fluoride Industry's Toxic Coup." *Food & Water Journal*, Summer 1998.

Griffiths, Joel, and Chris Bryson. "Fluoride, Teeth and the Atomic Bomb." *Waste Not*, Sept 1997.

Hertsgaard, Mark, and Phillip Frazer. "Fear of Fluoride." *Salon*, 17 Feb 1999.

Hileman, Bette. "Fluoridation of Water: Questions About Health Risks and Benefits Remain After More than 40 Years." *Chemical and Engineering News*, Aug 1988.

Huffington, Arianna. "A Little Arsenic Water With That Tainted Beef?" *Salon*, 9 Apr 2001.

Keeler, Barbara, and William Daily. "The Case Against Fluoride." *Santa Monica Mirror*, 8-14 Nov 2000.

League of California Cities. "Legislative Bulletin March 31, 2000." <www.cacities.org/Leg_Serv/bulletin/2000/html/Bulletin_13-2000.htm>.

Mercola, Dr. Joseph. "Is Fluoride Really As Safe As You Are Told?" Mercola.com, 2 Feb 2002.

Mullenix, Phyllis, *et al*. "Neurotoxicity of Sodium Fluoride in Rats." *Neurotoxicology and Teratology* 17.2 (1995).

Null, Gary, Ph.D. "Fluoride: The Deadly Legacy." Gary Null's Natural Living <www.garynull.com>.

O'Shea, Tim. "The New Agenda of American Dentistry." The Doctor Within <www. thedoctorwithin.com>.

Phillips, Peter. (Editor.) *Censored 1998: The News That Didn't Make the News*. New York: Seven Stories Press, 1998.

Rothbard, Murray N. "Fluoridation Revisited." LewRockwell.com, Jan 1993.

Shomon, Mary. "Fluoride Dangers to the Thyroid." Thyroid Disease at About.com <thyroid .about.com>, 7 Feb 2000.

Stauber, John C., and Sheldon Rampton. *Toxic Sludge Is Good for You!: Lies, Damn Lies and the Public Relations Industry*. Monroe, Maine: Common Courage Press, 1995.

Unsigned. "CDC: One in Three Suffer Arthritis, Joint Problems." Associated Press, 24 Mar 2002.

Valerian, Val. "Chronology of Fluoride." Leading Edge Research Group, 1997.

Yiamouyiannis, Dr. John. *Fluoride: The Aging Factor*. Ohio: Health Action Press, 1993.

Zaidi, A.S. "Rochester, Radiation, and Repression." *Z Magazine*, Apr 1997.

STRAIGHT TALK ABOUT SUICIDE

THOMAS S. SZASZ, M.D.

Suicide—like accident, illness, death, poverty, persecution, and war—has always been with us and has always been regarded as a part of life. Believing that a person's life belongs to God, not himself, the Jews declared it to be a grievous sin, and Christians and Muslims followed suit.

Enlightenment thought did not overtly repudiate this position. Instead, it supplemented it with a secular version of it. Suicide, declared the mad-doctors ("psychiatrists"), is due to a disease of the mind, which it is the duty of mad-doctors to prevent (by imprisoning/"hospitalizing" the madman/"patient"). The mainstream media and most people accept this ostensibly scientific doctrine as truth.

Although we now have more so-called rights than we have ever had—such as welfare rights, disability rights, patients' rights, the right to choice, the right to treatment, the right to reject treatment, *ad infinitum*—we have no right to suicide.

In the immediate aftermath of the attacks on the World Trade Center and the Pentagon, President Bush—with his disarmingly gauche use of language—called the act "cowardly" and the terrorists "cowards."

That characterization of our Muslim enemies was quickly abandoned in favor of our "scientific" clichés: brainwashing and mental illness. Declared George Will: "And although Americans are denouncing the terrorists' 'cowardice,' what is most telling and frightening is their lunatic fearlessness."

William Safire opted for brainwashing. He explained: "A more powerful weapon [than surprise] of radical Islam is its ability to erase from the brains of recruits the basic will to live. The normal survival instinct is replaced with a pseudo-religious fantasy of a killer's self-martyrdom leading to eternity in paradise surrounded by adoring virgins."

One of the effects of the September 11 attacks was that every politician and pundit suddenly became an expert about the fine points of Muslim theology. "This perversion of the world's great faiths," pontificated Safire, "produces suicide bombers. How to build a defense against the theological brainwashing that creates these human missiles? That is the challenge to Muslim clerics everywhere..."

How wrong can our most respected pundits be before we begin to view their expertise as we regard the expertise of the Enron accountants? The Muslim suicide bombers are a challenge to their victims, not to their teachers and paymasters. Any other interpretation is our collective folly, serving to indulge our love affair with a misguided concept of multiculturalism.

Are brainwashing, cowardice, and lunacy our only choices? Surely, it is not difficult to see an Arab youngster training to become a suicide bomber and becoming a celebrated patriot and martyr as engaging in what he considers a rationally motivated series of actions. From the point of view of the future terrorist, his family, and his society, his actions are just as rationally motivated as are the actions of a young American engaged in going to college, studying medicine, and becoming a surgeon.

I maintain that, from the point of view of the suicidal actor, planning to kill himself and carrying out the act are also rationally motivated. However, we regard this interpretation as so flagitious—so indecent—that, for most Americans, it is as good as taboo. The only socially acceptable view is that suicide is a "cry for help," uttered by a person who has a mental illness (depression) and denies that he is ill.

_CAUSED BY DEPRESSION?

A large, multi-story shopping mall in Syracuse, New York—the Carousel Center—has become one of the favorite places for young men and women to jump to their deaths. Every time this happens, the newspapers present the story as if the act were a symptom of—that is, were "due to"—the subject's mental illness. "Suicide jumpers often disordered," was the headline of a long report on the suicide of a young woman in April 2002. "[She] had been battling the disease [depression] for several years," her father said. The rest of the long, double-headed article—the other title was "Suicide-prevention counselor says barriers to jumping should be considered"—was devoted to telling the reader that (most) people who commit suicide, or think of doing so, suffer from "bipolar illness"; explaining that the disease is genetic and chemical in origin; and that it usually responds well to treatment with drugs. This and other newspapers never mention that persons suspected of being "suicidal," or who try to kill themselves and fail, are routinely incarcerated in prisons called "mental hospitals."

Muslim clerics engage in theological

I MAINTAIN THAT, FROM THE POINT OF VIEW OF THE SUICIDAL ACTOR, PLANNING TO KILL HIMSELF AND CARRYING OUT THE ACT ARE ALSO RATIONALLY MOTIVATED.

brainwashing. Does the mainstream American media—not to mention organized American psychiatry—engage in therapeutic brainwashing? Of course not. We call this "educating people about mental illness" and "eradicating the stigma of mental illness."

Kay Redfield Jamison—professor of psychiatry at John Hopkins University Medical School—is America's poster girl for suicide as a preventable and treatable illness. She advertises herself thusly: "As someone who studies, treats and suffers from a severe mental illness—manic depression"; preaches the psychiatric mantra: "Suicide is due to mental illness and mental illness is treatable"; and explains: "I drew up a clear arrangement with my psychiatrist and family that if I again become severely depressed they have the authority to approve, against my will if necessary, both electroconvulsive therapy, or ECT, an excellent treatment for certain types of severe depression, and hospitalization."

WE ARE SO BLIND TO THE ESSENTIALLY HUMAN (NON-"PATHOLOGICAL") NATURE OF VOLUNTARY DEATH THAT WE DENY THE REALITY OF WHAT PEOPLE THROUGHOUT HISTORY VIEWED AS "HEROIC SUICIDE."

Well and good. Does Jamison approve of other persons, similarly afflicted, having the right to reject psychiatric coercion and kill themselves? Certainly not.

We are so blind to the essentially human (non-"pathological") nature of voluntary death that we deny the reality of what people throughout history viewed as "heroic suicide." "Of all the 'isms' produced by the past centuries, fanaticism alone survives," declares memory-champion Elie Wiesel. "We have witnessed the downfall of Nazism, the defeat of fascism, and the abdication of communism. But fanaticism is still alive."

Our political-ideological prejudgments prevent us from acknowledging Zionism as the reason why some Palestinians choose to kill themselves for political reasons. Our psychiatric-ideological prejudgments prevent us from acknowledging the slings and arrows of outrageous fortune as the reason why some Americans choose to kill themselves for personal reasons.

We are as squeamish and superstitious about suicide as people used to be about demonic possession and witchcraft. And we will remain so until we begin to take seriously how we talk about it.

DID JESUS REALLY RISE FROM THE DEAD?

DAN BARKER

During the nineteen years I preached the Gospel, the resurrection of Jesus was the keystone of my ministry.[1] Every Easter I affirmed the Apostle Paul's admonition: "If Christ has not been raised, then our proclamation has been in vain and your faith has been in vain."[2] I wrote a popular Easter musical called "His Fleece Was White As Snow" with the joyous finale proclaiming: "Sing Hosanna! Christ is Risen! The Son has risen to shine on me!"[3]

But now I no longer believe it. Many Bible scholars[4] and ministers—including one-third of the clergy in the Church of England[5]—reject the idea that Jesus bodily came back to life. So do 30 percent of born-again American Christians![6]

Why? When the Gospel of John portrays the post-mortem Jesus on a fishing trip with his buddies, and the writer of Matthew shows him giving his team a mountain-top pep talk two days after he died, how can there be any doubt that the original believers were convinced he had bodily risen from the grave?

There have been many reasons for doubting the claim, but the consensus among critical scholars today appears to be that the story is a "legend." During the 60 to 70 years it took for the Gospels to be composed, the original story went through a growth period that began with the unadorned idea that Jesus, like Grandma, had "died and gone to heaven" and ended with a fantastic narrative produced by a later generation of believers that included earthquakes, angels, an eclipse, a resuscitated corpse, and a spectacular bodily ascension into the clouds.

> MANY BIBLE SCHOLARS AND MINISTERS—INCLUDING ONE-THIRD OF THE CLERGY IN THE CHURCH OF ENGLAND—REJECT THE IDEA THAT JESUS BODILY CAME BACK TO LIFE.

The earliest Christians believed in the "spiritual" resurrection of Jesus. The story evolved over time into a "bodily" resurrection.

Before discussing the legend in detail, let's look briefly at some of the other reasons for skepticism.

_CAN HISTORY PROVE A MIRACLE?

Philosopher Antony Flew, in a 1985 debate on the resurrection,[7] pointed out that history is the wrong tool for proving miracle reports. "The heart of the matter," said Flew, "is that the criteria by which we must assess historical testimony, and the general presumptions that make it possible for us to construe leftovers from the past as historical evidence, are such that the possibility of establishing, on purely historical grounds, that some genuinely miraculous event has occurred is ruled out."

When examining artifacts from the past, historians assume that nature worked back then as it does today; otherwise, anything goes. American patriot Thomas Paine, in *The Age of Reason,* asked: "Is it more probable that nature should go out of her course, or that a man should tell a lie? We have never seen, in our time, nature go out of her course; but we have good reason to believe that millions of lies have been told in the same time; it is, therefore, at least millions to one, that the reporter of a miracle tells a lie."

It is a fact of history and of current events that human beings exaggerate, misinterpret, or wrongly remember events. They have also fabricated pious fraud. Most believers in a religion understand this when examining the claims of *other* religions.

A messiah figure coming back to life—appearing out of thin air and disappearing—is a fantastic story, by anyone's standard, and that is what gives it its punch. If dead people today routinely crawled out of their graves and went back to work, a resurrection would have little value as proof of God's power. The fact that it is impossible or highly unlikely is what makes it a miracle.

And that is what removes it from the reach of history.

History is limited; it can only confirm events that conform to natural regularity. This is not an anti-supernaturalistic bias against miracles, as is sometimes claimed by believers. The miracles may have happened, but in order to *know* they happened, we need a different tool of knowledge. Yet except for faith (which is not a science), to make a case for the resurrection of Jesus, history is the only tool Christians have.

Examining a miracle with history is like searching for a planet with a microscope.

David Hume wrote: "No testimony is sufficient to establish a miracle unless that testimony be of such a kind that its falsehood would be more miraculous than the fact which it endeavours to establish."[8] Carl Sagan liked to say, "Extraordinary claims require extraordinary evidence." Such evidence is exactly what we *do not* have with the resurrection of Jesus.

At best (or worst), this should convince us not that the resurrection is disproved, but that disbelief in the resurrection is rationally justified. The incompatibility of miracles with the historical method is persuasive, especially to those not committed a priori to the truth of religious scripture, but we still need something more than this if we are to say with confidence that the bodily resurrection did not happen.

_DID JESUS EXIST?

A small number of scholars,[9] known informally as "mythicists," insist there is no convincing evidence for an historical Jesus at all. If the entire story is a myth, then he could hardly have risen from the dead.

The life of Jesus is not corroborated. Not a single word about Jesus appears outside of the New Testament in the entire first century, even though many writers documented first-hand the early Roman Empire in great detail, including careful accounts of the time and place where Jesus supposedly taught.[10] The little paragraph about Jesus that appears in Josephus' Antiquities (written after 90 CE) is regarded by liberal and conservative scholars to have been either entirely interpolated or drastically altered by a later generation of believers, probably by the dishonest Christian historian Eusebius in the fourth century.[11] (Whichever view is right, they both agree that early Christians tampered with documents, a fact that must bear on the reliability of the New Testament writings.)

The handful of second-century references to "Christ" is too late to be of much value.[12] They are brief second- or third-hand accounts of what some people by that time believed had happened in their distant past, and none of them mentions the name "Jesus." They are hearsay, not history.

The silence of Paul is also a problem. Paul wrote his letters many years before the Gospels, and it appears he was unaware of anything said in them about Jesus, except for some wording from a Last Supper ritual. Paul never met Jesus and never quoted the Jesus of the Gospels, even when that would have served his purposes. He sometimes disagreed with Jesus.[13] He never mentioned a single deed or miracle of Jesus. If Jesus had been a real person, certainly Paul, his main cheerleader, would have talked about him as a man. The "Christ" in Paul's epistles is mainly a supernatural figure, not a flesh and blood man of history.[14]

Mythicists notice that there are many pagan parallels to the resurrection story. The Greek god Dionysus was said to be the "Son of Zeus." He was killed, buried, and rose from the dead and now sits at the right hand of the father. His empty tomb at Delphi was long preserved and venerated by believers. The Egyptian Osiris, two millennia earlier, was said to have been slain by Typhon, to have risen again, and to have become ruler of the dead. Adonis and Attis also suffered and died to rise again.

The Persian god Mithra, revered by many Romans, was said to have been born of a virgin in a sacred birth-cave of the Rock on December 25, witnessed by shepherds and Magi bringing gifts. He raised the dead, healed the sick, made the blind see and the lame walk, and exorcised devils. Mithra celebrated a Last Supper with his twelve disciples before he died. His image was buried in a rock tomb, but it was withdrawn and he was said to live again. His triumph and ascension to heaven were celebrated at the spring equinox (Easter).[15]

Anybody who was anybody in those days was born of a virgin and ascended to heaven. The Roman historian Suetonius—whose brief second-century mention of "Chrestus" in Rome is sometimes offered as evidence of an historical Jesus (though few believe Jesus visited Rome, and "Chrestus" is not "Jesus")—also reported that Caesar Augustus bodily ascended into heaven when he died.[16]

Christianity appears to have been cut from the same fabric as pagan mythology, and some early Christians admitted it. Arguing with pagans around 150 CE, Justin Martyr said: "When we say that the Word, who is the first born of God, was produced without sexual union, and that he, Jesus Christ, our teacher, was crucified and died, and rose again, and ascended into heaven; we propound nothing different from what you believe regarding those whom you esteem sons of Jupiter [Zeus]."[17]

If early Christians, who were closer to the events than we are, said the story of Jesus is "nothing different" from paganism, can modern skeptics be faulted for suspecting the same thing?

Critics are not agreed on the degree of relevance of the pagan parallels to Jesus, and the number of true mythicists is a tiny minority among scholars, but it doesn't matter much. Even if Jesus did exist, that does not mean he rose from the dead.

The Jesus of history is not the Jesus of the New Testament. Many skeptics believe there might have existed a self-proclaimed messiah figure named Yeshua (there were many others[18]) on whom the later New Testament legend was loosely based, but they consider the exaggerated, miracle-working, resurrecting Jesus character to be a literary creation of a later generation of believers. The Gospels, written many decades after the fact, are a blend of fact and fantasy—historical fiction—and although the proportions of the blend may differ from scholar to scholar, no credible historians take them at 100 percent face value.

_NATURALISTIC EXPLANATIONS

Some critics have offered naturalistic explanations for the New Testament stories of the empty tomb. Maybe Jesus didn't actually die on the cross; he just passed out and woke up later—the "swoon theory."[19] Or perhaps the disciples hallucinated the risen Jesus. (They and "five hundred" others.) Or Mary went to the wrong tomb, finding it empty, mistaking

THE PERSIAN GOD MITHRA, REVERED BY MANY ROMANS, WAS SAID TO HAVE BEEN BORN OF A VIRGIN IN A SACRED BIRTH-CAVE OF THE ROCK ON DECEMBER 25, WITNESSED BY SHEPHERDS AND MAGI BRINGING GIFTS.

the "young man" for an angel. Or perhaps the body was stolen—the "conspiracy theory," an idea that boasts a hint of biblical support in that the only eyewitnesses (the Roman soldiers) said that that was exactly what happened.[20] Or perhaps Jesus' body was only temporarily stored in the tomb of Joseph of Arimathea (possibly with the two thieves) and was later reburied in a common grave, the usual fate of executed criminals.[21]

▌ "WHY HAVE *YOU* RULED OUT THE *NATURAL*?"

These hypotheses have various degrees of plausibility. In my opinion, none of them seems overly likely, but they are at *least* as credible as a corpse coming back to life, and they fit the biblical facts.

If a believer asks, "Why have you ruled out the supernatural?" I will say I have not ruled it out: I have simply given it the low probability it deserves along with the other possibilities. I might equally ask them, "Why have *you* ruled out the *natural?*"

The problem I have with some of the natural explanations is that they give the text too much credit. They tend to require almost as much faith as the orthodox interpretation. Combined with the historical objection and the mythicists' arguments (above), the existence of a number of plausible natural alternatives can bolster the confidence of skeptics, but it can't *positively* disprove the bodily resurrection of Jesus.

_INTERNAL DISCREPANCIES

The resurrection of Jesus is one of the few stories that is told repeatedly in the Bible—more than five times—so it provides an excellent test for the orthodox claim of scriptural inerrancy and reliability. When we compare the accounts, we see that they don't agree. (All of the following quotes are taken from the King James Version, unless otherwise noted.)

What time did the women visit the tomb?
Matthew: "as it began to dawn" (28:1)
Mark: "very early in the morning…at the rising of the sun" (16:2); "when the sun had risen" (New Revised Standard Version); "just after sunrise" (New International Version)
Luke: "very early in the morning" (24:1) "at early dawn" (New Revised Standard Version)
John: "when it was yet dark" (20:1)

Who were the women?
Matthew: Mary Magdalene and "the other Mary" (28:1)
Mark: Mary Magdalene, "the mother of James," and Salome (16:1)
Luke: Mary Magdalene, Joanna, "Mary the mother of James, and other women" (24:10)
John: Mary Magdalene (20:1)

What was their purpose?
Matthew: To see the tomb (28:1)
Mark: Had already seen the tomb (15:47), brought spices (16:1)
Luke: Had already seen the tomb (23:55), brought spices (24:1)

John: The body had already been spiced before they arrived (19:39,40)

Was the tomb open when they arrived?
Matthew: No (28:2)
Mark: Yes (16:4)
Luke: Yes (24:2)
John: Yes (20:1)

Who was at the tomb when they arrived?
Matthew: One angel (28:2-7)
Mark: One "young man" (16:5)
Luke: Two men (24:4)
John: Two angels (20:12)

Where were these messengers situated?
Matthew: Angel sitting on the stone (28:2)
Mark: Young man sitting inside, on the right (16:5)
Luke: Two men standing inside (24:4)
John: Two angels sitting on each end of the bed (20:12)

What did the messenger(s) say?
Matthew: "Fear not ye: for I know that ye seek Jesus, which was crucified. He is not here for he is risen, as he said. Come, see the place where the Lord lay. And go quickly, and tell his disciples that he is risen from the dead: and, behold, he goeth before you into Galilee; there shall ye see him: lo, I have told you." (28:5-7)
Mark: "Be not afrighted: Ye seek Jesus of Nazareth, which was crucified: he is risen; he is not here: behold the place where they laid him. But go your way, tell his disciples and Peter that he goeth before you into Galilee: there shall ye see him, as he said unto you." (16:6-7)
Luke: "Why seek ye the living among the dead? He is not here, but is risen: remember how he spake unto you when he was yet in Galilee, Saying, The Son of man must be delivered into the hands of sinful men, and be crucified, and the third day rise again." (24:5-7)
John: "Woman, why weepest thou?" (20:13)

Did the women tell what happened?
Matthew: Yes (28:8)
Mark: No. "Neither said they any thing to any man." (16:8)
Luke: Yes. "And they returned from the tomb and told all these things to the eleven, and to all the rest." (24:9, 22-24)
John: Yes (20:18)

When Mary returned from the tomb, did she know Jesus had been resurrected?
Matthew: Yes (28:7-8)
Mark: Yes (16:10,11)
Luke: Yes (24:6-9,23)
John: No (20:2)

When did Mary first see Jesus?
Matthew: Before she returned to the disciples (28:9)
Mark: Before she returned to the disciples (16:9,10)
John: After she returned to the disciples (20:2,14)

Could Jesus be touched after the resurrection?
Matthew: Yes (28:9)
John: No (20:17), Yes (20:27)

After the women, to whom did Jesus first appear?
Matthew: Eleven disciples (28:16)
Mark: Two disciples in the country, later to eleven (16:12,14)
Luke: Two disciples in Emmaus, later to eleven (24:13,36)
John: Ten disciples (Judas and Thomas were absent) (20:19, 24)
Paul: First to Cephas (Peter), then to the twelve (Twelve? Judas was dead.) (I Corinthians 15:5)

Where did Jesus first appear to the disciples?
Matthew: On a mountain in Galilee (60-100 miles away) (28:16-17)
Mark: To two in the country, to eleven "as they sat at meat" (16:12,14)
Luke: In Emmaus (about seven miles away) at evening, to the rest in a room in Jerusalem later that night (24:31, 36)
John: In a room, at evening (20:19)

Did the disciples believe the two men?
Mark: No (16:13)
Luke: Yes (24:34—it is the group speaking here, not the two)

What happened at that first appearance?
Matthew: Disciples worshipped, some doubted; Jesus said: "Go ye therefore, and teach all nations…" (28:17-20)
Mark: Jesus reprimanded them, said: "Go ye into all the world, and preach the gospel to every creature." (16:14-19)
Luke: Christ incognito, vanishing act, materialized out of thin air, reprimand, supper (24:13-51)
John: Passed through solid door, disciples happy, Jesus blesses them, no reprimand (21:19-23)

Did Jesus stay on earth for more than a day?
Mark: No (16:19). Compare 16:14 with John 20:19 to show that this was all done on Sunday
Luke: No (24:50-52). It all happened on Sunday
John: Yes, at least eight days (20:26, 21:1-22)
Acts: Yes, at least 40 days (1:3)

Where did the ascension take place?
Matthew: No ascension; book ends on mountain in Galilee
Mark: In or near Jerusalem, after supper (16:19)
Luke: In Bethany, very close to Jerusalem, after supper (24:50-51)
John: No ascension
Paul: No ascension
Acts: Ascended from Mount of Olives (1:9-12)

It is not just atheist critics who notice these problems. Christian scholars agree that the stories are discrepant. Culver H. Nelson: "In any such reading, it should become glaringly obvious that these materials often contradict one another egregiously. No matter how eagerly one may wish to do so, there is simply no way the various accounts of Jesus' post-mortem activities can be harmonized."[22]

E. Harvey: "All the Gospels, after having run closely together in their accounts of the trial and execution, diverge markedly when they come to the circumstance of the Resurrection. It's impossible to fit their accounts together into a single coherent scheme."[23] Thomas Sheehan agrees: "Despite our best efforts, the Gospel accounts of Jesus' post-mortem activities, in fact, cannot be harmonized into a consistent Easter chronology."[24]

IT IS NOT JUST ATHEIST CRITICS WHO NOTICE THESE PROBLEMS. CHRISTIAN SCHOLARS AGREE THAT THE STORIES ARE DISCREPANT.

The religiously independent (though primarily Christian) scholars in the Westar Institute, which includes more than 70 Bible scholars with a Ph.D or an equivalent, conclude: "The five gospels that report appearances (Matthew, Luke, John, Peter, Gospel of the Hebrews) go their separate ways when they are not rewriting Mark; their reports cannot be reconciled to each other. Hard historical evidence is sparse."[25]

I have challenged believers to provide a simple, non-contradictory, chronological narrative of the events between Easter Sunday and the ascension, without omitting a single biblical detail.[26] So far, without misinterpreting words or drastically rearranging passages, no one has given a coherent account. Some have offered "harmonies" (apparently not wondering why the work of a perfect deity should have to be harmonized), but none have met the reasonable request to simply tell the story.

_LEGEND

Urging us to consider who Jesus was, Christian apologist Josh McDowell offers three choices: "Liar, Lunatic, or Lord."[27] But this completely ignores a fourth option: "Legend." If the Jesus character is to some degree, if not completely, a literary creation, then it was others who put words in his mouth and it is grossly simplistic to take them at face value.

A legend begins with a basic story (true or false) that grows into something more embellished and exaggerated as the years pass. When we look at the documents of the resurrection of Jesus, we see that the earliest accounts are very simple, later retellings are more complex, and the latest tales are fantastic. In other words, they look exactly like a legend.

The documents that contain a resurrection story[28] are usually dated like this:

Paul:	50-55	(I Corinthians 15:3-8)
Gospel of Mark:	70	(Mark 16)
Gospel of Matthew:	80	(Matthew 28)
Gospel of Luke:	85	(Luke 24, also Acts 1:3-12)
Gospel of Peter:	85-90	(Fragment)
Gospel of John:	95	(John 20-21)

This is the general dating agreed upon by most scholars, including the Westar Institute. Some conservative scholars prefer to date them earlier, and others have moved some of them later, but this would not change the *order* of the writing,[29] which is more important than the actual dates when considering legendary growth. Shifting the dates changes the shape but not the fact of the growth curve.

I made a list of things I consider "extraordinary" (natural and supernatural) in the stories between the crucifixion and ascension of Jesus: earthquakes, angel(s), the rolling stone, dead bodies crawling from Jerusalem graves ("Halloween"[30]), Jesus appearing out of thin air ("Now you see him") and disappearing ("Now you don't"), the "fish story" miracle,[31] Peter's noncanonical "extravaganza" exit from the tomb (see below), a giant Jesus with head in the clouds, a talking cross, and a bodily ascension into heaven. Perhaps others would choose a slightly different list, but I'm certain it would include most of the same.

Then I counted the number of extraordinary events that appear in each account:

Writer	Extraordinary events
Paul	0
Mark	1
Matthew	4
Luke	5
Peter	6
John	8+

Putting these on a time graph produces the accompanying illustration.[32] Notice that the curve goes up as the years pass. The later resurrection reports contain more extraordinary events than the earlier ones, so it is clear that the story, at least in the telling, has evolved and expanded over time.

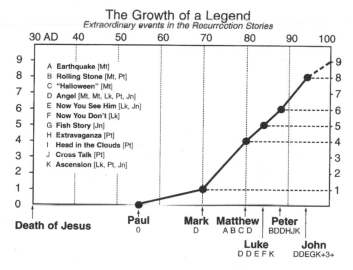

The Growth of a Legend
Extraordinary events in the Resurrection Stories

A Earthquake [Mt]
B Rolling Stone [Mt, Pt]
C "Halloween" [Mt]
D Angel [Mt, Mt, Lk, Pt, Jn]
E Now You See Him [Lk, Jn]
F Now You Don't [Lk]
G Fish Story [Jn]
H Extravaganza [Pt]
I Head in the Clouds [Pt]
J Cross Talk [Pt]
K Ascension [Lk, Pt, Jn]

Death of Jesus

Paul 0
Mark D
Matthew A B C D
Luke D D E F K
Peter B D D H J K
John D D E G K+3+

In finer detail, we can count the number of messengers at the tomb, which also grows over time, as well as the certainty of the claim that they were angels:

Paul	0 angels
Mark	1 young man, sitting
Matthew	1 angel, sitting
Luke	2 men, standing
Peter	2 men/angels, walking
John	2 angels, sitting

Other items fit the pattern. Bodily appearances are absent from the first two accounts, but show up in the last four accounts, starting in the year 80. The bodily ascension is absent from the first three stories, but appears in the last three, starting in the year 85.

This reveals the footprints of legend.

The mistake many modern Christians make is to view 30 CE backward through the distorted lens of 80-100 CE, more than a half century later. They forcibly superimpose the extraordinary tales of the late Gospels anachronistically upon the plainer views of the first Christians, pretending naively that all Christians believed exactly the same thing across the entire first century.

_PAUL'S ACCOUNT (YEAR 55)

How can we say that Paul reported no extraordinary events? Doesn't his account include an empty tomb and appearances of a dead man? Here is what Paul said in I Corinthians 15:3-8, around the year 55, the earliest written account of the resurrection:

"For I delivered unto you first of all that which I also received, how that

> Christ died for our sins
> in accordance with the Scriptures,
> and was **buried** [etaphe].
> And he was **raised** [egeiro] on the third day
> in accordance with the Scriptures
> and he **appeared** [ophthe] to Cephas [Peter]
> and then to the twelve.
> Afterward, he **appeared** to more than 500 brethren,
> most of whom are still alive,
> though some have fallen asleep.
> Afterward he **appeared** to James,
> and then to all the missionaries [apostles].
> Last of all, as to one untimely born,
> he **appeared** also to me."

This is a formula, or hymn, in poetic style that Paul claims he "received" from a believer reciting an earlier oral tradition. He edited the end of it, obviously. Viewing this passage charitably, it is possible that it came from just a few years after Jesus lived, although notice that Paul does not call him "Jesus" here. It is interesting that one of the arguments some apologists give for the authenticity of the New Testament is that it is written in a simple narrative style, unlike the poetic style of other myths and legends—yet the very first account of the resurrection is written in a poetic "legendary" style.

THE LATER RESURRECTION REPORTS CONTAIN MORE EXTRAORDINARY EVENTS THAN THE EARLIER ONES, SO IT IS CLEAR THAT THE STORY, AT LEAST IN THE TELLING, HAS EVOLVED AND EXPANDED OVER TIME.

This letter to the Corinthians was written at least a quarter of a century after the events to people far removed from the scene—Corinth is about 1,500 miles away by land. None of the readers, many or most not even born when Jesus supposedly died, would have been able to confirm the story. They had to take Paul's word alone that there were "500 brethren" who saw Jesus alive. Who were these 500 nameless people, and why didn't they or any of the thousands who heard their stories write about it? And isn't 500 a suspiciously round number? And why didn't Jesus appear to anyone who was not part of the in-crowd of believers? In any event, what Paul actually wrote here does not support a bodily resurrection. It supports legend.

First, notice how simple it is, this earliest resurrection story. No angelic messages, no mourning women, no earthquakes, no miracles, no spectacular bodily ascension into the clouds.

IN PAUL, WE HAVE NO EMPTY TOMB, NO RESURRECTION, AND NO BODILY APPEARANCES.

Nor is there an "empty tomb." The word "buried" is the ambiguous *etaphe*, which simply means "put in a grave (*taphos*)." Although a *taphos* could be a common dirt grave (the most likely destination of executed criminals) or a stone sepulchre (such as the one owned by Joseph of Arimathea), it is important to note that this passage does not use the word "sepulchre" (*mnemeion*) that first appears in Mark's later account.

Since Paul does not mention a tomb, we can hardly conclude with confidence he was thinking of an "empty tomb." Those who think he was talking of a tomb are shoehorning Mark's Gospel back into this plain hymn.

Neither is there a "resurrection" in this passage. The word "raised" is *egeiro*, which means to "wake up" or "come to." Paul did not use the word "resurrection" (*anastasis, anistemi*) here, though he certainly knew it. *Egeiro* is used throughout the New Testament to mean something simpler. "Now it is high time to awaken [*egeiro*] out of sleep"[33] was not written to corpses. "Awake [*egeiro*] thou that sleepest, and arise [*anistemi*] from the dead, and Christ shall give thee light"[34] was also written to breathing people, so Paul obviously means something non-physical here, even with his use of "resurrect," contrasted with *egeiro* (before you get up, you have to wake up). Matthew uses *egeiro* like this: "There arose a great tempest in the sea, insomuch that the ship was covered with waves: but he was asleep. And his disciples came to him and awoke [*egeiro*] him, saying, Lord, save us: we perish."[35] No one thinks Jesus "resurrected" from a boat.

Whatever Paul may have believed happened to Jesus, he did not say that his revived body came out of a tomb. It is perfectly consistent with Christian theology to think that the *spirit* of Jesus, not his body, was awakened from the grave, as Christians today believe that the *spirit* of Grandpa has gone to heaven while his body rots in the ground.

In fact, just a few verses later, Paul confirms this: "Flesh and blood cannot inherit the kingdom of God."[36] The physical body is not important to Christian theology.

But what about the post-mortem appearances Paul relates? Don't they suggest a risen body? Actually, the word "appeared" in this passage is also ambiguous and does not require a physical presence. The word *ophthe*, from the verb *horao*, is used for both physical sight as well as spiritual visions.

For example: "And a vision appeared [*ophthe*] to Paul in the night; There stood a man of Macedonia,... And after he had seen the vision [*horama*], immediately we endeavored to go into Macedonia..."[37] No one thinks the Macedonian was standing bodily in front of Paul when he "appeared" to him.

Paul includes Peter in his list of "appearances" by Christ, yet at the Transfiguration described in Matthew we find the same word used for an "appearance" to Peter that was *not* physical: "And after six days Jesus takes Peter, James, and John his brother, and brings them up into a high mountain apart, and was transfigured before them: and his face did shine as the sun, and his raiment was white as the light. And behold there appeared [*ophthe*] Moses and Elijah talking with him."[38] Did Moses and Elijah appear *physically* to Peter? Shall we start looking for their empty tombs? This is obviously some kind of *spiritual* appearance.

Besides, if we believe Mark and Matthew, Paul's first witness to the resurrection appearances was an admitted liar. In a court of law, Peter's reliability would be seriously compromised since he had repeatedly denied knowing Jesus just a couple of days earlier, after he had promised Jesus he would be loyal.[39] Paul himself was not above using a lie if it furthered his message: "Let God be true, but every man a liar... For if the truth of God hath more abounded through my lie unto his glory; why yet am I also judged a sinner?"[40]

Paul, needing to establish credentials with his readers, tacks onto the list that Christ "appeared also to me," so if we look at the description of that event, we can see what he means. Paul claimed that he had met Jesus on the road to Damascus, but notice that Jesus did not *physically* appear to Paul there. He was knocked off his horse and blinded. How could Jesus appear physically to a blind man? Paul's men admit they did not see anyone, hearing just a voice (Acts 9:7) or not hearing a voice (Acts 22:9), take your pick.[41] This "appearance" to Paul was supposedly years after Jesus ascended into heaven, which raises a good question: Where was Jesus all those years? Was his physical body hanging around in the clouds, hovering over the road to Damascus?

Clearly, Paul did not shake hands with Jesus, yet he includes his "appearance" in the list with the others. Elsewhere Paul elaborates on his roadside encounter: "For I neither received it of man, neither was I taught it, but...when it pleased God...to reveal his Son in me, that I might preach him among the heathen, immediately I conferred not with flesh and blood."[42] Notice he does not say, "I met Jesus physically," or, "I saw Jesus"—he says God "revealed his son *in me*." This was an *inner* experience, not a face-to-face meeting. This is exactly how many modern Christians talk about their own "personal relationship" with Jesus.

All of the "appearances" in I Corinthians 15:3-8 must be viewed as psychological "spiritual experiences," not physiological encounters with a revived corpse. In Paul, we have no empty tomb, no resurrection, and no bodily appearances.

_GOSPEL OF MARK (YEAR 70)

About fifteen years later, the next account of the resurrection appears in Mark, the first Gospel, written at least 40 years after the events. Almost all adults who were alive in the year 30 were dead by then.[43] No one knows who wrote Mark—the Gospels are all anonymous, and names were formally attached to them much later, around the year 180.[44] Whoever wrote Mark is speaking from the historical perspective of a second generation of believers, not as an eyewitness.

His account of the resurrection (16:1-8) is only eight verses long. The sixteen succeeding verses that appear in some translations (with snake handling and poison drinking) were a later addition by someone else (evidence that Christian tampering began early).

Mark's story is more elaborate than Paul's, but still very simple, almost blunt. If we consider the young man at the sepulchre "clothed in a long white garment" to be an angel, then we have one extraordinary event. Just one.

There are no earthquakes, no post-mortem appearances, and no ascension. In fact, there is *no belief* in the resurrection, and no preaching of a risen Christ. The book ends with the women running away: "...neither said they any thing to any man; for they were afraid," a rather limp finish considering the supposed import of the event.

Notice that the young man says that "he is risen [*egeiro*]." Like Paul, he avoids the word "resurrection."

_GOSPEL OF MATTHEW (YEAR 80)

In Matthew, a half century after the events, we finally get some of the fantastic stories of which modern Christians are so fond. The earthquake, the rolling stone, and the "Halloween" story appear for the first (and only) time. We also have a *bona fide* angel and post-mortem appearances.

_GOSPEL OF LUKE (YEAR 85)

Matthew and Luke were based to some degree on Mark, but they each added their own wrinkles. In Luke we have the "now you see him, now you don't" appearance and disappearance of Jesus, and a bodily ascension. We also have two angels, if we consider the men "in shining garments" to be angels.

_GOSPEL OF PETER (YEAR 85)

This is a fragment of an extracanonical Gospel—purportedly authored by Simon Peter (which means it was composed by a creative Christian)—that begins in the middle of what appears to be a resurrection story. The dating is controversial, but it certainly was composed no earlier than the 80s.

A crowd from Jerusalem visited the sealed tomb on the sabbath. On Easter morning, the soldiers observed the actual resurrection after the stone rolled by itself away from the entrance (no earthquake). In an extravaganza of light, two young men descended from the sky and went inside the tomb; then the two men whose heads reached to the sky carried out a third man who was taller, followed by a cross. A voice from heaven asked, "Have you preached to those who sleep?" and the cross answered, "Yes!" Then someone else entered the tomb. Later the women found a young man inside saying something similar to what was said in Mark. "Then the women fled in fear."

This is fantastic stuff.

HOW DID THE DISCIPLES SURVIVE THE PERSECUTION AND TORTURE TO LIVE LONG ENOUGH TO WRITE THOSE BOOKS?

_GOSPEL OF JOHN (YEAR 90-95)

The last of the canonical Gospels appears to be mainly independent of the others in style and content, which is why Mark, Matthew, and Luke, but not John, are called the "synoptic Gospels." John's resurrection story has real angels, bodily appearances (including a "now you see him" manifestation through shut doors), the "fish story" miracle, and an ascension.

The anonymous writer ends his Gospel with the claim that there were "many other things which Jesus did, the which, if they should be written every one, I suppose that even the world itself could not contain the books that should be written."[45] John is obviously exaggerating, but this is no surprise since he admits that his agenda is not simply to tell the facts: "And many other signs truly did Jesus in the presence of his disciples, which are not written in this book: But these are written, that ye might believe that Jesus is the Christ, the Son of God; and that believing ye might have life through his name."[46] This is not the work of an historian; it is propaganda: "that you might believe." Authors like this should be read with a grain of salt.

_DID THE DISCIPLES DIE FOR A LIE?

We often hear that the resurrection *must* have happened because the disciples were so confident that they endured torture and death for their faith (though there is no first-century evidence for this claim). But think about this. The Gospels were written between the years 70 and 100. Assume, charitably, that the writers were the actual disciples and that they were young men when they knew Jesus, perhaps 20 years old. (Matthew the tax collector and Luke the physician were perhaps older.) The life expectancy in that century was 45 years,[47] so people in their 60s would have been *ancient*. (As recently as the 1900 US Census, people 55 and older were counted as "elderly.") Mark would have been 65, Matthew at least 70, Luke at least 75, and John almost 90 when they sat down to write.

How did the disciples survive the persecution and torture to live long enough to write those books? Being martyred is no way to double your life expectancy. It makes more sense to think those anonymous documents were composed by a later generation of believers. They were not eyewitnesses.

_WHY DO SO MANY BELIEVE IN THE RESURRECTION?

In any open question, we should argue from what we do know to what we do not know. We do know that fervent legends and stubborn myths arise easily, naturally. We do not know that dead people rise from the grave. We do know that human memory is imperfect. We do not know that angels exist.

Some Christians argue that the period of time between the events and the writing was too short for a legend to have evolved; but we know this is not true. The 1981 legend of the Virgin Mary appearance at Medjugorje spread across Yugoslavia in just *two days,* confirmed by repeated corroborative testimony of real witnesses who are still alive. The place was visited almost immediately by international pilgrims, some claiming they were healed at the spot. Yet few Protestants believe the story. Shall we start looking for the empty tomb of Mary?

The legend of Elian Gonzales, the young Cuban refugee who was rescued off the coast of Florida in 1999, developed in a couple of weeks into an organized cult, complete with claims that he was the "Cuban Messiah" who would set his oppressed people free from the Castro Devil, sightings of the Virgin Mary in downtown Miami, tales of his protection by angels and dolphins (actually dolphin fish).

The extraordinary nineteenth-century stories of Mormon founder Joseph Smith were accepted as gospel fact within a few short years.

There was plenty of time for the legend of the resurrection of Jesus to evolve.

We do know that people regularly see deceased relatives and friends in dreams and visions. My own grandmother swore to me that she regularly saw my dead grandfather entering the house, smiling and waving at her, often accompanied by other dead relatives, opening and closing drawers. Should I have dug up my grandfather's grave to prove she was only dreaming or hallucinating in her grief? Would that have made any difference?

JESUS' EMPTY TOMB WAS NEVER VENERATED BY EARLY CHRISTIANS, WHICH IS ANOTHER PIECE OF EVIDENCE THAT IT DID NOT EXIST.

Yet some Christians insist that is exactly what would have happened if the story of Jesus were false. If the tomb were not empty, detractors could have easily silenced the rumors by producing the body. But this assumes that they cared enough to do such a thing—they didn't do it when Herod heard rumors that John the Baptist had been raised from the dead.[48] It was a crime to rob a grave, and who would have known where to find it? (Jesus' empty tomb was never venerated by early Christians, which is another piece of evidence that it did not exist.)

Also, it was at least seven weeks after the burial before the resurrection was first preached during Pentecost. By the time anyone might have cared to squelch the story, two or three months would have passed, and what happens to a dead body in that climate for that period of time? The body of Lazarus was "stinking" after only four days.[49] If someone had had the gumption to locate and illegally dig up the decayed body of Jesus and parade it through the streets, would the disciples have believed the unrecognizable rotting skeleton was really their Lord and Savior? I don't think so, any more than my grandmother would have been convinced she was deluded.

During one of my debates, Greg Boyd offered the simple argument that the resurrection *must* have happened because otherwise we have no explanation for the birth and tremendous growth of the Christian Church. Where there's smoke, there's fire, he insisted. But this argument can be equally applied to the "smoke" of other religions, such as Islam, with hundreds of millions of good people believing that the illiterate Muhammad miraculously wrote the Koran.

It can be applied to the "smoke" of Mormonism, with millions of moral and intelligent individuals believing the angel Moroni gave Joseph Smith gold tablets inscribed with the Book of Mormon. "Why should non-Mormons find the story hard to believe?" Robert J. Miller asks. "After all, it is no more plausible than dozens of stories in the Bible (for example, Jonah and the whale) that many Christians believe with no difficulty at all. The difference has very little to do with the stories themselves and a great deal to do with whether one approaches them as an insider or an outsider. Putting it a bit crudely perhaps, stories about *our* miracles are easy to believe because they're true; stories about *their* miracles are easy to dismiss because they're far-fetched and fictitious."[50]

It could also be applied to the Moonies, Jehovah's Witnesses, and many other successful religious movements. If smoke is evidence of fire, are they all true?

_SO WHAT DID HAPPEN?

If the story is not true, then how did it originate? We don't really know, but we can make some good guesses, based on what happened with other legends and religious movements, and what we know about human nature.

Assuming that the New Testament is somewhat reliable, Robert Price offers one sensible scenario. Peter's state of mind is the key. The disciples had expected Jesus to set up a kingdom on earth, but this did not happen. He was killed. They then expected Jesus to return, and this did not happen. Nothing was going right, and this created a cognitive dissonance. Peter, who had promised loyalty to Jesus and then denied him publicly a few hours before the crucifixion, must have been feeling horrible. (The day after "Good Friday" is called "Black Sabbath," the day the disciples were in mourning and shock.)

Imagine you had a horrible argument with a spouse or loved one where you said some unpleasant things you later regretted, but before you had a chance to apologize and make up, the person died. Picture your state of mind: grief, regret, shock, embarrassment, sadness, a desperate wish to bring the person back and make things right. That's how Peter must have felt.

Believing in God and the survival of the soul, Peter prays to Jesus: "I'm sorry. Forgive me." (Or something like that.) Then Peter gets an answer: "I'm here. I forgive you." (Or something like that.) Then Peter triumphantly tells his friends, "I talked with Jesus! He is not dead! I am forgiven," and his friends say, "Peter talked with Jesus? Peter met Jesus? He's alive! It's a *spiritual* kingdom!" (Or something like that.) Paul then lists Peter as the first person to whom Christ "appeared."

We don't need to know exactly what happened, only that things like this do happen. Look at the nineteenth-century Millerites, who evolved into the Seventh Day Adventists when the world did not end as they had predicted. Or the Jehovah's Witnesses, whose church rebounded after the failed prophecies of Charles Russell and Joseph Rutherford that the world would end in 1914, oops, they meant 1925. (They got creative and said Jesus actually returned to earth "spiritually.")

IF JESUS PHYSICALLY LEVITATED INTO THE SKY, WHERE IS HIS BODY NOW? DOES HE SOMETIMES NEED A HAIRCUT?

Robert Price elaborates: "When a group has staked everything on a religious belief, and 'burned their bridges behind them,' only to find this belief disconfirmed by events, they may find disillusionment too painful to endure. They soon come up with some explanatory rationalization, the plausibility of which will be reinforced by the mutual encouragement of fellow-believers in the group. In order to increase further the plausibility of their threatened belief, they may engage in a massive new effort at proselytizing. The more people who can be convinced, the truer it will seem. In the final analysis, then, a radical disconfirmation of belief may be just what a religious movement needs to get off the ground."[51]

There have been other plausible scenarios explaining the origin of the legend, but we don't need to describe them all. The fact that they exist shows that the historicity of the bodily resurrection of Jesus cannot be taken as a given.

_THE LEGEND IDEA IS RESPECTFUL

It is respectful of the humanity of the early Christians.

We do know that the human race possesses an immense propensity to create, believe, and propagate falsehood. So, what makes the early Christians exempt? Weren't they just people? Did they never make mistakes? Were they so superhuman that they always resisted the temptations of exaggeration and rhetoric? Did they have perfect memories? Given the discrepancies in their accounts, why not treat those early believers like ourselves, not as cartoon characters, but as real human beings with normal human fears, desires, and limitations? The fact that my grandmother was hallucinating did not make me love or respect her any less.

The legend idea is respectful of the historical method. We are not required to jettison natural regularity that makes history work. We can take the New Testament accounts as reports of what people sincerely *believed* to be true, not what is necessarily true. We can honor the question, "Do you believe everything you read?"

The legend idea is respectful of theology. If Jesus bodily ascended into physical clouds, then we are presented with a spatially limited flat-earth God sitting on a material throne of human size, with a right and left hand. If Jesus physically levitated into the sky, where is his body now? Does he sometimes need a haircut? If the bodily resurrection is viewed as a legendary embellishment, then believers are free to view their god as a boundless spiritual being, not defined in human dimensions as the pagan gods were.

Bible scholars conclude: "On the basis of a close analysis of all the resurrection reports, [we] decided that the resurrection of Jesus was not perceived initially to depend on what happened to his body. The body of Jesus probably decayed as do all corpses. The resurrection of Jesus was not an event that happened on the first Easter Sunday; it was not an event that could have been captured by a video camera.... [We] conclude that it does not seem necessary for Christians to believe the literal veracity of any of the later appearance narratives."[52]

Finally, the legend idea is respectful of the freedom to believe. If the resurrection of Jesus were proved as a blunt fact of history, then we would have no choice, no room for faith. You can't have the freedom to believe if you do not have the freedom *not* to believe.

Endnotes

1. Barker, Dan. *Losing Faith In Faith: From Preacher to Atheist.* Madison, WI: FFRF, Inc., 1992. **2.** I Corinthians 15:17. **3.** Barker, Dan. "His Fleece Was White As Snow." Manna Music, Inc., 1978. **4.** Including the Westar Institute, Santa Rosa, California, with 70+ Bible scholars and many books and publications. **5.** *Daily Telegraph* (London), 31 July 2002. **6.** Barna Research. "Americans' Bible Knowledge Is in the Ballpark, But Often off Base." www.barna.org, 12 July 2000. **7.** Habermas, Gary R., and Antony G. N. Flew. *Did Jesus Rise from the Dead? The Resurrection Debate.* Ed. by Terry L. Miethe. San Francisco: Harper & Row, 1987. Flew's remarks were inspired by David Hume's *First Enquiry.* **8.** Hume, David. 'Of Miracles,' pp.115-6. **9.** Including John Allegro, G.A. Wells, and Michael Martin (who leans towards Wells' view), and others. **10.** Philo of Alexandria (20 BCE-50 CE) wrote in careful detail about that region in that period of history. So did Justus of Tiberius and 40 other historians. **11.** See: Carrier, Richard. "The Formation of the New Testament Canon." <www.infidels.org/library/modern/ richard_carrier/NTcanon.html>, especially note 6. **12.** Including Suetonius, *Twelve Caesars,* 112 CE; Pliny the Younger, 112 CE; Tacitus, *Annals,* 117 CE, and scattered other references to a "wise king" or "hymn to Christ." **13.** For example, Jesus allowed for divorce (Matthew 5:31-32), while Paul did not (I Corinthians 7:10-11). **14.** Albert Schweitzer wrote: "There is nothing more negative than the result of the critical study of the life of Jesus.... The historical Jesus will be to our time a stranger and an enigma." Schweitzer, Albert. *The Quest of the Historical Jesus,* Macmillan, 1954. **15.** See: Walker, Barbara. *The Woman's Encyclopedia of Myths and Secrets.* Harper San Francisco, 1983: 663-5. **16.** *Twelve Caesars,* 112 CE. Here is all he said. The emperor Claudius "banished the Jews from Rome, since they had made a commotion because of Chrestus," and during the time of Nero "punishments were also inflicted on the Christians, a sect professing a new and mischievous religious belief." **17.** First Apology, ch. xxi. **18.** There was a Judas the Christ, a Theudas the Christ, and an Egyptian Jew Messiah, among others. **19.** See for example: Schonfield, Hugh. *The Passover Plot: A New Interpretation of the Life and Death of Jesus.* Bernard Geis Associates, 1965. **20.** Matthew 28:11-15. **21.** See: Lowder, Jeffery Jay. "Historical Evidence and the Empty Tomb Story: A Reply to William Lane Craig." <www.infidels.org/library/modern/jeff_lowder/empty.html>. **22.** Culver H. Nelson was Founding minister of the Church of the Beatitudes, Phoenix, Arizona. **23.** *New English Bible Companion to the New Testament.* Oxford University Press, 1988. **24.** Sheehan, Thomas. *The First Coming: How the Kingdom of God Became Christianity.* Random

House, 1986: 97. **25.** Funk, Robert W. and The Jesus Seminar. (Eds.) *The Acts of Jesus: What Did Jesus Really Do?* Santa Rosa, CA: Polebridge Press, 1998. **26.** *Op cit.*, Barker, *Losing Faith*: "Leave No Stone Unturned." Also online at <www.ffrf.org /lfif/stone.html>. **27.** McDowell, Josh. *More Than a Carpenter*. Carol Stream, IL: Tyndale House, 1987. **28.** There was also an appearance story in a lost book known as the Gospel of the Hebrews, probably written in the mid second century. We find a few quotes from this book in the writings of others. The appearance story was quoted by Jerome. Since it is not a complete resurrection account, it can't be compared with the others. **29.** Except perhaps for Peter, which might have been later than John. **30.** Matthew 27:52-53. **31.** John 21:1-14. **32.** The crucifixion is put at the year 30, though it was probably in the late 20s. **33.** Romans 13:11. **34.** Ephesians 5:14. **35.** Matthew 8:24-25. **36.** I Corinthians 15:50. **37.** Acts 16:9-10. *Horama* is from the same verb as *ophthe*. **38.** Matthew 17:1-3. **39.** Matthew 26:69-75; Mark 14:66-72. **40.** Romans 3:4,7. **41.** See: Barker, Dan. "Did Paul's Men Hear a Voice?" <www.infidels.org/library/ magazines/tsr/1994/1/1voice94.html>. **42.** Galatians 1:12-16. **43.** Coale, A., and P. Demeny. *Regional Model Life Tables and Stable Populations*, 2nd ed. Academic Press, 1983. This represents statistically exact results for Third World countries in the nine-

▌THERE WAS A JUDAS THE CHRIST, A THEUDAS THE CHRIST, ▌AND AN EGYPTIAN JEW MESSIAH, AMONG OTHERS.

teenth/early twentieth century with living conditions essentially the same as those in ancient Rome. Thanks to Richard Carrier for this data. **44.** Although names of various Gospels had been loosely assigned to the books by tradition in the early and mid second century, they were first formally attached to all of them by Irenaeus in 180. **45.** John 21:25. **46.** John 20:30-31. **47.** See note 43. **48.** Matthew 14:1-2. **49.** John 11:17,39. **50.** Miller, Robert J. *The Jesus Seminar and its Critics*. Santa Rosa, CA: Polebridge Press, 1999: 134. **51.** Price, Robert M. *Beyond Born Again*. Section II: "The Evangelical Apologists: Are They Reliable?," chapter 6: "Guarding An Empty Tomb." <www.infidels.org/library/modern/robert_price/beyond_born_again/chap6.html>. See also: Festinger, Leon. *When Prophecy Fails: A Social and Psychological Study*. Harper & Row, 1964. **52.** *Op cit.*, Funk: 533.

Editor's Note: With the permission of Dan Barker, this article employs an initial capital letter for the word "Bible." Dan prefers using lowercase. He explains: "I don't normally capitalize 'bible' because there are so many bibles, and they are not all the same book, or collection of books, or translation. I do capitalize it when it is a specific named version or translation, such as the 'King James Bible.' It's like 'the dictionary,' which I don't capitalize unless it is 'Webster's Dictionary' or 'The Random House Dictionary.'" However, in sticking with grammatical convention (*not* religious convention), I have opted for the big "B."

ISLAMIC CENSORSHIP
HOW ALLAH HAS NIPPED YOUR RIGHT TO KNOW
HOWARD BLOOM

Ever since October 18, 1899, when the American Anti-Imperialist League declared that "the subjugation of any people is 'criminal aggression,'" we've heard valid and disturbing complaints about how badly Western imperialism has damaged the nations of Africa, Asia, and South America. But imagine what life would have been like in the West if the tables of imperialism had been turned on us.

Suppose that Europe had been invaded by a power infinitely stronger than that of any piddling Euro-king in, let's say, 711 AD. Imagine that the armies of the imperialist invaders were so strong that they eventually overran the known earth, taking India, Russia, parts of China, Central Asia, Indonesia, Malaysia, and a slab of Africa as large as a daisy chain of Australias. Imagine that these international aggressors were determined to convert people to a more "advanced" way of life. Imagine that they used the persuaders of swords, gunpowder, and the biggest cannons this planet had ever seen. Imagine that the Mediterranean Sea was turned by navies of their New World Order to a pool of war for a millennium or more. Imagine that Spain, Portugal, Malta, Sicily, and the Italian provinces of Piedmont, Montferrat, and Liguria had fallen, and that Narbonne, in France, had been seized. Imagine that huge swatches of Eastern Europe—including Poland, Romania, and massive pizza slices of the Balkans and the Ukraine—had been swallowed entirely. Imagine that the monolithic masters of subjugation had sailed up the river Tiber and fought their way into Rome. Imagine that the Black Sea had been set aside by these conquerors as their "private lake."

Imagine that the coasts of Italy, England, and Ireland had been raided over and over again, the men killed, the women and children snatched as slaves. Imagine that the good-looking ones had been penned up with hundreds of others from around the world to feed a decadent dictator's sexual cravings. Imagine that the European sex-slaves had included not just pretty girls, but also the attractive younger boys.

Imagine that the imperialist powers had periodically swept parts of the European landscape for white babies, tearing them from their nursing mothers' nipples and raising the infants to be cannon fodder, forced to fight ferociously for the cause of the "higher" civilization. Imagine that this enthusiasm for the subjugation of Westerners, Asians, and Far Easterners had lasted more than 1,200 years. And imagine that you were not allowed to read about it. No book on these atrocities could be published in the English language.

You would be in the dark, forming opinions without a clue about your own people's history. If the old imperialist enslaver geared up to seize you once again, you would never know that he once had held you by the throat, and that his grip had rivaled in duration the life and death of civilizations. Your ability to assess the seriousness of new threats from the seasoned nation-crusher would be profoundly crippled.

Grisly science fiction? No. Every detail of this imperialist nightmare happened. The whole scenario is true.

We flatter ourselves when we claim to have been the biggest, baddest exploiters since the Fall of the Roman Empire. Yes, the West spent 195 years on eight crusades to take a territory (the Christian "Holy Land") the size of a postage stamp. Yes, the West filled the streets of Jerusalem in 1099 with so much blood it literally welled up to the European butchers' ankles. Yes, the West briefly held 75 percent of the globe's landmass under its thumb. Yes, the West used foreign kings and queens like Kleenex to wipe its control-snorting nose. And, yes, the West killed off tens of millions of Native Americans through starvation and disease, then snatched the Middle East like a rag doll and waggled it humiliatingly for nearly 50 years.

But we are mere midgets of Empire. We spent most of the last 1,500 years cooped up in a corner by the real giants of the capture-and-colonialization game.

If you are white, you are probably descended from one of the survivors who was *not* enslaved by these champions of people-chomping. Your ancestors are among the lucky ones who dodged being kidnapped and raised as battle-bots for a foreign power. Miguel Cervantes—the author of *Don Quixote*—was not so fortunate. He lost his left hand in a war of liberation against the predators, was captured, sold into slavery, and was kept in a central holding pen for Christian prisoners of the Empire for five years. The characters in Voltaire's *Candide* were forced to brave the Mediterranean Sea when it was patrolled by war fleets whose imperial propagandists bragged that their admirals totally "mastered" these waters. Voltaire's heroine, Cunegonde, was taken as a sex slave for a ruler of the rampaging military machine. Voltaire's fiction was a mere a reflection of Europe's longstanding reality.

> IMAGINE THAT THE COASTS OF ITALY, ENGLAND, AND IRELAND HAD BEEN RAIDED OVER AND OVER AGAIN, THE MEN KILLED, THE WOMEN AND CHILDREN SNATCHED AS SLAVES.

Even the young United States became involved, storming the parasitic exploiters' naval headquarters on the shores of Tripoli. The last European lands did not slip out of the oppressors' hands until 100 years ago. And some of those lands are now being fingered by the minions of tyranny once again.

Asia has not been so fortunate. Nor has Africa. In Mauritania and the Sudan, blacks are still enslaved by the thousands every year. Huge chunks of these continents remain a part of the old Empire, an Empire breathing heavily through its mask like Darth Vader, certain that its youth will bloom again. And convinced that in the next go-round, we won't stand a chance.

Those who've waged this assault on the West are the forces of Islam.

You've heard of our despicable Crusades. They went on for less than 200 years. The holy wars of Islam have ground on for over 1,300 years—65 generations. Islam's modern historians brag to their own people about "the history of Muslim rule in Europe." The scholars' goal? "To remind the Muslim Ummah of its glorious past"— and perhaps to hint at its glorious future. On an English-language Website designed to gather Western recruits to *Jihad* <www.jamatdawa.org>, Dr. Mohsin Farooqi crows with pride about the days when Islam's troops brought "terror to the Inhabitants of Corsica, Sardinia, Pisa and Genoa," "massacred the males" of Montferrat, and "devastated the cities and villages [of England and Ireland] and carried away booty and captives." Farooqi gloats over the fact that, "The terror of Muslim invaders along the old Danube highway hung over Europe for centuries," and that, "The yoke of Tatar Government remained on the necks of Russians for two hundred and fifty years."

Some of the Muslim world's most influential twenty-first century leaders say it is the sacred duty of Allah's 400 million men to resume the Empire's blessed campaigns, to yank all nations of this Earth into a global caliphate.

■ ■ ■ ■ ■ ■ ■ ■ ■ ■

Yet this thousand-year-plus *Jihad* against the West is not in your history books. It isn't on TV. And it isn't likely to be.

There is an Islamic loophole in our freedom of speech. In the 1990s, a British historical author, Paul Fregosi, was commissioned to write a book about the Islamic crusades against Europe. By April 1997, he had nearly finished the manuscript. Then his publisher, Little, Brown (a part of the AOL Time Warner media octopus), was approached very quietly by Islamic groups. Executives in the British offices of the publishing house had visions of bombs and cut throats dancing in their heads. They did what their polite Islamic visitors demanded. Without uttering a word to the public, they cancelled Paul Fregosi's book. The leading French news agency, Agence France-Presse, was the only media outlet with the guts to cover the tale. It did so in just one brief 254-word piece, then dropped the issue entirely. As an editor at Little, Brown told Fregosi: "We've got to play the game according to Muslim rules."

My publisher—Atlantic Monthly Press—was also threatened in June 1996 because my book, *The Lucifer Principle: A Scientific Expedition Into the Forces of History*, rips off the masks disguising violence in *every* society, including the societies of Islam. Arab pressure groups asked ever so politely that *The Lucifer Principle* be withdrawn from print and that nothing that I write be published again. They offered to boycott my publisher's products—all of them— worldwide. And they backed their warning with a call for my punishment in seventeen Islamic countries.

> WE FLATTER OURSELVES WHEN WE CLAIM TO HAVE BEEN THE BIGGEST, BADDEST EXPLOITERS SINCE THE FALL OF THE ROMAN EMPIRE.

In my case, punishment merely meant condemnation as a racist throughout the Islamic world, four years of denunciation on Islamic Websites from Michigan to Pakistan, an orchestrated campaign of negative readers' reviews on Amazon.com, an international letter-writing campaign to my publisher, and an attempt to stop the purchase or use of my books in universities and other places where they've gained popularity.

But if you want to know what *real* Islamic punishment means, ask the following people:

• *Satanic Verses* author Salman Rushdie, who has been in hiding since February 1989 because of a worldwide Islamic *fatwa* calling for his death issued by the late Ayatollah Khomeini. A militant Iranian group backed up the death sentence by offering a $2.8 million reward for Rushdie's murder. Despite reports to the contrary, the *fatwa* has *not* been lifted. In 1998, the Iranian parliament declared that only Allah or the person who issued the *fatwa* can rescind it. Since Khomeini is dead and Allah ain't talking, the death sentence remains technically in effect. The parliament did say that it would do nothing to enforce the murderous decree, but the multimillion-dollar bounty remains in effect, and radical Muslim groups have continued to say that they will rub Rushdie out. He has become somewhat more visible, but he still keeps a pretty low profile and doesn't announce public appearances in advance.

• Other people who've had a hand in the *Satanic Verses*. In issuing his *fatwa*, Khomeini called for the death not only of Rushdie but also of "all involved in its publication who were aware of its content." As of September 1998, according to the BBC, the book's Japanese translator had been stabbed to death, its Italian translator was non-fatally knifed, and its Norwegian publisher survived being shot.

• Writer, poet, and doctor Taslima Nasrin, whose 1992 novel *Laffa* [*Shame*] touched off deadly riots in her native Bangladesh and triggered a Muslim death sentence on her head (she's now in hiding in Sweden). Her comments on the Koran and the treatment of women in Islam have further enraged those who wish her harm. In September 2002, a court in Bangladesh found her guilty *in absentia* of offending Muslims and sentenced her to a year in prison.

• Playwright Terence McNally, who is the victim of a *fatwa* calling for his execution should he ever enter an Islamic nation. His crime: portraying Jesus as gay in *Corpus Christi*. Since Jesus is a minor prophet in Islam, an offense unto him is now apparently grounds for a Muslim death decree.

• Nigerian journalist Isioma Daniel, who wrote a column prior to her country's scheduled hosting of the 2002 Miss World Pageant. She dared to say: "The Muslims thought it was immoral to bring 92 women to Nigeria and ask them to revel in vanity. What would Mohammed think? In all honesty, he would probably have chosen a wife from one of them." These words triggered three days of riots that claimed the lives of more than 220 people. A government official in the Nigerian state of Zamfara issued a *fatwa* declaring: "Like Salman Rushdie, the blood of Isioma Daniel can be shed. It is binding on all Muslims, wherever they are, to consider the killing of the writer as a religious duty." Daniel is now hiding in the US.

• Amal Kashua, a mother of eight, and Amir (last name unknown). These two members of Israel's Muslim minority starred in the first Israeli Arab porn film. Both of them have been severely beaten by mobs, and Kashua's family has said that they will kill her.

• Nobel Prize-winning Egyptian novelist Naguib Mahfouz, whose neck carries a knife wound meant to end his life. His novel *Children of Gebalawi* (a/k/a/ *Children of the Alley*)—which indirectly depicts Mohammed, Jesus, and Moses as members of the working class—and his defense of Salman Rushdie led to the *fatwa*.

• Pulitzer Prize-winning cartoonist Doug Marlette. The creator of the comic strip *Kudzu* and syndicated political cartoons offered an acid take on Islamic terrorism. Taking off on the What Would Jesus Drive? ad campaign (which implies that Christ wouldn't tool around in a gas-guzzling SUV), his late-December 2002 cartoon showed a man in Middle Eastern garb behind the wheel of a Ryder truck. In the back is a nuclear missile, and across the top of the panel is the text: "What Would Mohammed Drive?" The cartoon didn't run in the print edition of the *Tallahassee Democrat* (where Marlette is on staff), but it did appear briefly on the newspaper's Website before being yanked off. Muslim groups howled, and Marlette was inundated with over 4,500 emails. "They all demanded an apology," he wrote. "Quite a few threatened mutilation and death."

It is too late to get the opinions of Islamist/feminist writer Konca Kuris, who was kidnapped, tortured, and killed by Hezbollah in the Turkish town of Konya in 1998, or of Turkish secularist and newspaper columnist Ahmet Taner Kislali, who died when a bomb went off beneath the hood of his car the following year.

While Paul Fregosi's book was being stifled and mine was under attack, Simon & Schuster, part of the Viacom media goliath, withdrew a children's book because the Islamic activists demanded it. The execs at S&S say that publishing *World Religions: Great Lives* by respected historian William Jay Jacobs had been an editorial mistake. The error? An illustration of the prophet Mohammed with a sword in his hand. Said the Muslim pressure groups, the painting was defamatory. Also, the section on Mohammed opens with this paragraph:

Muhammed. The Prophet (or "Messenger of God"). During his lifetime he was a man who loved beautiful women, fine perfume, and tasty food. He took pleasure in seeing the heads of his enemies torn from their bodies by the swords of his soldiers. He hated Christians and Jews, poets and painters, and anyone who criticized him. Once he had a Jewish prisoner tortured in

order to learn the location of the man's hidden treasure. Then, having uncovered the secret, he had his victim murdered and added the dead man's wife to the collection of women in his harem.

Because of this paragraph and the painting, the entire book—which contains biographies of 32 major figures of Judaism, Christianity, Islam, and Asian religions—was recalled, and it remains out of print. Simon & Schuster sent a letter of apology to the Council on Islamic-American Relations.

Was the portrayal of Mohammed in *World Religions: Great Lives* accurate? Mohammed ordered a minimum of 27 military raids, and personally led nine of them. That information comes from one of Islam's most popular modern biographies of Mohammed, a 120-page book published in Lahore, Pakistan, by Islamic Publications Ltd and distributed worldwide, but only in Islamic bookshops. The slender volume is Sarwat Saulat's *The Life of the Prophet*. Unless you are a potential convert to Islam, this is a book that Muslims do not want you to see.

The illustration that caused Great Lives: World Religions to be destroyed
CREDIT: *Great Lives: World Religions*, Simon & Schuster

The most influential twentieth-century interpreter of the Koran, the Ayatollah Khomeini, told all Muslims who would listen that military conquest was an obligation of all Godly men...including the Prophet Mohammed. "The leaders of our religion were all soldiers, commanders, and warriors," he wrote. "They put on military dress and went into battle in the wars that are described for us in our history; they killed, and they were killed. The Commander of the Faithful himself [Mohammed] (upon whom be peace) would place a helmet on his blessed head, don his coat of chain mail, and gird on a

AS AN EDITOR AT LITTLE, BROWN TOLD FREGOSI: "WE'VE GOT TO PLAY THE GAME ACCORDING TO MUSLIM RULES."

sword." So why was Simon & Schuster forced to withdraw a children's book that showed a picture of Mohammed with his sword in his hand? Because this is one of Islam's treasured views of its founder. But you are not allowed to know it.

In the late 1990s, a cabal of globally interlinked Islamic groups devised a strategy: "offer" major publishers access to "Islamic experts" who would screen books in advance. Said the letter the Islamic groups sent to my publisher: "We…invite the Atlantic Monthly Press to consult with Muslim Americans (we can provide a list of scholars) prior to the publication of materials that deal with Muslim issues in order to avert defamation in the future." These wise men would tell publishers in advance which manuscripts should *not* be published, which books—like Simon & Schuster's children's reader—would be offensive to the Muslim community. To put it differently, these Islamic censors would ever so gently prevent you and me from peering into the everyday beliefs and rhetoric of the worldwide Islamic community.

AS OF SEPTEMBER 1998, ACCORDING TO THE BBC, THE BOOK'S JAPANESE TRANSLATOR HAD BEEN STABBED TO DEATH, ITS ITALIAN TRANSLATOR WAS NON-FATALLY KNIFED, AND ITS NORWEGIAN PUBLISHER SURVIVED BEING SHOT.

Just to let Atlantic Monthly Press know it was not alone, the letter added that the publisher would merely be falling into line with what was becoming a common practice. The letter made it abundantly clear that "other publishers" had already caved in to the pressure groups' generous offer.

Publishers are heroes who stand up for truth, right? Except when their knees buckle and they kiss the floor in fear. Every publishing house approached with the pre-censorship deal kept silent. Many of them allowed the secret censors in. The press did not know it. Even the censorship watchdogs at the Authors Guild and the American Booksellers Association, sincerely pledged to uphold freedom of the press, didn't have a clue.

I knew it only because the Islamic groups had accidentally made me an insider when they attacked me back in 1991. *Omni Magazine* had printed an early version of a chapter from *The Lucifer Principle*, the book I was writing at the time. Muslim activists disliked the fact that the piece, "The Importance of Hugging," mentioned that it is taboo in many Muslim societies for a husband and a wife to hold hands, much less kiss, in public. The article cited scientific studies and research from an Arab sociologist indicating that this lack of physical affection may be one reason Islamic societies have a tendency to produce violence. The American Arab Anti-Discrimination Committee took exception to the very notion that Islamic violence exists, and picketed *Omni*'s offices for four days and nights.

I always thought Bob Guccione, Sr., the owner of *Omni* and *Penthouse*, had guts. Heck, back in the 1960s and 1970s, Guccione had peeled the cover off of one shabby CIA plot after another—a practice that could have put him in considerable danger. But when the Muslim activists showed up in the lobby of his building, Bob Sr. ordered his staff to keep their mouths shut. When *Omni* staffers were pelted with questions from reporters, none was allowed to utter even so much as a "no comment."

When reporters called *Omni* asking for my response to the protests, my phone number was kept secret and I was told nothing. That's the way Guccione wanted it. Why did his staff follow orders? Why were they so meek? Because high-level *Omni* employees were literally shaking with terror, wondering when an Islamic bomb would turn them from yuppies to Alpo splatter.

I had no idea the protests were taking place until a six-column headline about the demonstrations hit the *New York Post*. Then Pan Am Flight 103 was downed over Lockerbie, Scotland, by an Islamic terrorist's bomb, and the protestors swiftly and silently melted away.

Since then, the Islamic activists have learned that staging noisy protests doesn't pay. The big prize comes from arriving in "diplomatic" stealth. The mere presence of Islamic representatives in a publisher's office has the effect of a visit from enforcers of a Mafia don. People will do anything the Muslim delegation asks just to stay alive. And the victims will remain silent about the deals they make to buy Muslim activists off…as silent as if their tongues had been torn out.

There's a reason for this secrecy. Big-time authors, the ones who can make a publisher rich, hate censorship and will often refuse to sign with companies that are under a censor's thumb. If it's known that a publishing company has made a pre-censorship deal, that publishing house is shamed in public by elite organizations like the Authors Guild and the writers' international anti-censorship group PEN. So Viacom's Simon & Schuster; AOL Time Warner's Little, Brown; and even my publisher, the independent Atlantic Monthly Press, do not want these authors' groups to know a thing.

This fear of being caught in the act of censorship saved my book, *The Lucifer Principle*, from the shredder. After I'd spent four frantic days trying to find allies who would help defend *Lucifer*'s right to exist, my agent, Richard Curtis, put me in touch with the Authors Guild's chief attorney. He wrote a letter to Atlantic Monthly Press explaining that the Guild would be forced to notify its members if Atlantic surrendered to the pressure groups and yanked my book. Atlantic Monthly Press was caught between two perils. On the one hand, it could risk the worldwide amputation of cash flow threatened in the letter from the Muslims, who wrote that "we intend to inform 52 countries, members of the Organization of Islamic Conference and thousands of Islamic Centers in America, Canada and Europe to boycott all Atlantic Monthly Press publications." On the other hand, it could take a chance on being shunned by the top authors in North America, Britain, and Europe.

The executives at Atlantic Monthly Press compromised. They asked me to rewrite a key chapter on Islamic violence—this time citing every gory Koranic reference by sura and verse. The facts in *The Lucifer Principle* had already been triple-checked. But when I was forced to dig deeper, the resulting rewrite, with its 358 lines of footnotes, was far more damning to militant Islam than the original.

An author can be bankrupted and have his or her health destroyed by the pressures of a court case. Even a large organization like the Jewish Anti-Defamation League can be silenced by court actions. When I was under attack, I asked for aid from the ADL. One of its top officers told me, "We can't touch this. We're already in enough trouble." He referred to a court case leveled against the ADL in America by Muslim groups in 1993. That case dragged on until February 2002. Eleven years of bills from a squad of lawyers who each charge $300 or more per hour for their services add up fast. If that case had dragged on long enough, legal costs could have bled the ADL dry. As it was, it bled the ADL into silence.

Meanwhile, in 1997, when Paul Fregosi came under attack, I tracked down his home phone number in England and called him to offer support. He seemed confused about why his book had been hailed so enthusiastically by its publisher during its early manuscript stages, then had been abruptly turned down. I told him of my own experiences with Islamic pressure groups and tried to explain the force that had been brought to bear against his publisher. It was a hard story for him to believe. I gathered the facts and wrote them up to encourage journalists at publications like the *New York Times* and *The New Republic* to come to Fregosi's defense. It turned out that the problem was worse than I had realized. Television networks and film studios were also targets of Islamic censorship. Even Disneyland would later be attacked by a Cairo meeting of Arab Foreign Ministers, who put together a committee that included "representatives of the Arab League, American Arab-Islamic organisations and Palestinians" to police Disney's depiction of Jerusalem.

IN THE LATE 1990s, A CABAL OF GLOBALLY INTERLINKED ISLAMIC GROUPS DEVISED A STRATEGY: "OFFER" MAJOR PUBLISHERS ACCESS TO "ISLAMIC EXPERTS" WHO WOULD SCREEN BOOKS IN ADVANCE.

All of the media outlets I contacted shied away from the censorship story. Only *The American Reporter*, a Website dedicated to investigative journalism, printed an article on the subject. It deemed that bit of news so important that it led the day's edition with an editorial decrying Islamic efforts to muzzle the Western press.

Paul Fregosi's book, retitled *Jihad in the West: Muslim Conquests from the 7th to the 21st Centuries*, was eventually published by a small press in Buffalo, New York, that prides itself on its crusading efforts—Paul Kurtz's Prometheus Books. Kurtz is a veteran fighter against right-wing Christian fundamentalism and pseudoscience. He's the founder and chairman of the Committee for the Scientific Investigation of Claims of the Paranormal (CSICOP), founder and chairman of the Council for Secular Humanism, and President of the International Academy of Humanism. Which makes him one of the few publishers left who enjoys a good fight...especially one against religious extremists, no matter what god they are beholden to.

By the time *Jihad in the West* was ready for distribution, Fregosi had finally come to understand what he was up against. Prometheus' Webpage dedicated to Fregosi's book contains the following quote from him: "There's an intention to censor what's going on about Islam, more so than for any other religion."

Meanwhile, the Islamic censorship campaign moved from freedom of the press to freedom of speech—the freedom to talk out loud about Islam. Brigitte Bardot, the former sex goddess of the cinema, had become an activist for animal rights. She protested in two newspaper interviews with the French daily *Le Figaro* that ritual Islamic methods of slaughter were cruel. In 1997, she was taken to court in Paris for inciting racism by a French pro-Islamic group called The Movement Against Racism and for Friendship Between People. Bardot lost the case and was fined 2,000 francs. A lawyer for The Movement Against Racism and for Friendship Between People explained her interpretation of France's "liberty, equality, and fraternity" like this: "[R]acist insult is illegal.... [T]he law on freedom of the press...prohibits insults...for books,...public speeches and also private speeches between two people or private letters." Islam has claimed the right in France to sue you for what you say in confidence to your friends.

In 2002, the Islamic movement against Western freedom of speech was still gaining momentum. During an interview with the French magazine *Lire* (which means "To Read"), French novelist Michel Houellebecq called Islam "the most stupid religion" and went on to give his opinion of the Muslim holy book: "When you read the Koran, you give up. At least the Bible is very beautiful because Jews have an extraordinary literary talent." Offensive statements? Yes. Protected by the United Nations' Universal Declaration of Human Rights guaranteeing "freedom of opinion and expression; [including the] freedom to...seek, receive and impart information and ideas through any media"? Yes. Or so you'd think.

To quote an article written by Salman Rushdie—the great veteran of Islamic censorship—in the *Washington Post*, "[T]he largest mosques in Paris and Lyon, the National Federation of French Muslims and the World Islamic League—accused [Houellebecq] of 'making a racial insult' and of 'inciting religious hatred.'" These organizations pooled their considerable funds (think "oil money") and took Houellebecq to court. Houellebecq was eventually exonerated.

As this was happening, legendary Italian journalist Oriana Fallaci was also in court. Her offense? In the months after 9/11, she had written a book—*Anger and Pride* (a/k/a *Rage and Pride*)—trying to wake the West up to the goals of the people we trivialize as "terrorists"— the Osama bin Laden-style *mujahedin*, makers of Holy War. "You don't understand," she wrote, "you don't want to understand, that for those Reverse Crusaders the West is a world to conquer and subjugate to Islam." Some of her thoughts were quite harsh, as when she says that Muslims "multiply like rats" and that "the children of Allah spend their time with their bottoms in the air, praying five times a day." Fallaci received death threats. Several groups sued to ban the publication of her book in France. When Fallaci hired a lawyer, the attorney also was threatened with death. In November 2002, the case was thrown out of court on a technicality (it had been improperly filed). One of the groups has vowed to refile the complaint.

Then, as if to add a touch of irony, an American group supporting Muslim holy war claimed the protection of freedom of expression guaranteed by the American Bill of Rights. The Global Relief Fund, a Muslim charity organization operating out of Illinois, was added to the US government's list of terrorist organizations. The reason? Its publications—publications you are not meant to see—solicit donations for violent *Jihad* in hotspots all over the world. A lawyer and spokesman for the fund, Ashraf Nubani, was outraged. This was a denial of freedom of speech, and worse, of freedom of religion. Some of the statements the authorities considered bloodthirsty had come directly from the Koran, a book filled with phrases like the following:

Come fight in the way of Allah...kill them wherever you find them...then slay them; such is the recompense of the unbelievers. You shall soon be invited (to fight) against a people possessing mighty prowess; you will fight against them until they submit.... The punishment of those who wage war against Allah and His Apostle and strive with might and main for mischief through the land is: execution or crucifixion or the cutting off of hands and feet from opposite sides.... Say to the unbelievers if (now) they desist (from unbelief) their past would be forgiven them; but if they persist...fight them on until there is no more tumult or oppression and there prevail justice and faith in Allah altogether and everywhere.... Then Praise be to Allah Lord of the heavens and Lord of the earth Lord and Cherisher of all the worlds!

Said Nubani, "By quoting from foundation publications advocating that Muslims donate funds for *jihad* or struggle, the government is attacking Islam itself. You may not like it, but [financially supporting *jihad*] is part of the religion."

■ ■ ■ ■ ■ ■ ■ ■ ■ ■

By now, the number of Islamic facts you haven't been allowed to read is somewhere in the tens of thousands. If the secret pre-censors have their way, you may never understand why Osama bin Laden repeatedly vows to end 80 years of "humiliation and disgrace"—the 80 years since the global Islamic Empire of the Turks was carved up and its sinews slit, the 80 years in which the Holy Lands of Allah were divided into Algeria, Libya, Morocco, Iraq, Iran, Syria, Egypt, Saudi Arabia, and numerous others—all false Western creations designed to strip Islam of its military unity and of its worldwide might.

YOU MAY NEVER UNDERSTAND WHY ONE OF SUNNI ISLAM'S TOP CLERICS, SHEIKH YOUSEF AL-QARADHAWI, DECLARES ON HIS TELEVISION PROGRAMS THAT "ISLAM WILL RETURN TO EUROPE AS A CONQUEROR AND VICTOR."

You may never understand why one of Sunni Islam's top clerics, Sheikh Yousef Al-Qaradhawi, declares on his television programs that "Islam will return to Europe as a conqueror and victor." You may never hear about Khartoum, Sudan's imam Sheikh Muhammad Abd Al-Karim, who preaches to the congregation of his mosque that, "The Prophet said that the Muslims would take India…" And you may never be forewarned that an imam who presides over Saudi Arabia's mosque of King Fahd Defense Academy, Sheikh Muhammad bin Abd Al-Rahman Al-'Arifi, preaches and posts Website articles insisting, "We will control the land of the Vatican; we will control Rome and introduce Islam in it. Yes, the Christians, who carve crosses on the breasts of the Muslims in Kosovo—and before

then in Bosnia, and before then in many places in the world—will yet pay us the *Jiziya* [the tax Muslim rulers exact from unbelievers], in humiliation, or they will convert to Islam."

You may never understand the goals of the Middle Eastern military cells now planted in the cities of Belgium, Holland, France, Germany, Spain, and North America. You may never realize why Osama views Islamic mini-wars around the globe as part of a single battle for global purity, one that goes back in time to 640 AD. You may never know that Islamic militants are working mightily to gain control over "the Islamic Bomb" (i.e., Pakistan's atomic bombs) and over Pakistan's next-generation submarine-building shipyards…and the three 10,000-mile-range, missile-carrying subs those yards have built to date.

You will continue to read the propaganda about the West's horrible Crusades, and it is *true*. But you may never know about Islam's crusades against the West, and how much longer and more murderous they have been. Or how much more murderous their revival in an atomic, bio-savvy, wireless era may soon be.

THE VIRGIN OF MEDJUGORJE: A SHRINE FOR THE TWENTY-FIRST CENTURY

JONATHAN LEVY

The shrine of Medjugorje is an unpronounceable conundrum that in many ways symbolizes the current state of the Roman Catholic Church. The faithful believers, who number in the millions, are entranced by the simplistic messages received by the six Bosnian Croat seers, whose thousands of visions of the Virgin Mary since 1981 promote piety, world peace, and prayer. Critics find the whole mess beneath contempt, and Peter Hitchens' 1999 piece in *Salon* sums up that position quite nicely: "Stunningly politicized, painfully banal and too fraudulent for the Pope to recognize, the Virgin of Medjugorje stands for the bloody ethnic hatreds in the former Yugoslavia."[1] But fraud may be the least of the Virgin's problems; her devotees may also be unwittingly supporting a major child-sex tourism destination.

There is more to the Medjugorje story than prophesy versus profit; a pattern of depravity permeates the entire venture. Medjugorje is everything that is wrong with Catholicism, a microcosm of the universal church's failings. And the mainstream press unfortunately ignored the entire sordid story.

_MEDJUGORJE AND MODERNIZATION

Modernization theory proposes that increased structural complexity in society equates with greater efficiency; thus the more social differentiation, the more specialized we become and the better able to perform our tasks.[2] But is so-called progress really a one-way street? Or are some places just so cursed that modernization simply provides a better way to rape, murder, and swindle?

> ON JUNE 24, 1981, THE VIRGIN MARY—OR *GOSPA*, AS SHE IS REFERRED TO IN THE LOCAL DIALECT—APPEARED TO SIX CROATIAN TEENAGERS WHO HAD GONE OUT TO HAVE A SMOKE OR, AS WAS LATER REVISED BY THE LOCAL CLERICS, TO LOOK FOR LOST LAMBS.

The Dutch political sociologist Mart Bax spent well over fifteen years studying first-hand the town of Medjugorje in war-torn Bosnia Herzegovina. Medjugorje is not only an interesting religious-social phenomenon but has been the site of unprecedented growth, specialization, and globalization. More important, it is also the site of one of Catholicism's biggest draws on the international pilgrim circuit. In the late 1980s and early 1990s, Bax made scientific outings to Medjugorje on an annual basis to meet with his informants and make and record observations.

Medjugorje was a small agrarian hamlet in Herzegovina prior to 1981, notable only for being near the site of a massacre of Serbs by Croats in 1942. The Croats who allied themselves with Nazi Germany took revenge on the Serbs under whose rule the Croats had chafed after WWI. The Croats formed the paramilitary Ustasha organization, and with the help of Roman Catholic clergy, they sought to purge Croatia and Bosnia of the hated Serbs, who were Orthodox Christians. Operating from Medjugorje, the Ustasha rounded up the local Serbs and slaughtered several hundred, disposing of them in a ravine at a place called Suramanci.[3]

On June 24, 1981, the Virgin Mary—or *Gospa*, as she is referred to in the local dialect—appeared to six Croatian teenagers who had gone out to have a smoke or, as was later revised by the local clerics, to look for lost lambs.[4] What followed was a ten-year period of unprecedented growth and modernization fueled by a steady influx of pilgrims from Western Europe and America, freely spending hard currency and enhancing the local economy. Medjugorje prospered like never before despite the opposition of the local Bishop and the suspicions of the Yugoslav secret police.

The Virgin Mary, alias the Queen of Peace, brought prosperity to the town and its environs. Villagers expanded their homes into boarding houses to accommodate the pilgrims; concessionaires and tour guides sprang up; gift shops, hotels, and cafes were all built. Local villagers were pressed into service as laborers, technicians, and hospitality workers. Entrepreneurs operated taxis and other related businesses. Craftsman produced religious paraphernalia for sale to tourists.

Eventually, so-called Peace, or *Mir*, Centers were constructed along with new churches and a massive cathedral. And the miracles kept coming: Regular messages were received from the Virgin/*Gospa*; spontaneous healings of terminal illnesses were reported; pilgrims reported visions, interlocutions, and apparitions. It appeared to be a textbook case of modernization and globalization under the most benign of circumstances.

Evolutionary modernization had come to rural Yugoslavia. The development of Medjugorje as a shrine central to the worldwide Roman Catholic Church integrated Medjugorje into the global economy as a major tourist destination. By 1990, promoters of Medjugorje were claiming over eighteen million visitors.

Tito's government after World War II had been determined to rid Bosnia of fascist elements (the Ustasha) and their sympathizers in the Croat population. The Ustasha took to the mountains and carried on a low-level guerrilla conflict until 1957. On the surface it appeared that order had finally been reestablished, but old hatreds die hard. According to Bax, blood feuds continued in Bosnia. Likewise, the Franciscan Order, which had openly sided with the Ustasha during World War II, eventually returned to their churches and monasteries. The Franciscans[5] are a Roman Catholic religious order with a long history in Bosnia dating from the fourteenth century. They are essentially independent of the local archdiocese in Mostar. In 1972, the Franciscans built a new church in Medjugorje. By 1981, when the Virgin Mary appeared to six children there, the Franciscans were locked in an administrative dispute with the Bishop of Mostar over control of the village church and their activities.

The Franciscans immediately latched onto the six children and began collecting the messages the young seers received from the Virgin. The more general messages urging peace, fasting, and prayer were distributed worldwide. Other of the divine messages contained instructions to the local populace. Bax theorized that the Franciscans had two purposes in promoting the apparitions and messages: First, to prevent control by the Bishop of Mostar by establishing a viable religious shrine on the pilgrimage tour circuit. Second, to assert local control and pacification of the population and squelch blood feuds among local Croat clans, which had been endemic to the region.

Bax discovered that the Franciscans seemed remarkably well prepared to promote the apparitions worldwide. The Franciscan Order immediately sent their own experts to Medjugorje to validate the ongoing apparitions in 1981. More interesting is the global nature of the effort to promote Medjugorje. For over a decade, the international Medjugorje campaign was directed from Franciscan University at Steubenville, Ohio.[6] Tour promoters specialize in Medjugorje. One of largest such operations is run by Caritas, a cult-like group dedicated to Medjugorje that operates from an enclosed complex in rural Birmingham, Alabama.

A May 3, 2001, Fox News story aired locally on channel 19 in Cincinnati: A former Caritas member, Michael O'Neill, compared Caritas to Waco, and its founder, Terry Colafrancesco, to David Koresh. Colafrancesco, a former landscaper, began the Alabama-based sect in 1987. Caritas generates well over a million dollars in annual income and owns a 137-acre estate complete with swimming pool and ornate tabernacle. Fifty devoted followers work twelve-hour days running the publishing business that distributes Medjugorje tracts and staff a travel agency that specializes in pilgrimages to Medjugorje. The followers like Mike O'Neill, who was profiled by Fox News, live in run-down trailers. According to O'Neill, children often sleep on the floor, and members are paid a miserly wage.

Colafrancesco makes odd dictates, such as banning mayonnaise and marital sexual relations.[7] He is tied financially and emotionally to one of the Medjugorje visionaries, Marija Lunetti.[8] Of the six seers, Marija still experiences the most visions, touring the world and often witnessing apparitions of the Virgin in the drawing rooms of well-heeled donors. Caritas ex-members who sued Colafrancesco in an Alabama Court for misrepresentation and other torts were recently slapped with a multimillion-dollar countersuit for defamation and branded part of a satanic conspiracy. Caritas issued a remarkable 136-page document that blamed a mysterious "Satanic Network" for all their problems, including those with federal, state, and Catholic Church authorities. Colafrancesco claimed he even narrowly avoided an assassination attempt but was saved at the last minute by the intervention of "Our Lady."[9]

_MEDJUGORJE AND BARBARIZATION

Mart Bax found evidence of what he termed barbarization in Medjugorje following the breakdown of Yugoslav civil authority in 1991. Quoting the sociologist Norbert Elias, Bax wrote that the barbarizing process presupposed the civilizing processes.[10] Bosnia Herzegovina was the locale of 400 years of war between the Turks and Austrians; the area became a checkerboard of separate ethnicities—Serbs, Croats, and Muslims.

> OF THE SIX SEERS, MARIJA STILL EXPERIENCES THE MOST VISIONS, TOURING THE WORLD AND OFTEN WITNESSING APPARITIONS OF THE VIRGIN IN THE DRAWING ROOMS OF WELL-HEELED DONORS.

The founding of Yugoslavia in 1919 did little to quiet the region, as the Serbs dominated the government. Croats claimed they were discriminated against and formed armed bands of Ustasha; the Serbs retaliated by forming paramilitary groups known as Chetniks. The Second World War turned Bosnia into a huge battlefield where Croats and Muslims aligned with the Germans and fought Serbs and Communist Partisans. The Partisans were victorious, and Serbs again dominated Yugoslavia. By the late 1970s, the Croats, including those in Medjugorje, were forming Ustasha bands anew.

The establishment of the shrine in Medjugorje pacified the region. Bax reported that crime decreased and violence disappeared. The Queen of Peace brought millions of tourists, who pumped huge sums of money into the local economy. But as the state monopoly on power evaporated in 1991, Croat nationalism reasserted itself, often under the leadership of the Franciscans.[11] In Medjugorje and its environs, the Serbs and Muslims were quickly eliminated, but the civil war that was raging began to cut into the tourist trade. Tour groups were often waylaid or prevented from reaching their destination. Economically, the villagers had in many cases taken out loans to expand their homes. Croat clans controlled their rivalries as long as the money flowed in from tourists. By 1991, most of the boarding houses were empty except for those owned by the Ostojici clan, which had good connections. Other clans asked the Ostojici to share their good fortune; the Ostojici declined.

One of the most brutal aspects of the war in Medjugorje was not the conflict between Croats and Muslims or Serbs but between the Croats themselves. A blood feud was soon ignited in Medjugorje and its environs that killed 200 members of the village of 3,000 and caused another 600 to flee the region. The gullible pilgrims at the Medjugorje Peace Center did not even realize the feud was ongoing, although grisly atrocities, including mutilations and torture, were carried out on a regular basis between the warring clans in ghoulish nocturnal raids. Finally, elements of the regular Croatian Army that were aligned with one of the warring clans intervened against the Ostojici; 100 men were rounded up and quickly liquidated in one of the many ravines in the area.

BUT OTHER MEDJUGORJE PROMOTERS HAVE ALSO SUFFERED THE PRIESTLY WEAKNESS FOR LADS.

By the end of 1992, Medjugorje was again accessible to tourists. Houses were being built and repaired. Visitors were told Serb aggressors had done the damage to the village. But what is puzzling is the sheer barbarity of the dispute: Villagers cruelly mutilated and tortured each other; elderly people, women, and children were murdered; homes were ransacked and burned. Bax noted that as the violence became more grisly, it also became more organized. In regards to the mutilations, he notes they followed a fixed pattern, with more and more parts of bodies being removed as the intensity of the conflict increased. Homemade rocket launchers were used to chase out the Ostojici who remained. As for the Mother of God, the victors offered up prayers of thanks for her special grace and protection.[12]

_THE VIRGIN'S OTHER TRICKS

But finding better ways to conduct inter-clan warfare, mutilations, and ethnic cleansing was only one of the Virgin's tricks. There has always been the whiff of sexual scandal about Medjugorje. Even before the Catholic Church sex scandal/cover-up broke in the United States press early in 2002, there was Fr. Ken Roberts, the shining star and major promoter of the Medjugorje apparitions. Roberts was named one of the top 100 Catholics of the twentieth century by the *Daily Catholic*.[13]

Roberts, however, had a long struggle with his sexuality. According to the *St. Louis Post Dispatch*, Roberts—the author of the best-selling *From Playboy to Priest*—had a weakness for "young men." Criminal and civil sex abuse cases are still pending against Roberts, who began his career in 1966 and is currently laying low at the Our Lady of the Holy Spirit Center in Cincinnati, a Marian center.[14] Ironically, Father Ken still maintains cordial relations with one of his old Medjugorje contacts, Terry Colafrancesco of Caritas, who attended a recent birthday party for Roberts in Cincinnati.[15]

But other Medjugorje promoters have also suffered the priestly weakness for lads. According to the virulent anti-Medjugorje Website Unity Publishing, Fr. Richard Brown is a phony priest who visited Medjugorje and while there even heard visiting celebrity Martin Sheen's confession. "He [Brown] is a homosexual of the worst kind," the Website reports, "who first appeared on the Medjugorje circuit with wanted criminal Peter Miller and a suitcase full of condoms."[16] The aforementioned Peter K. Miller was a crooked tour guide whose assets were seized in 1995 by the California Attorney General following a court-ordered audit that turned up $1.3 million in missing customer payments.[17] Unity Publishing has also chronicled the story of accused pedophile David Hoop, a Medjugorje gift-shop owner, who, contemporaneously with Brown and Roberts, fled Bosnia after being accused of sexually molesting local boys.

Fr. Jozo Zovko, OFM, is one of the most charismatic promoters of Medjugorje and has been associated with the apparitions from the start. Fr. Jozo, as he is known by his admirers, was portrayed by Martin Sheen in the 1995 propaganda piece *Gospa*. Zovko, however, is a sexual predator whose priestly faculties have been suspended. According to a surprising article in the well-respected conservative Catholic newsweekly *The Wanderer*, Zovko reportedly is well known for having a penchant for oral sex performed by comely female pilgrims to Medjugorje.[18]

All this reached a proverbial head when the Croatian Rasputin was denied access to the Washington National Cathedral on November 20, 2002, after a seemingly successful whirlwind tour of the US. The next day, Zovko's peccadilloes became fodder for a juicy *Washington Post* article ("Bosnian Priest Barred at National Shrine; Prayer Service Organizers Cite Allegations of Disobedience, Sexual Abuse") that sent Zovko back to Bosnia with his tail between his legs and recriminations against a rival Medjugorje promoter, whom he blamed for blowing the whistle to the press.

Unnoticed was the almost simultaneous defrocking of another priest with Medjugorje connections on November 16, 2002. In a November 28 feature article, the *Pittsburgh Post Gazette* stated that Fr. Anthony Cippola was the subject of the extremely rare sanction personally imposed by John Paul II after Cippola had been accused repeatedly of child molestation (he was sanctioned as early as 1988). Cippola ignored the sanctions with seeming impunity and launched a career as a chaplain on cruises and tour guide to Medjugorje in 1995.

The strangest case is that of Brother Tom Falco, which was well documented by the media in Northern California beginning in late 1999. His court proceedings on criminal molestation allegations were covered by a local TV station. Falco, branded a phony priest by the press, was actually a real lay brother of a Medjugorje-based order, Oasis of Peace. The *San Jose Mercury News* reported that Falco lured a 15-year-old California boy to join him on a tour of Medjugorje, where Brother Tom drugged and sodomized the teenager.[19] Falco was described as a veteran pedophile and con man who somehow had gravitated towards Medjugorje. Two teen victims sued Falco, a Catholic travel agency who employed him, and the local California archdiocese. All of the defendants settled out of court except for Falco, who defaulted. Falco had more serious legal problems, a total of seven felony counts involving molestations of two teenage boys and drug and child pornography charges.[20]

But who is Brother Tom? Investigators for the police and the plaintiffs' attorney variously reported that he was in the witness protection program, a child pornographer, a phony priest, and a hardened criminal. The California Superior Court, however, could find no previous criminal record; indeed, it admitted difficulty finding *any* record of Tom Falco, alias Anthony Falcone. Falco for his part steadfastly claimed to be a monk or brother who was ordained near Medjugorje at the Oasis of Peace Monastery. Oasis of Peace is a curious institution— a Marian community that includes priests but also lay brothers like Falco who have taken vows of celibacy. Oddly, married couples are also allowed to be members. Oasis of Peace claims ecclesial recognition from the Italian Diocese of Sabina-Poggio Mirteto and is officially a "public association of the faithful."[21] Medjugorje is full of such communities, including an offshoot of Caritas of Birmingham.

As for Brother Tom, the Santa Cruz County Superior Court initially okayed a plea bargain in which the then-63-year-old "Brother" would serve no prison time. Without explanation, the court rejected the plea bargain (the presence of television cameras from KSBW-TV in the courtroom may have been a factor). Tom then inexplicably and perhaps unwisely entered an "open plea" to four felony charges, reduced from seven. The probation department recommended the middle term of six years, eight months.

The court has sealed much of Falco's sentencing report. However, one gets the feeling that there was a great deal of uneasiness about the case. The assistant district attorney wrote, "There is just not enough information about the defendant for us to know what he has done or how he lived his life…. [The] defendant has gone by a great many names." Brother Tom's only other known brushes with the law were misdemeanor marijuana convictions and as a victim of a vicious beating in Key West, Florida, that blinded him in one eye. Mention of Medjugorje and Oasis of Peace, as well as Falco's infiltration of a local diocese, was kept out of the open file. But a source close to the case indicates that the diocese knew Falco was a pedophile and pornographer yet gave him direct access to children at a parish school where his duties included helping the youngest children take their bathroom breaks.

_THE BREAKING STORY

The bloody-minded Croats—well documented by sociologist Mart Bax—are one thing, but what of the Medjugorje sex scandal? Is there a pattern, or are they simply isolated incidents? In two recent press stories, on either side of the Atlantic Ocean, the story of Medjugorje took a bizarre twist. First, on August 31, 2002, the *Portugal News*, an English-language newspaper for the largely British expatriate community in Portugal, reported on Portugal's pedophile problem in detail. Christine Dolan, described as a former CNN news reporter, was visiting the country, having just returned from an investigation of child trafficking and prostitution in the Balkans. The *Portugal News* reported: "She recently exposed a group of paedophile priests at the Marian shrine of Medjugorje, Yugoslavia, who had sexually abused hundreds of children and also made them available to sex tourists."[22]

> **"SHE RECENTLY EXPOSED A GROUP OF PAEDOPHILE PRIESTS AT THE MARIAN SHRINE OF MEDJUGORJE, YUGOSLAVIA, WHO HAD SEXUALLY ABUSED HUNDREDS OF CHILDREN AND ALSO MADE THEM AVAILABLE TO SEX TOURISTS."**

Dolan's credentials as a pedophile hunter are impeccable: She is the founder of the International Humanitarian Campaign Against Exploitation of Children,[23] a Washington, DC-based NGO (non-governmental organization), and is associated with the International Center for Missing and Exploited Children. Her previous reports have been presented at UN forums. Thus, Dolan's remark about a sex tourism industry at Medjugorje cannot be discounted. The mainstream press seemingly was oblivious to the story, though it involved a popular Catholic shrine that garners a reported one million visitors per year.

Perhaps the media was "pedophiled" out, since only a single local newspaper in the US, the *Woburn News* in Massachusetts, expanded on Dolan's investigation. Marie Coady, in her article "Shattered Innocence: The Millennium Holocaust," filled in the blanks regarding Dolan's mission in the Balkans and what she found at Medjugorje. Coady wrote:

Christine's [Dolan] investigation led her to discover an increasing number of children who are allegedly being sexually abused by so-called Catholic clerics within the confines of religious shrines, while managing to deceive their superiors. She recently exposed a group of pedophile priests at the Marian shrine of Medjugorje, Yugoslavia, who had sexually abused hundreds of children and also made them available to sex tourists.

Coady then graphically described a confrontation between Dolan and the ranking Franciscan monk at Medjugorje:

But when she [Dolan] confronted Fr. Svetozar Kraljevic, OFM, the priest who has had the longest association with the Shrine at Medjugorje and is their English-speaking representative, with her proof of what she had discovered, he referred to kids being drugged, raped and sodomized in a visionary's house as akin to a car accident.

The Coady article went on to describe the incredibly nonchalant attitude of the Franciscan Kraljevic towards sexual abuse allegations at the shrine: "[H]e simply shrugged and turned away." Bosnian and Interpol officials have had a similar non-reaction, since the shrine of Medjugorje has continued to operate with apparent impunity.

And therein lies the connection to Brother Tom. It was learned from a source close to Falco's civil case that the rape of the California teen was accomplished in the home of one of the Medjugorje visionaries, Mirijana. As Bax had discovered, the visionaries' families earned very good money renting the spare rooms attached to the seers' family homes. Should the talkative Virgin of Medjugorje have seen it coming, or was the incident covered by an umbrella insurance policy? In either event, the Church paid off the victim, and Falco went up the river to Corcoran Prison as a sex and drug offender.

But is there hard proof that Medjugorje really is a hotbed of pedophilia and barbarism, not to mention out and out fraud? The fraud is well documented; if the gullible continue to get fleeced, they have had plenty of warnings. As for barbarism, the sociologist Bax has a handle on that issue; the consensus is that one had better not give the villagers offense. There have been several suspicious disappearances in Medjugorje. An elderly Austrian woman and a priest vanished in 2001 in an incident the locals attributed to "satanic worshippers."[24] The villagers offered no explanation why their ethnic cleansing had included Serbs and Muslims but excluded Satanists. Other authorities have been keen to link Satanism, mind control, and Medjugorje but without the necessary corroboration to convince the major media outlets to go with the story.[25]

Dolan's report on the pedophilia allegation has been explained away by Medjugorje aficionados, also known as "Medj-heads," as a cheap shot. Is there really a sex tourism business in Medjugorje, as the former CNN reporter alleges? And if so, who can corroborate it? That may be up to the mercurial Brother Tom, who is due to be released from prison in 2003. He claims he was set up by the Church to take the fall for crimes he did not commit. Convicted pedophiles are generally not taken too seriously, but there is no explanation why the 63-year-old's rap sheet was clean as a whistle except for a couple of marijuana misdemeanors.

THERE HAVE BEEN SEVERAL SUSPICIOUS DISAPPEARANCES IN MEDJUGORJE.

The California media covered the Brother Tom case, but the Medjugorje connection was missed or misunderstood. When the Medjugorje sex scandal reappeared, the scandal-hungry major media studiously ignored the story. Maybe the sleight of hand of the Virgin is at work here, but if Brother Tom survives his prison term, he has promised to tell the rest of the story.

Endnotes

1. Hitchens, Peter. "Our Lady of Lies." *Salon*, 4 Oct 1999. **2.** Randall, Vicky, & Robin Theobald. *Political Change and Underdevelopment*. Durham, NC: Duke University Press, 1998: 28. **3.** Bax, Mart. *Medjugorje: Religion, Politics, and Violence in Rural Bosnia*. Amsterdam: Free University Press, 1995: 122-3. **4.** The approved Roman Catholic shrine of Fatima, Portugal, involved three shepherd children in 1917 coming upon an apparition of the Virgin Mary. The obvious intent of the Medjugorje children's handlers, Franciscan monks, was to associate Medjugorje with the approved shrines of Fatima and Lourdes. **5.** Order of the Franciscans Minor – OFM. **6.** Ohio and Indiana are the heartland of the international Medjugorje movement; besides the aforementioned Franciscan University at Steubenville, Ohio, there are major Medjugorje centers at Norwood, Ohio, the University of Dayton, Ohio, and at Notre Dame, Indiana. **7.** Interview with Mike O'Neill, April 2001. **8.** Treinen, Andy. "Local Man Escapes Cult." Fox 19 News (Cincinnati), 3 May 2001. **9.** *Caritas: Entering the Time of Persecution*, Sterret, Alabama. (copies available upon request, telephone 205-672-2000 ext. 315, 24 hours a day) **10.** *Op cit.*, Bax: 102. **11.** Bax, Mart. *Holy Mary and Medjugorje's Rocketeers: The Local Logic of an Ethnic Cleansing Process in Bosnia*. Ethnologia Europaea: 54. **12.** *Op cit.*, Bax, *Rocketeers*: 48. **13.** "Countdown of the Top 100 Catholics of the Twentieth Century." *The Daily Catholic*, 30 Sept 1999. Fr. Ken was number 51, to be exact, finishing well ahead of Cardinal Bernardin, Lech Walesa, and J.R.R. Tolkien. <www.dailycatholic.org/issue/99Sep/sep30top.htm>. **14.** "Dallas Priest Accused of Sexual Abuse Won't Stop Ministry." *St. Louis Post Dispatch*, 14 Nov 1998. **15.** Interview with Mike O'Neill. **16.** Unity Publishing Website. <www.unitypublishing.com/Apparitions/FruitsMed.html> [last visited 29 Oct 2002]. **17.** "Judge Freezes Funds of Agency Offering Religious Tours." *Los Angeles Times*, 22 April 1997. **18.** "Allegations of Molestation…Suspended Medjugorje Priest Launches Cross Country Tour." *The Wanderer*, 14 Nov 2002. **19.** "Fake Cleric Weaved Tale of Trust With Boys, Church." *San Jose Mercury News*, 2 April 2002. **20.** *People v. Anthony Falco*, Superior Court of Santa Cruz, California, Case No. S909470. **21.** <www.medjugorje.org/oasisofpeace.htm> [last visited October 29, 2002]. **22.** "Paedophile Problem Gains New Prominence." *The Portugal News*, 31 Aug 2002. **23.** <http://www.helpsavekids.org/>. **24.** "Zwei Oesterreichische Pilger in Bosnien-Herzegowina Vermisst [Two Austrian Pilgrims Missing in Bosnia]." Deutsche Presse-Agentur, 6 June 2001. **25.** Guyatt, David. *Masters of Persuasion*. Anguilla: World Watch Media, 2002: 5-8.

L. RON, SIRHAN, MANSON, AND ME

PAUL KRASSNER

When I was writing the script for a fake *Doonesbury* strip that would grace the cover of my magazine, *The Realist* ("Irreverence is our only sacred cow"), even though the masthead stated, "Fact Checker: None," I verified with a source in Mafia circles that Frank Sinatra had once delivered a suitcase full of money to Lucky Luciano in Havana after he was deported.

In 1967, I published "The Parts Left Out of the Kennedy Book." Jackie Kennedy had authorized William Manchester to write *The Death of a President*, but now she wanted portions of the manuscript excised. Unaware that I was utilizing an established literary form, apocrypha, I tried to nurture the utterly incredible in a context of credibility. Imitating Manchester's style, I began with a true item. During the 1960 primaries, Lyndon Johnson had attacked JFK on the grounds that his father, Joseph P. Kennedy, was a Nazi sympathizer while he was US Ambassador to Great Britain.

Then I improvised on stories—one involving Marilyn Monroe—that White House correspondents knew to be true but which had remained unpublished. Peeling off layer after layer of verisimilitude, I came closer and closer with each new paragraph to the climactic scene on Air Force One where Jackie walks in on LBJ, who is leaning over a casket and fucking the throat wound in Kennedy's corpse. This was not merely casual necrophilia, though. It had a serious purpose—to change the entry wound from the Grassy Knoll into an exit wound from the Texas Book Depository in order to fool the Warren Commission.

Well, it fooled a lot of *Realist* readers, too, if only for a moment, yet a moment in which they believed that the leader of the Western world, who had been escalating the war in Vietnam so severely, was actually totally insane. That issue reached a circulation of 100,000. Recently I met a 25-year-old woman who told me about that LBJ-JFK encounter, not knowing I had written it. She believed that the act of "neckrophilia" had actually occurred. What I had originally intended as a metaphorical truth has become, in her mind, a literal truth. Thanks to current realities, that piece of satire is now a credible urban myth.

When I moved from New York to San Francisco in 1971, I wanted to publish something in the thirteenth-anniversary issue that would top "The Parts Left Out of the Kennedy Book." I had observed a disturbing element being imposed upon the counterculture—various groups all trying to rip off the search for deeper consciousness—and I felt challenged to write a satirical piece about this phenomenon.

Scientology was one of the scariest of these organizations, if only because its recruiters were such aggressive zombies. Carrying their

behavior to its logical conclusion, they could become programmed assassins. I chose Sirhan Sirhan—in prison for killing presidential candidate Senator Robert F. Kennedy—as a credible allegory, since he was already known to have an interest in mysticism and self-improvement, from the secrets of the Rosicrucians to Madame Helena Blavatsky's Theosophy.

"PAUL," MY AUDITOR REPLIED, "THEY'RE NOT EVEN ATTACHED YET."

In a list of upcoming features for the anniversary issue, I included "The Rise of Sirhan Sirhan in the Scientology Hierarchy." Then I began to do my research. I was, after all, an investigative satirist. In fact, I even developed a source within the Scientology organization.

The goal of Scientology is to become a Clear—that is, a *complete* zombie—moving up to higher and higher levels by means of auditing sessions with an E-Meter, essentially a lie detector. John Godwin wrote in *Occult America* that the E-Meter "made lying difficult for the impressionable." I decided to try one at the San Francisco Center. The stares of the Scientology practitioners seemed to be tactical, their smiles unfelt. In confronting their guilts and fears through the medium of a machine, they had become machine-like themselves, and they responded like automatons. I took hold of the E-Meter's tin cans, one in each hand.

"Wow," I said, "I just felt a surge of energy go pulsating through me."

"Paul," my auditor replied, "they're not even attached yet."

"Well, such is the power of auto-suggestion."

There was no charge for the personality test by which prospective Scientologists screened themselves into "the world of the totally free." It consisted of 200 questions on topics ranging from fingernail-biting to jealousy. In *World Medicine*, David Delvin reported that when *his* answers were processed, he was told, "You've got quite a bit of agitation and you're moderately dispersed, but we can help you to standard tech.... So, you see, it's all *very* scientific—thanks to the fact that our founder is a man of science himself." Dr. Delvin confessed, "I hadn't the heart to tell him that his super-scientific system had failed to detect the fact that I had marked the 'don't know' column against all 200 questions in the test."

Founder L. Ron Hubbard's original thesis in his book *Dianetics* was that traumatic shock occurs not only during early childhood, but also during the pre-natal stage. In *Neurotica* magazine, G. Legman took off on that concept with his own cult, Epizootics, "demonstrating the basic cause of all neurosis in father's tight-fitting jockstrap." Not to be outdone by parody, Hubbard in 1952 turned Dianetics into Scientology, which traced trauma back to *previous* lives, not necessarily incarnations that were spent on this planet, either. In fact, Scientologists were forbidden to see the movie *2001* in order to avoid "heavy and unnecessary restimulation." By what? When Hal the computer says, "Unclear"?

In 1955, Hubbard incorporated Scientology as a religion, based in Washington, DC. This would enable its ministers to gain entry into hospitals and prisons, not to mention getting tax exemption. He issued the *Professional Auditors Bulletin*, a handbook for luring prospects into the Scientology fold. One example was the "illness research" method, taking out a newspaper ad, such as: "Polio victims—a charitable organization investigating polio desires to examine several victims of the after-effects of this illness. Phone so-and-so." Hubbard explained, "The interesting hooker in this ad is that anyone suffering from a lasting illness is suffering from it so as to attract attention and bring about an examination of it. These people will go on being examined endlessly."

Another example, under the subhead "Exploiting," was the "casualty contact" method, "requiring little capital and being highly ambulatory." All it needed was "good filing and a good personal appearance." Hubbard elaborated: "Every day in the daily papers, one discovers people who have been victimized one way or the other by life. One takes every daily paper he can get his hands on and cuts from it every story whereby he might have a pre-Clear. As speedily as possible, he makes a personal call on the bereaved or injured person. He should represent himself to the person or the person's family as a minister whose compassion was compelled by the newspaper story concerning the person. The goal is to move the customer from group processing to individual attention at a fee."

In 1962, Hubbard wrote to President John F. Kennedy, claiming that his letter was as important as the one Albert Einstein had sent to President Franklin D. Roosevelt about the atomic bomb. He insisted that "Scientology is very easy for the government to put into effect," and that "Scientology could decide the space race or the next war in the hands of America." Kennedy didn't respond—the bloody fool, daring not to answer a question he hadn't even asked.

The E-Meter was presented as a panacea that could cure such "psychosomatic" problems as arthritis, cancer, polio, ulcers, the common cold, and atomic radiation burns. In October 1962, the Food and Drug Administration was investigating Scientology, so Hubbard wrote that the E-Meter is "a valid religious instrument, used in Confessionals, and is in no way diagnostic and does not treat." Nevertheless, in January 1963, the FDA raided Scientology headquarters, seizing 100 E-Meters. Scientology claimed that this violated their freedom of religion, and Hubbard wrote to President Kennedy again. He wanted to meet with him so that they could "come to some amicable answers on religious matters." Again no response.

Then Hubbard wrote to Attorney General Robert Kennedy, "even though you are of a different faith," asking for protection of the Scientology religion. Bobby didn't respond, either. And there it was—my satirical angle—Hubbard's motivation for programming Sirhan Sirhan to kill Bobby Kennedy would be *revenge*. Hmmmmm. Had I accidentally stumbled into a real conspiracy when I thought I was merely making one up?

> THE E-METER WAS PRESENTED AS A PANACEA THAT COULD CURE SUCH "PSYCHOSOMATIC" PROBLEMS AS ARTHRITIS, CANCER, POLIO, ULCERS, THE COMMON COLD, AND ATOMIC RADIATION BURNS.

In Scientology, Kennedy could have been declared an "Enemy," subject to "Fair Game," a penalty described in a Hubbard Policy Letter whereby an Enemy "[m]ay be deprived of property or injured by any means by any Scientolgist. May be tricked, sued or lied to or destroyed." In October 1968, four months after the assassination of Senator Kennedy, Fair Game was "repealed," due to adverse publicity. "The practice of declaring people Fair Game will cease," Hubbard stated in a Policy Letter. "Fair Game may not appear on any Ethics Order. It causes bad public relations."

While Sirhan Sirhan found himself awaiting trial, he was given several psychological tests. In one of these, he couldn't provide a simple yes-or-no response to only two specific statements: "At one or more times in my life, I felt that someone was making me do things by hypnotizing me." And, "Someone has been trying to influence my mind." During the trial, psychiatrist Bernard Diamond used post-hypnotic suggestion to program Sirhan into climbing the bars of his cell. But there were two different accounts of that experiment.

In *Psychology Today*, Dr. Diamond stated: "He went over toward the guards and climbed the bars like a monkey. I asked him why. He answered in that cool way he affected, 'I am getting exercise.' Then I played the tape to prove to him that he had been under hypnosis to do just that. But he denied it and complained that I was bugging him."

However, in his book *RFK Must Die*, Robert Kaiser—who was also there—wrote: "Sirhan had no idea what he was doing up on the top of the bars. When he finally discovered that climbing was not his own idea, but Dr. Diamond's, he was struck with the plausibility of the idea that perhaps he had been programmed by someone else, in like manner, to kill Kennedy...."

When Scientology was kicked out of Australia, the official inquiry concluded: "It is only in name that there is any difference between authoritative hypnosis and most of the techniques of Scientology. Many Scientology techniques are in fact hypnosis techniques, and Hubbard has not changed their nature by changing their names."

At a Scientology meeting in Chicago, someone asked, "I understand that Scientology has been banned in England and Australia. Why was this done?" The reply: "Cool! I'm glad you asked that. You see, the kind of person who attacks Scientology is frightened of anything that offers real enlightenment to mankind. In Australia, the man who attacked Scientology was a so-called psychiatrist who was performing lobotomies with ice picks."

Even L. Ron Hubbard admitted the need for a "canceller," which was a contract with a patient stating that whatever the auditor said would not be literally interpreted by the patient or used in any way. So, immediately before patients were permitted to open their eyes at the end of a session, they were supposed to be told, "In the future, when I utter the word *Cancelled*, everything which I have said to you while you are in a therapy session will be cancelled and will have no force with you. Any suggestion I have made to you will be without force when I say the word *Cancelled*. Do you understand?"

When the word was used, it was not further amplified. Just that single word, *Cancelled*, would be uttered. Hubbard warned, "The canceller is vital. It prevents accidental positive suggestion. The patient may be suggestible or even in a permanent light hypnotic trance." Moreover, in his book *The Job*, William S. Burroughs stated: "Hubbard has refused to publish his advanced discoveries. There is every indication that the discoveries of Scientology are being used by the CIA and other official agencies."

> **I BEGAN TO WORK ON "THE RISE OF SIRHAN SIRHAN IN THE SCIENTOLOGY HIERARCHY," BASED ON THE ACTUAL CASE HISTORY OF A FRIEND WHO HAD BEEN ON THE CREW OF HUBBARD'S SEA ORG, A PARAMILITARY FLEET OF SHIPS.**

Ironically, using the Freedom of Information Act, Scientology obtained secret CIA documents which proposed mind-control experiments where hypnotized subjects would have an uncontrollable impulse to "commit a nuisance" on Groundhog Day on the steps of City Hall, in order to find out whether an unwilling subject could be quickly hypnotized, then be made to undergo amnesia by "durable and useful post-hypnotic suggestion." The CIA also collaborated with the US Army's "special operations division" in bacteriological and chemical "open air" tests in the streets and subway tunnels of New York City.

My ultimate fictional connection between Sirhan and Scientology was inadvertently suggested by Burroughs in *Evergreen* magazine:

Take a black militant and put him on the E-Meter. Tell him to mock up a nigger-killing Southern sheriff chuckling over the notches in his gun. The needle falls off the dial. He mocks up the sheriff again. The needle falls off the dial. Again, again, again, for two hours if need be. No matter how long it takes, the time will come when he mocks up the sheriff and there is no read on the E-Meter. He is looking at this creature calmly with slow heartbeat and normal blood pressure and seeing it for what it is. He has as-ised [Sheriff] Big Jim Clark. As-ising does not mean acceptance, submission, or resignation. On the contrary, when he can look at Big Jim with no reaction, he is infinitely better equipped to deal with the external manifestation, as a calm man fights better than an angry one. If you can't bring yourself to see the target, you can't hit it. When the needle reads off you are off target.

I began to work on "The Rise of Sirhan Sirhan in the Scientology Hierarchy," based on the actual case history of a friend who had been

on the crew of Hubbard's Sea Org, a paramilitary fleet of ships. Crew members wore maritime uniforms and had to sign an unusual contract:

I do hereby agree to enter into employment with the Sea Organization and, being of sound mind, do fully realize and agree to abide by its purpose, which is to get Ethics in on this Planet and the Universe and, fully and without reservation, subscribe to the discipline, mores and conditions of this group and pledge to abide by them. Therefore, I contract myself to the Sea Organization for the next billion years.

Give or take a few centuries. Anyway, my friend decided to leave Scientology, but he had surrendered his passport and, remaining true to his experience but simply changing his name, I wrote:

When Sirhan tried to get his passport back, he was required to stand in a corner, handcuffed, not allowed to speak to anyone, and given food only on someone's whim. Sirhan finally recanted, admitted that he didn't really want his passport returned, and he was forgiven. Hubbard apparently didn't bother to check the weather before pushing off. The ship sailed into a storm. Sirhan was at the helm. He couldn't stay on course, and Hubbard yelled at him. Sirhan shouted back—"Here, take the fuckin' wheel yourself!"—and he walked away. Hubbard threw a temper tantrum and began to cry.

Sirhan was nervous. He was afraid he would be declared a "Suppressive Person," with whom no Scientologists were allowed to associate. He could be "restrained or imprisoned." Moreover, the "homes, properties, places and abodes of Suppressives are all beyond any protection." When Sirhan considered how he had acted toward Hubbard, he realized that he might even be guilty of Treason: "May be turned over to civil authorities. Full background to be explored for purposes of prosecution."

But Sirhan was declared guilty neither of being a Suppressive Person nor of Treason. Rather, for punishment, he was forbidden to bathe or brush his teeth for the entire two-month cruise. When he got caught using soap and toothpaste, he was transferred to another job in London. He spent seven days a week, from 7 a.m. to midnight, at a salary of ten pounds per week, dictating 200 letters a day, urging dropouts to re-enroll in Scientology. Like all Scientologists, he received periodic security checks while he was working his way through the advanced courses. These were conducted by an Ethics Officer with an E-Meter. There were 150 questions. Here are some samples:

"Have you ever mistrusted your E-Meter? Do you think selling auditing is really a swindle? Have you ever written, then destroyed critical messages to L. Ron

Hubbard? Have you ever had any unkind thoughts about L. Ron Hubbard? Have you ever had sex with any other student or staff member? Have you ever used Dianetics or Scientology to force sex on someone? Have you ever raped anyone? Have you ever been raped? Have you ever been involved in an abortion? Do you have any bastards? Have you ever been sexually unfaithful? Have you ever practiced homosexuality? Have you ever practiced sodomy? Have you ever had intercourse with a member of your family? Have you practiced sex with children? Have you ever used hypnotism to practice sex with children? Have you ever practiced cannibalism? Have you ever slept with a member of a race of another color? Have you ever practiced sex with animals? Have you ever killed or crippled animals for pleasure? Have you ever had anything to do with pornography? Have you ever masturbated?

"Have you ever lived or worked under an assumed name? Have you ever been a newspaper reporter? Have you ever blackmailed anybody? Have you ever been blackmailed? Have you ever embezzled money? Have you ever forged a signature, check or document? Have you ever hit and run with a car? Have you ever murdered anyone? Have you ever hidden a body? Have you ever attempted suicide? Have you ever peddled dope? Have you ever been in prison? Do you think there's anything wrong with invading a pre-Clear's privacy? Have you permitted a pre-Clear to have secrets from you? Have you ever used hypnotism to procure sex or money? Have you ever been a prostitute? Have you ever taken money for giving anyone sexual intercourse? Have you ever had anything to do with Communism or been a Communist? Are you in communication with someone who understands more about Scientology than does L. Ron Hubbard? Do you know of any secret plans against Scientology? Have you ever coughed during Scientology lectures? Have you ever done anything your mother would be ashamed to find out? Do you have a secret you're afraid I'll find out? What unkind thoughts have you thought while I was doing this check?" And—Sirhan's favorite—"Have you ever tried to act normal?"

All that information could certainly be utilized as a source of blackmail. Hubbard had based Scientology's secret file system on that used by Nazi spy chief Richard Gehlen. The Ethics exam includes the following disclaimer which an auditor is supposed to read aloud: "While we cannot guarantee you that matters revealed in this check will be held forever secret, we can promise you faithfully that no part of it nor any answer you make here will be given to the police or state. No Scientologist will ever bear witness against you in court by reason of answers to this security check." However, one auditor swears that he has often seen pre-Clears' files with information circled, along with notations like, "We can use this." Indeed, one man had confessed to skimming $25,000 a year from his

business, but when he attempted to quit Scientology and get back $40,000 worth of future auditing he'd signed for after getting little sleep for four days, he was told that if he pursued his claim, they would reveal his tax-cheating to the Internal Revenue Service.

Nevertheless, Sirhan wrote to a friend, "Scientology works." He was back with the Sea Org. "I was put through some processes called Power and the darn things helped me get rid of so much tension, so much unreality, that I am still gaining from it. The funny thing is that I don't know why it is helping, and I guess that the more I study, the more I will find out about this technology that gets results. I am a month away from reaching the Clear level, and there are now six levels above that, and two more to come after that. It is all so incredible, but I am finding out who I am, where I fit in, what a group is, and most of all that I can go through something very, very difficult without running away or leaving it. I am on to something that will make me me and that is what I have always wanted. But I am not the master of my fate any longer until I'm out of this scene, which is getting more cloak and dagger every day. I am growing through the restrictions I and this ship have placed on me." Scientology's secret files held an awful lot of extremely intimate details about Sirhan's life, things he had admitted over the years in order to get "a clean needle" reading on the E-Meter, and they could certainly get people to do all sorts of things for fear of being exposed, but he wasn't concerned about that....

Then, in the course of my research, a strange thing happened. I learned of the *actual* involvement of Charles Manson with Scientology. In fact, there had been an E-Meter at the Spahn Ranch where his "family" stayed. Suddenly, I no longer had any reason to use Sirhan Sirhan as my protagonist. Reality will transcend allegory every time.

"HAVE YOU EVER RAPED ANYONE? HAVE YOU EVER BEEN RAPED? HAVE YOU EVER BEEN INVOLVED IN AN ABORTION? DO YOU HAVE ANY BASTARDS?"

Manson was abandoned by his mother and lived in various institutions since he was 8-years-old. He learned early how to survive in captivity. When he was fourteen, he got arrested for stealing bread and was jailed. He was suposed to go to reform school, but instead went to Boys Town in Nebraska. He ran away from Boys Town and got arrested again, beginning his life-long career as a prison inmate and meeting organized crime figures who became his role models. He tossed horseshoes with Frank Costello, hung around with Frankie Carbo, and learned how to play the guitar from Alvin "Creepy" Karpas.

Eventually, he was introduced to Scientology by fellow prisoners while he was at McNeil Island Penitentiary. He needed less deconditioning than his cellmates, who had spent more time in the outside world. One of his teachers said that, with Scientology, Charlie's ability to psych people out quickly was intensified so that he could zero

L. RON, SIRHAN, MANSON, AND ME
PAUL KRASSNER

in on their weaknesses and fears immediately. Thus, one more method was now stored in his manipulation tool-chest.

When Manson was released in 1967, he went to the Scientology Center in San Francisco. "Little Paul" Watkins, who accompanied him there, told me, "Charlie said to them, 'I'm Clear—what do I do now?' But they expected him to sweep the floor. Shit, he had done *that* in prison." In Los Angeles, he went to the Scientology *Celebrity* Center. Now this was more like it. Here he could mingle with the elite. I managed to obtain a copy of the original log entry: "7/31/68, new name, Charlie Manson, Devt., No address, In for processing = Ethics = Type III." The receptionist—who, by Type III, meant "psychotic"—sent him to the Ethics office, but he never showed up.

At the Spahn Ranch, Manson eclectically combined his version of Scientology auditing with post-hypnotic techniques he had learned in prison, with geographical isolation and subliminal motivation, with singalong sessions and encounter games, with LSD and mescaline, with transactional analysis and brainwashing rituals, with verbal probing and the sexual longevity that he had practiced upon himself for all those years in the privacy of his cell.

WHEN MANSON WAS RELEASED IN 1967, HE WENT TO THE SCIENTOLOGY CENTER IN SAN FRANCISCO.

Ultimately, in August 1969, he sent members of his well-progammed family off to slay actress Sharon Tate and her unborn baby, hairstylist and dealer to the stars Jay Sebring, would-be screenwriter Voytek Frykowski and his girlfriend, coffee heiress Abigail Folger. The next night, Manson accompanied them to kill supermarket mogul Leno LaBianca and his wife.

In 1971, my old friend, Ed Sanders, founder of the Fugs, the missing link between rock and punk, was covering the Manson trial for the *L.A. Free Press* and working on a book, *The Family*, about the case. I wrote to him for permisson to print any material that might be omitted from his book because the publisher considered it in bad taste or too controversial. Otherwise, I told him, I would have to make up those missing sections myself.

Sanders put a notice on the middle of one of his reports: "Oh, yes, before we ooze onward, I am not, nor shall I be, the author of any future article in *The Realist* titled 'The Parts I Left Out of the Manson Story, by Ed Sanders.'" He assured me that this was "a joke," but also, understandably, it was a safeguard.

I had known Ed for ten years. He was always on the crest of nonviolent political protest and outrageous cultural expression, such as *Fuck You: A Magazine of the Arts*. In 1961, he got arrested with others for trying to swim aboard the *Polaris* nuclear submarine. The next year he published a parody catalog listing actual relics, such as Allen Ginsberg's cold-cream jar containing one pubic hair. He sent the catalogs to universities and sold the items at outlandish prices. But now his courage and determination had taken a different path, and I flew to New York to pore through his Manson files. Sanders was a data addict, and his research notes were written in the form of quatrains. He had become an investigative poet.

When I returned to San Francisco, a young man with a child on his shoulders came to my house and rang the bell. I opened the door, and he served me with a subpoena. The Church of Scientology was accusing me of libel and conspiracy, simply for having *announced the title* of the upcoming article, "The Rise of Sirhan Sirhan in the Scientology Hierarchy"—which, ironically, I no longer planned to publish. They were suing me for three-quarters of a million dollars. I published their complaint in *The Realist*:

[This] was published for the purpose of exposing plaintiff to public hatred, contempt, ridicule, obliquy, and did cause it to be shunned and avoided, intended to injure plaintiff in the further proselytizing of the religion of Scientology and to heap embarrassment and humiliation upon it through the distribution of the aforesaid statement throughout the State of California, the United States of America and the world at large....

[The statement] was intended to be understood by the general public and readers, and was so understood by them, charging, asserting and imputing that the plaintiff is not involved in a religious movement, but rather some form of unlawful or unethical activity and that the plaintiff employs criminal methods in furthering its religion....

As a direct and proximate result of the foregoing, plaintiff has suffered pecuniary loss in that many members, prospective members and persons in the general public have not made or have decreased the amount of their fixed contributions, offerings and donations to plaintiff because of the defamatory statement.... Plaintiff does not know at this time the exact amount of the pecuniary loss resulting from the foregoing, and plaintiff prays leave to amend this allegation and insert the true amount of the loss when the same becomes known to it....

Defendants have conspired between themselves and with other established religions, medical and political organizations and persons presently unknown to plaintiff. By subtle covert and pernicious techniques involving unscrupulous manipulation of all public communication media, defendants and their co-conspirators have conspired to deny plaintiff its right to exercise religious beliefs on an equal basis with the established religious organizations of this country. These conspirators have utilized what has now become their modus operandi of hiring strangers to write libelous documents for them and then trying to hide behind them. Publication of said statement and the proposed article is one act in furtherance of that conspiracy.

Said conspirators and diverse other parties, members of the established social, religious and economic society of America today, have a conspiratorial party line whereby they harass, ridicule, defame and malign any new organizations, religious, social or economic, regardless of their merits, when it appears that they are about to become a threat to the established orders' source of funds or membership. Said conspirators thereby seriously protect their established order and economic well-being for their own selfish, economic, social and ideological reasons and thereby prevent dissemination of new ideas and freedom of speech....

By publishing their complaint, I allowed Scientology to reveal more about itself than anything I could have imagined about Sirhan. My attorney, James Wolpman, filed a petition to remove the suit to a federal court because of the constitutional question it raised concerning freedom of the press. It reached the interrogatories stage, with questions such as, "Have you ever spoken with or received communication from Sirhan Sirhan, his immediate family or his duly authorized agents or attorneys?" I refused to answer, on the grounds that it was privileged information.

Scientology eventually offered to settle out of court for $5,000, but I refused. Then they said they would drop the suit if I would publish an article in *The Realist* by Chick Corea, a jazz musician and Scientologist, but that wasn't quite the way I made my editorial decisions, and I refused again. Scientology finally dropped their lawsuit altogether. However, their records show that they had other plans for me. Under the heading "Operation Dynamite"—their jargon for a frame-up—a memo read:

Got CSW from SFO to not do this on Krassner. I disagree and will pass my comments on to DG I US as to why this should be done. SFO has the idea that Krassner is totally handled and will not attack us again. My feelings are that in PT, he has not got enough financial backing to get out *The Realist* or other publications and when that occurs, will attack again, maybe more covertly but attack, nonetheless.

Later on, I flew to Kansas City to participate in a symposium at the University of Missouri, where I would link up with Ken Kesey. He had written to me from Mexico about this event with Henry Kissinger, B.F. Skinner, and Buckminster Fuller. I in turn was supposed to contact Ed Sanders, who proceeded to compose a song about Kissinger. However, the Student Activities Office had sent Kesey a copy of the previous year's program. This year's program was honoring the memory of Robert F. Kennedy. So Sanders had to compose another song:

> If Robert Kennedy still were alive
> Things would be different today
> Richard Nixon would still be on Wall Street
> Selling Pepsi in Taiwan...
> The war would be over today
> And J. Edgar Hoover would be watching gangster movies
> In an old folks home....

Before singing it at the university, he announced, "In the course of my research in Los Angeles, it became evident that Robert Kennedy was killed by a *group* of people including Sirhan Sirhan." In *The Family*, he had written, in reference to the Process Church of the Final Judgment, to which Manson had ties: "It is possible that the

Process had a baleful influence on Sirhan Sirhan, since Sirhan is known, in the spring of '68, to have frequented clubs in Hollywood in occult pursuits. He has talked several times subsequent to Robert Kennedy's death about an occult group from London which he knew about and which he really wanted to go to London to see."

> **"MY CONTENTION IS THIS—THE REASON MANSON WAS LEFT ON THE STREET WAS BECAUSE OUR DEPARTMENT THOUGHT THAT HE WAS GOING TO ATTACK THE BLACK PANTHERS."**

Since the Process had been an offshoot of Scientology, this looked like it could be a case of satirical prophecy. I was tempted to return to my original premise involving Sirhan, but it was too late. I had already become obsessed with my Manson research. I was gathering piece after piece of a mind-boggling jigsaw puzzle, without having any model to pattern it after. It was clear that members of the Manson family had actually but unknowingly served as a hit-squad for a drug ring. Furthermore, conspiracy researcher Mae Brussell put me in contact with Preston Guillory, a former deputy sheriff, who told me:

We had been briefed for a few weeks prior to the actual raiding of Spahn Ranch. We had a sheaf of memos on Manson, that they had automatic weapons at the ranch, that citizens had complained about hearing machine-guns fired at night, that firemen from the local fire station had been accosted by armed members of Manson's band and told to get out of the area, all sorts of complaints like this.

We had been advised to put anything relating to Manson on a memo submitted to the station, because they were supposedly gathering information for the raid we were going to make. Deputies at the station of course started asking, 'Why aren't we going to make the raid sooner?' I mean, Manson's a parole violator, machine-guns have been heard, we know there's narcotics and we know there's booze. He's living at the Spahn Ranch with a bunch of minor girls in complete violation of his parole.

Deputies at the station quite frankly became very annoyed that no action was being taken about Manson. My contention is this—the reason Manson was left on the street was because our department thought that he was going to attack the Black Panthers. We were getting intelligence briefings that Manson was anti-black and he had supposedly killed a Black Panther, the body of which could not be found, and the department thought that he was going to launch an attack on the Black Panthers....

After the panel at the University of Missouri, Ed Sanders and I went to the cafeteria for lunch. Ed ordered a full vegetarian meal and then couldn't eat any of it. I had never seen him so shaken. It was because the Process people had been hassling him. He said he was having trouble sleeping. Occasionally he mumbled things to himself as though they were marginal notes describing the state of his depression.

I recalled that, in the summer of 1968, while the Yippies were planning a Festival of Life at the Democratic National Convention in Chicago, some zealots from the Process cult visited me in New York. They were hyper-anxious to meet Tim Leary and kept pestering me for his phone number. The Process, founded by Scientology dropouts, first came to the US from London in 1967. Members were called "mind benders" and proclaimed their "dedication to the elimination of the grey forces."

In January 1968, they became the Process Church of the Final Judgment, a New Orleans-based religious corporation. They claimed to be in direct contact with both Jesus and Lucifer, and had wanted to be called the Church of the Process of Unification of Christ and Satan, but local officials presumably objected to their taking the name of Satan in vain.

The Process struck me as a group of occult provocateurs, using radical Christianity as a front. They were adamantly interested in Yippie politics. They boasted to me of various rallies which their *vibrations alone* had transformed into riots. They implied that there was some kind of connection between the assassination of Bobby Kennedy and their mere presence on the scene. On the evening that Kennedy was killed at the Ambassador Hotel, he had been to a dinner party in Malibu with Roman Polanski and Sharon Tate.

> "AND THIS TIME," I SAID, GIVING MY BEST IMITATION OF CLINT EASTWOOD BRAVADO, "YOU CAN LEAVE THOSE *GOONS* OF YOURS AT HOME."

Bernard Fensterwald, head of the Committee to Investigate Assassinations, told me that Sirhan Sirhan had some involvement with the Process. Peter Chang, the district attorney of Santa Cruz, showed me a letter from a Los Angeles police official to the chief of police in San Jose, warning him that the Process had infiltrated biker gangs and hippie communes.

And Ed Sanders wrote in *Win* magazine:

[W]ord came out of Los Angeles of a current FBI investigation of the RFK murder, the investigation growing, as the source put it, out of "the Manson case." Word came from another source, this one in the halls of Government itself, that several police and investigatory jurisdictions have information regarding other murders that may have been connected to the Robert Kennedy shooting; murders that occurred after RFK's. A disturbing fact in this regard is that one agency in the Federal Bureaucracy (not the FBI) has stopped a multi-county investigation by its own officers that would have probed into such matters as the social and religious activities of Sirhan Sirhan in early '68, and into the allegations regarding RFK-connected murders.

In 1972, Paulette Cooper, author of *The Scandal of Scientology*, put me in touch with Lee Cole, a former Scientologist who was now working with the Process Church. I contacted him and flew to Chicago. Cole met me at the airport with a couple of huge men whose demeanor was somewhat frightening. They drove me to a motel, where I checked in, paying cash in advance. Cole arranged for a meeting with Sherman Skolnick, a local conspiracy researcher. He was in a wheelchair. Two men, one with a metal hook in place of his hand, carried him up the back stairway to my motel room. Cole kept peeking out the window for suspicious-looking cars. The scene was becoming more surrealistic every minute.

Early the next morning, the phone rang. It was Skolnick: "Paul, I'm sorry to wake you, but you're in extreme danger." I was naked, but with my free hand I immediately started putting my socks on. "That fellow from last night, Lee Cole, he's CIA." My heart was pounding. I got dressed faster than I had ever gotten dressed in my life, packed my stuff and ran down the back steps of the motel without even checking out. At another motel, I called Cole. He denied being with the CIA. We made an appointment to visit the Process headqarters. "And this time," I said, giving my best imitation of Clint Eastwood bravado, "you can leave those *goons* of yours at home."

The Process men were dressed all in black, with large silver crosses hanging from their necks. They called each other "Brother" and they had German shepherds that seemed to be menacing. The Brothers tried to convince me that Scientology, not the Process, was responsible for creating Charles Manson. But what else could I have expected?

Lee Cole's role was to provide information on Scientology to the Process. To prove that he wasn't with the CIA, he told *me* stuff about Scientology. For example, he described their plan to kidnap former boxing champion Joe Louis from a mental hospital, so that Scientology could get the credit for curing him. Back in San Francisco, I asked journalist Roland Jacopetti to check that one out, and he discovered that Scientology actually *did* have such a plan, although it had been aborted.

Not that belonging to the CIA and Scientology were mutually exclusive—infiltration is always a two-way street—but I called up Sherman Skolnick in Chicago, and he apologized for scaring me the way he did. "You know us conspiracy researchers," he chuckled. "We're paranoid."

On January 13, 2003, Sirhan Sirhan lost a Supreme Court appeal, part of his effort to get a new trial in the assassination of Senator Kennedy. The justices refused without comment to consider whether Sirhan's case could be impartially reviewed by some California courts. Sirhan claims that his lawyer at the trial in Los Angeles was working with the government to win his conviction. On that same day, Attorney General John Ashcroft endorsed giving religious organizations government money for social services, which many critics contend would be a blatant violation of the constitutional principle of separation of church and state. Of course, the Church of Scientology, which has high hopes for inclusion in this ripoff of taxpayer funds, is trying very hard to act normal.

MORMON RACISM
BLACK IS *NOT* BEAUTIFUL

RICHARD ABANES

> Editor's Note: This article has been adapted from the chapter of the same name in One Nation Under Gods: A History of the Mormon Church by Richard Abanes (Four Walls Eight Windows, 2002).

_PRIDE AND PREJUDICE

Mormonism and racism have for many years been synonymous terms to persons well acquainted with Latter-day Saint beliefs.[1] The prejudicial aspects of Mormonism, however, have been greatly obscured in recent decades thanks to a concerted effort by LDS leaders to portray their church as an equal-opportunity religion. This positive publicity push began in 1978, when in response to mounting social pressures, black males in the LDS church were granted access to Mormonism's priesthood. (They had previously been barred from that position.) But such a politically correct move could hardly eradicate the previous 148 years of Mormon racist/white supremacist teachings, all of which directly related to the LDS doctrine of pre-existence.

According to Latter-day Saint beliefs, everyone's place in the world (e.g., country of birth, socioeconomic status, etc.) is determined by their conduct in the pre-mortal world. This idea comes from Joseph Smith's *Book of Abraham*, which speaks of "the noble and great ones," who lived in the pre-existent realm as God's spirit children.[2] These admirable spirits served God well, followed his commands, and did the most with their talents before coming to earth. Consequently, they are rewarded by being born into favorable circumstances. To be specific, they are born as Mormons in America, or at the very least, somewhere in a predominantly Caucasian country. More righteous spirits are born with more advantages. Less commendable spirits, however, are born with fewer advantages, into lives of greater or lesser quality depending on how poorly they performed in the pre-earth world. Moreover, they are born as non-whites. This is their punishment for not having been all they could have been during the pre-existence.

Mormons also believe that performance in the pre-mortal realm not only determines one's race but also the darkness of one's skin within that race. The darker the race and the skin, the less righteously a spirit behaved during its pre-mortal life. Apostle Mark E. Petersen explained this doctrine during a 1954 Brigham Young University lecture:

[C]an we account in any other way for the birth of some of the children of God in darkest Africa, or in flood-ridden China, or among the starving hordes of India, while some of the rest of us are born here in the United States? We cannot escape the conclusion that because of performance in our pre-existence some of us are born as Chinese, some as Japanese, some as Latter-day Saints. These are rewards and punishments.... A Chinese, born in China with a dark skin, and with all the handicaps of that race seems to have little opportunity. But think of the mercy of God to Chinese people who are willing to accept the gospel. In spite of whatever they might have done in the pre-existence to justify being born over there as Chinamen, if they now, in this life, accept the gospel and live it the rest of their lives they can have the [Mormon] Priesthood.[3]

Of all the races and skin tones represented on earth, the lowest, most degrading form a spirit can receive, according to LDS teachings, is that of a black. This body, because of its extremely dark skin, has always been viewed as not being an "honourable body."[4] Latter-day Saint John J. Stewart, who in the 1960s was billed as one of the most widely-read Mormon authors, further explained that the less-than-admirable behavior of some of these pre-existent spirits also caused them to be born into filth, poverty, and degradation—e.g., ghettos or third world countries.[5] Such souls, according to Stewart, actually penalized themselves "as to their circumstances in this world."[6] Tenth LDS president Joseph Fielding Smith presented a similar message in his book *Doctrines of Salvation*:

There is a reason why one man is born black and with other disadvantages, while *another is born white* with great advantages. The reason is that we once had an estate before we came here, and were obedient, more or less, to the laws that were given us there. *Those who were faithful in all things there received greater blessings here, and those who were not faithful received less.*[7]

Blacks lucky enough to find themselves in more favorable conditions are enjoying God's mercy, says Stewart:

> THE DARKER THE RACE AND THE SKIN, THE LESS RIGHTEOUSLY A SPIRIT BEHAVED DURING ITS PRE-MORTAL LIFE.

There are Negroes born into families of wealth and refinement, others who are blessed with great talents, and there are those born into the lowest classes of society in Africa, in squalor and ignorance, living out their lives in a fashion akin to that of the animals. Does not this infinite variety of circumstance give further evidence of man's being assigned that station in life which he has merited by his performance in the pre-mortal existence?[8]

A person's skin color, more than anything else, is most commonly linked to one's actions during a great "rebellion," which supposedly took place in the pre-existent realm thousands (perhaps millions) of years ago. This celestial conflict, which culminated in a cosmic war between Lucifer and Christ, affected everyone in a very permanent

> "YOU SEE SOME CLASSES OF THE HUMAN FAMILY THAT ARE BLACK, UNCOUTH, UNCOMELY, DISAGREEABLE, AND LOW IN THEIR HABITS, WILD, AND SEEMINGLY DEPRIVED OF NEARLY ALL THE BLESSINGS OF THE INTELLIGENCE THAT IS GENERAL-LY BESTOWED UPON MANKIND." — BRIGHAM YOUNG

way. Those who bravely fought on Christ's side were born as privileged Mormon whites, while those who were indecisive and/or less valiant in the celestial struggle were born black.[9] They were born through the lineage of Cain, the son of Adam and Eve who murdered his brother, Abel. "Cain was cursed with a dark skin," said LDS apostle Bruce McConkie. "[H]e became the father of the Negroes."[10] Brigham Young propagated this doctrine as early as 1859, saying:

You see some classes of the human family that are black, uncouth, uncomely, disagreeable, and low in their habits, wild, and seemingly deprived of nearly all the blessings of the intelligence that is generally bestowed upon mankind…. Cain slew his brother…. [A]nd the Lord put a mark on him, which is the flat nose and black skin…. [T]hen, another curse is pronounced upon the same race—that they should be the "servant of servants;" and they will be, until that curse is removed.[11]

Prior to 1978, Latter-day Saints additionally believed that the greatest consequence of a substandard pre-mortal performance was the loss of one's right to both the Mormon priesthood and exaltation to godhood in the Celestial Kingdom. In reference to the priesthood, Mormon Elder George F. Richards made the following remarks:

The Negro is an unfortunate man. He has been given a black skin. But that is as nothing compared with that greater handicap that he is not permitted to receive the Priesthood and the ordinances of the temple, necessary to prepare men and women to enter into and enjoy a fullness of glory in the celestial kingdom [i.e., godhood].[12]

Joseph Fielding Smith agreed that the blacks could not hold the priesthood because they represented an inferior race "cursed with a

black skin."[13] He also taught that blacks, as added punishment, "have been made to feel their inferiority and have been separated from the rest of mankind from the beginning."[14] Most unfortunate for blacks, however, was the loss of priesthood blessings, which meant that no black could reproduce families in eternity like white Mormons.[15] Moreover, since priesthood membership is a prerequisite for holding any LDS church office, blacks also were effectively barred from assuming any position in the Latter-day Saint hierarchy.

But if blacks prior to 1978 could not attain godhood or hold any church office, then what could they look forward to as Mormons? Apostle Mark E. Petersen answered this question in 1954: "If that Negro is faithful all his days, he can enter the celestial kingdom. He will go there as a servant."[16] Mormons, realizing the controversial nature of such a doctrine, for many years sought to keep its existence quiet. Although discussed among long-time members and LDS leaders, it certainly was not to be shared with potential converts, unbelievers, or Mormon critics. Apostle Petersen, for instance, tried to suppress from public release the lecture in which he made the previous statement.[17] And during a missionary conference in Oslo, Norway, LDS European Mission president Alvin R. Dyer warned his listeners to not reveal what he had to say about blacks:

I want to talk to you a little bit now about something that is not missionary work, and what I say is NOT to be given to your investigators [i.e., potential converts] by any matter of means…. Why is it that you are white and not colored?… [Remember that] God is not unjust to cause a righteous spirit to be born as a cursed member of the black race.[18]

In 1966, Bruce McConkie (ordained an apostle in 1972) agreed with this teaching in his popular *Mormon Doctrine*, saying: "The negroes are not equal with other races where the receipt of certain spiritual blessings are concerned…. [B]ut this inequality is not of man's origin. It is the Lord's doing."[19] McConkie was merely echoing other Mormon leaders, such as Joseph Fielding Smith, who assured LDS critics: "It is not the authorities of the Church who have placed a restriction on him [i.e., the black man] regarding the holding of the Priesthood. It was not the Prophet Joseph Smith…. It was the Lord!"[20] LDS sociologist Dr. Lowery Nelson, who understood the ramifications of such a doctrine, wrote a 1947 protest letter to the church's First Presidency:

This doctrine pressed to its logical conclusion would say that Dr. George Washington Carver, the late eminent and saintly Negro scientist, is by virtue of the color of his skin, inferior even to the least admirable white person, not because of the virtues he may or may not possess, but because—through no fault of his—there is a dark pigment in his skin.[21]

Earlier this same year, the First Presidency had written to Nelson, telling him that his growing dissatisfaction with Mormonism was perhaps due to the erroneous idea that "all God's children stand in equal positions before Him in all things."[22]

Predictably, such teachings have produced nothing less than a sense of racial superiority among Mormons. In her book, *Mormonism, Mama, and Me*, Thelma Geer—a fourth-generation Mormon who eventually left the LDS church—recounted exactly what it was like growing up as a Mormon:

As a white Mormon, I proudly accepted the teaching that my fair skin and Mormon parentage signified that I had been one of God's most intelligent and obedient born-in-heaven spirit children.... As a reward for my superior attributes and attitudes, I had been singled out, trained, and qualified to be born a white Latter-day Saint, deserving of emulation, adulation, and eventual deification. All dark-skinned people, even darker-complexioned Caucasians...had been inferior spirits in heaven.[23]

> "IF THE WHITE MAN WHO BELONGS TO THE CHOSEN SEED MIXES HIS BLOOD WITH THE SEED OF CAIN, THE PENALTY, UNDER THE LAW OF GOD, IS DEATH ON THE SPOT. THIS WILL ALWAYS BE SO." — BRIGHAM YOUNG

Such a mindset inevitably led many Saints in the 1960s to conclude that segregation of the races, a point of heated controversy during the Civil Rights movement, was ordained of God. Mormon segregation, of course, included a prohibition on interracial marriage, which used to be considered one of the most heinous of deeds in the Mormon belief system. As the LDS *Juvenile Instructor* warned: "[W]e believe it to be a great sin in the eyes of our heavenly Father for a white person to marry a black one. And further, that it is a proof of the mercy of God that no such race appears able to continue for many generations."[24]

_SEGREGATION ACCORDING TO GOD

Despite evidence to the contrary, Mormons have consistently argued that their church's doctrine has never been, nor currently is, racist. Apostle Mark E. Petersen, for instance, stated in 1954 that he had absolutely no problem with blacks receiving an education, driving a Cadillac ("if they could afford it"), or obtaining other advantages. He then added: "But let them enjoy these things among themselves. I think the Lord segregated the Negro and who is man to change that segregation?"[25] In an ultimate example of blame-shifting, the 1963 volume titled *The Glory of Mormonism* argued that any suffering due to racism was more God's fault than anyone else's:

When God allows a spirit to take on a Negroid body, do you suppose He is unaware of the fact that he will suffer a social stigma? Therefore, if you say this Church is unjust in not allowing the Negro to bear the Priesthood, you must, to be consistent, likewise say that God is even more unjust in giving him a black skin.[26]

To Mormons one of the most sensitive aspects of segregation related to the intermarriage of blacks and whites. Brigham Young certainly left no doubt as to his thoughts on the subject, preaching:

"Shall I tell you the law of God in regard to the African race? If the white man who belongs to the chosen seed mixes his blood with the seed of Cain, the penalty, under the law of God, is death on the spot. This will always be so."[27] In a 1947 letter to a critic of Mormonism's racist views, the LDS First Presidency adamantly condemned any thoughts of interracial marriage:

Your ideas, as we understand them, appear to contemplate the intermarriage of the Negro and white races, a concept which has heretofore been most repugnant to most normal-minded people from the ancient patriarchs until now.... [T]here is a growing tendency, particularly among some educators, as it manifests itself in this area, toward the breaking down of race barriers in the matter of intermarriage between whites and blacks, but it does not have the sanction of the Church and is contrary to Church doctrine.[28]

Prior to 1978, particularly strong language was frequently used by LDS leaders who believed that even one drop of "Negro blood" would disqualify a person from holding the priesthood. Apostle Petersen explained:

We must not intermarry with the Negro. Why? If I were to marry a Negro woman and have children by her, my children would all be cursed as to the priesthood.... If there is one drop of Negro blood in my children, as I have read to you, they receive the curse.... There are 50 million Negroes in the United States. If they were to achieve complete absorption with the white race, think what that would do. With 50 million Negroes intermarried with us, where would the priesthood be?... Think what that would do to the work of the church![29]

Petersen additionally exhorted members of his white audience to avoid marrying not only blacks but also dark-skinned individuals, such as persons of Hawaiian, Japanese, or Chinese descent.[30] To combat the danger posed by interracial marriage, the First Presidency recommended that Mormons not communicate with blacks socially—even to share the LDS message of salvation:

No special effort has ever been made to proselyte among the Negro race, and social intercourse between the Whites and the Negroes should certainly not be encouraged because of leading to intermarriage, which the Lord has forbidden.[31]

Official LDS publications also presented highly racist mischaracterizations of blacks. One article in the Mormon church's *Juvenile Instructor*, for instance, alleged that blacks had the lowest intelligence of all humans, were the most barbarous of all people, advanced more slowly than anyone else, and were the least capable of improvement among the races.[32] This same article then described blacks as looking like someone, or something, that had been overcooked:

[A Negro] looks as though he has been put in an oven and burnt to a cinder.... His hair baked crisp, his nose melted to his face, and the color of his eyes runs into the whites. Some men look as if they had only been burned brown; but he appears to have gone a stage further, and been cooked until he was quite black.[33]

Up through the early 1970s, Mormon leaders continued to promote not only anti-black rhetoric but also highly offensive stereotypes and segregationist policies. Eventually, however, church leaders slowly realized that their view of blacks was harming Mormonism's expansion outside the United States. Moreover, the Civil Rights movement was placing Mormonism in a very bad light; so bad a light that protests against the church were beginning to occur. Organizations like the National Association for the Advancement of Colored People (NAACP) also were targeting the church as a hotbed of ongoing racism. The LDS ban on blacks in the priesthood would soon have to be lifted. But such steps of progress were not well-received by all Mormon leaders.

_WELCOME TO THE TEMPLE

After the death of the church's racially-progressive president David O. McKay in 1970, 93-year-old Joseph Fielding Smith inherited Mormonism's prophetic mantle. But he would only survive for two years (d. 1972), after which time Harold B. Lee took over the highest LDS office. Seventy-three-year-old Lee served an even shorter term, dying the following year on December 26, 1975. His successor was Spencer W. Kimball, a 78-year-old long-time church leader committed to seeing Mormonism spread throughout the world.

Kimball seemed to understand better than anyone that in order for Mormonism to continue its expansion, the church would need to change its policy on blacks. By the time he took over, the church had been enduring non-stop pressure to conform with America's realization that racial inequality had to end. Consider the following measures taken against the LDS church to break its racist restrictions:

> • The NAACP asked all Third World countries to deny visas to Mormon missionaries and representatives until their anti-black doctrine was repealed.
>
> • The Church of the Black Cross, under the leadership of Rev. Roy Flournoy, discouraged tourist travel to Utah and called for a boycott of Mormon goods, including Mormon Tabernacle Choir record albums.
>
> • A BYU basketball game was disrupted by a protest against the LDS church's policy on blacks.
>
> • A riot erupted at the University of Wyoming after black athletes were dismissed because they wore armbands protesting BYU's presence at the school.
>
> • Stanford University and the University of Washington canceled all sporting events with BYU.

> • Discrimination charges were brought against the LDS church for refusing to allow a black Boy Scout to be a patrol leader, a position reserved for white LDS youths in church-sponsored troops.

By the mid-1970s, the Mormon church had made a number of concessions due to increasing public pressure. They allowed a few blacks to join the Mormon Tabernacle Choir; black Boy Scouts were allowed to be patrol leaders in LDS-sponsored troops; and a few blacks were admitted to Brigham Young University. These token gestures within Mormonism might have remained just that had it not been for the fact that by the mid-1970s the church had expanded its missionary efforts to South America. There they were faced with an impossible task—distinguishing which converts, many of whom had very dark skin, had blacks in their ancestral line.

The intensity of the problem dramatically increased when Kimball announced plans in 1974 to build a new temple in Brazil; a temple that could only be entered by priesthood holders. Potential priesthood holders in Brazil numbered well into the tens of thousands, but

THE NAACP ASKED ALL THIRD WORLD COUNTRIES TO DENY VISAS TO MORMON MISSIONARIES AND REPRESENTATIVES UNTIL THEIR ANTI-BLACK DOCTRINE WAS REPEALED.

many of these same individuals were of a racially-mixed background. The crisis point was reached in 1978 as the temple neared completion. Apostle LeGrand Richards acknowledged to Kimball: "All those people with negro blood in them have been raising money to build a temple." Although his point hardly needed to be spelled out, Richards continued: "[I]f we don't change, then they can't even use it after they've got it."[34]

Kimball responded by asking each of the Twelve Apostles for their arguments for and against giving blacks the priesthood. One week later, on June 9, 1978, in a manner reminiscent of how Wilford Woodruff's 1890 Manifesto prohibiting polygamy was issued, Kimball released a document to the media announcing that blacks henceforth would be granted the LDS priesthood. Like the Manifesto, the 1978 policy change was billed as a "revelation" from God:

Aware of the promises made by the prophets and presidents of the Church who have preceded us that at some time, in God's eternal plan, all of our brethren who are worthy may receive the priesthood, and witnessing the faithfulness of those from whom the priesthood has been withheld, we have pleaded long and earnestly in behalf of these, our faithful brethren.... He has heard our prayers, and by revelation has confirmed that the long-promised day has come when every faithful, worthy man in the Church may receive the holy priesthood, with power to exercise its divine authority, and enjoy with his loved ones every blessing that flows therefrom, including the blessings of the temple. Accordingly, all worthy members of the

Church may be ordained to the priesthood without regard for race or color.[35]

Mormons, by and large, were pleased that God had changed his mind at such a convenient time in history. Even the more rigid, far right-wing Saints, although not too pleased, took the declaration in stride. After all, the doctrinal change would create a whole new world of opportunities not only in South America but in the formerly cursed continent of Africa. Lifting the ban also opened up missionary doors to the Caribbean, Central America, Haiti, and other lands where black ancestry is prominent in the population. As a result, millions of dollars began flowing into the church's coffers. Thus began Mormonism's move toward becoming one of the world's wealthiest religions.

Endnotes

1. Racism is resoundingly condemned in the Bible. Several passages, for example, plainly say that "God is no respecter of persons; but in every nation he that feareth him, and worketh righteousness, is accepted with him" (Acts 10:34-35, KJV). The Bible additionally says that there should be absolutely no race distinctions (Gal. 3:28). **2.** *Pearl of Great Price, Book of Abraham* 3:22. **3.** Petersen, Mark E. "Race Problems As They Affect the Church." Address At the Convention of Teachers of Religion On the College Level, delivered at Brigham Young University, Provo, Utah, 27 Aug 1954. On file at BYU Library, Special Collections. **4.** Hyde, Orson. *Speech of Orson Hyde, Delivered Before the High Priests' Quorum, in Nauvoo, April 27th, 1845, Upon the Course and Conduct of Mr. Sidney Rigdon.* Liverpool: James and Woodburn, 1845: 309. **5.** Stewart, John J. *The Glory of Mormonism.* Salt Lake City: Mercury Publishing Co., Inc., 1963: inside front flap book cover and 144. **6.** *Ibid.*: 145. **7.** Smith, Joseph Fielding. *Doctrines of Salvation,* vol. 1. Salt Lake City: Bookcraft, 1954: 61. **8.** *Op cit.,* Stewart: 152. **9.** Concerning this "rebellion in heaven," Mormon historian B.H. Roberts made the following statement: "Only those, however, who wickedly rebelled against God were adjudged to deserve banishment from heaven, and become the devil and his angels. Others there were, who may not have rebelled against God, and yet were so indifferent in their support of the righteous cause of our Redeemer, that they forfeited certain privileges and powers granted to those who were more valiant for God and correct principles. We have, I think, a demonstration of this in the seed of Ham.... I believe that race is the one through which it is ordained those spirits that were not valiant in the great rebellion in heaven should come; who through their indifference or lack of integrity to righteousness, rendered themselves unworthy of the Priesthood and its powers, and hence it is withheld from them to this day" (Roberts, B.H. "To the Youth of Israel." *The Contributor,* vol. 6: 296-7 [Salt Lake City: Junius F. Wells, 1885.]). According to apostle Bruce McConkie: "Those who were less valiant in pre-existence and who thereby had certain spiritual restrictions imposed upon them during mortality are known to us as the negroes" (McConkie, Bruce. *Mormon Doctrine.* Salt Lake City: Bookcraft, 1958 (second edition, 1966): 527). **10.** *Op cit.,* McConkie: 109; cf. *Pearl of Great Price, Book of Moses* 7:8 and *Pearl of Great Price, Book of Abraham* 1:21-26. **11.** Brigham Young, 9 Oct 1859. *Journal of Discourses,* vol. 7: 290. (Liverpool: Amasa Lyman, 1860; lithographed reprint of original edition, 1966.) **12.** Richards, George F. *Conference Report.* April 1939: 58. **13.** Smith, Joseph Fielding. *The Way to Perfection.* Salt Lake City: Genealogical Society of Utah, 1931: 101. Interestingly, Smith contradicted himself on this point by also writing: "The Latter-day Saints...have no animosity towards the Negro. Neither have they described him as belonging to an 'inferior race'" (Smith, Joseph Fielding. *Answers to Gospel Questions,* vol. 4. Salt Lake City: Deseret Book Company, 1979: 170.) **14.** *Op cit.,* Smith, *Way to Perfection*: 101-2. **15.** *Ibid.* **16.** Petersen, on file at BYU Library, Special Collections (see endnote #3). **17.** Wallace Turner gives the following account of what happened when Petersen found out his speech was being circulated: "This speech was delivered in a closed meeting. A copy of it came into the hands of James D. Wardle, the Salt Lake City barber who is a member of the Reorganized LDS church. Wardle has enjoyed many years of baiting his Utah Mormon townsmen, and made his copy available to Jerald Tanner, the LDS apostate who specializes in circulating anti-LDS materials. Tanner went to the LDS library, found a copy of the speech and assured himself that it was the same speech he had received from Wardle. But the church would not give him a copy he could take away with him. Using the Wardle copy as his source, Tanner began to circulate the address. At that time

Apostle Petersen was in England leading the mission there. In early 1965 he wrote to Tanner threatening to sue him if he did not stop publication and recall the previously issued copies of the speech. Tanner gleefully reproduced and circulated the letter. Since then Petersen has returned to Salt Lake City and no suit has been filed." (Turner, Wallace. *The Mormon Establishment.* Boston: Houghton Mifflin Company, 1966: 253-4). **18.** Dyer, Alvin R. "For What Purpose?" Missionary Conference in Oslo, Norway, 18 Mar 1961, printed in *The Negro in Mormon Theology,* 48-58. Quoted in Tanner, Jerald, and Sandra Tanner. *Mormonism: Shadow or Reality?* Salt Lake City: ULM, 1987: 264-5. **19.** *Op cit.,* McConkie: 527. **20.** Smith, Joseph Fielding. Mimeographed letter, 9 July 1963. Quoted in Stewart: 154. **21.** Nelson, Lowery. Letter to First Presidency, 8 Oct 1947. Quoted in Stewart: 146. **22.** LDS First Presidency. Letter to Lowery Nelson, 17 July 1947. Quoted in Stewart: 153. **23.** Geer, Thelma. *Mormonism, Mama & Me.* Chicago: Moody, 1986: 24-5. **24.** *Juvenile Instructor,* vol. 3: 165. Quoted in Tanner and Tanner: 266. **25.** Petersen (see endnote #3). **26.** *Op cit.,* Stewart: 155. **27.** Young, Brigham. *Journal of Discourses,* vol. 10: 110. (Liverpool: Daniel H. Wells, 1865; lithographed reprint of original edition.) **28.** LDS First Presidency. Letter to Lowery Nelson, 17 July 1947. Quoted in Stewart: 153-4. **29.** *Op cit.,* Petersen; cf. *op cit.,* Turner: 252. Both Ezra Taft Benson and Mark E. Petersen were sent on an extended mission to Europe. It is believed that they were sent abroad because of their outspoken ways and extremely conservative political views. **30.** "I think Hawaiians should marry Hawaiians," said Petersen. "[T]he Japanese ought to marry the Japanese, and the Chinese ought to marry Chinese, and the Caucasians should marry Caucasians" (*op cit.,* Turner: 253). **31.** LDS First Presidency. Letter to Virgil H. Sponberg, 5 May 1947. Quoted in Bush, Lester E. *Mormonism's Negro Doctrine: An Historical Overview.* Arlington, VA: Dialogue: A Journal of Mormon Thought, 1973: 42. This short booklet originally appeared as an article by the same title in the periodical *Dialogue: A Journal of Mormon Thought,* vol. 8 (spring 1973). **32.** "From Caucasian to Negro." *Juvenile Instructor,* vol. 3 (1868): 142. Quoted in Bush, 57-8, endnote 99. **33.** *Ibid.* **34.** Gottlieb, Robert, and Peter Wiley. *American Saints: The Rise of Mormon Power.* New York: G.P. Putnam's Sons, 1984: 184. **35.** Declaration 2, released to *Deseret News,* 9 June 1978: 1A. Printed in D&C, modern editions. For a highly detailed look at the events that led up to this so-called revelation, see Tanner, Sandra, and Jerald Tanner. "Blacks Receive LDS Priesthood: Pressure Forces Mormon President To Issue New 'Revelation.'" *Salt Lake City Messenger* 39 (July 1978). Online at <www.utlm.org/newsletters/no39.htm>.

CONTRIBUTORS

Religion journalist **Richard Abanes** has authored nearly a dozen books on cults, the occult, and new religious movements. More information may be obtained by contacting him through his religious information Website <www.abanes.com>.

Born and educated in Toronto, **James Bacque** has recently written two major books: *Crimes and Mercies* and *Other Losses* (both Little, Brown in Canada and the UK), which were published in eleven languages around the globe, selling 250,000+ copies. He has been the recipient of a front-page attack-dog review in the *New York Times Book Review* by well-known plagiarist Stephen E. Ambrose. Bacque's Website is at <www.jamesbacque.com>.

Dan Barker was an ordained evangelical minister, missionary, evangelist, and Christian songwriter before he abandoned religion in 1983. He is now Public Relations director of the Freedom From Religion Foundation <www.ffrf.org> in Madison, Wisconsin. Dan's story can be read in the autobiographical *Losing Faith in Faith: From Preacher to Atheist* (FFRF, Inc., 1992). He has also written *Just Pretend: A Freethought Book for Children* (FFRF, Inc., 1988), *Maybe Yes, Maybe No: A Guide for Young Skeptics* (Prometheus Books, 1990), and *Maybe Right, Maybe Wrong: A Guide for Young Thinkers* (Prometheus Books, 1992), as well as numerous articles for *Freethought Today*, the Foundation's newspaper. A professional musician and songwriter, Dan has produced an album of 34 historical and original freethought songs called *Friendly Neighborhood Atheist* (FFRF, Inc., 2000). He is married to Annie Laurie Gaylor. See <www.ffrf.org/lfif/biodan.html>.

Sandra Bisin is a French freelance journalist living in Paris.

Howard Bloom, a visiting scholar in the graduate department of psychology at NYU, is a longtime political and intellectual activist. He researched and wrote position papers for winning political candidates from the age of 20 on. Beginning in 1981, he fought the censorship forces of the religious right. And in 1984, he co-founded Music in Action, a national anti-censorship group that went toe to toe with Tipper Gore when she and a group of Senators' wives founded the PMRC and attacked rock music. Bloom is the author of *The Lucifer Principle: A Scientific Expedition Into the Forces of History* (Atlantic Monthly Press, 1997) and *Global Brain: The Evolution of Mass Mind From the Big Bang to the 21st Century* (John Wiley & Sons, 2000). He is also the founder of the International Paleopsychology Project, the founder of the Science of the Soul Initiative, a founding board member of the Epic of Evolution Society, and a Founding Council Member of the Darwin Project. His Website is at <www.howardbloom.net>.

William Blum left the State Department in 1967, abandoning his aspiration of becoming a Foreign Service Officer, because of his opposition to what the United States was doing in Vietnam. In 1969, he wrote and published an exposé of the CIA in which was revealed the names and addresses of more than 200 employees of the Agency. Blum has been a freelance journalist in the United States, Europe, and South America. In 1999, he received a Project Censored award for "exemplary journalism" for his article on how, in the 1980s, the United States gave Iraq the material to develop chemical and biological warfare capability. He is the author of *Killing Hope: US Military and CIA Interventions Since World War II* (Common Courage Press, 1995), *Rogue State: A Guide to the World's Only Superpower* (Common Courage Press, 2000), and *West-Bloc Dissident: A Cold War Political Memoir* (Soft Skull Press, 2002). Portions of his books can be read at <www.killinghope.org>.

Jakob S. Boeskov was born in Elsinore, Denmark, in 1973. He has drawn comics (*Flax Letter*) and participated in exhibitions around the globe. He has a degree in architecture from the Royal Danish Academy of Art and has used his academic distinctions in the tradition of famous "paper architects," such as Lebbeus Woods and Piranesi, to create "fictitious realities." New projects include creating fake wireless technology and fake advertising for the Ministry of Homeland Security (The Citizen Eye, Los Angeles 2002), and infiltrating China's first international weapons fair with a horrendous, fake weapon technology ("My Doomsday Weapon," first published in *Black Box Magazine*, 2003). His shocking and impressive art, ranging from personal writings to animation, drawings, and film, has been described as, "James Bond meets Ulrike Meinhof at a Situationist party." He is getting recognition as a unique social commentator and one of the most promising artists coming out of Scandinavia today.

Jeff Cohen is the founder of FAIR <www.fair.org>, the progressive media-watch organization based in New York. He has been a regular on national TV, including as an MSNBC commentator, a *News Watch* panelist on Fox News, and a cohost of *Crossfire* on CNN. His columns have appeared in dozens of dailies, including *USA Today*, the *Washington Post*, the *Los Angeles Times*, the *Boston Globe*, *Newsday*, the *Atlanta Journal-Constitution*, and the *Miami Herald*. For four years, he cowrote the nationally syndicated "Media Beat" column with Norman Solomon. He is the coauthor of a number of books, including *Wizards of Media Oz: Behind the Curtain of Mainstream News* (Common Courage Press, 1997) and *The Way Things Aren't: Rush Limbaugh's Reign of Error* (New Press, 1995).

Philip W. Cook is the author of *Abused Men: The Hidden Side of Domestic Violence* (Greenwood/Praeger, 1997), and Vice President of Stop Abuse For Everyone <www.safe4all.org>. His Website is at <www.abusedmen.com>.

Richard DeGrandpre is an independent scholar of drugs and other "technologies of the self." His books include *Ritalin Nation* (Norton, 1999) and *Digitopia* (Random House, 2001). He is also associate editor at *Adbusters* magazine <www.adbusters.org>.

Ovidio Diaz-Espino is the author of *How Wall Street Created a Nation: J.P. Morgan, Teddy Roosevelt and the Panama Canal* (Four Walls Eight Windows, 2001). He was born in Panama and has worked as a lawyer for several firms on Wall Street, including J.P. Morgan & Co.

Daniel Ellsberg grew up in Detroit and graduated from Harvard. He served as a company commander in the Marine Corps for two years, then completed a doctorate in economics at Harvard. In 1959, he joined the RAND Corporation's Economics Department as an analyst, and in 1964 he was recruited to serve in the Pentagon under Secretary of Defense Robert McNamara. Following two years in Vietnam for the State Department, Ellsberg eventually returned to RAND. In 1971, he made headlines around the world when he released the Pentagon Papers. Now a prominent speaker, writer, and activist, he lives in California and Washington, DC. His latest book is *Secrets: A Memoir of Vietnam and the Pentagon Papers* (Viking/Penguin, 2002). His Website is at <www.ellsberg.net>.

Daniel Forbes' <ddanforbes@aol.com> recent report on state and federal political malfeasance geared to defeat treatment-not-incarceration ballot initiatives was published by the Institute for Policy Studies <www.ips-dc.org/projects/drugpolicy/ohio.htm>. His contribution to this volume is an updated version of an article that appeared on DrugWar.com in September 2002 <www.drugwar.com/pforbesdea1.shtm>. Much of his work, including his series in *Salon* that led to his testimony before both the Senate and the House, is archived at <www.mapinc.org>.

Ritt Goldstein is a noted investigative journalist and former leader in the movement for US law enforcement accountability. He's broken stories such as "US Planning to Recruit One in 24 Americans as Citizen Spies" (*Sydney Morning Herald*, Australia) and "The Price of Oil?...War" (*CounterPunch* and the *SMH*). His articles are regularly showcased worldwide. Goldstein has lived in Sweden since 1997, seeking political asylum there; findings indicate he was the victim of life-threatening assaults in retaliation for his police accountability efforts. His application has been supported by the European Parliament, five of Sweden's seven major political parties, clergy, and Amnesty International and other rights groups. To date, his asylum claim has been refused on the grounds that "the US is an internationally recognized democracy with a just legal system," and the assaults he endured were pursued without "the authorization of police authorities." His first book, *In the Name of Justice*, awaits publication.

Lucy Gwin is author of *Going Overboard* (Viking Press, 1982), a memoir of her year as the solitary female deckhand in the Louisiana offshore oilfields, and editor of *Mouth* magazine <www.mouthmag.com>. Her bulletins from the freak front have appeared in both the mainstream and the disability-rights press. She lives in Topeka,

Kansas, of all places, where she fends off aggressive Christians and wishes a tornado would take her over the rainbow or anyway back East. She doesn't use email. Forget about it.

Thom Hartmann is a writer, former editor and reporter, entrepreneur, psychotherapist (and NLP Practitioner and NLP Trainer), and worldwide lecturer who lives in Vermont. His writings focus on the intersection of myth and stories—otherwise known as "culture"—and how those stories, when they become toxic, lead to problems with schools, democratic institutions, the environment, and even problems in life, relationships, and communities. His books include *Unequal Protection: The Rise of Corporate Dominance and the Theft of Human Rights* (Rodale Press, 2002), *Last Hours of Ancient Sunlight*, *The Greatest Spiritual Secret of the Century*, *Thom Hartmann's Complete Guide to ADD*, *Beyond ADD*, and *ADHD Secrets of Success*. His Websites are at <www.thomhartmann.com> and <www.unequalprotection.com>.

Jim Hougan is an award-winning investigative reporter, novelist, and documentary film-maker. A former Washington editor of *Harper's Magazine*, he is the author of *Kingdom Come* (a novel) and nonfiction books about the CIA and Watergate (*Spooks* and *Secret Agenda*).

John Kelly is a former research scientist and the first author with Phillip Wearne of *Tainting Evidence: Inside the Scandals at the FBI Crime Lab* (The Free Press, 1998), which was nominated for a Pulitzer Prize, and second author with Dr. Arjun Makhijani of *Why Japan* (Tokyo: Kyoikusha, 1985) about the US decision to drop the atomic bomb. More recently, he published an essay in the book *Into the Buzzsaw* (Prometheus Books, 2002) about the state of the US media. He has researched, written, and lectured about the CIA for some 20 years and is the former chairman of the Intelligence Study Group of the American Political Science Association. He served as editor and senior writer for the journal *The National Reporter*, which specialized in the CIA and other intelligence agencies. He has also served as an investigative associate producer and reporter for many television programs about the CIA, as well as having written stories which were made into programs. These programs included a six-part BBC series, *CIA*; BBC documentaries *CIA in Paradise* and *The Secret Wars of Ollie North*; a Channel 4 (UK) documentary, *Hidden Hand: CIA*; a three-hour BBC documentary, *Operation Gladio*; a three-part series on the CBS Evening News with Dan Rather about Ronald Rewald and the CIA; a two-part series on the ABC News Tonight with Peter Jennings about Rewald and the CIA; and an Australian Broadcasting Corporation documentary, *Conspiracy of Patriots*. He has worked as a freelance journalist and has published in or reported for *Penthouse*, the *Boston Globe*, the *San Francisco Examiner*, the *Oakland Tribune*, *The Nation*, Pacific News Service, the *Village Voice*, *LA Weekly*, *Le Monde*, *Le Monde Diplomatique*, *Jornal do Brasil*, the *Times of India*, the *Sydney Morning Herald*, and Kyodo News Service, among others. He recently served as Washington producer and writer for the award-winning Australian documentary *Shadow Play*, about the creation of the Suharto dictatorship in Indonesia; assistant director for a 40-minute documentary about the Armenian genocide begun in Turkey in 1915, for BBC-2's foreign affairs series, *Correspondent*; and, most recently, as an assistant producer for an award-winning Channel Four/TLC production investigating the causes of the collapse of the World Trade Center Twin Towers, which was broadcast in Britain and Europe as

How the Twin Towers Collapsed (December 2001) and in the US as *World Trade Center: Anatomy of a Collapse* (February 2002).

Russ Kick is the editor of the volume you're currently holding; *Everything You Know Is Wrong: The Disinformation Guide to Secrets and Lies*; *You Are Being Lied To: The Disinformation Guide to Media Distortion, Historical Whitewashes and Cultural Myths*; and *Hot Off the Net: Erotica and Other Sex Writings From the Internet*. He is the author of *Outposts, Psychotropedia*, and the upcoming *50 Things You're Not Supposed to Know* (The Disinformation Company, 2003). He's contributed to the *Village Voice*, Loompanics, the free-speech magazine *Gauntlet*, *The Murdering of My Years: Artists and Activists Making Ends Meet* (edited by Mickey Z.), and *Busted: Stone Cowboys, Narco-Lords and Washington's War on Drugs* (edited by Mike Gray). He's also editor-in-chief of the Disinformation Website <www.disinfo.com> and publisher-editor of The Memory Hole <www.thememoryhole.org>.

Lucy Komisar is a New York investigative and political journalist who reports on the offshore bank and corporate secrecy system and its role in moving and laundering the money of corporate crooks, arms and drug traffickers, dictators, corrupt officials, terrorists, covert action operatives, tax cheats, and other criminals. She is writing a book on the subject. Her articles from dozens of countries have appeared in major newspapers and magazines in the US and abroad. She unearthed and reported the classified memo proving that Henry Kissinger lied in his memoir about his meeting with Pinochet. Author: *Corazon Aquino: The Story of a Revolution*; *Down and Out in the USA: A History of Public Welfare*; and *The New Feminism*. Member of the Council on Foreign Relations in New York; past John D. and Catherine T. MacArthur grantee and John Simon Guggenheim fellow; theater critic and member of the Drama Desk (New York).

When *People* magazine called **Paul Krassner** "father of the underground press," he immediately demanded a paternity test. He edited *The Realist*, 1958-2001, blurring the line between observer and activist. He was a cofounder of the Yippies, and ran an abortion referral service while it was an illegal operation. In a poison-pen letter to *Life* magazine, the FBI wrote, "To classify Krassner as a social rebel is far too cute. He's a nut, a raving, unconfined nut." His new book is *Murder at the Conspiracy Convention and Other American Absurdities* (Barricade Books, 2002), with an introduction by George Carlin. His latest album is *Irony Lives!* (Artemis Records, 2002), with an introduction by Homer Simpson, which was suppressed by lawyers for Fox TV (but it can be found at <www.paulkrassner.com>). At the 14th annual Cannabis Cup in Amsterdam, he was inducted into the Counterculture Hall of Fame—"my ambition," he says, "since I was three years old."

Michael Levine is a veteran of 25 years of covert and deep-cover operations for the Drug Enforcement Administration and one of its most highly decorated officers. He is also a world-recognized, court-qualified expert witness, trial consultant, and lecturer in all matters relating to human intelligence, covert operations, narcotics trafficking, police procedures, RICO and conspiracy investigations, and the use of force; he has testified as an expert in over 500 civil and criminal trials internationally and domestically. As an author, his books include the *New York Times* bestseller *Deep Cover*, national bestseller *The Big White Lie*, fact-based fiction *Triangle of Death*, and

the community anti-drug plan *Fight Back*. He is also a contributor to the Cato Institute's *After Prohibition*. His biography, *Undercover*, was written by Donald Goddard and published by Times Books in 1988. His articles and interviews on the Drug War have been published in the *New York Times*, the *Los Angeles Times, USA Today, Esquire, Utne Reader, The Journal of Crime, Law and Social Change, Reason, Spin*, and many other newspapers and magazines throughout the US, Europe, and South America. In 1998, he was invited to address the United Nations Conference on Drugs and Minorities. He has served as consultant and on-air expert for various national television programs in both Spanish and English, including *60 Minutes, Crossfire, MacNeil/Lehrer NewsHour, Good Morning America*, the *Crier Report, Rivera Live, Contrapunto*, and Mike Wallace's *Twentieth Century* production *Losing the Drug War*, seen on the History Channel. He is also the host of the radio program Expert Witness <www.expertwitnessradio.org> (Kristina Borjesson, producer).

Jonathan Levy is an attorney involved in a class-action lawsuit against the Vatican Bank <www.vaticanbankclaims.com>, seeking restitution of World War II-era loot, and is also petitioning the United Nations to act against the Vatican's violations of the Convention on the Rights of the Child. His other diverse litigation involves fundraising fraud, cults, and other crimes all committed in the name of the Catholic Church. Levy has written extensively on abuses by the Catholic Church; his article "The Vatican Bank" is part of the collection *Everything You Know is Wrong* (The Disinformation Company, 2002).

Wayne Madsen is a Washington, DC-based investigative journalist and the Washington correspondent for Intelligence Online <www.intelligenceonline.com>. He is also a syndicated columnist. He is the author of *Genocide and Covert Operations in Africa 1993-1999* (Mellen Press) and has testified before the House International Relations Committee on the situation in the Democratic Republic of the Congo. He is a frequent commentator on national security issues on the Fox News Channel and has also appeared on *MacNeil/Lehrer NewsHour* and *60 Minutes*. He is a member of the National Press Club and the National Television Academy. He is a former US Naval officer and formerly worked at the National Security Agency (NSA) and the Department of State.

Nick Mamatas is the cowriter, along with Kap Su Seol, of the first English-language edition of *Kwangju Diary: Beyond Death, Beyond the Darkness of the Age*, (UCLA APM, 1999), which is based on Lee Jai-eui's first-hand account of the Kwangju uprising and massacre. He is also the author of *Northern Gothic* (Soft Skull Press, 2001), a novella of the Civil War draft riots and a 2002 Bram Stoker Award nominee. His reportage and essays have appeared in the *Village Voice, In These Times, Silicon Alley Reporter, Artbyte*, the previous Disinformation anthologies, and other magazines and Webzines. His short fiction has been published by *Razor*, the Hugo-nominated *Strange Horizons, Wide Angle*, Horrorfind.com, *Talebones*, and other magazines. He is currently at work on a Lovecraftian Beat road novel titled *Move Under Ground*. Visit his Website here: <www.kynn.com/wwnkd>.

Richard Metzger is a cofounder of The Disinformation Company, and is its creative director. He lives in Los Angeles.

Jim Naureckas has been the editor of *Extra!*, FAIR's bimonthly journal of media criticism, since 1990. He is the coauthor of *The Way Things Aren't: Rush Limbaugh's Reign of Error* (New Press, 1995) and coeditor of *The FAIR Reader* (Westview Press, 1996). Born in Libertyville, Illinois, in 1964, he became interested in censorship while covering the Iran-Contra scandal for the independent newspaper *In These Times*, and wondering why corporate media were missing so many stories.

A California native, born in 1951, **Michael Newton** has published 169 books under his own name and various pseudonyms since 1977. He began writing professionally as a "ghost" for author Don Pendleton on the best-selling *Executioner* series and continues his work on that series today. (With 86 episodes published to date, Newton has nearly tripled the number of Mack Bolan novels completed by creator Pendleton himself.) Newton's first book under his own name was *Monsters, Mysteries and Man* (1979), a survey of unexplained phenomena for younger readers. While 136 of Newton's published books have been novels—including Westerns, political thrillers, and psychological suspense—he is best known for nonfiction, primarily true crime and reference books. His firearms manual for writers, *Armed and Dangerous* (1990), remains a bestseller for Writer's Digest Books in its eighth printing. Newton's shorter work includes horror fiction, true crime articles, and case histories for Court TV's Crime Library online. His thirteen upcoming books, scheduled for release through 2005, include nine novels and four encyclopedias. He lives in Nashville, Indiana. His Website is at <www.michaelnewton.homestead.com>.

Stephanie Nolen is an international news reporter for the *Globe and Mail*, Canada's national newspaper. She has covered conflict on four continents, including the wars in Afghanistan and Somalia, and has done extensive reporting on the AIDS pandemic in sub-Saharan Africa. She is coauthor of *Shakespeare's Face*, about a seventeenth-century portrait which may be the only life image of the playwright; the book was first published in July 2002 and has since been reprinted in a half-dozen countries. Her first book, *Promised the Moon: The Untold Story of the First Women in the Space Race* (Penguin Canada), also appeared in 2002.

April Oliver is a former investigative producer in television news. An honors graduate of Princeton University's Woodrow Wilson School of International Affairs, she was an international affairs reporter for the *MacNeil/Lehrer NewsHour* for five years, covering conflicts in Nicaragua, South Africa, and China, among other hot spots. She has won numerous awards for her work in television, including the Cine Golden Eagle for her documentary hour *Assigment Africa*, and two national Emmy nominations for *Assignment Africa* and coverage of the Middle East Peace process. She was a Livingston Award finalist for the MacNeil/Lehrer program *Women in China*, and a joint recepient of the prestigious Joan Shorenstein Barone Award for CNN's coverage of the 1996 campaign trail and the Clinton White House coffee/teas fundraising scandal. In 1998, CNN fired her after she produced the controversial Tailwind report about the US using sarin nerve gas and targeting defectors in Laos during the Vietnam War. CNN settled the lawsuit Oliver filed against her former employers for defamation and fraud after a retired Chairman of the Joint Chiefs of Staff reconfirmed in a sworn deposition what she had reported. Oliver left television to attend George Mason University's School of Law. She graduated with honors in 2002.

Katherine Harris calls **Greg Palast** "twisted and maniacal," and a White House spokesman says, "We hate that sonovabitch." Palast is author of the best-seller *The Best Democracy Money Can Buy: An Investigative Reporter Exposes the Truth About Globalization, Corporate Cons and High-Finance Fraudsters* (Penguin Plume 2003), whose exposés can be seen on BBC Television's *Newsnight* and in the *Guardian* and *Observer* papers of Britain. The US-born reporter is a recipient of the Financial Times David Thomas Prize and, for his undercover investigation of Enron and other US corporations, the prize for top business story of the year (Britain). In the US, Palast's work is all but banned; a fate recognized by his award from California State University's Journalism School for reporting one of the most "Censored Stories of the Year" for 2001—President Bush's hindering the investigation of Saudi Arabian funding of terrorists prior to September 11, 2001. In 2003, the United Nations International Labor Organization released Palast's book, *Regulation and Democracy*, a policy guide for the control of privatized infrastructure industries (in conjunction with Pluto Press, London, 2003). Palast is now working on a film about Alaskan natives and the oil industry and completing a book of poetry to be published by Soft Skull Press (New York). Palast, who (with Oliver Shykles) contributed the opening essay to the Disinformation compendium *Everything You Know Is Wrong*, divides his time between New York and London.

Diane Petryk-Bloom has won seven awards for investigative journalism and feature writing, including honors from the New York Associated Press, the New York Newspaper Publisher's Association, the North Carolina Press Association, and the Georgia Associated Press. She was news editor of the *Sanford Herald* in Sanford, Florida; assistant city editor of the *Savannah Morning News* in Georgia; and editor of the *St. Ignace News* in northern Michigan. While reporting for the *New York Times'* regional paper in Hendersonville, North Carolina, her investigation of a school board pay scandal brought about reform of a corrupt system. She holds a Master's degree in journalism from Michigan State University and studied comparative journalism in Croatia. She also worked as a subeditor for the New Zealand national daily *The Dominion*. As a reporter for the *Press Republican* in Plattsburgh, New York, she was part of a team honored by the Associated Press for its localized and comprehensive 9/11 coverage.

Janine Roberts is the author of the forthcoming book *Glitter and Greed: Inside the Secret World of the Diamond Cartel* (The Disinformation Company, 2003)—the story of a 24-year investigation in five continents during which the author uncovered the inner secrets of an extraordinarily well-connected cartel with covert links to the White House. Go to her diamond Website <www.sparkle.plus.com> for more on diamonds or to purchase her feature-length film, *The Diamond Empire*, which helped to launch the "blood diamond" campaign when it documented allegations that De Beers itself had employed terrorists and had defrauded Sierra Leone.

Glenn J. Sacks writes about gender issues from the male perspective. His work has appeared in dozens of America's largest newspapers. He invites readers to visit his Website at <www.glennjsacks.com>.

Stephen Schlesinger is the Director of the World Policy Institute <www.worldpolicy.org>. He has been the Special Advisor to Secretary-General of Habitat II, United Nations (1995-97); visiting scholar, New York University, Taub Urban Research Center (1995-97); Director for International Organizations, New York State Department of Economic Development (1990-95); Special Assistant to and Director of Public Papers for Governor Cuomo (1983-1990); a member of election observer teams in Bulgaria, Guatemala, and Paraguay for the National Democratic Institute, Washington DC; chief political correspondent for the *New York Post* (1978); staff writer for *Time* magazine (1974-78); adjunct professor of American politics, New School for Social Research (1976-77); weekly columnist for the *Boston Globe* (1973-74); speechwriter for Sen. McGovern's campaign (1972); contributing writer to the *Village Voice* (1968-72); teaching fellow in English composition, Harvard University (1968); and special editor, *The Harvard Review* (Harvard 1963-64). He has provided commentary on CNN, the *Today Show*, Fox News, Japanese Television Fuji, and numerous radio shows, including NPR and Larry King. His writings include *Bitter Fruit: The Untold Story of the US Coup in Guatemala* (1982, with Stephen Kinzer), selected by the *New York Times* as one of the "notable" books of 1982 and reissued by Harvard University Press; *The New Reformers* (1975); and articles for the *New York Times* op-ed page, *Vogue*, *New York Magazine*, *Harper's*, the *Newsday* op-ed page, and the *Washington Post* Outlook section. He is currently writing a book on the 1945 San Francisco conference that founded the United Nations, entitled *Act of Creation*.

Terri Spahr Nelson is the author of *For Love of Country: Confronting Rape and Sexual Harassment in the US Military,* published by Haworth Press in 2002. She was the principal investigator of a five-year international research study on the same topic. Spahr Nelson is also a twice-decorated military veteran who worked in behavioral sciences. Currently, she specializes in sexual trauma treatment as a psychotherapist and has written and lectured to international audiences on related topics. She has also coauthored a popular booklet, "Coping with Sexual Assault: A Guide to Healing, Resolution and Recovery," printed in English, Spanish, Braille, and large print, with special editions for teens, college students, and professionals. Her Website is at <www.tsnelson.com>.

Robert Sterling is the editor of the Konformist <www.konformist.com>, the top underground Internet magazine dedicated to rebellion, konspiracy, and subversion. In 2001, he tricked Project Censored into giving the Konformist one of its prizes for alternative news coverage. More incredible was his ability to coax porn stars to strip for him on camera during "interviews" for the *Disinformation* TV series. He has borrowed $100 from Yippie leader Paul Krassner, joining Hunter S. Thompson and Abbie Hoffman in the hallowed list of deadbeat mooches off the famed *Realist* founder. The first issue of *Konformist Komix* should be out in 2003, featuring the wacky adventures of Kirby the Konspiracy Boy. Sterling is the author of "Uncle Ronnie's Sex Slaves" in *Apocalypse Culture II* (Feral House, 2001), a contributing editor at Disinformation's Website <www.disinfo.com>, and a contributor to the previous two Disinfo books, *You Are Being Lied To: The Disinformation Guide to Media Distortion, Historical Whitewashes and Cultural Myths* and *Everything You Know Is Wrong: The Disinformation Guide to Secrets and Lies.*

Many biological weapons are rapidly destroyed by bright sunlight. **The Sunshine Project** works to bring facts about biological weapons to light! We are an international non-profit organization with offices in Hamburg, Germany, and Austin, Texas, USA. We work against the hostile use of biotechnology in the post-Cold War era. We research and publish to strengthen the global consensus against biological warfare and to ensure that international treaties effectively prevent development and use of biological weapons. Our Website is at <www.sunshine-project.org>.

Thomas Szasz, A.B., M.D., D.Sc. (Hon.), L.H.D. (Hon.), is professor of psychiatry emeritus at the State University of New York Upstate Medical University, in Syracuse, New York. He is the author of 27 books, among them the classic *The Myth of Mental Illness* (New York: HarperCollins, 1961/1974) and, most recently, *Liberation By Oppression: A Comparative Study of Slavery and Psychiatry* (Transaction, 2002). Dr. Szasz, widely recognized as the world's foremost critic of psychiatric coercions and abuses, has received many awards for his defense of individual liberty and responsibility threatened by what he has called the "therapeutic state"—a new form of totalitarianism masquerading as medicine. A frequent and popular lecturer, he has addressed professional and lay groups, and has appeared on radio and television, in North, Central, and South America, as well as in Australia, Europe, Japan, and South Africa. His books have been translated into every major language. His Website is <www.szasz.com>.

Nancy Talanian began organizing against the USA PATRIOT Act in November 2001 as part of the Northampton (Massachusetts) Bill of Rights Defense Committee. The committee educated the community, worked with the city council toward the unanimous passage of a strongly worded resolution to defend civil liberties, and helped nearby communities do the same. Seeing the potential for a national movement, she developed a Website <www.bordc.org> that offers tools, tips, and information to other groups and communities. Her article in this volume is one of these tools. Her organization, now known as the Bill of Rights Defense Committee, provides ongoing support to city and county committees, student groups, unions, and religious organizations working to restore civil liberties threatened by the PATRIOT Act, various executive orders, and the Homeland Security Act.

William Turner is the FBI's first whistleblower—in 1961, he sought a congressional investigation of J. Edgar Hoover. Turning to investigative journalism, he became a senior editor of *Ramparts* magazine, which was for social justice and against the Vietnam War. He is the author of nine books—including *Hoover's FBI*—which have been published in English, Japanese, Russian, French, Spanish, and Polish editions. His current book is *Rearview Mirror: Looking Back at the FBI, the CIA, and Other Tails* (Penmarin Books, 2001).

Gary Webb has been an investigative journalist for around 25 years, focusing on government and private sector corruption. His controversial 1996 newspaper series "Dark Alliance"—which exposed the sale of cocaine and weapons by CIA-supported rebels to the street gangs of South Central Los Angeles—caused a nationwide outcry that is still reverberating today. His 1998 book, also called *Dark Alliance*, has received critical acclaim in the *San Francisco Chronicle*, the *Baltimore Sun*, and *The Nation*, along with several literary awards. Webb wrote for the *San Jose Mercury News* from 1988 to 1997. He worked as a statehouse correspondent for the *Cleveland Plain Dealer* and the *Kentucky Post* before that, and has won more than 30 journalism prizes. He was part of the *Mercury News* team that won the 1989 Pulitzer Prize for general news reporting. He has appeared on *Dateline NBC*, the *Montel Williams Show*, CNN, National Public Radio, C-SPAN, CBS *Morning News*, MSNBC, the BBC, British, Australian, and French TV, and dozens of syndicated and local talk radio shows from Bogota, Colombia to British Columbia. He now works as a consultant and researcher for the California Assembly. He has resurrected the "Dark Alliance" Website—which was pulled offline by the *Mercury News*—at <home.attbi.com/~gary.webb/>.

Mickey Z. is the author of *The Murdering of My Years: Artists and Activists Making Ends Meet* <www.murderingofmyyears.com>, *Saving Private Power: The Hidden History of "The Good War"*, and *Forgotten New York: Small Slices of a Big Apple*. His next book, *Seven Deadly Spins: How the US Sells War*, will be published by Common Courage Press. He is a regular contributor to Websites like ZNet, Dissident Voice, and Press Action, is the senior editor of *Wide Angle* <www.wideangleny.com>, and is the recipient of a 2002 writing grant from the Puffin Foundation. He lives in Astoria, NY, with his wife, Michele, and can be reached at <mzx2@earthlink.net>.

Richard Zacks' most recent book is *The Pirate Hunter: The True Story of Captain Kidd* (Hyperion, 2002), and it's **not** some lame Peter Pan/Hollywood account of peglegs and eyepatches. The real Captain Kidd was a New York privateer (1654-1701) who was hired to chase pirates and then double-crossed by his backers. This is an authentic nautical adventure. Zacks' first book, *History Laid Bare* (1994), delivered unusual accounts of sex, from Mark Twain's jokes about penis size to Joan of Arc's virginity tests. The *NY Times* gushed: "Zacks specializes in the raunchy and perverse." His second book, *An Underground Education* (100,000+ copies sold),

explored a huge range of topics from Edison's secret role in developing the first electric chair to Abe Lincoln's plan to ship out the freed slaves. The author, now researching the Barbary Pirates, lives in Pelham, NY, with his wife, Kristine, and their kids, Georgia and Ziggy. His Website is at <www.piratehunter.com>.

Howard Zinn grew up in New York City of working-class parents, was a shipyard worker at the age of eighteen, a bombardier in the Air Force at 21 (European theater, World War II), and went to New York University and Columbia under the G.I. Bill of Rights, receiving his Ph.D. in history and political science from Columbia in 1958. His doctoral dissertation, *LaGuardia in Congress*, was a Beveridge Prize publication of the American Historical Association. His first teaching job was at Spelman College in Atlanta, Georgia, a black women's college, where he taught for seven years, becoming involved in the Southern civil rights movement. After that he taught at Boston University, and was active in the movement against the war in Vietnam. He became a professor emeritus in 1988. He has written over a dozen books, his best known being *A People's History of the United States* (1980), which has sold over 700,000 copies. Some of his most recent books are *You Can't Be Neutral on a Moving Train* (a memoir; 1995), *The Zinn Reader* (1997), *The Future of History* (1999), and *Terrorism and War* (2002). In 2002, South End Press reprinted seven volumes of his early work. He has been a visiting professor in France and Italy, has lectured in Japan and South Africa, and his writings have been translated into many languages. He is also a playwright. His play *Emma*, on the anarchist-feminist Emma Goldman, has been produced in Boston, New York, London, and Tokyo, and his recent play *Marx in Soho* has been produced widely in the United States.

ARTICLE HISTORIES

"'A Truth So Terrible'" by James Bacque was written especially for this volume.

"The Agency and the Atom" by John Kelly is published for the first time in this volume.

"Are Secrecy Oaths a License to Lie?" by Daniel Ellsberg is published in print for the first time in this volume.

"Belgium: The Pedophilia Files" by Sandra Bisin was written especially for this volume.

"Bill of Rights, R.I.P." by Nancy Talanian originally appeared on the Website of the Bill of Right Defense Committee <www.bordc.org>. It is published in print for the first time in this volume.

"Corporations Claim the 'Right To Lie'" by Thom Hartmann is published in print for the first time in this volume.

"Creating Panama for Funds and Profit" by Ovidio Diaz-Espino was written especially for this volume.

"Cuban Political Prisoners ... in the United States" by William Blum is published in print for the first time in this volume.

"Did Jesus Really Rise From The Dead?" by Dan Barker is published for the first time in this volume. It is based on research done for Dan's public debates with Michael Horner (1996), John Morehead (1999), and Greg Boyd (2000). A transcription of the debate with Horner is online at <www.ffrf.org/debates/barker_horner.html>.

"Dirty Players of World Finance" by Lucy Komisar consists of previously published and unpublished articles. It appears here in its current form for the first time.

"The Enemy Within" by Terri Spahr Nelson was written especially for this volume.

"Exile on Mainstream" by Greg Palast was written especially for this volume.

"The Fluoridation Fraud" by Robert Sterling was written especially for this volume.

"Food-Drop Fiasco" by Russ Kick first appeared in the 2003 main catalog of Loompanics Unlimited.

"How I Crashed a Chinese Arms Bazaar With a Rifle That Doesn't Exist" by Jakob S. Boeskov is a shorter version of "My Doomsday Weapon" in *BLACK BOX* magazine #1 <www.blackboxmagazine.com>. It appears here in its current form for the first time.

"Inside Science's Closet" by Richard Zacks is comprised of excerpts from the "Science" chapter of *An Underground Education* (Doubleday, 1997). It appears here in its current form for the first time.

"Invasion of the Child-Snatchers" by Diane Petryk-Bloom was written especially for this volume.

"Islamic Censorship" by Howard Bloom is a heavily reworked, expanded version of an article that originally appeared on *Spin* magazine's Website. It was expanded especially for this volume.

"The Kwangju Uprising and the US" by Nick Mamatas was written especially for this volume.

"L. Ron, Sirhan, Manson, and Me" by Paul Krassner was written especially for this volume.

"The Lilly Suicides" by Richard DeGrandpre was published in much shorter form in *Adbusters* magazine <www.adbusters.org> and in its full form on their Website. It is published in print for the first time in this volume. It is part of a larger work, *The Cult of Pharmacology*, to be published by Duke University Press.

"Mainstream Media: The Drug War's Shills" by Michael Levine first appeared, in slightly different form, in *Into the Buzzsaw: Leading Journalists Expose the Myth of a Free Press*, edited by Kristina Borjesson (Prometheus Books, 2002).

"The Man Who Invented Normal" by Lucy Gwin was written especially for this volume.

"Mormon Racism" by Richard Abanes is comprised of excerpts from the chapter of the same title in *One Nation Under Gods: A History of the Mormon Church* (Four Walls Eight Windows, 2002).

"The Mysterious Decline of Men on Campus" by Philip W. Cook and Glenn J. Sacks was written especially for this volume.

"Mystery in Memphis" by Wayne Madsen is published for the first time in this volume.

"One Giant Leap—Backward" by Stephanie Nolen was first published in the *Globe and Mail* (Toronto), 12 Oct 2002. It is based on her book *Promised the Moon: The Untold Story of the First Women in the Space Race* (Penguin Books Canada, 2002).

"Operation Pipeline" by Gary Webb was first published as a report for the California State Assembly. It is published in book form for the first time in this volume. The introduction was written especially for this volume.

"The Others" by Howard Zinn was first published in *The Nation*.

"Our Back Pages" by Mickey Z. was written especially for this volume.

"The Pentagon's New Biochemical Warriors" by the Sunshine Project is comprised of articles previously published on the Project's Website <www.sunshine-project.org>. It appears here in its current form for the first time.

"Pieces of the 9/11 Puzzle" by Russ Kick was written especially for this volume.

"The Secret Behind the Creation of the United Nations" by Stephen Schlesinger was first published in *Cryptologia: A Quarterly Devoted to Cryptology* 19.3 (July 1995).

"Speer" by Daniel Ellsberg is published in print for the first time in this volume.

"Straight Talk About Suicide" by Thomas S. Szasz, M.D., first appeared in *Ideas on Liberty* 52 (Sept 2002).

"Suitable for Framing: Wayne Williams and the Atlanta Child Murders" by Michael Newton is published for the first time in this volume.

"US Homeland Security: A Bridge From Democracy to Dictatorship" by Ritt Goldstein was written especially for this volume.

"Unanswered Letters" by April Oliver was written especially for this volume.

"The Underside of De Beers Diamonds" by Janine Roberts is published for the first time in this volume.

"The Virgin of Medjugorje" by Jonathan Levy was written especially for this volume.

"War Against Terrorism or Expansion of the American Empire?" by William Blum is published in print for the first time in this volume.

"The Warren Report: Believe It or Not" by William W. Turner was written especially for this volume.

"Watergate Redux" by Jim Hougan was written especially for this volume.

"What Is a Terrorist?" by Jeff Cohen was first published by CommonDreams.org.

"The White House Campaign Against Drug Reform Initiatives" by Daniel Forbes is a heavily reworked, expanded version of an article that originally appeared on DrugWar.com. It was expanded especially for this volume.

"Why UN Inspectors Left Iraq in 1998" by Jim Naureckas first appeared in *Extra! Update* (Oct 2002), a publication of FAIR <www.fair.org>.